SEARCHING FOR GREAT IDEAS

Readings Past and Present,
Second Edition

Thomas Klein
Bruce Edwards
Thomas Wymer
Bowling Green State University

Harcourt Brace College Publishers

Forth Worth San Diego Philadelphia New York Orlando Austin San Antonio
Montreal Toronto London Sydney Tokyo

Publisher	Christopher P. Klein
Executive Editor	Michael Rosenberg
Developmental Editor	Adrienne Harton/Katie Frushour
Project Editor	John Haakenson
Production Manager	Diane Gray
Art Director	Garry Harman
Picture and Rights Editor	Beverly Wyatt
Permissions Editor	Aimé Merizon
Cover Image	Ron Lusk

Address for Editorial Correspondence: Harcourt Brace College Publishers, 301 Commerce Street, Suite 3700, Fort Worth, TX 76102.

Address for Orders: Harcourt Brace & Company, 6277 Sea Harbor Drive, Orlando, FL 32887-6777. 1-800-782-4479 (in Florida).

(Copyright Acknowledgments begin on page 630, which constitutes a continuation of this copyright page.)

Harcourt Brace College Publishers may provide complimentary instructional aids and supplements of supplement packages to those adopters qualified under our adoption policy. Please contact your sales representative for more information. If as an adopter or potential user you receive supplements you do not need, please return them to your sales representative or send them to:

Attn: Returns Department
Troy Warehouse
465 South Lincoln Drive
Troy, MO 63379

Printed in the United States of America

ISBN: 0-03-017718-9

Library of Congress Catalog Card Number: 96-79877

7 8 9 0 1 2 3 4 5 6 039 9 8 7 6 5 4 3 2 1

To the Instructor

Searching for Great Ideas: Readings Past and Present shares two guiding principles with its predecessor, *Great Ideas: Conversations Between Past and Present:* that the development of clear thinking, critical understanding, and effective writing skills requires nourishing food for thought, and that because the problems we face today are rooted in the past, we can understand them better when they are seen within a historical context. One of the most significant developments in the history of ideas which this text, like the previous one, attempts to reveal is changes in attitudes about the authority of the past. The new title clarifies this concern, while it preserves the essence of what the former text implied by the subtitle: a searching and continuing conversation about questions as well as answers to some of the most pressing problems of the last 3500 years.

To preserve that essence and realize it effectively, the text is designed around a number of features, many of which are new to this edition:

- Expanded chapter one to include critical writing as well as reading strategies to make the text more friendly to first-year composition instruction
- Reshaped the original second chapter into two chapters to emphasize the dual questions of the reported moral decline in the West and the problems of studying history
- Expanded chapter four on religion to include a consideration of the Islamic tradition, as well as an examination of the Judeo-Christian tradition
- Replaced the chapters on Existentialism and Psychology with one on art and imagination as great ideas and the preeminence of technology in what many are referring to as our "postmodern cyberfuture"
- 70% of the reading selections are new, expanding representation of minority and women writers to present a more complete perspective of the past
- Added chapter preludes in the form of a short essay from a very recent book or magazine to give students an opportunity to confront some of the major questions that the chapter will explore in a recognizable and contemporary setting
- Included three to five readings that demonstrate significant portions of the history of the idea and raise the major issues associated with that idea
- Added "Perspectives" section, which includes two to three works focusing on a currently controversial issue related to the idea
- Added a short story to most chapters

Several themes we felt were important enough in the first edition to preserve and reinforce here. First and most important, the book seeks to explore, define and even assert the evolving common heritage in America. We see the concerted efforts of various social communities, especially those reduced to silence in the past, to gain their human rights and to trumpet their voices and cultures as deserving a place in our public history as a healthy addition to an undeniably variegated culture. This second edition reemphasizes that struggle.

At times the struggle for self-definition and self-respect is exceedingly painful for all—given the strident voices and cultural differences that have lately arisen around issues of race, gender, and social-economic class. By juxtaposing traditional texts like the Declaration of Independence or Darwin's *Origin of Species* that have marked some of the familiar intellectual history of our country with newer voices like Nadine Gordimer and Joel Cracraft, we hope to strengthen our common heritage by inviting all participants thoughtfully into the marketplace of ideas. In a similar vein, we juxtapose Karl Marx with Toni Cade Bambara and the Jewish bible and New Testament with essays by Abraham Heschel and Dorothy Sayers.

Secondly, the readings in this text are embedded in our own reading of intellectual history. Informed debate grounded in a knowledge of history is superior to a mob's frenzy and one of the best means toward enlarging the numbers of individuals who can enjoy the rights of life, liberty and the pursuit of happiness. At the risk of oversimplification, we have created an informed reading of some of the dialectics that have shaped Western intellectual history, with documents contextualized in their times, in the belief that decontextualized judgment is dangerous folly. How can one understand Galileo's struggle with the Church to assert the truths of his own senses without understanding the enormous cultural momentum behind the traditional cosmology he was attempting to overturn? How can one understand the victories of American women and African-Americans over the last 30 years without appreciating the 19th-century pseudo-scientific claims about the biological inferiority of these two groups? And how can one understand, though not excuse, Neo-Nazi skinheads except by seeing the extent of their historical illiteracy and the severity of their social and economic marginalization?

In assembling essays and stories in historical context, we offer readings not as models of ideas or history. Rather, in the terms of our colleagues and critical thinking theorists Neil Browne and Stu Keeley, we ask students to confront these texts, even the most sacred of them, not as "sponges," but as "filters," examining assumptions, ambiguities, inferences, arguments, generalizations, fallacies and rhetorical strategies.

Thirdly, we believe that all study must be essentially moral, that it must always ask what are the conditions and problems we face as a society and a world, how these came to be, and how we can undertake to improve on them. Each chapter after the first three introductory ones presents an idea or theme around which all cultures struggle. For each, we raise moral questions like, What are the uses and misuses of reason? What is a just society? What is the role of religion in a moral society? How have science and technology enhanced and detracted from the common good? What does it mean to be a man or a woman today? What did it mean in the past? How do race and social/economic class affect the quest for the good society?

Fourthly, we commend the expansion of the canon over the last 20 years to include the voices of minorities and women, and have balanced the voice of the traditional and nontraditional to reflect this expansion. If education is in large part about learning to take an informed place in cultural conversations that shape our individual and collective destinities, familiarity with both kinds of writers is critical, for both of them raise the defining and critical questions we must investigate as a culture.

To the Student

Students sometimes ask, what can someone who lived centuries, even decades, ago possibly tell us about life in the modern, technological, tumultuous twenty-first century? What, indeed, could anyone "back then" have known about our particular challenges, problems, hopes, and dreams?

One answer to this compelling question begins first by asking another: *What is it about being human that is unique to any particular time or place?* That is, why should we assume automatically that someone who lived centuries ago did not share our aspirations, dreams, and problems? While admitting that our ancestors perhaps had to deal with their peculiar circumstances somewhat differently than we do, is there any reason to suspect that they prized peace, family, success, or vocation any less than we do?

The problem with assuming the past has nothing to say to us is summed up well by C. S. Lewis: "There is no magic about the past. People were no cleverer then than they are now; they made as many mistakes as we. But not the same mistakes. They will not flatter us in the errors we are already committing; and their own errors, being now open and palpable, will not endanger us" ("On the Reading of Old Books," *God in the Dock,* Grand Rapids, MI: Eerdmans, 1970, 202).

In other words, the past can serve as a barometer—a means of measuring the progress or lack thereof that the human community has made over time and through many different cultures. As we come to explore and understand what it means to be human, the past is for us an invaluable reference point, marking where we have been and how far we have to go in constructing a society that shares a common reverence for truth, life, justice, beauty, and the accompanying blessings of peace and harmony in a larger community.

In constructing *Searching for Great Ideas,* our aim has been to combat the view that because our times are "our" times, it follows that they are, therefore, definitively the best, the most enlightened, informed, important, and so on. Such notions are often based on the assumption—some would say *myth*—of "progress," that things naturally "get better" with the passage of time. But, reading texts from other eras alongside those from our own forces us to judge whether ideas, people, culture, and times do, in fact, "progress," or whether they can also regress.

The alternative to the kind of multicultural, transchronological reading we encourage in our book, is to live only in the "now," guided only by the current wisdom or the received popular knowledge; this is, in fact, what many of us are only too ready to do. Thus, it might be useful to suggest two modest principles employed to govern our selection of the texts for this revision, two principles, at least, that will increase our confidence in the validity or relevance of our inquiry.

The first is the simple belief that historical texts can speak to us out of their own times. With linguistic and historical research, we can provide the necessary contexts and backgrounds that allow us to see the past with tolerable clarity, maybe even as clearly as we see any phenomenon in our times. Even granting that every observer will bring prejudices or tendencies into the readings, a startlingly fresh wind can blow through the centuries when we read a selection without too much of our late twentieth-century bias getting in the way.

The second principle is the notion that multiple perspectives may be applied to a text, yielding different, but not necessarily mutually exclusive, interpretations. Because all of us operate from finite fields of vision that supply both unique perspective and characteristic blind spots, we can expect to find lively debate, which will include informed as well as uninformed, even dogmatic, opinions among those who are reading along with us. Together, we can find common ground upon which to build toward greater consensus as well as meaningful and respectful dissent.

What we want you to discover in this grand excursion into the past from the present is not a uniform response but an honest, individual encounter with challenging ideas; we want to encourage you to find meaning in the intersection of past and present, so that the future may be enriched by the insights of both.

To my father, *who in battling death, has exemplified the fortitude, courage and humility that he has taught me over his 86 years. To Dianne, whose level-headed wisdom has been a moral and intellectual compass for me. And to David, whose steady quest for a new career and life have taught me to respect the battles of young people today.*

—Tom Klein

To my father, *Bruce Edwards, Sr., who has exemplified in his life all the qualities of a parent, spouse, and citizen I would want exhibited in my own children, and my readers.*

—Bruce Edwards

To Penny, *whose support and patience during the development of this project have been indispensable.*

—Tom Wymer

Acknowledgments

A book this ambitious, comprehensive and inclusive depends on numerous persons. At the top of that list are those who over a decade ago encouraged and advised and taught the Great Ideas course: Kendall Baker, Jim Bissland, Alan Emery, Jim Litwin, and Ryan Tweney. Since those early days of what we call the Great Ideas Program at Bowling Green State University, over 150 sections of the course have been taught here, not to mention more at hundreds of universities here and around the world. To all who have come to our conference presentations, our monthly faculty lunches and so reliably taught our sections, we offer our thanks. In addition, Beth Casey, who currently runs the program, has been a constant source of encouragement and fresh ideas, as has Leigh Chiarelotte, Rev. Karen Thompson, Mary Catherine Harper and Mike Ryan.

We also thank Joan Edwards, for her frequently called upon proofreading, typing, and collating skills; George and Lisa Loper, for their continuing friendship and actualization of the Greatest of Ideas; and Rick Gebhardt, for his continuing support for the revision and vitality of this book and the Great Ideas curriculum.

Steve Krause's Great Ideas home page on the world wide web (http://ernie.bgsu.edu/~skrause/Great_Ideas.html) has been a source of constant stimulation, creativity and national visibility. Further, conversations with Neil Browne, Stu Keeley, Malcolm Campbell, Christine Shaerer-Cremean, Dave Cremean, Michael Peslikas, Scott Minar, Marjory Kinney, Roger Hall and Bill Phillips have kept us thinking.

Also, we appreciate the critical and careful responses from our reviewers: John Hanes, Duquesne University; Donald Heidt, College of the Canyons, Claudia Ingram, University of California at Los Angeles; Cary Ser, Miami-Dade Community Collge; Don Skiles, Chabot College; and Sally Young, University of Tennessee at Chattanooga.

Finally, thanks to our friends and editors at Harcourt Brace for making the second edition of *Searching for Great Ideas* possible: Tina Winslow, Adrienne Harton, Katie Frushour, Michael Rosenberg, John Haakenson, Diane Gray, and Garry Harman.

TABLE OF CONTENTS

Searching for Great Ideas

Chapter Preview

Ideas and Their Consequences
What is a "Great" Idea?
Understanding Great Ideas

Critical Reading and Writing Strategies for Exploring and Understanding Great Ideas
Reading as an Interactive Process
Sample Essay: Audre Lorde, "Fourth of July"

Critical Writing Strategies for Exploring and Understanding Your Own Ideas

Chapter 1

Searching for Great Ideas: The Reading and Writing Process

Ideas and Their Consequences

The late Richard Weaver, a rhetorician of considerable note in the twentieth century, passionately challenged his readers with the proposition that ideas have consequences. He believed that we do grave injury to our grasp of history and our sense of the future to ignore this fact. *Ideas have impact,* Weaver argued, not only on the eras in which they originate but *also beyond them.*

For instance, witness these curious phenomena: *Humanism* obviously did not die with the ancient Greeks but emerges again today in defense of the arts in congressional hearings; *the Copernican revolution in astronomy* continues to affect the way we "do" and how we "think about" science—and many other disciplines; women worldwide continue to draw on the insights into freedom and human dignity that erupted during the turbulent democratic revolutions in Europe and America in the eighteenth century in their quest for equality with men; and there continue to be devout *Jews, Christians, and Muslims* in the contemporary world, despite the millennia that have passed since their appearance as religious faiths among humankind.

Why did Weaver feel compelled to underscore these features of "ideas"? In essence, it was because he felt it a too common notion among people in his day that ideas were "mere" philosophical abstractions without true impact on the world, that ideas were only a part of some mental games played by intellectuals or academics—in sum, he feared that we were coming to believe that ideas were never connected to actions. What mattered was what people did, not what they thought, so the conventional wisdom went, according to Weaver. By contrast, he drew attention to the *actions* ideas themselves perform: how they influence, alter, undermine, determine, and shape the times; in short, how ideas originate and then affect the course of development of other ideas. For Weaver, no ideas are ever neutral, and all ideas have a beginning somewhere in time that can be noted and have a life that can be charted and that extends beyond their original frameworks and contexts.

Weaver's conception of the power of ideas and their continuing influence on our sense of individual identity and community membership is a useful one with which to begin this textbook. For *Searching for Great Ideas* finds its genesis in its authors' conviction that, indeed, ideas do have consequences and that "great" ideas (whatever they may be!) have greater and greater consequences not only for those who accept them as foundational to their communities and individual behavior, goals, and dreams—but also for those who come into contact with or are conquered by those who embrace them.

What Is a "Great" Idea?

That's a fair question. And one that we have wrestled with ourselves in writing the introductions to each chapter and in selecting the readings found within the covers of this book. One kind of answer to this question is that ideas are great if they *endure,* if they last more than one generation, or if they cross cultural and linguistic boundaries to have influence over more than one civilization or nation. Another answer might emphasize the *sheer numbers of people* who have been impacted by the idea and its subsequent formulations, that is, how much "power" the idea has had to shape government, education, various social institutions, or individual selfhood. Still another answer would draw attention to the *quality* of the idea, how it promotes peace or love or respect for difference or otherness or how it has helped generate many other ideas that partake of these human emotions and ideals.

However, none of these answers is ultimately sufficient by itself to capture in some neutral or objective way what is a "great" idea, at least not one that can be universally acknowledged by culture, time, and individual. For, on the other side of every idea is the compelling testimony of a person, community, or nation that has experienced the negative consequences of this idea or its later incarnations—as many of our selections will dramatize. It needs to be said that some ideas must be considered great not because they have been benevolent or humane innovations that have genuinely served the needs of human beings, but because they raise great moral dilemmas in the ways they have motivated and caused people to behave. Views of humanity that lead some civilizations to justify slavery or genocide, or new waves in technology that produce more and more efficient weapons to murder more and more are examples of ideas that are hardly "great" in a qualitative sense—but require our scrutiny all the more for their terrible impact on human society.

So it is that this book is entitled not *The Great Ideas,* but rather *Searching for Great Ideas.* In interacting with the texts we have chosen for this book—as an active reader and writer—you will join us and millions of other human sojourners who have sought to make sense of their own lives and times and to ask the great questions about origins and destinies, in a vast universe that yields what answers it does only to those earnestly seeking them.

Understanding Great Ideas

Now, it is well and good for us to offer our generalizations about what great ideas may or may not consist of. However, it is rather crucial that you yourself begin early to grapple with definitions and applications of "great" ideas, to see for yourself if what Weaver has suggested is also true of your era, place, and situation—that "ideas have consequences." Part of the power of ideas truly "great" in impact, endurance, or quality is how quickly they can become established and part of the "conventional wisdom" or "common sense" of one's own time and setting. Often it is those ideas whose impact is so pervasive that become difficult to "see" or articulate and which, therefore, we take for granted—for good or ill.

For instance, who among us in North America would today seriously question whether people accused of crimes should have a right to a defense attorney or a jury of their peers? Or that citizens ought to have a right to self-determination about where they can live or work? Or that worshippers should be allowed without government interference or persecution to congregate and proceed in their faith as their conscience dictates? Yet all these "commonplaces" were not always part of the core ideas of nations and communities in the Western world and, indeed, were often hard won, over many generations. And certainly one can find exceptions to these notions even in the West today and, as well, among non-Western nations.

It must also be pointed out that "great" ideas tend to consist of or are "nested" inside each other and, thus, form hierarchies or interlocking patterns of ideas that reinforce each other and depend upon one another for their impact and power. For instance, the "right to worship (or not worship) as one wishes" is predicated on the right to self-determination and personal privacy that privileges individual rights over state or institutional rights. Likewise, the idea that accused wrongdoers deserve "due process," or a right to defense, presumes that the idea "people are innocent until proven guilty" is valid itself.

One exercise that is useful for seeing this even more clearly is to consider the following 10 pairs of ideas and to try to determine which of the two (Column A or Column B) is the "foundational" idea and which is the "derivative" idea, or in other words, which is "nested" inside the other? (In some cases, it may not be easy to determine—for both may have come into being simultaneously.) But look carefully at each pair and decide, if you can, which seems "prior" to the other. You need not conclude whether either idea is "true," but only which seems to precede or imply the other and, therefore, has "influenced" the other or brought it into being.

Column A	Column B
1. the earth is round	planetary shape can be mathematically discerned
2. humankind manifests two genders	women are equal to men

Column A	Column B
3. all responsible citizens should vote	representative democracy is the best form of government
4. God is an omnipotent, omniscient being	God made the universe
5. capital punishment is wrong	society should treat its criminals with justice
6. scientific fact should rule over opinion	science can objectively account for phenomena
7. children should be reared by parents	the family structure of a father and mother is normative
8. marijuana should be legalized	individuals must have the maximum amount of free choice
9. all children have a right to literacy	literacy skills are crucial to national growth and stability
10. all monarchies are illegitimate	constitutional government is superior to dictatorial rule

If you identified either A or B as foundational, what was your reasoning? Did you discover that there may be other ideas or premises related to both that also must be considered in order to see the chronology or progression of ideas over time? Which of the 10 pairs does contemporary culture most take for granted? Why?

As you move through the readings in subsequent chapters, you will begin to see how these ideas developed and influenced the systems of personal identity, morality, government, behavior, and so on, among the peoples who first encountered them, and how people transformed them and then passed them on to others directly and indirectly.

Critical Reading and Writing Strategies for Exploring and Understanding Great Ideas

Reading as an Interactive Process

Ideas don't float around disattached. They become incarnate in the speech and texts of the cultures and societies in which they originate and flourish. Ideas that are great—enduring, influential, consequential—have been preserved in the oral narratives and written texts that have been passed down generationally from culture to culture, nation to nation, community to community, family to family. Most often in the modern, technological West, we have come to ideas through the experience of reading other texts and then creating our own ideas in response. Textuality is one large interlocking web of ideas—in fact, the word *text* is itself an ancient word that means *weaving.* A text is a woven product whose shape, pattern, length, etc., expresses the heart and mind not only of individual writers, but also of the communities that have shaped and continue to shape their experience. One speaks out of the many, the many speak through one. The weaving of ideas is both personal and individualistic as well as communal and corporate. "My" idea will always be related to those that have come before it and to those that will come after it; "great" ideas ultimately belong to no one person or group, and resist easy categorization and personal possession.

The weaving of texts and the reading of texts is a uniquely human and nearly universal activity, and to some degree all of us participate in the process of authoring and responding to texts. But "reading" is not merely a process of extracting meaning from an otherwise completely "visible" text nor of just decoding words and grammar and using some inner dictionary to "translate" the writer's thoughts into some objective package of ideas with which we're totally conversant; rather, it is a participation, a habitation within a writer's woven world, one to which we respond according to our own experiences, values, depth of insight, personal idiosyncrasies, and time period. Reading is thus an interactive process, as we attend first to the surface features of a text (e.g., vocabulary, topic, frame of reference), then move on to our own discerning of foundational and nested ideas and their levels of complexity, and on to how the writer has woven them to make meaning. Reading is also both an analytical and a synthetic process; that is, while I am "separating the text into component parts" or "classifying its features," I am also simultaneously attempting to "pull things together" into some coherent whole, examining my own stance and commitments, as well as my motives and predispositions. In the end, what I "discover" when I read depends almost as much on what I bring to a text as it does on what the writer has placed there.

If reading is an interactive, analytical, and synthetic process, then there ought to be some useful strategies that effective readers use to make connections, identify patterns, sort out the levels of ideas and their effects, and, finally, "make meaning." And there are. First of all, *one reading is never enough.* Use your initial encounter with a text to gain a general acquaintance with the subject matter and stance of the author in the text. Next, *do a second reading,* in which you employ the five important strategies, identified below, that good readers use to encounter ideas and make sense of them. Finally, *respond in writing* with engagement and discernment, using the activities of observation, evaluation, and responding and applying to help explore the author's world, and then to discover and articulate your own ideas and stance.

You probably already use these, at least unconsciously, whenever you are reading or writing about something. There is nothing magical about these strategies, and they, of course, could be employed in any order. But we will present them in a somewhat linear fashion and then illustrate them using a short, sample reading from the writer Audre Lorde. In many ways, these strategies are simply common-sensical ways of using your powers of observation, memory, and analysis on particular texts.

Five Strategies for Discerning Readers

1 *Locate* the main "thread" or topic—usually introduced in the title and opening two or three paragraphs of the text.

2 *Follow* this "thread" through subsequent paragraphs and sections by noticing the examples, illustrations, and arguments that the writer binds or weaves around this thread—listing them and evaluating them.

3 *Determine what is new* (ideas which you are encountering for the first time or which are presented in a fresh or startling way) or *given* (ideas with which you are familiar or count as conventional wisdom) in the text and how they affect your experience as a critical thinker.

4 *Characterize* this thread at critical junctures in your reading by highlighting significant sentences, words, or phrases in the text, or by noting transitional or summative phrases (for example, *therefore, as a result, consequently*), section headers, or paragraph breaks. How does the writer achieve her or his effects?

5 *Evaluate* the overall credibility and force of the author's ideas and experience. In what position are you placed by the text?

Sample Essay: Audre Lorde, "Fourth of July"

To see these strategies in action, read the following essay, "Fourth of July" by Audre Lorde.

Fourth of July
Audre Lorde

Audre Lorde (1934–1992) was, until her death, Official State Poet of New York and a well-known chronicler of the plight of African-American women in attempting to achieve recognition and equality in a democratic society. She served as a professor of English at Hunter College in New York City for many years and was the author of such works as *Between Ourselves* (1976) and *Zami: A New Spelling of My Name* (1982), from which this excerpt comes.

1 The first time I went to Washington, D.C., was on the edge of the summer when I was supposed to stop being a child. At least that's what they said to us all at graduation from the eighth grade. My sister Phyllis graduated at the same time from high school. I don't know what she was supposed to stop being. But as graduation presents for us both, the whole family took a Fourth of July trip to Washington, D.C., the fabled and famous capital of our country.

2 It was the first time I'd ever been on a railroad train during the day. When I was little, and we used to go to the Connecticut shore, we always went at night on the milk train, because it was cheaper. Preparations were in the air around our house before school was even over. We packed for a week. There were two very large suitcases that my father carried, and a box filled with food. In fact, my first trip to Washington was a mobile feast; I started eating as soon as we were comfortably ensconced in our seats, and did not stop until somewhere after Philadelphia. I remember it was Philadelphia because I was disappointed not to have passed by the Liberty Bell.

3 My mother had roasted two chickens and cut them up into dainty bite-size pieces. She packed slices of brown bread and butter and green pepper and carrot sticks. There were little violently yellow iced cakes with scalloped edges called "marigolds," that came from Cushman's Bakery. There was a spice bun and rock-cakes from Newton's, the West Indian bakery across Lenox Avenue from St. Mark's School, and iced tea in a wrapped mayonnaise jar. There were sweet pickles for us and dill pickles for my father, and peaches with the fuzz still on them, individually wrapped to keep them from bruising. And, for neatness, there were piles of napkins and a little tin box with a washcloth dampened with rosewater and glycerine for wiping sticky mouths.

4 I wanted to eat in the dining car because I had read all about them, but my mother reminded me for the umpteenth time that dining car food always cost too much money and besides, you never could tell whose hands had been playing all over that food, nor where those same hands had been just before. My mother never mentioned that Black people were not allowed into railroad dining cars headed south in 1947. As usual, whatever my mother did not like

and could not change, she ignored. Perhaps it would go away, deprived of her attention.

5 I learned later that Phyllis's high school senior class trip had been to Washington, but the nuns had given her back her deposit in private, explaining to her that the class, all of whom were white, except Phyllis, would be staying in a hotel where Phyllis "would not be happy," meaning, Daddy explained to her, also in private, that they did not rent rooms to Negroes. "We will take you to Washington, ourselves," my father had avowed, "and not just for an overnight in some measly fleabag hotel."

6 American racism was a new and crushing reality that my parents had to deal with every day of their lives once they came to this country. They handled it as a private woe. My mother and father believed that they could best protect their children from the realities of race in America and the fact of American racism by never giving them name, much less discussing their nature. We were told we must never trust white people, but why was never explained, nor the nature of their ill will. Like so many other vital pieces of information in my childhood, I was supposed to know without being told. It always seemed like a very strange injunction coming from my mother, who looked so much like one of those people we were never supposed to trust. But something always warned me not to ask my mother why she wasn't white, and why Auntie Lillah and Auntie Etta weren't, even though they were all that same problematic color so different from my father and me, even from my sisters, who were somewhere inbetween.

7 In Washington, D.C., we had one large room with two double beds and an extra cot for me. It was a back-street hotel that belonged to a friend of my father's who was in real estate, and I spent the whole next day after Mass squinting up at the Lincoln Memorial where Marian Anderson had sung after the D.A.R. refused to allow her to sing in their auditorium because she was Black. Or because she was "Colored," my father said as he told us the story. Except that what he probably said was "Negro," because for his times, my father was quite progressive.

8 I was squinting because I was in that silent agony that characterized all of my childhood summers, from the time school let out in June to the end of July, brought about by my dilated and vulnerable eyes exposed to the summer brightness.

9 I viewed Julys through an agonizing corolla of dazzling whiteness and I always hated the Fourth of July, even before I came to realize the travesty such a celebration was for Black people in this country.

10 My parents did not approve of sunglasses, nor of their expense.

11 I spent the afternoon squinting up at monuments to freedom and past presidencies and democracy, and wondering why the light and heat were both so much stronger in Washington, D.C., than back home in New York City. Even the pavement on the streets was a shade lighter in color than back home.

12 Late that Washington afternoon my family and I walked back down Pennsylvania Avenue. We were a proper caravan, mother bright and father brown,

the three of us girls step-standards in-between. Moved by our historical surroundings and the heat of the early evening, my father decreed yet another treat. He had a great sense of history, a flair for the quietly dramatic and the sense of specialness of an occasion and a trip.

13 "Shall we stop and have a little something to cool off, Lin?"

14 Two blocks away from our hotel, the family stopped for a dish of vanilla ice cream at a Breyer's ice cream and soda fountain. Indoors, the soda fountain was dim and fan-cooled, deliciously relieving to my scorched eyes.

15 Corded and crisp and pinafored, the five of us seated ourselves one by one at the counter. There was I between my mother and father, and my two sisters on the other side of my mother. We settled ourselves along the white mottled marble counter, and when the waitress spoke at first no one understood what she was saying, and so the five of us just sat there.

16 The waitress moved along the line of us closer to my father and spoke again. "I said I kin give you to take out, but you can't eat here. Sorry." Then she dropped her eyes looking very embarrassed, and suddenly we heard what it was she was saying all at the same time, loud and clear.

17 Straight-backed and indignant, one by one, my family and I got down from the counter stools and turned around and marched out of the store, and outraged, as if we had never been Black before. No one would answer my emphatic questions with anything other than a guilty silence. "But we hadn't done anything!" This wasn't right or fair! Hadn't I written poems about Bataan and freedom and democracy for all?

18 My parents wouldn't speak of this injustice, not because they had to accept it, but because they felt they should have anticipated it and avoided it. This made me even angrier. My fury was not going to be acknowledged by a like fury. Even my two sisters copied my parents' pretense that nothing unusual and anti-American had occurred. I was left to write my angry letter to the president of the united states all by myself, although my father did promise I could type it out on the office typewriter next week, after I showed it to him in my copybook diary.

19 The waitress was white, and the counter was white, and the ice cream I never ate in Washington, D.C. that summer I left childhood was white, and the white heat and the white pavement and the white stone monuments of my first Washington summer made me sick to my stomach for the whole rest of that trip and it wasn't much of a graduation present after all.

Here's how one reader applied our suggested reading strategies to her experience of reading this text.

1 *Locate* the main "thread" or topic.

The main thread in this essay is the author's reaction to a Fourth of July trip her family took to Washington, D.C., when she graduated from junior high. As an African American, Lorde finds her experience of the nation's capitol spoiled by the racism she and her family encounter when they stop for ice cream. The essay seems to be about the shock of recognizing how different she feels about herself, particularly about being "Black," after her trip when compared with how she felt before the trip. This thread is consistently evident and climaxes in the last line: "and the white stone monuments of my first Washington summer made me sick to my stomach for the whole rest of that trip . . ."

2 *Follow* this "thread."

Lorde begins her essay with a focus on her excitement about graduating from junior high and the prospect of visiting what she calls the "fabled" capitol. She has high expectations. She also knows that it is a transition point in her life—that she is "supposed to stop being a child." She wonders out loud about what her older sister, Phyllis, who also graduated, is "supposed to stop being." By the end of the essay, we see her grow from her negative experience—and it becomes both a memory she reflects upon as a young writer in her own diary, and, as well, a formative event that she chooses to write about as an adult.

3 *Determine what is new* or *given.*

What is "new" here is the seeing through Lorde's eyes how she discovered "color" as a factor in one's identity and how her parents did or didn't deal with this "discovery."

Lorde paints a picture of her parents as not preparing their daughters for the impact of racism on them as persons. She includes some very telling statements about her parents: "As usual, whatever my mother did not like and could not change, she ignored"; "But something always warned me not to ask my mother why she wasn't white . . ."; "Hadn't I written poems about Bataan and freedom and democracy for all!"; "We marched out . . . as if we had never been Black before." All of these sentences provide a window into her heart and help me understand better the experience, and not just the theory, of oppression that I have read in civics or history books.

What is "given" here is the basic notion of racism—a fact I know from other reading; the history of race relations not just during and after the Civil War, but of the 1950s and 1960s (twenty years before I was born!), is the context in which I read Lorde's essay. I am prepared to see "villains" but I was still shocked to hear once again how insensitive our culture had been. I, who got to see the end of apartheid in South Africa, still am surprised to be confronted by more anecdotes about our own apartheid in America.

4 *Characterize* this thread.

Lorde provides the reader with everyday detail that explains to the reader the anticipation and hope that accompanied her to Washington D.C. They "packed for a week" for their "mobile feast"; her mother "roasted two chickens and cut them up into dainty bite-sized pieces"; they brought "spice bun and rock-cakes" from a bakery. These elements provide very vivid images of her eighth-grade enthusiasm.

Later on, Lorde effectively shifts her point of view from this family preparation to the trip itself and her reflections on what her family had taught her about race in America, then on to the incident at the center of the essay—and the trip: the ice cream parlor, and then back to her family.

The repetition of the word "white" in the last paragraph drives home the point of how color became an issue for Lorde of great intensity thereafter—both her blackness and the whiteness of the privileged world to which she was refused entry.

5 *Evaluate* the overall credibility and force of the author's ideas and the position you are placed in by the text.

The title of the essay is ironic; for most Americans, at least white Americans, the Fourth of July represents a celebration of freedom, independence, and respect for country. Lorde's essay is a reminder and a challenge to us not to take for granted such freedoms, and to remember that not everyone is in a position to enjoy this "universal history" when they have been excluded from its benefit. The text places me, as part of the majority white culture, in the awkward position of wanting to identify with Lorde, amid proclaiming my innocence, but knowing that had I been in that era, I, too, might have "followed orders" and asked them to leave the ice cream parlor. The most chilling line in the essay comes toward the end: "Even my two sisters copied my parents' pretense that nothing unusual and anti-American had occurred." This means that racism could be taken for granted as part of the American landscape—part of the "Fourth of July"—and that her parents' basic strategy in dealing with it was unlike Dr. King's, a "passive nonresistance." Clearly, Audre Lorde learned to deal with it more effectively with her pen.

Critical Writing Strategies for Exploring and Understanding Your Own Ideas

Close, active reading alone will not necessarily result in a knowledgeable and authoritative ability to demonstrate what you have discovered to others. Reading and writing are interdependent and mutually beneficial activities that together provide you the best opportunity for understanding and evaluating the texts you read. Writing—along with public, classroom discussion—allows you to articulate and evaluate your discoveries, all the while measuring them against the readings others have given of the same material. In addition, it will allow you to become more aware of the strategies successful authors use to create meaning and achieve the effects they have on their readers. In the next 10 chapters of this textbook, you will encounter two kinds of writing tasks calculated to enrich your thinking about your reading.

First, at the end of each selection, you will find three sets of questions, each set designed to provoke a particular kind of reflection upon the respective text and to be recorded as a brief, paragraph-length response. Second, at the end of each chapter, you will find longer writing assignments that will assist you in synthesizing the varied ideas and contexts of the readings you've been assigned and in drawing conclusions about the cogency, impact, and relevance of these ideas for our times.

The shorter writing tasks attempt to focus your reading further, to prompt your expression, at least in part, of what you have already discovered in close reading, and to uncover what further insights may await you by having to put your thoughts on paper. These tasks thus allow you to explore, expand, and explain to yourself (as well as to debate with your classmates) the meanings and implications suggested by the texts you're asked to read. Their brevity and their focus permit you to complete your cycle of reading and reflecting with something concrete—something in writing that will potentially give your classroom discussion more substance and clarity.

The three modes or kinds of short writing tasks we employ are: *observing, evaluating,* and *responding and applying.* Writers use *observative questions* to probe a text, to clarify its meaning and intention, and to determine its main thesis and the implications of that thesis for the reader herself and for those in the text's original audience. An *observative text* will inevitably focus on the text itself, explaining as objectively as possible what it says—and why. *Evaluative questions* are employed by writers to argue in behalf of or against a particular point of view that is promoted or prompted by the text. An *evaluative text* "takes a stand"—marshalling evidence from the reading and the writer's own context to support a specific thesis, while anticipating possible objections and offering counter arguments to alternative views. *Responsive and application questions* allow the writer to respond directly to the readings in a personal way, deliberately examining his or her own feelings and associations, foregrounding them in a text, and applying the selection out of individual conviction and belief. A *responsive* or *applied text,* while informed and sensitive to context and to its audience, is a much more expressive attempt to react to or apply personally the ideas raised by a particular reading.

QUESTIONS FOR WRITING AND DISCUSSION

OBSERVING

1. How do Lorde's experiences as depicted in her essay clash with the expectations one might have for an essay entitled "Fourth of July"?
2. What signals are there that the title may be ironic?
3. How does Lorde use "color" in her essay as a symbol of privilege or exclusion?

EVALUATING

1. How does Lorde discover that the democratic principles on which her country is based, and which are symbolized in the monuments she encounters during her Washington, D.C., trip, may not apply to all peoples?
2. Do you believe her response to this discovery is appropriate? Why or why not?

RESPONDING AND APPLYING

1. What are your own memories of the Fourth of July?
2. What associations, common experiences, sensations of heritage and pride in the U.S.'s founding do you bring to Lorde's text?
3. How is the Fourth of July as an event or symbol changed or challenged by your experience of reading Lorde's text?

In summary, in the subsequent chapters of *Searching for Great Ideas* you will be asked to respond to these three kinds of short writing tasks, as illustrated in these about Audre Lorde's "Fourth of July."

Note that these categories of questions provide the basis for sound reading and interpretation of texts: *observative* questions ask for close reading, analysis, synthesis; *evaluative* questions ask for judgments, inferences, implications; *responsive* questions ask for personal thoughts and application of your discoveries to your own life.

How would *you* respond to these three types of questions?

The combination of the five reading strategies mentioned earlier and your completion of the three kinds of exploratory writing tasks will assist you in your continuing search for great ideas.

Let the search begin.

Chapter Preview

Chapter 2

CONFRONTING HISTORY: THE QUESTION OF MORAL DECLINE

The Closing of the Thompson Street Pool

Adam Gopnik

1 A Downtown friend writes:

2 Over on Thompson Street, about three blocks from where I live, there is a small outdoor pool for children: not exactly a wading pool, but hardly a swimming pool, either—the kind of pool that is known in New York as a "mini-pool." It's set in the middle of a chain-link-fenced asphalt playground on the northwest corner of Thompson and Spring. Across the street, on the east side of Thompson, are a Korean market and a chic-baby-clothing store and the rear entrance of 420 West Broadway—the famous five-story building that houses the Castelli, Sonnabend, and other galleries. A couple of basketball courts in the playground fill up every day at the end of school, and in summer fill up all day long; the kids who play here look a lot more proficient than the Knicks. There is also an open space where people bang tennis balls against a wall or play baseball with a soft rubber ball or just kick a soccer ball around. Once, I saw about fifteen Senegalese—you could tell they were Senegalese by their taut, angular look and their lilting French accents—arrive and try to play a soccer game, in about a twentieth of the space required. And then there is the pool; it sits up on a kind of dais, just behind and above the basketball courts.

3 What has always impressed me about the mothers and children who frequent the pool is how *still* they are. The children don't have the wired, joyful quality of the kids you see playing in fire-hydrant spray. Instead, the children and their mothers seem set in a frieze of elegant poses, like mothers and children on a tiny European beach. The pool itself is off-limits to grownups; we are not mini enough. When my wife and I first moved to the neighborhood, though, we used to look at the pool a little longingly on hot summer nights.

Back then, we couldn't afford to go away on weekends often, so on a Friday or Saturday night we'd get a couple of sodas and some pizza and just sit down on a bench outside the playground. "Benchampton," we called it.

4 The other evening, very late, we came back from Montauk on the Hampton Jitney and took a taxi home. Lower Broadway seemed filthier and more sordid than I had ever remembered it, or had imagined that it could be: the only people on the street were three homeless men, pushing their shopping carts from one garbage pile to another and dodging the indifferent traffic as they searched for cans. A single, self-confident rat waltzed down the street behind them. As we went up the steps of our building, we saw that someone had posted a sign there announcing that the Thompson Street pool was going to be closed by the city unless the community could raise twenty-five thousand dollars to keep it open. The sign also said that Anthony Dapolito would be collecting checks, over at the Vesuvio Bakery. First thing Monday morning, I went around to see Mr. Dapolito. On the way, I walked up Thompson Street, and saw that the pool was open, and was crowded, as usual.

5 The Vesuvio is a family bakery, and has been at 160 Prince Street for seventy-one years; the bread is very good, and very cheap—forty-five cents for a five-ounce loaf. (All its bread is still sold by the pound.) When I told Mr. Dapolito that I was from the neighborhood, he began to reminisce about the Broome Street stoopball team, back in the days when each block had its own stoopball style. (Our block's was to make up with craftiness what we lacked in power.) Then he explained what had happened to the Thompson Street pool. "I've been involved in the community forever," he said. "And I'm now its representative to the Parks Commission. Cuts came, and in June they said, 'We gotta close all the outdoor pools.' Well, then somebody turned up with money for the big pools, but all thirty-three mini-pools in the city had to be closed. I couldn't believe it. I mean, how are you going to have a summer without the pool? So a woman, Enid Braun, who's active in the community, asked them how much it would cost to keep the pool open for the summer. They said that it would be twenty-five thousand dollars. I said, 'Suppose we raise half, just enough to keep it going for a month.' The response has been fantastic. We got five, six thousand right away from local people and the local restaurants, and then Betsy Gotbaum, the Parks Commissioner, found a couple of thousand. We had the pool open again by July 6th. Right now, we've got enough money to keep it open until the middle of August, so things are looking O.K." He paused, his enthusiasm suddenly deflating, and then said, "Of course, the whole thing is past aggravation by now. You just feel helpless."

6 Twenty-five thousand dollars is not a lot of money. In SoHo, for example, twenty-five thousand dollars will buy you hardly any of the things that the neighborhood is famous around the world for. It will only get you fractions of those things, what the economists call "notional" properties: a quarter of a David Salle; about a hundred and fifty square feet of living space. Look beyond the neighborhood to the city as a whole and that twenty-five thousand dollars becomes even more insignificant: about two and a third innings pitched by Doc

Gooden, a dozen points by Patrick Ewing, less than a minute of "Miss Saigon." And look beyond the city to the country, and you see twenty-five thousand dollars gone in a few seconds of the flight of a Tomahawk cruise missile, or paying two hundred-thousandths of the cost of a Stealth bomber. I wonder if there is a bathroom in the palace of the al-Sabah family, whom we all chipped in to rescue, with fittings that cost less than twenty-five thousand dollars.

7 We are not poor as a people, yet somehow we have become bankrupt as a society. We are—to use an old-fashioned word—*ruined.* And yet how this ruin is possible—how it has come about—no one can explain. Our wealth may no longer be unlimited, but we surely remain a society of plenty. There is still plenty on our tables and on our roads. Plenty runs the Hampton Jitney, and stocks the Grand Union up on LaGuardia Place. But we have come to accept that in our public lives violence, impoverishment, squalor, and cruelty will rule, and that the most we can do is to keep them at bay until the middle of next month. We seem to have accepted two separate economies: one of abundance, ruling the way that many of us eat and sleep and entertain ourselves, and one of absolute hand-to-mouth impoverishment, ruling our civic life. I wrote out a check for Mr. Dapolito to help keep the Thompson Street pool open. By my reckoning, it should pay for about fifteen minutes worth of community.

QUESTIONS FOR WRITING AND DISCUSSION

OBSERVING

1. What do we learn about the writer's background, attitudes, and values?
2. What kind of neighborhood does the writer describe?

EVALUATING

1. Why is the writer concerned about the closing of the pool?
2. Why does the writer say that $25,000 is not a lot of money? Do you agree? What does paragraph 5 tell you about the writer's values, about what's important to him?
3. State the content of the last paragraph in your own words.
4. Explain what the writer is saying about the bankruptcy of our culture. Do you think he is right?

RESPONDING AND APPLYING

1. How would you measure the moral climate of a society? Against what standards would you judge the health of a culture? What minimum conditions of living would you require of the "good" society?

2. On a scale of 1 - 10, where 10 is best, how would you judge the effectiveness of our own society? Consider things like poverty, ignorance, injustice, abortion, the family, prejudice, illegitimacy, violence, and unemployment.
3. Those who state we have fallen into a moral state of decay imply that we have an admirable moral heritage to lose. If you agree, how would you describe that heritage?

The story of the Thompson Street pool is one small part of our nation's quest to heal itself. By writing the narrative, Adam Gopnik bears witness to an inequity in our society and, by inference, calls for change. Virtually no one who reads a daily newspaper or watches the evening news can escape the alarming possibility that our society is in a state of despair and decline. The incessant incidents of violence and crime (40% higher than they were a decade ago), of urban and family crisis (the numbers of illegitimate births continue to climb), and of prejudice and hatred are so disturbing that many of us opt to change the channel or flip to the sports page. Former Senator Robert Dole, the Republican majority leader during much of the 1990s, refers to media images of sex and violence as "nightmares of depravity . . . that undermine our character as a nation." Senator Richard Lugar calls the spread of gambling "a measure of the moral erosion taking place in our country" (*New York Times,* 14 Sept. 1995:A15).

The Chicago Tribune, in a series from summer 1995, reported that the erosion of the middle class is one sign of "a decaying civilization" corroding from its core (R. C. Longworth). To support his views, Longworth reports the growing numbers of poor: 18.5% of all families with children live in poverty now, compared with 11.4% in 1973. And the rich keep growing in number: the number of Americans earning more than $500,000 rose by 10 times in the 1980s, with inflation taken into account. Blue-collar wages have lagged inflation for 20 years, while divorce continues to soar. Downsizing of corporations and businesses is eroding job security.

Our youth are also in trouble. A recent Carnegie Foundation study found that one of five adolescents is growing up in poverty and one-half will live with only one parent at some time in their lives. Educational levels of eighth graders have remained stagnant, even though education needs in the workplace are increasing. And the suicide and homicide rates for those 10 - 14 years of age more than doubled from 1985 - 1992. What's more, young people demand counseling services more than any other group and most say they have no personal experience of lifelong committed relationships. Most feel overwhelmed by problems they feel they have inherited and are now being asked to resolve.

If these figures are not enough to depress you, consider the problems of African Americans. The infant death rate is twice as high as for white Americans. Blacks in inner cities, with a degenerating infrastructure, face inferior schools, joblessness, victimization by criminals, and squalor in their surroundings. Another study just found that one in three black men in their 20s are under supervision of the criminal justice system on any given day; four years ago, a similar study found one in four black men between the ages of 20 and 29 in prison, on parole, or supervised. Marc Mauer, the principal author of the report, said, "If one in three young white men were under criminal justice supervision, the nation would declare a national emergency" (*New York Times,* 5 Oct. 1995:A8). Perhaps the Million Man March of October 1995 led by Louis Farrakhan was just the beginning of that declaration.

The hunger for the moral society seems to take two forms. The liberals seek to right what they see as inequities based on race, gender, and class. They seek greater forms of tolerance, not to mention remedy, for the groups that have traditionally been pushed outside the mainstream, including women, gays and lesbians, and people of color. The conservatives seek a return of what they see as traditional values, including a strengthening of the family, a return of prayer in the schools, and an end to abortion.

For Charles Dickens, over a century ago, it was the best and worst of times. Many today feel that the worst has not only persisted, it has grown in ferocity, and they are tempted either to take drastic action to correct what they see as wrong or to become cynical and hopeless. In a recent *New Yorker* article, Michael Kelly describes one hopeful sign in relation to this supposed crisis: that the two sides described above may find convergence on a number of issues, such as the excesses of gangsta rap or pornography on the Internet:

> In this convergence, the moral society is one that allows all its citizens—and not just its upper-class ones—to lead decent lives. It is a society that protects people from violent crime, provides a healthy atmosphere in which to raise and educate children, affords working-class people housing in clean, safe neighborhoods, and recognizes the traditional family as the essential social unit. The moral society is unified by a shared commitment to civic responsibility and by common values that are rooted in religion and patriotism. It balances rights with responsibilities, and is not afraid to be judgmental—to demand that people adhere to a high standard of behavior. (*New Yorker* 17 July 1995:27–8)

Whether these times pose moral crises that are indeed unique or unprecedented, we are obligated to ask how this state came to pass and what we can do about it. Whether it is the strident voices that erupt around race relations, the increasing gap between rich and poor, or the alarming numbers of abortions and children born out of wedlock, we must investigate these moral questions and search for answers.

The readings in this chapter invite us to look in more depth at the question of moral decline. We do this not because we necessarily believe what these authors are saying, that we are in an unprecedented state of moral collapse. Rather, we want to pose the larger questions of whether things are really that much worse, what forces led us away from a "better" world (or to the perception that our world is so much worse than it used to be), how we can respond, and how study of the past can help us move toward social healing.

The opening reading is Peter Applebome's report of a Carnegie Corporation study, noting a disturbing failure by society to protect children and adolescents from poverty, violence, suicide, pregnancy, AIDS, and ignorance. If our children are victims of our worst faults, what does that bode for the future?

The second piece is the introduction from William Bennett's national bestseller, *The Book of Virtues: A Treasury of Moral Stories.* Currently codirector of Empower America, an organization "dedicated to preserving conservative principles and ideas," Bennett has led the fight to put an end to what many call moral decay. Recently, for example, he attacked Time-Warner's music division for the gangsta-rap music that contained lyrics advocating violence. *The Book of Virtues* is one of Bennett's attempts to reassert "moral literacy" at a time when schools, homes, and churches are having difficulties. In the final article, Howard Fineman of *Newsweek* profiles several "Virtuecrats," Bennett among them, in our nation's "yearning for civility."

Study Says Society Fails 19 Million Youths

Peter Applebome

1 At a time when there is widespread concern about the well-being of young children and the social problems of teen-agers, some 19 million young adolescents in between are increasingly falling between the cracks of society, according to a report by the Carnegie Corporation that was made public yesterday.

2 The report, entitled "Great Transitions: Preparing Adolescents for a New Century," said that young adolescents are facing critical decisions about their health, education and safety at ever younger ages and that society is failing to help them avoid dangers ranging from AIDS to suicide and from teen-age pregnancy to dropping out of school.

3 "What we tried to do was marshal statistics, push this out front and try to get people to really focus on the problems of early adolescence," said Ruby Takanishi, executive director of the Carnegie Council on Adolescent Development, which prepared the report over the last 10 years. "Everything in it argues that early adolescence, the years from 10 to 14, are much more risky business than they used to be."

4 The report says that one-third of 13-year-olds acknowledge that they have used illicit drugs, that educational achievement levels of eighth graders have remained stagnant while the educational needs of the workplace have increased, that the homicide rate for those 10 to 14 years of age more than doubled from 1985 to 1992 and that self-destructive violence, particularly the suicide rate, more than doubled from 1980 to 1992.

5 The report found that one of five adolescents are growing up in poverty and that one in two will live with only one parent at home at some time in their lives.

6 It calls for changes in schools, community services and family involvement to better meet the needs of young adolescents.

7 But David A. Hamburg, president of the Carnegie Corporation, said the main purpose of the report was to focus attention on what he said was the least studied and least understood phase of human development.

8 "This is the first comprehensive study of this age group," he said. "It has been the neglected phase, low on research priorities, low on educational priorities, low on service priorities. If I had to sum up what it's about, it would be in two words: neglected opportunities.

9 In education, the report called for smaller, more personal middle schools, even if that only meant breaking up large impersonal school buildings into smaller, more manageable units. It cited the successes of educational programs that use interdisciplinary approaches to study broad areas and integrate various disciplines rather than narrowly focused ones.

10 The report called for a much stronger life sciences program that could meet both the intellectual and the personal health needs of young adolescents. It called the health and life science curriculum "the weakest link in middle grade school reform," and urged the development of "one-stop" centers for counseling or health information at or near schools.

11 Smoking among eighth graders, defined as those who had smoked a cigarette within 30 days of the time they were polled, rose by 30 percent from 1991 to 1994, to 18.6 percent. Marijuana use more than doubled, to 13 percent. The firearms homicide rate more than doubled from 1985 to 1992, to 1.9 per 100,000 from eight-tenths of 1 percent. For black males, the rate increased to 8.4 per 100,000 from 3 in the same period.

12 Dr. Hamburg said it was clear that youngsters in inner city areas and poverty areas are far more vulnerable than those in more affluent areas. The report noted that by the year 2000, more than one-third of all young adolescents will be members of racial or ethnic minorities.

13 But he said the concerns and risks were common to all youths, particularly at a time of rising economic displacement, when parents are increasingly likely to work outside the home and only half of the nation's children can expect to grow up in an intact two-parent household.

14 Dr. Hamburg said that most of the report's recommendations could be put into effect through the redeployment of existing resources rather than the

addition of new ones, and that rigid analysis of which programs work would be necessary to justify additional expenditures in the current environment.

15 "We didn't put this in terms of utopian or hypothetical ideals," he said. "Generally, we can cite 5 or 10 or 20 examples of things that work, but it's on a scale that's much smaller than the nation requires."

QUESTIONS FOR WRITING AND DISCUSSION

OBSERVING

1. What are the most critical conclusions of the Carnegie Study?
2. Why did Carnegie study the young?

EVALUATING

1. What forces and events in our history do you think might have led to those changes? Which are cited in the article?
2. Why do you think adolescents have been neglected when it comes to research studies?
3. What solutions does Dr. Hamburg suggest and do you find them realistic?

RESPONDING AND APPLYING

1. Where would you put local, state, or national resources to solve the problems cited?

Introduction from The Book of Virtues

William J. Bennett

1 This book is intended to aid in the time-honored task of the moral education of the young. Moral education—the training of heart and mind toward the good—involves many things. It involves rules and precepts—the *do*s and *don't*s of life with others—as well as explicit instruction, exhortation, and training. Moral education *must* provide training in good habits. Aristotle wrote that good habits formed at youth make all the difference. And moral education must affirm the central importance of moral example. It has been said that there is nothing

more influential, more determinant, in a child's life than the moral power of quiet example. For children to take morality seriously they must be in the presence of adults who take morality seriously. And with their own eyes they must see adults take morality seriously.

2 Along with precept, habit, and example, there is also the need for what we might call moral literacy. The stories, poems, essays, and other writing presented here are intended to help children achieve this moral literacy. The purpose of this book is to show parents, teachers, students, and children what the virtues look like, what they are in practice, how to recognize them, and how they work.

3 This book, then, is a "how to" book for moral literacy. If we want our children to possess the traits of character we most admire, we need to teach them what those traits are and why they deserve both admiration and allegiance. Children must learn to identify the forms and content of those traits. They must achieve at least a minimal level of moral literacy that will enable them to make sense of what they see in life and, we may hope, help them live it well.

4 Where do we go to find the material that will help our children in this task? The simple answer is we don't have to reinvent the wheel. We have a wealth of material to draw on—material that virtually all schools and homes and churches once taught to students for the sake of shaping character. That many no longer do so is something this book hopes to change.

5 The vast majority of Americans share a respect for certain fundamental traits of character: honesty, compassion, courage, and perseverance. These are virtues. But because children are not born with this knowledge, they need to learn what these virtues are. We can help them gain a grasp and appreciation of these traits by giving children material to read about them. We can invite our students to discern the moral dimensions of stories, of historical events, of famous lives. There are many wonderful stories of virtue and vice with which our children should be familiar. This book brings together some of the best, oldest, and most moving of them.

6 Do our children know these stories, these works? Unfortunately, many do not. They do not because in many places we are no longer teaching them. It is time we take up that task again. We do so for a number of reasons.

7 First, these stories, unlike courses in "moral reasoning," give children some specific reference points. Our literature and history are a rich quarry of moral literacy. We should mine that quarry. Children must have at their disposal a stock of examples illustrating what we see to be right and wrong, good and bad—examples illustrating that, in many instances, what is morally right and wrong can indeed be known and promoted.

8 Second, these stories and others like them are fascinating to children. Of course, the pedagogy (and the material herein) will need to be varied according to students' levels of comprehension, but you can't beat these stories when it comes to engaging the attention of a child. Nothing in recent years, on television or anywhere else, has improved on a good story that begins "Once upon a time . . ."

9 Third, these stories help anchor our children in their culture, its history and traditions. Moorings and anchors come in handy in life; moral anchors and moorings have never been more necessary.

10 Fourth, in teaching these stories we engage in an act of renewal. We welcome our children to a common world, a world of shared ideals, to the community of moral persons. In that common world we invite them to the continuing task of preserving the principles, the ideals, and the notions of goodness and greatness we hold dear.

11 The reader scanning this book may notice that it does not discuss issues like nuclear war, abortion, creationism, or euthanasia. This may come as a disappointment to some. But the fact is that the formation of character in young people is educationally a different task from, and a prior task to, the discussion of the great, difficult ethical controversies of the day. First things first. And planting the ideas of virtue, of good traits in the young, comes first. In the moral life, as in life itself, we take one step at a time. Every field has its complexities and controversies. And so too does ethics. And every field has its basics. So too with values. This is a book in the basics. The tough issues can, if teachers and parents wish, be taken up later. And, I would add, a person who is morally literate will be immeasurably better equipped than a morally illiterate person to reach a reasoned and ethically defensible position on these tough issues. But the formation of character and the teaching of moral literacy come first, in the early years; the tough issues come later, in senior high school or after.

12 Similarly, the task of teaching moral literacy and forming character is not political in the usual meaning of the term. People of good character are not all going to come down on the same side of difficult political and social issues. Good people—people of character and moral literacy—can be conservative, and good people can be liberal. We must not permit our disputes over thorny political questions to obscure the obligation we have to offer instruction to all our young people in the area in which we have, as a society, reached a consensus: namely, on the importance of good character, and on some of its pervasive particulars. And that is what this book provides: a compendium of great stories, poems, and essays from the stock of human history and literature. It embodies common and time-honored understandings of these virtues. It is for everybody—all children, of all political and religious backgrounds, and it speaks to them on a more fundamental level than race, sex, and gender. It addresses them as human beings—as moral agents.

13 Every American child ought to know at least some of the stories and poems in this book. Every American parent and teacher should be familiar with some of them, too. I know that some of these stories will strike some contemporary sensibilities as too simple, too corny, too old-fashioned. But they will not seem so to the child, especially if he or she has never seen them before. And I believe that if adults take this book and read it in a quiet place, alone, away from distorting standards, they will find themselves enjoying some of this old, simple, "corny" stuff. The stories we adults used to know and forgot—or the stories we never did know but perhaps were supposed to know—are here. (Quick!—

what did Horatius do on the bridge? What is the sword of Damocles? The answers are in this book.) This is a book of lessons and reminders.

14 In putting this book together I learned many things. For one, going through the material was a mind-opening and encouraging rediscovery for me. I recalled great stories that I had forgotten. And thanks to the recommendations of friends, teachers, and the able prodding of my colleagues in this project, I came to know stories I had not known before. And, I discovered again how much books and education have changed in thirty years. In looking at this "old stuff" I am struck by how different it is from so much of what passes for literature and entertainment today.

15 Most of the material in this book speaks without hesitation, without embarrassment, to the inner part of the individual, to the moral sense. Today we speak about values and how it is important to "have them," as if they were beads on a string or marbles in a pouch. But these stories speak to morality and virtues not as something to be possessed, but as the central part of human nature, not as something to have but as something to be, the most important thing to be. To dwell in these chapters is to put oneself, through the imagination, into a different place and time, a time when there was little doubt that children are essentially moral and spiritual beings and that the central task of education is virtue. This book reminds the reader of a time—not so long ago—when the verities were the moral verities. It is thus a kind of antidote to some of the distortions of the age in which we now live. I hope parents will discover that reading this book with or to children can deepen their own, and their children's, understanding of life and morality. If the book reaches that high purpose it will have been well worth the effort.

16 A few additional notes and comments are in order. Although the book is titled *The Book of Virtues*—and the chapters are organized by virtues—it is also very much a book of vices. Many of the stories and poems illustrate a virtue in reverse. For children to know about virtue they must know about its opposite.

17 In telling these stories I am interested more in the moral than the historic lesson. In some of the older stories—Horatius at the bridge, William Tell, George Washington and the cherry tree—the line between legend and history has been blurred. But it is the instruction in the moral that matters. Some of the history that is recounted here may not meet the standards of the exacting historian. But we tell these familiar stories as they were told before, in order to preserve their authenticity.

18 Furthermore, I should stress that this book is by no means a definitive collection of great moral stories. Its contents have been defined in part by my attempt to present some material, most of which is drawn from the corpus of Western Civilization, that American schoolchildren, once upon a time, knew by heart. And the project, like any other, has faced several practical limitations such as space and economy (the rights to reprint recent stories and translations can be very expensive, while older material often lies in the public domain). The quarry of wonderful literature from our culture and others is deep, and I

have barely scratched the surface. I invite readers to send me favorite stories not printed here, in case I should attempt to renew or improve this effort sometime in the future.

19 This volume is not intended to be a book one reads from cover to cover. It is, rather, a book for browsing, for marking favorite passages, for reading aloud to family, for memorizing pieces here and there. It is my hope that parents and teachers will spend some time wandering through these pages, discovering or rediscovering some moral landmarks, and in turn pointing them out to the young. The chapters can be taken in any order; on certain days we need reminding of some virtues more than others. A quick look at the Contents will steer the reader in the sought-after direction.

20 The reader will notice that in each chapter the material progresses from the very easy to the more difficult. The early material in each chapter can be read aloud to, or even by, very young children. As the chapter progresses greater reading and conceptual proficiency are required. Nevertheless we urge younger readers to work their way through as far as possible. As children grow older they can reach for the more difficult material in the book. They can grow up (and perhaps even grow better!) with this book.

21 Finally, I hope this is an encouraging book. There is a lot we read of or experience in life that is not encouraging. This book, I hope, does otherwise. I hope it encourages; I hope it points us to "the better angels of our nature." This book reminds us of what is important. And it should help us lift our eyes. St. Paul wrote, "Whatever is true, whatever is honorable, whatever is right, whatever is pure, whatever is lovely, whatever is of good repute, if there is any excellence and anything worthy of praise, let your mind dwell on these things."

22 I hope readers will read this book and dwell on those things.

QUESTIONS FOR WRITING AND DISCUSSION

OBSERVING

1. What is the process of moral instruction, according to Bennett? How does he say one learns moral lessons, or fails to?
2. What moves Bennett to offer moral instruction?
3. Midway into Bennett's introduction to his book, he imagines a "moral sense" we used to have. What do you think he means?

EVALUATING

1. "Do as I say, not as I do" is a popular parental refrain. What does it mean and does it work? How successful is moral precept and moral admonition? Is there a difference between the two?

2. Bennett says we no longer are teaching stories of virtues and vice. Why might that be true? What might have taken their place? Some might know of educator E. D. Hirsch's attempts to respond to this crisis, or of Ted Sizer's Coalition for Essential Schools.
3. What moves Bennett to avoid what he calls the "political"? Do you think this is wise?
4. Using various literatures for deeply moral purposes is and has been one of the foundations of schooling. Why do you think Bennett's book has caught on at this time, when schooling for moral and liberal education is not by any means society's rallying call now?

RESPONDING AND APPLYING

1. Do you think stories, poems, and essays can succeed in moral education? Can you give examples of ways they can and have? What other kinds of moral education can you imagine?
2. What do you think Bennett means when he says good stories speak to our "moral sense"?

The Virtuecrats

Howard Fineman

1 Bill Bennett has to go, has to finish this interview in his office near the White House, has to catch a plane. Another week, another round of speeches, some big-buck and corporate, some public and political. Everyone wants a piece of him, and he's glad to oblige. His "Book of Virtues" remains hot beyond expectation: about a million hardcover copies in print. He's now a cottage industry of character education—a multimedia McGuffey. First, there is to be a sequel. "Maybe I'll call it 'Son of the Book of Virtues'," he jokes. Then, a series of virtue-teaching textbooks (elementary, junior high, senior high). Finally, inevitably, a deal in Hollywood, that precinct of sin that suddenly sees a market in virtue. Bennett will produce stories for film and television. "Some dramatizations, some animation," he says. The studio execs wanted to buy the right to "Virtue." He refused. He wants to write, maybe host: the Alistair Cooke of character ed. "I've got to maintain quality control," Bennett explains. "You can't crap this stuff up."

2 Certainly not: you must do right by virtue. After years of drilling dry holes, the former Reagan-era everything (chief of the humanities endowment, drug

czar, secretary of education) has hit a gusher. The fraying of America's social fabric—once considered the crotchety preoccupation of the cultural right—has become a national (even liberal) obsession. From the East Side of Manhattan to West L.A., Americans are agreeing that there are universally accepted principles of good character—"virtues" in Bennett's parlance—and that society is failing to teach them anymore.

3 Chaos, or the fear of it, has made Americans nostalgic for a more orderly age. The economy's perking along nicely, the world is more or less at peace, yet, in a new NEWSWEEK Poll, 76 percent of adults agree that "the United States is in moral and spiritual decline," and crime and drug abuse rank far ahead of jobs and health care as national concerns. The yearning for civility surfaces at town meetings. Democratic Rep. Ben Cardin of Maryland convened one near Baltimore recently. He had wanted to talk about the crime bill and health-care legislation. But voters in the high-school "multimedia center" (they don't call them libraries anymore) wanted to discuss something else. "No one today lives by the rules we were raised on," said one suburban mother in a sweat suit. "What happened to decency and respect?"

4 The craving for virtue goes beyond the debate over whose values are best—traditional families or single parents, gays or straights, Jews or Christians, black or white. It now seems painfully clear to most Americans that none of the traditional institutions is doing the job. Parents are absent or busy. "Neighbor" has been lost in the 'hood. "I Remember Mama" is long gone, replaced by Madonna music videos. Even religious institutions often seem more concerned with group grievances than individual behavior. Baby boomers, facing mortality and the even more frightening prospect of teenage kids, are finding that there is at least one absolute after all: good character.

5 The virtue crusade is creating a new kind of politics that could dominate the decade if economic or foreign crises don't intervene. It's already produced a new class of leaders from across the political spectrum—call them Virtuecrats—who view the formation of good character as an urgent aim of government. They are pushing politics away from world affairs and economics into something more personal, trying to win votes by vowing to erase a new kind of deficit. "The New Frontier of the '90s is an inner one," declares former Republican speechwriter and author Peggy Noonan. It doesn't seem to bother Virtuecrats that Americans decry the ethics lapses of the same government they are calling on to inculcate virtue. "It's just another example of the central paradox of our time," says White House aide William Galston, who wrote a prescient book called "Liberal Purposes" in 1991. "People hate the government, but they keep asking it to do things."

6 Nationally, Virtuecrats may be setting the stage for a Role Model candidacy that would seem to rule out the usual suspects in politics. For many Virtuecrats, the man of the moment is the presumptively virtuous Colin Powell. In the NEWSWEEK Poll, the retired general ranks just below Billy Graham as a role

model: 60 percent regard Powell as "excellent or good" in that regard, compared with 40 percent who see Clinton that way. And Powell is writing a memoir, due out next summer, which will be loaded with the character-building lessons of his up-from-the-ghetto life. "There's a huge amount of interest in Powell," says GOP strategist William Kristol, who was chief of staff to a founding Virtuecrat, former vice president Dan Quayle. "Colin Powell is a man of character, a straight arrow. And his military background gives him a claim to speak with authority."

7 Luckily for the Clintons, Bennett—and probably Powell—you don't have to score a perfect 10 in virtue to join in the crusade. Actually, a lack of shame could be an advantage. For Hillary, a "meaningful" life apparently includes reaping huge profits on the futures market with the help of friends. Ollie North won the GOP nomination for the Senate in Virginia last week by talking about family and character. At least to Republican conventioneers, it didn't seem to matter that he's an admitted liar and that a jury had found him guilty of shredding documents and illegally accepting a security system for his house. "It's not the politician's own character that gets him credit," says Mike Murphy, North's media adviser. "It's whether he's willing to stand up and *say* there is a moral crisis—in illegitimacy, crime, education."

8 Character crusades have occurred before in American politics. The public-school movement of the 1830s was launched in the name of civic virtue. Land-grant colleges were funded in the name not just of science but of "moral education," Bennett and Galston say. The most famous—and disastrous—effort to use government to make people virtuous was, of course, the temperance movement. It was launched at a time of social upheaval after the Revolution. The culmination was Prohibition, which lasted from 1919 to 1933, when the New Deal made filling jobs the paramount task of government.

9 Sobriety is easier to measure than good character. And specifying universal, incontestable standards of "virtue" isn't as simple as it seems from a glance at the Boy Scout manual. "Everybody's going to endorse these notions but defining them will create huge battles," predicts Yale law professor Stephen Carter. Virtuecrats are trying. In 1992, a group of educators and philosophers met in the mountains of Colorado and produced something they called the Aspen Declaration. It listed "Six Core Elements of Character" that should be inculcated by all "youth-influencing institutions": trustworthiness (including honesty and loyalty), respect, responsibility (including self-discipline and hard work), fairness, caring (compassion) and citizenship (including "obeying laws, staying informed and voting"). Bennett's list is similar, but with important additions: courage and faith; the latter, he says diplomatically, can be neutrally described as "reverence."

QUESTIONS FOR WRITING AND DISCUSSION

OBSERVING

1. What prompts the apparent national interest in virtue, according to Fineman?
2. What does history tell us about the success of moral crusades?

EVALUATING

1. Fineman presents "good character" as an "absolute"—what do you think he means?
2. What's the best way to attack moral decay, assuming it's spreading at an accelerating pace or is at an alarming level? What political, religious, or social means would you suggest?
3. Fineman examines the paradox where, according to a government official, we "hate the government" but "keep asking it to do things." Why do you think this might be true? What role do you think government can play in responding to moral problems? What is the role of the individual and private sector?

RESPONDING AND APPLYING

1. Based on your own experience, do you see a decline or absence of decency and respect? What basis do you have for comparison? Have you heard about our moral decline from adults, teachers, and parents? Have you seen it?
2. What persons, in public and private life, have acted as models in your own moral development? How responsive are you to the crusading spirit described in the article? Do you think the popularity of religious groups on and off campus is a sign of a return to morality? Do you see dangers therein?

CHAPTER WRITING ASSIGNMENTS

1. It's hard to open a newspaper or magazine and not see references to our society's moral decay. Do a study of various forms of media, including electronic. Where do you see claims of moral decline? Where do you see assertions of moral strength?
2. Do you accept the inference that we are in a state of moral decay? Why? Do you think our problems are really worse than those of peoples living in the past?
3. As you look at our culture, consider what kinds of persons we valorize. Besides rock musicians and sports stars, who do we look up to? And why? What values seem to undergird our construction of heroes?

4. Think about the moral content of your own education. Bennett would have us think more about the moral precepts and models that lead people to act morally. When, if ever, in school did you develop a moral sense? What classes or books helped you do this?

CHAPTER PREVIEW

Chapter Prelude
Tom Wolfe, "The Great Relearning Heralds the 21st Century"

Introductory Essay

Readings
Arthur Schlesinger, Jr., "The Challenge of Change"
Linda Simon, "The Naked Source"
Peter Burke, "What Is the New History?"
Judith Miller, from "One, by One, by One: Remembering the Holocaust"

Story
Steven Schwartz, "Madagascar"

Chapter Writing Assignments

Chapter 3

THE USES OF HISTORY: HOW WE LEARN FROM THE PAST

The Great Relearning Heralds 21st Century

Tom Wolfe

1 In 1968, in San Francisco, I came across a curious footnote to the psychedelic movement. At the Haight-Ashbury Free Clinic there were doctors who were treating diseases no living doctor had ever encountered before, diseases that had disappeared so long ago they had never even picked up Latin names, diseases such as the mange, the grunge, the itch, the twitch, the thrush, the scroff, the rot.

2 Why had they now returned? It had to do with the fact that thousands of young men and women had migrated to San Francisco to live communally in what I think history will record as one of the most extraordinary religious experiments of all time.

3 The hippies, as they became known, sought nothing less than to sweep aside all codes and restraints of the past and start out from zero. At one point Ken Kesey organized a pilgrimage to Stonehenge with the idea of returning to Anglo-Saxon civilization's point zero, which he figured was Stonehenge, and heading out all over again to do it better. Among the codes and restraints that people in the communes swept aside—quite purposely—were those that said you shouldn't use other people's toothbrushes or sleep on other people's mattresses without changing the sheets, or, as was more likely, without using any sheets at all or that you and five other people shouldn't drink from the same bottle of Shasta or take *tokes* from the same cigarette. And now, in 1968, they were relearning the laws of hygiene . . . by getting the mange, the grunge, the itch, the twitch, the thrush, the scroff, the rot.

4 This process, namely the relearning—following a Promethean and unprecedented start from zero—seems to be the *leitmotif* of our current interlude, here in the dying years of the 20th century.

5 "Start from zero" was the slogan of the Bauhaus School. The story of how the Bauhaus, a tiny artists' movement in Germany in the 1920s, swept aside the architectural styles of the past and created the glassbox face of the modern American city is a familiar one, and I won't retell it. But I should mention the soaring spiritual exuberance with which the movement began, the passionate conviction of the Bauhaus's leader, Walter Gropius, that by starting from zero in architecture and design man could free himself from the dead hand of the past. By the late 1970s, however, architects themselves were beginning to complain of the dead hand of the Bauhaus: The flat roofs, which leaked from rain and collapsed from snow, the tiny bare beige office cubicles, which made workers feel like component parts, the glass walls, which let in too much heat, too much cold, too much glare, and no air at all.

6 The relearning is now under way in earnest. The architects are busy rummaging about in what New York painter Richard Merkin calls the Big Closet. Inside the Big Closet, in promiscuous heaps, are the abandoned styles of the past. The current favorite rediscoveries: Classical, Secession, and Moderne (Art Deco). Relearning on the wing, the architects are off on a binge of eclecticism comparable to the Victorian period a century ago.

7 In politics, the 20th century's great start from zero was one-party socialism, also known as communism or Marxism-Leninism. Given that system's bad reputation in the West today (even among the French intelligentsia), it is instructive to read John Reed's "Ten Days That Shook the World"—before turning to Alexander Solzhenitzyn's "Gulag Archipelago."

8 The old strike hall poster of a Promethean worker in a blue shirt breaking his chains across his mighty chest was the vision of ultimate human freedom the movement believed in at the outset. For intellectuals in the West, the painful dawn began with the publication of the "Gulag Archipelago" in 1973. Solzhenitsyn insisted that the villain behind the Soviet concentration camp network was not Stalin or Lenin (who invented the term concentration camp) or even Marxism. It was instead the Soviets' peculiarly 20th-century notion that they could sweep aside not only the old social order but also its religious ethic, which had been millennia in the making ("common decency," Orwell called it) and reinvent morality . . . here . . . now . . . "at the point of a gun," in the famous phrase of the Maoists. Today the relearning has reached the point where even ruling circles in the Soviet Union and China have begun to wonder how best to convert communism into something other than, in Susan Sontag's phrase, Successful Fascism.

9 The great American Contribution to the 20th century's start from zero was in the area of manners and mores, especially in what was rather primly called "the sexual revolution." In every hamlet, even in the erstwhile Bible Belt, may be found the village brothel, no longer hidden in a house of blue lights or red lights behind a green door but openly advertised by the side of the road with a

thousand-watt back-lit plastic sign: *Totally All-Nude Girl Sauna Massage and Marathon Encounter Sessions Inside.*

10 Until several years ago pornographic movie theaters were as ubiquitous as the Seven-Eleven; these theaters included outdoor drive-ins with screens six, seven, eight stories high, the better to beam all the moistened folds and glistening nodes and stiffened giblets to a panting American countryside. But since then, in the last two years or so, the pornographic theaters have begun to be replaced by the pornographic videocassette, which could be brought into any home.

11 Up on the shelf in the den, next to the set of "The Encyclopaedia Britannica" and the great books, one now finds the cassettes: "Shanks Akimbo," "That Thing with the Cup." My favorite moment in Jessica Hahn's triumphal tour of Medialand this fall came when a 10-year-old girl, a student at a private school, wearing a buttercup blouse, a cardigan sweater, and her school uniform skirt, approached her outside a television studio with a stack of "Playboy" magazines featuring the famous Hahn nude form and asked her to autograph them. With the school's blessing, she intended to take the signed copies back to the campus and hold a public auction. The proceeds would go to the poor.

12 But in the sexual revolution, too, the painful dawn has already arrived, and the relearning is imminent. All may be summed up in a single term, requiring no amplification: AIDS.

13 The Great Relearning—if anything so prosaic as remedial education can be called great—should be thought of not as the end of the 20th century but the prelude to the 21st. There is no law of history that says a new century must start 10 or 20 years beforehand, but two times in a row it has worked out that way. The 19th began with the American and French revolutions of the late 18th. The 20th century began with the formulation of Marxism, Freudianism, and Modernism in the late 19th. And now the 21st begins with the Great Relearning.

14 The 21st century, I predict, will confound the 20th century notion of the Future as something exciting, unexpected or radiant; as Progress, to use an old word. It is already clear that the large cities, thanks to the Relearning, will not even look new.

15 Quite the opposite; the cities of 2007 will look more like the cities of 1927 than the cities of 1987. The 21st century will have a retrograde look and a retrograde mental atmosphere. People of the next century, snug in their Neo-Georgian apartment complexes, will gaze back with a ghastly awe upon our time. They will regard the 20th as the century in which wars became so enormous they were known as World Wars, the century in which technology leapt forward so rapidly man developed the capacity to destroy the planet itself—but also the capacity to escape to the stars on space ships if it blew.

16 But above all they will look back upon the 20th as the century in which their forebears had the amazing confidence, the Promethean hubris, to defy the gods and try to push man's power and freedom to limitless, god-like extremes.

They will look back in awe—without the slightest temptation to emulate the daring of those who swept aside all rules and tried to start from zero. Instead, they sink ever deeper into their Neo-Louis bergeres, content to live in what will be known as the Somnolent Century of the 20th Century's Hangover.

QUESTIONS FOR WRITING AND DISCUSSION

OBSERVING

1. What does Wolfe mean by "the relearning—following a Promethean and unprecedented start from zero" (paragraph 4)?
2. How do the examples from architecture, politics, manners and mores support this conclusion?

EVALUATING

1. What predictions does Wolfe make about the twenty-first century? How does he arrive at these predictions?
2. Do you see any flaws in his thinking? What assumptions is he making? Is he overstating his case?

RESPONDING AND APPLYING

1. What advantages do you see in questioning or rejecting the past? What historical events required a radical departure from the past? Which ones departed, but not as violently?
2. Can you identify with what Wolfe calls the "amazing confidence, the Promethean hubris" of the twentieth century? What examples of overweening pride come to your mind? Do you think more humility would help us as we venture into the twenty-first century?
3. What is your prescription for improvement and change?

This book is essentially historical. It invites readers to reflect on the circumstances and quality of our lives in the late twentieth century. As we do this reflecting, much like Tom Wolfe does in "The Great Relearning Heralds the 21st Century," most of us assume the role of historian. Given the stereotypical views of historians, that may surprise many of you. But whenever we make broad claims about our world, such as "The U.S. is the greatest power in the world," or "The corporations are taking too much power from the people," we wear the historian's cap, at least a small part of it. Even though many of us would insist that we're not interested in the study of history, we still pose as historians all the time and are fascinated by competing claims of interpretation: Should we see Columbus as a brave pioneer and explorer who opened the land to settlement and civilization, or as an exploiter who brought genocide to the native peoples?

Our purpose in Chapter Two was to raise important moral questions about the health of our society. The purpose of this chapter is to reflect on the very meaning of reflecting on history. Technically, this is called *historiography,* the study of the history and nature of history study. Confusing. Not really. Historiography poses questions like these: What does it mean to be an historian? What are the uses and values of studying history? What does the historian do in being a historian? In what way can and does each of us participate in the creation of a history? What makes us see the past in certain ways? How does our view of the past change from time to time, from perspective to perspective? Are all perspectives necessarily biased? Considering someone like Abraham Lincoln or Christopher Columbus, how and why do our views of the past change? How do they change and how do those changes affect our present lives? How can we trace the roots of the moral conditions of our society? How do we measure a moral climate? What was the moral climate like in the past? Are we capable of deciding or knowing? How do we as a culture see history and historians? Are we increasingly victims of historical amnesia? What causes us to forget? What are the costs of forgetting? Can we identify important historians? What in our society has replaced the storytellers, the novels and histories that at one time provided the major ways of knowing the world?

What follows is an important essay by Arthur Schlesinger, Jr., historian and author, special assistant and speech writer to several Democratic presidents, and winner of the Pulitzer Prize and the National Book Award. Schlesinger examines the accelerating pace of change and the ways in which it "compels us to perceive . . . the universe not as complete, but as unfinished." He helps us begin to answer questions about the uses of history in understanding the particular crises and demands of modern life. The next reading is by Linda Simon, a freelance writer, biographer, and director of the Writing Center at Harvard. Simon is critical of the way history is taught—she would have students engage in writing histories the way "real" historians do it, from primary experiences and documents, which she refers to as "naked sources."

Simon's article is followed by Peter Burke's piece on "the new history," a radical shift in the way we think of doing history. A Reader in Cultural History at the University of Cambridge, Burke describes the "new history" in his introduction to the book *New Perspectives on Historical Writing,* particularly the ways in which historians' lenses are changing, and how those lenses more broadly include diverse peoples and events. Finally, Judith Miller, a writer and reporter for *The New York Times,* confronts the "lava of memory" smoldering underneath the tranquil-seeming present, examining national forms of historical self-deception, the costs of which are repeating the worst forms of history. Finally, we conclude the chapter with Steven Schwartz's story "Madagascar," the account of a child of a Holocaust survivor. The father must decide how he will help his son remember the family's terrible past and, in so doing, is forced to consider the uses of the past.

The Challenge of Change

Arthur M. Schlesinger, Jr.

1 The last three centuries have seen dazzling revolutions in scientific theory and dazzling advances in the translation of theory into technology. This cumulative increase in the rate of change has been the decisive factor in the making of the modern world. The world has moved faster than ever before, and until recently it has moved fastest of all in the United States.

2 The American Revolution and the Industrial Revolution began at about the same time. From the start, Americans have rejoiced in unremitting technological change. Innovation was unrestrained by custom or tradition or timidity. "I simply experiment," said Ralph Waldo Emerson, the quintessential American, "an endless seeker with no Past at my back." It is hardly surprising that the first historian to emphasize the accelerating velocity of history should have been an American. "The world did not double or treble its movement between 1800 and 1900," Henry Adams wrote in 1909, "but; measured by any standard known to science—by horsepower, calories, volts, mass in any shape—the tension and vibration and volume and so-called progression of society were fully a thousand times greater in 1900 than in 1800." Acceleration left man and mind far behind. Adams's own education, the best an American could get in the 19th century, was, he concluded in the early 20th century, a total waste; the Harvard freshman he was in 1854 probably stood nearer to the thought of the year 1 than to that of the year 1904. "The law of acceleration," Adams said, "definite and constant as any law of mechanics, cannot be supposed to relax its energy to suit the convenience of man."

3 Adams's appeal to scientific law was both romantic and ironic. His notion that history could be reduced to mathematical physics was a delusion, or perhaps an elaborate joke. Still, as metaphor, his point is powerful. William James, who patiently explained to Adams why the second law of thermodynamics did not apply to history, agreed that humanity had experienced only the most preliminary impact of science and technology. "Think how many absolutely new scientific conceptions have arisen in our own generation," he wrote, "how many new problems have been formulated that were never thought of before, and then cast an eye upon the brevity of science's career. . . . Is it credible that such a mushroom knowledge, such a growth overnight as this *can* represent more than the minutest glimpse of what the universe will really prove to be when adequately understood? No! our science is a drop, our ignorance a sea."

4 Humans have lived on earth for possibly 800 lifetimes, most of which they spent in caves. "Some five or six score people," James said, "if each . . . could speak for his own generation, would carry us away to the black unknown of the human species, to days without a document or monument to tell their tale." Movable type appeared only eight lifetimes ago, industrialization in the last

three lifetimes. The static societies that consumed most of human history perceived no great difference between present and past. Society subsisted on the existing stock of wisdom for a long time. The functional need for new ideas was limited. Tradition was sacred and controlling.

5 The last two lifetimes have seen more scientific and technological achievement than the first 798 put together. The shift to a swiftly changing society has not greatly affected the surfaces of daily living. The New York of the 1980's resembles the New York of the 1930's more than the New York of the 1930's resembles the New York of the 1880's. But the shift has profoundly altered inner perceptions and expectations. It has placed traditional roles and institutions under severe and incomprehensible strain. It has cast off reference points and rituals that had stabilized and sanctified life for generations. It has left the experience of elders useless to the tribulations of the young. Children, knowing how different their own lives will be, no longer look to parents as models and authorities; rather, parents now learn from their children.

6 The pace of change grows ever faster. A boy who saw the Wright brothers fly for a few seconds at Kitty Hawk in 1903 could have watched Apollo 11 land on the moon in 1969. The first rockets were launched in the 1920's; today, astronauts roam outer space. The first electronic computer was built in 1946; today, the world rushes from the mechanical into the electronic age. The double helix was first unveiled in 1953; today, biotechnology threatens to remake mankind. The first atomic bomb fell in 1945; today, the world shudders under the threat of nuclear obliteration.

7 The acceleration of change compels us to perceive life as motion, not as order; the universe not as complete, but as unfinished. For people of buoyant courage, like William James, the prospect was exhilarating. Henry Adams saw change as irreversible, but contemplated the future with foreboding. Others, in the midst of flounder and flux, strive to resurrect the old ways.

8 The hunger for stability is entirely natural. Change is scary; uncharted change, demoralizing. If the law of acceleration is not to spin the world out of control, society must cherish its lifelines into the past. That is why, even in this age of whirl, so much of the old abides. People instinctively defend the self against disruption. "In this matter of belief," said James, "we are all extreme conservatives." When new facts finally drive out old opinions, we take care to graft the new perception on the ancient stock with "a minimum of jolt, a maximum of continuity." Everyone becomes his own Landmarks Preservation Commission. We seek with T. S. Eliot the still point in the turning world.

9 Traditions endure, from which, consciously or not, we draw sustenance. It is not fashionable these days for historians to talk about "national character." But of course persisting traits, values, folkways, create a palpable national identity. The reader of Alexis de Tocqueville is constantly astonished to recognize the lineaments of modern America in his great work, though Tocqueville visited a predominantly agricultural nation of 13 million people a century and a half ago. Even J. Hector St. John de Crèvecoeur still astonishes by the contemporaneity

of his 18th-century answer to his own famous question: "What then is the American, this new man?"

10 "*He* is an American, who, leaving behind him all his ancient prejudices and manners, receives new ones from the new mode of life he has embraced, the new government he obeys, and the new rank he holds. . . . Here individuals of all nations are melted into a new race of men, whose labours and posterity will one day cause great changes in the world. Americans are the western pilgrims, who are carrying with them that great mass of arts, sciences, vigour, and industry which began long since in the east; they will finish the great circle. . . . The American is a new man, who acts upon new principles; he must therefore entertain new ideas, and form new opinions."

11 The law of acceleration hurtles us into the inscrutable future. But it cannot wipe clean the slate of the past. History haunts even generations who refuse to learn history. Rhythms, patterns, continuities, drift out of time long forgotten to mold the present and to color the shape of things to come. Science and technology revolutionize our lives, but memory, tradition and myth frame our response. Expelled from individual consciousness by the rush of change, history finds its revenge by stamping the collective unconscious with habits, values, expectations, dreams. The dialectic between past and future will continue to form our lives.

12 These reflections are not presented in any confidence that history is the cure for all that ails us. Still, the past helps explain where we are today and how we got there. Knowledge of what Americans have been through in earlier times will do us no harm as we grope through the darkness of our own days. During the Soviet blockade of Berlin in 1948, when forebodings of a third World War swept Washington, a young assistant secretary exclaimed to Secretary of State George C. Marshall at a panicky staff meeting, "How in the world can you remain so calm during this appalling crisis?" Marshall replied, calmly, "I've seen worse."

13 Americans have indeed seen worse. History, by putting crisis in perspective, supplies the antidote to every generation's illusion that its own problems are uniquely oppressive. Troubles impending always seem worse than troubles surmounted, but this does not prove that they really are. Nuclear weapons excepted, the problems of the 1980's are modest compared to the problems that confronted George Washington's generation in achieving independence and fashioning a free state, or to the problems that confronted Abraham Lincoln's generation in bringing the Republic through the glare of civil war, or to the problems that confronted Franklin Roosevelt's generation in surviving the worst depression and winning the greatest war in American history. "So hot? my little Sir," said Emerson, warning us not to mistake the sound of a popgun for the crack of doom.

14 Nuclear weapons, however, are the fatal exception. They introduce a qualitatively new factor into the historical process. For the first time in the life

of humanity, the crack of doom becomes a realistic possibility. So history embraces discontinuity as well as continuity. Knowledge of the past should inoculate against hysteria but should not instill complacency. History walks on a knife edge.

15 No one knew the risks of history better than Henry Adams. Humanity, Adams well understood, had been subjected to a succession of technological shocks, each of which by itself would have taken decades to digest and control. Every shock increased the velocity of history. The nuclear shock threatens the end of history. "Man has mounted science and is now run away with," Adams wrote to his brother on 11 April 1862, a few days after the Battle of Shiloh, while the Monitor and the Merrimack were maneuvering around Newport News. "I firmly believe that before many centuries more, science will be the master of man. The engines he will have invented will be beyond his strength to control. Some day science shall have the existence of mankind in its power, and the human race commit suicide by blowing up the world."

QUESTIONS FOR WRITING AND DISCUSSION

OBSERVING

1. What is Schlesinger's thesis regarding the impact of science and technology on society? How has our attitude toward tradition and our elders changed over the last 200 years?
2. What does Schlesinger mean when he writes "society must cherish its lifeline into the past . . . people instinctively defend the self against disruption"?
3. Schlesinger concludes by quoting Henry Adams: "Science will be the master of man." What does that mean?

EVALUATING

1. Why do you think Schlesinger sees a demise in the ways we traditionally have learned from older role models?
2. Argue that science has or hasn't gotten out of hand, and speculate about what we can do about it.

RESPONDING AND APPLYING

1. Schlesinger claims parents look more to their children as "models and authorities" than the other way around. Do you find this to be true? Might it be truer in some things than others?
2. Schlesinger is a passionate advocate of the uses of history. What is your experience in that regard? Has the study of history been useful to you? Has such a study been related to life in the present?

The Naked Source

Linda Simon

1 It is true that my students do not know history. That annals of the American past, as students tell it, are compressed into a compact chronicle: John Kennedy and Martin Luther King flourish just a breath away from FDR and Woodrow Wilson, who themselves come right on the heels of Jefferson and Lincoln. The far and distant past is more obscure still.

2 Some, because they are bright and inquisitive, have learned names, dates, and the titles of major events. But even these masters of Trivial Pursuit often betray their ignorance of a real sense of the past. Teachers all have favorite one-liners that point to an abyss in historical knowledge. Mine is: Sputnik *who?*

3 There is no debate here. Students do not know history. Students should learn history. There is less agreement about what they should know, why they should know it, and far less agreement about how they should pursue this study of the past.

4 When I ask my students why they need to know history, they reply earnestly: We need to learn history because those who do not know history are doomed to repeat the mistakes of the past. They have heard this somewhere, although no one can attribute the remark. And if they are told that George Santayana said it, they know not who Santayana was, although if you care to inform them they will dutifully record his name, dates (1863–1952), and the title of the work (*The Life of Reason*) in which the remark was made.

5 Is that so? I ask. What will not be repeated?

6 Inevitably they respond emotionally with the example of the Holocaust. Some have watched an episode of a PBS series. Some have seen the film *The Diary of Anne Frank*. Such genocide, they reply, will not be repeated because we know about it. Undaunted by examples of contemporary genocide, they remain firm in their conviction. Genocide, they maintain. And the Great Depression.

7 The Great Depression has made a big impact on the adolescent imagination. Given any work of literature written at any time during the 1930s, some students will explain it as a direct response to the Great Depression. Wasn't everyone depressed, after all? And aren't most serious works of literature grim, glum, dark, and deep? There you have it.

8 But now we know about the Great Depression. And so it will not, cannot, happen again.

9 I am not persuaded that requiring students to read Tacitus or Thucydides, Carl Becker or Francis Parkman, Samuel Eliot Morison or Arnold Toynbee will remedy this situation, although I believe that students, and we, might well benefit from these writers' illumination. What students lack, after all, is a sense of historical-mindedness, a sense that lives were lived in a context, a sense that events (the Battle of Barnet, for example) had consequences (if men were slain

on the battlefield, they could not return to the farm), a sense that answers must generate questions, more questions, and still more subtle questions.

10 As it is, students learning history, especially in the early grades, are asked prescribed questions and are given little opportunity to pursue their own inquiry or satisfy their own curiosity. The following questions are from current high school texts:

> Has the role of the present United Nations proved that the hopes and dreams of Woodrow Wilson were achievable? If so, how? If not, why?
>
> What were the advantages of an isolationist policy for the United States in the nineteenth century? Were there disadvantages?

11 Questions such as these perpetuate the idea that history is a body of knowledge on which students will be tested. The first question, in other words, asks students: Did you read the section in the text on the role of the United Nations? Did you read the section on Wilson's aims in proposing the League of Nations? Can you put these two sections together?

12 The second question asks students: Did you understand the term *isolationist?* Did you read the section on U.S. foreign relations in the nineteenth century? Can you summarize the debate that the authors of the textbook recount?

13 Questions such as these perpetuate the idea that history can uncover "facts" and "truth," that history is objective, and that students, if only they are diligent, can recover "right answers" about the past. Questions such as these ignore the role of historians. Even those bright students who can recall dates and events rarely can recall the name of a historian, much less any feeling about who this particular man or woman was. For many students, historical facts are things out there, like sea shells or autumn leaves, and it hardly matters who fetches them. The sea shell will look the same whether it is gathered in Charles Beard's pocket or Henri Pirenne's.

14 What students really need to learn, more than "history," is a sense of the historical method of inquiry. They need to know what it is that historians do and how they do it. They need to understand the role of imagination and intuition in the telling of histories, they need to practice, themselves, confronting sources, making judgments, and defending conclusions.

15 When I ask my freshmen what they think historians do, they usually offer me some lofty phrases about "influencing the course of future events." But what I mean is: what do historians do after breakfast? That is a question few of my students can answer. And they are surprised when I read them the following passage by British historian A. L. Rowse from his book *The Use of History.*

> You might think that in order to learn history you need a library of books to begin with. Not at all: that only comes at the end. What you need at the beginning is a pair of stout walking shoes, a pencil and a notebook; perhaps I should add a good county guide covering the area you mean to explore . . . and a map of the country . . . that gives you field footpaths and a wealth of things of interest, marks churches and historic buildings and ruins, wayside

> crosses and holy wells, prehistoric camps and dykes, the sites of battles. When you can't go for a walk, it is quite a good thing to study the map and plan where you would like to go. I am all in favour of the open-air approach to history; the most delightful and enjoyable, the most imaginative and informative, and—what not everybody understands—the best training.

16 It is the best training because it gives the would-be historian an encounter with the things that all historians look at and puzzle over: primary sources about the past. Historians look at battlefields and old buildings, read letters and diaries and documents, interview eyewitnesses or participants in events. And they ask questions of these sources. Gradually, after asking increasingly sophisticated questions, they make some sense, for themselves, of what once happened.

17 What professional historians do, however, is not what most students do when they set out to learn history within the confines of a course. Instead of putting students face to face with primary sources, instructors are more likely to send them to read what other people say about the past. Students begin with a library of books of secondary sources, or they may begin with a text. But that, cautions Rowse, should come "at the end." Instead of allowing students to gain experience in weighing evidence and making inferences, the structures of many courses encourage them to amass information. "I found it!" exclaim enthusiastic students. They need to ask, "But what does it mean?"

18 They need to ask that question of the kinds of sources that historians actually use. Instead of reading Morison's rendering of Columbus's voyages, for example, students might read Columbus himself: his journal, his letters to the Spanish monarchs. Then they can begin to decide for themselves what sort of man this was and what sort of experience he had. Morison—as excellent a historian as he is—comes later. With some sense of the sources that Morison used, students can begin to evaluate his contribution to history, to understand how he drew conclusions from the material available to him, to see how "facts" are augmented by historical intuition. They can begin to understand, too, that the reconstruction of the past is slow and painstaking work.

19 Courses that cover several decades or even millennia may give students a false impression of historical inquiry. Historians, like archaeologists or epidemiologists, move slowly through bumpy and perilous terrain. They are used to travelling for miles only to find themselves stranded at a dead end. Once, in the archives of Westminster Abbey, I eagerly awaited reading a fragment of a letter from King Henry VI (after all, that is how it was described in the card catalog), only to lift out of an envelope the corner of a page, about an inch across, with the faintest ink-mark the only evidence that it had, five hundred years before, been a letter at all.

20 Slowly the historian assembles pieces of the past. A household expense record might be the only artifact proving that a certain medieval woman existed. How much can be known about her? How much can be known by examining someone's checkbook today? Yet historians must make do with just such

odd legacies: wills and land deeds, maps and drawings, family portraits or photographs. Can you imagine the excitement over the discovery of a diary or a cache of letters? At last, a text. But the diary may prove a disappointment, a frustration. William James recorded the title of a book he may have been reading or the name of a visitor. Didn't he understand that a historian or biographer would need the deep, reflective ruminations of which we know he was more than capable?

21 Students have not had these experiences. When they are asked to write, they write *about* history. The research paper or the term paper seems to many of them another form of test—this time a take-home drawn out over weeks. Even if they have learned that "voice" and "audience" are important for a writer, they see history papers as different. They must be objective; they must learn proper footnoting and documentation. They must compile an impressive bibliography. Most important, they must find something out. The research paper produces nothing so much as anxiety, and the student often feels overwhelmed by the project.

22 They might, instead, be asked to write history as historians do it. They might be introduced to archives—in their college, in their community, in their state capital. They might be encouraged to interview people, and to interview them again and again until they begin to get the kind of information that will enlighten them about a particular time or event. They might be encouraged to read newspapers on microfilm or the bound volumes of old magazines that are yellowing in the basement of their local library. And then they might be asked to write in that most challenging form: the historical narrative.

23 "I can recall experiencing upon the completing of my first work of history," George Kennan wrote once, ". . . a moment of panic when the question suddenly presented itself to me: What is it that I have done here? Perhaps what I have written is not really history but rather some sort of novel, the product of my own imagination,—an imagination stimulated, inspired and informed, let us hope, by the documents I have been reading, but imagination nevertheless." Most historians share Kennan's reaction.

24 Students, of course, can never discover the boundary between "fact" and imaginative construction unless they have contact with primary sources. They cannot know where the historian has intervened to analyze the information he or she has discovered. "Most of the facts that you excavate," Morison wrote in "History as A Literary Art," "are dumb things; it is for you to make them speak by proper selection, arrangement, and emphasis." Morison suggested that beginning historians look to such writers as Sherwood Anderson and Henry James for examples of the kind of palpable description and intense characterization that can make literature—historical or fictional—come alive.

25 Students need to be persuaded that they are writing literature, not taking a test, when they set out to be historians. Their writing needs to be read and evaluated not only for the facts that they have managed to compile, but for the sense of the past that they have conveyed. They need to discover that the past

was not only battles and elections, Major Forces and Charismatic Leaders, but ordinary people, growing up, courting, dancing to a different beat, camping by a river that has long since dried up, lighting out for a territory that no longer exists. Except in the imagination of historians, as they confront the naked source, unaided.

QUESTIONS FOR WRITING AND DISCUSSION

OBSERVING

1. Simon refers to the "abyss in historical knowledge." What is she referring to?
2. Why does Simon think we should know history? How does her thinking compare to the reasons apparently behind much teaching of history and social science?
3. What does the author mean by "historical-mindedness" and how does that differ from "history as a body of knowledge"? Why does she quote Rowse?

EVALUATING

1. Why do you think so many are historically illiterate today?
2. What would a course in history taught by Simon look like?

RESPONDING AND APPLYING

1. How did you learn history? Were there any positive experiences that stand out? What is your worst horror story? How do the media portray the teaching of history?
2. If you were to become the kind of historian Simon describes, what questions and topics would you want to pursue?
3. If your school has any kind of archives, what do they contain? Have you ever examined an archive, family or otherwise? How did you find it?

What Is the New History?

Peter Burke

1 The phrase "the new history" is best known in France. *La nouvelle histoire* is the title of a collection of essays edited by the distinguished French medievalist Jacques Le Goff. Le Goff has also helped edit a massive three-volume collection of essays, concerned with "new problems," "new approaches," and "new objects." In these cases it is clear what the new history is: it is a history "made in France," the country of *la nouvelle vague* and *le nouveau roman,* not to mention *la nouvelle cuisine.* More exactly, it is the history associated with the so-called *école des Annales,* grouped around the journal *Annales: économies, sociétés, civilisations.*

2 What is this *nouvelle histoire?* A positive definition is not easy; the movement is united only in what it opposes, and the pages which follow will demonstrate the variety of the new approaches. It is therefore difficult to offer more than a vague description, characterizing the new history as total history (*histoire totale*) or as structural history. Hence there may be a case for imitating medieval theologians faced with the problem of defining God, and opting for a *via negativa,* in other words for defining the new history in terms of what it is not, of what its practitioners oppose.

3 The new history is history written in deliberate reaction against the traditional "paradigm," that useful if imprecise term put into circulation by the American historian of science Thomas Kuhn. It will be convenient to describe this traditional paradigm as "Rankean history," after the great German historian Leopold von Ranke (1795-1886), although he was less confined by it than his followers were. (Just as Marx was not a Marxist, Ranke was not a Rankean.) We might also call this paradigm the common-sense view of history, not to praise it but to make the point that it has often—too often—been assumed to be *the* way of doing history, rather than being perceived as one among various possible approaches to the past. For the sake of simplicity and clarity, the contrast between old and new history might be summed up in seven points.

4 1. According to the traditional paradigm, history is essentially concerned with politics. In the confident Victorian phrase of Sir John Seeley, Regius Professor of History at Cambridge, "History is past politics: politics is present history." Politics was assumed to be essentially concerned with the state; in other words it was national and international rather than local. However, it did include the history of the Church as an institution and also what the military theorist Karl von Clausewitz defined as "the continuation of policies by other means," that is, war. Although other kinds of history—the history of art, for example, or the history of science—were not altogether excluded by the traditional paradigm, they were marginalized in the sense of being considered peripheral to the interests of "real" historians.

5 The new history, on the other hand, has come to be concerned with virtually every human activity. "Everything has a history," as the scientist J. B. S. Haldane once wrote; that is, everything has a past which can in principle be reconstructed and related to the rest of the past. Hence the slogan "total history," so dear to the *Annales* historians. The first half of the century witnessed the rise of the history of ideas. In the last thirty years we have seen a number of remarkable histories of topics which had not previously been thought to possess a history, for example, childhood, death, madness, the climate, smells, dirt and cleanliness, gestures, the body, femininity, reading, speaking, and even silence. What had previously been considered as unchanging is now viewed as a "cultural construction," subject to variation over time as well as in space.

6 The cultural relativism implicit here deserves to be emphasized. The philosophical foundation of the new history is the idea that reality is socially or culturally constituted. The sharing of this idea, or assumption, by many social historians and social anthropologists helps explain the recent convergence between these two disciplines, referred to more than once in the chapters which follow. This relativism also undermines the traditional distinction between what is central in history and what is peripheral.

7 2. In the second place, traditional historians think of history as essentially a narrative of events, while the new history is more concerned with the analysis of structures. One of the most famous works of history of our time, Fernand Braudel's *Mediterranean,* dismisses the history of events (*histoire événementielle*) as no more than the foam on the waves of the sea of history. According to Braudel, economic and social changes over the long term (*la longue durée*) and geo-historical changes over the very long term are what really matter. Although there has recently been something of a reaction against this view and events are no longer dismissed as easily as they used to be, the history of structures of various kinds continues to be taken very seriously.

8 3. In the third place, traditional history offers a view from above, in the sense that it has always concentrated on the great deeds of great men, statesmen, generals, or occasionally churchmen. The rest of humanity was allocated a minor role in the drama of history. The existence of this rule is revealed by reactions to its transgression. When the great Russian writer Alexander Pushkin was working on an account of a peasant revolt and its leader Pugachev, Tsar Nicholas's comment was that "such a man has no history." In the 1950s, when a British historian wrote a thesis about a popular movement in the French Revolution, one of his examiners asked him, "Why do you bother with these bandits?"

9 On the other hand, a number of the new historians are concerned with "history from below," in other words with the views of ordinary people and with their experience of social change. The history of popular culture has received a great deal of attention. Historians of the Church are beginning to examine its history from below as well as from above. Intellectual historians too have shifted their attention away from great books, or great ideas—their equivalent of great men—to the history of collective mentalities or to the history of

discourses or "languages," the language of scholasticism, for example, or the language of the common law.

10 4. In the fourth place, according to the traditional paradigm, history should be based on the documents. One of Ranke's greatest achievements was his exposure of the limitations of narrative sources—let us call them chronicles—and his stress on the need to base written history on official records, emanating from governments and preserved in archives. The price of this achievement was the neglect of other kinds of evidence. The period before the invention of writing was dismissed as "prehistory." However, the "history from below" movement in its turn exposed the limitations of this kind of document. Official records generally express the official point of view. To reconstruct the attitudes of heretics and rebels, such records need to be supplemented by other kinds of source.

11 In any case, if historians are concerned with a greater variety of human activities than their predecessors, they must examine a greater variety of evidence. Some of this evidence is visual, some of it oral. There is also statistical evidence: trade figures, population figures, voting figures, and so on. The heyday of quantitative history was probably the 1950s and 1960s, when some enthusiasts claimed that only quantitative methods were reliable. There has been a reaction against such claims, and to some extent against the methods as well, but interest in a more modest quantitative history continues to grow. In Britain, for example, an Association for History and Computing was founded in 1987.

12 5. According to the traditional paradigm, memorably articulated by the philosopher-historian R. G. Collingwood, "When an historian asks 'Why did Brutus stab Caesar?' he means 'What did Brutus think, which made him decide to stab Caesar?'" This model of historical explanation has been criticized by more recent historians on a number of grounds, principally because it fails to take account of the variety of historians' questions, often concerned with collective movements as well as individual actions, with trends as well as events.

13 Why, for example, did prices rise in sixteenth-century Spain? Economic historians do not agree in their answer to this question, but their various responses (in terms of silver imports, population growth and so on) are very far from Collingwood's model. In Fernand Braudel's famous study of the sixteenth-century Mediterranean, first published in 1949, only the third and last part, devoted to the history of events, asks questions remotely like Collingwood's, and even here the author offers a very different kind of answer, emphasising the constraints on his protagonist, King Philip II, and the king's lack of influence on the history of his time.

14 6. According to the traditional paradigm, History is objective. The historian's task is to give readers the facts, or as Ranke put it in a much-quoted phrase, to tell "how it actually happened." His modest disclaimer of philosophical intentions was interpreted by posterity as a proud manifesto for history without bias. In a famous letter to his international team of contributors to the *Cambridge Modern History,* published from 1902 onwards, its editor, Lord Acton, urged them that "our Waterloo must be one that satisfies French and

English, Germans and Dutch alike" and that readers should be unable to tell where one contributor laid down his pen and another took it up.

15 Today, this ideal is generally considered to be unrealistic. However hard we struggle to avoid the prejudices associated with colour, creed, class or gender, we cannot avoid looking at the past from a particular point of view. Cultural relativism obviously applies as much to historical writing itself as to its so-called objects. Our minds do not reflect reality directly. We perceive the world only through a network of conventions, schemata and stereotypes, a network which varies from one culture to another. In this situation, our understanding of conflicts is surely enhanced by a presentation of opposite viewpoints, rather than by an attempt, like Acton's, to articulate a consensus. We have moved from the ideal of the Voice of History to that of heteroglossia, defined as "varied and opposing voices." It is therefore quite appropriate that this volume should itself take the form of a collective work and that its contributors should speak different mother tongues.

16 Rankean history was the territory of the professionals. The nineteenth century was the time when history became professionalized, with its departments in universities and its trade journals like the *Historische Zeitschrift* and the *English Historical Review.* Most of the leading new historians are also professionals, with the distinguished exception of the late Philippe Ariès, who liked to describe himself as "a Sunday historian." One way to describe the achievements of the *Annales* group is to say that they have shown that economic, social and cultural history can meet the exacting professional standards set by Ranke for political history.

17 All the same, their concern with the whole range of human activity encourages them to be interdisciplinary in the sense of learning from and collaborating with social anthropologists, economists, literary critics, psychologists, sociologists, and so on. Historians of art, literature and science, who used to pursue their interests more or less in isolation from the main body of historians, are now making more regular contact with them. The history-from-below movement also reflects a new determination to take ordinary people's views of their own past more seriously than professional historians used to do. The same is true for some forms of oral history. In this sense too heteroglossia is essential to the new history.

QUESTIONS FOR WRITING AND DISCUSSION

OBSERVING

1. Burke starts off trying to define the "old approach to doing history," the traditional paradigm. From your own experiences in history classes and from what Burke says, what do you think he means by the old history?

2. Write a one-line summary for each of the seven points. Which do you think is/are the most important?
3. Burke talks of the old history in terms of marginalization. What does he mean? What is "total history"? How does he respond to the criticism of "cultural relativism"?

EVALUATING

1. What do you think the significance is of the change Burke describes, from the "view from above" to including the rest of humanity? What political implications, as far as the distribution of power is concerned, do you see?
2. Describe some of the challenges the new history might face. What problems would a historian today face that a traditional one would not have to worry about? What happens when history is no longer assumed to be "objective"?
3. What do you think Burke means by "heteroglossia"?

RESPONDING AND APPLYING

1. Describe your own history education in the terms Burke presents.
2. Examine a history text you've used or found. What model of history does it represent?

from One, by One, by One: Remembering the Holocaust

Judith Miller

1 My grandmother was a tiny, deceptively frail-looking woman with white hair, a fierce temperament, and an infuriating habit of speaking to my father in Russian or Yiddish, neither of which I understood. Despite decades in this country, she never mastered more than a smattering of English.

2 Given our language gap, she and I did not speak much. But as a child, I spent hours in silent wonderment watching her furiously chop beets and onions for what my father proclaimed "the world's greatest borscht." She had been poor beyond description in Russia. As a child, she had witnessed a series of vicious pogroms. She was a shrewd woman, with intelligent eyes, who had never gone to school. She had lost two of her seven children to disease and misfortune.

3 My father said that when he was a boy his mother loved to sing and dance. But there seemed to be little joy left in her by the time I was born. The only pleasure she relished was cooking for us, and making sure that we ate every bite.

4 On one such occasion at our home in Miami Beach, the whole family was assembled in the kitchen, watching television, as my grandmother pulverized an onion for that evening's soup. The broadcaster interrupted his newscast to announce that there had just been a terrible airplane crash moments before the program had begun. It was feared that all on board—more than one hundred people—had perished.

5 My normally loquacious father fell silent. My Irish Catholic mother, who was terrified of flying even in the calmest of skies, gasped.

6 Grandmother Lena stopped chopping for a moment. Turning to my father, all but ignoring my mother and me, she asked in broken English: "How many Jews were on board?"

7 My grandmother had suffered in Europe. And she had responded to her suffering in a very European way. The conclusion she drew from her own experience, even after she got to freedom and safety in America, was that concern about her fellow human beings had to be rationed. No human tragedy could be measured as such. It was the fate of her people that mattered. If an airliner went down, she would dole out her sympathy based on the number of Jews on board.

8 Born an American, I drew the opposite conclusions. My experience with Judaism and Jewish activities taught me—as Hyman Bookbinder never tired of reminding me—that there could be no Jewish welfare without general well-being. I concluded that the Holocaust suggests that Jews and all threatened minorities need allies in their societies, that no minority can survive in political and cultural isolation.

9 So at times while writing this book, I found myself losing patience with the debate over whether the Holocaust was, or was not, a uniquely Jewish experience. Of course the Holocaust was unique and, yes, it happened to the Jews. The Jews were singled out for total eradication, and for senseless, even counterproductive slaughter, since the genocide required resources that the Germans diverted from their war effort. But the Holocaust was a tragedy for Western civilization as well.

10 Could anyone not believe that it called into question the underpinnings of "civilized" society? Could anyone doubt that it undermined for a long time to come the spiritual authority of the Catholic Church and other churches that put their institutional interests above the tenets of their faith? Was it possible to have older European friends and not know that the war had destroyed their families and their world?

11 No, most of the "others," as they are often callously called, did not die in gas chambers. Their suffering is not comparable to that of the Jews as a people. Except for Gypsies, no other group was singled out for total extermination by

the Nazis. But that does not mean that the memory of their tragedy matters less or is any less compelling. The war that produced the Holocaust was a universal tragedy not only because six million Jews were deliberately killed. It was a universal catastrophe because the allegedly civilized world let it happen.

12 Western Europe today seems prosperous, self-assured, and tranquil enough. But beneath the crust, the lava of memory smolders. Only when a society is forced to confront these memories—by a Jenninger speech in Germany, a Waldheim election in Austria, or a Barbie trial in France—does the bitterness, the hatred, and the anti-Semitism, along with the guilt and defensiveness, burst forth with what seems astonishing power and vehemence.

13 In every country, every culture I explored, irrespective of national character or political ideology, a particularly national form of self-deception has usually triumphed over self-revelation. The need to evade has most often transcended illumination.

14 It does not help to quote Santayana—that those who refuse to learn from history are bound to repeat it. For history, as Geoffrey Hartman astutely observed, sends decidedly mixed messages. Was it inevitable that Jews in Germany, the most successful and among the most assimilated in Europe, would be singled out as vermin fit only for extermination?

15 The so-called "lessons" of the war and the Holocaust are now being written and rewritten. But the Holocaust does not "teach." It is not a religion or an ideology. It cannot provide a moral or political framework for living one's life. The Holocaust exhausts. It defies. It negates. And it raises frightening questions, such as what did the Jews of Europe do to incur such wrath? How could Europe's most cultured people have devised the West's most efficient, neatly implemented genocide? Why did so many people follow Hitler? Why did relatively few resist?

16 While the vehicles of remembrance differ from society to society, the mechanisms of suppression tend to be similar. Cultures suppress what they would like to forget in remarkably similar ways, even when the events themselves are strikingly different. Events such as Stalin's brutal collectivization and purges in the USSR, the Dreyfus affair and Klaus Barbie's crimes and collaboration in France, Kurt Waldheim's war service in Austria, Wounded Knee or My Lai for Americans, or the Holocaust almost everywhere, are not comparable. But that does not imply that they cannot and will not be compared. One thing they have in common is the desire of the people and societies responsible for them to forget them or evade responsibility for them. They become alike in the way in which we come to think of them, or to suppress them.

17 Cultures tend to employ the same vehicles to suppress pain and unpleasant memories as individuals: denial, the shifting of blame, rationalization, and relativization.

18 In almost every country, denial, the least sophisticated form of suppression, is the easiest to combat. The unabashed revisionists who deny that the Holocaust took place have no intellectual credibility in Europe or the United States;

their audience has been extremely limited and is likely to remain so. Even the Soviet Union does not deny that there was a Final Solution for Jews; it has simply chosen not to emphasize their disproportionate slaughter and suffering.

19 Shifting blame is also a common form of amnesia; the Austrians have most finely perfected it as a technique for blaming others and exonerating themselves for their political and moral failings. But shifting blame, which enables the perpetrator to see himself as a victim, is a common defense mechanism throughout Western Europe and the Soviet Union. The Soviets blame the Nazis in part for the mass suffering Stalin inflicted on them. In its own national mythology, France failed to resist not because it was a nation that had not wanted to fight another war, but because it had been so quickly "overwhelmed" by Germany.

20 Rationalization and relativization are the most common, insidious, and hence problematic forms of the suppression of memory. Examples in Europe and the United States abound. The United States did not do more to rescue Jews because priority had to be placed on winning the war. True as far as it goes, but that is not the sole explanation. Or there was no "proof" of what the Germans were doing to the Jews until it was too late. Completely untrue, as historians Walter Laqueur and David Wyman have devastatingly demonstrated. As for the American officials who read the reports and heard the intelligence and saw the aerial reconnaissance pictures of Auschwitz, what they read and heard and saw was, as Deborah Lipstadt concluded, "Beyond Belief."

21 Relativization, what Lipstadt has called the "yes, but" syndrome, is one of the trickier forms of rationalization. "Yes, six million Jews were killed by the Germans, but the United States also committed mass murder. Did they not drop a second (implicitly unnecessary) nuclear weapon on Nagasaki? Yes, the Germans slaughtered Jews, but was Hitler not a response to Stalin? Yes, the Germans massacred Jews, but did the Soviet Union not kill more than a million Germans on the eastern front? Yes, the Jewish genocide in Europe was horrific, but was not Pol Pot's slaughter of his own people—between one and three million, no one will ever know for sure—equally reprehensible?"

22 Tragedies will always be compared. Saying that the Holocaust was unique will not prevent that. For it is natural, as Israeli scholar Yehuda Bauer has argued, for the Holocaust to be placed in historical context, to be compared with events before and after. "If what happened to the Jews was unique, then [the Holocaust] took place outside of history, and it becomes a mysterious event, an upside-down miracle, so to speak, an event of religious significance in the sense that it is not man-made," he wrote of the problematic nature of the Holocaust. If, on the other hand, "it is not unique, then where are the precedents or parallels?"

23 It is also understandable, as the scholar James Young noted, that Holocaust imagery would be applied to other genocides and slaughters, even if they predated the Final Solution. The Armenians, for example, describe their suffering at the hands of the Turks as the "Armenian Holocaust," though their tragedy occurred twenty-five years before Germany's extermination of the Jews. To the

extent that Nazism and the Holocaust have come to symbolize evil, Armenians and other victims of racial or religious hatred will inevitably seek to appropriate that symbol as a metaphor for their own despair. That the Palestinians should seek to portray themselves as the modern-day historical equivalent of Jews and the Israelis as Nazis is understandable. That the West should fail to note the differences or to challenge the analogy is not. On the other hand, it is equally unacceptable for American Jews and Israelis to discount Palestinian suffering simply because the plight of Palestinians is not comparable to that of the slaughtered Jews.

24 The expression of one's tragedy in the metaphor of another people's sorrow does not imply that the tragedies are equal in intent or scale. But the sloppy use of Holocaust language to evoke the imagery of Nazi terror for noncomparable situations has contributed, often inadvertently, to the relativization of the Jewish genocide. Even Elie Wiesel, who has argued most eloquently for the uniqueness of the Holocaust, has warned in writing and speeches of the dangers of a "nuclear holocaust."

25 Imprecise language is a culprit in many cultures. In France, where love of the nuance of language borders on obsession, the use of the term *déporté,* "deported," masks a historically painful distinction. The Jew who was deported as part of the Final Solution becomes the linguistic equal of the Resistance hero who made a conscious decision to fight fascism. Both were deported. And the fate of neither is revealed in this word.

26 The American penchant for calling victims "martyrs" also blurs. John F. Kennedy, for example, was called a martyr because he was killed when he went to Texas in 1963 to campaign. Martyrs are those who choose to die for their beliefs—like Masha Bruskina. The children of Izieu did not choose Auschwitz. Most of the six million Jews who died in Europe had no choice. The use of the term "martyr" may be well intentioned, since it attempts to add some posthumous grandeur to the slaughter. But it distorts as it tries to give a meaning to the inexplicable.

27 In some countries, the memory of trauma remains more tenacious than in others. The durability of a memory depends in part on the nature of what is being remembered. Wounded Knee and My Lai were unpardonable massacres, but what is more often recalled is the broader context in which they occurred—the dispossession of the Indians and the war in Vietnam.

28 The quality and veracity of memory also depend on who is doing the remembering. Some nations and cultures are simply better than others at remembering. Jews, for example, are geniuses at transmitting memory. They have done so not only by making memory a fundamental touchstone of the faith. They have also devised powerful family-based rituals for sharing the memory of suffering and victory. The Passover seder occurs once a year—not often enough to become routinized and boring and not so infrequently as to be unfamiliar. Through recitation of a well-known story—accompanied by food and wine that help evoke the period—Jews are reminded not only of their bondage and humiliation as slaves in Egypt but of their glorious liberation and Exodus,

their long and arduous journey into independence and the promised land. And unlike the Christian churches, where Christ's sacrifice is commemorated in public services, the Passover seder is held not in a public place, but in the home, where most of our most powerful memories reside.

29 Armenians, too, are skilled at remembrance. A people like the Jews whose history is laced with suffering, Armenians have traditionally placed a premium on transmitting the memory of their trauma as a means of perpetuating a sense of cultural identity, a bond shared by all their scattered flock.

30 Some societies remember better because they value history—the French, for example, who study themselves and perpetually take their national pulse. For some countries, such as the Soviet Union, history is a form of political legitimation. So emphasis is placed on remembrance, even if what is being remembered is partly mythology.

31 As I was writing, I occasionally asked myself: Since remembering the past, particularly painful episodes is so arduous, why bother? Does it really matter that Europeans do not dwell on the war? Will the world be any worse off if the United States does not commemorate the Holocaust?

32 Knowing and remembering the evil in history and in each of us might not prevent a recurrence of genocide. But ignorance of history or suppression of memory removes the surest defense we have, however inadequate, against such gigantic cruelty and indifference to it. There is always a danger of overreaction—the fear that every form of cruelty will inexorably lead to a new Holocaust. But that Europeans and Americans failed to react quickly and decisively to Pol Pot's genocide in Cambodia is alarming evidence that the memory of the Holocaust has not sufficiently sensitized Western democracies to the consequences of violations of human rights elsewhere in the world. On a much smaller scale, the delayed and initially weak response by Western intellectuals to Iran's death warrant against writer Salman Rushdie suggests that even those who should be most aware of the dangers of intolerance are not yet equipped to act as moral and intellectual guardians of the precious freedoms and liberties we enjoy.

33 The memory of evil has not transformed human nature. A new generation of flawed men and women now control the awesomely destructive weapons of the new age. One need not talk of "nuclear holocaust" to be concerned about the consequences of the proliferation and potential use of such weapons anywhere on the planet. The two superpowers that are the custodians of atomic arsenals should pay the closest attention to World War II and the Holocaust.

34 How best can this be done? How can the memory of the Holocaust be transmitted most effectively?

35 No single vehicle of memory is perfect; there is no perfect solution waiting for well-intentioned societies to discover and implement. Each has impressive limitations.

36 Consider, for example, the writing and teaching of history. In France, Robert Paxton's pioneering book on Vichy helped shape young French historians who have, in turn, helped the French confront the past more boldly. In the

Soviet Union, historians are being given access, often for the first time, to a wealth of archival material that may enable them to learn much about their wartime past, if the present political trends continue, that is, if Gorbachev prevails and does not shift direction. But while the work of historians affects a society's intellectuals, it is far harder to translate their work and its significance to the society at large.

37 Historical films and docudramas such as Marcel Ophuls's *The Sorrow and the Pity* and Claude Lanzmann's *Shoah* are effective. But these works, too, are seen mostly by highly educated people. Television's mega-mini-series *Holocaust* and other efforts to translate the Holocaust for mass audiences have proven far more effective at imparting knowledge about and interest in the event. But they risk romanticizing and trivializing history's most complex phenomenon. And in the end, even celluloid is fleeting. The raw power of *Holocaust* has faded dramatically over time as film techniques have advanced and the sophistication of audiences has grown.

38 Then there are commemorations. They are most common in Germany and the Soviet Union. In the United States, commemorations tend to focus on joyous occasions: the Fourth of July celebration, the Bicentennial, Thanksgiving. But while Americans commemorate Memorial Day, the country has no special national commemoration for the Civil War.

39 In Germany, where commemorations have become part of a veritable industry of *Angst,* the results are mixed. If poorly conceived or insensitively conducted, like the harebrained gathering at Bitburg, commemorations can be counterproductive, prompting defensiveness and amnesia rather than collective introspection. My experience in Fulda indicated that commemorations can be effective catalysts of memory for those who have experienced an event. But they often seem to be less effective for those too young to remember what is being commemorated.

40 Another prompter of memory is war-crimes trials and judicial proceedings against those who committed atrocities. But given the age of the perpetrators, such trials will soon end. And even when they are held, the distance from the event, coupled with the failing memory of the victims, sometimes results in doubts about the process itself. In the case of Klaus Barbie, legitimate concerns were raised by respected French officials and intellectuals about whether this trial of a German Gestapo officer in Lyons was a truly useful vehicle for exploring France's role in the war. On the other hand, the transcripts of such trials provide an enduring, permanent record of atrocities, a document that can be used as ammunition against those who may one day seek to challenge the existence or scale of the Nazi Holocaust.

41 Not only the perpetrators of war crimes are dying, the victims are too. And when they are gone, we will lose the single most valuable and emotionally compelling source of information about that horrific event. Menachem Rosensaft once noted that he could never feel the pain his parents felt. No matter how many times he had heard about the camps, he would never really know what it had been like to wake up to the black sun of Auschwitz.

42 Similarly, we can never know what he has felt. For watching and listening to his parents has given him and other children of survivors a special relationship to the Holocaust. They do not draw from the traumas the same conclusions as their parents, of course, but the so-called "second generation" has a proximity to the suffering that most of us cannot share.

43 Perhaps the closest we can come is to watch a survivor speak to us on film. I have never met "Helen K." or "Leon S.," who shared their painful memories with the video archivists at Yale. But I shall never forget their words either. And I continue to believe that their own stories, told to us in their own hauntingly painful, sometimes contradictory words, can do more to make future generations begin to understand the incomprehensible than any other single vehicle of memory. These portraits would not be possible without video technology, the same technology that Rabbi Hier and the other Holocaust entrepreneurs are using to stage the Holocaust shows they hope will broaden their audience. But unlike the sound-and-light shows, the video archives are highly personal documents. They "repersonalize" those who suffered. The victims become people, not numbers.

44 These personal accounts of the Holocaust are not history; they cannot be substituted for factual accounts of the events and analyses of how they could have occurred. But they accomplish something that few history texts can: they stir our emotions; they make us feel the survivor's pain, the bystander's confusion. In attempting to understand the Holocaust, empathy counts for much.

45 The quantity of instruction about the Holocaust has been increasing and its quality improving. But the lessons of history being imparted vary widely and are difficult to regulate or monitor in Germany, the United States, and other countries where national education is the responsibility of states and even smaller political entities. Such decentralization prompts healthy differences and divergent approaches to remembrance. But it also means that the national government is limited in terms of how it can promote memory and what kind of memory it can promote through the schools. Education, moreover, is a protracted, undramatic process that often holds too little attraction for societies like the United States, where quick fixes and prompt results are more highly valued.

46 Many thoughtful Jews have argued that political tests of strength—such as the Waldheim election in Austria and the Bitburg affair in America—are educational and help spark debate, and hence enliven memory. The Waldheim election surely had that effect in the United States and in Western Europe. But Austrians argue, and public opinion surveys support their view, that the Waldheim election had the opposite effect on the Austrians. The Waldheim affair made Austrians more defensive about the past, not less so. It made them feel more, not less, like victims. It made them close their minds to the unpleasant truths they were hearing. It did not illuminate. The confrontational nature of this vehicle of memory made people shun the past, rather than explore it.

47 Moreover, the Germans, the French, and even the Dutch savored the Waldheim scandal in Austria to some extent. It enabled them to compare themselves and their postwar remembrance records favorably. There is no indication

that the Waldheim affair made those countries more reflective about their own moral failings during the war. Ultimately, the Waldheim controversy may prompt a future generation of Austrians to debate the past more candidly, to become more politically sensitive and less anti-Semitic, especially once their national embarrassment subsides. But there is little proof that it has had this effect to date.

48 The Soviet Union is the master of another vehicle of memory—official rewriting of history. Though such rewriting is much denigrated in the West, all governments, even nonauthoritarian ones, make judgments about how much they want their citizens to know about the past. The opening of the archives in the Soviet Union is in some ways the Soviet version of American government's Freedom of Information Act and sunshine laws. But while the Soviets have taken steps to open the vaults of an exceedingly painful, often disgraceful past, the inherent weakness of this official mechanism of memory is that the process can and may be stopped as abruptly as it began. If a society takes the view that memory should be the purview of the state, the search for facts and explanations will remain subservient to political objectives and regimes.

49 There are more creative efforts at prompting memory being tried in the United States than in any other country. America's diversity and its pluralism have given birth to a thousand different remembrance projects, even a moving Holocaust "comic" book, which is intelligent and brutally poignant, not funny at all. What such efforts may lack in taste, they compensate for in sincerity, originality, and enthusiasm.

50 What fosters memory of the Holocaust? Essentially, any intellectual tool, any mechanism, any tradition that reduces its abstraction will do so, any way of making individuals and peoples and nations remember that before the Holocaust was a national and international catastrophe, it was a family tragedy, an individual loss. History books and education are important. But my memory of a single infant's leather shoe encased in glass at Yad Vashem in Jerusalem is as powerful.

51 Abstraction is memory's most ardent enemy. It kills because it encourages distance, and often indifference. We must remind ourselves that the Holocaust was not six million. It was one, plus one, plus one. . . . Only in understanding that civilized people must defend the one, by one, by one . . . can the Holocaust, the incomprehensible, be given meaning.

QUESTIONS FOR WRITING AND DISCUSSION

OBSERVING

1. What universal questions and issues does Miller think the Holocaust raises?
2. What distinctions between Jews and non-Jews does Miller make and why does she make them?

3. Why is memory important for Miller? Why do cultures suppress memory and why is this important to Miller? Explain the four vehicles "to suppress pain and unpleasant memories" that cultures employ.

EVALUATING

1. Can you draw a parallel between the vehicles countries and individuals use to suppress memory?
2. What examples in American history of these vehicles can you think of? Which ones does Miller cite?
3. What dangers does Miller see in applying Holocaust language and imagery to other genocides?

RESPONDING AND APPLYING

1. Miller says some societies remember more and better because they value history. How do you think we stand on that question? What forms does this remembering take?
2. Many ask, Why bother to remember the evil in history? What's your answer to that question?

Madagascar

Steven Schwartz

Steven Schwartz was born in 1950 in Chester, Pennsylvania, and attended Miami University. He received his undergraduate degree from the University of Colorado and his M.F.A. from the University of Arizona. Schwartz has had a variety of jobs, including catering manager, community educator in juvenile rights, and faculty member at Colorado State University, Fort Collins. He has also won a number of awards for his fiction, including the Breakthrough Award, the O. Henry Festival Short Fiction Prize, the Syndicated Fiction Award from International P.E.N., and the Nelson Algren Award for "Madagascar." Schwartz has published two collections of stories: *To Leningrad in Winter: Stories* (1985) and *Lives of the Fathers;* he has had work represented in anthologies including The O. Henry Awards in both 1983 and 1993.

Schwartz has said that "Most crucial for me in fiction writing is that moment when a story loses its husk—an autobiographical covering—and becomes autobiographical in spirit but fictional in fact: an ongoing effort to join memory with imagination." In the story that follows, Schwartz has done more than joined memory to imagination: he has delved into the crucial role memory plays in our lives, charting the ways in which we will behave and believe. For the 1993 O'Henry Awards collection, Schwartz wrote this comment to accompany this story:

" 'Madagascar' grew out of a family story. My uncle, a German Jew, crisscrossed fourteen borders escaping from the Nazis during the early part of World War II. He wound up in Holland and, as the story goes, hid in a baker's oven there. I first heard this story when I was five (my brother passed it on to me), and I suppose my imagination had worked on it ever since. One afternoon years afterward when I was stuck writing, wandering around the house looking for a distraction, I turned on the TV. Two historians were discussing an early plan of Hitler's to send the Jews to Madagascar and then ransom them. It was enough—the spark needed—to awaken the old family story of my uncle: an encoded tale of survivors and war, joined with my own concerns about fathers and sons." (Wm. Abrahams, ed., Prize Stories 1993 The O. Henry Awards, Anchor/Doubleday, 1993)

1 This is a story I know so well.

2 My father, who is twenty-one, is on his way home from finding food for his family. He has traded a gold brooch for a bottle of milk, some vegetables, and a little meat. With his blue eyes and blond hair, my father is the only one in the family who has any chance to pass for gentile on the streets. He makes sure to sit on a public bench, to pick out a paper from the trash and look comfortable, then go on. Among the many edicts against Jews—no traveling in motor cars, no leaning out windows, no using balconies open to the street, no going outside after dark—is one that forbids them to sit on park benches.

3 On the way home he takes another chance, meeting his fiancée in South Amsterdam. Before the deportations started they were to be married; now they must wait until the war ends, each of them hidden in different areas of the city.

4 After dark when he returns to the apartment cellar where his father, mother, and sister hide, he sees the Gestapo drive up. It is May 26, 1943. Tomorrow he will learn that the Great Raid has taken away all the remaining Jews, those in rest homes, in mental institutions, in orphanages, those too sick to walk, those who have cooperated with the Germans thinking it would spare them. Even the entire Jewish Council will be shipped to the labor camps. Now he knows nothing, only that he must avoid the house, that if he is caught out after curfew he will be imprisoned or shot. He steps into a bakery where the baker—a gentile though trusted friend of the family—offers to hide my father. If someone has informed on the family and the Gestapo do not find all the members, the baker knows they will search the whole block; they have been through here before. They will check the back room, the bins of flour, the attic above. They will tap the floor and walls for any hollow spaces. But, ironically, they will not check the ovens.

5 The baker tells my father to climb into an oven no longer in use. At first my father resists. He is afraid. Afraid he will die in there. But there is no other way. The Gestapo will not think to look in such an obvious yet unlikely place.

6 My father crawls in. The sirens stop. His family is taken away to Majdanek, never to return. He lives in the oven until the end of the war, coming out every two hours when business has slowed sufficiently so that he may stretch. Some days the baker stays so busy that my father must be inside for three, four, and once even six hours. Without room to turn over or extend his legs, he remains curled up in a ball. On one occasion, much to his humiliation, he must go to the bathroom in his pants. The baker and his wife kindly provide him with a long apron while his trousers are washed in back. In the oven, he makes up waltzes in his head and has long, complex discussions with himself, marshaling arguments for each side, as to which of the two Strausses, father or son, is the true Waltz King, despite the son being known by the title. He re-creates each note of their compositions and discusses the works with a panel of experts, but always delays the final vote another day so he may weigh the evidence more carefully and reconsider the merits of "Joy and Greetings," "Lorelei-Rheinklange," "Shooting Stars," and a hundred others.

7 After the war my father will listen to music in a high-backed chair. The record player during my childhood, a hi-fi, will be near a whisper in volume, perhaps the loudness at which he originally heard the melodies in his head. When I come into the room, he does not mind being disturbed, but asks me to sit and listen with him. I am ten. "Ah, now," he says raising his hand when the French horns begin to play. "Our favorite part." I do not know if "our" includes me or someone else or if he just speaks of himself in the plural. Soon he closes his eyes, smiles, and extends his hand for mine. Although we are sitting down, me at his feet, our arms sway together, my father waltzing with me from this position. Softly he releases my hand, tells me I have good timing and to remember practice practice practice. Mastering the clarinet is no easy task—even for a bright ten-year-old. He rises from his chair, pulls down the sides of his coat—on Sunday afternoons he wears a jacket and tie at home—returns the record to its sleeve, closes the lid of the hi-fi, and stands with his hands behind his back for a few seconds as though making a silent prayer. Then he says, "Ephram, would you like to accompany me on a walk in the park?" I have my coat on within five seconds.

8 In ninth grade, I am caught shoplifting. I steal a silver pen from a drugstore. I am taken to the police station in Haverford, the small town where we live outside of Philadelphia and where my father teaches European history at Haverford College. My mother is in New York visiting her sisters, so I must call my father. The department secretary informs me that he should return from class within the hour.

9 "Are you at home, Ephram?"

10 "I'm at the police station," I say, shocked by my own admission. Perhaps I want to confess right away and get it over with, not hide the shame I feel, or perhaps I want to boast.

11 Without comment, she makes a note of my situation and promises she will get the message to my father immediately.

12 While I wait for my father in front of the sergeant's desk, on a plastic chair of a faded aqua color, I think how I've wanted to succeed at something, most recently sports. The basketball game I made sure my father attended, positive I would be put in since we were playing a much weaker team, we wound up only narrowly winning, coming from behind. I sat on the bench the whole time. "Very stirring match," my father said afterward, walking me to the car, his arm around me. He knew I felt bad, of course, but there was nothing he could do, nothing I could do.

13 I lack the speed and agility to be first string; and by this season I've lost interest in sports, don't even try out for the team, and instead have fallen in with a group of kids who hang out at the edge of the parking lot, wear pointed shoes with four-inch Cuban heels, pitch quarters during lunch, comb their hair in ducktails (a style that requires me to sleep with my hair parted the opposite way so that the curls will straighten out by morning), and who generally get in trouble for everything from smoking cigarettes to belching "The Star-Spangled Banner" in back of Spanish class. It is 1964. School has become intolerable.

14 My father soon comes to the police station. I am released into his custody and we leave the old armory building of massive, buff sandstone, me in a blue corduroy coat that says Haverford Panthers, my father with his walking stick and tweed overcoat, a cream-colored scarf tucked under his chin. He puts his hand lightly behind me and I involuntarily sink back against his open palm, no easy feat going down a flight of steps. I keep expecting him to ask me what happened. Though I know he won't raise his voice, he never does, let alone physically punish me, I anticipate a lecture, as is his custom when I've misbehaved, which to be honest has not happened all that often. An only child, I have learned how to fulfill my parents' wishes better than my own. They have little reason to find fault with me, so trained am I in the most subtle of ways—a raised eyebrow from my father, a frown from my mother—to find fault with myself first.

15 "Why don't we walk a little bit, Ephram." We stop at the post office. My father buys a roll of stamps and some airmail envelopes for letters to Holland. We have no relatives over there anymore but he keeps a regular correspondence with friends and some members of the Amsterdam Symphony. Before the war he, too, had studied the clarinet and planned to become a professional musician, a source of conflict with his father who wanted my father to have a career in business like himself. When I was younger I always eagerly awaited the letters from Holland so I could steam off the stamps for my collection.

16 We sit down on a bench in front of the post office. It is December but the sun is bright enough for us to rest a moment outdoors.

17 I am prepared to apologize, no longer able to stand my father's silence. At the same time I want to explain that school offers me nothing but hypocrisy, lies, false values, and mushheaded teachers who haven't read a book themselves in years, and that I know this frustration has something to do with what I've done. But before I have the chance, he says he wants to tell me something

about the war, one subject in which I am intensely interested because I always hope he will speak, as he rarely does, of his own experience.

18 "You may not know," he says, "that Hitler had several plans for the Jews. The camps came much later, after he had ruled out other possibilities, such as selling Jews to different countries. He also considered sending the Jews to the island of Madagascar. He wanted to permanently exile them there. Not destroy them, just isolate them on a remote island. This was to be his answer to the Jewish question. I have imagined many times what this situation may have been. I see the beaches, I see the shops, I see the clothes my mother and father wear there—light fabrics, colorful, soft cotton, a little lace on holidays. The sea is blue, the houses white. My mother does not like the heat, but my father welcomes it every morning by doing calisthenics on the balcony. They have settled here, done well, as Jews will do most anywhere, even in Nazi Madagascar. But you see how childish this is of me, don't you? That I want there to be a refuge in the midst of such undeniable evil. Perhaps it is why I decided to study history after the war. I have the liberty to make sense of the many possible pasts historians can always imagine—but the duty to choose only one. Sometimes I fail to honor my task because it is too unbearable. I do not think you are in a very happy period of your life now, Ephram. We are perhaps letting you down, your mother and I. I hope, though, that you will see I am far from perfect and struggle to make meaning of things as much as you do. It is my wish only that you will not harm others in the process, nor assault your own dignity. Leave yourself a small measure of respect in reserve. Always. You see, even in my worst memories—and I know nothing that can be worse for a man than to remember his mother and father and sister while he walks free in the world—even here I have left myself an escape to Madagascar. So allow yourself the same opportunity and do not think so poorly of your own promise that you must succumb to the disgrace of crime. You are bright, imaginative, resourceful. Surely there is a way out of whatever hell it is you too experience. I do not doubt that you can do better than this."

19 Chastened, I sit in silence with my father while we drive home. After his intercession, charges will be dropped by the drugstore. My mother learns nothing of the incident, and I soon separate from the group of misfits I've joined earlier. I also give up the clarinet when I discover—as my teacher agrees—that I feel nothing for the instrument.

20 My college roommate freshman year is named Marshall X. Tiernan. I have chosen to go to a small liberal arts college in Ohio that is not too far from Haverford but far enough so I feel I'm leaving home. Every Tuesday afternoon he asks if I can vacate the room for three hours and fifteen minutes (exactly) so he can listen to music.

21 "I don't mind if you listen while I'm here," I tell him.

22 He shakes his head. He must have privacy. Marshall X. Tiernan, reedy and tall as elephant grass but not nearly so uncultivated, has an enormous collection of classical records that takes up one quarter of our room. He is studying to be

an engineer. Unlike the rest of the men in my dorm, who in the fall of 1968 have grown their hair long and wear patched jeans and army surplus coats, Marshall dresses in Arrow shirts with buttondown collars and keeps a well-inked pen protector in his pocket. He has an unfortunate stutter and does not socialize beyond a fellow engineering student he knows from home. We have a respectful relationship, but I can't say that Marshall is a friend.

23 I agree to leave him alone on Tuesday afternoons, but one time I come back early. I have forgotten some notes that I need to take with me to the library. Expecting to hear music outside the door, I hear nothing and decide to go in. On the bed, with large padded earphones, is Marshall, his thin body rigid as slate. He sees me but does not acknowledge that I am here. His clothes, the sheets, everything is drenched with sweat. His legs tremble, a kind of seizure starts. When the record ends, a composition by Satie, Marshall sits up, quickly strips the bed, throws the sheets in the closet (Tuesday the maids bring new linen), changes his clothes, and returns to his desk to study.

24 We do not discuss the incident.

25 Shortly afterward he drops out of school and moves home. I have the privacy of my own room, a lucky situation that enables me to spend time alone with Jessica, whom I've met at an antiwar meeting. One night while I am telling her, with some amusement I am sorry to say, about Marshall X. Tiernan, I suddenly stop. Jessica says later the look on my face is as if I've seen a ghost, for that is what happens. I suddenly see—no, *feel*—a twenty-one-year-old man curled painfully in a baker's oven, his body kept alive by music.

26 Thanksgiving vacation my sophomore year I bring Jessica home with me. Several years older than I and a senior in anthropology, she helps my mother with Thanksgiving dinner, talks at length with my father who retains a lifelong interest in Margaret Mead, and makes such a positive impression on them both that my mother whispers to me as we are about to leave for the airport, "*She's a jewel.*"

27 But at school I sink into a profound depression. My grades plummet and although Jessica tries to stand by me, I manage to chase even her away. She finds her own apartment yet continues to call every day to check up on me. I become more withdrawn, however, and after a while I ask her to stop phoning. I watch television and eat chocolate donuts, drink milk from the carton and stare at the dark smudge marks my lips leave on the spout.

28 My father appears one afternoon, a surprise visit, he says. I know by the look on his face, though, that he has come because of Jessica. I burst into tears when I see him.

29 "What has happened, Ephram?" he says.

30 But I don't know what has happened, only that I can no longer study, I don't care about school and have no chance of passing finals; I don't care if I flunk out.

31 "Your mother is very worried. She wanted to come with me but I thought it best if I came alone. Is there anything I can do to help you? Is there something

wrong in school, you don't like your courses, the pressure perhaps of too many hours . . ."

32 "I haven't been to class in weeks," I say. "I can't go. Even a trip to the store is overwhelming." I start to cry again. "I want to go home. I want to go back with you."

33 "But what will you do back there?" my father says. "There is nothing at home for you now. You have your studies here, your friends."

34 I look at my father. As always, he is dressed neatly, and warmly, a blue blazer and gray slacks, a wool vest under his coat. Meanwhile, my apartment remains a mess, dishes in the sink, clothes everywhere, my hair unwashed.

35 "I'll find a job, I'll work and make money."

36 "And live at home?"

37 "Yes, what's wrong with that?"

38 My father pauses. "I don't know. I would think that you'd enjoy the freedom of living on your own."

39 "I have freedom and privacy at home. You've never told me what to do or when to come in. I'm not happy here."

40 "But Ephram, changing the place you live will not solve your problems. You need to get to the bottom of this."

41 "I don't care, I just want to go home! Can't you understand that?" I am almost screaming. "I have to go back. I can't make it here!"

42 For the rest of the winter, I work in a bubble gum factory near Philadelphia. It is miserable, but the more miserable the better because I feel as if I deserve the punishment of tedious, demeaning work for failing in school. I am paid minimum wage, $1.85 an hour. So much sugar hangs in the air—we throw bags of it into a mixing contraption resembling the gigantic maw of a steam shovel—that the people who have worked for years at the factory have lost many of their teeth. The gum itself comes out on long (and unsanitary) splintered boards that I carry to racks, which are taken to another station where these long tubular strips of bubble gum—more like waxy pink sausages than gum at this stage—are cut into bite-size pieces with a tool akin to a large pizza wheel.

43 One day at the beginning of spring I receive a letter from the draft board. According to their records my student deferment has expired; I am now eligible to be considered for military service.

44 My father comes home early from his office hour at school. He himself hates the war, the senseless bombing and killing. He has marched with his college's students and protested the presence on campus of recruiters from a chemical company that makes napalm. He has, in fact, been more active than I, who have withdrawn into the routine and oblivion of factory labor, for which there are no deferments.

45 "What are your plans?" my father asks.

46 "I don't know. Canada, I suppose, if all else fails."

47 "And what is 'all else'?"

48 "A medical deferment."

49 "On what basis?"

50 "My mental condition."

51 "But you have never been to a psychiatrist. You have no history."

52 "I don't know then." I shrug. I feel numb, resigned. Why not basic training and then the jungles of Southeast Asia? Could it be much worse than the bubble gum factory?

53 "You will not go. That is all there is to it. We will make sure of that."

54 "And how will you do that?"

55 "We'll hide you, if necessary."

56 I look at my father and almost laugh. But I can see he is serious, alarmed.

57 "What are you talking about—hide me? Where?"

58 He picks up his newspaper and folds it back once, twice, three times until he has a long strip of news in front of him. It is the idiosyncratic way he likes to read the paper—folding it like a map until he is down to a small, tight square of information the size of a wallet or obituary. I think that it must make him feel some control over the world's chaotic events to read about them in such miniature, compressed spaces.

59 My mother brings in a stuck jar for one of us to loosen, and my father puts down his newspaper, which pops open on his lap like an accordion. I am still thinking about his wanting to hide me, aware that the draft has touched off buried fears for him, a flashback to the war, some instinctive response to the personal terror of his family being taken away from him. "I'll get out of it, Dad," I say. "Don't worry. I won't go."

60 "Don't worry, don't worry, is that what you think is the problem here? You have put yourself in this position, though I begged you not to. What is there to do now but worry!" He stands up. "I am *sick* with worry, if you must know. This is my fault. I should have demanded you stay in school, not let you come here!"

61 I have never heard him raise his voice like this. His body begins to tremble, and from the kitchen my mother hurries in with her hand over her heart. "What is going on here?" she says. "What are you arguing about?"

62 "Nothing," my father answers. "The argument is finished," and he goes into his study and closes the door—a sight I am used to from childhood. I hear him weep but rather than sadness I feel a great relief; finally, something I've done has touched him.

63 I do not get drafted but receive a high number in the first lottery. The long and tiresome depression, the deadness I have felt, is replaced with the exhilaration of a survivor, a life reclaimed. I make plans to visit Europe, use the money I've saved from the bubble gum factory to travel for three months. Guidebooks about England, France, Spain, and Italy cover my bed. I pore over them and come up with a tentative itinerary. But when I actually get to Europe, I find I make a detour from England to Holland. I locate the Jewish quarter where my father hid during the war, find his school—the Vossius Gymnasium—and then what I've come for: the bakery. It is still there, although the original owners who saved my father have long ago died. I explain to the current owners who I

am; they tell me in broken English that yes, they have heard what happened here during the war, they know about my father and the Koops, who saved him; the story is legend. "Does the oven still exist by any chance?" I ask.

64 They take me to the back, outside to a shed. It is here, covered with a tablecloth. I ask them if I can be by myself for a few moments and they say certainly, no one will disturb me.

65 A squat and solid object, the oven stands only chest high. I pull open the door and look inside. The opening is deeper than it is wide, the height a little less than two feet. I hoist myself up to sit on the edge. Then I swing my legs around and push my body in feet first. My neck is back against the left edge. I cannot go any farther. My shoulder sticks out too much even when I bend my knees into my chest. I do not understand how he did this, but I am determined to fit inside, so I slide out again and try to enter without my shoes and without my jacket. I tuck my legs under and pull my head inside, my back curved tight as an archer's bow. I hook my finger through the match hole and close the door. The stove smells of mildew and carbon; the scaled roughness of the iron ceiling grates against my cheek. It is pitch black except for the match hole through which I can see. I put my eye up to it and watch. Soon I hear footsteps and I feel frightened, but the footsteps recede into the distance and the bakery becomes silent.

66 Many years later my parents come out to celebrate the occasion of our son's fifth birthday. My father helps Philip build the space station they have brought him. I watch them play together, my father with no awareness of the world around him other than this mission to be his grandson's assistant.

67 While my mother and Judith, my wife, put Philip to bed, my father and I have coffee on the porch. It is a cool summer night and we are in Boulder, Colorado, where the shimmering night sky looks, to my parents, like a planetarium. Judith works in the university's office of communications, while I teach literature. Like my father, I have become a professor.

68 "What are you going to do now?" I ask him. He is on transitional retirement, half-time teaching, and is scheduled to leave the college next year. "Will you finally go to Europe?"

69 "Perhaps," he says, "but your mother's back may not permit it."

70 I nod. The trip out here has cost her a great deal of pain, which she has accepted stoically. If she walks for more than half an hour or sits for that long, the result is the same, inflammation.

71 "Have you thought of going yourself?" I ask.

72 "I could not leave your mother for that long. She would not be well enough."

73 My father sits with the hiking boots he has bought for this trip out west laced tight on his feet. They are spanking new and he has already cleaned them of mud from our climb this afternoon. I take pleasure in seeing him so fond of the mountains, so open to the world out here. "You and I could go," I say. "Together. A nurse could help mother if we went next summer."

74 "I will give it some thought," my father says, but I can see that the veil has already dropped—the complex configuration of blank terror that can still scare me with its suddenness, the yearning on his face vanished. He has gone to Madagascar. He empties the coffee he has spilled in the saucer back into his cup. "I have made a mess here," he says, replacing the dry saucer underneath. He stands up. Pulls down the sides of his jacket. Despite the hiking boots, he has dressed for dinner. "Would you like to go for a walk with me, Ephram?"

75 Yes, I say, and get my coat, eager as always.

76 Last summer Judith and I took Philip to Europe because I wanted to show him where his grandfather grew up. Though the bakery was no longer there—an insurance office now—I described everything about the original building, and the oven. I held him in my arms while he listened with intelligence and care, and I kissed his long lashes and felt his soft cheek against mine. I wondered what he knew that I would never know about him, what pleased him that could not be spoken. When would he grow past me, leave his fatherland, hack and chop and hew whole forests until he could find one piece of hallowed ground to plant the seed of his own self?

77 One night in our hotel I could not sleep and began to write: "Every son's story about his father is, in a sense, written to save himself from his father. It is told so that he may go free and in the telling the son wants to speak so well that he can give his father the power to save himself from his own father." I wrote this on a note card, put it in an airmail envelope, and planned to send it with its Amsterdam postmark to my father.

78 The following morning a call from my mother let us know that my father had suffered a stroke. We flew home immediately, and I rushed to see him in the hospital while Judith waited with Philip at the house. My mother was there by his bed. An IV bottle was connected to his wrist. His other arm I saw had purplish bruises from all the injections and from the blood samples taken. The effects of the stroke made him confuse the simplest objects, or draw on archaic uses—a pen became a plume. A part of his brain had lost the necessary signals for referencing things and faces with words, and now dealt in wild compensatory searches to communicate. When he spoke of Judith he referred to her as my husband, called me "ram" trying to pronounce Ephram, and, saddest of all, could not understand why I had so much trouble understanding him. He had once spoken three languages fluently, and to see him in this state was more of a shock than I could bear. When he fell asleep, I left his room to speak with the doctor, a neurologist who explained to me that a ruptured blood vessel was causing the illogical and distorted speech. Bleeding in the brain. The image for me was vivid, his brain leaking, his skull swelling from the fluid's pressure inside, and all one could do was wait.

79 One day while I sat and read by his bed, he said my name clearly and asked if I could help him get dressed. He had a white shirt and tie in the closet. He spoke with difficulty from the stroke, although his condition had improved and we all believed he would be released soon. I dressed him and because he was

cold I put my sweater over his shoulders and tied the arms in front so he looked like a college man again. While he sat up in bed I held onto his hand to steady him, reminded of how we used to waltz together when I was ten. I said something to him that I had carried around with me for a long while, something that had no basis in fact, only in the private burden of a son traversing the globe for a father's loss. "I'm sorry if I've disappointed you," I told him and he answered me in speech slowed by his stroke, "I forget everything, Ephram." I nodded, but then cried later at his funeral because I thought and hoped he had meant to say forgive.

QUESTIONS FOR WRITING AND DISCUSSION

OBSERVING

1. Who tells the story? What do we find out about him early in the story? What is his relationship with his father?
2. What is the father's Holocaust experience and how does it become significant for the narrator?
3. The story begins with a flashback to Holland in 1943. Why do you think the author begins here? It then adds seven sections or episodes. List and summarize each of these. Then, consider why you think the author included these.
4. The narrator's roommate in college is a black student, Marshall X. Tiernan. What role and significance do you suppose he has in the story?

EVALUATING

1. How does the study and knowledge of history figure in the story? Reread paragraph 18; what does it say about the varieties of history? What does the father mean when he says, "I have the liberty to make sense of the many possible pasts historians can always imagine—but the duty to choose only one."?
2. Why do you think the narrator drops out of school?
3. What parallels do you see between the narrator's and his father's life? Why do you think he wants to get in the oven his father was in?
4. Why do you think the narrator wants to tell his son about the oven?
5. What do you think the story's theme is?

RESPONDING AND APPLYING

1. In paragraph 77, the narrator reflects on the way each generation sees the stories of the past generations. What do you think he is saying?

2. At the story's end, the narrator wants to hear his father say he forgives everything. What do you think he means?
3. In what sense do you write your own story to "save" yourself from the story of your father or mother?
4. This story is about a son and his father, primarily. Do you think anything would be significantly different if the narrator had been a woman? Could we as easily say, "Every daughter's story about her mother is written to save herself from her mother?"

CHAPTER WRITING ASSIGNMENTS

1. Wolfe makes a strong case for building the future on a strong foundation of the past. What problems do you see with that position? How would important changes happen if we all did that? What changes seem most important in this century? How did those who shaped these changes build on or reject the past?
2. What forces today make it hard to reclaim our history? How do electronic media affect our relationship to the past? Do you think young people are any more disinterested in thinking and knowing the past than they were before television and the Internet?
3. Interview your peers or parents regarding their history education with an eye to determining the uses and abuses of history education. What were their best experiences? Their worst? What lessons or readings or discussions can they recall?
4. Interview a history teacher: what led him or her to become a historian? What is a historian to this person? What are the special problems of teaching history?
5. Investigate the national effort to develop a set of history standards. What need motivated such an effort? Why did the first published draft receive such criticism from such people as Lynn Cheney when she was at the National Endowment for the Humanities?

CHAPTER PREVIEW

Chapter Prelude
C. S. Lewis, "Meditation in a Toolshed"

Introductory Essay

Readings
The Hebrew Scriptures
Genesis 1–3; 12; Exodus 1–3; 19–20; Psalm 8, 23
The New Testament Scriptures
Matthew 5–7; 26–28; Luke 15
From The Qur'an
Sūrahs 1, 19, 55, 76

Story
Max Lucado, "A Tale of Two Trees"

Perspectives
Three Faiths, A Common Father
Abraham Heschel, "The Spirit of Judaism"
Dorothy L. Sayers, "The Greatest Drama Ever Staged"
M. S. Modood, "Islam, My Faith, A Personal Statement"

Chapter Writing Assignments

Chapter 4

SPIRITUALITY AND RELIGION: MONOTHEISM AND WESTERN CULTURE

Meditation in a Toolshed

C. S. Lewis

1 I was standing today in the dark toolshed. The sun was shining outside and through the crack at the top of the door there came a sunbeam. From where I stood that beam of light, with the specks of dust floating in it, was the most striking thing in the place. Everything else was almost pitch-black. I was seeing the beam, not seeing things by it.

2 Then I moved, so that the beam fell on my eyes. Instantly the whole previous picture vanished. I saw no toolshed, and (above all) no beam. Instead I saw, framed in the irregular cranny at the top of the door, green leaves moving on the branches of a tree outside and beyond that, 90 odd million miles away, the sun. Looking along the beam, and looking at the beam are very different experiences.

3 But this is only a very simple example of the difference between looking at and looking along. A young man meets a girl. The whole world looks different when he sees her. Her voice reminds him of something he has been trying to remember all his life, and ten minutes casual chat with her is more precious than all the favours that all other women in the world could grant. He is, as they say, 'in love'. Now comes a scientist who describes this young man's experience from the outside. For him it is all an affair of the young man's genes and a recognised biological stimulus. That is the difference between looking *along* the sexual impulse and looking *at* it.

4 When you have got into the habit of making this distinction you will find examples of it all day long. The mathematician sits thinking, and to him it seems that he is contemplating timeless and spaceless truths about quantity. But the cerebral physiologist, if he could look inside the mathematician's head, would

find nothing timeless and spaceless there—only tiny movements in the grey matter. The savage dances in ecstasy at midnight before Nyonga and feels with every muscle that his dance is helping to bring the new green crops and the spring rain and the babies. The anthropologist, observing that savage, records that he is performing a fertility ritual of the type so-and-so. The girl cries over her broken doll and feels that she has lost a real friend; the psychologist says that her nascent maternal instinct has been temporarily lavished on a bit of shaped and coloured wax.

5 As soon as you have grasped this simple distinction, it raises a question. You get one experience of a thing when you look along it and another when you look at it. Which is the 'true' or 'valid' experience? Which tells you most about the thing? And you can hardly ask that question without noticing that for the last fifty years or so everyone has been taking the answer for granted. It has been assumed without discussion that if you want the true account of religion you must go, not to religious people, but to anthropologists; that if you want the true account of sexual love you must go, not to lovers, but to psychologists; that if you want to understand some 'ideology' (such as medieval chivalry or the nineteenth-century idea of a 'gentleman'), you must listen not to those who lived inside it, but to sociologists.

6 The people who look *at* things have had it all their own way; the people who look *along* things have simply been brow-beaten. It has even come to be taken for granted that the external account of a thing somehow refutes or 'debunks' the account given from inside. 'All these moral ideals which look so transcendental and beautiful from inside', says the wiseacre, 'are really only a mass of biological instincts and inherited taboos.' And no one plays the game the other way round by replying, 'If you will only step inside, the things that look to you like instincts and taboos will suddenly reveal their real and transcendental nature.'

7 That, in fact, is the whole basis of the specifically 'modern' type of thought. And is it not, you will ask, a very sensible basis? For, after all, we are often deceived by things from the inside. For example, the girl who looks so wonderful while we're in love, may really be a very plain, stupid, and disagreeable person. The savage's dance to Nyonga does not really cause the crops to grow. Having been so often deceived by looking along, are we not well advised to trust only to looking at?—in fact to discount all these inside experiences?

8 Well, no. There are two fatal objections to discounting them *all.* And the first is this. You discount them in order to think more accurately. But you can't think at all—and therefore, of course, can't think accurately—if you have nothing to think *about.* A physiologist, for example, can study pain and find out that it 'is' (whatever *is* means) such and such neural events. But the word *pain* would have no meaning for him unless he had 'been inside' by actually suffering. If he had never looked *along* pain he simply wouldn't know what he was looking *at.* The very subject for his inquiries from outside exists for him only because he has, at least once, been inside.

9 This case is not likely to occur, because every man has felt pain. But it is perfectly easy to go on all your life giving explanations of religion, love, morality, honour, and the like, without having been inside any of them. And if you do that, you are simply playing with counters. You go on explaining a thing without knowing what it is. That is why a great deal of contemporary thought is, strictly speaking, thought about nothing—all the apparatus of thought busily working in a vacuum.

10 The other objection is this: let us go back to the toolshed. I might have discounted what I saw when looking along the beam (i.e., the leaves moving and the sun) on the ground that it was 'really only a strip of dusty light in a dark shed'. That is, I might have set up as 'true' my 'side vision' of the beam. But then that side vision is itself an instance of the activity we call seeing. And this new instance could also be looked at from outside. I could allow a scientist to tell me that what seemed to be a beam of light in a shed was 'really only an agitation of my own optic nerves'. And that would be just as good (or as bad) a bit of debunking as the previous one. The picture of the beam in the toolshed would now have to be discounted just as the previous picture of the trees and the sun had been discounted. And then, where are you?

11 In other words, you can step outside one experience only by stepping inside another. Therefore, if all inside experiences are misleading, we are always misled. The cerebral physiologist may say, if he chooses, that the mathematician's thought is 'only' tiny physical movements of the grey matter. But then what about the cerebral physiologist's own thought at that very moment? A second physiologist, looking at it, could pronounce it also to be only tiny physical movements in the first physiologist's skull. Where is the rot to end?

12 The answer is that we must never allow the rot to begin. We must, on pain of idiocy, deny from the very outset the idea that looking *at* is, by its own nature, intrinsically truer or better than looking *along*. One must look both *along* and *at* everything. In particular cases we shall find reason for regarding the one or the other vision as inferior. Thus the inside vision of rational thinking must be truer than the outside vision which sees only movements of the grey matter; for if the outside vision were the correct one all thought (including this thought itself) would be valueless, and this is self-contradictory. You cannot have a proof that no proofs matter. On the other hand, the inside vision of the savage's dance to Nyonga may be found deceptive because we find reason to believe that crops and babies are not really affected by it. In fact, we must take each case on its merits. But we must start with no prejudice for or against either kind of looking. We do not know in advance whether the lover or the psychologist is giving the more correct account of love, or whether both accounts are equally correct in different ways, or whether both are equally wrong. We just have to find out. But the period of brow-beating has got to end.

QUESTIONS FOR WRITING AND DISCUSSION

OBSERVING

1. In this essay, Lewis distinguishes between "looking *at*" and "looking *along*." What is the distinction he is making? Do you agree with him that our culture tends to value one more than the other?
2. Do you regard one way of looking—either *at* or *along*—more valuable or reliable than the other for determining what is true of something? Does Lewis make it an "either-or" matter or does he adopt a "both-and" perspective?

EVALUATING

1. Lewis says the two ways of looking are "very different experiences"; how different are they in *your* experience?
2. Think of something you tend to look *at* or *along* exclusively; what difference would it make in what you saw or how you judged its worth if you exchanged viewpoints?

RESPONDING AND APPLYING

1. Do you think contemporary society tends to discount the subjective or religious in favor of the objective and scientific? Is there good reason to do so?
2. Does science seem to rely on "evidence," and religion on "faith"? Is this a fair characterization of both realms of experience and inquiry? Does it strike you that it is difficult to credibly approach the topic of *spirituality*—of whether there is a world *beyond this one* that impinges upon it or whether there is a *world within us* that bears meditation and scrutiny for insights into what or who I am?

C. S. Lewis, famous for his *Chronicles of Narnia* and many other works of fiction and nonfiction dealing with the quest for knowledge about God and the meaning of the universe, poses some challenging questions in his short essay about the nature of "looking," and what we can see—and not see—depending upon the vantage point we take. Ultimately, Lewis' essay calls upon us to examine carefully what we claim as knowledge, especially knowledge about the supernatural or preternatural—*about spirituality and religion*—and how to identify our assumptions and presuppositions that determine "what" we can even see.

As a beginning point, the essay helps illustrate how important and foundational the spiritual search, as both "looking 'at' *and* 'along'," is in the fabric of our lives even at the edge of the twenty-first century. The following questions and the means by which we answer them often turn on how we are "looking": What does it mean to be human? How do I live an ethical life? How do I live in community with others? How do I raise a family, and what is a family anyway? Is there a God/supreme being or beings? Is there a life after death? If so—or if not—how should we live in response to this news?

It is clear that in terms of spiritual search and the very vocabulary of faith, the West has been primarily influenced by the traditions represented in two monotheistic faiths, Judaism and Christianity, and, subsequently—and increasingly at the end of the twentieth century—by their encounter with a third, Islam. In this chapter, we will explore the topic of spirituality by looking closely at some representative *Scriptures* from each of these major faiths—with a heavier emphasis and selection from Judaism and Christianity, whose foundation is in the book many call "The Bible" and which consists of two large units, the Hebrew Scriptures and the New Testament. Both the Bible and the Qur'an, the Holy Scriptures of Islamic faith, present a spirituality based upon "monotheism," by which we refer to a system of belief in which the object of worship is one, single god or supreme being—a personal-infinite god, as theologians might say.

The God of the Bible and of the Qur'an reveals himself (yes, the masculine pronoun is preeminent in both texts) as a "self" or a "person" to humankind through words, actions, and events and prescribes both a code of behavior and a destiny for those who would follow him. Such a deity, traditionally referred to with the masculine pronoun, has a "will" that his creation should conform to, and, as such, he may be petitioned, obeyed, disobeyed, and so on. Such a monotheism is promoted in distinction to a polytheism ("many gods," like those who populate Greek and Roman myth) or a pantheism (a belief system in which deity subsumes and/or corresponds to all living, organic, or sentient beings—all is God—and is not, as in a monotheistic system, a "someone" who stands outside creation or the created order but is "within" it).

In some sense the Scripture selections featured here themselves are more profound stories than any that appear in the other chapters of this book, narratives that speak to the heart of what Judaism, Christianity, or Islam are about: a story written by God in history with human characters interacting with God and their fellow creatures in a grand and divine drama. For our Perspectives section in this chapter, we will instead present three "believers," speaking about their faith and its meaning for their own lives—personal testimony, if you will, about *looking at and along* their respective faiths.

What the main texts, the ancient texts presented here, share is an "Abrahamic origin," that is, each faith may be traced back to the life and times of a historical personage by the name of Abraham, whose encounter with God is first recorded in the Book of Genesis, and in many ways forms the paradigm for both Christianity and Islam. Abraham is not only a major character and influential, even dominant, thematically in the Hebrew Scriptures, but he also serves a major theological role in the New Testament Scriptures and in the sacred text of Islam, the Qur'an.

By reading some primary Biblical and Qur'anic texts, you may encounter firsthand the dynamics of these faiths and how they have shaped the peoples and nations in which their theological foundations have taken hold. The fact is, these texts continue to influence the cultures in which they are read in both direct and subtle ways; even when they are not received literally as authoritative documents that compel their readers to "obey" their directives, the stories, characters, and themes of the Bible and the Qur'an shape the contexts and social norms in which they are found. It is impossible to underestimate the profound effect the Bible in particular has had on Western art and literature, as well as the politics and social order of Western civilization. The same can certainly be said of the Qur'an in the contemporary Middle East, and increasingly in the West as well.

Reading any ancient text—including the Bible and the Qur'an—can be a perilous tightrope walk between two extremes. The first extreme is dismissing an ancient text out of hand because it *is* old—that is, seemingly out of date or irrelevant because of the wide time span between the composition of the text and your reading of it. The second extreme is reading into the ancient text all of our twentieth century preconceptions and biases about the age in which it is written, thus precluding the possibility of its speaking out of its own age to ours directly. Unfortunately, the tightrope walk we speak of is unavoidable, short of time-travel, and all the more perilous when we are reading sacred texts like these.

Understanding Sacred Texts

Sacred texts are those writings that are revered by a community of readers as documents that speak unique, universal truths about our lives as human beings—usually, though not always, because they are thought to be communications from a divine being. It is important to note that the sacredness of a given text is therefore only partly a function of what it contains; the reverance paid to any putatively sacred text is intimately related to the way it is *used* and *received* in a particular reading community. For instance, those inside a particular faith have a different vantage point with which to view such a text than those outside it; what may be to you perhaps a merely interesting literary or political or historical text may be an essential, transcendently significant one that makes certain demands to someone else. The moral/political/social impact of a text always depends in large measure, then, upon the "acceptance" of its authority as a divinely inspired or uniquely insightful document. Nevertheless, even a text that is no longer held as "sacred" by a majority of people within a culture can continue to have a profound influence on their way of looking at the world and how a society should function. In general, these six characteristics of sacred texts should be noted:

1 Sacred texts usually profess to be a product of *revelation* (divine inspiration) or *personal illumination* (contemplative discovery). For instance, the Bible authors often claim divine authorship of their words, while the insights of Gautama Buddha are usually traced to his disciplined meditation.

2 Sacred texts offer a *prescriptive pattern of life* (a set of moral codes, a "path," a list of duties, etc.) that set the believer apart from the society in which she or he lives. The Law of Moses and its elaborations in the Sermon on the Mount, the Parables of Jesus, and the numerous letters from the Apostle Paul clearly represent exhortations and moral governance that demand certain kinds of behavior and exclude others. The Qur'an provides Muslims with a patterned lifestyle that includes religious observance, for example, five prayer sessions a day with the body positioned reverently toward the sacred site of Mecca and a code of ethics that envelopes and shapes their family lives and the responses to moral challenges in the societies in which they live.

3 Sacred texts tend to be *anachronistic* (deliberately out of step with "the times") by offering a worldview that calls in question the predominant or existing one in the culture. The Pentateuch, the first five books of the Hebrew Scriptures that are traditionally ascribed to Moses, like the Qur'an, are defiantly monotheistic, presenting a holy, righteous God who opposes the often violent and unethical polytheism of the pagan world; present-day Islam, Judaism, and Christianity continue to offer alternative frameworks to the status quo or more secular creeds to guide believers in their moral decision-making.

4 Sacred texts often are *offensive to the sensibilities within the culture in which their authority is evoked.* This occurs usually by demanding that its readers return to an old or embrace a new standard of behavior or conduct that is in direct conflict with prevailing norms. This is true not only in the times in which the sacred text is written, but also in the contemporary present. For instance, the Bible is increasingly criticized by feminist readers for its apparently "patriarchal orientation" in which certain social roles and positions of authority are presented exclusively as male or masculine domains as well as its exclusive use of a masculine deity—issues which also affect Western perceptions of Islamic tradition. Nevertheless, some social reformers in many Third World cultures continue to find comfort in the Bible's championing of compassion toward all humankind and the rights of individuals for their attempts to liberate their population from undemocratic and oppressive governments.

5 Sacred texts are *sometimes obscure, demand careful interpretation, and inspire considerable debate not only between believers and skeptics, but also among believers.* The reasons for this are various, but they involve such matters as: the imperfection of language as an instrument for conveying a truth that is sometimes inherently mysterious; the ancient languages in which the texts are found sometimes present scholars with puzzles and difficulties of lexicon and syntax that make passages ambiguous; and the original process of collecting, copying, and preserving such texts are often beset by problems that are only partially offset by the care which sacred texts naturally elicit.

6 Sacred texts usually *generate a large body of secondary literature that is dedicated to their interpretation—both in terms of what they meant originally to their intended readers and how they can be applied to the present.* The Talmud, for instance, is a collection of ancient rabbinical writing providing the basis for religious authority in traditional Judaism. For some believers, these secondary texts sometimes take on an importance approaching the ancient text itself and become one of the means by which believers define, debate, and defend orthodoxy.

With these principles in mind, it is time to encounter these ancient texts.

HEBREW SCRIPTURES

Genesis 1–3, 12; Exodus 1–3, 19–20; Psalms 8, 23.

The Hebrew Scriptures are traditionally classified according to three divisions: (1) The Law (Torah); (2) The Prophets, which contains both history and prophecy, that is, foretelling of events and exhortation to the people of Israel; and (3) The Writings, which contains the wisdom literature of ancient Israel, including the Psalms, the Book of Job, and the Proverbs of Solomon. The narratives of the Hebrew Scriptures essentially comprise the story of God's mighty acts in history and his holy character as seen through the eyes of Jewish faith. These events include the creation of the world and call of Abraham, God's special envoy to the world (Genesis); God's special covenant or agreement with a chosen people, the descendents of Israel, led by Moses (Exodus); God's passion for justice and righteousness in the earth (most of the Prophets); and God's desire for love and mercy in the nation of Israel and the world at large (the Proverbs and the Psalms).

All of the Hebrew Scriptures were originally composed in the Hebrew language and come to us in English through the work of translators. The importance of these works is indicated in the care of transmission and the continuing effort of accurate and sensitive translation of its meaning into countless world languages. The events depicted in the Pentateuch are variously dated by Biblical scholars and archaeologists. Beginning with the person of Abraham, the first Bible character, chronologically speaking, whose identity might be subjected to historical corroboration, we might set the events of Genesis 12 around 1900 B.C.E. The fully developed Law emerges with Moses somewhere around 1300 B.C.E. And the events in the life of David presented in the Psalms included in our readings are approximately 900 B.C.E.

In reading the short excerpts from the Bible that we have provided in our text, you may find it helpful to get a complete Bible to study in order to gain the larger context that will help you interpret the events and people encountered there. In *Genesis* the reader is presented with a world created by God in unspoiled beauty and grandeur and its human creatures placed by God in the Garden of Eden to serve Him in peace and harmony, only to have their world shattered through the introduction of temptation and sin. Expelled from the Garden, humankind multiplies and travels over the earth but is not abandoned by God, who calls men and women out of their native lands to do His will and forge a new nation with a new ethic, compared with cultures around it. Abraham and his family are among the first to be singled out in the Biblical story, as God promises to him that his many descendants will occupy a land and become a blessing to the whole world. This is the people of Israel.

Exodus thus tells the story of Israel's formation as a nation under slavery, the raising up of a leader (Moses) who leads them out of their slavery in Egypt and out to meet their God at the foot of Mount Sinai. Soon after committing themselves to the covenant, they break the covenant. Interceding for his people, Moses renews the covenant with Yahweh, the name by which God reveals Himself in Exodus 3, "I Am Who I Am," an everlasting, personal being, outside of time, who nevertheless cares for and identifies with the plight of peoples trapped in despair. As heirs of God's covenant with Abraham, the chosen people are called out by a jealous God, and their rigid monotheism, a belief in a personal-infinite God who is both separate from His creation but immanent in it, distinguishes them from their idolatrous, polytheistic neighbors. The so-called pagan world in which the Israelites found themselves was often a nightmare of cruelty, slavery, inhumane treatment of women and children, and general savagery. Bound together with the Law compiled by Moses, Israel is called to be faithful to the covenant of their fathers and to be holy as God is holy.

The Psalms of King David of Israel (ca. 930 B.C.E.) celebrate the dealings of God with the people of Israel and offer repentance, praise, and honor to the God they worship. David is a well-known Biblical figure whose exploits as a lowly shepherd boy who rises up to defend his people against the taunts of the giant, Goliath, and who is eventually anointed as King of Israel, have made his name legendary in Western culture. Not only a skilled soldier and leader, David is traditionally thought of as a remarkably talented musician whose songs and psalms could enchant the soul and soothe the violent passions of the beast in humans. The two selections from the Psalms provide a glimpse of Israel's view of humankind's place in God's universe (Psalm 8) and their reverence for God as shepherd of their lives—a poignant image drawn from David's youth (Psalm 23).

The first five books of the Hebrew Scriptures—Genesis through Deuteronomy—have been traditionally ascribed, as we noted earlier, to Moses. In fact, there has been an ongoing debate in Biblical scholarship since the middle of the nineteenth century about the historical authenticity of the books, given their supernaturalism and emphasis on divine intervention in the affairs of humankind, and the disputed claims of Mosaic authorship. Much post-Enlightenment Biblical scholarship of the late eighteenth century through the nineteenth century had begun to question and reinterpret many of the miraculous accounts found in the Bible from a non-miraculous, "natural law" perspective, attempting to make the Biblical narrative more "scientific" and less susceptible to unwarranted or ill-informed religious use. Likewise, the debate regarding Mosaic authorship has often centered around the unity and coherence of Genesis as a literary document, for instance, its use of different names to refer to God in the narrative, a fact that leads many Biblical scholars to conclude that Genesis is the product of several authors over a longer period of time. For some believers, the key issue here is as much a theological one as a historical one; since many conservative Jewish and Christian sects rest the authority of the Bible as a whole upon the inerrancy and infallibility of each section of Scripture, the skepticism among leading Biblical scholars regarding Mosaic authorship—something some readers think the Bible in its present form clearly claims—is a special problem.

from Genesis

I. The Origin of the World and of Mankind

1. The Creation and the Fall

The First Account of the Creation[a]

1 2 **1** In the beginning God created the heavens and the earth. ·Now the earth was a formless void, there was darkness over the deep, and God's spirit hovered over the water.

3 4 5 God said, 'Let there be light', and there was light. ·God saw that light was good, and God divided light from darkness. ·God called light 'day', and darkness he called 'night'. Evening came and morning came: the first day.

6 7 8 God said, 'Let there be a vault[b] in the waters to divide the waters in two'. And so it was. ·God made the vault, and it divided the waters above the vault from the waters under the vault. ·God called the vault 'heaven'. Evening came and morning came: the second day.

9 10 God said, 'Let the waters under heaven come together into a single mass, and let dry land appear'. And so it was. ·God called the dry land 'earth' and the mass of waters 'seas', and God saw that it was good.

---

[1] a. Ascribed to the 'priestly' source. . . . b. For the ancient Semites, the 'arch' or 'vault' of the sky was a solid dome holding the upper waters in check.

11 God said, 'Let the earth produce vegetation: seed-bearing plants, and fruit 12 trees bearing fruit with their seed inside, on the earth'. And so it was. •The earth produced vegetation: plants bearing seed in their several kinds, and trees bearing fruit with their seed inside in their several kinds. God saw that it was good. 13 •Evening came and morning came: the third day.

14 God said, 'Let there be lights in the vault of heaven to divide day from night, and let them indicate festivals, days and years. 15 •Let there be lights in the vault of heaven to shine on the earth.' And so it was. 16 •God made the two great lights:[c] the greater light to govern the day, the smaller light to govern the night, and the stars. 17 •God set them in the vault of heaven to shine on the earth, 18 •to govern the day and the night and to divide light from darkness. God saw that it was good. 19 •Evening came and morning came: the fourth day.

20 God said, 'Let the waters teem with living creatures, and let birds fly above the earth within the vault of heaven'. And so it was. 21 •God created great sea-serpents and every kind of living creature with which the waters teem, and every kind of winged creature. God saw that it was good. 22 •God blessed them, saying, 'Be fruitful, multiply, and fill the waters of the seas; and let the birds multiply upon the earth'. 23 •Evening came and morning came: the fifth day.

24 God said, 'Let the earth produce every kind of living creature: cattle, reptiles,[d] and every kind of wild beast'. And so it was. 25 •God made every kind of wild beast, every kind of cattle, and every kind of land reptile. God saw that it was good.

26 God said, 'Let us[e] make man[f] in our own image, in the likeness of ourselves, and let them be masters of the fish of the sea, the birds of heaven, the cattle, all the wild beasts and all the reptiles that crawl upon the earth'.

27 God created man in the image of himself,
in the image of God he created him,
male and female he created them.

28 God blessed them, saying to them, 'Be fruitful, multiply, fill the earth and conquer it. Be masters of the fish of the sea, the birds of heaven and all living animals on the earth.' 29 •God said, 'See, I give you all the seed-bearing plants that are upon the whole earth, and all the trees with seed-bearing fruit; this shall be your food. 30 •To all wild beasts, all birds of heaven and all living reptiles on the earth I give all the foliage of plants for food.' And so it was. 31 •God saw all he had made, and indeed it was very good. Evening came and morning came: the sixth day.

---

c. Their names are omitted deliberately: the sun and the moon were worshipped by neighbouring peoples, and here they are treated as no more than lamps to light the earth and regulate the calendar. d. 'Things which crawl', a general term for small mammals, reptiles, amphibians and insects. e. Perhaps the plural of majesty; the common name for God was *Elohim*, a plural form. But possibly the plural form implies a discussion between God and his heavenly court. f. Man, *adam*, is a collective noun ('mankind'), hence the plural in 'Let them be masters of . . .'.

1 2 **2** Thus heaven and earth were completed with all their array. •On the seventh day God completed the work he had been doing. He rested on the seventh 3 day after all the work he had been doing. •God blessed the seventh day and made it holy, because on that day he had rested after all his work of creating.
4 Such were the origins of heaven and earth when they were created.

THE SECOND ACCOUNT OF THE CREATION.[a] PARADISE

5 At the time when Yahweh God made earth and heaven •there was as yet no wild bush on the earth nor had any wild plant yet sprung up, for Yahweh God had 6 not sent rain on the earth, nor was there any man to till the soil. •However, a 7 flood was rising from the earth and watering all the surface of the soil. •Yahweh God fashioned man of dust from the soil. Then he breathed into his nostrils a breath of life, and thus man became a living being.

8 Yahweh God planted a garden in Eden which is in the east, and there he 9 put the man he had fashioned. •Yahweh God caused to spring up from the soil every kind of tree, enticing to look at and good to eat, with the tree of life and 10 the tree of the knowledge of good and evil in the middle of the garden. •A river flowed from Eden to water the garden, and from there it divided to make four 11 streams.[b] The first is named the Pishon, and this encircles the whole land of 12 Havilah where there is gold. •The gold of this land is pure; bdellium[c] and onyx 13 stone are found there. •The second river is named the Gihon, and this encircles 14 the whole land of Cush. •The third river is named the Tigris, and this flows to 15 16 the east of Ashur. The fourth river is the Euphrates. •Yahweh God took the man 17 and settled him in the garden of Eden to cultivate and take care of it. •Then Yahweh God gave the man this admonition, 'You may eat indeed of all the trees in the garden. Nevertheless of the tree of the knowledge of good and evil you are not to eat, for on the day you eat of it you shall most surely die.'

18 Yahweh God said, 'It is not good that the man should be alone. I will make 19 him a helpmate.' •So from the soil Yahweh God fashioned all the wild beasts and all the birds of heaven. These he brought to the man to see what he would call 20 them; each one was to bear the name the man would give it. •The man gave names to all the cattle, all the birds of heaven and all the wild beasts. But no 21 helpmate suitable for man was found for him. •So Yahweh God made the man fall into a deep sleep. And while he slept, he took one of his ribs and enclosed 22 it in flesh. •Yahweh God built the rib he had taken from the man into a woman, 23 and brought her to the man. •The man exclaimed:

> 'This at last is bone from my bones,
> and flesh from my flesh!
> This is to be called woman,[d]
> for this was taken from man.'

---

[2] a. From the 'Yahwistic' source. . . . b. Verses 10–14 are intended to fix the locality of Eden. However, the rivers Pishon and Gihon are unknown, and the two 'lands' named are probably not the regions designated elsewhere by the same names. c. An aromatic resin. d. In Hebrew a play on the words *ishshah* (woman) and *ish* (man).

24 This is why a man leaves his father and mother and joins himself to his wife, and they become one body.

25 Now both of them were naked, the man and his wife, but they felt no shame in front of each other.

The Fall

1 3 The serpent was the most subtle of all the wild beasts that Yahweh God had made. It asked the woman, 'Did God really say you were not to eat from any 2 of the trees in the garden?' •The woman answered the serpent, 'We may eat the 3 fruit of the trees in the garden. •But of the fruit of the tree in the middle of the 4 garden God said, "You must not eat it, nor touch it, under pain of death".' Then 5 the serpent said to the woman, 'No! You will not die! •God knows in fact that on the day you eat it your eyes will be opened and you will be like gods, know-6 ing good and evil.' •The woman saw that the tree was good to eat and pleasing to the eye, and that it was desirable for the knowledge that it could give. So she took some of its fruit and ate it. She gave some also to her husband who was 7 with her, and he ate it. •Then the eyes of both of them were opened and they realised that they were naked. So they sewed fig-leaves together to make themselves loin-cloths.

8 The man and his wife heard the sound of Yahweh God walking in the garden in the cool of the day, and they hid from Yahweh God among the trees 9 of the garden. •But Yahweh God called to the man. 'Where are you?' he asked. 10 'I heard the sound of you in the garden;' he replied 'I was afraid because I was 11 naked, so I hid.' •'Who told you that you were naked?' he asked 'Have you been 12 13 eating of the tree I forbade you to eat?' •The man replied, 'It was the woman 14 you put with me; she gave me the fruit, and I ate it'. •Then Yahweh God asked the woman, 'What is this you have done?' The woman replied, 'The serpent tempted me and I ate'.

Then Yahweh God said to the serpent, 'Because you have done this,

'Be accursed beyond all cattle,
all wild beasts.
You shall crawl on your belly and eat dust
every day of your life.
15 I will make you enemies of each other:
you and the woman,
your offspring and her offspring.
It will crush your head
and you will strike its heel.'

16 To the woman he said:

'I will multiply your pains in childbearing,
you shall give birth to your children in pain.
Your yearning shall be for your husband,
yet he will lord it over you.'

17 To the man he said, 'Because you listened to the voice of your wife and ate from the tree of which I had forbidden you to eat,

'Accursed be the soil because of you.
With suffering shall you get your food from it
every day of your life.
18 It shall yield you brambles and thistles,
and you shall eat wild plants.
19 With sweat on your brow
shall you eat your bread,
until you return to the soil,
as you were taken from it.
For dust you are
and to dust you shall return.'

20 The man named his wife 'Eve' because she was the mother of all those who live.[a] 21 ·Yahweh God made clothes out of skins for the man and his wife, and they put them on. 22 ·Then Yahweh God said, 'See, the man has become like one of us, with his knowledge of good and evil. He must not be allowed to stretch his hand out next and pick from the tree of life also, and eat some and live for ever.' 23 ·So Yahweh God expelled him from the garden of Eden, to till the soil from which he had been taken. 24 ·He banished the man, and in front of the garden of Eden he posted the cherubs, and the flame of a flashing sword, to guard the way to the tree of life.

II. The Story of Abraham

The Call of Abraham

1 **12** Yahweh said to Abram, 'Leave your country, your family and your father's house, for the land I will show you. 2 ·I will make you a great nation; I will bless you and make your name so famous that it will be used as a blessing.

3 'I will bless those who bless you:
I will curse those who slight you.
All the tribes of the earth
shall bless themselves by you.'

4 So Abram went as Yahweh told him, and Lot went with him. Abram 5 was seventy-five years old when he left Haran. ·Abram took his wife Sarai, his nephew Lot, all the possessions they had amassed and the people they had acquired in Haran. They set off for the land of Canaan, and arrived there.

6 Abram passed through the land as far as Shechem's holy place, the Oasis 7 of Moreh. At that time the Canaanites were in the land. ·Yahweh appeared to Abram and said, 'It is to your descendants that I will give this land'. So Abram 8 built there an altar for Yahweh who had appeared to him. ·From there he

---

[3] a. The name Eve is explained as derived from the Hebrew verb, 'to live'.

moved on to the mountainous district east of Bethel, where he pitched his tent, with Bethel to the west and Ai to the east. There he built an altar to Yahweh and
9 invoked the name of Yahweh. •Then Abram made his way stage by stage to the Negeb.

Abraham in Egypt

10 When famine came to the land Abram went down into Egypt, to stay there for
11 the time, since the land was hard pressed by the famine. •On the threshold of
12 Egypt he said to his wife Sarai, 'Listen! I know you are a beautiful woman. When the Egyptians see you they will say, "That is his wife", and they will kill me but
13 spare you. •Tell them you are my sister, so that they may treat me well because
14 of you and spare my life out of regard for you.' •When Abram arrived in Egypt
15 the Egyptians did indeed see that the woman was very beautiful. When Pharaoh's officials saw her they sang her praises to Pharaoh and the woman was
16 taken into Pharaoh's palace. •He treated Abram well because of her, and he received flocks, oxen, donkeys, men and women slaves, she-donkeys and camels.
17 •But Yahweh inflicted severe plagues on Pharaoh and his household because of
18 Abram's wife Sarai. •So Pharaoh summoned Abram and said, 'What is this you
19 have done to me? Why did you not tell me she was your wife? •Why did you say, "She is my sister", so that I took her for my wife? Now, here is your wife. Take
20 her and go!' •Pharaoh committed him to men who escorted him back to the frontier with his wife and all he possessed.

from Exodus

I. The Liberation From Egypt

A. Israel in Egypt

The Prosperity of the Hebrews in Egypt

1 2 **1** These are the names of the sons of Israel who went with Jacob to Egypt,
3 each with his family: •Reuben, Simeon, Levi and Judah, •Issachar, Zebulun
4 5 and Benjamin, •Dan and Naphtali, Gad and Asher. •In all, the descendants of
6 Jacob numbered seventy persons. Joseph was in Egypt already. •Then Joseph
7 died, and his brothers, and all that generation. •But the sons of Israel were fruitful and grew in numbers greatly; they increased and grew so immensely powerful that they filled the land.

The Hebrews Oppressed

8 Then there came to power in Egypt a new king who knew nothing of Joseph.
9 'Look,' he said to his subjects 'these people, the sons of Israel, have become so

10 numerous and strong that they are a threat to us. ·We must be prudent and take steps against their increasing any further, or if war should break out, they might add to the number of our enemies. They might take arms against us and so es-
11 cape out of the country.' ·Accordingly they put slave-drivers over the Israelites to wear them down under heavy loads. In this way they built the store-cities of
12 Pithom and Rameses[a] for Pharaoh. ·But the more they were crushed, the more
13 they increased and spread, and men came to dread the sons of Israel. ·The Egyp-
14 tians forced the sons of Israel into slavery, ·and made their lives unbearable with hard labour, work with clay and with brick, all kinds of work in the fields; they forced on them every kind of labour.

15 The king of Egypt then spoke to the Hebrew midwives, one of whom was
16 named Shiphrah, and the other Puah. ·'When you midwives attend Hebrew women,' he said 'watch the two stones[b] carefully. If it is a boy, kill him; if a girl,
17 let her live.' ·But the midwives were God-fearing: they disobeyed the command
18 of the king of Egypt and let the boys live. ·So the king of Egypt summoned the
19 midwives. 'Why' he asked them 'have you done this and spared the boys?' ·'The Hebrew women are not like Egyptian women,' they answered Pharaoh 'they
20 are hardy, and they give birth before the midwife reaches them.' ·God was kind to the midwives. The people went on increasing and grew very powerful; ·since the midwives reverenced God he granted them descendants.

22 Pharaoh then gave his subjects this command: 'Throw all the boys born to the Hebrews into the river, but let all the girls live'.

B. Early Life and Call of Moses

The Birth of Moses

1 2 There was a man of the tribe of Levi who had taken a woman of Levi as his
2 wife. ·She conceived and gave birth to a son and, seeing what a fine child he
3 was, she kept him hidden for three months. ·When she could hide him no longer, she got a papyrus basket for him; coating it with bitumen and pitch, she
4 put the child inside and laid it among the reeds at the river's edge. ·His sister stood some distance away to see what would happen to him.

5 Now Pharaoh's daughter went down to bathe in the river, and the girls attending her were walking along by the riverside. Among the reeds she noticed
6 the basket, and she sent her maid to fetch it. ·She opened it and looked, and saw a baby boy, crying; and she was sorry for him. 'This is a child of one of the He-
7 brews' she said. ·Then the child's sister said to Pharaoh's daughter, 'Shall I go and find you a nurse among the Hebrew women to suckle the child for you?'
8 ·'Yes, go' Pharaoh's daughter said to her; and the girl went off to find the baby's
9 own mother. ·To her the daughter of Pharaoh said, 'Take this child away and suckle it for me. I will see you are paid.' So the woman took the child and

[1] a. The residence of Rameses II in the Delta; either Tanis or Qantir. b. The exact meaning is uncertain.

10 suckled it. ·When the child grew up, she brought him to Pharaoh's daughter who treated him like a son; she named him Moses because, she said, 'I drew him out of the water'.[a]

MOSES ESCAPES TO MIDIAN

11 Moses, a man by now, set out at this time to visit his countrymen, and he saw what a hard life they were having; and he saw an Egyptian strike a Hebrew, one 12 of his countrymen. ·Looking round he could see no one in sight, so he killed the 13 Egyptian and hid him in the sand. ·On the following day he came back, and there were two Hebrews, fighting. He said to the man who was in the wrong, 14 'What do you mean by hitting your fellow countryman?' ·'And who appointed 15 you' the man retorted ·'to be prince over us, and judge? Do you intend to kill me as you killed the Egyptian?' Moses was frightened. 'Clearly that business has come to light' he thought. ·When Pharaoh heard of the matter he would have killed Moses, but Moses fled from Pharaoh and made for the land of Midian.[b] And he sat down beside a well.

16 Now the priest of Midian had seven daughters. They came to draw water 17 and fill the troughs to water their father's sheep. ·Shepherds came and drove them away, but Moses came to their defence and watered their sheep for them. 18 ·When they returned to their father Reuel, he said to them, 'You are back early 19 today!' 'An Egyptian protected us from the shepherds;' they said 'yes, and he 20 drew water for us and watered the flock.' ·'And where is he?' he asked his 21 daughters. 'Why did you leave the man there? Ask him to eat with us.' ·So Moses 22 settled with this man, who gave him his daughter Zipporah in marriage. ·She gave birth to a son, and he named him Gershom because, he said, 'I am a stranger in a foreign land'.

The Call of Moses

GOD REMEMBERS ISRAEL

23 During this long period the king of Egypt died. The sons of Israel, groaning in their slavery, cried out for help and from the depths of their slavery their cry 24 came up to God. ·God heard their groaning and he called to mind his covenant 25 with Abraham, Isaac and Jacob. ·God looked down upon the sons of Israel, and he knew . . .

THE BURNING BUSH

1 **3** Moses was looking after the flock of Jethro, his father-in-law, priest of Midian. He led his flock to the far side of the wilderness and came to Horeb,[a] 2 the mountain of God. ·There the angel of Yahweh appeared to him in the shape

---

[2] a. Folk-derivation of the name Moses from *mashah,* to draw out. b. Midian lies S. of Edom and E. of the Gulf of Aqaba.

[3] a. Sinai; the alternative name used in the 'Elohistic' tradition.

of a flame of fire, coming from the middle of a bush. Moses looked; there was
3 the bush blazing but it was not being burnt up. •'I must go and look at this
4 strange sight,' Moses said 'and see why the bush is not burnt.' •Now Yahweh saw him go forward to look, and God called to him from the middle of the
5 bush. 'Moses, Moses!' he said. 'Here I am' he answered. •'Come no nearer' he
6 said. 'Take off your shoes, for the place on which you stand is holy ground. I am the God of your father,' he said 'the God of Abraham, the God of Isaac and the God of Jacob.' At this Moses covered his face, afraid to look at God.

The Mission of Moses

7 And Yahweh said, 'I have seen the miserable state of my people in Egypt. I have heard their appeal to be free of their slave-drivers. Yes, I am well aware of their
8 sufferings. •I mean to deliver them out of the hands of the Egyptians and bring them up out of that land to a land rich and broad, a land where milk and honey flow, the home of the Canaanites, the Hittites, the Amorites, the Perizzites, the
9 Hivites and the Jebusites. •And now the cry of the sons of Israel has come to me,
10 and I have witnessed the way in which the Egyptians oppress them, so come, I sent you to Pharaoh to bring the sons of Israel, my people, out of Egypt.'

11 Moses said to God, 'Who am I to go to Pharaoh and bring the sons of Israel
12 out of Egypt?' •'I shall be with you,' was the answer 'and this is the sign by which you shall know that it is I who have sent you . . . After you have led the people out of Egypt, you are to offer worship to God on this mountain.'

The Divine Name Revealed

13 Then Moses said to God, 'I am to go, then, to the sons of Israel and say to them, "The God of your fathers has sent me to you". But if they ask me what his name
14 is, what am I to tell them?' •And God said to Moses, 'I Am who I Am. This' he added 'is what you must say to the sons of Israel: "I Am has sent me to you".'
15 •And God also said to Moses, 'You are to say to the sons of Israel: "Yahweh,[b] the God of your fathers, the God of Abraham, the God of Isaac, and the God of Jacob, has sent me to you". This is my name for all time; by this name I shall be invoked for all generations to come.

Moses Instructed for His Mission

16 'Go and gather the elders of Israel together and tell them, "Yahweh, the God of your fathers, has appeared to me,—the God of Abraham, of Isaac, and of Jacob; and he has said to me: I have visited you and seen all that the Egyptians are do-
17 ing to you. •And so I have resolved to bring you up out of Egypt where you are oppressed, into the land of the Canaanites, the Hittites, the Amorites, the Perizzites, the Hivites and the Jebusites, to a land where milk and honey flow."
18 •They will listen to your words, and with the elders of Israel you are to go to the king of Egypt and say to him, "Yahweh, the God of the Hebrews, has come to

b. The formula, 'I Am who I Am' becomes, in the third person, Yahweh, 'He is'.

meet us. Give us leave, then, to make a three days' journey into the wilderness
19 to offer sacrifice to Yahweh our God." •For myself, knowing that the king of
20 Egypt will not let you go unless he is forced by a mighty hand, •I shall show my power and strike Egypt with all the wonders I am going to work there. After this he will let you go.

The Egyptians to Be Plundered

21 I will give this people such prestige in the eyes of the Egyptians that when
22 you go, you will not go empty-handed. •Every woman will ask her neighbour and the woman who is staying in her house for silver ornaments and gold. With these you will adorn your sons and daughters; you will plunder the Egyptians.' . . .

III. The Covenant at Sinai

A. The Covenant and the Decalogue

The Israelites Come to Sinai

1 **19** Three months after they came out of the land of Egypt . . . on that day
2 the sons of Israel came to the wilderness of Sinai.[a] •From Rephidim they set out again; and when they reached the wilderness of Sinai, there in the wilderness they pitched their camp; there facing the mountain Israel pitched camp.

Yahweh Promises a Covenant

3 Moses then went up to God, and Yahweh called to him from the mountain, say-
4 ing, 'Say this to the House of Jacob, declare this to the sons of Israel, •"You yourselves have seen what I did with the Egyptians, how I carried you on eagle's
5 wings and brought you to myself. •From this you know that now, if you obey my voice and hold fast to my covenant, you of all the nations shall be my very
6 own for all the earth is mine. •I will count you a kingdom of priests, a conse-
7 crated nation." Those are the words you are to speak to the sons of Israel.' •So Moses went and summoned the elders of the people, putting before them
8 all that Yahweh had bidden him. •Then all the people answered as one, 'All that Yahweh has said, we will do.' And Moses took the people's reply back to Yahweh.

Preparing for the Covenant

9 Yahweh said to Moses, 'I am coming to you in a dense cloud so that the people may hear when I speak to you and may trust you always'. And Moses took the people's reply back to Yahweh.

---

[19] a. According to tradition, Mount Sinai was at Jebel Musa, in the southern region of the Sinai peninsula.

10 Yahweh said to Moses, 'Go to the people and tell them to prepare them-
11 selves today and tomorrow. Let them wash their clothing and ·hold themselves in readiness for the third day, because on the third day Yahweh will descend on
12 the mountain of Sinai in the sight of all the people. ·You will mark out the limits of the mountain and say, "Take care not to go up the mountain or to touch the
13 foot of it. Whoever touches the mountain will be put to death. No one must lay a hand on him: he must be stoned or shot down by arrow, whether man or beast; he must not remain alive." When the ram's horn sounds a long blast, they are to go up the mountain.'

14 So Moses came down from the mountain to the people and bade them pre-
15 pare themselves; and they washed their clothing. ·Then he said to the people, 'Be ready for the third day; do not go near any woman'.

THE THEOPHANY ON SINAI

16 Now at daybreak on the third day there were peals of thunder on the mountain and lightning flashes, a dense cloud, and a loud trumpet blast, and inside the
17 camp all the people trembled. ·Then Moses led the people out of the camp to
18 meet God; and they stood at the bottom of the mountain. ·The mountain of Sinai was entirely wrapped in smoke, because Yahweh had descended on it in the form of fire. Like smoke from a furnace the smoke went up, and the whole
19 mountain shook violently. ·Louder and louder grew the sound of the trumpet.
20 Moses spoke, and God answered him with peals of thunder. Yahweh came down on the mountain of Sinai, on the mountain top, and Yahweh called Moses
21 to the top of the mountain; and Moses went up. ·Yahweh said to Moses, 'Go down and warn the people not to pass beyond their bounds to come and look
22 on Yahweh, or many of them will lose their lives. ·The priests, the men who do approach Yahweh,[b] even these must purify themselves, or Yahweh will break
23 out against them.' ·Moses answered Yahweh, 'The people cannot come up the mountain of Sinai because you warned us yourself when you said, "Mark
24 out the limits of the mountain and declare it sacred"'. ·'Go down,' said Yahweh to him 'and come up again bringing Aaron with you. But do not allow the priests or the people to pass beyond their bounds to come up to Yahweh, or he
25 will break out against them.' ·So Moses went down to the people and spoke to them . . .

THE DECALOGUE[a]

1 **20** Then God spoke all these words. He said, ·'I am Yahweh your God who
2 brought you out of the land of Egypt, out of the house of slavery.

3 'You shall have no gods except me.

---

b. But see ch. 29, which treats the investiture of priests as a later occurrence.

[20] a. This is the priestly version of the Ten Commandments: another version, the Deuteronomic, is found in Dt 5, and it is the second which has been adopted by the Church.

4 'You shall not make yourself a carved image or any likeness of anything in
5 heaven or on earth beneath or in the waters under the earth; ·you shall not bow down to them or serve them. For I, Yahweh your God, am a jealous God and I punish the father's fault in the sons, the grandsons, and the great-grandsons of
6 those who hate me; ·but I show kindness to thousands of those who love me and keep my commandments.

7 'You shall not utter the name of Yahweh your God to misuse it,[b] for Yahweh will not leave unpunished the man who utters his name to misuse it.

8 9 'Remember the sabbath day and keep it holy. ·For six days you shall labour
10 and do all your work, ·but the seventh day is a sabbath for Yahweh your God. You shall do no work that day, neither you nor your son nor your daughter nor your servants, men or women, nor your animals nor the stranger who lives with
11 you. ·For in six days Yahweh made the heavens and the earth and the sea and all that these hold, but on the seventh day he rested; that is why Yahweh has blessed the sabbath day and made it sacred.

12 'Honour your father and your mother so that you may have a long life in the land that Yahweh your God has given to you.

13 'You shall not kill.

14 'You shall not commit adultery.

15 'You shall not steal.

16 'You shall not bear false witness against your neighbour.

17 'You shall not covet your neighbour's house. You shall not covet your neighbour's wife, or his servant, man or woman, or his ox, or his donkey, or anything that is his.'

18 'All the people shook with fear at the peals of thunder and the lightning flashes, the sound of the trumpet, and the smoking mountain; and they kept
19 their distance. ·'Speak to us yourself' they said to Moses 'and we will listen; but
20 do not let God speak to us, or we shall die.' ·Moses answered the people, 'Do not be afraid; God has come to test you, so that your fear of him, being always
21 in your mind, may keep you from sinning'. ·So the people kept their distance while Moses approached the dark cloud where God was.

B. The Book of the Covenant

Law Concerning the Altar

22 Yahweh said to Moses, 'Tell the sons of Israel this, "You have seen for your-
23 selves that I have spoken to you from heaven. ·You shall not make gods of silver or gods of gold to stand beside me; you shall not make things like this for yourselves.

24 "You are to make me an altar of earth, and sacrifice on this the holocausts and communion sacrifices from your flocks or herds. In every place in which I

b. Either in a false oath or irreverently.

25 have my name remembered I shall come to you and bless you. ·If you make me an altar of stone, do not build it of dressed stones; for if you use a tool on it, you
26 profane it. ·You shall not go up to my altar by steps for fear you expose your nakedness."

from Psalms

Psalm 8

The Munificence of the Creator

[a]For the choirmaster   On the . . . of Gath[a]   Psalm   Of David

1 Yahweh, our Lord,
how great your name throughout the earth!

Above the heavens is your majesty chanted
2 by the mouths of children, babes in arms.
You set your stronghold firm against your foes
to subdue enemies and rebels.

3 I look up at your heavens, made by your fingers,
at the moon and stars you set in place—
4 ah, what is man that you should spare a thought for him,
the son of man that you should care for him?

5 Yet you have made him little less than a god,
you have crowned him with glory and splendour,
6 made him lord over the work of your hands,
set all things under his feet,

7 sheep and oxen, all these,
yes, wild animals too,
8 birds in the air, fish in the sea
travelling the paths of the ocean.

9 Yahweh, our Lord,
how great your name throughout the earth!

---

[8] a. A musical instrument, or the name of a tune.

Psalm 23

The Good Shepherd

Psalm Of David

1 Yahweh is my shepherd,
I lack nothing.

2 In meadows of green grass he lets me lie.
To the waters of repose he leads me;
3 there he revives my soul.

He guides me by paths of virtue
for the sake of his name

4 Though I pass through a gloomy valley,
I fear no harm;
beside me your rod and your staff
are there, to hearten me.

5 You prepare a table before me
under thc eyes of my enemies,
you anoint my head with oil,
my cup brims over.

6 Ah, how goodness and kindness pursue me,
every day of my life,
my home, the house of Yahweh,
as long as I live!

QUESTIONS FOR WRITING AND DISCUSSION

OBSERVING

1. Describe the relationships evident between God and humankind, and then between man and woman in this creation account. In what way are man and woman related to nature? Is there any clue in the text as to what it means to be "made in God's image"?
2. Explain how each of the specific promises offered by God in Genesis 12 to *Abram* (which means "father" in Hebrew, and by which he was known before referred to as "Abraham," i.e., "father of many nations.") may fit into the formation of Israel as a nation as depicted in Exodus.

3. Moses is "called" by God in Exodus 3. What is the significance of Moses asking God his name? Argue that this event is significant in preparing Moses for his task and lends him authority when he later confronts his people after his greater, Mount Sinai experience? (Exodus 19 - 20).
4. Consider carefully the questions raised by Psalm 8. In answering his questions, how does the psalmist's poetry reveal his conception of men and women and their position before God? In what ways is it parallel with the relationships depicted in Genesis 1 - 2? In what ways is it different?
5. Psalm 23, the famous "shepherd" psalm, portrays God as a tender comforter of individual believers. Point out specific imagery in the psalm that reinforces this theme and suggest reasons why it would have been a particularly endearing metaphor for God's dealings with the ancient Israelites.

EVALUATING

1. How important is it that a society has a common history or belief about its origins or destiny? In what way has the Book of Genesis seemed to have served that role in the United States? Defend your answer.
2. Archaeological expeditions have been launched many times in the past two centuries to recover possible evidence of the events described in the Book of Genesis, for example, the flood and some remnant of the Ark. What would be the historical significance if such evidence was indisputably found? Argue the question of whether such data—if verified—would alter the way a majority of readers view the Bible.
3. It is sometimes said that the Ten Commandments (Exodus 20:1 - 17) provide the foundation for much of what many would regard as "traditional American values." Provide evidence that these "laws" present a basis for family life, and ethics in a community or nation.
4. Do you believe there is such a thing as "sin"? Why or why not? If so, define the term and describe in your own words what constitutes the outside standard by which one can recognize and label any particular action as "sin"? If not, how do you account for the origin of the idea of sin and its use in Western history?
5. In what way can the religious message of a psalm like Psalm 23 be comforting and reassuring even if one is not an adherent of the faith from which it emerges? It is possible to find solace in the faith of others who do not share yours in every specific detail?

RESPONDING AND APPLYING

1. There are stories throughout history of bargains with the devil. Consider how the serpent tempts Eve. Why would she or anyone find it appealing to "be like God"? If you were presented with the seemingly diabolical proposition of becoming "like God," how would you respond? Why?
2. From your point of view, is Genesis a credible account of "the way the universe began . . ."? If not, what accounts for your twentieth-century

skepticism? If so, how do you reconcile certain scientific theories that appear to explain the existence of the cosmos?
3. Look at each of the Ten Commandments individually. How might they be grouped? What purpose does each serve in the building of a nation or community? How does each contribute to the goal of stability and mutual concern? Explain as well how the more "religious" commandments (Exodus 20:3-8) fit in?
4. Write a psalm of your own, modelled on the sample psalms here, that expresses your own sense of wonderment (like Psalm 8) or comfort (Psalm 23)—or which parodies the theme, form, or style of one of these psalms.
5. In what way does the poetic form of the psalms make the reading of them more or less difficult than other Biblical passages? Does their presence in the Bible surprise you? Why or why not?

New Testament Scriptures

Matthew 5–7, 26–28; Luke 15

The use of the word "testament" to distinguish between the Hebrew Scriptures and what Christians refer to as "the New Testament" is derived from the idea of a covenant or agreement between God and a group of people in which each has stated responsibilities. The Hebrew Scriptures report the unique covenant made between God and the people of Israel through Moses, while the Christian Scriptures (hereafter, "NT," short for "New Testament") report a second covenant that Christians believe God made with the whole world through Jesus Christ. (One clear distinction between Jews and Christians is their understanding of the relationship between these two covenants and whether one has supplanted or takes precedence over the other; Muslims, on the other hand, believe the Qur'an supersedes both.)

The New Testament, read by Christians as a fulfillment of and companion volume to the Hebrew Scriptures, includes four "gospels" that are essentially quasi-biographical narratives about the life and teaching of Jesus Christ, one historical work (Acts of the Apostles), and twenty-two letters written by early Christian leaders to their converts in various locations in Europe and Asia. The general focus of these Scriptures is the life, death, and resurrection of Jesus Christ, whom Christians regard as the unique Son of God and the fulfillment of Hebrew prophecies about a coming Messiah. At the same time they also paint a portrait of the early church and its battle for survival in an often hostile environment.

The Book of Matthew is regarded by many scholars as the most "Jewish" gospel, charting Jesus' lineage back to David and Abraham, emphasizing his association with the Kingdom of God and stressing His unique sonship and Messiahship. In contrast, the Book of Luke is often referred to as a work written for a Greco-Roman audience, because of its more philosophical, contemplative nature. The explicit thesis of Matthew's gospel is that Jesus is the logical conclusion and fulfillment of the Hebrew covenant and is the expected Messiah. The "Sermon on the Mount" seems deliberately designed as a contrast to the then contemporary interpretation of the Torah, which Jesus regarded as a misconstruing of the Mosaic teaching with a return to a more balanced, traditional interpretation. Though the "Sermon on the Mount," presented in Matthew 5-7, is the ethical center of Jesus' teaching, it is only part of the larger purpose in his message, which stresses a coming kingdom and his unique part in its establishment.

It might be pointed out here that in Matthew 5-7, Jesus is entering into the kind of debate alluded to earlier in the introductory essay to the readings, namely, an attempt to define (or redefine) "orthodoxy." In effect, while Jesus' teaching style was basically modelled on the rabbinical tradition with which he was familiar, nevertheless "he taught as one having authority" (Matthew 7:29). This "authority" focused not as much on his ability to debate rival teachers as on his personal integrity and powerful presence. In some ways, Jesus was the original "populist," a public speaker appealing to his hearers with stories and simple, homely images—all poignant contrasts to the sometimes legalistic style more common to the Judaism in place during his lifetime, a feature evident in the selections from Luke's gospel. In other ways, he was simply an original—a charismatic and dynamic individual unafraid to challenge the status quo with outspoken pronouncements about his own authority ("Ye have heard it said . . . but I say unto you"). This is but one manifestation of how Christianity would depart from the ethical monotheisms of Judaism; Jesus overtly claimed to be God—appropriating names and symbols previously attributed only to Yahweh, the God of Abraham, Isaac, and Jacob, the God of Moses and David. In short, whatever readers may make of him, Jesus clearly claimed a power and authority that labeled him a blasphemer among the Scribes and Pharisees of the first-century Jewish community. The Betrayal, Trial, Crucifixion, and Resurrection narratives of Matthew 26-28 attest to the violently different opinions that abounded on his character and mission. These excerpts thus focus on the completion of Jesus' ministry, which, in summary form, was that he came to teach, to be crucified as an atoning sacrifice for humankind's original sin against God, but rose from the dead to confirm his identity as the unique Son of God and to usher in a new kingdom which he now reigns over as King from a heavenly throne.

from Matthew

The Sermon on the Mount[a]

The Beatitudes

1 **5** Seeing the crowds, he went up the hill. There he sat down and was joined
2 by his disciples. ·Then he began to speak. This is what he taught them:

3 'How happy are the poor in spirit;
theirs is the kingdom of heaven.
4 Happy *the gentle:*[b]
they shall have the earth for their heritage.
5 Happy those who mourn:
they shall be comforted.
6 Happy those who hunger and thirst for what is right:
they shall be satisfied.
7 Happy the merciful:
they shall have mercy shown them.
8 Happy the pure in heart:
they shall see God.
9 Happy the peacemakers:
they shall be called sons of God.
10 Happy those who are persecuted in the cause of right:
theirs is the kingdom of heaven.

11 'Happy are you when people abuse you and persecute you and speak all kinds
12 of calumny against you on my account. ·Rejoice and be glad, for your reward will be great in heaven; this is how they persecuted the prophets before you.

Salt of the Earth and Light of the World

13 'You are the salt of the earth. But if salt becomes tasteless, what can make it salty again? It is good for nothing, and can only be thrown out to be trampled underfoot by men.

14 'You are the light of the world. A city built on a hill-top cannot be hidden.
15 No one lights a lamp to put it under a tub; they put it on the lampstand where
16 it shines for everyone in the house. ·In the same way your light must shine in the sight of men, so that, seeing your good works, they may give the praise to your Father in heaven.

---

[5] a. In this discourse, which occupies three ch. of this gospel, Mt has included sayings which probably originated on other occasions (cf. their parallels in Lk). b. Or 'the lowly'; the word comes from the Greek version of Ps 37.

The Fulfilment of the Law

17 'Do not imagine that I have come to abolish the Law or the Prophets. I have 18 come not to abolish but to complete them. •I tell you solemnly, till heaven and earth disappear, not one dot, not one little stroke, shall disappear from the Law 19 until its purpose is achieved. •Therefore, the man who infringes even one of the least of these commandments and teaches others to do the same will be considered the least in the kingdom of heaven; but the man who keeps them and teaches them will be considered great in the kingdom of heaven.

The New Standard Higher than the Old

20 'For I tell you, if your virtue goes no deeper than that of the scribes and Pharisees, you will never get into the kingdom of heaven.

21 'You have learnt how it was said to our ancestors: *You must not kill*[c] and if 22 anyone does kill he must answer for it before the court. •But I say this to you: anyone who is angry with his brother will answer for it before the court; if a man calls his brother "Fool"[d] he will answer for it before the Sanhedrin;[e] and if 23 a man calls him "Renegade"[f] he will answer for it in hell fire. •So then, if you are bringing your offering to the altar and there remember that your brother has 24 something against you, •leave your offering there before the altar, go and be reconciled with your brother first, and then come back and present your offering. 25 •Come to terms with your opponent in good time while you are still on the way to the court with him, or he may hand you over to the judge and the judge to 26 the officer, and you will be thrown into prison. •I tell you solemnly, you will not get out till you have paid the last penny.

27 28 'You have learnt how it was said: *You must not commit adultery.*[g] •But I say this to you: if a man looks at a woman lustfully, he has already committed 29 adultery with her in his heart. •If your right eye should cause you to sin, tear it out and throw it away; for it will do you less harm to lose one part of you than 30 to have your whole body thrown into hell. •And if your right hand should cause you to sin, cut it off and throw it away; for it will do you less harm to lose one part of you than to have your whole body go to hell.

31 'It has also been said: *Anyone who divorces his wife must give her a writ* 32 *of dismissal.*[h] •But I say this to you: everyone who divorces his wife, except for the case of fornication, makes her an adulteress; and anyone who marries a divorced woman commits adultery.

33 'Again, you have learnt how it was said to our ancestors: *You must not* 34 *break your oath, but must fulfil your oaths to the Lord.*[i] •But I say this to you: 35 do not swear at all, either by *heaven,* since that is God's throne; •or by *the earth,* since that is *his footstool;* or by Jerusalem, since that is *the city of the* 36 *great king.* •Do not swear by your own head either, since you cannot turn a

---

c. Ex 20:13. d. Translating an Aramaic term of contempt. e. The High Court at Jerusalem. f. Apostasy was the most repulsive of all sins. g. Ex 20:14. h. Dt 24:1. i. Ex 20:7.

37 single hair white or black. All you need say is "Yes" if you mean yes, "No" if you mean no; anything more than this comes from the evil one.

38 39 'You have learnt how it was said: *Eye for eye and tooth for tooth.*[j] •But I say this to you: offer the wicked man no resistance. On the contrary, if anyone 40 hits you on the right cheek, offer him the other as well; •if a man takes you to 41 law and would have your tunic, let him have your cloak as well. •And if anyone 42 orders you to go one mile, go two miles with him. •Give to anyone who asks, and if anyone wants to borrow, do not turn away.

43 'You have learnt how it was said: *You must love your neighbor* and hate 44 your enemy.[k] •But I say this to you: love your enemies and pray for those who 45 persecute you; •in this way you will be sons of your Father in heaven, for he causes his sun to rise on bad men as well as good, and his rain to fall on honest 46 and dishonest men alike. •For if you love those who love you, what right have 47 you to claim any credit? Even the tax collectors[l] do as much, do they not? •And if you save your greetings for your brothers, are you doing anything excep-48 tional? Even the pagans do as much, do they not? •You must therefore be perfect just as your heavenly Father is perfect.

Almsgiving in Secret

1 **6** 'Be careful not to parade your good deeds before men to attract their no-2 tice; by doing this you will lose all reward from your Father in heaven. •So when you give alms, do not have it trumpeted before you; this is what the hypocrites do in the synagogues and in the streets to win men's admiration. I tell 3 you solemnly, they have had their reward. •But when you give alms, your left 4 hand must not know what your right is doing; •your almsgiving must be secret, and your Father who sees all that is done in secret will reward you.

Prayer in Secret

5 'And when you pray, do not imitate the hypocrites: they love to say their prayers standing up in the synagogues and at the street corners for people to 6 see them. I tell you solemnly, they have had their reward. •But when you pray, *go to your private room and, when you have shut your door, pray*[a] to your Father who is in that secret place, and your Father who sees all that is done in secret will reward you.

How to Pray. The Lord's Prayer

7 'In your prayers do not babble as the pagans do, for they think that by using 8 many words they will make themselves heard. •Do not be like them; your Fa-9 ther knows what you need before you ask him. •So you should pray like this:

---

j. Ex 21:24. k. The quotation is from Lv 19:18; the second part of this commandment, not in the written Law, is an Aramaic way of saying 'You do not have to love your enemy'. l. They were employed by the occupying power and this earned them popular contempt.

[6] a. Not a direct quotation but an allusion to the practice common in the O.T., see 2 K 4:33.

'Our Father in heaven,
may your name be held holy,
your kingdom come,
10 your will be done,
on earth as in heaven.
11 Give us today our daily bread.
12 And forgive us our debts,
as we have forgiven those who are in debt to us.
13 And do not put us to the test,
but save us from the evil one.

14 Yes, if you forgive others their failings, your heavenly Father will forgive you
15 yours; ·but if you do not forgive others, your Father will not forgive your failings either.

Fasting in Secret

16 'When you fast do not put on a gloomy look as the hypocrites do: they pull long faces to let men know they are fasting. I tell you solemnly, they have had their
17 reward. ·But when you fast, put oil on your head and wash your face, so that no
18 one will know you are fasting except your Father who sees all that is done in secret; and your Father who sees all that is done in secret will reward you.

True Treasures

19 'Do not store up treasures for yourselves on earth, where moths and wood-
20 worms destroy them and thieves can break in and steal. ·But store up treasures for yourselves in heaven, where neither moth nor woodworms destroy them
21 and thieves cannot break in and steal. ·For where your treasures is, there will your heart be also.

The Eye, the Lamp of the Body

22 'The lamp of the body is the eye. It follows that if your eye is sound, your whole
23 body will be filled with light. ·But if your eye is diseased, your whole body will be all darkness. If then, the light inside you is darkness, what darkness that will be!

God and Money

24 'No one can be the slave of two masters: he will either hate the first and love the second, or treat the first with respect and the second with scorn. You cannot be the slave both of God and of money.

Trust in Providence

25 'That is why I am telling you not to worry about your life and what you are to eat, nor about your body and how you are to clothe it. Surely life means more
26 than food, and the body more than clothing! ·Look at the birds in the sky. They

do not sow or reap or gather into barns; yet your heavenly Father feeds them.
27 Are you not worth much more than they are? •Can any of you, for all his worry-
28 ing, add one single cubit to his span of life? •And why worry about clothing?
29 Think of the flowers growing in the fields: they never have to work or spin; •yet I assure you that not even Solomon in all his regalia was robed like one of these.
30 •Now if that is how God clothes the grass in the field which is there today and thrown into the furnace tomorrow, will he not much more look after you, you
31 men of little faith? So do not worry; do not say, "What are we to eat? What are
32 we to drink? How are we to be clothed?" •It is the pagans who set their hearts
33 on all these things. Your heavenly Father knows you need them all. •Set your hearts on his kingdom first, and on his righteousness, and all these other things
34 will be given you as well. So do not worry about tomorrow; tomorrow will take care of itself. Each day has enough trouble of its own.

Do not Judge

1 2 7 'Do not judge, and you will not be judged; •because the judgments you give are the judgments you will get, and the amount you measure out is the
3 amount you will be given. •Why do you observe the splinter in your brother's
4 eye and never notice the plank in your own? •How dare you say to your brother, "Let me take the splinter out of your eye", when all the time there is a plank in
5 your own? •Hypocrite! Take the plank out of your own eye first, and then you will see clearly enough to take the splinter out of your brother's eye.

Do not Profane Sacred Things

6 'Do not give dogs what is holy;[a] and do not throw your pearls in front of pigs, or they may trample them and then turn on you and tear you to pieces.

Effective Prayer

7 'Ask, and it will be given to you; search, and you will find; knock, and the door
8 will be opened to you. •For the one who asks always receives; the one who searches always finds; the one who knocks will always have the door opened to
9 him. •Is there a man among you who would hand his son a stone when he
10 asked for bread? •Or would hand him a snake when he asked for a fish? •If you, then, who are evil, know how to give your children what is good, how much more will your Father in heaven give good things to those who ask him!

The Golden Rule

11 'So always treat others as you would like them to treat you; that is the meaning of the Law and the Prophets.

---

[7] a. The meat of animals which have been offered in sacrifice in the Temple; the application is to the parading of holy beliefs and practices in front of those who cannot understand them.

The Two Ways

12 'Enter by the narrow gate, since the road that leads to perdition is wide and spacious, and many take it; •but it is a narrow gate and a hard road that leads to life, and only a few find it.

False Prophets

13 'Beware of false prophets[b] who come to you disguised as sheep but underneath are ravenous wolves. •You will be able to tell them by their fruits. Can people pick grapes from thorns, or figs from thistles? •In the same way, a sound tree 14 produces good fruit but a rotten tree bad fruit. •A sound tree cannot bear bad 15 fruit, nor a rotten tree bear good fruit. •Any tree that does not produce good 16 fruit is cut down and thrown on the fire. •I repeat, you will be able to tell them by their fruits.

The True Disciple

17 'It is not those who say to me, "Lord, Lord", who will enter the kingdom of 18 heaven, but the person who does the will of my Father in heaven. •When the day[c] comes many will say to me, "Lord, Lord, did we not prophesy in your name, cast out demons in your name, work many miracles in your name?" 19 •Then I shall tell them to their faces: I have never known you; *away from me, you evil men!*'

20 'Therefore, everyone who listens to these words of mine and acts on them 21 will be like a sensible man who built his house on rock. •Rain came down, floods rose, gales blew and hurled themselves against that house, and it did not 22 fall: it was founded on rock. •But everyone who listens to these words of mine 23 and does not act on them will be like a stupid man who built his house on sand. 24 •Rain came down, floods rose, gales blew and struck that house, and it fell; and 25 what a fall it had!'

The Amazement of the Crowds

26 Jesus had now finished what he wanted to say, and his teaching made a deep 27 impression on the people •because he taught them with authority, and not like their own scribes.[d] . . .

VII. Passion and Resurrection

The Conspiracy Against Jesus

1 2 **26** Jesus had now finished all he wanted to say, and he told his disciples, 'It will be Passover, as you know, in two days' time, and the Son of Man will be handed over to be crucified'.

---

b. Lying teachers of religion. c. The day of Judgment. d. Doctors of the law, who buttressed their teaching by quotation from the scriptures and traditions.

3 Then the chief priests and the elders of the people assembled in the palace 4 of the high priest, whose name was Caiaphas, ·and made plans to arrest Jesus 5 by some trick and have him put to death. ·They said, however, 'It must not be during the festivities; there must be no disturbance among the people'.

The Anointing at Bethany

6 7 Jesus was at Bethany in the house of Simon the leper, when ·a woman came to him with an alabaster jar of the most expensive ointment, and poured it on his 8 head as he was at table. ·When they saw this, the disciples were indignant; 9 'Why this waste?' they said ·'This could have been sold at a high price and the 10 money given to the poor'. ·Jesus noticed this. 'Why are you upsetting the woman?' he said to them. 'What she has done for me is one of the good works[a] 11 indeed! You have the poor with you always, but you will not always have 12 me. ·When she poured this ointment on my body, she did it to prepare me for 13 burial. ·I tell you solemnly, wherever in all the world this Good News is proclaimed, what she has done will be told also, in remembrance of her'.

Judas Betrays Jesus

14 Then one of the Twelve, the man called Judas Iscariot, went to the chief priests 15 16 and said, 'What are you prepared to give me if I hand him over to you?' They paid him thirty silver pieces,[b] and from that moment he looked for an opportunity to betray him.

Preparations for the Passover Supper

17 Now on the first day of Unleavened Bread[c] the disciples came to Jesus to say, 'Where do you want us to make the preparations for you to eat the passover?' 18 ·'Go to so-and-so in the city' he replied 'and say to him, "The Master says: My time is near. It is at your house that I am keeping Passover with my disciples." ' 19 ·The disciples did what Jesus told them and prepared the Passover.

The Treachery of Judas Foretold

20 21 When evening came he was at table with the twelve disciples. ·And while they were eating he said, 'I tell you solemnly, one of you is about to betray me'. 22 ·They were greatly distressed and started asking him in turn, 'Not I, Lord, 23 surely?' ·He answered, 'Someone who has dipped his hand into the dish with 24 me, will betray me. ·The Son of Man is going to his fate, as the scriptures say he will, but alas for that man by whom the Son of Man is betrayed! Better for that 25 man if he had never been born!' ·Judas, who was to betray him, asked in his turn, 'Not I, Rabbi, surely?' 'They are your own words' answered Jesus.

---

[26] a. As 'good works', charitable deeds were reckoned superior to almsgiving. b. 30 shekels, the price fixed for a slave's life. Ex 21:32. c. Unleavened bread was normally to be eaten during the seven days which followed the Passover supper; here the writer appears to mean the first day of the whole Passover celebration.

The Institution of the Eucharist

26 Now as they were eating,[d] Jesus took some bread, and when he had said the blessing he broke it and gave it to the disciples. 'Take it and eat;' he said 'this is 27 my body.' •Then he took a cup, and when he had returned thanks he gave it to 28 them. 'Drink all of you from this,' he said •'for this is my blood, the blood of the 29 covenant, which is to be poured out for many for the forgiveness of sins. •From now on, I tell you, I shall not drink wine until the day I drink the new wine with you in the kingdom of my Father.'

Peter's Denial Foretold

30 31 After psalms had been sung[e] they left for the Mount of Olives. •Then Jesus said to them, 'You will all lose faith in me this night,[f] for the scripture says: *I shall* 32 *strike the shepherd and the sheep of the flock will be scattered,*[g] •but after my 33 resurrection I shall go before you to Galilee'. •At this, Peter said, 'Though all 34 lose faith in you, I will never lose faith'. •Jesus answered him, 'I tell you solemnly, this very night, before the cock crows, you will have disowned me three 35 times'. •Peter said to him, 'Even if I have to die with you, I will never disown you'. And all the disciples said the same.

Gethsemane

36 Then Jesus came with them to a small estate called Gethsemane; and he said 37 to his disciples, 'Stay here while I go over there to pray'. •He took Peter and the two sons of Zebedee with him. And sadness came over him, and great dis-38 tress. Then he said to them, 'My soul is sorrowful to the point of death. Wait 39 here and keep awake with me.' •And going on a little further he fell on his face and prayed. 'My Father,' he said 'if it is possible, let this cup pass me by. Never-40 theless, let it be as you, not I, would have it.' •He came back to the disciples and found them sleeping, and he said to Peter, 'So you had not the strength to keep 41 awake with me one hour? •You should be awake, and praying not to be put to 42 the test. The spirit is willing, but the flesh is weak.' •Again, a second time, he went away and prayed: 'My Father,' he said 'if this cup cannot pass by without 43 my drinking it, your will be done!' •And he came back again and found them 44 sleeping, their eyes were so heavy. •Leaving them there, he went away again 45 and prayed for the third time, repeating the same words. •Then he came back to the disciples and said to them, 'You can sleep on now and take your rest. Now the hour has come when the Son of Man is to be betrayed into the hands of sin-46 ners. •Get up! Let us go! My betrayer is already close at hand.'

The Arrest

47 He was still speaking when Judas, one of the Twelve, appeared, and with him a large number of men armed with swords and clubs, sent by the chief priests

---

d. The Passover supper itself, for which exact rules for the blessing of bread and wine were laid down. The 'eating' of v. 21 is the first course, which came before the Passover itself. e. The psalms of praise which end the Passover supper. f. 'be brought down'; the regular expression for the losing of faith through a difficulty or blow to it. g. Zc 13:7.

48 and elders of the people. •Now the traitor had arranged a sign with them. 'The
49 one I kiss,' he had said 'he is the man. Take him in charge.' •So he went straight
50 up to Jesus and said, 'Greetings, Rabbi', and kissed him. •Jesus said to him, 'My
friend, do what you are here for'. Then they came forward, seized Jesus and
51 took him in charge. •At that, one of the followers of Jesus grasped his sword and
52 drew it; he struck out at the high priest's servant, and cut off his ear. •Jesus then
53 said, 'Put your sword back, for all who draw the sword will die by the sword.
54 •Or do you think that I cannot appeal to my Father who would promptly send
55 more than twelve legions of angels to my defence? •But then, how would the
scriptures be fulfilled that say this is the way it must be?' •It was at this time that
Jesus said to the crowds, 'Am I a brigand, that you had to set out to capture me
with swords and clubs? I sat teaching in the Temple day after day and you never
56 laid hands on me.' •Now all this happened to fulfill the prophecies in scripture.
Then all the disciples deserted him and ran away.

JESUS BEFORE THE SANHEDRIN

57 The men who had arrested Jesus led him off to Caiaphas the high priest, where
58 the scribes and the elders were assembled. •Peter followed him at a distance,
and when he reached the high priest's palace, he went in and sat down with
the attendants to see what the end would be.

59 The chief priests and the whole Sanhedrin were looking for evidence
60 against Jesus, however false, on which they might pass the death-sentence. •But
they could not find any, though several lying witnesses came forward. Eventu-
61 ally two stepped forward •and made a statement, 'This man said, "I have power
62 to destroy the Temple of God and in three days build it up"'. •The high priest
then stood up and said to him, 'Have you no answer to that? What is this evi-
63 dence these men are bringing against you?' •But Jesus was silent. And the high
priest said to him, 'I put you on oath by the living God to tell us if you are the
64 Christ, the Son of God'. •'The words are your own' answered Jesus. 'Moreover,
I tell you that from this time onward you will see the *Son of Man seated at*
65 *the right hand of the Power* and *coming on the clouds of heaven.*' •At this, the
high priest tore his clothes and said, 'He has blasphemed. What need of wit-
66 nesses have we now? There! You have just heard the blasphemy. •What is your
opinion?' They answered, 'He deserves to die'.

67 Then they spat in his face and hit him with their fists; others said as they
68 struck him, •'Play the prophet, Christ! Who hit you then?'

PETER'S DENIALS

69 Meanwhile Peter was sitting outside in the courtyard, and a servant-girl came
70 up to him and said, 'You too were with Jesus the Galilean'. •But he denied it in
71 front of them all. 'I do not know what you are talking about' he said. •When he
went out to the gateway another servant-girl saw him and said to the people
72 there, 'This man was with Jesus the Nazarene'. •And again, with an oath, he de-
73 nied it, 'I do not know the man'. •A little later the bystanders came up and said
74 to Peter, 'You are one of them for sure! Why, your accent gives you away.' •Then
he started calling down curses on himself and swearing, 'I do not know the

75 man'. At that moment the cock crew, ·and Peter remembered what Jesus had said, 'Before the cock crows you will have disowned me three times'. And he went outside and wept bitterly.

Jesus is Taken Before Pilate

1 **27** When morning came, all the chief priests and the elders of the people 2 met in council to bring about the death of Jesus. ·They had him bound, and led him away to hand him over to Pilate,[a] the governor.

The Death of Judas

3 When he found that Jesus had been condemned, Judas his betrayer was filled with remorse and took the thirty silver pieces back to the chief priests and elders. 'I have sinned;' he said 'I have betrayed innocent blood.' 'What is that to 4 us?' they replied 'That is your concern.' 5 ·And flinging down the silver pieces in 6 the sanctuary he made off, and went and hanged himself. ·The chief priests picked up the silver pieces and said, 'It is against the Law to put his into the 7 treasury; it is blood-money'. ·So they discussed the matter and bought the pot-8 ter's field with it as a graveyard for foreigners, ·and this is why the field is called 9 the Field of Blood today. ·The words of the prophet Jeremiah[b] were then fulfilled: *And they took the thirty silver pieces, the sum at which the precious* 10 *One was priced by children of Israel, ·and they gave them for the potter's field, just as the Lord directed me.*

Jesus Before Pilate

11 Jesus, then, was brought before the governor, and the governor put to him this 12 question, 'Are you the king of the Jews?' Jesus replied, 'It is you who say it'. ·But when he was accused by the chief priests and the elders he refused to answer 13 at all. ·Pilate then said to him, 'Do you not hear how many charges they have 14 brought against you?' ·But to the governor's complete amazement, he offered no reply to any of the charges.

15 At festival time it was the governor's practice to release a prisoner for the 16 people, anyone they chose. ·Now there was at that time a notorious prisoner 17 whose name was Barabbas. ·So when the crowd gathered, Pilate said to them, 'Which do you want me to release for you: Barabbas, or Jesus who is called 18 Christ?' ·For Pilate knew it was out of jealousy that they had handed him over.

19 Now as he was seated in the chair of judgment, his wife sent him a message, 'Have nothing to do with that man; I have been upset all day by a dream I had about him'.

20 The chief priests and the elders, however, had persuaded the crowd to de-21 mand the release of Barabbas and the execution of Jesus. ·So when the governor spoke and asked them, 'Which of the two do you want me to release for

---

[27] a. The Jews had to approach the Roman governor for confirmation and execution of any sentence of death. b. Actually a free quotation from Zc 11:12–13.

22 you?' they said, 'Barabbas'. •'But in that case,' Pilate said to them 'what am I to 23 do with Jesus who is called Christ?' They all said, 'Let him be crucified!' •'Why?' 24 he asked 'What harm has he done?' But they shouted all the louder, 'Let him be crucified!' Then Pilate saw that he was making no impression, that in fact a riot was imminent. So he took some water, washed his hands in front of the crowd 25 and said, 'I am innocent of this man's blood. It is your concern.' •And the 26 people, to a man, shouted back, 'His blood be on us and on our children!' •Then he released Barabbas for them. He ordered Jesus to be first scourged[c] and then handed over to be crucified.

Jesus is Crowned with Thorns

27 The governor's soldiers took Jesus with them into the Praetorium and collected 28 the whole cohort round him. •Then they stripped him and made him wear a 29 scarlet cloak, •and having twisted some thorns into a crown they put this on his head and placed a reed in his right hand. To make fun of him they knelt to him 30 saying, 'Hail, king of the Jews!' •And they spat on him and took the reed and 31 struck him on the head with it. •And when they had finished making fun of him, they took off the cloak and dressed him in his own clothes and led him away to crucify him.

The Crucifixion

32 On their way out, they came across a man from Cyrene, Simon by name, and en-33 listed him to carry his cross. •When they had reached a place called Golgotha,[d] 34 that is, the place of the skull, •they gave him wine to drink mixed with gall, 35 which he tasted but refused to drink. •When they had finished crucifying him 36 they shared out his clothing by casting lots, •and then sat down and stayed there keeping guard over him.

37 Above his head was placed the charge against him; it read: 'This is Jesus, 38 the King of the Jews'. •At the same time two robbers were crucified with him, one on the right and one on the left.

The Crucified Christ is Mocked

39 40 The passers-by jeered at him; they shook their heads •and said, 'So you would destroy the Temple and rebuild it in three days! Then save yourself! If you are 41 God's son, come down from the cross!' •The chief priests with the scribes and 42 elders mocked him in the same way. •'He saved others;' they said 'he cannot save himself. He is the king of Israel; let him come down from the cross now, 43 and we will believe in him. •He puts his trust in God; now let God rescue him if 44 he wants him. For he did say, "I am the son of God".' •Even the robbers who were crucified with him taunted him in the same way.

---

c. The normal prelude to crucifixion. d. The Aramaic form of the name of which Calvary is the more familiar Latin equivalent.

The Death of Jesus

45 From the sixth hour there was darkness over all the land until the ninth hour.[e] 46 And about the ninth hour, Jesus cried out in a loud voice, 'Eli, Eli, lama sabachthani?' that is, '*My God, my God, why have you deserted me?*'[f] 47 ·When some of those who stood there heard this, they said, 'The man is calling on Elijah', and 48 one of them quickly ran to get a sponge which he dipped in vinegar[g] and, putting it on a reed, gave it him to drink. 49 ·'Wait!' said the rest of them 'and see if Elijah will come to save him.' 50 ·But Jesus, again crying out in a loud voice, yielded up his spirit.

51 At that, the veil of the Temple[h] was torn in two from top to bottom; the earth quaked; the rocks were split; 52 ·the tombs opened and the bodies of many holy men rose from the dead, 53 ·and these, after his resurrection, came out of the tombs, entered the Holy City and appeared to a number of people. 54 ·Meanwhile the centurion, together with the others guarding Jesus, had seen the earthquake and all that was taking place, and they were terrified and said, 'In truth this was a son of God.'

55 And many women were there, watching from a distance, the same women who had followed Jesus from Galilee and looked after him. 56 ·Among them were Mary of Magdala, Mary the mother of James and Joseph, and the mother of Zebedee's sons.

The Burial

57 When it was evening, there came a rich man of Arimathaea, called Joseph, who had himself become a disciple of Jesus. 58 ·This man went to Pilate and asked for the body of Jesus. Pilate thereupon ordered it to be handed over. 59 ·So Joseph took the body, wrapped it in a clean shroud 60 ·and put it in his own new tomb which he had hewn out of the rock. He then rolled a large stone across the entrance of the tomb and went away. 61 ·Now Mary of Magdala and the other Mary were there, sitting opposite the sepulchre.

The Guard at the Tomb

62 Next day, that is, when Preparation Day[i] was over, the chief priests and the Pharisees went in a body to Pilate 63 ·and said to him, 'Your Excellency, we recall that this impostor said, while he was still alive, "After three days I shall rise again". 64 ·Therefore give the order to have the sepulchre kept secure until the third day, for fear his disciples come and steal him away and tell the people, "He has risen from the dead". This last piece of fraud would be worse than what went before.' 65 ·'You may have your guard' said Pilate to them. 'Go and make all as secure as you know how.' 66 ·So they went and made the sepulchre secure, putting seals on the stone and mounting a guard.

---

e. From mid-day to 3 P.M. f. Ps 22:1. g. The rough wine drunk by Roman soldiers. h. There were two curtains in the Temple; most probably this was the inner curtain which guarded the Most Holy Place. i. The day before the sabbath.

THE EMPTY TOMB. THE ANGEL'S MESSAGE

1 **28** After the sabbath, and towards dawn on the first day of the week, Mary 2 of Magdala and the other Mary went to visit the sepulchre. ·And all at once there was a violent earthquake, for the angel of the Lord, descending from 3 heaven, came and rolled away the stone and sat on it. ·His face was like light-4 ning, his robe white as snow. ·The guards were so shaken, so frightened of him, 5 that they were like dead men. ·But the angel spoke; and he said to the women, 'There is no need for you to be afraid. I know you are looking for Jesus, who 6 was crucified. ·He is not here, for he has risen, as he said he would. Come and 7 see the place where he lay, ·then go quickly and tell his disciples, "He has risen from the dead and now he is going before you to Galilee; it is there you will see 8 him". Now I have told you.' ·Filled with awe and great joy the women came quickly away from the tomb and ran to tell the disciples.

APPEARANCE TO THE WOMEN

9 And there, coming to meet them, was Jesus. 'Greetings' he said. And the 10 women came up to him and, falling down before him, clasped his feet. ·Then Jesus said to them, 'Do not be afraid; go and tell my brothers that they must leave for Galilee; they will see me there'.

PRECAUTIONS TAKEN BY THE LEADERS OF THE PEOPLE

11 While they were on their way, some of the guard went off into the city to tell 12 the chief priests all that had happened. ·These held a meeting with the elders and, after some discussion, handed a considerable sum of money to the soldiers 13 with these instructions, 'This is what you must say, "His disciples came during 14 the night and stole him away while we were asleep". ·And should the governor come to hear of this, we undertake to put things right with him ourselves and 15 to see that you do not get into trouble.' ·The soldiers took the money and carried out their instructions, and to this day that is the story among the Jews.

APPEARANCE IN GALILEE. THE MISSION TO THE WORLD

16 Meanwhile the eleven disciples set out for Galilee, to the mountain where Jesus 17 had arranged to meet them. ·When they saw him they fell down before him, 18 though some hesitated. ·Jesus came up and spoke to them. He said, 'All author-19 ity in heaven and on earth has been given to me. ·Go, therefore, make disciples of all the nations; baptise them in the name of the Father and of the Son and of 20 the Holy Spirit,[a] ·and teach them to observe all the commands I gave you. And know that I am with you always; yes, to the end of time.'

---

[28] a. This formula is perhaps a reflection of the liturgical usage of the writer's own time.

from Luke

The Three Parables of God's Mercy

1 **15** The tax collectors and the sinners, meanwhile, were all seeking his com-
2 pany to hear what he had to say, ·and the Pharisees and the scribes com-
3 plained. 'This man' they said 'welcomes sinners and eats with them.' ·So he
spoke this parable to them:

The Lost Sheep

4 'What man among you with a hundred sheep, losing one, would not leave the
5 ninety-nine in the wilderness and go after the missing one till he found it? And
6 when he found it, would he not joyfully take it on his shoulders ·and then,
when he got home, call together his friends and neighbours? "Rejoice with
7 me," he would say "I have found my sheep that was lost." ·In the same way, I
tell you, there will be more rejoicing in heaven over one repentant sinner than
over ninety-nine virtuous men who have no need of repentance.'

The Lost Drachma

8 'Or again, what woman with ten drachmas would not, if she lost one, light a
9 lamp and sweep out the house and search thoroughly till she found it? ·And
then, when she had found it, call together her friends and neighbours? "Rejoice
10 with me," she would say "I have found the drachma I lost." ·In the same way, I
tell you, there is rejoicing among the angels of God over one repentant sinner.'

The Lost Son (the 'Prodigal') and the Dutiful Son

11 12 He also said, 'A man had two sons. ·The younger said to his father, "Father, let
me have the share of the estate that would come to me". So the father divided
13 the property between them. ·A few days later, the younger son got together
everything he had and left for a distant country where he squandered his
money on a life of debauchery.

14 'When he had spent it all, that country experienced a severe famine, and
15 now he began to feel the pinch, ·so he hired himself out to one of the local in-
16 habitants who put him on his farm to feed the pigs. ·And he would willingly
have filled his belly with the husks the pigs were eating but no one offered him
17 anything. Then he came to his senses and said, "How many of my father's paid
18 servants have more food than they want, and here am I dying of hunger! ·I will
leave this place and go to my father and say: Father, I have sinned against
19 heaven and against you; ·I no longer deserve to be called your son; treat me as
20 one of your paid servants." ·So he left the place and went back to his father.

21 'While he was still a long way off, his father saw him and was moved with
pity. He ran to the boy, clasped him in his arms and kissed him tenderly. ·Then
his son said, "Father, I have sinned against heaven and against you. I no longer
22 deserve to be called your son." ·But the father said to his servants, "Quick! Bring
out the best robe and put it on him; put a ring on his finger and sandals on his

23 feet. •Bring the calf we have been fattening, and kill it; we are going to have a 24 feast, a celebration, •because this son of mine was dead and has come back to life; he was lost and is found." And they began to celebrate.

25 'Now the elder son was out in the fields, and on his way back, as he drew 26 near the house, he could hear music and dancing. •Calling one of the servants 27 he asked what it was all about. •"Your brother has come" replied the servant "and your father has killed the calf we had fattened because he has got him 28 back safe and sound." •He was angry then and refused to go in, and his father 29 came out to plead with him; •but he answered his father, "Look, all these years I have slaved for you and never once disobeyed your orders, yet you never of-30 fered me so much as a kid for me to celebrate with my friends. •But, for this son of yours, when he comes back after swallowing up your property—he and his women—you kill the calf we had been fattening."

31 'The father said, "My son, you are with me always and all I have is yours. 32 But it was only right we should celebrate and rejoice, because your brother here was dead and has come to life; he was lost and is found." '

QUESTIONS FOR WRITING AND DISCUSSION

OBSERVING

1. What evidence is there in the Sermon on the Mount that Jesus was attempting to introduce a completely "new" ethic here? What does he mean when he says that he came not to "abolish" the Law [of Moses] and the Prophets, but to "fulfill" them (Matthew 5:17)?
2. Many of the sayings recounted in Matthew 5–7 have made their way into popular speech as code words and catch phrases, for example, "Judge not, lest you be judged." Make a list of those you recognize and explain how their meaning may have changed since they were first recorded here.
3. How do the parables recorded in Luke's gospel (e.g., "The Prodigal Son") attempt to soften or "humanize" the God that Jesus was trying to portray to his hearers? What traits of God does Jesus try to emphasize?

EVALUATING

1. The Sermon on the Mount ends with a comment that the people were "amazed" at Jesus' teaching, since he taught with "authority." Does this text command that same response today? Why or why not?
2. The betrayal, crucifixion, and resurrection narratives of Matthew 26–28 are among the most evocative and influential texts in Western culture, as artists and writers of the centuries since have attempted to depict these events and dramatize their significance. What accounts for the power and endurance of his story and its effects on art, literature, music, and drama?

Is it the poignancy of his sacrificial heroism? Is it the significance of his teaching? Speculate on the source of Jesus' continuing and influential presence in the traditions and faith of twentieth-century inhabitants.

3. Had Jesus presently come to the twentieth century, what do you think he would find most troubling and most in need of attention? Imagine a "sermon" he might address to a crowd of people in your hometown or in the middle of your college campus. What would be the theme and focus of his teaching?

RESPONDING AND APPLYING

1. Which of Jesus' sayings in the Sermon on the Mount strikes you as most out of step with contemporary American society, that is, which of them would seem impossible to implement or follow in our culture? Which ones are attractive to you? Why?
2. It is said by some Christians that Christianity is not "views" (an elaborate religious system of laws and rules) but "news" (the declaration of Christ's unique status as God's son who came to redeem humankind from its hatred and alienation from God). How useful is this notion in understanding the life of Christ? In reading Matthew 5–7, 26–28, and Luke 15 is there any indication that this is the way the gospel writers understood Jesus' ministry?
3. The term *fundamentalist* is sometimes used to describe a person who seems dogmatically and rigidly committed to a "conservative" religious point of view. Is fundamentalism a derogatory term? If so, does the term have any positive connotations? Can fundamentalists exist outside of religious faith? For instance, can there be fundamentalist democrats, feminists, or scientists? How might political, social, or scientific fundamentalism differ from religious fundamentalism? Is there a fundamentalist Marxist? A fundamentalist republican?

FROM THE QUR'AN

Sūrahs 1, 19, 76

The Qur'an (commonly known among Westerners as the Koran and after the Bible probably the most influential book in the world) is the sacred text of the world's Muslims and the source of doctrine and practice in the Islamic faith; The word *islam* means "surrender" or "submission" and refers to the total commitment due the one true God, Allah; closely related to the word for "peace," *islam* also implies the sense of peace—within oneself, with God, and toward humanity—that should follow from this surrender. Islam was born in the Arabian peninsula in the early seventh century and now, like Judaism and Christianity, has adherents worldwide, with recent estimates of their numbers ranging from 900 million to 1.5 billion. Its most revered place of worship, located in present-day Saudi Arabia, is Mecca, the site of the Kaaba, an altar believed to have been dedicated to the worship of God by Abraham.

Muslims describe the central tenets of their faith as the "five pillars of Islam": (1) the Creed, or the commitment to the doctrine that "there is only one God and that Mohammed is His prophet"; (2) the Prayers, to be performed five times a day by by each individual wherever he or she may be; (3) the Fasting, total abstinence from food, liquids, and sexual intimacy during the daylight hours for the entire month of Ramadan; (4) the Poor Due, the "purifying" of one's possessions by contributing a portion to the needy; (5) the Pilgrimage, the journey to Mecca, a once in a lifetime obligation for those physically and financially able to perform it.

The Qur'an contains the revelations of the prophet Mohammed (570–632 C.E.), whom Muslims regard as the "last prophet," sent by God to confirm and renew the work of previous prophets, which includes the Torah of Moses, the Psalms of David, and the Bible of Jesus. These other texts, Muslims believe, survive only in corrupted forms, the original and authentic versions having been lost, while the Qur'an is believed to survive in its original form as dictated directly by Allah to Mohammed over a period of 22 years and recited by him to his followers, who first memorized, then began to write it down. They were collected into their present form by Mohammed's secretary, Zaid ibn Thabit, and have been passed down unchanged since.

Because of its complexity, it is less a sustained narrative of a people or a set of individual protagonists in the way the Hebrew Scriptures or the New Testament is and less easy to excerpt or paraphrase coherently. The Qur'an admonishes the reader with the precepts of "the one, true God" who created humankind, revealed himself through various messengers and prophets, and who intends to judge the human race at the end of time. The Western reader will find references to familiar Biblical characters like Noah, Abraham, Ismail (Isaac), Joseph, Moses, Jonah, and also Mary and Jesus, but rarely are their full stories told—it seems often as though the reader is expected to be familiar with them. Such characters may serve as brief examples; often they are mentioned to make a particular moral point, somctimes providing a significant detail missing from the biblical narrative (God's reason for rejecting Cain's sacrifice, for example, is more clearly stated in Sūrah 5); and sometimes they seem to be brought up to correct a point of difference with the Bible (Sūrah 19 makes it clear that Jesus, while a great prophet, was not the son of God).

Each chapter or portion of the Qur'an is called a Sūrah, which means "degree" or "step." The Sūrahs offered below (1, 19, 76) were chosen to illustrate two aspects of the full text: (1) how Allah is understood and worshipped by Muslims, that is, what attributes he is said to possess and what he expects of his followers; (2) how the Qur'an attempts to frame the historical relationships that exist between Islam and both Judaism and Christianity. Sūrah 1, "The Opening," opens the Qur'an and underscores in its epigram, "In the Name of Allah, Most Gracious, Most Merciful," the spirit that Muslims believe ought to shape all human activity. This phrase appears at the beginning of each subsequent Sūrah, and the whole Sūrah precedes every Muslim prayer. Indeed, in its centrality to Islamic faith and culture, Sūrah 1 resonates both with the Hebrew text, "Hear O Israel, the Lord our God, the Lord is One. Love the Lord your God with all your heart and with all your soul and with all your strength" (Deuteronomy 6:4-5), and with the New Testament "Lord's Prayer" (Matthew 6:9-13). Sūrah 19, "Maryam," reflects Islamic thought on the role and identity of the mother of Jesus in Christian tradition. Mary is here portrayed from a Muslim point of view and precedes the introduction of Jesus Christ. Jesus is depicted as indeed born of a virgin and as a worthy prophet, but not the unique Son of God portrayed in the New Testament. This Sūrah deals, however, not just with Mary and Jesus but with how a number of the messengers of Allah overcame problems in their personal relations in their struggle to carry out his will. Thus, we are presented as well with the relations of Yahya (John the Baptist) with his father Zakariya, Abraham with his unbelieving father, Moses with his brother Aaron, Ismail with his family, and Idris in the high station to which he was called. Sūrah 76, "Man" or "Time," introduces the theme of humankind's creation and then quickly focuses on the contrasts between those who choose good and those who choose evil, the believing and the unbelieving, and their respective destinies. Included with these texts are selections from the translator's explanatory notes.

Sūrah 1

Al Fatīḥah (The Opening)

1 *In the Name of Allah, Most Gracious, Most Merciful*[1]

2 Praise be to Allah
The Cherisher and Sustainer of the Worlds;

3 Most Gracious, Most Merciful;

4 Master of the Day of Judgment.

---

[1] The Arabic words *"Raḥmān* and *Raḥīm,"* translated "Most Gracious" and "Most Merciful" are both intensive forms referring to different aspects of Allah's attribute of Mercy. The Arabic intensive is more suited to express Allah's attributes than the superlative degree in English. The latter implies a comparison with other beings, or with other times or places, while there is no being like unto Allah, and He is independent of Time and Place. Mercy may imply pity, long-suffering, patience, and forgiveness, all of which the sinner needs and Allah Most Merciful bestows in abundant measure. But there is a Mercy that goes before even the need arises, the Grace which is ever watchful, and flows from Allah Most Gracious to all His creatures, protecting them, preserving them, guiding them, and leading them to clearer light and higher life. For this reason the attribute *Raḥmān* (Most Gracious) is not applied to any but Allah, but the attribute *Raḥīm* (Merciful), is a general term, and may also be applied to Men.

5 Thee do we worship,[2]
And Thine aid we seek.

6 Show[3] us the straight way,

7 The way of those on whom
Thou hast bestowed Thy Grace,
Those whose (portion)
Is not wrath,
And who go not astray[4]

Sūrah 19

Maryam (Mary)

In the name of Allah, Most Gracious, Most Merciful.

1 Kāf Hā Yā 'Ayn Ṣād[5]

---

[2] On realizing in our souls Allah's love and care, His grace and mercy, and His power and justice (as Ruler of the Day of Judgement), the immediate result is that we bend in the act of worship, and see both our shortcomings and His all-sufficient power. The emphatic form means that not only do we reach the position of worshipping Allah and asking for His help, but we worship Him alone and ask for His aid only. For there is none other than He worthy of our devotion and able to help us. The plural "we" indicates that we associate ourselves with all who seek Allah, thus strengthening ourselves and strengthening them in a fellowship of faith.

[3] If we translate by the English word "guide," we shall have to say: "Guide us to and in the straight Way." For we may be wandering aimlessly, and the first step is to find the Way; and the second need is to keep in the Way: Our own wisdom may fail in either case. The straight Way is often the narrow Way, or the steep Way, which many people shun (90:11). By the world's perversity the straight Way is sometimes stigmatized and the crooked Way praised. How are we to judge? We must ask for Allah's guidance. With a little spiritual insight we shall see which are the people who walk in the light of Allah's grace, and which are those that walk in the darkness of Wrath. This also would help our judgement.

[4] Are there two categories?—those who are in the darkness of Wrath and those who stray? The first are those who deliberately break God's law; the second those who stray out of carelessness or negligence. Both are responsible for their own acts or omissions. In opposition to both are the people who are in the light of Allah's Grace: for His Grace not only protects them from active wrong (if they will only submit their will to Him) but also from straying into paths of temptation or carelessness. The negative *ghayr* should be construed as applying not to the way, but as describing men protected from two dangers by Allah's Grace.

[5] This is the only Sūrah which begins with these five Abbreviated Letters, *Kāf, Hā, Yā, 'Ayn, Ṣād.* I offer this suggestion with some diffidence. The suggestion of the *Tafsīr Kabīr* is that the letters stand for attributes of Allah: K. for *Kafī* (the One sufficient in Himself); H. for *Hādī* (He who guides); Y. for *Yād* (Hand as a symbol of Power and Authority; *Cf.* 48:10, "The Hand of Allah is above their hands"); 'A for *'Alīm* (the All-Knowing); and Ṣ for *Ṣādiq* (The True One).

2 (This is) a recital
Of the Mercy of thy Lord
To His Servant Zakarīya.

3 Behold! he cried
To his Lord in secret,

4 Praying: "O my Lord!
Infirm indeed are my bones,
And the hair of my head
Doth glisten with gray:
But never am I unblest,
O my Lord, in my prayer[6]
To Thee!

5 "Now I fear (what)
My relatives (and colleagues)
(Will do) after me:
But my wife is barren:
So give me an heir
As for Thyself—

6 "(One that) will (truly)
Represent me, and represent
The posterity of Jacob;
And make him, O my Lord!
One with whom Thou art
Well-pleased!"

7 (His prayer was answered):
"O Zakarīya We give thee
Good news of a son:
His name shall be Yaḥyā:
On none by that name
Have We conferred distinction before."[7]

---

[6] This preface shows the fervent faith of Zakarīya. Zakarīya was a priest of the Most High Allah. His office was the Temple, and his relatives were his colleagues. But he found in them no true spirit of the service of Allah and man. He was filled with anxiety as to who would uphold the godly ideas he had in mind, which were strange to his worldly colleagues.

[7] This was John the Baptist, the forerunner of Jesus. In accordance with his father's prayer he, and Jesus for whom he prepared the way, renewed the Message of Allah, which had been corrupted and lost among the Israelites. The Arabic form Yaḥyā suggests "Life." The Hebrew form is Johanan, which means "Jehovah has been Gracious."

8 He said: "O my Lord!
How shall I have a son,
When my wife is barren
And I have grown quite decrepit
From old age?"

9 He said: "So (it will be):[8]
Thy Lord saith, 'That is
Easy for Me: I did
Indeed create thee before,
When thou hadst been nothing!' "

10 (Zakarīya) said: "O my Lord!
Give me a sign."
"Thy Sign," was the answer,
"Shall be that thou
Shalt speak to no man
For three nights,
Although thou art not dumb."

11 So Zakarīya came out
To his people
From his chamber:
He told them by signs
To celebrate Allah's praises
In the morning
And in the evening.

12 (To his son came the command):
"O Yaḥyā! take hold
Of the Book with might":
And We gave him Wisdom
Even as a youth.

13 And pity (for all creatures)
As from Us, and purity:
He was devout,

---

[8] Who is the "He" in this clause? As I have construed it, following the majority of Commentators, it means the angel who brought the message from Allah. *Cf.* 19:21 below. But some Commentators construe it to refer to Zakarīya. In that case the meaning will be: Zakarīya after a little reflection said (in his wonder) "So:", *i.e.* "Can it really be so? Can I really have a son in my old age?" The speech following, "Thy Lord saith," etc., will then be that of the angel-messenger.

14 And kind to his parents,
And he was not overbearing
Or rebellious.

15 So Peace on him
The day he was born
The day that he dies,
And the day that he
Will be raised up
To life (again)!

Section 2.

16 Relate in the Book
(The story of) Mary,[9]
When she withdrew
From her family
To a place in the East.[10]

17 She placed a screen
(To screen herself) from them;
Then We sent to her
Our angel, and he appeared
Before her as a man
In all respects.

18 She said: "I seek refuge
From thee to (Allah)
Most Gracious: (come not near)
If thou dost fear Allah."

19 He said: "Nay, I am only
A messenger from thy Lord,
(To announce) to thee
The gift of a holy son."

---

[9] *Cf.* the story of Mary as related in 3:42-51. Here the whole theme is different: it is the personal side of the spiritual experiences of the worshippers of Allah in relation to their families or environment.

[10] To a private eastern chamber, perhaps in the Temple. She went into privacy, from her people and from people in general, for prayer and devotion. It was in this state of purity that the angel appeared to her in the shape of a man. She thought it *was* a man. She was frightened, and she adjured him not to invade her privacy.

20 She said: "How shall I
Have a son, seeing that
No man has touched me,
And I am not unchaste?"

21 He said: "So (it will be):
Thy Lord saith, 'That is
Easy for Me: and (We
Wish) to appoint him
As a Sign unto men
And a Mercy from Us':
It is a matter
(So) decreed."

22 So she conceived him,
And she retired with him
To a remote place.

23 And the pains of childbirth
Drove her to the trunk
Of a palm tree:
She cried (in her anguish):
"Ah! would that I had
Died before this! would that
I had been a thing
Forgotten and out of sight!"

24 But (a voice) cried to her
From beneath the (palm tree):
"Grieve not! for thy Lord
Hath provided a rivulet
Beneath thee;

25 "And shake towards thyself
The trunk of the palm tree;
It will let fall
Fresh ripe dates upon thee.

26 "So eat and drink
And cool (thine) eye.
And if thou dost see
Any man, say, 'I have
Vowed a fast to (Allah)
Most Gracious, and this day

Will I enter into no talk
With any human being.' "

27 At length she brought
The (babe) to her people,
Carrying him (in her arms).
They said: "O Mary!
Truly an amazing thing
Hast thou brought![11]

28 "O sister of Aaron![12]
Thy father was not
A man of evil, nor thy
Mother a woman unchaste!"

29 But she pointed to the babe.[13]
They said: "How can we
Talk to one who is
A child in the cradle?"

30 He said: "I am indeed
A servant of Allah:
He has given me
Relevation and made me
A prophet;

31 "And He hath made me
Blessed wheresoever I be,
And hath enjoined on me
Prayer and Charity as long
As I live.[14]

---

[11] The amazement of the people knew no bounds. In any case they were ready to think the worst of her, as she disappeared from her kin for some time. But now she comes, shamelessly parading a babe in her arms! How she had disgraced the house of Aaron, the fountain of priesthood! We may suppose that the scene took place in the Temple in Jerusalem, or in Nazareth.

[12] Aaron, the brother of Moses, was the first in the line of Israelite priesthood. Mary and her cousin Elisabeth (mother of Yaḥyā) came of a priestly family, and were therefore "sisters of Aaron" or daughters of 'Imrān (who was Aaron's father).

[13] What could Mary do! How could she explain? Would they, in their censorious mood, accept her explanation? All she could do was to point to the child, who, she knew, was no ordinary child. And the child came to her rescue. By a miracle he spoke, defended his mother, and preached—to an unbelieving audience.

[14] There is a parallelism throughout the accounts of Jesus and Yaḥyā, with some variations. Both the parallelisms and the variations are interesting. For instance Jesus declares at the very outset that he is a servant of Allah, thus negativing the false notion that he was Allah or the son of Allah. The

32 "(He) hath made me kind
To my mother, and not
Overbearing or miserable;[15]

33 "So peace is on me
The day I was born,
The day that I die,
And the Day that I
Shall be raised up
To life (again)!"

34 Such (was) Jesus the son
Of Mary: (it is) a statement
Of truth, about which
They (vainly) dispute.

35 It is not befitting
To (the majesty of) Allah
That He should beget
A son. Glory be to Him!
When He determines
A matter, He only says
To it, "Be," and it is.

36 Verily Allah is my Lord
And your Lord: Him
Therefore serve ye: this is
A Way that is straight.

37 But the sects differ
Among themselves: and woe
To the Unbelievers because
Of the (coming) Judgment
Of a momentous Day!

---

greatness of Yaḥyā is described in 19:12-13 in terms that are not applied to Jesus, but the verses 19:14-15 as applied to Yaḥyā are in almost identical terms with those applied to Jesus here (19:32-33). Devotion in Prayer and Charity is a good description of the Church of Christ at its best, and pity, purity, and devotion in Yaḥyā are a good description of the ways leading to Prayer and Charity, just as John led to Jesus.

[15] Overbearing violence is not only unjust and harmful to those on whom it is practised; it is perhaps even more harmful to the person who practises it, for his soul becomes turbid, unsettled, and ultimately unhappy and wretched—the state of those in Hell. Here the negative qualities are "not overbearing or miserable." As applied to John they were "not overbearing or rebellious." John bore his punishment from the State without any protest or drawing back.

38 How plainly will they see
And hear, the Day that
They will appear before Us!
But the unjust today
Are in error manifest![16]

39 But warn them of the Day
Of Distress,[17] when
The matter will be determined:
For (behold,) they are negligent
And they do not believe!

40 It is We Who will inherit[18]
The earth, and all beings
Thereon: to Us will they
All be returned.

Section 3.

41 (Also) mention in the Book
(The story of) Abraham:
He was a man of Truth.
A prophet.

42 Behold, he said to his father:[19]
"O my father! why
Worship that which heareth not
And seeth not, and can
Profit thee nothing?

43 "O my father! to me
Hath come knowledge which
Hath not reached thee:
So follow me: I will guide
Thee to a Way that
Is even and straight.

---

[16] *Cf.* 1:22, and that whole passage, where the Resurrection is described.

[17] *Ḥasrah:* Sighs, sighing, regrets, distress.

[18] *Cf.* 3:180, n. 485; 15:23 n. 1964. Material property passes from one to another: when one dies another inherits it. Allah gives life and death, and all that survives after physical death goes back to Allah, the original source of all things.

[19] The reference to Abraham here is in relation to his tender solicitude for his father, who had not received the light of Unity, and to whom Abraham wanted to be a guide and friend.

44 "O my father! serve not
Satan: for Satan is
A rebel against (Allah)
Most Gracious.

45 "O my father! I fear
Lest a Penalty afflict thee
From (Allah) Most Gracious,
So that thou become
To Satan a friend."

46 (The father) replied: "Dost thou
Hate my gods, O Abraham?
If thou forbear not, I will
Indeed stone thee:
Now get away from me
For a good long while!"[20]

47 Abraham said: "Peace be
On thee: I will pray
To my Lord for thy forgiveness:[21]
For He is to me
Most Gracious.

48 "And I will turn away
From you (all) and from those
Whom ye invoke besides Allah:
I will call on my Lord:
Perhaps, by my prayer to my Lord,
I shall be not unblest!

49 When he had turned away
From them and from those

---

[20] Note the gentle persuasive tone of Abraham in his speeches in 19:42-45 (for we may suppose those sentences to sum up a long course of arguments) and in 19:47-48, contrasted with the brusque and repellent one of the father's reply in this verse. The one was the outcome of the true Light which had come to Abraham from Allah, as the other was the outcome of Pagan arrogance and the worship of brute force. The spiritual lesson from this episode of Abraham's life may be stated in four propositions: (1) the pious son is dutiful to his father and wishes him well in all things, material and spiritual; (2) if the father refuses Allah's Light, the son will do his utmost to bring such Light to the father; (3) having received the Light, the son will never renounce that Light, even if he has to forfeit his father's love and renounce his home; (4) even if the father repels him and turns him out, his answer will be a soft answer, full of love and forgiveness on the one hand, but firmness on behalf of Truth on the other.

[21] *Cf.* 9:114, where this promise of Abraham to pray for his father is referred to, and its limitations pointed out.

Whom they worshipped besides
Allah, We bestowed on him
Isaac and Jacob, and each one
Of them We made a prophet.

50 And We bestowed
Of Our Mercy on them,
And We granted them
Lofty honour on the tongue
Of truth.

Section 4.

51 Also mention in the Book
(The story of) Moses:
For he was specially chosen,
And he was a messenger
And a prophet.

52 And We called him
From the right side[22]
Of Mount (Sinai), and made
Him draw near to Us,
For mystic (converse).

53 And, out of Our Mercy,[23]
We gave him his brother
Aaron, (also) a prophet.

54 Also mention in the Book
(The story of) Ismā'īl:
He was (strictly) true
To what he promised,[24]
And he was a messenger
(And) a prophet.

---

[22] The *right side* of the mountain may mean that Moses heard the voice from the right side of the mountain as he faced it: or it may have the figurative meaning of "right" in Arabic, *i.e.,* the side which was blessed or sacred ground. (R).

[23] Moses was diffident, and reluctant to go to Pharaoh as he had an impediment in his tongue, and he asked that his brother Aaron should be associated with him in his mission. Allah in His Mercy granted his request: 20:25-36.

[24] Ismā'īl was *Dhabīḥ Allah, i.e.,* the chosen sacrifice of Allah in Muslim tradition. When Abraham told him of the sacrifice, he voluntarily offered himself for it, and never flinched from his promise, until the sacrifice was redeemed by the substitution of a ram under Allah's commands. He was the fountainhead of the Arabian Ummah, and in his posterity came the Prophet of Allah. The Ummah and the Book of Islam reflect back the prophethood on Ismā'īl.

55 He used to enjoin
On his people Prayer
And Charity, and he was
Most acceptable in the sight
Of his Lord.

56 Also mention in the Book
The case of Idrīs:[25]
He was a man of truth
(And sincerity), (and) a prophet:

57 And We raised him
To a lofty station.

58 Those were some
Of the prophets on whom
Allah did bestow His Grace—
Of the posterity of Adam,
And of those whom We
Carried (in the Ark)
With Noah, and of
The posterity of Abraham[26]
And Israel—of those
Whom We guided and chose;
Whenever the Signs
Of (Allah) Most Gracious
Were rehearsed to them,
They would fall down
In prostrate adoration.
And in tears.

59 But after them there followed
A posterity who missed
Prayers and followed after lusts:

---

[25] Idrīs is mentioned twice in the Qur'ān, *viz.:* here and in 21:85, where he is mentioned among those who patiently preserved. His identification with the Biblical Enoch, who "walked with God" (Gen. v. 21-24), may or may not be correct. Nor are we justified in interpreting verse 57 here as meaning the same thing as in Gen. v. 24 ("God took him"), that he was taken up without passing through the portals of death. All we are told is that he was a man of truth and sincerity, and a prophet, and that he had a high position among his people. It is this point which brings him in the series of men just mentioned: he kept himself in touch with his people, and was honoured among them. Spiritual progress need not cut us off from our people, for we have to help and guide them. He kept to truth and piety in the highest station.

[26] The earlier generations are grouped into three epochs from a spiritual point of view: (1) from Adam to Noah, (2) from Noah to Abraham, and (3) from Abraham to an indefinite time, say to the time when the Message of Allah was corrupted and the need arose for the final Message of Unity and Truth. Israel is another name for Jacob.

Soon, then, will they
Face Destruction—

60 Except those who repent
And believe, and work
Righteousness: for these
Will enter the Garden
And will not be wronged
In the least—

61 Gardens of Eternity, those
Which (Allah) Most Gracious
Has promised to His servants
In the Unseen: for His promise
Must (necessarily) come to pass.

62 They will not there hear
Any vain discourse, but
Only salutations of Peace:[27]
And they will have therein
Their sustenance,[28] morning
And evening.

63 Such is the Garden which
We give as an inheritance
To those of Our Servants
Who guard against evil.

64 (The angels say:)
"We descend not but
By command of thy Lord:
To Him belongeth what is
Before us, and what is
Behind us, and what is
Between: and thy Lord
Never doth forget"—

---

[27] *Salām,* translated "Peace," has a much wider signification. It includes (1) a sense of security and permanence, which is unknown in this life; (2) soundness, freedom from defects, perfection, as in the word *salim;* (3) preservation, salvation, deliverance, as in the word *sallama;* (4) salutation, accord with those around us; (5) resignation, in the sense that we are satisfied and not discontented; besides (6) the ordinary meaning of Peace, *i.e.,* freedom from any jarring element. All these shades of meaning are implied in the word *Islām.* (R).

[28] *Rizq:* literally sustenance or means of subsistence, the term covers all the means of perfect satisfaction of the body and soul. Morning and evening *i.e.,* early and late, all the time, always. (R).

65 "Lord of the heavens
And of the earth,
And of all that is
Between them: so worship Him,
And be constant and patient
In His worship: knowest thou
Of any who is worthy
Of the same Name as He?"

Section 5.

66 Man says: "What!
When I am dead, shall I
Then be raised up alive?"

67 But does not man
Call to mind that We
Created him before
Out of nothing?

68 So, by thy Lord,
Without doubt, We shall gather
Them together, and (also)
The Evil Ones (with them);
Then shall We bring them
Forth on their knees
Round about Hell;

69 Then shall We certainly
Drag out from every sect
All those who were worst
In obstinate rebellion
Against (Allah) Most Gracious.

70 And certainly We know best
Those who are most worthy
Of being burned therein.

71 Not one of you but will[29]
Pass over it: this is,

---

[29] Three interpretations are possible: (1) The general interpretation is that every soul must pass through or by or over the Fire. Those who have had *Taqwā* (see n. 26 to 2:2) will be saved by Allah's Mercy, while unrepentant sinners will suffer the torments in ignominy. (2) If we refer the pronoun "you" to those "in obstinate rebellion" in verse 69 above, both leaders and followers in sin, this verse only applies to the wicked. (3) Some refer this verse to the Bridge over Hell, the Bridge *Sirāt,* over which all must pass to their final destiny. This Bridge is not mentioned in the Qur'ān. (R).

With thy Lord, a Decree
Which must be accomplished.

72 But We shall save those
Who guarded against evil,
And We shall leave
The wrongdoers therein,
(Humbled) to their knees.

73 When Our Clear Signs
Are rehearsed to them,
The Unbelievers say to those
Who believe, "Which of the two
Sides is best in point of
Position? which makes the best
Show in Council?"

74 But how many (countless)
Generations before them
Have We destroyed,
Who were even better
In equipment and in glitter
To the eye?

75 Say: "If any man go
Astray, (Allah) Most Gracious
Extends (the rope) to them.
Until, when they see
The warning of Allah (being
Fulfilled)—either in punishment
Or in (the approach of)
The Hour—they will
At length realise who is
Worst in position, and (who)
Weaker in forces!

76 "And Allah doth advance
In guidance those who seek
Guidance: and the things
That endure. Good Deeds,
Are best in the sight
Of thy Lord, as rewards,
And best in respect of
(Their) eventual returns."

77 Hast thou then seen
The (sort of) man who
Rejects Our Signs, yet
Says: "I shall certainly
Be given wealth and children?"

78 Has he penetrated to
The Unseen, or has he
Taken a contract with
(Allah) Most Gracious?

79 Nay! We shall record
What he says, and We
Shall add and add
To his punishment.

80 To Us shall return
All that he talks of,
And he shall appear
Before Us bare and alone.

81 And they have taken
(For worship) gods other than
Allah, to give them
Power and glory!

82 Instead, they shall reject
Their worship, and become
Adversaries against them.

Section 6.

83 Seest thou not that We
Have set the Evil Ones on
Against the Unbelievers,
To incite them with fury?[30]

84 So make no haste
Against them, for We

---

[30] Under the laws instituted by Allah, when evil reaches a certain stage of rebellion and defiance, it is left to gather momentum and to rush with fury to its own destruction. It is given a certain amount of respite, as a last chance: but failing repentance, its days are numbered. The godly therefore should not worry themselves over the apparent worldly success of evil, but should get on with their own duties in a spirit of trust in Allah.

But count out to them
A (limited) number (of days).

85 The day We shall gather
The righteous to (Allah)
Most Gracious, like a band
Presented before a king for honours.

86 And We shall drive
The sinners to hell,
Like thirsty cattle
Driven down to water—

87 None shall have the power
Of intercession, but such a one
As has received permission (or promise)
From (Allah) Most Gracious.

88 They say: "(Allah) Most Gracious
Has begotten a son!

89 Indeed ye have put forth
A thing most monstrous![31]

90 As if the skies are ready
To burst, the earth
To split asunder, and
The mountains to fall down
In utter ruin.

91 That they should invoke
A son for (Allah) Most Gracious.

92 For it is not consonant
With the majesty of (Allah)
Most Gracious that He
Should beget a son.

93 Not one of the beings
In the heavens and the earth

---

[31] The belief in Allah begetting a son is not a question of words or of speculative thought. It is a stupendous blasphemy against Allah. It lowers Allah to the level of an animal. If combined with the doctrine of vicarious atonement, it amounts to a negation of Allah's justice and man's personal responsibility. It is destructive of all moral and spiritual order, and is condemned in the strongest possible terms.

But must come to (Allah)
Most Gracious as a servant.

94 He does take an account
Of them (all), and hath
Numbered them (all) exactly.

95 And every one of them
Will come to Him singly
On the day of Judgment.

96 On those who believe
And work deeds of righteousness,
Will (Allah) Most Gracious
Bestow Love.

97 So have We made
The (Qur'ān) easy
In thine own tongue,
That with it thou mayest give
Glad tidings to the righteous,
And warnings to people
Given to contention.

98 But how many (countless)
Generations before them
Have We destroyed? Canst thou
Find a single one of them
(Now) or hear (so much
As) a whisper of them?

Sūrah 76

Al Insān (Man), or *Al Dahr* (The Time)

In the name of Allah, Most Gracious, Most Merciful.

1 Has there not been
Over Man a long period

Of Time,[32] when he was
Nothing—(not even) mentioned?

2 Verily We created
Man from a drop
Of mingled sperm,
In order to try him:
So We gave him (the gifts),
Of Hearing and Sight.

3 We showed him the Way:
Whether he be grateful
Or ungrateful (rests
On his will).

4 For the Rejecters
We have prepared
Chains, Yokes, and
A Blazing Fire.

5 As to the Righteous.
They shall drink
Of a Cup (of Wine)
Mixed with *Kāfūr*[33]

6 A Fountain where
The Devotees of Allah
Do drink, making it
Flow in unstinted abundance.

7 They perform (their) vows,
And they fear a Day
Whose evil flies far and wide.

8 And they feed, for the love
Of Allah, the indigent,
The orphan, and the captive—

---

[32] *Dahr* is Time as a whole, or for a long period. Time used to be deified by the Pagan Arabs. . . . An analogy can be found in the Greek ideas connected with Chronos or Kronos, themselves a blend of different myths. Kronos (or Time), they said, was the father of Zeus himself.

[33] *Kāfūr* is literally Camphor. It is a fountain in the Realms of Bliss, It is a seasoning added to the Cup of pure, beatific Wine, which causes no intoxication (56:18–19), but stands for all that is wholesome, agreeable, and refreshing, Camphor is cool and refreshing, and is given as a soothing tonic in Eastern medicine. In minute doses its odour and flavour are also agreeable. (R).

9 (Saying), "We feed you
For the sake of Allah alone:
No reward do we desire
From you, nor thanks."

10 "We only fear a Day
Of distressful Wrath
From the side of our Lord."

11 But Allah will deliver
Them from the evil
Of that Day, and will
Shed over them a Light
Of Beauty and
A (blissful) Joy.

12 And because they were
Patient and constant, He will
Reward them with a Garden
And (garments of) silk.

13 Reclining in the (Garden)
On raised thrones,
They will see there neither
The sun's (excessive heat)
Nor (the moon's) excessive cold.

14 And the shades of the (Garden)
Will come low over them,
And the bunches (of fruit),
There, will hang low
In humility.

15 And amongst them will be
Passed round vessels of silver
And goblets of crystal—

16 Crystal-clear, made of silver:
They will determine
The measure thereof
(According to their wishes).

17 And they will be given
To drink there of a Cup

(Of Wine) mixed[34]
With *Zanjabīl*—

18 A fountain there,
Called *Salsabīl.*[35]

19 And round about them
Will (serve) youths
Of perpetual (freshness):
If thou seest them,
Thou wouldst think them
Scattered Pearls.

20 And when thou lookest,
It is there thou wilt see
A Bliss and
A Realm Magnificent.

21 Upon them will be
Green Garments of fine silk
And heavy brocade,
And they will be adorned
With Bracelets of silver;
And their Lord will
Give to them to drink
Of a Wine
Pure and Holy.

22 "Verily this is a Reward
For you, and your Endeavour
Is accepted and recognised."

---

[34] *Cf.* above, 76:5-6, where the Cup of *Kāfūr* (Camphor) was mentioned for coolness and refreshment to the Righteous, who had just passed the great Event of Judgement. The second state is symbolised by verses 12-14, when they enter the Garden in Garments of Silk, and find that their former humility in the probationary life is rewarded with high honour in the new world they have entered. The third stage is in verses 15-21, where they settle down in Bliss, with Garments of fine silk and heavy brocades, with Ornaments and Jewels, with an ordered Feast of set service, and the Cup of *Zanjabīl.* This literally means Ginger. In Eastern medicine Ginger is administered to give warmth to the body and zest to the taste; this is appropriate for the Royal Feast which is now figured forth. (R).

[35] *Salsabīl* literally means: "Seek the Way." The Way is now open to the presence of the Most High. The Banquet is spread. Get thyself ready. It is a "Realm Magnificent" (verse 20) in a new spiritual world. (R).

Section 2.

23 It is We Who
Have sent down the Qur'ān
To thee by stages.

24 Therefore be patient
With constancy to the Command
Of thy Lord, and hearken not
To the sinner or the ingrate
Among them.

25 And celebrate the name
Of thy Lord morning
And evening,

26 And part of the night,
Prostrate thyself to Him;
And glorify Him
A long night through.

27 As to these, they love
The fleeting life,
And put away behind them[36]
A Day (that will be) hard.

28 It is We Who created
Them, and We have made
Their joints strong;
But, when We will,
We can substitute
The like of them
By a complete change.

29 This is an admonition:
Whosoever will, let him
Take a (straight) Path
To his Lord.

---

[36] *Fleeting life: Cf.* 75:20. *They:* the immediate reference was to the Pagan Quraysh; the general reference is to the Unbelievers of all ages. They reject, or at least put away the thought of, a Hereafter, a Day that will be hard, for the easy pleasures of a fleeting life.

30 But ye will not,
Except as Allah wills:
For Allah is full of
Knowledge and Wisdom.

31 He will admit
To His Mercy Whom He will;
But the wrongdoers—
For them has He prepared
A grievous Penalty.

QUESTIONS FOR WRITING AND DISCUSSION

OBSERVING

1. Given the information provided here, sketch a view of Allah as perceived from within the heart of Islam. What are his attributes? What is the relationship of humankind to Him and His will?
2. How would you describe the form or "style" of the Sūrahs reflected here? How hard or challenging are they to make sense of? In what ways do they reflect the characteristics of "sacred texts" discussed earlier? In what ways do they differ?
3. Isolate references in the Sūrahs to any Biblical characters with whom you are familiar; what new or elaborated characteristics of the anecdotes about them do you see?

EVALUATING

1. What do these Sūrahs have in common with Hebrew or Christian tradition in terms of the character of the God they present? Where do they differ?
2. How does the subject matter of the Qur'an vary from what you find in the Hebrew Scriptures and New Testament as reflected in these excerpts? What is especially delightful or interesting to you? Troubling or thought-provoking?
3. Based upon your reading of these Sūrahs, if you were asked to judge how Muslims should relate to Jews and Christians, how would you answer?

RESPONDING AND APPLYING

1. To what degree does reading these Sūrahs give you insight into what it means to be a Muslim? Can the reading of any "sacred" work provide that insight? Why or why not?
2. What, if anything, seems uniquely "sacred" about any of the Qur'anic texts represented here? If you are a Jew or a Christian, what new insight

or reflection do you have upon your own faith by reading these portions of the Qur'an?

3. If you do not count yourself a member of any of the three faiths represented in this chapter, what reflection do you have upon the historical circumstances revolving around the themes and goals of the three as reflected in their sacred texts?

Max Lucado, "A Tale of Two Trees"

Max Lucado is a contemporary pastor/preacher whose disarming "retellings" of familiar Biblical stories have won him a vast and popular audience. In this brief tale, Lucado attempts to "defamiliarize" three distinct themes and represent them in fresh ways: the biblical creation story, the journey of Israel toward nationhood, and the ministry and death of Christ, all linked by the presence of two "trees."

A Tale of Two Trees

Max Lucado

I

1 Formless masses. Floating. Disconnected. Divine artist. Earthly dream.

2 Light! Sun rays piercing through jungle trees. Sunsets volcanic with explosions of gold. Soft sheets of moonlight soothing a weary ocean.

3 Beings! Snorting. Flying. Splashing. Bleating. Gnawing. Clawing. Digging.

4 Sound! Horses' hoofbeats. Cawing crows. Hyena laughter. Cannoning thunder. Chirping chicks. Rat-tat-tatting rain.

5 Nothingness converted.

6 Then silence . . . as an unseen Sculptor molds mud and dust. Lions motionlessly watching. Sparrows perched, peering downward. Clouds hovering. Inquisitive kangaroos. Curious caribou. Snooping centipedes.

7 "What's he making?"

8 "An animal?"

9 Giraffes peeking through leaves. Squirrels chattering gossip. Pausing. Wondering. Jibbering.

10 "A mountain?"

11 A sudden breeze, surprisingly warm, whistles through the leaves scattering dust from the lifeless form. And with the breath of fresh air comes the

difference. Winging on the warm wind is his image. Laughter is laid in the sculpted cheeks. A reservoir of tears is stored in the soul. A sprinkling of twinkle for the eyes. Poetry for the spirit. Logic. Loyalty. Like leaves on an autumn breeze, they float and land and are absorbed. His gifts become a part of him.

12 His Majesty smiles at his image. "It is good."

13 The eyes open.

14 Oneness. Creator and created walking on the river bank. Laughter. Purity. Innocent joy. Life unending.

15 Then the tree.

16 The struggle. The snake. The lie. The enticement. Heart torn, lured. Soul drawn to pleasure, to independence, to importance. Inner agony. Whose will?

17 The choice. Death of innocence. Entrance of death. The fall.

18 Tearstains mingling with fruit-stains.

II

19 The Quest.

20 "Abram, you will father a nation! And Abram—tell the people I love them."

21 "Moses, you will deliver my people! And Moses—tell the people I love them."

22 "Joshua, you will lead the chosen ones! And Joshua—tell the people I love them."

23 "David, you will reign over the people! And David—tell the people I love them."

24 "Jeremiah, you will bear tidings of bondage! But Jeremiah, remind my children, remind my children that I love them."

25 Altars. Sacrifices. Rebelling. Returning. Reacting. Repenting. Romance. Tablets. Judges. Pillars. Bloodshed. Wars. Kings. Giants. Law. Hezekiah. Nehemiah. Hosea . . . God watching, never turning, ever loving, ever yearning for the Garden again.

III

26 Empty throne: Spirit descending. Hushed angels.

27 A girl . . .

a womb . . .

an egg.

28 The same Divine Artist again forms a body. This time his own. Fleshly divinity. Skin layered on spirit. Omnipotence with hair. Toenails. Knuckles. Molars. Kneecaps. Once again he walks with man. Yet the Garden is now thorny. Thorns that cut, thorns that poison, thorns that remain lodged, leaving bitter wounds. Disharmony. Sickness. Betrayal. Fear. Guilt.

The lions no longer pause. The clouds no longer hover. The birds scatter too quickly. Disharmony. Competition. Blindness.

29 And once again, a tree.

Once again the struggle. The snake. The enticement. Heart torn, lured. 30 Once again the question, "Whose will?"

31 Then the choice. Tearstains mingle with bloodstains. Relationship restored. Bridge erected.

32 Once again he smiles. "It is good."

33 For just as death came by the means of a man, in the same way the rising from death comes by means of a man. For just as all people die because of their 34 union with Adam, in the same way all will be raised to life because of their union with Christ.[1]

QUESTIONS FOR WRITING AND DISCUSSION

OBSERVING

1. What use does Lucado make of the Genesis creation story? How does he refocus it or transform it to suit his narrative purpose?
2. What is the "quest" of the second division? And what is the importance of the list of characters he cites?
3. What is the relationship of the third division to the rest of the text? How does it offer a climax to the story?

EVALUATING

1. How effective are the author's lists of images and fragments in conveying the sense of wonder and power he wishes to express?
2. What is the relationship of the "two trees" referred to in the title? What trees is Lucado talking about?
3. What relationship or "bridge" is restored according to the author? What is it that is declared "good" by tale's end?

RESPONDING AND APPLYING

1. It could be said that Lucado tries to make "sound bites" out of the Biblical stories he uses in order to make them seem fresher or more accessible. Choose another portion of Scripture—from any of the three faiths we've looked at in this chapter—and write your own Lucado-esque text.

[1] 1 Corinthians 15:21, 22 TEV

2. Since Lucado's "Tale" ends with Christian Scripture, he clearly intends for it to be the "last word" in his three-part tale. How effective is this choice? If you are not a Christian, does it diminish the impact of the tale? Why or why not?

PERSPECTIVES

Three Faiths, A Common Father

The three texts that follow are all written from the standpoint of a believer, that is, each author speaks out of her or his faith and attempts to explain or articulate its meaning and vitality for them individually. As you read each, practice Lewis' multiperspectival approach—look *at* and *along;* also note not only what is said, but how the authors express their notions of faith and lifestyle. How and why do they differ in their "telling" of their respective journeys of faith? How convincing are they in articulating the vitality of their faith in the modern world? With which of the three would you be inclined to want to have a further conversation?

ABRAHAM HESCHEL (1907–1972), "THE SPIRIT OF JUDAISM"

Born in 1907 in Warsaw, Poland, *Abraham Heschel* came to United States in 1940 and spent more than 30 years as a professor of Jewish ethics and mysticism, most of them at the Theological Seminary of America in New York City, educating four generations of students in the impact and meaning of Judaism in the modern Western world. The author of more than 20 works of history, theology, and poetry, his works have been translated into German, French, Hebrew, Yiddish, Spanish, and Polish and circulated throughout the world.

The Spirit of Judaism

Abraham Heschel

1 Is there a unique expression for the spirit of Judaism? Is there a term that would convey its singular nature?

2 Let us turn to the text of the Ten Commandments, the most representative monument of Jewish teaching, and see whether such a term can be found.

The Ten Commandments have been translated into all tongues, and its vocabulary has become part of the literature of all nations. Reading that famous text in any translation, Greek, Latin or English, we are struck by a surprising fact. All words of the Hebrew text have been easily rendered by English equivalents. There is a word for *pesel:* a graven image; there are words for *shamayim,* for example, and *erets:* heaven and earth. The whole text has been faithfully translated into English and yet it reads as if it were originally written in English. But, lo and behold! There is one Hebrew word for which no English equivalent has been found and which remained untranslated: *Sabbath.* "Remember the Sabbath Day." In the Greek of the Septuagint we read *Sabbaton;* in the Latin of the Vulgate *Sabbatum;* in Aramaic *Shabbatha;* in the King James version the *Sabbath.*

3 Perhaps Sabbath is the idea that expresses what is most characteristic of Judaism.

4 What is the Sabbath? A reminder of every man's royalty; an abolition of the distinction of master and slave, rich and poor, success and failure. To celebrate the Sabbath is to experience one's ultimate independence of civilization and society, of achievement and anxiety. The Sabbath is an embodiment of the belief that all men are equal and that equality of men means the nobility of men. The greatest sin of man is to forget that he is a prince.

5 The Sabbath is an assurance that the spirit is greater than the universe, that beyond the good is the holy. The universe was created in six days, but the climax of creation was the seventh day. Things that come into being in the six days are good, but the seventh day is holy. The Sabbath is *holiness in time.*

6 What is the Sabbath? The presence of eternity, a moment of majesty, the radiance of joy. The soul is enhanced, time is a delight, and inwardness a supreme reward. Indignation is felt to be a desecration of the day, and strife the suicide of one's additional soul. Man does not stand alone, he lives in the presence of the day.

The Art of Surpassing Civilization

7 Lift up your eyes and see: who created these. Six days a week we are engaged in conquering the forces of nature, in the arts of civilization. The seventh day is dedicated to the remembrance of creation and the remembrance of redemption, to the liberation of Israel from Egypt, to the exodus from a great civilization into a wilderness where the word of God was given. By our acts of labor during the six days we participate in the works of history; by sanctifying the seventh day we are reminded of the acts that surpass, ennoble and redeem history.

8 The world is contingent on creation, and the worth of history depends on redemption. To be a Jew is to affirm the world without being enslaved to it; to be a part of civilization and to go beyond it; to conquer space and to sanctify time. Judaism is *the art of surpassing civilization,* sanctification of time, sanctification of history.

9 Civilization is on trial. Its future will depend upon how much of the Sabbath will penetrate its spirit.

10 The Sabbath, as experienced by man, cannot survive in exile, a lonely stranger among days of profanity. It needs the companionship of the other days. All days of the week must be spiritually consistent with the seventh day. Even if we cannot reach a plane where all our life would be a pilgrimage to the seventh day, the thought and appreciation of what the day may bring to us should always be present in our minds. The Sabbath is the counterpoint of living; the melody sustained throughout all agitations and vicissitudes which menace our conscience; our awareness of God's presence in the world. It teaches us to sense the delights of spirit, the joys of the good, the grandeur of living in the face of eternity.

11 What the Sabbath is among the days, the consecrated man, the *talmid chacham,* is among us, the common people. The consecrated man is he who knows how to sanctify time. Not deceived by the splendor of space, he remains attentive to the divine tangent at the whirling wheel of living.

12 The Sabbath is more than a day, more than a name for a seventh part of the week. It is eternity within time, *the spiritual underground of history.*

13 In the language of the Jew, living *sub specie aeternitatis* means living *sub specie Sabbatis.* Every Friday eve we must kindle the lights in the soul, enhance our mercy, deepen our sensitivity.

14 The Sabbath is one day, *Shabbesdikeit* is what should permeate all our days. *Shabbesdikeit* is spirituality, the epitome and spirit of Judaism.

15 The great dream of Judaism is not to raise priests, but a people of priests; to consecrate all men, not only some men.

16 "And why was not the tribe of Levi granted a share in the land of Israel? . . . Because it was dedicated to the worship of God and His ministry. The vocation of the tribe of Levi was to teach the multitude the upright ways of the Lord and His righteous judgments. . . . But not the tribe of Levi alone was consecrated thus. Every human being born into this world whose spirit stirs him and whose intellect guides him to dedicate himself to the Lord in order to minister to Him and worship Him and to come to know Him, and who acts in conformity with God's design and disembarrasses himself of the devious ways which men have sought out, becomes sanctified with supreme sanctity."

The Meaning of Jewish Existence

17 There is a high cost of living to be paid by a Jew. He has to be exalted in order to be normal in a world that is neither propitious for nor sympathetic to his survival. Some of us, tired of sacrifice and exertion, often wonder: Is Jewish existence worth the price? Others are overcome with panic; they are perplexed, and despair of recovery.

18 The meaning of Jewish existence, the major theme of any Jewish philosophy, is baffling. To fit it into the framework of personal intellectual predilec-

tions or current fashions of our time would be a distortion. The claim of Israel must be recognized *before* attempting an interpretation. As the ocean is more than what we know about it, so Judaism surpasses the content of all philosophies of it. We have not invented it. We may accept or reject, but should not distort it.

19 It is as an individual that I am moved by an anxiety for the meaning of my existence as a Jew. Yet when I begin to ponder about it, my theme is not the problem of one Jew but of all Jews. And the more deeply I probe, the more strongly I realize the scope of the problem: It embraces not only the Jews of the present but also those of the past and those of the future, the meaning of Jewish existence in all ages.

20 What is at stake in our lives is more than the fate of one generation. In this moment *we,* the living, are Israel. The tasks begun by the patriarchs and prophets, and carried out by countless Jews of the past, are now entrusted to us. No other group has superseded them. We are the only channel of Jewish tradition, those who must save Judaism from oblivion, those who must hand over the entire past to the generations to come. We are either the last, the dying, Jews or else we are those who will give new life to our tradition. Rarely in our history has so much depended upon one generation. We will either forfeit or enrich the legacy of the ages. . . .

Israel—A Spiritual Order

21 Why is our belonging to the Jewish people a sacred relation? Israel is a *spiritual order* in which the human and the ultimate, the natural and the holy enter a lasting covenant, in which kinship with God is not an aspiration but a reality of destiny. For us Jews there can be no fellowship with God without the fellowship with the people Israel. Abandoning Israel, we desert God.

22 Jewish existence is not only the adherence to particular doctrines and observances, but primarily the living *in* the spiritual order of the Jewish people, the living *in* the Jews of the past and *with* the Jews of the present. It is not only a certain quality in the souls of the individuals, but primarily the existence of the community of Israel. It is neither an experience nor a creed, neither the possession of psychic traits nor the acceptance of a theological doctrine, but the living in a holy dimension, in a spiritual order. Our share in holiness we acquire by living in the Jewish community. What we do as individuals is a trivial episode, what we attain as Israel causes us to grow into the infinite.

23 The meaning of history is to be a sanctuary in time, and every one of us has his part in the great ritual. The ultimate meaning of human deeds is not restricted to the life of him who does these deeds and to the particular moment in which they occur.

24 Religious living is not only a private concern. Our own life is a movement in the symphony of ages. We are taught to pray as well as to live in the first person plural. We do a mitsvah "in the name of all Israel." We act both as

individuals and as the community of Israel. All generations are present, as it were, in every moment.

25 Israel is the tree, we are the leaves. It is the clinging to the stem that keeps us alive. There has perhaps never been more need of Judaism than in our time, a time in which many cherished hopes of humanity lie crushed. We should be pioneers as were our fathers three thousand years ago. The future of all men depends upon their realizing that the sense of holiness is as vital as health. By following the Jewish way of life we maintain that sense and preserve the light for mankind's future visions.

26 It is our destiny to live for what is more than ourselves. Our very existence is an unparalleled symbol of such aspiration. By being what we are, namely Jews, we mean more to mankind than by any particular service we may render.

27 We have faith in God and faith in Israel. Though some of its children have gone astray, Israel remains the mate of God. We cannot hate what God loves. Rabbi Aaron the Great used to say: "I wish I could love the greatest saint as the Lord loves the greatest rascal."

28 Israel exists not in order to be, but in order to cherish the vision of God. Our faith may be strained but our destiny is anchored to the ultimate. Who can establish the outcome of our history? Out of the wonder we came and into the wonder we shall return.

The Dignity of Israel

29 Belonging to Israel is in itself a spiritual act. It is utterly inconvenient to be a Jew. The very survival of our people is a ***kiddush hashem*** [sanctification of the Divine Name]. We live in spite of peril. Our very existence is a refusal to surrender to normalcy, to security and comfort. Experts in assimilation, the Jews could have disappeared even before the names of modern nations were known. Still we are patient and cherish the will to perpetuate our essence.

30 We are Jews as we are men. The alternative to our existence as Jews is spiritual suicide, disappearance. It is *not* a change into something else. Judaism has allies but not substitutes. Jewish faith consists of attachment to God, attachment to Torah, and attachment to Israel.

31 There is a unique association between the people and the land of Israel. Even before Israel becomes a people, the land is preordained for it. What we have witnessed in our own days is a reminder of the power of God's mysterious promise to Abraham and a testimony to the fact that the people kept its promise, "If I forget thee, O Jerusalem, let my right hand wither" (Psalms 137:5). The Jew in whose heart the love of Zion dies is doomed to lose his faith in the God of Abraham who gave the land as an earnest of the redemption of all men.

32 The people of Israel groaned in distress. Out of Egypt, the land of plentiful food, they were driven into the wilderness. Their souls were dried away; there

was nothing at all: no flesh to eat, no water to drink. All they had was a promise: to be led to the land of milk and honey. They were almost ready to stone Moses. "Wherefore hast thou brought us out of Egypt, to kill us and our children and our cattle with thirst?" they cried. But, after they had worshipped the golden calf—when God had decided to detach Himself from His people, not to dwell any more in their midst, but to entrust an angel with the task of leading them out of the wilderness to the Promised Land—Moses exclaimed: "If Thou Thyself dost not go with us, take us not out of the wilderness" (Exodus 33:15). This, perhaps, is the secret of our history: *to choose to remain in the wilderness rather than to be abandoned by Him.*

33 Israel's experience of God has not evolved from search. Israel did not discover God. Israel was discovered by God. Judaism is *God's quest for man.* The Bible is a record of God's approach to His people. More statements are found in the Bible about God's love for Israel than about Israel's love for God.

34 We have not chosen God; He has chosen us. There is no concept of a chosen God but there is the idea of a chosen people. The idea of a chosen people does not suggest the preference for a people based upon a discrimination among a number of peoples. We do not say that we are a superior people. The "chosen people" means a people approached and chosen by God. The significance of this term is genuine in relation to God rather than in relation to other peoples. It signifies not a quality inherent in the people but a relationship between the people and God.

35 Harassed, pursued with enmity and wrong, our fathers continued to feel joy in being Jews. "Happy we are. How good is our destiny, how pleasant our lot, how beautiful our heritage." What is the source of that feeling?

36 The quest for immortality is common to all men. To most of them the vexing question points to the future. Jews think not only of the end but also of the beginning. As parts of Israel we are endowed with a very rare, a very precious consciousness, the consciousness that we do not live in a void. We never suffer from harrowing anxiety and fear of roaming about in the emptiness of time. We own the past and are, hence, not afraid of what is to be. We remember where we came from. We were summoned and cannot forget it, as we wind the clock of eternal history. We remember the beginning and believe in an end. We live between two historic poles: Sinai and the Kingdom of God.

37 Upon thy walls, O Jerusalem,
I have set watchmen,
All the day and all the night
They shall never be silent.
Ye that stir the Lord to remember,
Take no rest,
And give Him no rest
Till He establishes Jerusalem,
And makes it a praise in the earth.
Isaiah 62:6–7

QUESTIONS FOR WRITING AND DISCUSSION

OBSERVING

1. According to the author, what *is* the "spirit of Judaism"? What examples, illustrations, or categories of religion or philosophy does he use to explain and establish his case?
2. What does the author gain by discussing the "spirit" of Judaism? Is the term *spirit* meant to be contrasting to the religion or the practice of Judaism in some way? Why or why not?
3. What does Heschel think the contributions of Judaism are to the modern world or to the West? How is this contribution measured?

EVALUATING

1. How is Judaism foundational to both Christianity and Islam? Could either exist in the present without Judaism?
2. Contemporary Judaism is often classified by one of three descriptors, each representing a distinctive form of practice: Reform, Conservative, and Orthodox. Look up these terms in an encyclopedia or dictionary of religion and then place the author's text in one of these categories. Which category does it best represent, if any? Why?
3. This essay was first published in 1955, after the Holocaust but before recent political and geographical changes in the Middle East. If it were written today, how would its content—or its tone—be altered? Write a new conclusion to the essay with current events in mind.

RESPONDING AND APPLYING

1. Does Judaism define a creed, a nationality, a race, or some combination of the three? What consequences are there for identifying this faith as one with the other categories? Does one mean something different when she or he says, "I am a Jew," than when she or he says, "I am a Christian" or "I am a Muslim"? Explore this question.
2. Is there, following the author's line of thought, a "spirit" of Christianity and of Islam? Write a brief summary statement of what a Christian or Muslim author might say in response to this question.
3. Imagine a conversation between Abraham and Jesus Christ and Mohammed. On what would they agree? On what would they differ? Could Abraham be a Christian or a Muslim? Why or why not?

Dorothy L. Sayers, "The Greatest Drama Ever Staged"

Dorothy L. Sayers (1893-1957) is best known as the creator of the popular detective characters Lord Peter Wimsey and Harriet Vane, who solve crimes in such Sayers mystery novels as *Strong Poison* and *Gaudy Night.* In a varied career, Sayers was one of the first women to obtain a degree from the venerable Oxford University, England's oldest institution of higher learning. She later worked as a teacher at several women's schools and had a successful career as a translator; particularly successful was her "modern" translation of the works of the medieval poet Dante. What many of her readers do not know about her is that she was also a formidable theologian and wrote religious drama and poignant editorials about the recovery of orthodox Christian faith in Britain.

Sayers argues in the essay presented here, "The Greatest Drama Ever Staged," that many believe that the Christian faith needs to be "updated" and that it has been hindered by "dogma," which is intended to be firm through the centuries without change. The key to Christianity's vitality is reaffirming that dogma, which she posits is exciting and ever relevant. In this essay, Sayers achieves a clear and concise presentation of what the basic tenets of orthodox Christian faith involve in the twentieth century.

The Greatest Drama Ever Staged

Dorothy L. Sayers

1 Official Christianity, of late years, has been having what is known as "a bad press." We are constantly assured that the churches are empty because preachers insist too much upon doctrine—"dull dogma," as people call it. The fact is the precise opposite. It is the neglect of dogma that makes for dullness. The Christian faith is the most exciting drama that ever staggered the imagination of man—and the dogma *is* the drama.

2 That drama is summarized quite clearly in the creeds of the Church, and if we think it dull it is because we either have never really read those amazing documents, or have recited them so often and so mechanically as to have lost all sense of their meaning. The plot pivots upon a single character, and the whole action is the answer to a single central problem: *What think ye of Christ?* Before we adopt any of the unofficial solutions (some of which are indeed excessively dull)—before we dismiss Christ as a myth, an idealist, a demagogue, a

liar, or a lunatic—it will do no harm to find out what the creeds really say about Him. What does the Church think of Christ?

3 The Church's answer is categorical and uncompromising, and it is this: That Jesus Bar-Joseph, the carpenter of Nazareth, was in fact and in truth, and in the most exact and literal sense of the words, the God "by whom all things were made." His body and brain were those of a common man; His personality was the personality of God, so far as that personality could be expressed in human terms. He was not a kind of demon pretending to be human; He was in every respect a genuine living man. He was not merely a man so good as to be "like God"—He *was* God.

4 Now, this is not just a pious commonplace; it is no commonplace at all. For what it means is this, among other things: that for whatever reason God chose to make man as he is—limited and suffering and subject to sorrows and death—He had the honesty and the courage to take His own medicine. Whatever game He is playing with His creation, He has kept His own rules and played fair. He can exact nothing from man that He has not exacted from Himself. He has Himself gone through the whole of human experience, from the trivial irritations of family life and the cramping restrictions of hard work and lack of money to the worst horrors of pain and humiliation, defeat, despair, and death. When He was a man, He played the man. He was born in poverty and died in disgrace and thought it well worthwhile.

5 Christianity is, of course, not the only religion that has found the best explanations of human life in the idea of an incarnate and suffering god. The Egyptian Osiris died and rose again; Aeschylus in his play, *The Eumenides,* reconciled man to God by the theory of a suffering Zeus. But in most theologies, the god is supposed to have suffered and died in some remote and mythical period of prehistory. The Christian story, on the other hand, starts off briskly in St. Matthew's account with a place and a date: "When Jesus was born in Bethlehem of Judea in the days of Herod the King." St. Luke, still more practically and prosaically, pins the thing down by a reference to a piece of government finance. God, he says, was made man in the year when Caesar Augustus was taking a census in connexion with a scheme of taxation. Similarly, we might date an event by saying that it took place in the year that Great Britain went off the gold standard. About thirty-three years later (we are informed) God was executed, for being a political nuisance, "under Pontius Pilate"—much as we might say, "when Mr. Joynson-Hicks was Home Secretary." It is as definite and concrete as all that.

6 Possibly we might prefer not to take this tale too seriously—there are disquieting points about it. Here we had a man of Divine character walking and talking among us—and what did we find to do with him? The common people, indeed, "heard Him gladly"; but our leading authorities in Church and State considered that He talked too much and uttered too many disconcerting truths. So we bribed one of His friends to hand Him over quietly to the police, and we tried Him on a rather vague charge of creating a disturbance, and had Him publicly flogged and hanged on the common gallows, "thanking God we were rid

of a knave." All this was not very creditable to us, even if He was (as many people thought and think) only a harmless crazy preacher. But if the Church is right about Him, it was more discreditable still; for the man we hanged was God Almighty.

7 So that is the outline of the official story—the tale of the time when God was the underdog and got beaten, when He submitted to the conditions He had laid down and became a man like the men He had made, and the men He had made broke Him and killed Him. This is the dogma we find so dull—this terrifying drama of which God is the victim and hero.

8 If this is dull, then what, in Heaven's name, is worthy to be called exciting? The people who hanged Christ never, to do them justice, accused Him of being a bore—on the contrary; they thought Him too dynamic to be safe. It has been left for later generations to muffle up that shattering personality and surround Him with an atmosphere of tedium. We have very efficiently pared the claws of the Lion of Judah, certified Him "meek and mild," and recommended Him as a fitting household pet for pale curates and pious ladies. To those who knew Him, however, He in no way suggested a milk-and-water person; *they* objected to Him as a dangerous firebrand. True, He was tender to the unfortunate, patient with honest inquirers, and humble before Heaven; but He insulted respectable clergymen by calling them hypocrites; He referred to King Herod as "that fox"; He went to parties in disreputable company and was looked upon as a "gluttonous man and a wine-bibber, a friend of publicans and sinners"; He assaulted indignant tradesmen and threw them and their belongings out of the Temple; He drove a coach-and-horses through a number of sacrosanct and hoary regulations; He cured diseases by any means that came handy, with a shocking casualness in the matter of other people's pigs and property; He showed no proper deference for wealth or social position; when confronted with neat dialectical traps, He displayed a paradoxical humour that affronted serious-minded people, and He retorted by asking disagreeably searching questions that could not be answered by rule of thumb. He was emphatically not a dull man in His human lifetime, and if He was God, there can be nothing dull about God either. But He had "a daily beauty in His life that made us ugly," and officialdom felt that the established order of things would be more secure without Him. So they did away with God in the name of peace and quietness.

9 *"And the third day He rose again."* What are we to make of that? One thing is certain: if He was God and nothing else, His immortality means nothing to us; if He was man and no more, His death is no more important than yours or mine. But if He really was both God and man, then when the man Jesus died, God died too; and when the God Jesus rose from the dead, man rose too, because they were one and the same person. The Church binds us to no theory about the exact composition of Christ's Resurrection Body. A body of some kind there had to be, since man cannot perceive the Infinite otherwise than in terms of space and time. It may have been made from the same elements as the body that disappeared so strangely from the guarded tomb, but it was not that

old, limited moral body, though it was recognizably like it. In any case, those who saw the risen Christ remained persuaded that life was worth living and death a triviality—an attitude curiously unlike that of the modern defeatist, who is firmly persuaded that life is a disaster and death (rather inconsistently) a major catastrophe.

10 Now, nobody is compelled to believe a single word of this remarkable story. God (says the Church) has created us perfectly free to disbelieve in Him as much as we choose. If we do disbelieve, then He and we must take the consequences in a world ruled by cause and effect. The Church says further, that man did, in fact, disbelieve, and that God did, in fact, take the consequences. All the same, if we are going to disbelieve a thing, it seems on the whole to be desirable that we should first find out what, exactly, we are disbelieving. Very well, then: "The right Faith is, that we believe that Jesus Christ is God *and* Man. Perfect God and perfect Man, of a reasonable soul and human flesh subsisting. Who although He be God and Man, yet is He not two, but one Christ." There is the essential doctrine, of which the whole elaborate structure of Christian faith and morals is only the logical consequence.

11 Now, we may call that doctrine exhilarating or we may call it devastating; we may call it revelation or we may call it rubbish; but if we call it dull, then words have no meaning at all. That God should play the tyrant over man is a dismal story of unrelieved oppression; that man should play the tyrant over man is the usual dreary record of human futility; but that man should play the tyrant over God and find Him a better man than himself is an astonishing drama indeed. Any journalist, hearing of it for the first time, would recognize it as news; those who did hear it for the first time actually called it news, and good news at that; though we are apt to forget that the word Gospel ever meant anything so sensational.

12 Perhaps the drama is played out now, and Jesus is safely dead and buried. Perhaps. It is ironical and entertaining to consider that once at least in the world's history those words might have been spoken with complete conviction, and that was upon the eve of the Resurrection.

QUESTIONS FOR WRITING AND DISCUSSION

OBSERVING

1. Sayers begins her essay on a negative note: "Official Christianity . . . has been having what is known as a 'bad press.'" What does she mean by "Official" Christianity? In what way does her aggressive beginning prepare the reader for her argument that "The Christian faith is the most exciting drama that ever staggered the imagination of man"?

EVALUATING

1. In Sayers' answer to what she considers the essential question of Christianity, "What think ye of Christ?" she lists such possibilities as myth, idealist, demagogue, liar, or lunatic, and then explains the historic creeds of Christianity (paragraph 2). Summarize her explanation.
2. Sayers emphasizes in her essay that whatever else the "dogma" or teaching about Christ is, it is a very good story or drama and that it may be revelation or rubbish but it is not dull. What incidents and personality traits of Christ does she cite to establish her point?

RESPONDING AND APPLYING

1. Imagine that you are a first-century journalist asked to cover the itinerant ministry of the man called Jesus Christ. Write an account of a typical day of traveling with Jesus and his disciples as you might for a twentieth-century national newspaper.
2. Consider yourself an anthropologist who is attempting to explain the religious behavior of Christians to an audience completely unfamiliar with the Christian tradition. Interview friends or relatives who consider themselves Christians, visit a church service, or watch a broadcast of a Christian evangelist. Write a factual account of this experience and then offer an objective, "clinical" report of this experience to your readers.

M. S. MODOOD, "ISLAM, MY FAITH: A PERSONAL STATEMENT"

M. S. Modood, a Muslim who moved to Britain from Pakistan in 1961, offers a "personal statement" on what his Islamic faith and heritage mean to him and how Islam offers a critique of and an alternative to Western society.

Islam, My Faith: A Personal Statement

M. S. Modood

1 My intellectual starting-point is the proposition that the world has a Creator. None of us has willed ourselves into existence; indeed when I came into existence in the belly of my mother, it was weeks before she was even aware of the

fact. Our parents may have willed the act of sex, but they had no control over what, if anything, was being created. If we do not choose to be created and have no say over what we will be, it follows that He who wills Creation must lie outside the created world.

2 Some have held that the Creator is hidden, beyond our grasp, or chooses not to be known. Muslims believe that man is created out of matter, but is infused with the spirit of God, his Creator. We have therefore the potential to receive communications from God and to understand the purpose of Creation. Reason makes us aware that Nature is ordered, not chaotic, that every element, even the tiniest microbe, contributes to a greater ecology and purpose; yet while Reason reveals the presence of purpose, at the same time it makes us aware of the limits of our knowledge. Reason sets in motion a chain of questions and answers, but is of itself unable—at least for ordinary mortals—to come up with any ultimate answers. Faith alone—based on direct communication from Creator to created—can give us the answers and complete the train of reflection set in motion by Reason.

3 All made things work best when the manufacturer's instructions are followed. To use a car or a lawn-mower in ways that run contrary to the manufacturer's instructions is to abuse it and to risk malfunction and even total breakdown. So it is with Man: our proper functioning depends upon carefully adhering to the dos and don'ts, the step-by-step instructions, of the manufacturer's manual. It is therefore our duty to seek to discover and to obey the Word of the Creator.

4 Muslims believe that all the prophets are part of a single message, and that when properly understood they will be seen not to be contradicting each other but to be giving emphasis to an aspect of a single universal Truth: God's guidance to Man on how to live on the earth and secure eternity in heaven by means of this life.

5 Islam is sometimes described by commentators as a young or middle-aged religion. This is far from our own self-understanding. We believe that there is only one religion and that Islam is the clearest statement of God's repeated attempts to communicate the Truth to wayward mankind. We hold Adam to be the first Muslim and we honour all the prophets as prophets of Islam, and respect all the scriptures as divine messages. The Qur'an, however, is the perfect statement and corrects all previous misinterpretations and misunderstandings including, of course, the relationship between Jesus, peace be upon him, and God. Our confidence in the Qur'an is strengthened by the fact that, unlike the Bible, it has been perfectly guarded so there are no different texts in competition with one another, nor new editions which rest on nothing more than linguistic or theological fashions.

6 A full, learned understanding of the Qur'an is, however, dependent upon a knowledge of the tradition of which it is the climax. Where the Qur'an is silent, or needs interpretation, or takes something for granted, one must look to the wider tradition in order to understand it. Let me give a simple example: the

Qur'an speaks of 'Adam and his wife,' yet Muslims have no hesitation in supposing that the unnamed spouse is called Hawa (Eve).

7 For me, 'the five pillars of Islam' is something of a misnomer. For what is referred to as the first pillar, the profession of faith (*kalma* or *shahada*), is not a pillar but the foundation upon which all else rests. Faith in God as our Creator, in Muhammad, peace be upon him, as the ultimate prophet and model human being, and the Qur'an as the word of God is the foundation of Islam. Unlike the Christian trinity, God, the Qur'an and Muhammad are not joined in one being but form a unity of purpose.

8 On this foundation rests the four pillars: prayer (*namaz* or *salat*), fasting (*roza* or *sawm*), almsgiving (*zakat*) and pilgrimage (*hajj*). Each of these involves time, effort and some economic cost (including that of lost opportunities). If they did not, they would not be worth doing for they are expressions of love and thus a form of giving, though also, like love, a form of receiving. For on these pillars rests perfect internal harmony and social peace—a harmony and peace that is only possible if one is leading the life for which one was created, like a perfect ball-bearing.

9 I came to Britain in 1961, full of admiration for the British. In the early days I used to fear that the superiority and attractions of the West would prove too much for a simple-minded people and that we would sell our faith for a share in the obvious advantages of Western civilisation. Thirty years on I no longer have this fear. Early in this century Muhammad 'Abduh, a distinguished religious leader and scholar at Al-Azhar, the centre of Muslim learning in Cairo, after a visit to Europe wrote: "In Europe I saw Islam but no Muslims; in Egypt I see many Muslims but no Islam." Even today the standard of public service, rule of law, democracy, freedom to dissent, and equality in Britain far exceed anything that is found in a Muslim country where dictatorship and brutish coercion, bribery, nepotism and deceit are usual. Yet familiarity with the West increasingly reveals to us—through the many stories in the media about child abuse, rape of the elderly, routine sexual greed and exploitation—the rottenness that lies at the core of this civilisation, contact with which makes us embrace our faith with greater certitude and welcome British converts.

10 All Muslims long for the creation of truly Muslim societies and polities; but it is our conviction that these will arise from the purity, integrity and strength that flows from submission to God, not from an imitation of the West. It is my sincere belief that this example of faith, modelled on Muhammad, peace be upon him, is the greatest service that Muslims can render Britain and indeed the world. For the wickedness of the human heart will be defeated, not by social reform alone, but by the discipline of faith.

11 He is the Lord of the Universe, nothing is possible without His knowledge and His will. Islam is complete faith in His sovereignty and justice and complete submission to His will.

QUESTIONS FOR WRITING AND DISCUSSION

OBSERVING

1. The author begins his statement with his "intellectual starting point." What is this starting point and how does it shape the rest of what he has to say?
2. Why does the author say the term "the five pillars of Islam" is something of a misnomer? How does he reinterpret it?
3. Compare and contrast the author's discussion of Nature and Reason; what part does each play in shaping or limiting knowledge in his view?

EVALUATING

1. The author says "Muslims hold Adam to be the first Muslim." What is the meaning of this statement? Could a Jew or a Christian say something analogous about Adam with respect to their faith? Why or why not?
2. What does the author intend when he cites the statement, "In Europe I saw Islam but no Muslims; in Egypt I see many Muslims but no Islam"? How does it lie at the center of his contrast between the Western democracy he witnesses in Britain and the ideal society he envisions?
3. What would the "truly Muslim societies" the author refers to look like in your opinion?

RESPONDING AND APPLYING

1. What is your general impression of Islam from your personal experience? How does this personal testimony affect that impression, either positively or negatively? Why?
2. The author claims a different status of accuracy and stability for the Qur'an than he believes is true for the Bible, which, according to him, is affected by "linguistic or theological fashion." What is this difference, and how does his statement affect your appreciation for either text?
3. The author refers to the "rottenness at the core of this civilization." Do you agree that Western civilization is corrupt at its heart and needs some kind of religious order to bring it equilibrium?

CHAPTER WRITING ASSIGNMENTS

1. There are a number of other creation stories extant from the ancient world, including several whose accounts bear some similarity to Genesis, but most of which are even less specific and detailed. To what extent is Genesis 1–2 a "mythological" or a "scientific" account of the origin of the universe? Why or why not? What details would make it more "scientific" for twentieth-century readers? In responding, consider its possible purpose for (1) its original readers; (2) those who today accept it at face value; (3) those outside the community of believers?

2. Write an EVALUATING essay that explores the impact of the Law of Moses, the Sermon on the Mount, or any aspect of Islamic thought or practice on our culture. To what extent is our legal and judicial system based upon these teachings? Do you regard their influence as beneficial or detrimental? To what extent is their influence being eroded or altered? In view of the way our culture is headed, are you optimistic or pessimistic about the twenty-first century?
3. Moses is seen as a prototypical "hero" by most cultures—daring, courageous, clever, and wise. Consider this tribute to the historical Moses' impact on Hebrew culture and the world's ethical system by theologican John Wenham: "No sense can be made of the history of the world unless Moses is recognized, not only as a historical figure, but as one of the greatest figures of all time. It can be safely said that the appearance in the world of the ethical monotheism of Judaism represents the most far-reaching influence in the whole history of mankind" ("Moses and the Pentateuch," New Bible Commentary, 43). Do you agree with this assessment? Why or why not?
4. The Passover is a significant, sacred event to Israel. What is Passover about? How does it fit into Israel's later history as a family observance? How is it related to the Easter celebration that Christians observe? Are there similar traditions in your household that link the family to the past as a cherished and celebrated moment? In what way?
5. Write a tongue-in-cheek essay that "discovers" laws, stories, or principles "inadvertently left out" of the Ten Commandments, Sermon on the Mount, or the Sūrahs of the Qur'an. Title your essay, "The Lost Book of Moses," "The Missing Notes from the Sermon on the Mount," or "The Recovered Sūrha," and recreate those twentieth-century circumstances that elicit new or different versions of the guidelines these sacred texts presented to their times.
6. If you count yourself a believer in God, craft an essay that explains your reasons for your faith to a sympathetic but skeptical nonbeliever. You may cite personal experience, but try to keep your essay based in historical and/or biblical evidence as much as possible.

OR

If you count yourself a nonbeliever in God, craft an essay that explains your reasons for your lack of faith to a sympathetic but skeptical believer. You may cite personal experience, but, again, try to keep your essay based in historical and/or biblical evidence as much as possible.

7. Science and religious faith are often assumed to be in conflict. Each "side" tends to identify the other with being either "unscientific" or "superstitious." Considering the views C. S. Lewis offers in his "Meditation in a Toolshed," answer these questions: Do science and religion necessarily contradict? Can they be reconciled? Should one have more authority than the others? Craft an essay that might be titled, "Toward a Harmony of Science and Religion" or "Refuting the Claims of Religion from a Scientific Point of View." Is one of the three faiths discussed in this chapter easier to reconcile with science than the others? Consider in your essay either (1) that the claims of science take precedence over the claims of religion; (2) that the claims of religion take precedence over those of science; or

(3) that there is some synthesis of these two positions which parcels out different realms of authority depending upon the issues being raised. Whichever view you take, assume that your reader will not necessarily be sympathetic to your point of view and thus present evidence accordingly.

8. What *harmonies* among Judaism, Christianity, and Islam have you observed in this chapter. What *differences* have you observed? How might someone choose among them or combine them? Are there irreconcilable distinctives between them? Which ones? How, if at all, do you think their respective view of deity and humankind differ? Which faith, if any of the three, is more appealing or explains more for you? What is problematic about all three? Write an essay that explores these questions.
9. Interview a believer, an agnostic, and an atheist, asking them all the same series of questions, focusing their attention on such issues as (1) how do they know there is (or isn't) a supreme deity; (2) how do they determine how to make ethical choices in their personal views and what role does their "religious" views play in this decision-making; (3) what are their views on what happens after death. Write an essay that explores the differing means by which they arrive at their conclusions.

CHAPTER PREVIEW

Chapter Prelude
Peter Marin, "Secularism's Blind Faith"

Introductory Essay

Readings
Plato, "Allegory of the Cave"
Marcus Tullium Cicero, "On Natural Law"
John Stuart Mill, "Nature"
Jean Paul Sartre, "Existentialism"

Story
Franz Kafka, "The Problem of Our Laws"

Perspectives
Morality and Rational Judgment
Mary Midgley, "Trying Out One's New Sword"
Patricia M. King, "How Do We Know? Why Do We Believe? Learning to Make Reflective Judgments"

Chapter Writing Assignments

Chapter 5

PHILOSOPHY AND RATIONALITY

Secularism's Blind Faith

Peter Marin

1 The great dream at the heart of modern American secularism has always been that religion would slowly wither away, giving way, as it did so, to reason, to a morality rooted not in a fear of God or the hope of heaven but in reflection, a sense of kinship, and a belief in the common good. Values once maintained through oppression or fear would rise naturally from human reason, instinct, and sympathy. The religious divisions and hatred separating us from one another would disappear, and the senses of gratitude and awe traditionally felt for God would be transferred to the human world and provide a foundation for a universalized community. As we know, none of this came to be, or is likely to come to be. The struggle to live ethically without God has left us not with the just and moral order we imagined but with disorder and confusion.

2 Something has gone radically wrong with secularism. The problem has more than its share of irony, for secularism, in the end, has converted itself into a kind of religion. Our hallowed tradition of skepticism and tolerance has grown into its near opposite, and it now partakes of precisely the same arrogance, the same irrationality and passion for certainty, the same pretense to unquestioned virtue against which its powers were once arrayed. In the desperate way we cling to belief, in our contempt for those who do not believe what we believe, secularism has, indeed, taken on the trappings of a faith—and a narrow one at that.

3 All of this, I suppose, should come as no surprise. Certain ideas fundamental to much of modern secularism—especially those associated with progress, improvement, "uplift," or rehabilitation—have their most obvious and deepest roots in religious ways of seeing the world. Analyze the positions of secular, liberal, or left-wing Americans on any of our contemporary national debates and you can find, clearly preserved, many of the assumptions and attitudes held by the Puritans toward community, deviance, sinners, and rectitude.

4 Remember, in this context, what we saw at the last Democratic Convention, and then at the Inauguration: Bill Clinton surrounded by secular academics and experts of all kinds, ready to right society's various wrongs with an endless series of schemes and interventions, an extended twelve-step program for the nation with the role of "higher power" played by the state. Our secular claims to moral authority, our postures of superiority and virtue, our belief in the use of a "moral" government to correct errant behavior—all of this is the secular form of what in the nineteenth century was brought to frontier towns by the preachers and the other members of the "civilizing classes." Now the transition is complete: the state has become the church, and it's all happened in the name of ends so virtuous, so pure, so astonishingly assured, they might have been handed down by God.

5 The attitudes I am describing—a passion for totalizing thought, a conviction that we know better than others what is good for them—cut across almost the entire range of contemporary secularism. They're present, obviously, in the Marxist notions of the new man, in the speech and behavior codes now enacted on campuses, and in the fury with which abortion-rights defenders denounce as charlatans or knaves all those who persist in thinking of the fetus as a person and alive. All of the positions I've named may indeed be defensible on one ground or another, but what's important is *how* they're held: with a monstrous certainty that assumes first the tone of self-righteousness and then the form of coercion or tyranny.

6 I remember that a few years ago someone discovered, behind an abandoned California abortion mill, hundreds of discarded fetuses in Dumpsters. As best I can recall, a Christian group approached state officials and asked to say some kind of prayer when the fetuses were buried. But this proved too much for certain secularists. They went to court and argued against the rights of the Christians to say their prayer and petitioned the judge to declare the fetuses "waste human tissue."

7 *Waste human tissue!* This is what we've come to as secularists. This is what we fight for in court. I honestly doubt that souls exist and rise, and I've never believed there exists a God who listens to our prayers. But so what? I can understand the human horror or grief one might feel at the desecration in a Dumpster of life-to-be or what-might-have-been-life. Is a reverence for that life-to-be, or sorrow at its degradation, so out of the question that we must forbid its expression in prayer? Here, juxtaposed with one another, we have the illusions of religion and the "mature realism" of secularism. And which one seems more frightening, more dangerous, closer to death than life: the religious notion that the soul of a fetus floats up to God, or the secular notion that nothing more is involved here than a discarded appendix?

8 Pick up, if you will, almost any copy of *The Nation,* or *Mother Jones,* or *The Village Voice.* In those dissident publications you'd hope to find, in one form or another, some kind of alternative wisdom to hold over and against the conservative or religious points of view now on the rise. But that is not what's there.

Though I sometimes write for these magazines, I now find it increasingly difficult to read them. There's an implicit sense of superiority in almost every word, a denunciatory tone attached to all disagreement, a furious self-righteousness that accompanies all criticism, turning it into a battle between the saved and the sinner. Everything is put forth as if fundamental matters had been settled, as if truth had been revealed, as if our own particular points of view—socialism, say, or feminism—are somehow coeval with reason itself, have emerged from history as absolute truths magically vouchsafed to us from the future.

9 I do not mean to demean here the extraordinary ideas or glorious ideals which still lie, half-forgotten and largely unexpressed, at the heart of secular belief. The role secularism has played in the last couple of hundred years has usually been an honorable one, powered by deep and transformative passions and hopes. But along the way we've bred out of secularism the deep seriousness and the humility that once informed it, and also the senses of tragedy, complexity, and ambiguity which, at its best, marked it as a legitimate response to the mindlessness of others. And we've somehow picked up the baggage of those mindless others: a readiness to force upon people through law what reason cannot teach them, and a sense of superiority or virtue that makes us contemptuous of others. Whether it is the state of education or children born out of wedlock or divorce rates or moral confusion in our communities, we steer forever away from the possibility that something in our system of beliefs may be in some small way to blame.

10 The astonishing thing about all this is that such certainty, such freedom from self-doubt, should persist at the heart of secularism even after the past century, after countless examples of the ways in which predominantly secular ideologies—I am thinking here of Marxism, Stalinism, the Maoists in China—have failed to produce the results that were anticipated or promised. What we should have learned has something to do with fallibility, with humility, with the endless human capacity for error. It ought to have sent us rushing back to examine the fundamental assumptions we've made about the world, the pretty castles and palaces we've etched in the air. We know now, or ought to know, that men are as ready to kill in God's absence as they are in his name: that reason, like faith, can lead to murder, that the fanaticism long associated with religion was not born there, but has its roots deeper down in human nature.

QUESTIONS FOR WRITING AND DISCUSSION

OBSERVING

1. Values are abstract ideas that individuals or groups use to guide conduct, to define what is important to them. What values do you think can be said to "rise naturally from human reason, instinct, and sympathy"?

2. In what ways does Marin suggest that secularism has become like a religion?
3. Explain Marin's distinction between the question of what moral or ethical positions one has and how he or she defends them.

EVALUATING

1. Is it possible to establish a basis on which to "live ethically without God"—or for a society to do so without all believing in the same god? Can reason establish a certain basis for moral value? To what extent do a people's laws embody such values?
2. If not a certain basis for moral value, can reason establish a basis that we can call at least adequate? That is, assuming a people are of good will, how can they arrive at agreement on basic principles of right and wrong?
3. If people continue to disagree about moral values, we cannot expect them to stop trying to convince each other of their position, but is it possible to arrive at some consensus on which disagreements can be tolerated and which must not?
4. In what kind of context might dogmatism, the authoritative assertion of principles that may not be questioned, be necessary?
5. In what contexts is it possible for certainty to become monstrous? What is the relation between faith and certainty, reason and certainty?
6. What is it that generates the conviction in some that their view of things is "settled, as if truth had been revealed, as if our own particular points of view . . . are somehow coeval with reason itself"?

RESPONDING AND APPLYING

1. To what extent do you think such conviction is a social construct, the product of a narrow group of like-thinking individuals who simply reenforce each other's prejudices?
2. Perhaps the only alternative to religious or rational certainty is a numbing skepticism, an abandonment of any possibility of discovering truth. What alternatives can you imagine?

THE CRADLE OF RATIONALISM

The problem that Peter Marin raises—the conflict between traditional religion and a more humanistic and secular rationalism, including the tendency toward dogmatism in both, far from being a recent aberration—can be found among the Greeks from the sixth through the fourth centuries B.C.E., at the very beginning of rationalism.

The Greek world provided a favorable combination of conditions for the emergence of the new strategy for the discovery of truth and meaning that is rationalism. The Greeks' mountainous land with its many relatively isolated valleys contributed to the development of a spirit of individuality, exhibited both in the appreciation of heroism fostered by their warrior cultures and in the growth of numerous independent city-states. But at the same time, their irregular coastlines with countless harbors and the opportunities for exchange and colonization offered by the many islands in the highly navigable and relatively placid Aegean Sea helped them develop a sense of cultural unity that was also highly cosmopolitan.

Though the Greeks were deeply religious and they believed in an afterlife of sorts, their values were centered on this life and on developing their capacities to enjoy it. This point is made explicitly in Book XI of Homer's *Odyssey* when Odysseus, having performed a sacrifice to call up some of the dead for consultation on how he can return home, speaks with the ghost of Achilles, the greatest warrior to fight in the Trojan War. Odysseus wonders why Achilles seems so unhappy, since the position of so great a man among the dead must be royal. Achilles answers, "Better, I say, to break sod as a farm hand / for some poor country man, on iron rations, / than lord it over all the exhausted dead." In other words, he would rather be the poorest of day laborers and alive, than king of all the dead.

The Greeks came, in fact, to cultivate the joy of living in all its possible dimensions: not only the natural joy that begins with merely drawing breath, but also the pleasures that come from wealth and power, as well as the deeper delight and fullness that come from pursuits like human love and eventually art, literature, and philosophy.

The variety of the Greeks' very anthropomorphic gods may also have inspired rationalism in other ways. Like humans, the Greek gods were capable of lofty justice and munificence as well as petty spitefulness and unpredictability. This lack of consistency seemed to leave unsatisfied the emerging desire in some thinkers for a more coherent sense of order in the universe. What the gods had not given, humanity would have to work out for itself.

The Gifts and Burdens of Rationalism

It is the process initiated by the Greeks of working out the answers to such needs by means of rational thinking that has so profoundly affected our understanding not only of philosophy, but of such areas of learning and practice as politics, law, art, architecture, logic, poetry, drama, history, biography, language, oratory, mathematics, science, and even athletic competition. Perhaps most important, the rational tradition has led us to see these areas not as fixed institutions given for all time by the gods, but as human creations capable of continuing revision and development.

Such gifts to culture, however, carry with them considerable potential for conflict, not only among philosophers, but also between philosophers and the defenders of traditional forms of spirituality. This potential emerged clearly as early as the second half of the fifth century B.C.E. in the very cradle of rational thought. We can see something of the conflict Marin describes, for example, in the plays of the classical Greek dramatist Sophocles, who seems to have seen his own time as undergoing a crisis of faith. As the chorus laments in *Oedipus the King,* "Nowhere Apollo's golden glory now— / the gods, the gods go down" (Sophocles, *The Three Theban Plays,* Trans. Robert Fagles, New York: Penguin, 1982). What seems to be undermining the old traditional beliefs are the new more humanist and secularist forces of statism (that is, the belief in the absolute authority of the corporate political entity) and rationalism. In *Antigone,* written in the middle of the Periclean Age (460–430 B.C.E.), at the height of the Athenian empire, the political power that creates and enforces human law, embodied in the person of Creon, king of Thebes, is pitted against Antigone, who fights for divine law, "that Justice, dwelling with the gods . . . the great unwritten, unshakable traditions [that] are alive, not just today or yesterday; they live forever, from the first of time." In this struggle, Creon is shown to be in the wrong, and Sophocles reveals his belief in the precedence of the authority of divinity and tradition over that of human reason and will.

A similar conflict occurs in *Oedipus,* written 13 years later during the first years of the disastrous Pelopponesian War. Oedipus not only does all he can to flee the oracle that says he will kill his father and bed his mother, he denies its validity: "all those prophecies I feared. . . . They're nothing, worthless." Rejecting the authority of the oracles and with them the notion of a world ruled by the will of the gods, he calls himself "the son of Chance," preferring to conceive of the world as one in which a smart man can play the odds and make his own destiny. The outcome of the play proves Oedipus wrong and reaffirms the power of the oracles, and Sophocles again makes clear his stand on the side of traditional faith in the crisis of values in his time.

But although some philosophers are antireligious, there is no necessary opposition or antipathy to spirituality in rationalism. Indeed, the three major religious traditions we have included in this text have all produced important philosophers who are believers in divinity as well. As an alternative way of knowing, however, rationalism can be, and often has been, perceived as irreverent or impious, whether or not it was in fact. Perhaps this is because there is a potential for impiety inevitable in rationalism: in seeking another way to answer questions that the religious tradition sees as either given or unanswerable, rationalism and humanism imply, intentionally or not, that the traditional answers are somehow inadequate. Thus rationalism becomes identified with secularism and, especially in times of great economic, social, or political stress, with what Marin calls secularism's "hallowed tradition of skepticism and tolerance," which can be seen as a threat to orthodoxy. Socrates, who may be seen as the originator of that hallowed tradition, is a case in point. However skeptical he may have been, he still believed in the gods, as he says, "in a sense higher than that in which any of my accusers believe in them"; nevertheless he was condemned to death for teaching what the Athenians saw as impiety and for corrupting Athenian youth with unorthodox ideas.

PLATO, "THE ALLEGORY OF THE CAVE" *FROM* THE REPUBLIC

When *Socrates* (470–399 B.C.E.), Plato's (c. 427–347 B.C.E.) mentor and the first of the great Classical Greek philosophers, began to teach late in the fifth century B.C.E., he already had two centuries of Greek philosophical tradition behind him. That tradition had degenerated, however, into a combination of gamesmanship and commercialism—or so Socrates believed. These characteristics were centered in a group of thinkers called Sophists, the intellectual Pharisees of the time. Today, they would be equivalent to lawyers or law professors because they worked for pay and because they taught their students how to win an argument, no matter which side they argued, two practices that Socrates abhorred. Socrates believed that one should teach out of a pure love of knowledge and that the purpose of argument and inquiry was not to persuade but to arrive at the truth. He remains a symbol of several principles central to Greek humanism: a belief in the primary importance of the human intellect and in its capacity to perfect itself and to attain truth and a commitment to the life of the mind and to the highest standards of intellectual honesty.

Socrates is a difficult figure to describe accuratcly, however, because he never wrote anything himself, and what we know of him comes only from the reports of others, especially Plato, who was his greatest student. This problem is magnified by Plato's practice of using Socrates as the voice for his own ideas, which may or may not accurately reflect the teachings of Socrates. A few facts, however, are generally agreed on. Socrates was uncompromisingly committed to philosophy as a way of life. He made philosophy highly personal, emphasizing that its basis was self-knowledge and that the beginning of self-knowledge was an awareness of one's own ignorance. Only from this basis could objective analysis begin. His self-proclaimed purpose was to be a kind of gadfly, who stung people into an awareness of their own blindness. He questioned most matters of conventional wisdom: virtue, ethics, justice, piety, and so forth and did so in a time of social disorder when such questions were greatly feared. Although he developed a small, but dedicated, group of followers, he was far from popular; indeed, he was sentenced to death by Athens' democratic court on charges of not believing in the traditional gods, of introducing gods of his own, and of corrupting the youth. Thus, he was the victim of popular anti-intellectualism and was the first great martyr of humanism.

Plato's most widely read work over the centuries, the *Republic,* is concerned with articulating the nature of justice and with describing what a truly just society would be. This is the world's first major work of political philosophy; many have called it the greatest ever, and it describes the world's first fully developed utopia. Although the word *utopia* has Greek roots, it was coined as a pun in the sixteenth century A.D. by the English humanist Thomas More. *Ou topos* means "no place," and *eu topos* means "good place"; thus, *utopia* means both an imaginary and an ideal society. It represents a peculiarly humanistic concept because it is not an ideal place established by a divinity, like Eden or some Paradise yet to come, and it is not a mere dream of a state of pleasure and ease. Rather, it is a rational model of a society that human beings might construct.

Plato conceived of the state as a commonwealth, something owned not by kings and rulers, but by the people as a whole (in Latin, this concept of the state would be described as "a public thing," *res publica,* which is the source of the English word *republic*). The central problem in such a state is ensuring that the best and wisest rule. Plato believed in neither the effectiveness of traditional aristocracy where family connections determined one's right to power nor in the effectiveness of democracy where lottery and popular election determined one's right to rule. Rather, he believed that some people understand what a just state is better than others and that some people are better qualified to rule than others. He also believed that the public masses are not the best judges of who their governors ought to be. In an attempt to describe those individuals who are wisest and best qualified to rule and to explain their relation to the rest of humanity, Plato wrote what has come to be called "The Allegory of the Cave," the best known passage in the *Republic* (Book 7) and the best known of all his passages. Socrates converses here with Glaucon, Plato's brother.

The Allegory of the Cave

Plato

1 Next said I, here is a parable to illustrate the degrees in which our nature may be enlightened or unenlightened. Imagine the condition of men living in a sort of cavernous chamber underground, with an entrance open to the light and a long passage all down the cave. Here they have been from childhood, chained by the leg and also by the neck, so that they cannot move and can see only what is in front of them, because the chains will not let them turn their heads. At some distance higher up is the light of a fire burning behind them; and between the prisoners and the fire is a track with a parapet built along it, like the screen at a puppetshow, which hides the performers while they show their puppets over the top.

2 I see, said he.

3 Now behind this parapet imagine persons carrying along various artificial objects, including figures of men and animals in wood or stone or other materials, which project above the parapet. Naturally, some of these persons will be talking, others silent.

4 It is a strange picture, he said, and a strange sort of prisoners.

5 Like ourselves, I replied; for in the first place prisoners so confined would have seen nothing of themselves or of one another, except the shadows thrown by the fire-light on the wall of the Cave facing them, would they?

6 Not if all their lives they had been prevented from moving their heads.

7 And they would have seen as little of the objects carried past.

8 Of course.

9 Now, if they could talk to one another, would they not suppose that their words referred only to those passing shadows which they saw?

10 Necessarily.

11 And suppose their prison had an echo from the wall facing them? When one of the people crossing behind them spoke, they could only suppose that the sound came from the shadow passing before their eyes.

12 No doubt.

13 In every way, then, such prisoners would recognize as reality nothing but the shadows of those artificial objects.

14 Inevitably.

15 Now consider what would happen if their release from the chains and the healing of their unwisdom should come about in this way. Suppose one of them set free and forced suddenly to stand up, turn his head, and walk with eyes lifted to the light; all these movements would be painful, and he would be too dazzled to make out the objects whose shadows he had been used to see. What do you think he would say, if someone told him that what he had formerly seen was meaningless illusion, but now, being somewhat nearer to reality and turned towards more real objects, he was getting a truer view? Suppose further that he were shown the various objects being carried by and were made to say, in reply to questions, what each of them was. Would he not be perplexed and believe the objects now shown him to be not so real as what he formerly saw?

16 Yes, not nearly so real.

17 And if he were forced to look at the fire-light itself, would not his eyes ache, so that he would try to escape and turn back to the things which he could see distinctly, convinced that they really were clearer than these other objects now being shown to him?

18 Yes.

19 And suppose someone were to drag him away forcibly up the steep and rugged ascent and not let him go until he had hauled him out into the sunlight, would he not suffer pain and vexation at such treatment, and, when he had come out into the light, find his eyes so full of its radiance that he could not see a single one of the things that he was now told were real?

20 Certainly he would not see them all at once.

21 He would need, then, to grow accustomed before he could see things in that upper world. At first it would be easiest to make out shadows, and then the images of men and things reflected in water, and later on the things themselves. After that, it would be easier to watch the heavenly bodies and the sky itself by night, looking at the light of the moon and stars rather than the Sun and the Sun's light in the day-time.

22 Yes, surely.

23 Last of all, he would be able to look at the Sun and contemplate its nature, not as it appears when reflected in water or any alien medium, but as it is in itself in its own domain.

24 No doubt.

25 And now he would begin to draw the conclusion that it is the Sun that produces the seasons and the course of the year and controls everything in the visible world, and moreover is in a way the cause of all that he and his companions used to see.

26 Clearly he would come at last to that conclusion.

27 Then if he called to mind his fellow prisoners and what passed for wisdom in his former dwelling-place, he would surely think himself happy in the change and be sorry for them. They may have had a practice of honouring and commending one another, with prizes for the man who had the keenest eye for the passing shadows and the best memory for the order in which they followed or accompanied one another, so that he could make a good guess as to which was going to come next. Would our released prisoner be likely to covet those prizes or to envy the men exalted to honour and power in the Cave? Would he not feel like Homer's Achilles, that he would far sooner "be on earth as a hired servant in the house of a landless man" or endure anything rather than go back to his old beliefs and live in the old way?

28 Yes, he would prefer any fate to such a life.

29 Now imagine what would happen if he went down again to take his former seat in the Cave. Coming suddenly out of the sunlight, his eyes would be filled with darkness. He might be required once more to deliver his opinion on those shadows, in competition with the prisoners who had never been released, while his eyesight was still dim and unsteady; and it might take some time to become used to the darkness. They would laugh at him and say that he had gone up only to come back with his sight ruined; it was worth no one's while even to attempt the ascent. If they could lay hands on the man who was trying to set them free and lead them up, they would kill him.

30 Yes, they would.

31 Every feature of this parable, my dear Glaucon, is meant to fit our earlier analysis. The prison dwelling corresponds to the region revealed to us through the sense of sight, and the fire-light within it to the power of the Sun. The ascent to see the things in the upper world you may take as standing for the upward journey of the soul into the region of the intelligible; then you will be in possession of what I surmise, since that is what you wish to be told. Heaven

knows whether it is true; but this, at any rate, is how it appears to me. In the world of knowledge, the last thing to be perceived and only with great difficulty is the essential Form of Goodness. Once it is perceived, the conclusion must follow that, for all things, this is the cause of whatever is right and good; in the visible world it gives birth to light and to the lord of light, while it is itself sovereign in the intelligible world and the parent of intelligence and truth. Without having had a vision of this Form no one can act with wisdom, either in his own life or in matters of state.

32 So far as I can understand, I share your belief. . . .

33 You will see, then, Glaucon, that there will be no real injustice in compelling our philosophers to watch over and care for the other citizens. We can fairly tell them that their compeers in other states may quite reasonably refuse to collaborate: there they have sprung up, like a self-sown plant, in despite of their country's institutions; no one has fostered their growth, and they cannot be expected to show gratitude for a care they have never received. "But," we shall say, "it is not so with you. We have brought you into existence for your country's sake as well as for your own, to be like leaders and kingbees in a hive; you have been better and more thoroughly educated than those others and hence you are more capable of playing your part both as men of thought and as men of action. You must go down, then, each in his turn, to live with the rest and let your eyes grow accustomed to the darkness. You will then see a thousand times better than those who live there always; you will recognize every image for what it is and know what it represents, because you have seen justice, beauty, and goodness in their reality; and so you and we shall find life in our commonwealth no mere dream, as it is in most existing states, where men live fighting one another about shadows and quarrelling for power, as if that were a great prize; whereas in truth government can be at its best and free from dissension only where the destined rulers are least desirous of holding office."

QUESTIONS FOR WRITING AND DISCUSSION

OBSERVING

1. An allegory is a narrative in the form of an extended metaphor where everything about the imagined situation corresponds to something about life as seen by the writer. Plato's cave, for example, represents the general condition of our lives; the individuals in it represent ourselves, etc. Briefly identify what each element of the situation corresponds to according to Socrates' explanation.
2. Notice that the ascent out of the cave described here is not an easy one. Not only is there the climb out into the sunlight, but a descent back down into the darkness follows, as well as a further struggle to lead others into

the light. Moreover, Socrates argues, it is proper to compel those who have stepped into the light to return to the darkness in order to help their benighted fellows. What does this suggest about Plato's concepts of learning and of governance?

EVALUATING

1. Putting aside what they were teaching and which one you may consider the more correct, who do you think is the better teacher: Christ, as depicted in the Sermon on the Mount, or Socrates, as depicted in the *Republic?*
2. Plato's Socrates says that only those who have had "a vision" of "the essential Form of Goodness" can act with wisdom. This sounds like a religious vision and is one of many similarities that could be noted between Socrates and religious figures such as Moses, Christ, or Mohammed: all four committed their lives to the pursuit of a vision of goodness, all believed in a higher reality, both Socrates and Christ were martyred for their beliefs, to name a few of the most obvious. Why then has one been considered a philosopher, the others religious leaders? Using Socrates and one of these three religious figures as types, define what you think are the essential differences between philosophy and religion.
3. Plato seems to think that the community has the right to expect individuals to share their wisdom with that community, a right that in a just society corresponds to individuals' debt to the community for the guidance it has given them. Do you think that argument is convincing?

RESPONDING AND APPLYING

1. Plato describes the individual who has achieved a higher vision as one who has been "drag[ged] . . . away forcibly up the steep and rugged ascent and . . . hauled out into the sunlight." Would most people have to be dragged this way, or do you think most would be eager to "see the light"? Which of these two groups do you think you most likely belong to, and why?
2. Do you think there is such a thing as "the essential Form of Goodness" (some translate this as the "absolute" Good)? If you knew, or thought you knew, the absolute Good, what responsibilities would you feel toward your community? If you did not have such knowledge, how would you feel about those who wanted to guide you to such knowledge?
3. Knowledge of absolute goodness aside, do you think you owe anything to your town or state or nation? How would you define the nature of that indebtedness, if any, and the indebtedness of others toward you as a member of the community?
4. Although democracy is generally considered a development of humanistic philosophy, the emphasis on excellence in traditional philosophy carries with it a tendency toward elitism which to some seems at odds with democracy. That tendency is especially apparent in the *Republic,* where

the superiority, indeed the right to rule, of an intellectual elite is emphasized. How do you see this emphasis on these kinds of excellence in relation to democracy? How have possible conflicts between the two entered into American culture? You might consider some of the politicians who in their time were considered intellectuals, like Thomas Jefferson, Woodrow Wilson, Adlai Stevenson, or Eugene McCarthy. Or consider the attitudes you have noticed in your community toward various kinds of excellence, like attitudes toward "jocks" and "brains."

MARCUS TULLIUS CICERO, "ON NATURAL LAW" *FROM* THE LAWS

A man of many talents—rhetorician, orator without peer, and lawyer (indeed the most successful attorney, defending or prosecuting, of his time), politician, reformer, and statesman, man of letters and philosopher—*Marcus Tullius Cicero* (106–43 B.C.E.) is credited with having forged the Latin language into the vehicle of learning and literature that would serve western Europe for the next 1,700 years. And he did so as a leading participant in one of the most exciting and dangerous times in history, as the Roman Republic, torn between a decayed and corrupt aristocracy and the forces of radical demagoguery and dictatorship, suffered its last days. He died the year after Julius Caesar's assassination.

Not the most original of philosophers, he nevertheless produced in more than a dozen books written during the last decade of his life an eloquent synthesis of much of the best of Greek and Roman thought of the previous three or four centuries. This is apparent in this selection from *The Laws* (*De Legibus*), which reflects a way of thinking much closer to that of Aristotle (384–322 B.C.E.), Plato's great successor, though it is written in the form of a Platonic dialogue. This was a wise choice since Aristotle was far less accomplished a stylist than Plato. Philosophically, however, Aristotle agreed with Plato that the quest for knowledge is a fundamental human activity and that rational analysis and rigorous deduction are crucial needs for that quest, but he rejected Plato's dualism, the belief that real being lies in an ideal world somewhere beyond the shadows that make up the material world of sense experience. Aristotle believed conversely that sense experience, rightly analyzed, yields reliable knowledge; that form is inherent in and inseparable from matter; and that every being or object possesses its own identifiable nature or essence. Thus, Aristotle established the basis for the belief in what came to be called natural law. Cicero makes use of this concept nearly three centuries later as he seeks one of the fundamental goals of rationalism, to define the universal principles of right living, the moral foundation of human law, in a time when an ancient tradition of rule by law was gradually being replaced by a system of rule by men.

On Natural Law

Cicero

1 Out of all the material of the philosophers' discussions, surely there comes nothing more valuable than the full realization that we are born for Justice, and that right is based, not upon men's opinions, but upon Nature. This fact will immediately be plain if you once get a clear conception of man's fellowship and union with his fellow-men. For no single thing is so like another, so exactly its counterpart, as all of us are to one another. Nay, if bad habits and false beliefs did not twist the weaker minds and turn them in whatever direction they are inclined, no one would be so like his own self as all men would be like all others. And so, however we may define man, a single definition will apply to all. This is a sufficient proof that there is no difference in kind between man and man; for if there were, one definition could not be applicable to all men; and indeed reason, which alone raises us above the level of the beasts and enables us to draw inferences, to prove and disprove, to discuss and solve problems, and to come to conclusions, is certainly common to us all, and, though varying in what it learns, at least in the capacity to learn it is invariable. For the same things are invariably perceived by the senses, and those things which stimulate the senses, stimulate them in the same way in all men; and those rudimentary beginnings of intelligence to which I have referred, which are imprinted on our minds, are imprinted on all minds alike; and speech, the mind's interpreter, though differing in the choice of words, agrees in the sentiments expressed. In fact, there is no human being of any race who, if he finds a guide, cannot attain to virtue.

2 XI. The similarity of the human race is clearly marked in its evil tendencies as well as in its goodness. For pleasure also attracts all men; and even though it is an enticement to vice, yet it has some likeness to what is naturally good. For it delights us by its lightness and agreeableness; and for this reason, by an error of thought, it is embraced as something wholesome. It is through a similar misconception that we shun death as though it were a dissolution of nature, and cling to life because it keeps us in the sphere in which we were born; and that we look upon pain as one of the greatest of evils, not only because of its cruelty, but also because it seems to lead to the destruction of nature. In the same way, on account of the similarity between moral worth and renown, those who are publicly honoured are considered happy, while those who do not attain fame are thought miserable. Troubles, joys, desires, and fears haunt the minds of all men without distinction, and even if different men have different beliefs, that does not prove, for example, that it is not the same quality of superstition that besets those races which worship dogs and cats as gods, as that which torments other races. But what nation does not love courtesy, kindliness, gratitude, and remembrance of favours bestowed? What people does not hate and despise the

haughty, the wicked, the cruel, and the ungrateful? Inasmuch as these considerations prove to us that the whole human race is bound together in unity, it follows, finally, that knowledge of the principles of right living is what makes men better.

3 If you approve of what has been said, I will go on to what follows. But if there is anything that you care to have explained, we will take that up first.

4 *A.* We have no questions, if I may speak for both of us.

5 XII. *M.* The next point, then, is that we are so constituted by Nature as to share the sense of Justice with one another and to pass it on to all men. And in this whole discussion I want it understood that what I shall call Nature is (that which is implanted in us by Nature); that, however, the corruption caused by bad habits is so great that the sparks of fire, so to speak, which Nature has kindled in us are extinguished by this corruption, and the vices which are their opposites spring up and are established. But if the judgments of men were in agreement with Nature, so that, as the poet says, they considered "nothing alien to them which concerns mankind," then Justice would be equally observed by all. For those creatures who have received the gift of reason from Nature have also received right reason, and therefore they have also received the gift of Law, which is right reason applied to command and prohibition. And if they have received Law, they have received Justice also. Now all men have received reason; therefore all men have received Justice. Consequently Socrates was right when he cursed, as he often did, the man who first separated utility from Justice; for this separation, he complained, is the source of all mischief. For what gave rise to Pythagoras' famous words about friendship?[1] . . . From this it is clear that, when a wise man shows toward another endowed with equal virtue the kind of benevolence which is so widely diffused among men, that will then have come to pass which, unbelievable as it seems to some, is after all the inevitable result—namely, that he loves himself no whit more than he loves another. For what difference can there be among things which are all equal? But if the least distinction should be made in friendship, then the very name of friendship would perish forthwith; for its essence is such that, as soon as either friend prefers anything for himself, friendship ceases to exist.

6 Now all this is really a preface to what remains to be said in our discussion, and its purpose is to make it more easily understood that Justice is inherent in Nature. After I have said a few words more on this topic, I shall go on to the civil law, the subject which gives rise to all this discourse.

7 XIII. *Q.* You certainly need to say very little more on that head, for from what you have already said, Atticus is convinced, and certainly I am, that Nature is the source of Justice.

---

[1] Whether the quotation from Pythagoras was given by Cicero or not we cannot tell, nor can we be sure what "famous words" are referred to. The well-known sayings, "the possessions of friends are owned in common," and "a friend is a second self," are credited to him, as well as several other aphorisms on the subject. (See Porphyrius, *De Vita Pythag.* §33.)

8 *A.* How can I help being convinced, when it has just been proved to us, first, that we have been provided and equipped with what we may call the gifts of the gods; next, that there is only one principle by which men may live with one another, and that this is the same for all, and possessed equally by all; and, finally, that all men are bound together by a certain natural feeling of kindliness and good-will, and also by a partnership in Justice? Now that we have admitted the truth of these conclusions, and rightly, I think, how can we separate Law and Justice from Nature?

9 IV. *M.* Once more, then, before we come to the individual laws, let us look at the character and nature of Law, for fear that, though it must be the standard to which we refer everything, we may now and then be led astray by an incorrect use of terms, and forget the rational principles on which our laws must be based.

10 *Q.* Quite so, that is the correct method of exposition.

11 *M.* Well, then, I find that it has been the opinion of the wisest men that Law is not a product of human thought, nor is it any enactment of peoples, but something eternal which rules the whole universe by its wisdom in command and prohibition. Thus they have been accustomed to say that Law is the primal and ultimate mind of God, whose reason directs all things either by compulsion or restraint. Wherefore that Law which the gods have given to the human race has been justly praised; for it is the reason and mind of a wise lawgiver applied to command and prohibition.

12 *Q.* You have touched upon this subject several times before. But before you come to the laws of peoples, please make the character of this heavenly Law clear to us, so that the waves of habit may not carry us away and sweep us into the common mode of speech on such subjects.

13 *M.* Ever since we were children, Quintus, we have learned to call, "If one summon another to court,"[2] and other rules of the same kind, laws. But we must come to the true understanding of the matter, which is as follows: this and other commands and prohibitions of nations have the power to summon to righteousness and away from wrong-doing; but this power is not merely older than the existence of nations and States, it is coeval with that God who guards and rules heaven and earth. For the divine mind cannot exist without reason, and divine reason cannot but have this power to establish right and wrong. No written law commanded that a man should take his stand on a bridge alone, against the full force of the enemy, and order the bridge broken down behind him; yet we shall not for that reason suppose that the heroic Cocles[3] was not obeying the law of bravery and following its decrees in doing so noble a deed. Even if there was no written law against rape at Rome in the reign of Lucius Tarquinius, we cannot say on that account that Sextus Tarquinius did not break

---

[2] A familiar quotation from the Laws of the Twelve Tables, the earliest written code of Roman law.

[3] Haratius Cocles, the famous warrior who held a bridge over the Tiber against the Etruscans.

that eternal Law by violating Lucretia, the daughter of Tricipitinus! For reason did exist, derived from the Nature of the universe, urging men to right conduct and diverting them from wrongdoing, and this reason did not first become Law when it was written down, but when it first came into existence; and it came into existence simultaneously with the divine mind. Wherefore the true and primal Law, applied to command and prohibition, is the right reason of supreme Jupiter.

14 V. *Q.* I agree with you, brother, that what is right and true is also eternal, and does not begin or end with written statutes.

15 *M.* Therefore, just as that divine mind is the supreme Law, so, when [reason] is perfected in man, [that also is Law; and this perfected reason exists] in the mind of the wise man; but those rules which, in varying forms and for the need of the moment, have been formulated for the guidance of nations, bear the title of laws rather by favour than because they are really such. For every law which really deserves that name is truly praiseworthy, as they prove by approximately the following arguments. It is agreed, of course, that laws were invented for the safety of citizens, the preservation of States, and the tranquillity and happiness of human life, and that those who first put statutes of this kind in force convinced their people that it was their intention to write down and put into effect such rules as, once accepted and adopted, would make possible for them an honourable and happy life; and when such rules were drawn up and put in force, it is clear that men called them "laws." From this point of view it can be readily understood that those who formulated wicked and unjust statutes for nations, thereby breaking their promises and agreements, put into effect anything but "laws." It may thus be clear that in the very definition of the term "law" there inheres the idea and principle of choosing what is just and true. I ask you then, Quintus, according to the custom of the philosophers: if there is a certain thing, the lack of which in a State compels us to consider it no State at all, must we consider this thing a good?

16 *Q.* One of the greatest goods, certainly.

17 *M.* And if a State lacks Law, must it for that reason be considered no State at all?

18 *Q.* It cannot be denied.

19 *M.* Then Law must necessarily be considered one of the greatest goods.

20 *Q.* I agree with you entirely.

21 *M.* What of the many deadly, the many pestilential statutes which nations put in force? These no more deserve to be called laws than the rules a band of robbers might pass in their assembly. For if ignorant and unskilful men have prescribed deadly poisons instead of healing drugs, these cannot possibly be called physicians' prescriptions; neither in a nation can a statute of any sort be called a law, even though the nation, in spite of its being a ruinous regulation, has accepted it. Therefore Law is the distinction between things just and unjust, made in agreement with that primal and most ancient of all things, Nature; and in conformity to Nature's standard are framed those human laws which inflict punishment upon the wicked but defend and protect the good.

22 VI. *Q.* I understand you completely, and believe that from now on we must not consider or even call anything else a law.

23 *M.* Then you do not think the Titian or Apuleian Laws were really laws at all?

24 *Q.* No; nor the Livian Laws either.

25 *M.* And you are right, especially as the Senate repealed them in one sentence and in a single moment. But the Law whose nature I have explained can neither be repealed nor abrogated.

QUESTIONS FOR WRITING AND DISCUSSION

OBSERVING

1. Cicero, like Plato, is trying to define justice and seeking for some standard that this idea can be based on that will raise discussion above the clash of mere opinion. What is that standard and how does he define it? What is the basis for his belief that this is a universal standard?
2. What connections does Cicero see between right reason, law, and justice?

EVALUATING

1. Cicero defines his ideal of friendship as a condition in which a person "loves himself no whit more than he loves another," a condition that sounds much like the Christian ideal of loving one another. Do you prefer to think in terms of the rational or the religious basis for this ideal, and why? Which do you think is likely to have the stronger effect on the mass of humanity, and why?
2. Do you think Cicero is defining and applying the words "reason" and "nature" consistently?

RESPONDING AND APPLYING

1. If, as Atticus sums it up, "there is only one principle by which men may live with one another, . . . this is the same for all and possessed equally by all," how does Cicero seem to account for the great variety of law to be found in different times and lands? How would you account for it?
2. What advantages and dangers can you see in Cicero's claim that an unjust law is not a "Law" at all or in his belief that law and justice are universal concepts?

JOHN STUART MILL, *FROM* NATURE

Rational philosophy in the Western world suffered rather a hiatus during the early years of the Christian Era, until the Middle Ages when philosopher-theologians like Thomas Aquinas attempted to synthesize the religious and philosophical traditions. In the Christian world, the conviction developed that while the more mystical articles of faith were dependent on revelation, the basic truths necessary for living justly could not only be found in revelation but discovered, indeed established with equally convincing authority, through a combination of systematic thinking and simple observation. Reason, in other words, was thought to be compatible with faith and religion.

The authority of reason began to be seriously threatened, at least with regard to its pronouncements about the natural world, in the seventeenth century with the rise of science, which produced a series of discoveries demonstrating that the great thinkers of the past had been dead wrong about a number of "truths" thought to be self-evident (for more about this, See Chapter 6). Nevertheless the belief that human reason was capable of establishing universal principles of justice and morality persisted, and philosophers and theologians continued to speak of natural law as a viable moral concept. This probably had to do with the fact that the new sciences of the seventeenth century, astronomy and physics, while challenging reigning rational concepts of cosmological order, seemed less of a threat to the social and moral order. The latter threat came with the new nineteenth-century sciences, geology and biology, which suggested to poet Alfred Tennyson that "Nature, red in tooth and claw / With ravine, shrieked against [humanity's] creed," as he described it in 1850, nearly a decade before Charles Darwin's *Origin of Species.* It was this spirit that led more systematic thinkers to challenge the concept of a rational moral law based on nature.

The writings of *John Stuart Mill* (1806–1873) are characterized by brilliance of logic and thoroughness of argument. He tackled many of the key political, economic, aesthetic, and religious problems of his age with a clarity that has come to have a profound effect on twentieth-century thinking. Schooled at home by his father, utilitarian philosopher James Mill, young John could read Greek by age 3; he could read Latin and was proficient in arithmetic by age 8; and he had mastered logic by age 12. As he writes in his *Autobiography* (1873), by the time he was 14 he had more than a two-decade advantage over his peers. Mill is best known for his essays *On Liberty* (1859), a classic defense of minority rights, and "On the Subjection of Women" (1869), which contains virtually all the major arguments that would be applied in defense of women's rights for the next century. In *Nature,* written between 1850 and 1858 but not published until 1874, the year after his death, he critiques natural law theories, which were the basis of some of the most widely held beliefs that opposed change in attitudes that might depart from traditional values.

from Nature
John Stuart Mill

1 Nature, natural, and the group of words derived from them, or allied to them in etymology, have at all times filled a great place in the thoughts and taken a strong hold on the feelings of mankind. That they should have done so is not surprising when we consider what the words, in their primitive and most obvious signification, represent; but it is unfortunate that a set of terms which play so great a part in moral and metaphysical speculation should have acquired many meanings different from the primary one, yet sufficiently allied to it to admit of confusion. The words have thus become entangled in so many foreign associations, mostly of a very powerful and tenacious character, that they have come to excite, and to be the symbols of, feelings which their original meaning will by no means justify; and which have made them one of the most copious sources of false taste, false philosophy, false morality, and even bad law. . . .

2 According to the Platonic method, which is still the best type of such investigations, the first thing to be done with so vague a term is to ascertain precisely what it means. It is also a rule of the same method, that the meaning of an abstraction is best sought for in the concrete—of a universal in the particular. Adopting this course with the word Nature, the first question must be, what is meant by the "nature" of a particular object—as of fire, of water, or of some individual plant or animal? Evidently the ensemble or aggregate of its powers or properties: the modes in which it acts on other things (counting among those things the senses of the observer) and the modes in which other things act upon it; to which, in the case of a sentient being, must be added its own capacities of feeling or being conscious. The nature of the thing means all this, means its entire capacity of exhibiting phenomena. And since the phenomena which a thing exhibits, however much they vary in different circumstances, are always the same in the same circumstances, they admit of being described in general forms of words, which are called the *laws* of the thing's nature. Thus it is a law of the nature of water that, under the mean pressure of the atmosphere at the level of the sea, it boils at 212° Fahrenheit.

3 Such, then, is a correct definition of the word nature. But this definition corresponds only to one of the senses of that ambiguous term. It is evidently inapplicable to some of the modes in which the word is familiarly employed. For example, it entirely conflicts with the common form of speech by which nature is opposed to art, and natural to artificial. For in the sense of the word nature which has just been defined, and which is the true scientific sense, art is as much nature as anything else; and everything which is artificial is natural—art has no independent powers of its own: art is but the employment of the pow-

ers of nature for an end. Phenomena produced by human agency, no less than those which as far as we are concerned are spontaneous, depend on the properties of the elementary forces, or of the elementary substances and their compounds. The united powers of the whole human race could not create a new property of matter in general, or of any one of its species. We can only take advantage for our purposes of the properties which we find. A ship floats by the same laws of specific gravity and equilibrium as a tree uprooted by the wind and blown into the water. . . .

4 It thus appears that we must recognize at least two principal meanings in the word nature. In one sense, it means all the powers existing in either the outer or the inner world and everything which takes place by means of those powers. In another sense it means, not everything which happens, but only what takes place without the agency, or without the voluntary and intentional agency, of man. This distinction is far from exhausting the ambiguities of the word; but it is the key to most of those on which important consequences depend.

5 Such, then, being the two principal senses of the word nature, in which of these is it taken, or is it taken in either, when the word and its derivatives are used to convey ideas of commendation, approval, and even moral obligation?

6 It has conveyed such ideas in all ages. *Naturum sequi*[1] was the fundamental principle of morals in many of the most admired schools of philosophy. . . .

7 Yet idle as it is to exhort people to do what they cannot avoid doing, and absurd as it is to prescribe as a rule of right conduct what agrees exactly as well with wrong, nevertheless a rational rule of conduct *may* be constructed out of the relation which it ought to bear to the laws of nature in this widest acceptation of the term. Man necessarily obeys the laws of nature, or, in other words, the properties of things, but he does not necessarily *guide* himself by them. . . . If, therefore, the useless precept to follow nature were changed into a precept to study nature—to know and take heed of the properties of the things we have to deal with, so far as these properties are capable of forwarding or obstructing any given purpose—we should have arrived at the first principle of all intelligent action, or rather at the definition of intelligent action itself. And a confused notion of this true principle is, I doubt not, in the minds of many of those who set up the unmeaning doctrine which superficially resembles it. . . . But the maxim of obedience to nature, or conformity to nature, is held up not as a simply prudential but as an ethical maxim, and by those who talk of *jus naturae,* even as a law, fit to be administered by tribunals and enforced by sanctions. Right action must mean something more and other than merely intelligent action; yet no precept beyond this last can be connected with the word nature in the wider and more philosophical of its acceptations. We must try it, therefore, in the other sense, that in which nature stands distinguished from art

[1] *Naturam Sequi:* follow nature.

and denotes, not the whole course of the phenomena which come under our observation, but only their spontaneous course.

8 Let us then consider whether we can attach any meaning to the supposed practical maxim of following nature in this second sense of the word, in which nature stands for that which takes place without human intervention. In nature as thus understood, is the spontaneous course of things when left to themselves the rule to be followed in endeavoring to adapt things to our use? But it is evident at once that the maxim, taken in this sense, is not merely, as it is in the other sense, superfluous and unmeaning, but palpably absurd and self-contradictory. For while human action cannot help conforming to nature in the one meaning of the term, the very aim and object of action is to alter and improve nature in the other meaning. If the natural course of things were perfectly right and satisfactory, to act at all would be a gratuitous meddling, which, as it could not make things better, must make them worse. Or if action at all could be justified, it would only be when in direct obedience to instincts, since these might perhaps be accounted part of the spontaneous order of nature; but to do anything with forethought and purpose would be a violation of that perfect order. If the artificial is not better than the natural, to what end are all the arts of life? To dig, to plow, to build, to wear clothes are direct infringements of the injunction to follow nature.

9 The consciousness that whatever man does to improve his condition is in so much a censure and a thwarting of the spontaneous order of nature has in all ages caused new and unprecedented attempts at improvement to be generally at first under a shade of religious suspicion as being in any case uncomplimentary, and very probably offensive, to the powerful beings (or, when polytheism gave place to monotheism, to the all-powerful Being) supposed to govern the various phenomena of the universe, and of whose will the course of nature was conceived to be the expression. Any attempt to mold natural phenomena to the convenience of mankind might easily appear an interference with the government of those superior beings; and though life could not have been maintained, much less made pleasant, without perpetual interferences of the kind, each new one was doubtless made with fear and trembling until experience had shown that it could be ventured on without drawing down the vengeance of the gods.

10 Feelings of this sort, though repressed on ordinary occasions by the contrary current of life, are ready to break out whenever custom is silent and the native promptings of the mind have nothing opposed to them but reason; and appeals are continually made to them by rhetoricians, with the effect, if not of convincing opponents, at least of making those who already hold the opinion which the rhetorician desires to recommend better satisfied with it. For in the present day it probably seldom happens that anyone is persuaded to approve any course of action because it appears to him to bear an analogy to the divine government of the world, though the argument tells on him with great force, and is felt by him to be a great support, in behalf of anything which he is already inclined to approve.

11 In sober truth, nearly all the things which men are hanged or imprisoned for doing to one another are nature's everyday performances. Killing, the most criminal act recognized by human laws, nature does once to every being that lives, and in a large proportion of cases after protracted tortures such as only the greatest monsters whom we read of ever purposely inflicted on their living fellow creatures. If by an arbitrary reservation we refuse to account anything murder but what abridges a certain term supposed to be allotted to human life, nature also does this to all but a small percentage of lives, and does it in all the modes, violent or insidious, in which the worst human beings take the lives of one another. Nature impales men, breaks them as if on the wheel, casts them to be devoured by wild beasts, burns them to death, crushes them with stones like the first Christian martyr, starves them with hunger, freezes them with cold, poisons them by the quick or slow venom of her exhalations, and has hundreds of other hideous deaths in reserve such as the ingenious cruelty of a Nabis or a Domitian[2] never surpassed. All this nature does with the most supercilious disregard both of mercy and of justice, emptying her shafts upon the best and noblest indifferently with the meanest and worst; upon those who are engaged in the highest and worthiest enterprises, and often as the direct consequence of the noblest acts; and it might almost be imagined as a punishment for them. She mows down those on whose existence hangs the well-being of a whole people, perhaps the prospects of the human race for generations to come, with as little compunction as those whose death is a relief to themselves or a blessing to those under their noxious influence. Such are nature's dealings with life.

12 But, it is said, all these things are for wise and good ends. On this I must first remark that whether they are so or not is altogether beside the point. Supposing it true that, contrary to appearances, these horrors when perpetrated by nature promote good ends, still, as no one believes that good ends would be promoted by our following the example, the course of nature cannot be a proper model for us to imitate. Either it is right that we should kill because nature kills, torture because nature tortures, ruin and devastate because nature does the like, or we ought not to consider at all what nature does, but what it is good to do. . . .

13 It may be possible to believe with Plato that perfect goodness, limited and thwarted in every direction by the intractableness of the material, has done this because it could do no better. But that the same perfectly wise and good Being had absolute power over the material and made it, by voluntary choice, what it is—to admit this might have been supposed impossible to anyone who has the simplest notions of moral good and evil. Nor can any such person, whatever kind of religious phrases he may use, fail to believe that if Nature and Man are both the works of a Being of perfect goodness, that Being intended Nature as a scheme to be amended, not imitated, by Man. . . .

---

[2] Nabis, tyrant of Sparta, who seized power in 207 B.C.E., after Sparta's defeat by the Achaean League, had a reputation as a cruel monster. Domitian was a Roman emperor, Titus Flavius Domitianus (A.D. 81–96), who in the late period of his reign became unstable, ruthless, and revengeful.

14 The scheme of nature regarded in its whole extent cannot have had, for its sole or even principal object, the good of human or other sentient beings. What good it brings to them is mostly the result of their own exertions. Whatsoever in nature gives indication of beneficent design proves this beneficence to be armed only with limited power; and the duty of man is to co-operate with the beneficent powers, not by imitating but by perpetually striving to amend the course of nature—and bringing that part of it over which we can exercise control more nearly into conformity with a high standard of justice and goodness.

15 Is it necessary to recognize in these forms of speech another distinct meaning of the word nature? Or can they be connected, by any rational bond of union, with either of the two meanings already treated of? At first it may seem that we have no option but to admit another ambiguity in the term. All inquiries are either into what is, or into what ought to be: science and history belonging to the first division, art, morals, and politics to the second. But the two senses of the word nature first pointed out agree in referring only to what is. In the first meaning, nature is a collective name for everything which is. In the second, it is a name for everything which is of itself, without voluntary human intervention. But the employment of the word nature as a term of ethics seems to disclose a third meaning, in which nature does not stand for what is but for what ought to be, or for the rule or standard of what ought to be. A little consideration, however, will show that this is not a case of ambiguity; there is not here a third sense of the word. Those who set up nature as a standard of action do not intend a merely verbal proposition; they do not mean that the standard, whatever it be, should be *called* nature; they think they are giving some information as to what the standard of action really is. Those who say that we ought to act according to nature do not mean the mere identical proposition that we ought to do what we ought to do. They think that the word nature affords some external criterion of what we should do; and if they lay down as a rule for what ought to be a word which in its proper signification denotes what is, they do so because they have a notion, either clearly or confusedly, that what is constitutes the rule and standard of what ought to be.

16 When it is asserted or implied that nature, or the laws of nature, should be conformed to, is the nature which is meant nature in the first sense of the term, meaning all which is—the powers and properties of all things? But in this signification there is no need of a recommendation to act according to nature, since it is what nobody can possibly help doing, and equally whether he acts well or ill. There is no mode of acting which is not conformable to nature in this sense of the term, and all modes of acting are so in exactly the same degree. Every action is the exertion of some natural power, and its effects of all sorts are so many phenomena of nature, produced by the powers and properties of some of the objects of nature, in exact obedience to some law or laws of nature.

QUESTIONS FOR WRITING AND DISCUSSION

OBSERVING

1. List the common definitions of nature that Mill examines.
2. What do you make of Mill's assertion that appeals to the moral qualities of nature are often made not so much to convince opponents as to make those who already hold the opinion better satisfied with their conclusions? Does this suggest that such appeals carry no logical, only emotional weight?
3. Why would it be a "dangerous responsibility" to pick and choose among the works of nature for "some more definite indication of the Creator's designs"?

EVALUATING

1. Mill argues that those who use the word *nature* as a term of ethics "think that the word nature affords some external criterion of what we should do, . . . that what is constitutes the rule and standard of what ought to be." Is there any sense in which this could be true?
2. One of Mill's conclusions with regard to the definition of nature as "things as they would be, apart from human intervention," is that "if Nature and Man are both the works of a Being of perfect goodness, that Being intended Nature as a scheme to be amended, not imitated by Man." Are there contexts in which you could argue that Mill's conclusions are questionable? On what basis can we argue logically that certain aspects of nature ought to be preserved? Are these cases in which we are asserting some value inherent in nature, which as moral beings we are to follow, or ones in which we are simply acknowledging our need as intelligent beings to better understand the properties of things so that we can act prudently?

RESPONDING AND APPLYING

1. Mill argues that misunderstandings and misapplications of the word *nature* have been the source of "false taste, false philosophy, false morality, and even bad law." Can you cite any examples from your own experience where you think forms of the word were used in ways that led to questionable conclusions? Have you heard it applied, for example, as a basis for judgment of art or with regard to moral and social issues like relations between the genders, family structure, the right or wrong of homosexuality or pedophilia? In what senses is "nature" or "natural" being applied in each case? Is it valid in any of these cases?
2. If Mill is right, are we, in our quest for morality, thrust back on the uncertainty Cicero called the clash of mere opinions? Do we require some external standard of rectitude grounded either in nature or revelation to provide a basis for morality, or are there other options that can form the basis for the assurance—if we cannot have certainty—that our sense of morality can grow in some hopeful direction?

JEAN-PAUL SARTRE, "EXISTENTIALISM"

Mill's questioning of the notion of a natural moral law is symptomatic of a process of radical questioning that has been going on for the last two centuries. Although skepticism, as we pointed out at the beginning of this chapter, is part of the hallowed tradition of rationalism, it sometimes seems to have overwhelmed rationalism itself. It may be more accurate, however, to say that it has redefined rationalism.

An important assumption of traditional rationalism is that Truth is "out there" somewhere, really existing in the world, or in the human mind itself, or as Plato believed in some eternal realm of the ideal. Additional assumptions are that human reason has the power to discover this Truth—as mid-nineteenth century British poet, critic, and educator Matthew Arnold insisted, "the prescriptions of reason are absolute, unchanging, of universal validity"—and that life ought to be the individual and social struggle to make that Truth manifest in the world. This is an orientation grounded in what philosophers call ontology, the study of Being. Beginning in the late eighteenth century, this faith in a stable, for many an eternal, reality has been increasingly shaken, and even for many who held on to the belief in a transcendent reality, faith was equally shaken in reason as a means of discovering or understanding it. Developments such as political revolutions, the Industrial Revolution, the promotion of democracy and individualism, rapid population growth and population shifts, unstable class structures, and world wars have undermined traditional notions of social order; advances in science have undermined traditional notions of the origin and future of the cosmos, of the nature of life and of humanness; and all such changes have undermined the authority of reason. Indeed, the failure of this ontologically based faith in reason as a way to understand Being is sometimes almost comically apparent: Arnold illustrates his bold declaration quoted above of the absolute validity of reason by an example that we of the late twentieth century world of binary information can especially appreciate: "To count by tens is the easiest way of counting." This is only one of numerous "truths" thought to be self-evident, which have been exposed as historical developments long peculiar to Western culture, not universal truths.

Such blows to notions of self-evident truth, of course, heightened insecurity and anxiety, but they were also accompanied by growth in technology, in education, in social consciousness, in personal and political freedom, and more subtly by a gradual but major shift that is still going on in philosophical orientation: from a concentration on Being to one on Becoming. Gradually the world is coming less to be seen as made as is, at some fixed point in or just before time, with the essence or nature of things fixed and the power of perceiving and comprehending them defined for all time. Rather there has been emerging a way of conceiving of the world as forever coming into being; of seeing the cosmos as process, event, dynamics, not some agglomeration of ordered things. The work of existential philosopher *Jean-Paul Sartre* (1905–1980) illustrates how one modern thinker struggled to understand rationally the problem of maintaining a sense of ethics in such a world, one where the traditional certainties no longer seemed to exist.

Having concentrated his studies in psychology and philosophy, Sartre taught at a variety of universities in France until World War II broke out, when he was briefly taken as a prisoner. He managed to convince the Nazis to release him, but, like fellow existentialist Albert Camus (1913–1960), a close friend until some time after the war when the two broke over Sartre's growing sympathy with Marxism, Sartre was a leader in the French Resistance to the Nazi occupation. This was a time in France when it looked like the Third Reich would fulfill Hitler's promise to last a thousand years. The average citizen had but two choices: to acquiesce (that is, to collaborate, to submit, to be silent) or to resist. In such a context, being authentic as Sartre defined it (that is, reevaluating one's values, making responsible and thoughtful choices) seemed absurd, for the likelihood of failure, torture, and death far outweighed that of success. Nevertheless, many chose to resist, and some individuals managed to re-create a sense of humanity out of nothing but their own will.

Although he began writing before the war, Sartre's most productive period came during and shortly after the war, when he wrote his most famous plays, *The Flies* (1943) and *No Exit* (1947), and his major philosophical treatise, *Being and Nothingness* (1943). One of the best known existential philosophers, Sartre is especially famous for a definition of a fundamental tenet of this approach to thought and analysis, which is also a characteristic expression of a philosophy of becoming: "existence precedes essence." The significance of this statement derives from its reversal of the traditional rational idea that essences are preexistent realities. For Sartre, we are before we are anything in particular; our essence is something we define by our acts, especially by our choices; development is a creative process; and the only thing essential about humanity is our capacity—and our responsibility—to engage honestly in that process of self-definition. He explores these ideas in a famous lecture delivered in 1946 and printed below. It was published in England under the title "Existentialism and Humanism."

Existentialism

Jean-Paul Sartre

1 Man is nothing else but what he makes of himself. Such is the first principle of existentialism. It is also what is called subjectivity, the name we are labeled with when charges are brought against us. But what do we mean by this, if not that man has a greater dignity than a stone or table? For we mean that man first exists, that is, that man first of all is the being who hurls himself toward a future and who is conscious of imagining himself as being in the future. Man is at the start a plan which is aware of itself, rather than a patch of moss, a piece of garbage, or a cauliflower; nothing exists prior to this plan; there is nothing in heaven; man will be what he will have planned to be. Not what he will want to be. Because by the word "will" we generally mean a conscious decision, which is subsequent to what we have already made of ourselves. I may want to belong to a political party, write a book, get married; but all that is only a manifestation of an earlier, more spontaneous choice that is called "will." But if existence really does precede essence, man is responsible for what he is. Thus, existentialism's first move is to make every man aware of what he is and to make the full responsibility of his existence rest on him. And when we say that a man is responsible for himself, we do not only mean that he is responsible for his own individuality, but that he is responsible for all men.

2 The word "subjectivism" has two meanings, and our opponents play on the two. Subjectivism means, on the one hand, that an individual chooses and makes himself; and, on the other, that it is impossible for man to transcend human subjectivity. The second of these is the essential meaning of existentialism. When we say that man chooses his own self, we mean that every one of us does likewise; but we also mean by that that in making this choice he also chooses all men. In fact, in creating the man that we want to be, there is not a single one of our acts which does not at the same time create an image of man as we think he ought to be. To choose to be this or that is to affirm at the same time the value of what we choose, because we can never choose evil. We always choose the good, and nothing can be good for us without being good for all.

3 If, on the other hand, existence precedes essence, and if we grant that we exist and fashion our image at one and the same time, the image is valid for everybody and for our whole age. Thus, our responsibility is much greater than we might have supposed, because it involves all mankind. If I am a workingman and choose to join a Christian trade union rather than be a Communist, and if by being a member, I want to show that the best thing for man is resignation, that the kingdom of man is not of this world, I am not only involving my own case—I want to be resigned for everyone. As a result, my action has involved all humanity. To take a more individual matter, if I want to marry, to have children, even if this marriage depends solely on my own circumstances or passion or

wish, I am involving all humanity in monogamy and not merely myself. Therefore, I am responsible for myself and for everyone else. I am creating a certain image of man of my own choosing. In choosing myself, I choose man.

4 This helps us understand what the actual content is of such rather grandiloquent words as anguish, forlornness, despair. As you will see, it's all quite simple.

5 First, what is meant by anguish? The existentialists say at once that man is anguish. What that means is this: the man who involves himself and who realizes that he is not only the person he chooses to be, but also a lawmaker who is, at the same time, choosing all mankind as well as himself, cannot help escape the feeling of his total and deep responsibility. Of course, there are many people who are not anxious; but we claim that they are hiding their anxiety, that they are fleeing from it. Certainly, many people believe that when they do something, they themselves are the only ones involved, and when someone says to them, "What if everyone acted that way?" they shrug their shoulders and answer, "Everyone doesn't act that way." But really, one should always ask himself, "What would happen if everybody looked at things that way?" There is no escaping this disturbing thought except by a kind of double-dealing. A man who lies and makes excuses for himself by saying "not everybody does that," is someone with an uneasy conscience, because the act of lying implies that a universal value is conferred upon the lie.

6 Anguish is evident even when it conceals itself. This is the anguish that Kierkegaard called the anguish of Abraham. You know the story: an angel has ordered Abraham to sacrifice his son; if it really were an angel who has come and said, "You are Abraham, you shall sacrifice your son," everything would be all right. But everyone might first wonder, "Is it really an angel, and am I really Abraham? What proof do I have?" . . .

7 Now, I'm not being singled out as an Abraham, and yet at every moment I'm obliged to perform exemplary acts. For every man, everything happens as if all mankind had its eyes fixed on him and were guiding itself by what he does. And every man ought to say to himself, "Am I really the kind of man who has the right to act in such a way that humanity might guide itself by my actions?" And if he does not say that to himself, he is masking his anguish.

8 There is no question here of the kind of anguish which would lead to quietism, to inaction. It is a matter of a simple sort of anguish that anybody who has had responsibilities is familiar with. For example, when a military officer takes the responsibility for an attack and sends a certain number of men to death, he chooses to do so, and in the main he alone makes the choice. Doubtless, orders come from above, but they are too broad; he interprets them, and on this interpretation depend the lives of ten or fourteen or twenty men. In making a decision he cannot help having a certain anguish. All leaders know this anguish. That doesn't keep them from acting; on the contrary, it is the very condition of their action. For it implies that they envisage a number of possibilities, and when they choose one, they realize that it has value only because it is chosen. We shall see that this kind of anguish, which is the kind that

existentialism describes, is explained, in addition, by a direct responsibility to the other men whom it involves. It is not a curtain separating us from action, but is part of action itself.

9 When we speak of forlornness, a term Heidegger was fond of, we mean only that God does not exist and that we have to face all the consequences of this. This existentialist is strongly opposed to a certain kind of secular ethics which would like to abolish God with the least possible expense. About 1880, some French teachers tried to set up a secular ethics which went something like this: God is a useless and costly hypothesis; we are discarding it; but, meanwhile, in order for there to be an ethics, a society, a civilization, it is essential that certain values be taken seriously and that they be considered as having an *a priori* existence. It must be obligatory, *a priori,* to be honest, not to lie, not to beat your wife, to have children, etc., etc. So we're going to try a little device which will make it possible to show that values exist all the same, inscribed in a heaven of ideas, though otherwise God does not exist. In other words—and this, I believe, is the tendency of everything called reformism in France—nothing will be changed if God does not exist. We shall find ourselves with the same norms of honesty, progress, and humanism, and we shall have made of God an outdated hypothesis which will peacefully die off by itself.

10 The existentialist, on the contrary, thinks it very distressing that God does not exist, because all possibility of finding values in a heaven of ideas disappears along with Him; there can no longer be an *a priori* Good, since there is no infinite and perfect consciousness to think it. Nowhere is it written that the Good exists, that we must be honest, that we must not lie; because the fact is we are on a plane where there are only men. Dostoievsky said, "If God didn't exist, everything would be possible." That is the very starting point of existentialism. Indeed, everything is permissible if God does not exist, and as a result man is forlorn, because neither within him nor without does he find anything to cling to. He can't start making excuses for himself.

11 If existence really does precede essence, there is no explaining things away by reference to a fixed and given human nature. In other words, there is no determinism, man is free, man is freedom. On the other hand, if God does not exist, we find no values or commands to turn to which legitimize our conduct. So, in the bright realm of values, we have no excuse behind us, nor justification before us. We are alone, with no excuses.

12 That is the idea I shall try to convey when I say that man is condemned to be free. Condemned, because he did not create himself, yet, in other respects is free; because, once thrown into the world, he is responsible for everything he does. The existentialist does not believe in the power of passion. He will never agree that a sweeping passion is a ravaging torrent which fatally leads a man to certain acts and is therefore an excuse. He thinks that man is responsible for his passion.

13 Some other interpretation might have been drawn from this series of setbacks; for example, that he might have done better to turn carpenter or

revolutionist. Therefore, he is fully responsible for the interpretation. Forlornness implies that we ourselves choose our being. Forlornness and anguish go together.

14 As for despair, the term has a very simple meaning. It means that we shall confine ourselves to reckoning only with what depends upon our will, or on the ensemble of probabilities which make our action possible. When we want something, we always have to reckon with probabilities. I may be counting on the arrival of a friend. The friend is coming by rail or streetcar; this supposes that the train will arrive on schedule, or that the streetcar will not jump the track. I am left in the realm of possibility; but possibilities are to be reckoned with only to the point where my action comports with the ensemble of these possibilities, and no further. The moment the possibilities I am considering are not rigorously involved by my action, I ought to disengage myself from them, because no God, no scheme, can adapt the world and its possibilities to my will. When Descartes said, "Conquer yourself rather than the world," he meant essentially the same thing. . . .

15 Given that men are free and that tomorrow they will freely decide what man will be, I cannot be sure that, after my death, fellow-fighters will carry on my work to bring it to its maximum perfection. Tomorrow, after my death, some men may decide to set up Fascism, and the others may be cowardly and muddled enough to let them do it. Fascism will then be the human reality, so much the worse for us.

16 Actually, things will be as man will have decided they are to be. Does that mean that I should abandon myself to quietism? No. First, I should involve myself; then, act on the old saw, "Nothing ventured, nothing gained." Nor does it mean that I shouldn't belong to a party, but rather that I shall have no illusions and shall do what I can. For example, suppose I ask myself, "Will socialization, as such, ever come about?" I know nothing about it. All I know is that I'm going to do everything in my power to bring it about. Beyond that, I can't count on anything. Quietism is the attitude of people who say, "Let others do what I can't do." The doctrine I am presenting is the very opposite of quietism, since it declares, "There is no reality except in action." Moreover, it goes further, since it adds, "Man is nothing else than his plan; he exists only to the extent that he fulfills himself; he is therefore nothing else than the ensemble of his acts, nothing else than his life.". . .

17 From these few reflections it is evident that nothing is more unjust than the objections that have been raised against us. Existentialism is nothing else than an attempt to draw all the consequences of a coherent atheistic position. It isn't trying to plunge man into despair at all. But if one calls every attitude of unbelief despair, like the Christians, then the word is not being used in its original sense. Existentialism isn't so atheistic that it wears itself out showing that God doesn't exist. Rather, it declares that even if God did exist, that would change nothing. There you've got our point of view. Not that we believe that God exists, but we think that the problem of His existence is not the issue. In this

sense existentialism is optimistic, a doctrine of action, and it is plain dishonesty for Christians to make no distinction between their own despair and ours and then to call us despairing.

QUESTIONS FOR WRITING AND DISCUSSION

OBSERVING

1. "Man is nothing else but what he makes of himself." What does that mean in terms of religion, politics, family, and self? What would a diametrically opposite position be?
2. We are "responsible for all men. . . . In fact, in creating the man that we want to be, there is not a single one of our acts which does not at the same time create an image of man as we think he ought to be." Explain these statements. What kind of relationship to the world does this position imply?
3. Characterize Sartre's atheism as stated in this essay. How does he arrive at atheism, and what are the implications? Is Sartre's position as stated in the essay's first two paragraphs necessarily opposed to religion? Where does he most directly reject God?

EVALUATING

1. Much of Sartre's essay is a defense against claims of subjectivism. Other thinkers attack Sartre for his nihilism, utter gloominess, and anarchy. How would you evaluate his position against one or several of these attacks? Take the position that Sartre, in this essay, is not a pessimist.
2. How would Sartre address a Jewish, a Christian, or a Moslem critic of his position? Defend Sartre against such a critic.

RESPONDING AND APPLYING

1. The opening paragraph argues that most of us are not responsible for our own attitudes, that we have not made ourselves, that we are what others (family, peers, country, and God) have made of us. By allowing other persons or forces to create us, we would, according to Sartre, have committed a form of intellectual suicide. How would you acknowledge those sides of yourself that you were not fully responsible for forming? For example, to what degree is your religious affiliation or your attitudes on capital punishment, abortion, or flag burning convenient rather than carefully thought out?
2. Sartre belongs to the atheistic school of existentialism, whereas others like Miguel de Unamuno (1864-1936), Martin Buber (1878-1965), Gabriel Marcel (1889-1973), and Paul Tillich (1886-1965) see no necessary con-

tradiction between existentialism and religious faith. To be "existential," how do you think such a faith would have to differ from that of the more traditional believer?

3. What other examples in contemporary culture can you think of that reveal the shift described in the Sartre introduction and exemplified in his essay to a concern for reality as becoming? What problems, controversies, or solutions has this example inspired?

FRANZ KAFKA, "THE PROBLEM OF OUR LAWS"

Franz Kafka (1883-1924) was born in Prague, Czechoslovakia, where he earned a doctorate in law from the German university there. Although he was a brilliant law student, he never practiced; instead, he went to work for a government insurance agency. Twice engaged to the same woman, Kafka experienced a stormy five-year relationship with her, during which time he completed many of his most famous stories, including "The Metamorphosis," and most of his novel *The Trial.*

A corrosive and all-consuming alienation pervaded his life, which probably accounted for the brooding sense of isolation and nightmare in the lives of his fictional characters. He was a Jew and was, thus, separated from the predominantly Christian society, and as a religious skeptic, he failed to identify with his family's Judaism. He lacked a sense of his national identity because he was a German-speaking minority in the Slavic Austro-Hungarian monarchy; and as the often sickly son (he had a tubercular condition) of an oppressive father, he grew away from close attachments to his family. Increasingly, he believed himself to be a victim, but he could not comprehend who was punishing him and what wrongs he had committed to deserve the suffering.

The stories that follow come close to the ancient form of fiction called parable. A parable is a short allegory; that is, it tells a story about one thing while suggesting something else. The characters in the parables of Christ demonstrate his teachings; the story of the prodigal son, for example, shows how God is willing to forgive repentant sinners. Though these pieces from Kafka seem much like parables, one important feature distinguishes them from the parables we are used to: while Christ's parables usually are either specifically explained or appear in a context that makes their meaning reasonably clear (the story of the prodigal son appears as part of Christ's answer to complaints about his spending so much time with sinners), we have only our own sense of history to use in interpreting Kafka.

The Problem of Our Laws

Franz Kafka

1 Our laws are not generally known; they are kept secret by the small group of nobles who rule us. We are convinced that these ancient laws are scrupulously administered; nevertheless it is an extremely painful thing to be ruled by laws that one does not know. I am not thinking of possible discrepancies that may arise in the interpretation of the laws, or of the disadvantages involved when only a few and not the whole people are allowed to have a say in their interpretation. These disadvantages are perhaps of no great importance. For the laws are very ancient; their interpretation has been the work of centuries, and has itself doubtless acquired the status of law; and though there is still a possible freedom of interpretation left, it has now become very restricted. Moreover the nobles have obviously no cause to be influenced in their interpretation by personal interests inimical to us, for the laws were made to the advantage of the nobles from the very beginning, they themselves stand above the laws, and that seems to be why the laws were entrusted exclusively into their hands. Of course, there is wisdom in that—who doubts the wisdom of the ancient laws?—but also hardship for us; probably that is unavoidable.

2 The very existence of these laws, however, is at most a matter of presumption. There is a tradition that they exist and that they are a mystery confided to the nobility, but it is not and cannot be more than a mere tradition sanctioned by age, for the essence of a secret code is that it should remain a mystery. Some of us among the people have attentively scrutinized the doings of the nobility since the earliest times and possess records made by our forefathers—records which we have conscientiously continued—and claim to recognize amid the countless number of facts certain main tendencies which permit of this or that historical formulation; but when in accordance with these scrupulously tested and logically ordered conclusions we seek to adjust ourselves somewhat for the present or the future, everything becomes uncertain, and our work seems only an intellectual game, for perhaps these laws that we are trying to unravel do not exist at all. There is a small party who are actually of this opinion and who try to show that, if any law exists, it can only be this: The Law is whatever the nobles do. This party see everywhere only the arbitrary acts of the nobility, and reject the popular tradition, which according to them possesses only certain trifling and incidental advantages that do not offset its heavy drawbacks, for it gives the people a false, deceptive, and overconfident security in confronting coming events. This cannot be gainsaid, but the overwhelming majority of our people account for it by the fact that the tradition is far from complete and must be more fully inquired into, that the material available, prodigious as it looks, is still too meager, and that several centuries will have to pass before it becomes really adequate. This view, so comfortless as far as the present is concerned, is lightened only by the belief that a time will eventually come when

the tradition and our research into it will jointly reach their conclusion, and as it were gain a breathing space, when everything will have become clear, the law will belong to the people, and the nobility will vanish. This is not maintained in any spirit of hatred against the nobility; not at all, and by no one. We are more inclined to hate ourselves, because we have not yet shown ourselves worthy of being entrusted with the laws. And that is the real reason why the party who believe that there is no law have remained so few—although their doctrine is in certain ways so attractive, for it unequivocally recognizes the nobility and its right to go on existing.

3 Actually one can express the problem only in a sort of paradox: Any party that would repudiate not only all belief in the laws, but the nobility as well, would have the whole people behind it; yet no such party can come into existence, for nobody would dare to repudiate the nobility. We live on this razor's edge. A writer once summed the matter up in this way: The sole visible and indubitable law that is imposed upon us is the nobility, and must we ourselves deprive ourselves of that one law?

QUESTIONS FOR WRITING AND DISCUSSION

OBSERVING

1. What is the narrator's attitude toward the laws and toward the nobles who administer them? Is there any ambivalence in either of these attitudes?
2. The narrator speaks in the first paragraph of some of his people having derived from the study of history and tradition "certain main tendencies" which have been refined into a set of "scrupulously tested and logically ordered conclusions" which they apply in order "to adjust ourselves somewhat for the present or the future." Thus, he describes their attempt to understand on their own the laws that they have been barred from knowing more directly. What sort of individuals does this group of people represent?
3. What is the "small party" of which the narrator speaks in the second paragraph? Why do they take exception to the nobility, and why do the majority of the people reject the nobility's position? What do the majority do and why?
4. For many, the "tradition sanctioned by age" tends to give credibility to the laws, however painful they may be. What comfort is given to people by this attitude, especially when the people generally do not believe themselves to be "worthy of being entrusted with the laws"?

EVALUATING

1. What does Kafka mean by "our laws"? Is there a religious and moral, as well as legal and political, sense to the term? Show how one of these

senses applies throughout the story, or argue that the ambiguity is functional in that the law can mean many things.

2. Critics have commented that when Kafka read his parables and stories aloud, his audience almost always laughed. What irony and humor, often of an unreal, surrealist variety, permeate this parable? What is the source of the irony and humor?

RESPONDING AND APPLYING

1. What makes this parable almost immediately comprehensible to a modern audience?
2. The "razor's edge" these people live on involves their unwillingness "to repudiate the nobility." Kafka's language suggests not that they are afraid of some sort of reprisals from the nobility, but that they fear that repudiating the nobility will leave them without any law at all. Do you think human society can survive without the sense that its laws are grounded in some absolute authority, be it God or reason?

PERSPECTIVES: MAKING RATIONAL MORAL JUDGMENTS

One of the most crucial ways that rational thinking bears on our lives, both personally and socially, is our making of moral judgments. Is it possible to make valid moral judgments at all, and if we can, why should any one person's judgments have any bearing on what anyone else should think? Are there ways of approaching these questions rationally that can give us, if not certainty, at least some sense of confidence in our judgments? The two essays that follow may give us some help in thinking about these issues.

MARY MIDGLEY, "TRYING OUT ONE'S NEW SWORD"

The problems we have in dealing rationally with a world in which certainties are vague or nonexistent are especially apparent when we are called upon to pass judgment on other cultures. Does the ideal of a multicultural world in which differences are tolerated mean that we cannot make rational judgments about other cultures? There is a body of contemporary thought, pioneered by anthropologists like Claude Levi-Strauss and Margaret Mead, which attempts to devalue and dismantle any set of criteria that might be used to evaluate another culture's beliefs, customs, and practices. In contrast to these postmodernist approaches, *Mary Midgley* (1919–) seeks approaches through which we can establish relationships among different cultures and even different species. A professional philosopher and former senior lecturer at the University of Newcastle-upon-Tyne, Midgley has written several books on ethics, including *Heart and Mind: The Varieties of Moral Experience* (1981) from which comes the selection included here, *Can't We Make Moral Judgments?* (1991), *The Ethical Primate: Humans, Freedom, and Morality* (1996), and *Utopias, Dolphins, and Computers: Some Problems in Philosophical Plumbing* (1996). In addition, she has written extensively on the theoretical issues in the relationship between humans and animals, her works including *Beast and Man: The Roots of the Human Race* (1980), *Animals and Why They Matter* (1983), and *Evolution as a Religion: Strange Hopes and Stranger Fears* (1985).

Trying Out One's New Sword

Mary Midgley

1 All of us are, more or less, in trouble today about trying to understand cultures strange to us. We hear constantly of alien customs. We see changes in our lifetime which would have astonished our parents. I want to discuss here one very short way of dealing with this difficulty, a drastic way which many people now theoretically favour. It consists in simply denying that we can ever understand any culture except our own well enough to make judgements about it. Those who recommend this hold that the world is sharply divided into separate societies, sealed units, each with its own system of thought. They feel that the respect and tolerance due from one system to another forbids us ever to take up a critical position to any other culture. Moral judgement, they suggest, is a kind of coinage valid only in its country of origin.

2 I shall call this position 'moral isolationism'. I shall suggest that it is certainly not forced upon us, and indeed that it makes no sense at all. People usually take it up because they think it is a respectful attitude to other cultures. In fact, however, it is not respectful. Nobody can respect what is entirely unintelligible to them. To respect someone, we have to know enough about him to make a *favourable* judgement, however general and tentative. And we do understand people in other cultures to this extent. Otherwise a great mass of our most valuable thinking would be paralysed.

3 To show this, I shall take a remote example, because we shall probably find it easier to think calmly about it than we should with a contemporary one, such as female circumcision in Africa or the Chinese Cultural Revolution. The principles involved will still be the same. My example is this. There is, it seems, a verb in classical Japanese which means 'to try out one's new sword on a chance

wayfarer'. (The word is *tsujigiri,* literally 'crossroads-cut'.) A samurai sword had to be tried out because, if it was to work properly, it had to slice through someone at a single blow, from the shoulder to the opposite flank. Otherwise, the warrior bungled his stroke. This could injure his honour, offend his ancestors, and even let down his emperor. So tests were needed, and wayfarers had to be expended. Any wayfarer would do—provided, of course, that he was not another Samurai. Scientists will recognize a familiar problem about the rights of experimental subjects.

4 Now when we hear of a custom like this, we may well reflect that we simply do not understand it; and therefore are not qualified to criticize it at all, because we are not members of that culture. But we are not members of any other culture either, except our own. So we extend the principle to cover all extraneous cultures, and we seem therefore to be moral isolationists. But this is, as we shall see, an impossible position. Let us ask what it would involve.

5 We must ask first: Does the isolating barrier work both ways? Are people in other cultures equally unable to criticize *us?* This question struck me sharply when I read a remark in *The Guardian* by an anthropologist about a South American Indian who had been taken into a Brazilian town for an operation, which saved his life. When he came back to his village, he made several highly critical remarks about the white Brazilians' way of life. They may very well have been justified. But the interesting point was that the anthropologist called these remarks 'a damning indictment of Western civilization'. Now the Indian had been in that town about two weeks. Was he in a position to deliver a damning indictment? Would we ourselves be qualified to deliver such an indictment on the Samurai, provided we could spend two weeks in ancient Japan? What do we really think about this?

6 My own impression is that we believe that outsiders can, in principle, deliver perfectly good indictments—only, it usually takes more than two weeks to make them damning. Understanding has degrees. It is not a slapdash yes-or-no matter. Intelligent outsiders can progress in it, and in some ways will be at an advantage over the locals. But if this is so, it must clearly apply to ourselves as much as anybody else.

7 Our next question is this: Does the isolating barrier between cultures block praise as well as blame? If I want to say that the Samurai culture has many virtues, or to praise the South American Indians, am I prevented from doing *that* by my outside status? Now, we certainly do need to praise other societies in this way. But it is hardly possible that we could praise them effectively if we could not, in principle, criticize them. Our praise would be worthless if it rested on no definite grounds, if it did not flow from some understanding. Certainly we may need to praise things which we do not *fully* understand. We say 'there's something very good here, but I can't quite make out what it is yet'. This happens when we want to learn from strangers. And we can learn from strangers. But to do this we have to distinguish between those strangers who are worth learning from and those who are not. Can we then judge which is which?

8 This brings us to our third question: What is involved in judging? Now plainly there is no question here of sitting on a bench in a red robe and sentencing people. Judging simply means forming an opinion, and expressing it if it is called for. Is there anything wrong about this? Naturally, we ought to avoid forming—and expressing—*crude* opinions, like that of a simple-minded missionary, who might dismiss the whole Samurai culture as entirely bad, because non-Christian. But this is a different objection. The trouble with crude opinions is that they are crude, whoever forms them, not that they are formed by the wrong people. Anthropologists, after all, are outsiders quite as much as missionaries. Moral isolationism forbids us to form *any* opinions on these matters. Its ground for doing so is that we don't understand them. But there is much that we don't understand in our own culture too. This brings us to our last question: If we can't judge other cultures, can we really judge our own? Our efforts to do so will be much damaged if we are really deprived of our opinions about other societies, because these provide the range of comparison, the spectrum of alternatives against which we set what we want to understand. We would have to stop using the mirror which anthropology so helpfully holds up to us.

9 In short, moral isolationism would lay down a general ban on moral reasoning. Essentially, this is the programme of immoralism, and it carries a distressing logical difficulty. Immoralists like Nietzsche are actually just a rather specialized sect of moralists. They can no more afford to put moralizing out of business than smugglers can afford to abolish customs regulations. The power of moral judgement is, in fact, not a luxury, not a perverse indulgence of the self-righteous. It is a necessity. When we judge something to be bad or good, better or worse than something else, we are taking it as an example to aim at or avoid. Without opinions of this sort, we would have no framework of comparison for our own policy, no chance of profiting by other people's insights or mistakes. In this vacuum, we could form no judgements on our own actions.

10 Now it would be odd if Homo sapiens had really got himself into a position as bad as this—a position where his main evolutionary asset, his brain, was so little use to him. None of us is going to accept this sceptical diagnosis. We cannot do so, because our involvement in moral isolationism does not flow from apathy, but from a rather acute concern about human hypocrisy and other forms of wickedness. But we polarize that concern around a few selected moral truths. We are rightly angry with those who despise, oppress or steamroll other cultures. We think that doing these things is actually *wrong*. But this is itself a moral judgement. We could not condemn oppression and insolence if we thought that all our condemnations were just a trivial local quirk of our own culture. We could still less do it if we tried to stop judging altogether.

11 Real moral scepticism, in fact, could lead only to inaction, to our losing all interest in moral questions, most of all in those which concern other societies. When we discuss these things, it becomes instantly clear how far we are from doing this. Suppose, for instance, that I criticize the bisecting Samurai, that I say his behaviour is brutal. What will usually happen next is that someone will protest, will say that I have no right to make criticisms like that of another

culture. But it is most unlikely that he will use this move to end the discussion of the subject. Instead, he will justify the Samurai. He will try to fill in the background, to make me understand the custom, by explaining the exalted ideals of discipline and devotion which produced it. He will probably talk of the lower value which the ancient Japanese placed on individual life generally. He may well suggest that this is a healthier attitude than our own obsession with security. He may add, too, that the wayfarers did not seriously mind being bisected, that in principle they accepted the whole arrangement.

12 Now an objector who talks like this is implying that it *is* possible to understand alien customs. That is just what he is trying to make me do. And he implies, too, that if I do succeed in understanding them, I shall do something better than giving up judging them. He expects me to change my present judgement to a truer one—namely, one that is favourable. And the standards I must use to do this cannot just be Samurai standards. They have to be ones current in my own culture. Ideals like discipline and devotion will not move anybody unless he himself accepts them. As it happens, neither discipline nor devotion is very popular in the West at present. Anyone who appeals to them may well have to do some more arguing to make *them* acceptable, before he can use them to explain the Samurai. But if he does succeed here, he will have persuaded us, not just that there was something to be said for them in ancient Japan, but that there would be here as well.

13 Isolating barriers simply cannot arise here. If we accept something as a serious moral truth about one culture, we can't refuse to apply it—in however different an outward form—to other cultures as well, wherever circumstance admit it. If we refuse to do this, we just are not taking the other culture seriously. This becomes clear if we look at the last argument used by my objector—that of justification by consent of the victim. It is suggested that sudden bisection is quite in order, *provided* that it takes place between consenting adults. I cannot now discuss how conclusive this justification is. What I am pointing out is simply that it can only work if we believe that *consent* can make such a transaction respectable—and this is a thoroughly modern and Western idea. It would probably never occur to a Samurai; if it did, it would surprise him very much. It is *our* standard. In applying it, too, we are likely to make another typically Western demand. We shall ask for good factual evidence that the wayfarers actually do have this rather surprising taste—that they are really willing to be bisected. In applying Western standards in this way, we are not being confused or irrelevant. We are asking the questions which arise *from where we stand,* questions which we can see the sense of. We do this because asking questions which you can't see the sense of is humbug. Certainly we can extend our questioning by imaginative effort. We can come to understand other societies better. By doing so, we may make their questions our own, or we may see that they are really forms for the questions which we are asking already. This is not impossible. It is just very hard work. The obstacles which often prevent it are simply those of ordinary ignorance, laziness and prejudice.

14 If there were really an isolating barrier, of course, our own culture could never have been formed. It is no sealed box, but a fertile jungle of different

influences—Greek, Jewish, Roman, Norse, Celtic and so forth, into which further influences are still pouring—American, Indian, Japanese, Jamaican, you name it. The moral isolationist's picture of separate, unmixable cultures is quite unreal. People who talk about British history usually stress the value of this fertilizing mix, no doubt rightly. But this is not just an odd fact about Britain. Except for the very smallest and most remote, all cultures are formed out of many streams. All have the problem of digesting and assimilating things which, at the start, they do not understand. All have the choice of learning something from this challenge, or, alternatively, of refusing to learn, and fighting it mindlessly instead.

15 This universal predicament has been obscured by the fact that anthropologists used to concentrate largely on very small and remote cultures, which did not seem to have this problem. These tiny societies, which had often forgotten their own history, made neat, self-contained subjects for study. No doubt it was valuable to emphasize their remoteness, their extreme strangeness, their independence of our cultural tradition. This emphasis was, I think, the root of moral isolationism. But, as the tribal studies themselves showed, even there the anthropologists were able to interpret what they saw and make judgements—often favourable—about the tribesmen. And the tribesmen, too, were quite equal to making judgements about the anthropologists—and about the tourists and Coca-Cola salesmen who followed them. Both sets of judgements, no doubt, were somewhat hasty, both have been refined in the light of further experience. A similar transaction between us and the Samurai might take even longer. But that is no reason at all for deeming it impossible. Morally as well as physically, there is only one world, and we all have to live in it.

QUESTIONS FOR WRITING AND DISCUSSION

OBSERVING

1. Midgley employs a logical tactic called *reductio ad absurdum,* reducing a proposition to absurdity. Starting from the moral isolationist position which denies "that we can ever understand any culture except our own well enough to make judgements about it," she shows how this must necessarily mean that if we cannot judge other cultures we cannot judge either our own culture or our own personal actions; moral isolationism, if consistent with its own principles, would ban moral reasoning altogether. Explain how she develops this chain of reasoning and argue whether or not it is convincing. To what other propositions does she apply this tactic?
2. While arguing that we cannot avoid judging other cultures, Midgley admits that we ought to avoid crude and simple-minded judgments. Do any clear criteria, either explicit or implied, emerge from her discussion that help us distinguish between those crude judgments and more acceptable ones? List and discuss as many as you can spot.

3. Notice that the moral isolationist Midgley describes is not a morally apathetic person (apathy is a conceivable basis for moral isolationism, but a different one). The type she speaks of argues from the principle of respect for the differences between cultures. How does Midgley show that such a position is contradictory?

EVALUATING

1. Midgley argues that respect for another is based on knowledge and understanding of that other. Do you agree? Do we owe some respect to all human beings and cultures? Do we owe equal respect to all human beings and cultures?
2. In arguing her position, Midgley creates an opponent, a moral isolationist to whom she attributes specific arguments, which she in turn answers. This is a form of dialectic, a word brought up in the introduction to Plato. Do you think the argument would have been clearer or otherwise more effective if it had been cast in the form of a dialog? Try doing so and argue which is the most effective form.

RESPONDING AND APPLYING

1. How would you define the concepts of human rights and of international human rights? Ought there to be any difference between the two concepts? Whether or not there should be a difference, international politics, it could be argued, makes some difference a practical necessity. Pick an example where this seems to be the case and argue whether or not tolerance of difference is appropriate, and whether that tolerance is driven by a rationally consistent notion of human rights or by politics. Do you think the United States has been consistent in its support for human rights issues worldwide?
2. Compare Midgley's claim that "the power of moral judgement is . . . a necessity" with Sartre's that in choosing his own self, a person chooses all men, that "in creating the man that we want to be . . . [we] create an image of man as we think he ought to be." How do both claims relate to Midgley's argument that if we accept something as a serious moral truth in another culture and refuse to apply it to our own, "we just are not taking the other culture seriously"?

PATRICIA M. KING, "HOW DO WE KNOW? WHY DO WE BELIEVE? LEARNING TO MAKE REFLECTIVE JUDGMENTS"

Patricia M. King (1950–) in many ways fulfills the trends we have been speaking of with regard to rationalism. Making rational judgments is not so much a matter of one's personal philosophy, although that might enter into the process, as one of maturity and intellectual development. Thinking clearly and making intelligent judgments about complex issues is not an arbitrary process, however beset with uncertainty it may be; it is something that one can learn and that can best be understood in terms of a developmental model. An associate professor in the Department of Higher Education and Student Affairs at Bowling Green State University, she is one of the creators of the reflective judgment model of adult intellectual development. Originally published in the journal *Liberal Education* in 1992, this article is based on the work later published in the book she co-authored with Karen Strohm Kitchener, *Developing Reflective Judgment: Understanding and Promoting Intellectual Growth and Critical Thinking in Adolescents and Adults* (1994). It offers us a glimpse behind textbooks since its intended readers are not students but college and university educators.

How Do We Know? Why Do We Believe?

Patricia M. King

1 How do we know? Why do we believe? What is the evidence? Here, whatever the subject matter, we are at the heart of the intellectual process, concerned with the phenomenon of humans thinking, the processes whereby they establish a fact, put two or more of them together, come to conclusions as to their meaning, and perhaps even soar with some leap of imagination to a thought that has never been thought before.[1]

2 How do college students learn to answer these questions and reach meaningful conclusions in informed and convincing ways? What kinds of skills and understandings do they need to do so? In its 1991 report, *The Challenge of Connecting Learning,* the Association of American Colleges examined the kinds of thinking skills ("habits of mind") associated with liberal learning. These include the ability ". . . to state why a question or argument is significant and for whom; what the difference is between developing and justifying a position and merely asserting one; and how to develop and provide warrants for their own interpretations and judgments."[2]

3 Clarifying educational goals such as these is a critical first step toward teaching college students how to make thoughtful, reasoned judgments. Such goals provide direction and clarity for our educational efforts; without them, our efforts risk being either badly off the mark or diluted by ambiguity. . . .

---

[1] *Integrity in the College Curriculum* (Washington: Association of American Colleges, 1985), 15.

[2] *The Challenge of Connecting Learning* (Washington: Association of American Colleges, 1991), 14.

4 Students' assumptions are elucidated in the reflective judgment model of adult intellectual development that Karen Strohm Kitchener and I first described in 1981.[3] This model provides a foundation for understanding how college faculty and staff members can responsibly assist students to question their assumptions about knowing and learning and to make more reflective judgments.

5 No single model of intellectual development can capture and describe adequately all of the complexities of human reasoning. Models, however, can provide heuristic tools that teachers may use to help understand some basic differences in the ways students reason and make judgments. They also can help teachers learn how to take these differences into account in encouraging students to think more reflectively and make more reasoned judgments. We offer the reflective judgment model here as one such heuristic tool.

6 The term "reflective thinking" was used by John Dewey to describe the thinking process people use when faced with questions of controversy or doubt for which their current understanding or solution, for whatever reason, no longer is satisfactory.[4] According to Dewey, a "reflective judgment" is the end goal of good thinking: the judgment or solution that brings closure to the problem (if only temporarily).

7 While reflective and critical thinking can (and should!) be directed toward a variety of types of problems, the reflective judgment model specifically focuses on controversial problems where real doubt exists about correct solutions (or best resolutions). Evaluating the merits of alternative proposals to stimulate the economy, weighing competing interpretations of national or international political events, and deciding how to reduce pollution while respecting economic interests are examples of what C. W. Churchman refers to as "ill-structured" problems.[5] Questions such as these are full of the kinds of doubts to which Dewey referred because they can be neither described with a high degree of completeness nor solved with a high degree of certainty. Other types of intellectual problems—such as calculating interest payments on a loan, converting units of measure between metric and English standards, and balancing a checkbook—can be described more completely and solved with higher certainty; these are called "well-structured" problems. The reflective judgment model describes a sequence of changes in thinking that affects the ways students justify their beliefs and make judgments about ill-structured problems.

---

[3] Karen S. Kitchener and Patricia M. King, "Reflective Judgment: Concepts of Justification and Their Relationship to Age and Education," *Journal of Applied Developmental Psychology* 2 (1981): 89–116.

[4] John Dewey, *How We Think: A Restatement of the Relation of Reflective Thinking to the Educative Process* (Lexington, Mass.: D. C. Heath and Company, 1933).

[5] C. W. Churchman, *The Design of Inquiring Systems: Basic Concepts of Systems and Organizations* (New York: Basic Books, 1971).

The Reflective Judgment Model

8 For the last fifteen years, several colleagues and I have studied the ways people explain and justify their interpretations and judgments about controversial topics. We have found that individuals' answers to questions of what and how they know are related to their fundamental assumptions about knowledge itself and that these assumptions change during people's college years.

9 The reflective judgment model describes a developmental sequence of increasingly complex and adequate ways of understanding and resolving ill-structured problems. It demonstrates how a person's basis of judgment (the way a belief is justified) is rooted in his or her assumptions about knowledge itself.[6] These epistemic assumptions are implicit in individuals' decisions to look for or ignore the facts of a situation, in the strategies they use to gain information about a problem, in their attempts to understand divergent interpretations, and in the degree of certainty they feel about whether a problem has been solved. This model attempts to make these assumptions explicit and to show how they evolve over time.

10 In the steps toward reflective thinking described by the model, people become better able to evaluate knowledge claims and to explain and defend a point of view on a controversial issue. This developmental progression in reasoning is described by seven distinct sets of assumptions about knowledge and how it is acquired; each set of assumptions, called a "stage," is associated with a different strategy for solving ill-structured problems. Following each of the descriptions below, a verbatim quotation (printed in italics) from a Reflective Judgment Interview (RJI)—the instrument we use to assess reflective judgment—is given to illustrate the type of reasoning associated with these assumptions.

11 The early stages, 1 and 2, are characterized by the assumption that knowledge is gained through direct, personal observation or through the word of an authority figure and is therefore assumed to be absolutely correct and certain: *"I figure if it's on the news, it's got to be true or they wouldn't put it on."* Thinking consistent with these assumptions is considered "pre-reflective."

12 This level of assumed correctness and certainty is less apparent in subsequent stages, but some vestiges remain. In Stage 3, for example, absolute answers are assumed to exist but to be temporarily inaccessible. *"Right now, they are finding things about the pyramids that can't be explained. Right now they are just guessing. . . . Until there is evidence that people can give to convince everybody one way or another, it's just a guess. Then it will be*

---

[6] While several developmental theorists informed the initial conceptualization of this model—most notably William G. Perry, Jr., in *Forms of Intellectual and Ethical Development in the College Years: A Scheme* (New York: Holt, Rinehart & Winston, 1968) and J. Broughton in *The Development of Natural Epistemology in Adolescence and Early Adulthood* (unpublished doctoral dissertation, Harvard University, 1975)—the stage descriptions summarized here are derived from extensive sets of interviews with many individuals of varied ages and educational levels.

knowledge." People who use these assumptions to guide their reasoning tend to view all problems as though they were defined with a high degree of certainty and completeness; as a result, they are unable to differentiate between well- and ill-structured problems. Moreover, until this absolutely convincing evidence is in, no one can claim to "know" beyond his or her own personal impressions: ***"It doesn't matter what you believe or what I believe because until one of them finds an answer, then I'm just going to believe what I want to believe."***

13 Stage 4 reasoning is less whimsical: Evidence emerges as an important ingredient in the construction of knowledge claims, along with the acknowledgment that the evidence itself cannot be known with absolute certainty. Pragmatic reasons such as incorrect calibration of measurement tools, the loss of data over time, or the lack of a first-person account are used to explain this lack relationship to context and evidence, and some interpretations may be judged as being in some way better than others. These stages reflect the assumption that one's understanding of the world is not "given" but must be actively constructed and interpreted and that knowledge must be understood in relationship to the context in which it was generated. An additional assumption made at this level is that some interpretations or knowledge claims may be judged more plausible than others. Criteria that might be used in making such evaluations include conceptual soundness, coherence, degree of fit with the data, meaningfulness, usefulness, and parsimony. "[*One judges arguments by looking at such things as*] ***how well thought out the positions are, at what level one chooses to argue the position, what kinds of reasoning and evidence one would use to support it, how it fits into the rest of one's world view or rational explanation, how consistently one argues on this topic compared with other topics.***" Individuals who make judgments in this way are exhibiting good "reflective thinking."

The Development of Reflective Judgment

14 Unlike other models of reflective or critical thinking, the reflective judgment model is grounded in the underlying assumptions of the cognitive developmental perspective articulated by Piaget and Kohlberg. As such, this model also reflects assumptions about the process of learning to think and reason more effectively. Because these assumptions hold special implications for teaching reflective thinking—or reflective inquiry, a concept introduced by Barry Kroll elsewhere in this *Liberal Education*—I want to describe them briefly.

15 *Assumption 1:* Individuals actively attempt to interpret and make sense of what they experience. Examining an interpretation from the perspective of the individual who constructed it often reveals an internal logic to the explanation. Cognitive-developmental theories attempt to describe patterns (for example, common themes or assumptions) that can be seen in individuals' explanations.

In the reflective judgment model, the observed patterns correspond to stages (sets of epistemic assumptions) described above. The importance of engaging students in the process of making meaningful interpretations is evident in the *Integrity* passage that opens this article.

16 *Assumption 2:* People's ways of making meaning develop over time. Just as young children solve problems using different strategies than do older children, so young adults understand their worlds and reason differently than older adults, including college teachers. Earlier ways of making meaning mature over time, providing the foundation for later ways of making meaning.

17 More mature structures, furthermore, are assumed to offer more complex, complete, and adequate ways of interpreting experience; some of these ways might include considering more pieces of information at one time, evaluating contradictory pieces of information, or critiquing one's own as well as others' ideas. Earlier ways of thinking are revised when individuals realize these ways have become inadequate, necessitating the creation of new ways of understanding.

18 Such changes in how one thinks—which can be tantamount to a change in one's world view—reflect no small intellectual accomplishment. Some students describe this change as nothing less than a personal metamorphosis: "I used to think that everything printed in a book must be *true;* now I realize how naive I was!" This individual was acknowledging that she now thinks in qualitatively different terms about sources of knowledge and her own role in evaluating the truth of given statements. This reevaluation of "old ways of thinking" is presumably what the authors of *The Challenge of Connecting Learning* had in mind when they noted, "Faculty members must take seriously what students believe about a given subject and engage their prior knowledge so that *new learning restructures the old, complicating and correcting it rather than merely living side by side with it.*"[7]

19 *Assumption 3:* Interaction with the environment affects an individual's development (in this case, intellectual development or reflective thinking). That is, environmental factors such as the types of intellectual challenges offered, quality of feedback, and opportunities for practice without fear of failing or being penalized affect how well a person learns to reason to conclusions. Although the direction of cognitive changes—that is, toward greater complexity and adequacy—is predictable, the rate of change for any individual fluctuates, depending in part on the characteristics of the environment, including the perceived amount of stimulation and support. In Dewey's words, "We never educate directly, but indirectly by means of the environment. Whether we permit chance environments to do the work, or whether we design environments for the purpose makes a great difference."[8]

---

[7] *The Challenge of Connecting Learning,* 13 (emphasis added).

[8] John Dewey, *Democracy and Education* (New York: Macmillan, 1916), 22.

20 *Assumption 4:* An emerging assumption is that individuals do not function "in a stage." Rather, individuals tend to exhibit a range of responses across stages. How an individual performs at a given point in time—that is, what particular stage characteristics he or she is evidencing—will depend on a variety of factors: how well the person was feeling or concentrating at the time, whether the person was distracted by another concern, the difficulty of the task presented, and the type of feedback and support offered.[9] Teachers who wish to assess students' developmental levels should not rely on single examples of students' reasoning. A given example may be indicative of the level at which a student typically reasons, but it may underestimate the level at which she or he could function in other circumstances or learning environments. . . .

Although a central goal of many educational programs is for students to be able to reason using the types of reasoning skills associated with the higher stages of reflective judgment, it is important to accept and respect people at whatever developmental levels they may be experiencing. While the characteristics of early stages are not consistent with true reflective thinking, nevertheless they are reflections of students' assumptions about knowledge and how knowledge is gained—assumptions that some students genuinely use to solve controversial problems. These assumptions provide building blocks for subsequent ways of understanding and resolving problems. Therefore, teachers must show emotional acceptance for all students whose reasoning they are challenging and understand that a strong internal logic exists in the patterns of reasoning at each stage (including the early stages, which often appear illogical). This understanding may make the student more receptive when the teacher points out the insufficiencies of earlier ways of reasoning and more willing to take the kinds of intellectual risks associated with abandoning old, comfortable ways of thinking. . . .

QUESTIONS FOR WRITING AND DISCUSSION

OBSERVING

1. How is it that King thinks the reflective judgment model will help college educators carry out their function? What is a heuristic tool?
2. Define the key terminology used here. What is reflective judgment; what are well-structured and ill-structured problems?
3. How is the question of how we make judgments related to what philosophers call the epistemological questions: what can we know and how do we know?

---

[9] For references on stage theory, please contact the author.

4. Among the examples offered of student responses, which do you think sounds most like your most typical responses?

EVALUATING

1. Do you agree that the reflective judgment model provides a sequence of ways of understanding and resolving (at least temporarily) ill-structured problems that are both "increasingly complex and adequate"?
2. The fourth assumption behind the model is that individuals do not function "in a stage," rather in a range of stages. Part of what may cause this variance is the degree of confidence we have in our own learning and understanding in various fields or concerning various issues. In what areas do you feel most confident of your ability to make judgments when "experts" disagree? In what areas do you feel least confident?

RESPONDING AND APPLYING

1. Look back at one or more of the essays in this chapter and consider at what level of reflective thinking each should be placed. Defend your decisions.
2. One of the goals of education indicated here is to help students understand "what the difference is between developing and justifying a position and merely asserting one; and how to develop and provide warrants for their own interpretations and judgments." How capable do you think you are in these areas? Do you usually distinguish between your own opinions and judgments?
3. Some teachers are inappropriately dogmatic, but often students who complain that their views are not accepted by teachers do not realize that their view was only an opinion, not a judgment. On the other hand, a teacher may reject a student's weakly argued idea in a way that fails to understand that he or she has not yet advanced to a stage of reflective thinking that permits an understanding of the teacher's response. Look back on your experience as a student and consider which teachers you admired the most and which most contributed to your intellectual growth. Were they the same or different ones? If the same, do you think they had an intuitive grasp of something like the reflective judgment model or is there something else that you think accounts for their success? Do you think this model can help teachers find that compromise between building students' self-confidence and challenging them to grow? Do you think students should be made aware of models like this to help them understand teachers' goals? How much would that depend on what stage of judging the students were in?
4. Do you believe that the types of reasoning skills associated with what King calls "the higher stages of reflective judgment" are most appropriate for all ill-structured problems? Are there some answers that we should accept

from authority of some type? Of what type? Are there some questions we ought not to ask or pursue?

5. If you were asked to state your educational philosophy, do you think that the reflective judgment model offers a good basis for developing it? If not, would you prefer some modification of this model, or would you base your philosophy on entirely different goals?

CHAPTER WRITING ASSIGNMENTS

1. Look again at the questions following the preview piece for this chapter. Having worked your way through this chapter, having examined and expressed your own views and listened to a variety of others' views, do you feel better equipped to answer and defend any of them? Do you feel at least better equipped to set about seeking answers? Which essays do you think helped you the most?
2. The language of traditional rationalism usually contains words and phrases like *universal* or *eternal truth, self-evidence, order, tradition, hierarchy, objectivity, simplicity, clarity;* in discourse shaped by the new rationalism, we find instead the likes of *process, dynamics, emergence, self-organization, complexity, subjectivity, chaos, models, uncertainty, anxiety, authenticity.* Which do you think more accurately represents the real world? Which view do you think creates a better world?
3. The language of these two views of reality, you may have discovered in considering the preceding question, is not always clearly different. Both, for example, have a conception of *order* in the world and in society, but those conceptions can be quite different. Choose an important word the two might use with significantly different meanings and explain those meanings. In addition to *order,* you might consider such words as *faith, freedom* (the Anglican Prayer Book refers to God as "He in whose service is perfect freedom"), *justice,* even *truth* or *reality* if you are very ambitious.
4. Another concept sometimes closely identified with rationalism is humanism. Here is how art historian Erwin Panofsky defines it: "The conviction of the dignity of man, based on both the insistence on human values (rationality and freedom) and the acceptance of human limitations (fallibility and frailty); from this two postulates result—responsibility and tolerance" (*Meaning and the Visual Arts,* Garden City, NY: Doubleday, 1955, 2). Review the documents you have read here, and measure each against Panofsky's definition. How well do each of the writers included here fit this definition? Do you think such a view is compatible with a religious view?
5. Which viewpoint, a rationalistic or a religious one, do you think is the more dogmatic, which the more tolerant? If you are thinking critically, this question should have inspired questions in return like: Which denomination of which religion? Which form of rationalism? Granting the wide variance in both, the excesses and beauties each has produced, is it still possible to make cautious generalizations in this regard about either?

Another approach to this question is to set up an imaginary dialog or debate between Christ, Moses, or Mohammed on one side and one of the writers in this chapter on the other. Which of these two individuals appears the more dogmatic, the more tolerant?

6. Which viewpoint, a rationalistic or a religious one, do you think more able to establish a basis for people of divergent views in a multicultural society to get along peaceably? Which seems to offer the better means for resolving differences?

Chapter Preview

Chapter Prelude
John Brockman, "The Emerging Third Culture"

Introductory Essay

Readings
Galileo Galilei, *from* "The Starry Messenger"
Charles Darwin, *from* "Origin of Species"
Stephen Jay Gould, "Women's Brains"
Robert Jay Lifton, "This World Is Not This World"

Story
Frederick Pohl, "Day Million"

Perspectives
Science and Scientific Controversies
Stephen Jay Gould, "Sex Drugs, Disasters and the Extinction of Dinosaurs"
Joel Cracraft, "The Scientific Response to Creationism"

Chapter Writing Assignments

Chapter 6

THE SCIENTIFIC REVOLUTION

The Emerging Third Culture

John Brockman

1 The third culture consists of those scientists and other thinkers in the empirical world who, through their work and expository writing, are taking the place of the traditional intellectual in rendering visible the deeper meanings of our lives, redefining who and what we are.

2 In the past few years, the playing field of American intellectual life has shifted, and the traditional intellectual has become increasingly marginalized. A 1950s education in Freud, Marx, and modernism is not a sufficient qualification for a thinking person in the 1990s. Indeed, the traditional American intellectuals are, in a sense, increasingly reactionary, and quite often proudly (and perversely) ignorant of many of the truly significant intellectual accomplishments of our time. Their culture, which dismisses science, is often nonempirical. It uses its own jargon and washes its own laundry. It is chiefly characterized by comment on comments, the swelling spiral of commentary eventually reaching the point where the real world gets lost.

3 In 1959 C. P. Snow published a book titled *The Two Cultures.* On the one hand, there were the literary intellectuals; on the other, the scientists. He noted with incredulity that during the 1930s the literary intellectuals, while no one was looking, took to referring to themselves as "the intellectuals," as though there were no others. This new definition by the "men of letters" excluded scientists such as the astronomer Edwin Hubble, the mathematician John von Neumann, the cybereticist Norbert Wiener, and the physicists Albert Einstein, Niels Bohr, and Werner Heisenberg.

4 How did the literary intellectuals get away with it? First, people in the sciences did not make an effective case for the implications of their work. Second, while many eminent scientists, notably Arthur Eddington and James Jeans, also wrote books for a general audience, their works were ignored by the

self-proclaimed intellectuals, and the value and importance of the ideas presented remained invisible as an intellectual activity, because science was not a subject for the reigning journals and magazines.

5 In a second edition of *The Two Cultures,* published in 1963, Snow added a new essay, "The Two Cultures: A Second Look," in which he optimistically suggested that a new culture, a "third culture," would emerge and close the communications gap between the literary intellectuals and the scientists. In Snow's third culture, the literary intellectuals would be on speaking terms with the scientists. Although I borrow Snow's phrase, it does not describe the third culture he predicted. Literary intellectuals are not communicating with scientists. Scientists are communicating directly with the general public. Traditional intellectual media played a vertical game: journalists wrote up and professors wrote down. Today, third-culture thinkers tend to avoid the middleman and endeavor to express their deepest thoughts in a manner accessible to the intelligent reading public.

6 The recent publishing successes of serious science books have surprised only the old-style intellectuals. Their view is that these books are anomalies—that they are bought but not read. I disagree. The emergence of this third-culture activity is evidence that many people have a great intellectual hunger for new and important ideas and are willing to make the effort to educate themselves.

7 The wide appeal of the third-culture thinkers is not due solely to their writing ability; what traditionally has been called "science" has today become "public culture." Stewart Brand writes that "Science is the only news. When you scan through a newspaper or magazine, all the human interest stuff is the same old he-said-she-said, the politics and economics the same sorry cyclic dramas, the fashions a pathetic illusion of newness, and even the technology is predictable if you know the science. Human nature doesn't change much; science does, and the change accrues, altering the world irreversibly." We now live in a world in which the rate of change is the biggest change. Science has thus become a big story.

8 Scientific topics receiving prominent play in newspapers and magazines over the past several years include molecular biology, artificial intelligence, artificial life, chaos theory, massive parallelism, neural nets, the inflationary universe, fractals, complex adaptive systems, superstrings, biodiversity, nanotechnology, the human genome, expert systems, punctuated equilibrium, cellular automata, fuzzy logic, space biospheres, the Gaia hypothesis, virtual reality, cyberspace, and teraflop machines. Among others. There is no canon or accredited list of acceptable ideas. The strength of the third culture is precisely that it can tolerate disagreements about which ideas are to be taken seriously. Unlike previous intellectual pursuits, the achievements of the third culture are not the marginal disputes of a quarrelsome mandarin class: they will affect the lives of everybody on the planet.

9 The role of the intellectual includes communicating. Intellectuals are not just people who know things but people who shape the thoughts of their gen-

eration. An intellectual is a synthesizer, a publicist, a communicator. In his 1987 book *The Last Intellectuals,* the cultural historian Russell Jacoby bemoaned the passing of a generation of public thinkers and their replacement by bloodless academicians. He was right, but also wrong. The third-culture thinkers are the new public intellectuals.

10 America now is the intellectual seedbed for Europe and Asia. This trend started with the prewar emigration of Albert Einstein and other European scientists and was further fueled by the post-Sputnik boom in scientific education in our universities. The emergence of the third culture introduces new modes of intellectual discourse and reaffirms the preeminence of America in the realm of important ideas. Throughout history, intellectual life has been marked by the fact that only a small number of people have done the serious thinking for everybody else. What we are witnessing is a passing of the torch from one group of thinkers, the traditional literary intellectuals, to a new group, the intellectuals of the emerging third culture.

QUESTIONS FOR WRITING AND DISCUSSION

OBSERVING

1. If literary intellectuals are culture one and scientists are culture two, what constitutes the third culture as C. P. Snow defined it in 1963? The third culture as Brockman defines it today?
2. In what sense, according to Brockman, has what traditionally has been called "science" become "public culture"?

EVALUATING

1. Though science has become "public culture," according to Brockman it has done so largely in spite of the literary intellectuals, who are still "not speaking to scientists." Do you agree that science remains isolated from other aspects of intellectual culture?
2. Implicit in Brockman's discussion are a number of fundamental issues with regard not only to scientific ideas but to all the great ideas: Where do they come from? Who initiates them? Who transmits them? Who are their audiences? How do we identify them? And, of course, why should we study them, or perhaps better, do we have any responsibility to seek to understand them? Do you think Brockman illuminates these issues? Has your attitude toward or understanding of these more fundamental issues, not so much the ideas themselves, changed at all since you began working with this text?

RESPONDING AND APPLYING

1. From your own experience, how would you describe the attitudes of your teachers of the traditional humanities—literature, language, the plastic and musical arts, history, philosophy—toward science? Interested, fascinated, ignorant, indifferent? How often do issues related to science enter into the discussions they lead?
2. How would you describe your own attitude toward science? Interested, fascinated, indifferent, frightened, intimidated? To what extent do you think your attitudes have been shaped by your teachers (both in terms of their attitudes and the quality of science instruction you have received), parents, the various media you are exposed to?
3. Consider the list Brockman provides of "scientific topics receiving prominent play in newspapers and magazines over the past several years." Do any of these topics especially interest you? If so, would you describe the motivation behind your interest as intellectual curiosity or something more practical like the expectation that knowledge of this area will affect your prospects for a career, health, happiness, survival, etc.?
4. Considering that list again, how many of those topics do you think likely to be involved somehow in questions of public policy about which you, as a member of a democratic society, might have a part in deciding? To what extent do you think your education and understanding equip you to partake in such decisions?

SCIENCE AND THE COPERNICAN REVOLUTION

If time travelers from at least a century ago were to visit our world today, the most immediately apparent changes would be those brought about by science. They would see it in our skylines, our roads and automobiles, the microwave ovens and electric can openers in our homes, the incredible bulk of information available in the print and electronic media; a closer look would reveal a marked change in such areas as the speed of worldwide travel, our average life expectancy, our ability to exterminate a large selected group of people, and our potential for annihilating our entire species. But not all the changes brought about by science are physical; some are abstract. Many of Western humanity's basic assumptions and beliefs, indeed the notions of what differentiates belief from fact, have been shaped by the scientific revolution. Yet there are no subjects in which American students seem less interested than the sciences, except perhaps mathematics, which is one of the fundamental tools of science.

Indeed, if Brockman is correct, disinterest is only a reflection of the ignorance of most of the so-called intellectuals of the Western world, including most of America's teachers. Although the usefulness of science is widely recognized and our fascination with the technology resulting from its applications increases, relatively few of us have had our curiosity really piqued by any scientific idea, and still fewer understand the vital connections that have developed over the centuries between the seemingly dry facts of science and our notions of beauty, goodness, and spirit.

The value of an understanding of science, however, extends far beyond our capacities for intellectual curiosity or cultural growth. We are bombarded daily with messages that relate or appeal to science and that can profoundly affect our economic and political lives; and numerous individuals and organizations profit mightily by attempting to distort our view of science, both exaggerating and undermining its truth claims, feeding on both our overconfidence and our insecurities. It is crucial to our well-being as individuals and as members of a democratic society that we understand enough about science to assess the many claims made in its name. A broader understanding of science, therefore, including its background and development as a discipline, its methods of exploring and establishing truths about nature, as well as some of its current controversies, is necessary for a fuller appreciation of and some sense of control over how it bears on our lives.

The word *science* comes from the Latin word *scientia,* meaning simply "knowledge," but the word has developed numerous additional meanings, of which two are particularly important. First, with ancient Greek and Roman philosophical movements, "science" came to mean a systematic approach to knowledge in general; hence, the study of nature had to be called "natural science" to distinguish it from the many other knowledge disciplines. Second, some four hundred years ago, the most common modern meaning began to emerge from the scientific revolution, and "science" came to mean a systematic approach to the knowledge of the natural world based on reason and experiment.

Science Before the Scientific Revolution

Human culture, from its darkest beginnings, is full of technological discoveries, a part of science in the very broadest sense: the domestication of animals and of plants, the molding and firing of clay, the use of the wheel, the craft of shipbuilding, the invention of writing, the smelting of bronze and then of iron, and many more; each step profoundly affected developments in civilization and culture. But these discoveries, as far as known, were largely fortuitous, certainly not through any systematic study of nature. Systematic observation of nature seems to have begun when priestly groups in cultures from China to Egypt, from Mesopotamia to Pre-Columbian America, began to catalog the motions of the heavenly bodies to establish the times for planting and harvesting. Technological developments and systematic observation by themselves, however, do not make science in the modern sense, although any increase in the body of knowledge, any addition of system to its method of accumulation, helps lay the foundation from which science can develop.

Judaism made significant, though somewhat indirect, contributions to that foundation. If the Bible is, as some have said, less a book than a collection of books, it can be described as the world's first great library. Its focus, however, was on systematic approaches to theology and moral philosophy and to some extent history but not to science. In addition, Judaism, like many cultures, had its own lore about the practical concerns of life, and much of that lore would later be seen to be scientifically justified—the dietary laws, for example, no doubt protected Jews from many diseases. Even so, the Biblical authors' justification for those laws was always theological—they were God's commands—not scientific in the modern sense. Nevertheless, the Judaic tradition fostered a profound respect for learning, which was preserved and expanded in its applications as Western culture developed. For this reason, many of the world's greatest scholars have been Jews, and in our own century, they are perhaps the most fully represented ethnic group among Nobel Prize laureates in the sciences.

The rise of humanism, associated primarily with the height of Greek civilization in the fifth century B.C.E., marked a major increase in the systematic study of nature. Ionian Greek scholars in the sixth century B.C.E. were among the first to look for naturalistic rather than theological explanations for objects and events in nature. For example, lightning to Homer in the eighth century B.C.E. was the action of an angry Zeus, but to the sixth century B.C.E. philosopher Anaximander, it was the result of pent up wind escaping suddenly from clouds. The Greeks also developed a rhetorical tradition, inspired perhaps by their democratic institutions, that demanded not only reason but demonstration, a principle that when applied to nature meant physical demonstration. But anything like real experimentation was rare, and observations often continued to be explained in terms of theological or highly questionable rationalistic assumptions. For example, Pythagoras, who in the sixth century B.C.E. produced the famous theorem that the square of the hypotenuse of a right triangle is equal to the sum of the squares of the two sides, saw this and other relations as indications that mathematics revealed the basic principles of all things, an idea dear to the hearts of many modern scientists. But he saw those relations as mystic, and his "school" was as much a cult as an institution of learning. In the fourth century B.C.E., Aristotle saw motion as a natural attribute of all physical objects, which were believed to be composed of four fundamental substances: earth and water, whose natural motions were downward, and air and fire, whose natural motions were upward. To account for the heavenly bodies, Aristotle posited the existence of a perfect fifth element whose natural motion was circular and eternal. As obviously wrong as these ideas may appear to us now, they came to be generally accepted and remained so for the next two thousand years. Nevertheless, Aristotle's observations were often highly accurate, especially in the biological sciences in which he created the basis for modern classification systems (he recognized, for example, that whales and porpoises were mammals), contributions for which Charles Darwin, some 2200 years later, would acknowledge his indebtedness.

The contributions of humanism to science culminated in the establishment of the library of Alexandria in Egypt about 300 B.C.E., which stood for seven centuries and which Carl Sagan describes as "the brain and glory of the greatest city on the planet, the first true research institute in the history of the world." In addition to the 70 Hebrew scholars who produced the Septuagint, the Greek translation of the Torah, Alexandria's large community of scholars included Archimedes (third century B.C.E.), engineer and physicist who discovered how to mathematically describe and experimentally determine the density of an object; Euclid (third century B.C.E.), mathematician and physicist whose geometry is still taught today almost intact; Eratosthenes (third century B.C.E.), mathematician and astronomer who deduced that the earth is round and computed its diameter to within only a small percent error; Galen (second century B.C.E.), anatomist and physician who became the Western world's major medical authority for nearly two millennia; Ptolemy (second century C.E.), astronomer and geographer who created a model for describing the motions of heavenly bodies that prevailed in the Western world for the next millennium and a half; Hypatia, a woman reputed to be the greatest mathematician of her time, expert in numerous other areas of learning, slain in 415 C.E. at the instigation of St. Cyril, Bishop of Alexandria, by a fanatical Christian mob, some 25 years after Cyril's predecessor, in a similar spirit of anti-intellectualism, had instigated the burning of the great library in Alexandria.

As significant as the contributions of Greek humanism to science were, they fell short of initiating any scientific revolution because they caused no fundamental change in how humanity looked at or acted in the world. New theoretical knowledge emerged rarely and remained largely within a small elite group of scholars, and any new technology was likewise too little known or too rare to inspire any faith in the fruits of scientific progress. As a result, science languished in the Roman Empire, where interest flourished in certain practical areas of learning—politics, the law, rhetoric, architecture—but where little of the Greek interest in learning for its own sake prevailed.

Although Christianity contributed little directly to the growth of science, it would be a mistake to define the relation of Christianity with science in terms of the extreme opposition suggested by the murder of Hypatia. In fact, the concept of the Incarnation, the belief that God became flesh in Christ, uniting the human and the divine, provided the basis for the argument that God thereby acknowledged the value and dignity of the flesh and of the material world; the view of the world as a stable cosmos regulated by a benevolent deity encouraged Christians to look for system and regularity in the visible world. The study of nature could not, therefore, be evil. Even so, the material world was still seen as lower than that of the spiritual, and although the Church did not oppose natural science, it did nothing to encourage it. Until the sixteenth century, there was not much in the way of any other significant forces encouraging science.

In fact, in the late Classical period, as Rome began its protracted fall and as barbarian invaders threatened its borders, interest in science declined further. Christian monastics did preserve some ancient learning, but the proportion saved was small. The library at Alexandria, for example, is reported to have contained 123 plays by Sophocles alone. Seven survive today. For the survival of Greek science, we are more indebted to Near Eastern culture than to Christian. For example, developments by Indian mathematicians Brahmagupta (c. 628), Mahavira (c. 850), and Bhaskara (1114-1185) and by Persian poet, mathematician, and astronomer Omar Khayyám advanced algebra well beyond what the Greeks had achieved and beyond anything the Western world would achieve until the seventeenth century. In fact, Aristotle's work was all but lost to the West until the twelfth century when many of his works were translated into Latin from Arabic manuscripts found in libraries in Islamic Spain.

Because of interest stimulated by these translations in the High Middle Ages, the twelfth and thirteenth centuries, science in the tradition of systematic philosophy and theology began to be studied in universities modeled to some degree on the academies established by Plato and Aristotle. The medieval universities were created primarily to train clergymen and, as a result, there was much less of the spirit of free inquiry that had characterized the Classical academies and much more emphasis on mastering an established body of learning and dogma. Nevertheless, these academies provided the basis for an international community of scholars through whom new knowledge could spread. Science, in the modern sense, began to emerge when a few scholars began independently to observe nature closely and, perhaps most importantly, to conduct controlled observations and to design experiments that tested the "truths" they had been taught. Such investigations did not trigger a revolution in ideas, however; the process was much more gradual. Indeed, it was some five hundred years later when the findings of the Polish astronomer Copernicus began to undermine many of the basic assumptions that were used to explain the operations of the universe.

Authority and the Scientific Revolution

One of the most basic of medieval assumptions on the operation of the universe relates to a problem Owen Barfield describes as the twentieth century's "chronological snobbery," that is, our tendency to devalue the past, to see the present, the modern world, as the most civilized, informed, advanced, and important of all time. This is unquestionably a fault, but it is a relatively new fault. For most of human existence, at least for as long as language has permitted the preservation and transmission of the past, chronological snobbery has worked in the opposite direction. The greatest value has been attached to the old, to what was thought to have been established from the beginning of time, to what has withstood the test of time. In fact, one of the ways in which science has been most revolutionary is precisely in reversing this attitude. That is why a central issue surrounding the scientific revolution was the question of which authority establishes "truth."

Up to the beginning of the scientific revolution in the sixteenth and seventeenth centuries, the prime authority for truth, scientific or otherwise, was traditional in that the presumed validity of any idea was dependent on texts handed down from the ancients. Although the two major acknowledged sources of knowledge, revelation and reason, might seem to be ongoing processes, their major manifestations were in fact seen to have already taken place: revelation was embodied in the Bible; reason was embodied in the texts of the great philosophers, especially Aristotle. In effect, the Judeo-Christian concept of honoring sacred texts had been applied as well to the surviving texts of ancient philosophers—a little less rigorously, however, for in any dispute between the sacred and the worldly realms, revelation, the authority for which was divine, took precedence over reason, the authority for which was human. After the work of the great medieval philosophers, especially Thomas Aquinas, revelation and reason were seen as largely compatible, as parts of a grand system, and any gaps within it were considered as indications of the weakness of human reason, not as flaws in the system itself. No fundamentally new knowledge was expected, or desired, to emerge. Those who wanted to know the truth were to consult the ancient texts and those texts commenting on them, and any new contribution would only be in the form of further commentary.

This medieval synthesis was a tenuous one and was held together primarily by the embodiment of these traditional sources of authority in institutions. That is, knowledge was officially approved by both church and state; arguments might arise over whether church or state should exert authority in a particular case (indeed, much of medieval history concerns the working out, sometimes violently, of their rival claims), but both institutions would agree on the principle of the authority of the ancient traditions. Both saw knowledge as part of a grand and essentially coherent system because they saw authority as part of that grand system, both of which were ordained by God. Especially to those in powerful positions, whether in church or state, all authority, that of clergy over laity, of king over noble and subject, of master over servant, and of man over woman, was grounded in the past and the more ancient, the better. Any notion of change, certainly any fundamental change, was subversive, for to question any one authority was to threaten all.

During the early stages of the rise of modern science, those in authority had cause to feel threatened. When Galileo's *The Starry Messenger* was published in 1610, the Protestant Reformation was already a century old, the age of exploration (da Gama, Columbus, and Magellan) was a century and a half old, both of which introduced profound changes in a culture reluctant to change. In addition, for some time before the fall of Constantinople a century and a half earlier, a small flood of Greek scholars had been migrating to Western Europe; with the aid of ancient manuscripts unknown in the West, they initiated a revival of Plato that gradually began to challenge the dominance of Aristotle and to open a new era of philosophical speculation. In addition, Europe was far from politically stable. In fact, the religious, social, and political order all seemed threatened, and those in power struggled to maintain the old order not merely to hold on to their privileged positions but, as many sincerely believed, to keep the fabric of society from unraveling altogether.

The resulting instability and insecurity surrounding the concept of authority explains the basis for the resistance to the scientific revolution and why, in fact, it was a revolution. That resistance must be understood and kept in historical perspective in order to avoid the bewilderment often suffered by modern readers confronting relatively ancient scientific texts: why do writers like Galileo have so much trouble presenting ideas and observations that are taken for granted today? First, these authors were usually writing not to a general audience interested in scientific information but to a body of scholars wedded to a different way of looking at the phenomena in question. Second, because of the habit of bowing to tradition, the authority of the past, the audience was usually reluctant to even consider a new approach, and the writer had to take special care to be convincing without being insulting or seeming to be presumptuous. Third, there was often no common body of belief, not even a faulty theory, to explain the phenomena in question, and the writer was forced to build his field from its very foundations. Galileo is one of the more lucid of the early science writers in part because he did not have to deal with this third problem: he had a coherent theory to react against, the Ptolemaic system, and Copernicus had already laid the new foundations for change. But in order to understand the scientific revolution in general and the Copernican revolution in particular, we need to understand a little more about the systems of cosmological thought contending against each other.

The Old Versus the New Model for the Universe

The scientific revolution is commonly said to have begun in the middle of the sixteenth century with the publication of Copernicus' *De Revolutionibus Orbium Coelestium (Concerning the Revolutions of Celestial Bodies)* (1543). Copernicus was the first to argue on a sound mathematical basis for the universe being heliocentric, centered around the Sun, as opposed to the Ptolemaic system, which for more than fourteen centuries had embodied the dominant view, that the Earth was the center of the universe. This initial struggle in the scientific revolution, between Ptolemaic and Copernican views of the universe, illustrates the degree to which fundamental spiritual values become linked, rightly or wrongly, to the way the physical universe is conceived.

The Ptolemaic system of the universe provided a picture of order, a series of concentric circles (actually they were conceived of as spheres) with Earth at the center, surrounded in turn by the spheres of the Moon, Mercury, Venus, the Sun, Mars, Jupiter, Saturn, and finally the outermost sphere of the fixed stars (see Figure 1). Beyond that was the empyreum, the realm of God and the an-

FIGURE 6–1

The system of the world in broad outline according to the Medieval astronomers, from Armitage, A., *Sun, Stand Thou Still: The Life and Work of Copernicus,* New York: Henry Schuman, 1947, 140.

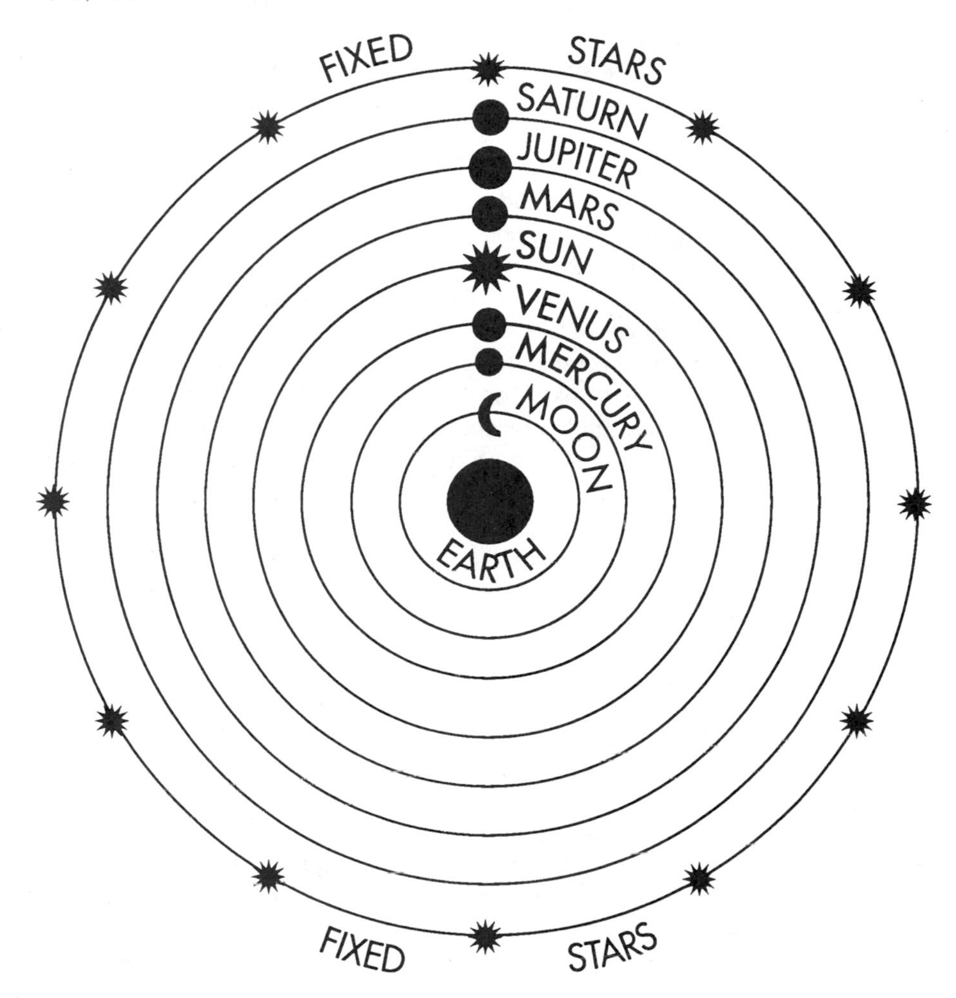

gels. As odd as it may appear today, the Ptolemaic system was for a millennium and a half a practical and satisfying view of the universe.

On the practical level, the Ptolemaic system satisfied common sense because everything in the heavens does seem to revolve around the Earth. Also, it helped explain other obvious phenomena, like the difference between the "fixed" stars, that is, those that maintain so constant a relation to each other that they are identified by their groupings or constellations, and the "planets," literally (in Greek) "wanderers," which move independently across the backdrop of the fixed stars. The Ptolemaic view was also useful because it provided a model on the basis of which the motions of the heavenly bodies could be predicted fairly accurately. Thus, it served the needs of navigation by providing reliable signposts, of agriculture by helping to mark the seasons, and of daily life by providing the basis for a calendar.

More than a practical way of viewing the universe, however, the Ptolemaic system developed into the symbol of an elaborate body of values by satisfying other needs:

1 It satisfied reason, that is, that notion of the higher kind of common sense handed down primarily from the Greeks that drew logical deductions from supposedly self-evident truths. Ptolemy accepted Aristotle's Earth-centered view, including his rationalistic notion that the heavens constituted a realm of perfection, that the sphere of the Moon marked the division between the higher and perfect celestial realm and the dull, "sublunary," imperfect world of the Earth. The "self-evident" basis for this logic was the association of matter with heaviness, lowness, and imperfection on the one hand and of spirit with lightness, height, and perfection on the other. Thus, in this scheme, there is movement from base matter on Earth to purified matter in the heavenly bodies to pure spirit in the empyreum. Bodies in the realm of perfected matter, according to Aristotle, were perfect spheres with smooth shining surfaces, unlike the irregular and imperfect surface of the Earth, and they moved eternally in that most perfect of two-dimensional forms, the circle.

2 It satisfied the need for a spiritual order. Although Ptolemy was not Christian, his system lent itself very well to, and by the Middle Ages had been incorporated fully into, Christian cosmology. It was easy to equate the philosophical concept of earthly imperfection with the religious concept of sin; indeed, many writers described the Earth's surface not just in terms of the idea that irregularity meant imperfection, but in terms of the metaphor of a diseased body; its irregularities were the outward signs of spiritual corruption. Moreover, Earth was at the literal bottom of the universe, an appropriate place for fallen humanity. In fact, hell was imagined to be either on a physical level with us, on the opposite side of the globe, or in the only lower place one could get, beneath the surface.

3 It answered the need for traditional authority. Ptolemy himself was, of course, an ancient whose model was based largely on that even more ancient (by about 500 years) and most respected of philosophers, Aristotle. Moreover, the Bible in no way contradicted Ptolemy's model and in an occasional passage seemed to support the idea of the sun moving around the Earth: most notably Joshua's prayer, which God answered, that the sun stand still so his army could have more time to slaughter the Amorites (Joshua 10:12–14).

4 It answered the need for beauty. Renaissance theories of beauty placed great emphasis on geometric form and mathematical proportion. Certain geometric figures, especially the circle, and certain ratios were thought to be inherently pleasing to the eye, and some artists, Leonardo da Vinci, for example, had worked out elaborate systems for describing the proper proportions of the ideal human figure. Many of the same rationalistic and aesthetic assumptions lie behind both da Vinci's theories of anatomical proportions and the diagram of the Ptolemaic universe. It may seem surprising, but science has always had an aesthetic side. The great scientific theories are distinguished by what scientists like to call their "elegance," a quality of simplicity and coherence in complexity that is really impossible to distinguish from what artists call the beautiful (Einstein once said that his theory of relativity simply had to be true; it was too beautiful not to be). Indeed, the Ptolemaic cosmology, in its wonderfully symmetrical system of concentric circles, seemed to possess this kind of elegance. And this was an elegance, like all beautiful things, that seemed to extend beyond itself to embrace within its material order the rational and spiritual order described above. It must have, indeed, seemed in the sixteenth century too beautiful not to be true.

With all of these needs that the Ptolemaic system fulfilled, that there could be any reason to challenge its authority seems surprising, but there were in fact many. Although it was quite literally the picture of simplicity in broad outline, in practice it was curiously complex. Because the planets do in fact circle the sun, accounting for their motions in an Earth-centered system required complicated adjustments (eccentrics and epicycles, they were called) that were only approximately accurate and that became increasingly complicated as inaccuracies multiplied over time. To those in the late sixteenth century who looked at it closely, the Ptolemaic system seemed to be losing its elegance, like a symphony played by an orchestra going increasingly out of tune.

The system created by the Polish astronomer Copernicus, though clearly superior to Ptolemy's from a modern scientific perspective, did not have an immediate impact on the world. The reasons for this are many. As can be seen by comparing Copernicus' system (Figure 2) with Ptolemy's system (Figure 1), the two did not really appear much different at first glance; indeed, Copernicus continued to adhere to some of the old rationalistic assumptions in his preference for perfect circles. Published in Latin, *De Revolutionibus* had as its audience a small scholarly and clerical community, which limited both its spread and its threat to authority. Copernicus, moreover, did not agree to the publication of his work until he was dying so that when it appeared he would be unavailable for attack. In addition, he confined himself almost entirely to purely astronomical issues, avoiding the theological and philosophical ramifications of his system. He did provide a valuable new mathematical model for computing the positions of planets, but that model only further limited his audience to a relatively few scholars. Last, there was still not a body of sufficiently accurate and generally accepted observations against which the Copernican model could be readily tested; thus, it could be seen as merely speculative.

Nevertheless, Copernicus's work had attracted the attention of a small scientific community, and by the first decade of the seventeenth century, that work began to bear fruit. Three names stand out in this regard. First was Tycho

FIGURE 6–2

The system of the world in broad outline according to Copernicus, from Armitage, A., *Sun, Stand Thou Still: The Life and Work of Copernicus,* New York: Henry Schuman, 1947, 141.

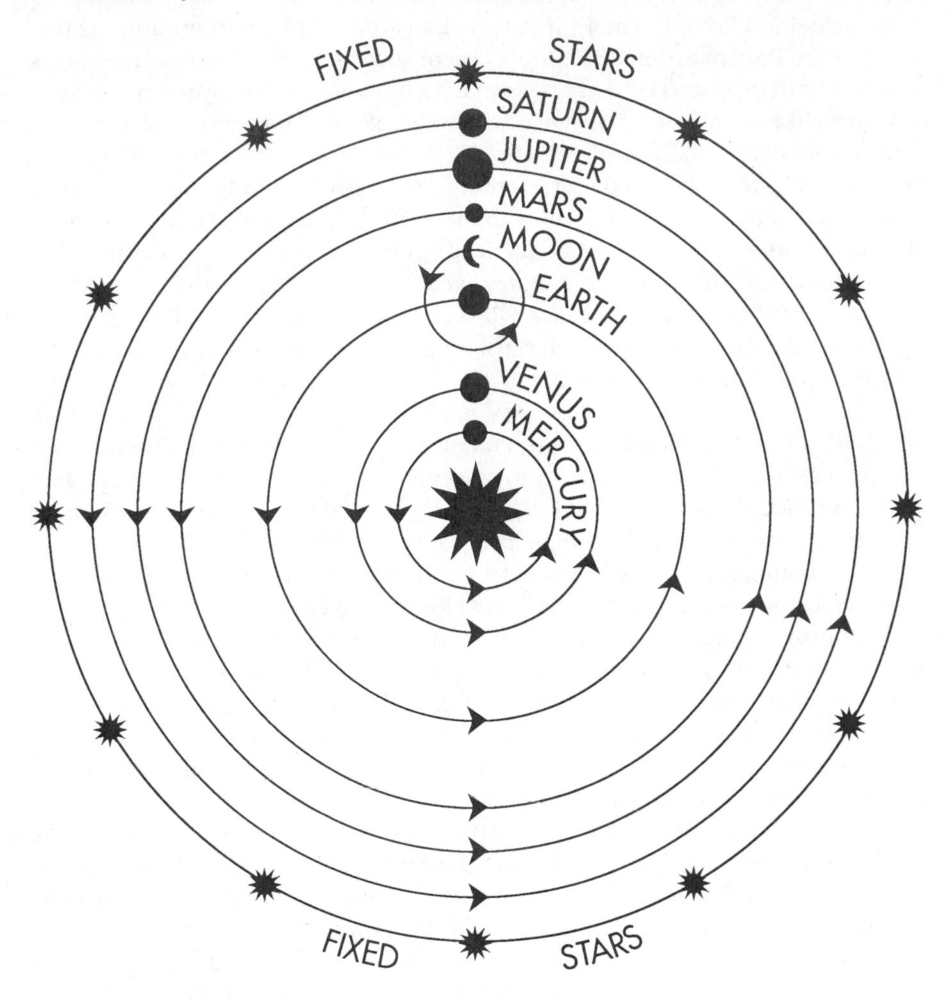

Brahe, a Danish exile in Prague who accumulated the most accurate set of data on planetary positions available before the invention of the telescope. Next was Johannes Kepler, the German astronomer who, with the aid of Tycho's data, determined that the planetary orbits were not circular but elliptical (Kepler's First Law of Planetary Motion) and that, in its orbit, a planet sweeps out equal areas in equal times (Kepler's Second Law). The third name is Galileo.

GALILEO GALILEI, *FROM* THE STARRY MESSENGER

Galileo Galilei (1564 - 1642) raised the scientific revolution to a new level, partly because of his success in reaching a wider audience. Though he understood and extended Copernicus' mathematical analyses of planetary positions, he rested the bulk of his arguments on direct observation through his own specially designed telescope. And since the telescope was so obviously valuable in navigation and warfare, its use rapidly spread, so that anyone who read his book could also confirm his observations. The radical process of challenging authority through an appeal to direct observation of nature, which we associate with modern science, was suddenly raised to a level where institutional authority could no longer ignore it.

Born in Pisa in 1564, Galileo received the standard classical and religious education of the well-to-do of his time, but he began to surpass that standard education when he went to the University of Pisa. There he studied medicine and upset his professors by challenging the major classical authorities in that field, Aristotle and Galen. He then studied mathematics at Florence, where he took his degree. By the age of 24 he was a lecturer in mathematics at Pisa, and three years later, in 1592, he accepted the chair of mathematics at the University of Padua, where he remained for the next eighteen years. During his lifetime he made major contributions to science in his experiments with magnetism and hydrostatics, while his understanding of the implications of his experiments with falling bodies and the pendulum laid the groundwork for Newton's discovery of the laws of motion a half century later. But it was his work in astronomy that attracted the greatest immediate attention, beginning with the publication in 1610 of his *Sidereus nuncius* (*The Starry Messenger*). Here Galileo showed how his observations with the telescope confirmed the Copernican system: he demonstrated that the Moon has mountains, valleys, and other geologic features much like Earth; he discovered four moons circling Jupiter, just as the Moon circles Earth; he showed that Venus had phases like the Moon that were consistent with its position relative to the Earth and the Sun according to the Copernican system. In short, Earth was not, as the Ptolemaic system claimed, unique in form or position—it was another planet.

Church authorities took exception to Galileo's arguments, and attacks on him appeared maintaining that those arguments contradicted scripture. Galileo attempted to answer these attacks in letter which he directed in 1615 to Christina, Grand Duchess of Tuscany, because he thought her to be a friend and a power in court, and because he hoped she would respond to the chance he was offering her to become the patron saint of science. And science needed a patron saint, for Galileo recognized that the crisis he faced was more than a personal one: the question was whether "in discussions of physical problems we ought to begin . . . from the authority of scriptural passages" or "from sense-experiences and necessary demonstrations";

and in cases where such demonstrations are more complicated than common observers can comprehend, which authority takes precedence, a theologian or an astronomer-mathematician.

Although later scholars thought he did an effective job of arguing his case, a year later the Roman Catholic Church condemned the Copernican system, laying a ban against teaching it which would remain in effect until 1821. Galileo tried to get around that ban by presenting the controversy in 1632 in the form of a debate between two characters in a fictional setting, *Dialogo . . . sopra i due massimi sistemi del mondo (Dialogue over the Two Chief World Systems.* His hope was that the author's position apart from the debate would protect him, partly because he would present the contending arguments and leave the decision up to the reader, and partly because a friend of his had in the meantime become Pope Urban VIII, who Galileo was led to believe encouraged the project. But the dialog approach did not save him. This may have had something to do with the fact that he placed the defense of the Aristotelian-Ptolemaic system in the mouth of a character named Simplicio, which in Italian means "simpleton." The next year, the 69-year-old Galileo was tried by the Inquisition, convicted of violating the ban of 1616, and forced under threat of torture to confess his error and recant his position; in addition, he was placed under a kind of house arrest that lasted until his death nine years later. His works, moreover, were placed on the Index of forbidden works, where they remained until 1835.

In 1893, Pope Leo XIII in his encyclical *Providentissimus Deus* stated the official Church position on the relations of science and religion, which was in substance little different from Galileo's as presented in the letter to Christina, though no reference was made to Galileo himself. In 1979, Pope John Paul II requested a Vatican commission to reconsider the Galileo case, and on October 31, 1992, he acted on its report, formally admitting that the Church had erred. In the meantime, Galileo had become a heroic and lasting symbol in the struggle for freedom in the pursuit of knowledge.

from The Starry Messenger

Galileo Galilei

1 Great indeed are the things which in this brief treatise I propose for observation and consideration by all students of nature. I say great, because of the excellence of the subject itself, the entirely unexpected and novel character of these things, and finally because of the instrument by means of which they have been revealed to our senses.

2 Surely it is a great thing to increase the numerous host of fixed stars previously visible to the unaided vision, adding countless more which have never before been seen, exposing these plainly to the eye in numbers ten times exceeding the old and familiar stars.

3 It is a very beautiful thing, and most gratifying to the sight, to behold the body of the moon, distant from us almost sixty earthly radii,[1] as if it were no farther away than two such measures—so that its diameter appears almost thirty times larger, its surface nearly nine hundred times, and its volume twenty-seven thousand times as large as when viewed with the naked eye. In this way one may learn with all the certainty of sense evidence that the moon is not robed in a smooth and polished surface but is in fact rough and uneven, covered everywhere, just like the earth's surface, with huge prominences, deep valleys, and chasms.

4 Again, it seems to me a matter of no small importance to have ended the dispute about the Milky Way by making its nature manifest to the very senses as well as to the intellect.[2] Similarly it will be a pleasant and elegant thing to demonstrate that the nature of those stars which astronomers have previously called "nebulous" is far different from what has been believed hitherto. But what surpasses all wonders by far, and what particularly moves us to seek the attention of all astronomers and philosophers, is the discovery of four wandering stars[3] not known or observed by any man before us. Like Venus and Mercury, which have their own periods about the sun, these have theirs about a certain star that is conspicuous among those already known, which they sometimes precede and sometimes follow, without ever departing from it beyond certain limits. All these facts were discovered and observed by me not many days ago with the aid of a spyglass which I devised, after first being illuminated by divine grace. Perhaps other things, still more remarkable, will in time be discovered by me or by other observers with the aid of such an instrument, the form and construction of which I shall first briefly explain, as well as the occasion of its having been devised. Afterwards I shall relate the story of the observations I have made.

5 About ten months ago a report reached my ears that a certain Fleming[4] had constructed a spyglass by means of which visible objects, though very distant

---

[1] The original text reads "diameters" here and in another place. That this error was Galileo's and not the printer's has been convincingly shown by Edward Rosen. The slip was a curious one, as astronomers of all schools had long agreed that the maximum distance of the moon was approximately sixty terrestrial radii. Still more curious is the fact that neither Kepler nor any other correspondent appears to have called Galileo's attention to this error; not even a friend who ventured to criticize the calculations in this very passage.

[2] In a section not included here Galileo explains how the telescope reveals that the Milky Way, about which there had been considerable speculation, is in fact "a congeries of innumerable stars."

[3] In the terminology of his time Galileo often calls any celestial body a "star," using "fixed star" and "wandering star" to distinguish between stars and planets. The "four wandering stars" moving "about a certain star" are the four largest moons circling the planet Jupiter.

[4] Credit for the original invention is generally assigned to Hans Lipperhey, a lens grinder in Holland who chanced upon this property of combined lenses and applied for a patent on it in 1608.

from the eye of the observer, were distinctly seen as if nearby. Of this truly remarkable effect several experiences were related, to which some persons gave credence while others denied them. A few days later the report was confirmed to me in a letter from a noble Frenchman at Paris, Jacques Badovere, which caused me to apply myself wholeheartedly to inquire into the means by which I might arrive at the invention of a similar instrument. This I did shortly afterwards, my basis being the theory of refraction. First I prepared a tube of lead, at the ends of which I fitted two glass lenses, both plane on one side while on the other side one was spherically convex and the other concave. Then placing my eye near the concave lens I perceived objects satisfactorily large and near, for they appeared three times closer and nine times larger than when seen with the naked eye alone. Next I constructed another one, more accurate, which represented objects as enlarged more than sixty times. Finally, sparing neither labor nor expense, I succeeded in constructing for myself so excellent an instrument that objects seen by means of it appeared nearly one thousand times larger and over thirty times closer than when regarded with our natural vision.

6 It would be superfluous to enumerate the number and importance of the advantages of such an instrument at sea as well as on land. But forsaking terrestrial observations, I turned to celestial ones, and first I saw the moon from as near at hand as if it were scarcely two terrestrial radii away. After that I observed often with wondering delight both the planets and the fixed stars, and since I saw these latter to be very crowded, I began to seek (and eventually found) a method by which I might measure their distances apart. . . .

7 Now let us review the observations made during the past two months, once more inviting the attention of all who are eager for true philosophy to the first steps of such important contemplations. Let us speak first of that surface of the moon which faces us. For greater clarity I distinguish two parts of this surface, a lighter and a darker; the lighter part seems to surround and to pervade the whole hemisphere, while the darker part discolors the moon's surface like a kind of cloud, and makes it appear covered with spots. Now those spots which are fairly dark and rather large are plain to everyone and have been seen throughout the ages; these I shall call the "large" or "ancient" spots, distinguishing them from others that are smaller in size but so numerous as to occur all over the lunar surface, and especially the lighter part. The latter spots had never been seen by anyone before me. From observations of these spots repeated many times I have been led to the opinion and conviction that the surface of the moon is not smooth, uniform, and precisely spherical as a great number of philosophers believe it (and the other heavenly bodies) to be, but is uneven, rough, and full of cavities and prominences, being not unlike the face of the earth, relieved by chains of mountains and deep valleys. The things I have seen by which I was enabled to draw this conclusion are as follows.

Lipperhey had discovered how lenses commonly available for spectacles could be used to produce a magnification of about three times. Galileo developed the idea and technology to produce much higher magnification in the first astronomical quality telescopes.

8 On the fourth or fifth day after new moon, when the moon is seen with brilliant horns, the boundary which divides the dark part from the light does not extend uniformly in an oval line as would happen on a perfectly spherical solid, but traces out an uneven, rough, and very wavy line as shown in the figure below. Indeed, many luminous excrescences extend beyond the boundary into the darker portion, while on the other hand some dark patches invade the illuminated part. Moreover a great quantity of small blackish spots, entirely separated from the dark region, are scattered almost all over the area illuminated by the sun with the exception only of that part which is occupied by the large and ancient spots. Let us note, however, that the said small spots always agree in having their blackened parts directed toward the sun, while on the side opposite the sun they are crowned with bright contours, like shining summits. There is a similar sight on earth about sunrise, when we behold the valleys not yet flooded with light though the mountains surrounding them are already ablaze with glowing splendor on the side opposite the sun. And just as the shadows in the hollows on earth diminish in size as the sun rises higher, so these spots on the moon lose their blackness as the illuminated region grows larger and larger.

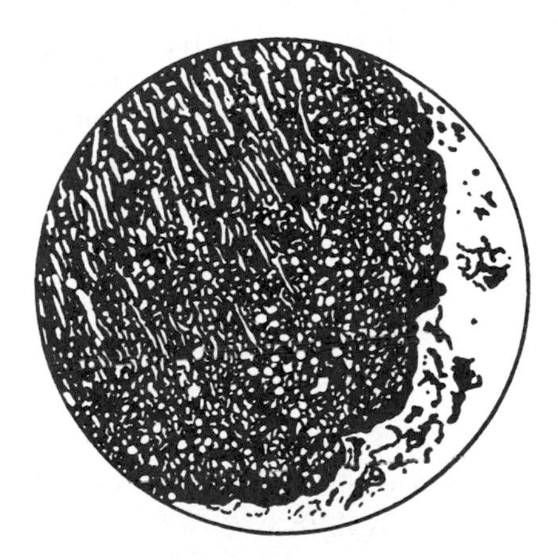

9 Again, not only are the boundaries of shadow and light in the moon seen to be uneven and wavy, but still more astonishingly many bright points appear within the darkened portion of the moon, completely divided and separated from the illuminated part and at a considerable distance from it. After a time these gradually increase in size and brightness, and an hour or two later they become joined with the rest of the lighted part which has now increased in size. Meanwhile more and more peaks shoot up as if sprouting now here, now there, lighting up within the shadowed portion; these become larger, and finally they too are united with that same luminous surface which extends ever further. An illustration of this is to be seen in the figure above. And on the earth, before the rising of the sun, are not the highest peaks of the mountains illuminated by the sun's rays while the plains remain in shadow? Does not the light go

on spreading while the larger central parts of those mountains are becoming illuminated? And when the sun has finally risen, does not the illumination of plains and hills finally become one? But on the moon the variety of elevations and depressions appears to surpass in every way the roughness of the terrestrial surface, as we shall demonstrate further on. . . .

10 We have now briefly recounted the observations made thus far with regard to the moon, the fixed stars, and the Milky Way. There remains the matter which in my opinion deserves to be considered the most important of all—the disclosure of four PLANETS never seen from the creation of the world up to our own time, together with the occasion of my having discovered and studied them, their arrangements, and the observations made of their movements and alterations during the past two months. I invite all astronomers to apply themselves to examine them and determine their periodic times, something which has so far been quite impossible to complete, owing to the shortness of the time. Once more, however, warning is given that it will be necessary to have a very accurate telescope such as we have described at the beginning of this discourse.

11 On the seventh day of January in this present year 1610, at the first hour of night, when I was viewing the heavenly bodies with a telescope, Jupiter presented itself to me; and because I had prepared a very excellent instrument for myself, I perceived (as I had not before, on account of the weakness of my previous instrument) that beside the planet there were three starlets, small indeed, but very bright. Though I believed them to be among the host of fixed stars, they aroused my curiosity somewhat by appearing to lie in an exact straight line parallel to the ecliptic, and by their being more splendid than others of their size. Their arrangement with respect to Jupiter and each other was the following:

East * * O * **West**

that is, there were two stars on the eastern side and one to the west. The most easterly star and the western one appeared larger than the other. I paid no attention to the distances between them and Jupiter, for at the outset I thought them to be fixed stars, as I have said.[5] But returning to the same investigation on January eighth—led by what, I do not know—I found a very different arrangement. The three starlets were now all to the west of Jupiter, closer together, and at equal intervals from one another as shown in the following sketch:

East O * * * **West**

---

[5] The reader should remember that the telescope was nightly revealing to Galileo hundreds of fixed stars never previously observed. His unusual gifts for astronomical observation are illustrated by his having noticed and remembered these three merely by reason of their alignment, and recalling them so well that when by chance he happened to see them the following night he was certain that they had changed their positions. No such plausible and candid account of the discovery was given by the rival astronomer Simon Mayr, who four years later claimed priority.

12 At this time, though I did not yet turn my attention to the way the stars had come together, I began to concern myself with the question how Jupiter could be east of all these stars when on the previous day it had been west of two of them. I commended to wonder whether Jupiter was not moving eastward at that time, contrary to the computations of the astronomers, and had got in front of them by that motion.[6] Hence it was with great interest that I awaited the next night. But I was disappointed in my hopes, for the sky was then covered with clouds everywhere.

13 On the tenth of January, however, the stars appeared in this position with respect to Jupiter:

East * * O West

that is, there were but two of them, both easterly, the third (as I supposed) being hidden behind Jupiter. As at first, they were in the same straight line with Jupiter and were arranged precisely in the line of the zodiac. Noticing this, and knowing that there was no way in which such alterations could be attributed to Jupiter's motion, yet being certain that these were still the same stars I had observed (in fact no other was to be found along the line of the zodiac for a long way on either side of Jupiter), my perplexity was now transformed into amazement. I was sure that the apparent changes belonged not to Jupiter but to the observed stars, and I resolved to pursue this investigation with greater care and attention.

14 And thus, on the eleventh of January, I saw the following disposition:

East * * O West

There were two stars, both to the east, the central one being three times as far from Jupiter as from the one farthest east. The latter star was nearly double the size of the former, whereas on the night before they had appeared approximately equal.

15 I had now decided beyond all question that there existed in the heavens three stars wandering about Jupiter as do Venus and Mercury about the sun, and this became plainer than daylight from observations on similar occasions which followed. Nor were there just three such stars; four wanderers complete their revolutions about Jupiter, and of their alterations as observed more precisely later on we shall give a description here. Also I measured the distances between them by means of the telescope, using the method explained before. Moreover I recorded the times of the observations, especially when more than one was made during the same night—for the revolutions of these planets are so speedily completed that it is usually possible to take even their hourly variations. . . .

---

[6] Jupiter was at this time in "retrograde" motion; that is, the earth's motion made the planet appear to be moving westward among the fixed stars.

16 Such are the observations concerning the four Medicean planets recently first discovered by me, and although from these data their periods have not yet been reconstructed in numerical form, it is legitimate at least to put in evidence some facts worthy of note. Above all, since they sometimes follow and sometimes precede Jupiter by the same intervals, and they remain within very limited distances either to east or west of Jupiter, accompanying that planet in both its retrograde and direct movements in a constant manner, no one can doubt that they complete their revolutions about Jupiter and at the same time effect all together a twelve-year period about the center of the universe. That they also revolve in unequal circles is manifestly deduced from the fact that at the greatest elongation[7] from Jupiter it is never possible to see two of these planets in conjunction, whereas in the vicinity of Jupiter they are found united two, three, and sometimes all four together. It is also observed that the revolutions are swifter in those planets which describe smaller circles about Jupiter, since the stars closest to Jupiter are usually seen to the east when on the previous day they appeared to the west, and vice versa, while the planet which traces the largest orbit appears upon accurate observation of its returns to have a semimonthly period.

17 Here we have a fine and elegant argument for quieting the doubts of those who, while accepting with tranquil mind the revolutions of the planets about the sun in the Copernican system, are mightily disturbed to have the moon alone revolve about the earth and accompany it in an annual rotation about the sun. Some have believed that this structure of the universe should be rejected as impossible. But now we have not just one planet rotating about another while both run through a great orbit around the sun; our own eyes show us four stars which wander around Jupiter as does the moon around the earth, while all together trace out a grand revolution about the sun in the space of twelve years.

18 And finally we should not omit the reason for which the Medicean stars appear sometimes to be twice as large as at other times, though their orbits about Jupiter are very restricted. We certainly cannot seek the cause in terrestrial vapors, as Jupiter and its neighboring fixed stars are not seen to change size in the least while this increase and diminution are taking place. It is quite unthinkable that the cause of variation should be their change of distance from the earth at perigee and apogee, since a small circular rotation could by no means produce this effect, and an oval motion (which in this case would have to be nearly straight) seems unthinkable and quite inconsistent with the appearances. But I shall gladly explain what occurs to me on this matter, offering it freely to the judgment and criticism of thoughtful men. It is known that the interposition of terrestrial vapors makes the sun and moon appear large, while the fixed stars and planets are made to appear smaller. Thus the two great luminaries are seen larger when close to the horizon, while the stars appear smaller and for the

---

[7] By this is meant the greatest angular separation from Jupiter attained by any of the satellites.

most part hardly visible. Hence the stars appear very feeble by day and in twilight, though the moon does not, as we have said. Now from what has been said above, and even more from what we shall say at greater length in our *System,* it follows that not only the earth but also the moon is surrounded by an envelope of vapors, and we may apply precisely the same judgment to the rest of the planets. Hence it does not appear entirely impossible to assume that around Jupiter also there exists an envelope denser than the rest of the aether, about which the Medicean planets revolve as does the moon about the elemental sphere. Through the interposition of this envelope they appear larger when they are in perigee by the removal, or at least the attenuation, of this envelope.

19 Time prevents my proceeding further, but the gentle reader may expect more soon.

QUESTIONS FOR WRITING AND DISCUSSION

OBSERVING

1. Describe the major contributions to knowledge that Galileo claims to make in *The Starry Messenger* (summarized in his first paragraphs), and explain how each contribution opposes the accepted opinion at the time.
2. Choose one of Galileo's major points (for example, that the surface of the moon is rough and uneven), and summarize how his observations support his conclusions.

EVALUATING

1. Argue whether Galileo is an effective communicator according to the features of his presentation. Consider his tone, use of evidence, clarity of argument, handling of opposing views, and sense of audience.
2. Given that Galileo's new information would be seen by many to undermine the basis for faith in God, argue whether he should have withheld this information, presented it in a different manner, or done just what he did.

RESPONDING AND APPLYING

1. Is your own scientific knowledge based on direct experience or on something else? Choose some particular scientific issue or principle of interest to you and consider how much of your knowledge is based on faith in the processes of investigation and peer review (the validation by other scientists of the reliability of experimental methods, the logic of argument, and the honesty of the investigators involved in advancing any scientific conclusions).

2. How effective is your own judgment in distinguishing between solid conclusions based on sound observations, reasonable speculations based on limited knowledge, and nonsense? In what areas do you think it important for you or people in general to make such distinctions better?
3. Galileo still held with Copernicus that the Sun was the center not only of the solar system but of the universe. How do you suppose he would feel if he knew that the Sun is in fact only a medium-sized star two thirds of the way out on one spiral arm of a galaxy of a hundred billion stars, itself only a medium-sized galaxy in a universe of another hundred billion galaxies? How does this knowledge of your physical place in the universe affect your philosophical or theological view of your own significance or purpose?

Charles Darwin, *from* The Origin of Species

Although *Charles Darwin* (1809-1882) was the grandson of Erasmus Darwin (1731-1802), one of the earlier thinkers to speculate about an evolutionary universe, as a young man he had little interest in science and not much commitment to anything else. He pursued medical training for a while but found its study boring and its practice (surgery) gruesome. He turned to the ministry by default rather than by any great desire, taking his B.A. from Cambridge in 1831, when he was offered the opportunity to sail with H.M.S. *Beagle* on a five-year, round-the-world voyage of discovery. This was the experience that made him a scientist.

During his voyage, Darwin was especially impressed with the unusual varieties of life that were found in isolated places like Australia, the Galapagos Islands, and New Zealand, and he began to think seriously about their origins. Fairly soon after his return, by 1837 or 1838, he had worked out his major ideas, but these were not printed until 1859. Part of the reason for this delay was Darwin's reclusive spirit, but part also was the intellectual climate of the time, which did not make easy the argument for a natural process of biological development.

The reasons for this intellectual climate had their origins in the previous century. During the eighteenth century, many thinkers had developed a sense of reconciliation between science and religion based largely on the discoveries of Newton at the end of the seventeenth century and a set of assumptions involving what is called "the argument from design." Newton's major contribution in this regard was his study of motion, which suggested that all actions were controlled by universal laws. The argument from design, one of several traditional "proofs" of the existence of God, states that the existence of order in the universe necessarily implies a divine source of that order: more specifically, after Newton, mathematically precise and experimentally demonstrable natural law was seen as proof of the existence of a divine lawgiver. These beliefs were linked with a mechanical model of the universe. That is, the universe was a grand mechanism created by God, who also created the natural laws governing its operations. As a mechanism, the universe was a static structure, most commonly described in terms of a clock, designed so that every part had a predetermined function, and "change" referred only to the revolutions of parts within that structure.

This view not only seemed to satisfy reason, but seemed compatible with the Biblical version of Creation as well. Because the world was an essentially fixed structure, it was not critical to determine when it was created; therefore, Biblical chronology was as good as any (the standard date for creation was 4004 B.C.E., computed early in the eighteenth century from Biblical genealogies by the Anglican Bishop Ussher). Indeed, for some, the growth of science seemed to contribute to a kind of "natural theology," a process defined in the title of the major work summing up these ideas for the eighteenth century, William Paley's *Natural Theology, or Evidences of the Existence and Attributes of the Deity Collected from the Appearances of Nature* (1802). For thinkers like Paley, who used the image of a watch to represent organisms, the more one looked at the incredible intricacies of the machinery of natural design, the perfect adaptations of organisms to survive in their environment, the more one must be convinced by these "evidences" of the wisdom and benevolence of the divine watchmaker, their creator.

What has been described above can be referred to as the static or clock model of the universe, which as a scientific model is analogous to the Ptolemaic universe. Just as the Copernican revolution brought about the displacement of the Ptolemaic system in the sixteenth and seventeenth centuries, in the nineteenth century, the Darwinian revolution, the emergence of an evolutionary or developmental model, brought about the displacement of the static model. The similarities between these two revolutions are that they struck a major blow to humanity's anthropocentric assumptions about the universe and they extended concepts of natural physical laws in important new dimensions. The crucial difference between the two is that the Copernican revolution extended this sense of law spatially, to the planets and stars, applying to the entire physical universe, whereas the Darwinian revolution extended this sense of law temporally, describing the processes by which the universe came to be as we know it, processes operating since the unimaginably distant past by the same laws that govern the present.

What drove science to exploring a new model in this case was similar to what caused the Copernican revolution, the gradual accumulation of new information that seemed increasingly incompatible with the old model. The sources of that information were the newly developing sciences of geology and paleontology.

The crucial geological discovery was what has been called "deep time." Geologists realized, first of all, that "sedimentary" rock had been created by the accumulation of sediments in the bottom of seas and other low-lying areas over so long a period of time that the weight of accumulations above had compressed the sediments into rock. Indeed, there were whole series of layers (or strata) of such sedimentary rock hundreds of feet thick that would have required even longer periods of time to create. Moreover, some of those whole series of strata, originally laid down horizontally, had been somehow turned vertical, been worn down, and had hundreds of feet of new horizontal strata laid on top of them, creating a kind of giant multilayered underground "T" that geologists call an "unconformity" and that would have required even vaster expanses of time to create. These are the kinds of observations that led to the conception of deep time, the recognition that the world might be a thousand, maybe ten thousand *times* as old as Bishop Ussher's Biblically based estimate. (Today's estimates would be more than 70,000 times as old—the earth is now believed to have formed 4.3 to 4.6 billion years ago, the universe from 12-15 billion years ago.)

Paleontology, the study of fossils, the petrified remains of organic life embedded in rocks, also uncovered a number of incompatibilities with the static model. Just as geology reveals a kind of dynamic history of earth in deep time, the fossils embedded in rocks reveal a similar kind of history of organic life. In broad outline, this history suggests a long period in which there was no life at all followed by periods during which increasingly complex life forms appeared. The movement toward more complex forms, however, which some might find a reassuring sign of rational order, is not one-directional or consistent. Regression seems to take place as well as progress, and whole orders of living creatures sometimes disappear. Indeed, the oft-cited extinction of the dinosaurs is only the best known of several mass extinctions found in the fossil record.

During the early 1800s, still long before Darwin's *Origin of Species,* geology (which then included paleontology) split into two camps, although this division was not clear at the time. The first group, which today we would call creationists, clung to the static model, associating themselves with a few central concepts: special creation, the belief that God miraculously created the material world, including every living thing in it, at a specific point in time or at a series of specific points corresponding to the Biblical days of Creation; fixity of species, the belief that each living species as created by God is capable of wide variation within itself but is incapable of divergence into any other species; catastrophism, the belief that marked changes in the geological record were signs of specific catastrophes, like Noah's Flood, instituted by God. Some of those who supported this model were willing to expand their notion of the scale of time somewhat beyond the Biblical estimate of a 6000-year-old earth, but few accepted the idea of an earth existing on the scale of deep time.

The second group, which today we would call evolutionists, though taking no consistent position on the ultimate origin of the universe or of life, insisted on the scientific principle of explaining natural phenomena, including the origins of species in the world, in terms of natural causes. They too associated themselves with a few central concepts: uniformitarianism, the belief that nature operates according to the same laws today as it did any time in the past (this concept is defined in the subtitle of the major work by Charles Lyell, a major influence on Darwin, *Principles of Geology, Being an Attempt to Explain the Former Changes of the Earth's Surface, by Reference to Causes Now in Operation,* 1830); gradualism, the belief that changes, even those that appear "sudden" relative to deep time, took place slowly by the gradual accumulation of small changes over long periods of time, not by sudden catastrophes; mutability of species, the belief that the great variety of organic life on earth came to be, as in the concept of gradualism, by the slow accumulation of small changes in species and their transformation into others.

The crucial problem with the early evolutionary model was the lack of any reasonable scientific mechanism for the transformation of species. Many speculations were offered: that an organism's "need" somehow generated new organs or that the use or disuse of an organ generated its development or disappearance, but these mechanisms lacked clear evidence to support them. Darwin's chief contribution was describing a convincing mechanism and effectively illustrating it through his own extensive observations.

The great variety of life forms Darwin observed seemed directly analogous to the wide variations within species that were produced in domestic breeding programs for animals like pigeons and dogs, a process involving *artificial* selection of desired traits. For Darwin to propose that such a process could account naturally for the development of the wide variety of species on earth, he needed only the concept of deep time, already provided by geology, and the postulation of a mechanism for the *natural* selection of favorable variations.

A central element in defining the mechanism of natural selection came to Darwin by way of an economist, Thomas Malthus, whose *Essay on the Principle of Population* (1798) argued that in human society, population tended to increase more rapidly than the means of subsistence. In Malthus' mathematical terms, "Population, when unchecked, increases in a geometrical ratio [2, 4, 8, 16, 32, . . .]. . . . The means of subsistence could not possibly be made to increase faster than in an arithmetical ratio [2, 4, 6, 8, 10, . . .]." Malthus was making a point about the limits to human progress, but Darwin saw this kind of population pressure in a broader biological perspective. It established the basic condition of a "struggle for existence" in which varieties of a species with traits favorable to their survival have a greater chance of passing on those traits to their progeny.

Darwin's central purpose was to extend Lyell's efforts in geology to biology, to explain earlier changes in plant and animal life "by reference to causes now in operation," and his argument was inescapably logical. Given the problem of geometrical population increase—indeed, in nature many species have a reproductive potential not on the 2 × 2 scale illustrated above, but on a 1000 × 1000 scale—there must be a great struggle for survival. Given the wide variability of features within a species, some of those features must be more conducive to survival than others. Assuming that beneficial features can be inherited, some traits would tend, therefore, to be "naturally selected" and passed to descendants. Given the wide dispersion of species over a variety of changing environments and given the hundreds of millions of years provided by deep time, members of a species must have diverged into new species, eventually producing the almost infinite variety of life alive today and observable in the fossil record.

Darwin's major scientific impact has been the establishment of evolution as the chief unifying principle in biology, a principle that has stood up well in absorbing major new developments, in areas ranging from geology and paleontology, which originally inspired the new model, to genetics and molecular biology. His influence, however, has extended far beyond biology, for better and for worse. Among the worst extensions of Darwinism was the misapplication of the concept of the survival of the fittest to economics, thereby justifying in the name of science the most rapacious forms of capitalism, something Darwin never suggested (discussed later in the chapter on Economics). Others misapplied evolutionary theory in arguing that certain races were more "highly evolved" than others or even that men were more highly evolved than women, issues that are examined in the readings after the Darwin selection. More fruitful extensions by astrophysicists and nuclear physicists have applied the evolutionary model to trace the development of the universe back to its origin in the Big Bang, which is believed to mark the very beginning of time.

Perhaps the greatest impact of evolutionary theory on culture as a whole, however, has been its philosophical and theological implications, including those stemming from its extension to human origins. Darwin himself did not extend the theory to humanity until the *Descent of Man, and Selection in Relation to Sex* (1871), but his critics anticipated and opposed it almost immediately after the publication of the *Origin of Species.* To Darwin's critics, the inevitable implication of that extension would be to debase and despiritualize humanity, to see us as just another animal species, however highly evolved, the accidental result of the operations of natural law, not the crowning glory of creation for which everything else was made. To many who championed Darwin, these implications were seen as liberating humanity from its ancient prejudices and its false sense of superiority: just as the Copernican revolution destroyed our geocentrism, the Darwinian revolution destroyed our anthropocentrism. Still, others managed to reconcile their religious beliefs to an evolutionary model by conceiving of creation as ultimately directed by God but operating through natural law in a process continuing throughout all time; thus, change is the law of life and of the whole universe, including human nature. Before leaping too far into the broader implications of these ideas, however, we would do well to look carefully at their humbler origins in the observations of a scientist who did his best to leave the philosophical and theological debates to others.

from The Origin of Species[1]

Charles Darwin

CHAPTER IV

Natural Selection; or the Survival of the Fittest

SUMMARY OF CHAPTER

1 If under changing conditions of life organic beings present individual differences in almost every part of their structure, and this cannot be disputed; if there be, owing to their geometrical rate of increase, a severe struggle for life at some age, season, or year, and this certainly cannot be disputed; then, considering the infinite complexity of the relations of all organic beings to each other and to their conditions of life, causing an infinite diversity in structure, constitution, and habits, to be advantageous to them, it would be a most extraordinary fact if no variations had ever occurred useful to each being's own welfare, in the same manner as so many variations have occurred useful to man. But if variations useful to any organic being ever do occur, assuredly individuals thus characterised will have the best chance of being preserved in the struggle for life; and from the strong principle of inheritance, these will tend to produce offspring similarly characterised. This principle of preservation, or the survival of the fittest, I have called Natural Selection. It leads to the improvement of each creature in relation to its organic and inorganic conditions of life; and consequently, in most cases, to what must be regarded as an advance in organisation. Nevertheless, low and simple forms will long endure if well fitted for their simple conditions of life.

2 Natural selection, on the principle of qualities being inherited at corresponding ages, can modify the egg, seed, or young, as easily as the adult. Amongst many animals, sexual selection[2] will have given its aid to ordinary selection, by assuring to the most vigorous and best adapted males the greatest number of offspring. Sexual selection will also give characters useful to the males alone, in their struggles or rivalry with other males; and these characters will be transmitted to one sex or to both sexes, according to the form of inheritance which prevails.

3 Whether natural selection has really thus acted in adapting the various forms of life to their several conditions and stations, must be judged by the

---

[1] The present text is excerpted from the sixth edition of the *Origin* (1872), the last edition during Darwin's lifetime.

[2] Sexual selection, a special form of natural selection, refers to the patterns of mating choices within a species. The female peacock, for example, seems to prefer males with the largest and brightest expanse of tail feathers, a preference that selects and develops that feature within the males of that species.

general tenor and balance of evidence given in the following chapters. But we have already seen how it entails extinction; and how largely extinction has acted in the world's history, geology plainly declares. Natural selection, also leads to divergence of character; for the more organic beings diverge in structure, habits, and constitution, by so much the more can a large number be supported on the area,—of which we see proof by looking to the inhabitants of any small spot, and to the productions naturalised in foreign lands. Therefore, during the modification of the descendants of any one species, and during the incessant struggle of all species to increase in numbers, the more diversified the descendants become, the better will be their chance of success in the battle for life. Thus the small differences distinguishing varieties of the same species, steadily tend to increase, till they equal the greater differences between species of the same genus, or even of distinct genera. . . .

4 Natural selection, as has just been remarked, leads to divergence of character and to much extinction of the less improved and intermediate forms of life. On these principles, the nature of the affinities, and the generally well-defined distinctions between the innumerable organic beings in each class throughout the world, may be explained. It is a truly wonderful fact—the wonder of which we are apt to overlook from familiarity—that all animals and all plants throughout all time and space should be related to each other in groups, subordinate to groups, in the manner which we everywhere behold—namely, varieties of the same species most closely related, species of the same genus less closely and unequally related, forming sections and sub-genera, species of distinct genera much less closely related, and genera related in different degrees, forming sub-families, families, orders, sub-classes and classes. The several subordinate groups in any class cannot be ranked in a single file, but seem clustered round points, and these round other points, and so on in almost endless cycles. If species had been independently created, no explanation would have been possible of this kind of classification; but it is explained through inheritance and the complex action of natural selection, entailing extinction and divergence of character. . . .

5 The affinities of all the beings of the same class have sometimes been represented by a great tree. I believe this simile largely speaks the truth. The green and budding twigs may represent existing species; and those produced during former years may represent the long succession of extinct species. At each period of growth all the growing twigs have tried to branch out on all sides, and to overtop and kill the surrounding twigs and branches, in the same manner as species and groups of species have at all times overmastered other species in the great battle for life. The limbs divided into great branches, and these into lesser and lesser branches, were themselves once, when the tree was young, budding twigs, and this connection of the former and present buds by ramifying branches may well represent the classification of all extinct and living species in groups subordinate to groups. Of the many twigs which flourished when the tree was a mere bush, only two or three, now grown into great branches, yet survive and bear the other branches; so with the species which

lived during long-past geological periods, very few have left living and modified descendants. From the first growth of the tree, many a limb and branch has decayed and dropped off; and these fallen branches of various sizes may represent those whole orders, families, and genera which have now no living representatives, and which are known to us only in a fossil state. As we here and there see a thin straggling branch springing from a fork low down in a tree, and which by some chance has been favoured and is still alive on its summit, so we occasionally see an animal like the Ornithorhynchus or Lepidosiren,[3] which in some small degree connects by its affinities two large branches of life, and which has apparently been saved from fatal competition by having inhabited a protected station. As buds give rise by growth to fresh buds, and these, if vigorous, branch out and overtop on all sides many a feebler branch, so by generation I believe it has been with the great Tree of Life, which fills with its dead and broken branches the crust of the earth, and covers the surface with its ever-branching and beautiful ramifications. . . .

Chapter X

On the Imperfection of the Geological Record

6 In the sixth chapter I enumerated the chief objections which might be justly urged against the views maintained in this volume. Most of them have now been discussed. One, namely the distinctness of specific forms, and their not being blended together by innumerable transitional links, is a very obvious difficulty. I assigned reasons why such links do not commonly occur at the present day under the circumstances apparently most favourable for their presence, namely, on an extensive and continuous area with graduated physical conditions. I endeavoured to show, that the life of each species depends in a more important manner on the presence of other already defined organic forms, than on climate, and, therefore, that the really governing conditions of life do not graduate away quite insensibly like heat or moisture. I endeavoured, also, to show that intermediate varieties, from existing in lesser numbers than the forms which they connect, will generally be beaten out and exterminated during the course of further modification and improvement. The main cause, however, of innumerable intermediate links not now occurring everywhere throughout nature, depends on the very process of natural selection, through which new varieties continually take the places of and supplant their parent-forms. But just in proportion as this process of extermination has acted on an enormous scale, so must the number of intermediate varieties, which have formerly existed, be truly enormous. Why then is not every geological formation and every stratum full of such intermediate links? Geology assuredly does

[3] Ornithorhynchus, the duck-billed platypus: Lepidosiren, a South American lungfish.

not reveal any such finely-graduated organic chain; and this, perhaps, is the most obvious and serious objection which can be urged against the theory. The explanation lies, as I believe, in the extreme imperfection of the geological record.

7 In the first place, it should always be borne in mind what sort of intermediate forms must, on the theory, have formerly existed. I have found it difficult, when looking at any two species, to avoid picturing to myself forms *directly* intermediate between them. But this is a wholly false view: we should always look for forms intermediate between each species and a common but unknown progenitor; and the progenitor will generally have differed in some respects from all its modified descendants. To give a simple illustration: the fantail and pouter pigeons are both descended from the rock-pigeon; if we possessed all the intermediate varieties which have ever existed, we should have an extremely close series between both and the rock-pigeon; but we should have no varieties directly intermediate between the fantail and pouter; none, for instance, combining a tail somewhat expanded with a crop somewhat enlarged, the characteristic features of these two breeds. These two breeds, moreover, have become so much modified, that, if we had no historical or indirect evidence regarding their origin, it would not have been possible to have determined, from a mere comparison of their structure with that of the rock-pigeon, C. livia, whether they had descended from this species or from some allied form, such as C. oenas.

8 So, with natural species, if we look to forms very distinct, for instance to the horse and tapir, we have no reason to suppose that links directly intermediate between them ever existed, but between each and an unknown common parent. The common parent will have had in its whole organisation much general resemblance to the tapir and to the horse; but in some points of structure may have differed considerably from both, even perhaps more than they differ from each other. Hence, in all such cases, we should be unable to recognise the parent-form of any two or more species, even if we closely compared the structure of the parent with that of its modified descendants, unless at the same time we had a nearly perfect chain of the intermediate links.

9 It is just possible by the theory, that one of two living forms might have descended from the other; for instance, a horse from a tapir; and in this case *direct* intermediate links will have existed between them. But such a case would imply that one form had remained for a very long period unaltered, whilst its descendants had undergone a vast amount of change; and the principle of competition between organism and organism, between child and parent, will render this a very rare event; for in all cases the new and improved forms of life tend to supplant the old and unimproved forms.

10 By the theory of natural selection all living species have been connected with the parent-species of each genus, by differences not greater than we see between the natural and domestic varieties of the same species at the present day; and these parent-species, now generally extinct, have in their turn been similarly connected with more ancient forms; and so on backwards, always

converging to the common ancestor of each great class. So that the number of intermediate and transitional links, between all living and extinct species, must have been inconceivably great. But assuredly, if this theory be true, such have lived upon the earth.

On the Lapse of Time, as Inferred from the Rate of Deposition and Extent of Denudation

11 Independently of our not finding fossil remains of such infinitely numerous connecting links, it may be objected that time cannot have sufficed for so great an amount of organic change, all changes having been effected slowly. It is hardly possible for me to recall to the reader who is not a practical geologist, the facts leading the mind feebly to comprehend the lapse of time. He who can read Sir Charles Lyell's grand work on the Principles of Geology, which the future historian will recognise as having produced a revolution in natural science, and yet does not admit how vast have been the past periods of time, may at once close this volume. Not that it suffices to study the Principles of Geology, or to read special treatises by different observers on separate formations, and to mark how each author attempts to give an inadequate idea of the duration of each formation, or even of each stratum. We can best gain some idea of past time by knowing the agencies at work, and learning how deeply the surface of the land has been denuded, and how much sediment has been deposited. As Lyell has well remarked, the extent and thickness of our sedimentary formations are the result and the measure of the denudation which the earth's crust has elsewhere undergone. Therefore a man should examine for himself the great piles of superimposed strata, and watch the rivulets bringing down mud, and the waves wearing away the sea-cliffs, in order to comprehend something about the duration of past time, the monuments of which we see all around us. . . .

On the Poorness of Palaeontological Collections

12 Now let us turn to our richest geological museums, and what a paltry display we behold! That our collections are imperfect is admitted by every one. The remark of that admirable paleontologist, Edward Forbes, should never be forgotten, namely, that very many fossil species are known and named from single and often broken specimens, or from a few specimens collected on some one spot. Only a small portion of the surface of the earth has been geologically explored, and no part with sufficient care, as the important discoveries made every year in Europe prove. No organism wholly soft can be preserved. Shells and bones decay and disappear when left on the bottom of the sea, where sediment is not accumulating.

13 . . . Those who believe that the geological record is in any degree perfect, will undoubtedly at once reject the theory. For my part, following out Lyell's metaphor, I look at the geological record as a history of the world imperfectly kept, and written in a changing dialect; of this history we possess the last volume alone, relating only to two or three countries. Of this volume, only here and there a short chapter has been preserved; and of each page, only here and

there a few lines. Each word of the slowly-changing language, more or less different in the successive chapters, may represent the forms of life, which are entombed in our consecutive formations, and which falsely appear to have been abruptly introduced. On this view, the difficulties above discussed are greatly diminished, or even disappear. . . .

CHAPTER XV

Recapitulation and Conclusion

14 As this whole volume is one long argument, it may be convenient to the reader to have the leading facts and inferences briefly recapitulated.

15 That many and serious objections may be advanced against the theory of descent with modification through variation and natural selection, I do not deny. I have endeavored to give to them their full force. Nothing at first can appear more difficult to believe than that the more complex organs and instincts have been perfected, not by means superior to, though analogous with, human reason, but by the accumulation of innumerable slight variations, each good for the individual possessor. Nevertheless, this difficulty, though appearing to our imagination insuperably great, cannot be considered real if we admit the following propositions, namely, that all parts of the organisation and instincts offer, at least, individual differences—that there is a struggle for existence leading to the preservation of profitable deviations of structure or instinct—and, lastly, that gradations in the state of perfection of each organ may have existed, each good of its kind. The truth of these propositions cannot, I think, be disputed.

16 Now let us turn to the other side of the argument. Under domestication we see much variability, caused, or at least excited, by changed conditions of life; but often in so obscure a manner, that we are tempted to consider the variations as spontaneous. Variability is governed by many complex laws,—by correlated growth, compensation, the increased use and disuse of parts, and the definite action of the surrounding conditions. There is much difficulty in ascertaining how largely our domestic productions have been modified; but we may safely infer that the amount has been large, and that modifications can be inherited for long periods. As long as the conditions of life remain the same, we have reason to believe that a modification, which has already been inherited for many generations, may continue to be inherited for an almost infinite number of generations. On the other hand, we have evidence that variability when it has once come into play, does not cease under domestication for a very long period; nor do we know that it ever ceases, for new varieties are still occasionally produced by our oldest domesticated productions.

17 Variability is not actually caused by man; he only unintentionally exposes organic beings to new conditions of life, and then nature acts on the organisation and causes it to vary. But man can and does select the variations given to him by nature, and thus accumulates them in any desired manner. He thus

adapts animals and plants for his own benefit or pleasure. He may do this methodically, or he may do it unconsciously by preserving the individuals most useful or pleasing to him without any intention of altering the breed. It is certain that he can largely influence the character of a breed by selecting, in each successive generation, individual differences so slight as to be inappreciable except by an educated eye. This unconscious process of selection has been the great agency in the formation of the most distinct and useful domestic breeds. That many breeds produced by man have to a large extent the character of natural species, is shown by the inextricable doubts whether many of them are varieties or aboriginally distinct species.

18 There is no reason why the principles which have acted so efficiently under domestication should not have acted under nature. In the survival of favoured individuals and races, during the constantly-recurrent Struggle for Existence, we see a powerful and ever-acting form of Selection. The struggle for existence inevitably follows from the high geometrical ratio of increase which is common to all organic beings. This high rate of increase is proved by calculation,—by the rapid increase of many animals and plants during a succession of peculiar seasons, and when naturalised in new countries. More individuals are born than can possibly survive. A grain in the balance may determine which individuals shall live and which shall die,—which variety or species shall increase in number, and which shall decrease, or finally become extinct. As the individuals of the same species come in all respects into the closest competition with each other, the struggle will generally be most severe between them; it will be almost equally severe between the varieties of the same species, and next in severity between the species of the same genus. On the other hand the struggle will often be severe between beings remote in the scale of nature. The slightest advantage in certain individuals, at any age or during any season, over those with which they come into competition, or better adaptation in however slight a degree to the surrounding physical conditions, will, in the long run, turn the balance.

19 With animals having separated sexes, there will be in most cases a struggle between the males for the possession of the females. The most vigorous males, or those which have most successfully struggled with their conditions of life, will generally leave most progeny. But success will often depend on the males having special weapons, or means of defense, or charms; and a slight advantage will lead to victory. . . .

20 If then, animals and plants do vary, let it be ever so slightly or slowly, why should not variations or individual differences, which are in any way beneficial, be preserved and accumulated through natural selection, or the survival of the fittest? If man can by patience select variations useful to him, why, under changing and complex conditions of life, should not variations useful to nature's living products often arise, and be preserved or selected? What limit can be put to this power, acting during long ages and rigidly scrutinising the whole constitution, structure, and habits of each creature,—favouring the good and rejecting the bad? I can see no limit to this power, in slowly and beautifully adapting

each form to the most complex relations of life. The theory of natural selection, even if we look no farther than this, seems to be in the highest degree probable. I have already recapitulated, as fairly as I could, the opposed difficulties and objections: now let us turn to the special facts and arguments in favour of the theory. . . .

21 It can hardly be supposed that a false theory would explain, in so satisfactory a manner as does the theory of natural selection, the several large classes of facts above specified. It has recently been objected that this is an unsafe method of arguing; but it is a method used in judging of the common events of life, and has often been used by the greatest natural philosophers. The undulatory theory of light has thus been arrived at; and the belief in the revolution of the earth on its own axis was until lately supported by hardly any direct evidence. It is no valid objection that science as yet throws no light on the far higher problem of the essence or origin of life. Who can explain what is the essence of the attraction of gravity? No one now objects to following out the results consequent on this unknown element of attraction; notwithstanding that Leibnitz formerly accused Newton of introducing "occult qualities and miracles into philosophy."

22 I see no good reason why the views given in this volume should shock the religious feelings of any one. It is satisfactory, as showing how transient such impressions are, to remember that the greatest discovery ever made by man, namely, the law of the attraction of gravity, was also attacked by Leibnitz, "as subversive of natural, and inferentially of revealed, religion." A celebrated author and divine has written to me that "he has gradually learnt to see that it is just as noble a conception of the Deity to believe that He created a few original forms capable of self-development into other and needful forms, as to believe that He required a fresh act of creation to supply the voids caused by the action of His laws." . . .

23 But the chief cause of our natural unwillingness to admit that one species has given birth to clear and distinct species, is that we are always slow in admitting great changes of which we do not see the steps. The difficulty is the same as that felt by so many geologists, when Lyell first insisted that long lines of inland cliffs had been formed, the great valleys excavated, by the agencies which we see still at work. The mind cannot possibly grasp the full meaning of the term of even a million years; it cannot add up and perceive the full effects of many slight variations, accumulated during an almost infinite number of generations.

24 Although I am fully convinced of the truth of the views given in this volume under the form of an abstract, I by no means expect to convince experienced naturalists whose minds are stocked with a multitude of facts all viewed, during a long course of years, from a point of view directly opposite to mine. It is so easy to hide our ignorance under such expressions as the "plan of creation," "unity of design," &c., and to think that we give an explanation when we only re-state a fact. Any one whose disposition leads him to attach more weight to unexplained difficulties than to the explanation of a certain number

of facts will certainly reject the theory. A few naturalists, endowed with much flexibility of mind, and who have already begun to doubt the immutability of species, may be influenced by this volume; but I look with confidence to the future,—to young and rising naturalists, who will be able to view both sides of the question with impartiality. Whoever is led to believe that species are mutable will do good service by conscientiously expressing his conviction; for thus only can the load of prejudice by which this subject is overwhelmed be removed. . . .

25 Authors of the highest eminence seem to be fully satisfied with the view that each species has been independently created. To my mind it accords better with what we know of the laws impressed on matter by the Creator, that the production and extinction of the past and present inhabitants of the world should have been due to secondary causes, like those determining the birth and death of the individual. When I view all beings not as special creations, but as the lineal descendants of some few beings which lived long before the first bed of the Cambrian system was deposited, they seem to me to become ennobled. Judging from the past, we may safely infer that no one living species will transmit its unaltered likeness to a distant futurity. And of the species now living very few will transmit progeny of any kind to a far distant futurity; for the manner in which all organic beings are grouped, shows that the greater number of species in each genus, and all the species in many genera, have left no descendants, but have become utterly extinct. We can so far take a prophetic glance into futurity as to foretell that it will be the common and widely-spread species, belonging to the larger and dominant groups within each class, which will ultimately prevail and procreate new and dominant species. As all the living forms of life are the lineal descendants of those which lived long before the Cambrian epoch, we may feel certain that the ordinary succession by generation has never once been broken, and that no cataclysm has desolated the whole world. Hence we may look with some confidence to a secure future of great length. And as natural selection works solely by and for the good of each being, all corporeal and mental endowments will tend to progress towards perfection.[4]

QUESTIONS FOR WRITING AND DISCUSSION

OBSERVING

1. Point out as many specific references as you can find to comparisons Darwin makes between artificial and natural selection.

---

[4] We are not sure what exactly Darwin meant by "progress towards perfection," but modern understanding sees it as a tendency toward better adaptation of organisms toward their environment, not a claim that evolution leads to perfection. In fact, natural selection often produces highly imperfect "solutions."

2. Explain the meaning of the following words and their importance to Darwin's argument: variation, improvement, diversification, the tree of life.

EVALUATING

1. Define "intermediate forms," and argue, as would Darwin, that their apparent absence would not undermine his theory. How does this concept relate to the imperfection of the fossil record?
2. On the basis that the fossil record does not now and is not likely ever to "yield the infinitely many fine gradations between past and present species required on the theory," argue that Darwin's theory can or cannot be maintained. What is the usefulness of a theory like evolution that cannot ever be fully proven?

RESPONDING AND APPLYING

1. In a passage added by Darwin since the original 1859 edition of his work, he compares certain theological attacks on his theory to Leibniz's reaction to Newton's concept of gravity. He might as well have compared himself to Galileo—certainly it will be easier for us to consider that comparison. Is it valid to do so? What is the difference, if any, between a religiously based attack on Galileo and one on Darwin?
2. Evolutionary theory has undergone several modifications since Darwin as a result of new knowledge, some of which might have surprised Darwin. Given the encouraging tone of his conclusion, how do you think he would have responded to the information that further examination of the fossil record has revealed several mass extinctions, in some of which more than 90% of plant and animal species on land and in the sea were wiped out? How does that knowledge affect you?

STEPHEN JAY GOULD, "WOMEN'S BRAINS"

A Professor of Geology at Harvard University and Curator of Invertebrate Paleontology and Alexander Agassiz Professor of Zoology in Harvard's Museum of Comparative Zoology, *Stephen Jay Gould* (1941–) is one of the most lucid of modern writers on the sciences. His books include *Ever Since Darwin* (1977), *Ontogeny and Phylogeny* (1977), *The Panda's Thumb* (1980), *The Mismeasure of Man* (1981), *Hen's Teeth and Horse's Toes* (1983), *The Flamingo's Smile* (1985), *Time's Arrow, Time's Cycle* (1987), *Bully for Brontosaurus* (1991), *Eight Little Piggies* (1993), and *Dinosaur in a Haystack* (1995). "This View of Life," his column appearing for over a decade in the journal *Natural History,* won the 1980 National Magazine Award for Essays and Criticism and is the source for many of the essays later collected in several of the books listed above. His two essays that follow exhibit an approach peculiar to the last half of the twentieth century in the way they consider the viability of a scientific theory. These essays could not have been written without the change that occurred in the first half of this century in the way science itself is viewed, a change that constitutes, in fact, another kind of scientific revolution.

Despite Blaise Pascal's warning in 1648 that scientific knowledge is always provisional, that its certainty is dependent on the unlikely possibility that we have examined all relevant cases, science grew in the eighteenth and nineteenth centuries under the assumption that it was delivering the eternal truths of nature. The history of science was, therefore, seen as the progressive displacement of the darkness of ignorance and superstition by the light of scientific truth. Ironically, although science began by questioning all claims to authority, it established itself as the new authority; although it was originally an outgrowth of humanism, it forgot the humanist doctrine of human fallibility. It was inevitable, however, that eventually the new scientific knowledge would radically displace, not old superstition, but not-so-old science.

This began to happen most noticeably in the late 1890s, when an explosion of radically new knowledge began that over the next few decades would include the structure of the atom, relativity, the interchangeability of matter and energy, and much more. Each of these reorientations was not based simply on an acquisition of new data, but each was a revolution in its own right.

For example, by the first decade of the twentieth century, scientists realized that the atom had an internal structure much like a solar system, with the major part of its mass concentrated in a very small central nucleus and with the major part of its volume made up of electrons in orbit around the nucleus. However, theories that attempted to account for the motion of these electrons using mechanical laws failed utterly. As has been discussed, the discovery late in the seventeenth century, based primarily on Newton, that nature operated according to precise, mathematically definable laws had an enormous impact on science and culture. Equally momentous was the discovery early in the twentieth century, as Nobel laureate Richard P. Feynman puts it, "that Newton's laws of motion were quite wrong in atoms."[1]

Gould's "Women's Brains," illustrates some of the changes that resulted from these revelations, changes in how science itself is perceived. Science is not a process of pure induction, a body of conclusions that emerge inevitably and necessarily from the data. Its hypotheses emerge instead from a variety of sources, including cultural presuppositions and pure guesswork. Scientific theories of a particular time, therefore, can be as near *or* far from universal truth and as much a unique expression of a culture as its art, literature, music, religion, or philosophy.

[1] Feynman, R. P., *QED: The Strange Theory of Light and Matter,* Princeton: Princeton U.P., 1985, p. 5.

Women's Brains

Stephen Jay Gould

1 In the prelude to *Middlemarch,* George Eliot lamented the unfulfilled lives of talented women:

> Some have felt that these blundering lives are due to the inconvenient indefiniteness with which the Supreme Power has fashioned the natures of women: if there were one level of feminine incompetence as strict as the ability to count three and no more, the social lot of women might be treated with scientific certitude.

2 Eliot goes on to discount the idea of innate limitation, but while she wrote in 1872, the leaders of European anthropometry were trying to measure "with scientific certitude" the inferiority of women. Anthropometry, or measurement of the human body, is not so fashionable a field these days, but it dominated the human sciences for much of the nineteenth century and remained popular until intelligence testing replaced skull measurement as a favored device for making invidious comparisons among races, classes, and sexes. Craniometry, or measurement of the skull, commanded the most attention and respect. Its unquestioned leader, Paul Broca (1824–80), professor of clinical surgery at the Faculty of Medicine in Paris, gathered a school of disciples and imitators around himself. Their work, so meticulous and apparently irrefutable, exerted great influence and won high esteem as a jewel of nineteenth-century science.

3 Broca's work seemed particularly invulnerable to refutation. Had he not measured with the most scrupulous care and accuracy? (Indeed, he had. I have the greatest respect for Broca's meticulous procedure. His numbers are sound. But science is an inferential exercise, not a catalog of facts. Numbers, by themselves, specify nothing. All depends upon what you do with them.) Broca depicted himself as an apostle of objectivity, a man who bowed before facts and cast aside superstition and sentimentality. He declared that "there is no faith, however respectable, no interest, however legitimate, which must not accommodate itself to the progress of human knowledge and bend before truth." Women, like it or not, had smaller brains than men and, therefore, could not equal them in intelligence. This fact, Broca argued, may reinforce a common prejudice in male society, but it is also a scientific truth. L. Manouvrier, a black sheep in Broca's fold, rejected the inferiority of women and wrote with feeling about the burden imposed upon them by Broca's numbers:

> Women displayed their talents and diplomas. They also invoked philosophical authorities. But they were opposed by *numbers* unknown to Condorcet or to John Stuart Mill. These numbers fell upon poor women like a sledge hammer, and they were accompanied by commentaries and sarcasms more ferocious than the most misogynist imprecations of certain church fathers. The theolo-

gians had asked if women had a soul. Several centuries later, some scientists were ready to refuse them a human intelligence.

4 Broca's argument rested upon two sets of data: the larger brains of men in modern societies, and a supposed increase in male superiority through time. His most extensive data came from autopsies performed personally in four Parisian hospitals. For 292 male brains, he calculated an average weight of 1.325 grams; 140 female brains averaged 1.144 grams for a difference of 181 grams, or 14 percent of the male weight. Broca understood, of course, that part of this difference could be attributed to the greater height of males. Yet he made no attempt to measure the effect of size alone and actually stated that it cannot account for the entire difference because we know, a priori, that women are not as intelligent as men (a premise that the data were supposed to test, not rest upon):

> We might ask if the small size of the female brain depends exclusively upon the small size of her body. Tiedemann has proposed this explanation. But we must not forget that women are, on the average, a little less intelligent than men, a difference which we should not exaggerate but which is, nonetheless, real. We are therefore permitted to suppose that the relatively small size of the female brain depends in part upon her physical inferiority and in part upon her intellectual inferiority.

5 In 1873, the year after Eliot published *Middlemarch,* Broca measured the cranial capacities of prehistoric skulls from L'Homme Mort cave. Here he found a difference of only 99.5 cubic centimeters between males and females, while modern populations range from 129.5 to 220.7. Topinard, Broca's chief disciple, explained the increasing discrepancy through time as a result of differing evolutionary pressures upon dominant men and passive women:

> The man who fights for two or more in the struggle for existence, who has all the responsibility and the cares of tomorrow, who is constantly active in combating the environment and human rivals, needs more brain than the woman whom he must protect and nourish, the sedentary woman, lacking any interior occupations, whose role is to raise children, love, and be passive.

6 In 1879, Gustave Le Bon, chief misogynist of Broca's school, used these data to publish what must be the most vicious attack upon women in modern scientific literature (no one can top Aristotle). I do not claim his views were representative of Broca's school, but they were published in France's most respected anthropological journal. Le Bon concluded:

> In the most intelligent races, as among the Parisians, there are a large number of women whose brains are closer in size to those of gorillas than to the most developed male brains. This inferiority is so obvious that no one can contest it for a moment; only its degree is worth discussion. All psychologists who have studied the intelligence of women, as well as poets and novelists, recognize today that they represent the most inferior forms of human evolution and that they are closer to children and savages than to an adult, civilized man. They

> excel in fickleness, inconstancy, absence of thought and logic, and incapacity to reason. Without doubt there exist some distinguished women, very superior to the average man, but they are as exceptional as the birth of any monstrosity, as, for example, of a gorilla with two heads; consequently, we may neglect them entirely.

7 Nor did Le Bon shrink from the social implications of his views. He was horrified by the proposal of some American reformers to grant women higher education on the same basis as men:

> A desire to give them the same education, and, as a consequence, to propose the same goals for them, is a dangerous chimera. . . . The day when, misunderstanding the inferior occupations which nature has given her, women leave the home and take part in our battles; on this day a social revolution will begin, and everything that maintains the sacred ties of the family will disappear.

Sound familiar?[1]

8 I have reexamined Broca's data, the basis for all this derivative pronouncement, and I find his numbers sound but his interpretation ill-founded, to say the least. The data supporting his claim for increased difference through time can be easily dismissed. Broca based his contention on the samples from L'Homme Mort alone—only seven male and six female skulls in all. Never have so little data yielded such far ranging conclusions.

9 In 1888, Topinard published Broca's more extensive data on the Parisian hospitals. Since Broca recorded height and age as well as brain size, we may use modern statistics to remove their effect. Brain weight decreases with age, and Broca's women were, on average, considerably older than his men. Brain weight increases with height, and his average man was almost half a foot taller than his average woman. I used multiple regression, a technique that allowed me to assess simultaneously the influence of height and age upon brain size. In an analysis of the data for women, I found that, at average male height and age, a woman's brain would weigh 1,212 grams. Correction for height and age reduces Broca's measured difference of 181 grams by more than a third, to 113 grams.

10 I don't know what to make of this remaining difference because I cannot assess other factors known to influence brain size in a major way. Cause of death has an important effect: degenerative disease often entails a substantial diminution of brain size. (This effect is separate from the decrease attributed to age alone.) Eugene Schreider, also working with Broca's data, found that men killed in accidents had brains weighing, on average, 60 grams more than men dying of infectious diseases. The best modern data I can find (from American hospitals) records a full 100-gram difference between death by degenerative

---

[1] When I wrote this essay, I assumed that Le Bon was a marginal, if colorful, figure. I have since learned that he was a leading scientist, one of the founders of social psychology, and best known for a seminal study on crowd behavior, still cited today (*La psychologie des foules,* 1895), and for his work on unconscious motivation.

arteriosclerosis and by violence or accident. Since so many of Broca's subjects were very elderly women, we may assume that lengthy degenerative disease was more common among them than among the men.

11 More importantly, modern students of brain size still have not agreed on a proper measure for eliminating the powerful effect of body size. Height is partly adequate, but men and women of the same height do not share the same body build. Weight is even worse than height, because most of its variation reflects nutrition rather than intrinsic size—fat versus skinny exerts little influence upon the brain. Manouvrier took up this subject in the 1880s and argued that muscular mass and force should be used. He tried to measure this elusive property in various ways and found a marked difference in favor of men, even in men and women of the same height. When he corrected for what he called "sexual mass," women actually came out slightly ahead in brain size.

12 Thus, the corrected 113-gram difference is surely too large; the true figure is probably close to zero and may as well favor women as men. And 113 grams, by the way, is exactly the average difference between a 5 foot 4 inch and a 6 foot 4 inch male in Broca's data. We would not (especially us short folks) want to ascribe greater intelligence to tall men. In short, who knows what to do with Broca's data? They certainly don't permit any confident claim that men have bigger brains than women.

13 To appreciate the social role of Broca and his school, we must recognize that his statements about the brains of women do not reflect an isolated prejudice toward a single disadvantaged group. They must be weighed in the context of a general theory that supported contemporary social distinctions as biologically ordained. Women, blacks, and poor people suffered the same disparagement, but women bore the brunt of Broca's argument because he had easier access to data on women's brains. Women were singularly denigrated but they also stood as surrogates for other disenfranchised groups. As one of Broca's disciples wrote in 1881: "Men of the black races have a brain scarcely heavier than that of white women." This juxtaposition extended into many other realms of anthropological argument, particularly to claims that, anatomically and emotionally, both women and blacks were like white children—and that white children, by the theory of recapitulation, represented an ancestral (primitive) adult stage of human evolution. I do not regard as empty rhetoric the claim that women's battles are for all of us.

14 Maria Montessori did not confine her activities to educational reform for young children. She lectured on anthropology for several years at the University of Rome, and wrote an influential book entitled *Pedagogical Anthropology* (English edition, 1913). Montessori was no egalitarian. She supported most of Broca's work and the theory of innate criminality proposed by her compatriot Cesare Lombroso. She measured the circumference of children's heads in her schools and inferred that the best prospects had bigger brains. But she had no use for Broca's conclusions about women. She discussed Manouvrier's work at length and made much of his tentative claim that women, after proper correction of the data, had slightly larger brains than men. Women, she concluded,

were intellectually superior, but men had prevailed heretofore by dint of physical force. Since technology has abolished force as an instrument of power, the era of women may soon be upon us: "In such an epoch there will really be superior human beings, there will really be men strong in morality and in sentiment. Perhaps in this way the reign of women is approaching, when the enigma of her anthropological superiority will be deciphered. Woman was always the custodian of human sentiment, morality and honor."

15 This represents one possible antidote to "scientific" claims for the constitutional inferiority of certain groups. One may affirm the validity of biological distinctions but argue that the data have been misinterpreted by prejudiced men with a stake in the outcome, and that disadvantaged groups are truly superior. In recent years, Elaine Morgan has followed this strategy in her *Descent of Women,* a speculative reconstruction of human prehistory from the woman's point of view—and as farcical as more famous tall tales by and for men.

16 I prefer another strategy. Montessori and Morgan followed Broca's philosophy to reach a more congenial conclusion. I would rather label the whole enterprise of setting a biological value upon groups for what it is: irrelevant and highly injurious. George Eliot well appreciated the special tragedy that biological labeling imposed upon members of disadvantaged groups. She expressed it for people like herself—women of extraordinary talent. I would apply it more widely—not only to those whose dreams are flouted but also to those who never realize that they may dream—but I cannot match her prose. In conclusion, then, the rest of Eliot's prelude to *Middlemarch:*

> The limits of variation are really much wider than anyone would imagine from the sameness of women's coiffure and the favorite love stories in prose and verse. Here and there a cygnet is reared uneasily among the ducklings in the brown pond, and never finds the living stream in fellowship with its own oary-footed king. Here and there is born a Saint Theresa, foundress of nothing, whose loving heartbeats and sobs after an unattained goodness tremble off and are dispersed among hindrances instead of centering in some long-recognizable deed.

QUESTIONS FOR WRITING AND DISCUSSION

OBSERVING

1. In discussing Paul Broca's work, Gould makes a crucial distinction: "science is an inferential exercise, not a catalog of facts." Illustrate this point by briefly describing the accuracy of Broca's method of data collection and the accuracy of his conclusions drawn from the data.
2. Maria Montessori accepted some of Broca's conclusions but not others. On what basis does she seem to have made this distinction?

EVALUATING

1. Gould's discussion reveals how social presuppositions can dictate supposedly scientific results and lead to contradictions. Why, for example, is Gustave Le Bon concerned about the social consequences of giving women the same education as men if women are intellectually inferior to men? Can you think of any other such contradictions in similar arguments? For example, Nazis argued that Jews were racially inferior to "Aryans" and at the same time claimed that Jews were taking over the world, an indication, one would suppose in applying evolutionary principles in this way to "races," of their superior fitness.
2. Summarize the arguments you have heard for the inferiority of any racial, ethnic, sexual, or economic group, and argue that the scientific basis for those claims is based on presuppositions.

RESPONDING AND APPLYING

1. Suppose Broca had discovered that the women's brains he weighed were heavier than the men's. How do you think he would have responded? Would he have remained the objective scientist and bent before the truth, or would he have found a way to interpret the data consistent with his belief that "women are, on average, a little less intelligent than men"? To what extent can you be found guilty of interpreting data to support your own presuppositions?
2. Although most anthropologists and archaeologists accept the fact that human life arose in Africa, most held to the theory "that the complex thinking and behavior necessary for major cultural changes arose in Europe no earlier than 35,000 years ago." The results of excavations carried out between 1986 and 1990 in Zaire published recently (see *Science News,* 147[1995]: 260) reveal that "Humans in Africa invented sophisticated [tool] technologies long [at least 89,000 years ago] before their European counterparts, who have often been credited with initiating modern culture." To what extent do you think the previous theory was influenced by racist assumptions? What other scientific conclusions do you think might have been influenced by similarly biased assumptions?
3. Gould points out that "individious comparisons among races, classes, and sexes," even after skull measurement had been discredited, continued to be made on the "scientific" basis of intelligence testing. What do you know about the controversies surrounding the validity of intelligence tests? Has the practice of intelligence testing touched you in any way? Has your reading of Gould's essay changed the way you look at this practice?
4. Gould warns against the dangers of attaching value to biological groups, of implying that some are inherently better than others. List the biologically based groups to which you belong. Imagine a "scientific" argument to support the inferiority or superiority of one, and describe your life in a society in which belief in that argument is widespread.

Robert Jay Lifton, "This World Is Not This World" *from* The Nazi Doctors: Medical Killing and the Psychology of Genocide

Perhaps more than any other person working in the medical or psychological sciences, *Robert Jay Lifton* (1926–) has chronicled the experiences of extreme violence and suffering caused by "educated" men and women who are distinctly products of an "advanced" technological age. Whether it be those who survived the atomic bombing of Hiroshima, the pilots who dropped bombs on Vietnam, the medical personnel who became indispensible to Hitler's "final solution," or the planners who have amassed more than 40,000 nuclear warheads, Lifton has used his psychiatric training to become an intimate witness to man's inhumanity to man.

A doctor of medicine himself, Lifton is Distinguished Professor of Psychiatry and Psychology at John Jay College and the Graduate Center of the City University of New York. The twelve books he has written collectively reveal how human the commission of even the most unspeakable atrocities can be. He undertook the study for one of his most important books, *The Nazi Doctors: Medical Killing and the Psychology of Genocide* (1986), the first chapter of which appears below, as a logical consequence of his work on survivors and perpetrators of monstrous evil and because he is a Jew. His friends, however, advised him to stay away from the topic, fearing that in conducting the study, which would require many years and immersion in gruesome atrocities, condemnation might be replaced by kinds of insight that would somehow lessen the horror. Lifton responded by saying that "to avoid probing the sources of evil seemed to me, in the end, a refusal to call forth our capacity to engage and combat it. Such avoidance contains not only fear of contagion but an assumption that Nazis or any other evil has no relationship whatsoever to the rest of us—to more general human capacities." In other words, the scientist can help us make sense of acts by "ordinary" people (for example, the killing of more than one million children) that seem incomprehensible.

Scientists, being after all ordinary people, have often served as instruments of evil policies, and it is especially ironic that during the twentieth century practitioners of the medical sciences, the healing arts, have appeared prominently in such roles. One can note Soviet psychiatrists who lock up dissidents, Chilean doctors serving as torturers, South African doctors who cover up reports of blacks killed in prison, or doctors of many nationalities including our own who have worked to develop the most insidious instruments of mind control and chemical and biological warfare. But Lifton realized there was a significant new element to be examined in Nazi doctors, their "biological visions that justified genocide as a means of national and racial healing." Only a person schooled in the science of psychology could begin to make sense of the foundations of a virulently anti-Semitic racial ideology.

Just as pseudoscience was used in the nineteenth century to reinforce sexism (summarized in Gould's "Women's Brains"), a racial ideology built on what seemed a solid science to millions was used to exterminate an entire culture of Jews in Europe. The fact that hundreds of thousands of educated persons—lawyers, doctors, civil servants, and professors—participated, not to mention the millions who watched and did nothing, begs for an explanation. Part of that explanation is that the ideology of hate was convincing because it was dressed in a metaphor of "scientific" healing.

This World Is Not This World

Robert Jay Lifton

Approaching Auschwitz

1 I gained an important perspective on Auschwitz from an Israeli dentist who had spent three years in that camp. We were completing a long interview, during which he had told me about many things, including details of SS dentists' supervision of prisoners' removal of gold fillings from the teeth of fellow Jews killed in the gas chambers. He looked about the comfortable room in his house with its beautiful view of Haifa, sighed deeply, and said, "This world is not this world." What I think he meant was that, after Auschwitz, the ordinary rhythms and appearances of life, however innocuous or pleasant, were far from the truth of human existence. Underneath those rhythms and appearances lay darkness and menace.

2 The comment also raises the question of our capacity to approach Auschwitz. From the beginning there has been enormous resistance on the part of virtually everyone to knowledge of what the Nazis were doing and have done there. That resistance has hardly abated, whatever the current interest in what we call "the Holocaust." Nor have more recent episodes of mass slaughter done much to overcome it. For to permit one's imagination to enter into the Nazi killing machine—to begin to experience that killing machine—is to alter one's relationship to the entire human project. One does not want to learn about such things.

3 Psychologically speaking, nothing is darker or more menacing, or harder to accept, than the participation of physicians in mass murder. However technicized or commercial the modern physician may have become, he or she is still supposed to be a healer—and one responsible to a tradition of healing, which

all cultures revere and depend upon. Knowledge that the doctor has joined the killers adds a grotesque dimension to the perception that "this world is not this world." During my work I gained the impression that, among Germans and many others, this involvement of physicians was viewed as the most shameful of all Nazi behavior.

4 When we think of the crimes of Nazi doctors, what come to mind are their cruel and sometimes fatal human experiments. Those experiments, in the precise and absolute violation of the Hippocratic oath, mock and subvert the very idea of the ethical physician dedicated to the well-being of patients. I shall examine those human experiments from the standpoint of the regime's medical and political ideology.

5 Yet when we turn to the Nazi doctor's role in Auschwitz, it was not the experiments that were most significant. Rather it was his participation in the killing process—indeed his supervision of Auschwitz mass murder from beginning to end. This aspect of Nazi medical behavior has escaped full recognition—even though we are familiar with photographs of Nazi doctors standing at the ramp and performing their notorious "selections" of arriving Jews, determining which were to go directly to the gas chamber and which were to live, at least temporarily, and work in the camp. Yet this medicalized killing had a logic that was not only deeply significant for Nazi theory and behavior but holds for other expressions of genocide as well.

6 In this book I will examine both the broad Nazi "biomedical vision" as a central psychohistorical principle of the regime, and the psychological behavior of individual Nazi doctors. We need to look at both dimensions if we are to understand more about how Nazi doctors—and Nazis in general—came to do what they did.

7 The very extremity of Auschwitz and related Nazi murder renders it close to unreality. A distinguished European physician, who had struggled with Nazi brutality for forty years—first as an inmate of Auschwitz and other camps and then as an authority on medical consequences of that incarceration—said to me very quietly at the end of a long interview, "You know, I still can't really believe that it happened—that a group of people would round up all of the Jews in Europe and send them to a special place to kill them." He was saying that the Auschwitz "other world" is beyond belief. The wonder is that there is not an even greater tendency than actually exists to accept the directly false contention that Nazi mass murder did not take place.

8 Also at issue for us here is the relationship of Nazi doctors to the human species. Another Auschwitz survivor who knew something about them asked me, "Were they *beasts* when they did what they did? Or were they *human beings?*" He was not surprised by my answer: they were and are men, which is my justification for studying them; and their behavior—Auschwitz itself—was a product of specifically *human* ingenuity and cruelty.

9 I went on to tell this survivor of the ordinariness of most Nazi doctors I had interviewed. Neither brilliant nor stupid, neither inherently evil nor particularly

ethically sensitive, they were by no means the demonic figures—sadistic, fanatic, lusting to kill—people have often thought them to be. My friend replied, "But it is *demonic* that they were *not* demonic." He could then raise his second question, really the one he had in mind in the first place: "How did they become killers?" That question can be addressed, and this book is in the way of an answer.

10 What my survivor friend was struggling with—what I have struggled with throughout this study—is the disturbing psychological truth that participation in mass murder need not require emotions as extreme or demonic as would seem appropriate for such a malignant project. Or to put the matter another way, ordinary people can commit demonic acts.

11 But that did not mean that Nazi doctors were faceless bureaucratic cogs or automatons. As human beings, they were actors and participants who manifested certain kinds of behavior for which they were responsible, and which we can begin to identify.

12 There are several dimensions, then, to the work. At its heart is the transformation of the physician—of the medical enterprise itself—from healer to killer. That transformation requires us to examine the interaction of Nazi political ideology and biomedical ideology in their effects on individual and collective behavior. That in turn takes us to the significance of medicalized killing for Nazi mass murder in general—and for large-scale killing and genocide on the part of others. Finally, the work has relevance for broad questions of human control over life and death—for physicians everywhere, for science and scientists and other professionals in general, for institutions of various kinds—and also for concepts of human nature and ultimate human values. I can no more than touch on most of these general issues, having made a decision to focus on Nazi doctors and medicalized killing, and then on issues of mass murder. But my hope is that others will find here experience that might help them explore any of the searing moral issues implicit in this study.

13 That hope raises the important question of specificity and generality. I believe that one must stress the specificity of the Nazi killing project, especially concerning Jews: its unique characteristics, and the particular forces that shaped it. But having done that, one must also search for larger *principles* suggested by that unique project. No other event or institution can or should be equated with Auschwitz; but nor should we deny ourselves the opportunity to explore its general relevance for genocide and for situations of a very different order in which psychological and moral questions may be considerably more ambiguous. . . .

Medicalized Killing

14 In Nazi mass murder, we can say that a barrier was removed, a boundary crossed: that boundary between violent imagery and periodic killing of victims

(as of Jews in pogroms) on the one hand, and systematic genocide in Auschwitz and elsewhere on the other. My argument in this study is that the medicalization of killing—the imagery of killing in the name of healing—was crucial to that terrible step. At the heart of the Nazi enterprise, then, is the destruction of the boundary between healing and killing.

15 Early descriptions of Auschwitz and other death camps focused on the sadism and viciousness of Nazi guards, officers, and physicians. But subsequent students of the process realized that sadism and viciousness alone could not account for the killing of millions of people. The emphasis then shifted to the bureaucracy of killing: the faceless, detached bureaucratic function originally described by Max Weber, now applied to mass murder.[1] This focus on numbed violence is enormously important, and is consistent with what we shall observe to be the routinization of all Auschwitz function.

16 Yet these emphases are not sufficient in themselves. They must be seen in relation to the visionary motivations associated with ideology, along with the specific individual-psychological mechanisms enabling people to kill. What I call "medicalized killing" addresses these motivational principles and psychological mechanisms, and permits us to understand the Auschwitz victimizers—notably Nazi doctors—both as part of a bureaucracy of killing and as individual participants whose attitudes and behavior can be examined.

17 Medicalized killing can be understood in two wider perspectives. The first is the "surgical" method of killing large numbers of people by means of a controlled technology making use of highly poisonous gas; the method employed became a means of maintaining distance between killers and victims. This distancing had considerable importance for the Nazis in alleviating the psychological problems experienced (as attested over and over by Nazi documents) by the *Einsatzgruppen* troops who carried out face-to-face shooting of Jews in Eastern Europe—problems that did not prevent those troops from murdering 1,400,000 Jews.[2]

18 I was able to obtain direct evidence on this matter during an interview with a former *Wehrmacht* neuropsychiatrist who had treated large numbers of *Einsatzgruppen* personnel for psychological disorders. He told me that these disorders resembled combat reactions of ordinary troops: severe anxiety, nightmares, tremors, and numerous bodily complaints. But in these "killer troops," as he called them, the symptoms tended to last longer and to be more severe. He estimated that 20 percent of those doing the actual killing experienced these symptoms of psychological decompensation. About half of that 20 percent associated their symptoms mainly with the "unpleasantness" of what they

---

[1] See Raul Hilberg, *The Destruction of the European Jews* (Chicago: Quadrangle, 1967 [1961]); Richard L. Rubenstein, *The Cunning of History: Mass Death and the American Future* (New York: Harper & Row, 1975); Arendt, *Eichmann* [1]. Hilberg's expanded edition of his classic work was too recent to consult fully for this book; see *The Destruction of the European Jews,* 3 vols., rev. and definitive ed. (New York: Holmes & Meier, 1985).

[2] Hilberg, *Destruction* [7], 256.

had to do, while the other half seemed to have moral questions about shooting people in that way. The men had greatest psychological difficulty concerning shooting women and children, especially children. Many experienced a sense of guilt in their dreams, which could include various forms of punishment or retribution. Such psychological difficulty led the Nazis to seek a more "surgical" method of killing.

19 But there is another perspective on medicalized killing that I believe to be insufficiently recognized: *killing as a therapeutic imperative.* That kind of motivation was revealed in the words of a Nazi doctor quoted by the distinguished survivor physician Dr. Ella Lingens-Reiner. Pointing to the chimneys in the distance, she asked a Nazi doctor, Fritz Klein, "How can you reconcile that with your [Hippocratic] oath as a doctor?" His answer was, "Of course I am a doctor and I want to preserve life. And out of respect for human life, I would remove a gangrenous appendix from a diseased body. The Jew is the gangrenous appendix in the body of mankind."[3]

20 The medical imagery was still broader. Just as Turkey during the nineteenth century (because of the extreme decline of the Ottoman empire) was known as the "sick man of Europe," so did pre-Hitler ideologues and Hitler himself interpret Germany's post-First World War chaos and demoralization as an "illness," especially of the Aryan race. Hitler wrote in *Mein Kampf,* in the mid-1920s, that "anyone who wants to cure this era, *which is inwardly sick and rotten, must first of all summon up the courage to make clear the causes of this disease.*"[4] The diagnosis was racial. The only genuine "culture-creating" race, the Aryans, had permitted themselves to be weakened to the point of endangered survival by the "destroyers of culture," characterized as "the Jew." The Jews were agents of "racial pollution" and "racial tuberculosis," as well as parasites and bacteria causing sickness, deterioration, and death in the host peoples they infested. They were the "eternal bloodsucker," "vampire," "germ carrier," "peoples' parasite," and "maggot in a rotting corpse."[5] The cure had to be radical: that is (as one scholar put it), by "cutting out the 'canker of decay,' propagating the worthwhile elements and letting the less valuable wither away, . . . [and] 'the extirpation of all those categories of people considered to be worthless or dangerous.'"[6]

---

[3] A slightly different, published version is found in Ella Lingens-Reiner, *Prisoners of Fear* (London: Gollancz, 1948), 1-2.

[4] Adolf Hitler, *Mein Kampf* (Boston: Houghton Mifflin, 1943 [1925-26]), 435.

[5] Ibid., 150, 300-308, 312-13. For scholarly treatments of Hitler's (and earlier) metaphors for the Jews, see Eberhard Jäckel, *Hitler's Weltanschauung: A Blueprint for Power* (Middletown, Conn.: Wesleyan University Press, 1972 [1969]); Rudolph Binion, *Hitler Among the Germans* (New York: Elsevier, 1976); Lucy S. Dawidowicz, *The War Against the Jews, 1933-1945* (New York: Holt, Rinehart & Winston, 1975), 19-21, 55-56; Uriel Tal, *Christians and Jews in Germany: Religion, Politics and Ideology in the Second Reich, 1870-1914* (Ithaca: Cornell University Press, 1975), 259-89.

[6] Hans Buchheim, quoted in Helmut Krausnick, "The Persecution of the Jews," in Krausnick et al., *Anatomy of the SS State* (New York: Walker, 1968 [1965]), 15.

21 Medical metaphor blended with concrete biomedical ideology in the Nazi sequence from coercive sterilization to direct medical killing to the death camps. The unifying principle of the biomedical ideology was that of a deadly racial disease, the sickness of the Aryan race; the cure, the killing of all Jews.

22 Thus, for Hans Frank, jurist and General Governor of Poland during the Nazi occupation, "the Jews were a lower species of life, a kind of vermin, which upon contact infected the German people with deadly diseases." When the Jews in the area he ruled had been killed, he declared that "now a sick Europe would become healthy again."[7] It was a religion of the will—the will as "an all-encompassing metaphysical principle";[8] and what the Nazis "willed" was nothing less than total control over life and death. While this view is often referred to as "social Darwinism," the term applies only loosely, mostly to the Nazi stress on natural "struggle" and on "survival of the fittest." The regime actually rejected much of Darwinism; since evolutionary theory is more or less democratic in its assumption of a common beginning for all races, it is therefore at odds with the Nazi principle of inherent Aryan racial virtue.[9]

23 Even more specific to the biomedical vision was the crude genetic imagery, combined with still cruder eugenic visions. Here Heinrich Himmler, as high priest, spoke of the leadership's task as being "like the plant-breeding specialist who, when he wants to breed a pure new strain from a well-tried species that has been exhausted by too much cross-breeding, first goes over the field to cull the unwanted plants."[10]

24 The Nazi project, then, was not so much Darwinian or social Darwinist as a vision of absolute control over the evolutionary process, over the biological human future. Making widespread use of the Darwinian term "selection," the Nazis sought to take over the functions of nature (natural selection) and God (the Lord giveth and the Lord taketh away) in orchestrating their own "selections," their own version of human evolution.

25 In these visions the Nazis embraced not only versions of medieval mystical anti-Semitism but also a newer (nineteenth- and twentieth-century) claim to "scientific racism." Dangerous Jewish characteristics could be linked with alleged data of scientific disciplines, so that a "mainstream of racism" formed from "the fusion of anthropology, eugenics, and social thought."[11] The resulting "racial and social biology" could make vicious forms of anti-Semitism seem intellectually respectable to learned men and women.

---

[7] Hilberg, *Destruction* [7], 12.

[8] J. P. Stern, *Hitler: The Führer and the People* (Glasgow: Fontana/Collins, 1971), 70. The celebration of that religious impulse was epitomized by the gigantic Nuremberg rally of 1934, whose theme, "The Triumph of the Will," became the title of Leni Riefenstahl's noted film. Riefenstahl, in an interview with an assistant of mine, made clear that Hitler himself provided that slogan.

[9] Mosse, *German Ideology* [5], 103.

[10] Himmler, quoted in Krausnick, "Persecution" [12], 14.

[11] George L. Mosse, *Toward the Final Solution: A History of European Racism* (New York: Fertig, 1978), 77.

QUESTIONS FOR WRITING AND DISCUSSION

OBSERVING

1. What does Lifton mean when he says, "The reversal of healing and killing became an organizing principle of the work"? What, in other words, was the logic behind Nazi killing? Why does Lifton see sadism as an incomplete explanation?
2. How does Lifton interpret the Israeli dentist's words, "This world is not this world"? How does his interpretation explain our resistance to or hesitation in studying evil?
3. Lifton is asked whether the Nazi doctors were humans or beasts. What is his answer and what is the significance of the question? What interpretation of Arendt's phrase, "the banality of evil," does Lifton offer?
4. What is the relation between Nazi "scientific racism" and Darwinism?

EVALUATING

1. Describe some of the reactions of the doctors to Lifton's questions. Why did many try to characterize themselves as decent folks?
2. What role did "distancing" have in "medicalized killing"? In what sense is the same distancing characteristic of life in our industrialized culture?
3. What value do you see in studying genocides like those that occurred in Cambodia in the late 1970s or Armenia in the early part of this century?

RESPONDING AND APPLYING

1. Could anything like what Lifton describes happen again? What tendencies to totalitarianism do you see today in the United States? How does science or pseudoscience enter into these tendencies?
2. Albert Camus, speaking from his own experiences during World War II as a member of the French anti-Nazi underground, has stated that we must strive to be neither victims nor executioners, that we must avoid institutions and actions that create these categories. Is this possible? Before answering, carefully consider the ways you can be victimized and can victimize others, however distanced you may be.
3. Do you think the Holocaust was a Jewish or a human tragedy?
4. In 1932, a study of the long-term effects of syphilis on the human body was begun by the U.S. Public Health Service in the area around Tuskegee, Alabama, which at the time had the highest syphilis rate in the nation. The subjects, poor and uneducated blacks, 425 of them with some form of the disease and a control group of 200 without, were offered free medical treatment for everything except—this they were not told—syphilis. At the time, treatments for syphilis were uncertain and dangerous, but by 1942 penicillin was found to be safe and almost totally effective against the disease, and shortly after the end of the war, the drug was readily available.

Yet treatment for syphilis continued to be withheld from the subjects of this study for the next 25 years, until an alert Associated Press correspondent called attention to the situation in 1971. By then the subjects were either dead or too far advanced in the disease for even penicillin to help. How do you suppose the "distancing" achieved by the medical doctors involved in this experiment (and by the larger medical community as well, since the study's findings were published periodically in medical journals for years) compares with that achieved by Nazi doctors? Do you think these American doctors might have seen their work in terms of something like the "therapeutic imperative" found among Nazi doctors? What do you imagine their logic might have been?

FREDERIK POHL, "DAY MILLON"

Frederik Pohl (1919–) is truly one of the grand old men of American science fiction, having worked as a magazine editor (*Astonishing Stories* and *Super Science Stories* in the early 1940s; *If, Galaxy,* and *Worlds of Tomorrow* in the 1960s), as a book editor for Ace and Bantam in the early 1970s, and most especially as a writer, from the 1930s to the present, authoring some 50 novels and collections of shorter work and still going strong. His best known works include *The Space Merchants,* with C. M. Kornbluth (1953), *Drunkard's Walk* (1960), *Man Plus* (1976), *Gateway* (1977), *JEM* (1979), and *The Way the Future Was: A Memoir* (1979), an autobiographical account of the rise of American science fiction. "Day Million," first published in *Rogue Magazine* in 1966, attacks the narrowmindedness, prejudice, and resistance to change the narrator assumes in his audience. This is an expression of a well-established tradition in science fiction that advocates progress and the expansion of knowledge and sees such resistance to change as the enemy. The issues raised in the story carry into the present well, relating to problems like uncontrolled population growth, narrow notions of racism and of what is permissible behavior sexually, even the purpose of work in a high-tech society. The context of a future so vastly different from our present calls for broader notions of right and wrong, suggesting that perhaps all values are cultural artifacts, not universal and unchanging truths.

Day Million

Frederik Pohl

1 On this day I want to tell you about, which will be about ten thousand years from now, there were a boy, a girl and a love story.

2 Now, although I haven't said much so far, none of it is true. The boy was not what you and I would normally think of as a boy, because he was a hundred and eighty-seven years old. Nor was the girl a girl, for other reasons. And the love story did not entail that sublimation of the urge to rape, and concurrent postponement of the instinct to submit, which we at present understand in such matters. You won't care much for this story if you don't grasp these facts at once. If, however, you will make the effort you'll likely enough find it jam-packed, chockful and tip-top crammed with laughter, tears and poignant sentiment which may, or may not, be worthwhile. The reason the girl was not a girl was that she was a boy.

3 How angrily you recoil from the page! You say, who the hell wants to read about a pair of queers? Calm yourself. Here are no hot-breathing secrets of perversion for the coterie trade. In fact, if you were to see this girl you would not guess that she was in any sense a boy. Breasts, two; reproductive organs, female. Hips, callipygean; face hairless, supra-orbital lobes non-existent. You would term her female on sight, although it is true that you might wonder just what species she was a female of, being confused by the tail, the silky pelt and the gill slits behind each ear.

4 Now you recoil again. Cripes, man, take my word for it. This is a sweet kid, and if you, as a normal male, spent as much as an hour in a room with her you would bend heaven and Earth to get her in the sack. Dora—We will call her that; her "name" was omicron-Dibase seven-group-totter-oot S Doradus 5314, the last part of which is a colour specification corresponding to a shade of green—Dora, I say, was feminine, charming and cute. I admit she doesn't sound that way. She was, as you might put it, a dancer. Her art involved qualities of intellection and expertise of a very high order, requiring both tremendous natural capacities and endless practice; it was performed in null-gravity and I can best describe it by saying that it was something like the performance of a contortionist and something like classical ballet, maybe resembling Damilova's dying swan. It was also pretty damned sexy. In a symbolic way, to be sure; but face it, most of the things we call "sexy" are symbolic, you know, except perhaps an exhibitionist's open clothing. On Day Million when Dora danced, the people who saw her panted, and you would too.

5 About this business of her being a boy. It didn't matter to her audiences that genetically she was male. It wouldn't matter to you, if you were among them, because you wouldn't know it—not unless you took a biopsy cutting of

her flesh and put it under an electron-microscope to find the XY chromosome—and it didn't matter to them because they didn't care. Through techniques which are not only complex but haven't yet been discovered, these people were able to determine a great deal about the aptitudes and casements of babies quite a long time before they were born—at about the second horizon of cell-division, to be exact, when the segmenting egg is becoming a free blastocyst—and then they naturally helped those aptitudes along. Wouldn't we? If we find a child with an aptitude for music we give him a scholarship to Julliard. If they found a child whose aptitudes were for being a woman, they made him one. As sex had long been dissociated from reproduction this was relatively easy to do and caused no trouble and no, or at least very little, comment.

6 How much is "very little"? Oh, about as much as would be caused by our own tampering with Divine Will by filling a tooth. Less than would be caused by wearing a hearing aid. Does it still sound awful? Then look closely at the next busty babe you meet and reflect that she may be a Dora, for adults who are genetically male but somatically female are far from unknown even in our own time. An accident of environment in the womb overwhelms the blueprints of heredity. The difference is that with us it happens only by accident and we don't know about it except rarely, after close study; whereas the people of Day Million did it often, on purpose, because they wanted to.

7 Well, that's enough to tell you about Dora. It would only confuse you to add that she was seven feet tall and smelled of peanut butter. Let us begin our story.

8 On Day Million, Dora swam out of her house, entered a transportation tube, was sucked briskly to the surface in its flow of water and ejected in its plume of spray to an elastic platform in front of her—ah—call it her rehearsal hall.

9 "Oh, hell!" she cried in pretty confusion, reaching out to catch her balance and finding herself tumbled against a total stranger, whom we will call Don.

10 They met cute. Don was on his way to have his legs renewed. Love was the farthest thing from his mind. But when, absentmindedly taking a shortcut across the landing platform for submarinites and finding himself drenched, he discovered his arms full of the loveliest girl he had ever seen, he knew at once they were meant for each other. "Will you marry me?" he asked. She said softly, "Wednesday," and the promise was like a caress.

11 Don was tall, muscular, bronze and exciting. His name was no more Don than Dora's was Dora, but the personal part of it was Adonis in tribute to his vibrant maleness, and so we will call him Don for short. His personality colour-code, in Angstrom units, was 5,290, or only a few degrees bluer than Dora's 5,314—a measure of what they had intuitively discovered at first sight; that they possessed many affinities of taste and interest.

12 I despair of telling you exactly what it was that Don did for a living—I don't mean for the sake of making money, I mean for the sake of giving purpose and

meaning to his life, to keep him from going off his nut with boredom—except to say that it involved a lot of travelling. He travelled in interstellar spaceships. In order to make a spaceship go really fast, about thirty-one male and seven genetically female human beings had to do certain things, and Don was one of the thirty-one. Actually, he contemplated options. This involved a lot of exposure to radiation flux—not so much from his own station in the propulsive system as in the spillover from the next stage, where a genetic female preferred selections, and the sub-nuclear particles making the selections she preferred demolished themselves in a shower of quanta. Well, you don't give a rat's ass for that, but it meant that Don had to be clad at all times in a skin of light, resilient, extremely strong copper-coloured metal. I have already mentioned this, but you probably thought I meant he was sunburned.

13 More than that, he was a cybernetic man. Most of his ruder parts had been long since replaced with mechanisms of vastly more permanence and use. A cadmium centrifuge, not a heart, pumped his blood. His lungs moved only when he wanted to speak out loud, for a cascade of osmotic filters rebreathed oxygen out of his own wastes. In a way, he probably would have looked peculiar to a man from the 20th century, with his glowing eyes and seven-fingered hands. But to himself, and of course to Dora, he looked mighty manly and grand. In the course of his voyages Don had circled Proxima Centauri, Procyon and the puzzling worlds of Mira Ceti; he had carried agricultural templates to the planets of Canopus and brought back warm, witty pets from the pale companion of Aldebaran. Blue-hot or red-cool, he had seen a thousand stars and their ten thousand planets. He had, in fact, been travelling the starlanes, with only brief leaves on Earth, for pushing two centuries. But you don't care about that, either. It is people who make stories, not the circumstances they find themselves in, and you want to hear about these two people. Well, they made it. The great thing they had for each other grew and flowered and burst into fruition on Wednesday, just as Dora had promised. They met at the encoding room, with a couple of well-wishing friends apiece to cheer them on, and while their identities were being taped and stored they smiled and whispered to each other and bore the jokes of their friends with blushing repartee. Then they exchanged their mathematical analogues and went away, Dora to her dwelling beneath the surface of the sea and Don to his ship.

14 It was an idyll, really. They lived happily ever after—or anyway, until they decided not to bother any more and died.

15 Of course, they never set eyes on each other again.

16 Oh, I can see you now, you eaters of charcoal-broiled steak, scratching an incipient bunion with one hand and holding this story with the other, while the stereo plays d'Indy or Monk. You don't believe a word of it, do you? Not for one minute. People wouldn't live like that, you say with a grunt as you get up to put fresh ice in a drink.

17 And yet there's Dora, hurrying back through the flushing commuter pipes toward her underwater home (she prefers it there; has had herself somatically

altered to breathe the stuff). If I tell you with what sweet fulfillment she fits the recorded analogue of Don into the symbol manipulator, hooks herself in and turns herself on . . . if I try to tell you any of that you will simply stare. Or glare; and grumble, what the hell kind of love-making is this? And yet I assure you, friend, I really do assure you that Dora's ecstasies are as creamy and passionate as any of James Bond's lady spies', and one hell of a lot more so than anything you are going to find in "real life." Go ahead, glare and grumble. Dora doesn't care. If she thinks of you at all, her thirty-times-great-great-grandfather, she thinks you're a pretty primordial sort of brute. You are. Why, Dora is farther removed from you than you are from the australopithecines of five thousand centuries ago. You could not swim a second in the strong currents of her life. You don't think progress goes in a straight line, do you? Do you recognize that it is an ascending, accelerating, maybe even exponential curve? It takes hell's own time to get started, but when it goes it goes like a bomb. And you, you Scotch-drinking steak-eater in your relaxacizing chair, you've just barely lighted the primacord of the fuse. What is it now, the six or seven hundred thousandth day after Christ? Dora lives in Day Million, the millionth day of the Christian Era. Ten thousand years from now. Her body fats are polyunsaturated, like Crisco. Her wastes are haemodialysed out of her bloodstream while she sleeps—that means she doesn't have to go to the bathroom. On whim, to pass a slow half-hour, she can command more energy than the entire nation of Portugal can spend today, and use it to launch a weekend satellite or remould a crater on the Moon. She loves Don very much. She keeps his every gesture, mannerism, nuance, touch of hand, thrill of intercourse, passion of kiss stored in symbolic-mathematical form. And when she wants him, all she has to do is turn the machine on and she has him.

18 And Don, of course, has Dora. Adrift on a sponson city a few hundred yards over her head, or orbiting Arcturus fifty light-years away, Don has only to command his own symbol-manipulator to rescue Dora from the ferrite files and bring her to life for him, and there she is; and rapturously, tirelessly they love all night. Not in the flesh, of course; but then his flesh has been extensively altered and it wouldn't really be much fun. He doesn't need the flesh for pleasure. Genital organs feel nothing. Neither do hands, nor breasts, nor lips; they are only receptors, accepting and transmitting impulses. It is the brain that feels; it is the interpretation of those impulses that makes agony or orgasm, and Don's symbol manipulator gives him the analogue of cuddling, the analogue of kissing, the analogue of wild, ardent hours with the eternal, exquisite and incorruptible analogue of Dora. Or Diane. Or sweet Rose, or laughing Alicia; for to be sure, they have each of them exchanged analogues before, and will again.

19 Rats, you say, it looks crazy to me. And you—with your aftershave lotion and your little red car, pushing papers across a desk all day and chasing tail all night—tell me, just how the hell do you think you would look to Tiglath-Pileser, say, or Attila the Hun?

QUESTIONS FOR WRITING AND DISCUSSION

OBSERVING

1. How would you describe the tone of this story? What are the effects of the narrator's addressing the reader? What responses does the narrator seem to expect from the reader, and how does he correct them? Do you find yourself identifying with the audience in this story, with either of the two major characters, with the narrator (the strong presence of the narrator's voice and person as well as the audience responses within the story make them kinds of characters), or with none of the above? Could you argue that the narrator and the imagined audience are in fact the major characters in the story?
2. The narrator says that in his present it is "the six or seven hundred thousandth day after Christ" (1966 is in fact a little over the 700,000th) and that the story's present is "the millionth day of the Christian Era," which would come out about 2730, just 764 years later. Why then does he next say, "Ten thousand years from now," repeating the phrase he used in the story's first paragraph (that would be nearly day 4.4 million)?

EVALUATING

1. There is much in this story that may seem sexist, but it first appeared in and was written for the primarily audience of *Rogue Magazine,* a publication much like *Playboy* or *Penthouse.* In what way is Pohl playing to that audience, in what ways satirizing it?
2. In the future, Pohl imagines it is possible to determine Dora's sexual preference at a pre-embryonic stage and to make appropriate alterations to his/her apparent gender. What assumptions lie behind these capabilities—about the physical basis for certain kinds of behavior, for example, or the degree of certainty of knowledge about those physical conditions?

RESPONDING AND APPLYING

1. What would a traditional rationalist think about such things as sex change, or sex being completely dissociated from reproduction, or sexual activity being completely dissociated from actual physical contact with another person? Would such a person feel similarly about cybernetic human beings, mixtures of man and machine like Don, or about genetic alterations for special capabilities, like Dora's gills, or for the sake of appearance, like the unusual skin colors of both?
2. As you may know, the human genome project has been advancing apace, in fact ahead of the pace projected when it began in 1990, which makes many of the capabilities suggested in Pohl's story closer to reality than even he imagined. And the disturbing implications of these developments

have not gone unrecognized. Noted writer in bioethics Leon R. Kass has pointed out that the new biotechnologies

> are in a decisive respect unique in that the object upon which they operate is man himself. The technologies of energy or food production, of communication, of manufacture, and of motion greatly alter the implements available to man and the conditions under which he uses them. In contrast, the biomedical technology works to change the user himself. . . . Indeed, both those who welcome and those who fear the advent of human engineering ground their hopes and fears in the same prospect, that *man can, for the first time, re-create himself.* (*Toward a More Natural Science: Biology and Human Affairs,* 1985, 18; Kass' italics.)

Given such possibilities, what action would you recommend? Stop all genetic research? Stop all research on human genetic materials? Somehow control the application of the results of such research?

3. Would you support or object to the application of genetic manipulations, assuming they are possible, to problems of birth defects like Down syndrome, hemophilia, dwarfism, or sickle cell anemia? How about genetically based susceptibility to diseases like certain kinds of cancer, schizophrenia, or alcoholism? How possible do you think it is to distinguish clearly between the therapeutic (curing a diseased condition) and the eugenic (improving the individual or the race) applications of genetics? Cosmetic surgery in certain cases, for example, has been legally judged to be therapeutic; if such conditions could be identified and corrected genetically prior to birth, should they be?

PERSPECTIVES

Scientific Controversy and Pseudoscience

We focus here not so much on the many ethical issues science may generate, but on some of the more strictly scientific ones. Let us grant that science can be quite wrong, as Gould demonstrated in "Women's Brains," but how can we distinguish between good and bad science, between theories we can recognize as useful contributions to knowledge, ones that are interesting but not of much use, and ones which are not science at all, though they may claim our attention in what appears to be the language of science?

STEPHEN JAY GOULD, "SEX, DRUGS, DISASTERS, AND THE EXTINCTION OF DINOSAURS"

Science, by its nature, is full of controversy. It develops consensus on many issues as it moves along, but its cutting edge always appears in those areas of uncertainty where a real possibility exists that greater certainty can emerge, and occasionally its supposed consensus is shattered in what are often called scientific revolutions. In those cutting areas especially, however, we find competing explanations and the opportunity for surprise. *Stephen Jay Gould* gives us a good example of such competing claims in the essay that follows.

The judgments Gould expresses here are based on the work of two modern historians of science, Karl R. Popper and Thomas S. Kuhn. In such works as *The Logic of Scientific Discovery* (1934) and *Conjectures and Refutations: The Growth of Scientific Knowledge* (1962), Popper argues that scientific knowledge is never complete and, most important, can never be proven. Scientific theories are essentially conjectures that can be tested: consistently negative results can prove a theory false (in Popper's terms, an experiment can "falsify" the theory), but positive results can only provisionally "confirm" or corroborate the theory, which may mean it is true only in this case, or that class of cases, but never absolutely or certainly. Popper continues:

> Those among our theories which turn out to be highly resistant to criticism, which appear to us at a certain moment of time to be better approximations to truth than other known theories, may be described, together with the reports of their tests, as "the science" of that time. Since none of them can be positively justified [i.e., proven], it is essentially their critical and progressive character—the fact that we can *argue* about their claim to solve our problems better than their competitors—which constitutes the rationality of science.[1]

Thus, science differs from other areas of knowledge in that it deals with problems that can be solved; it proposes hypotheses that can be tested and confirmed or, as Gould does with Broca's theory in "Women's Brains," that can be falsified.

Kuhn, in *The Structure of Scientific Revolutions* (1962), offers a similar conception of scientific knowledge in slightly different terms. He defines "normal science" in any particular area for any particular time as a coherent body of knowledge possessing two characteristics: it is generally accepted by the scientific community, and it is "sufficiently open-ended to leave all sorts of problems for the redefined

[1] Popper, K. R., *Conjectures and Refutations: The Growth of Scientific Knowledge,* New York: Basic Books, 1962, vii.

group of practitioners to resolve"[2]; that is, it generates more science. Gould uses a combination of Popper's and Kuhn's criteria to decide among competing theories that may account for the extinction of the dinosaurs.

Sex, Drugs, Disasters, and the Extinction of Dinosaurs

Stephen Jay Gould

1 Science, in its most fundamental definition, is a fruitful mode of inquiry, not a list of enticing conclusions. The conclusions are the consequence, not the essence.

2 My greatest unhappiness with most popular presentations of science concerns their failure to separate fascinating claims from the methods that scientists use to establish the facts of nature. Journalists, and the public, thrive on controversial and stunning statements. But science is, basically, a way of knowing—in P. B. Medawar's apt words, "the art of the soluble." If the growing corps of popular science writers would focus on *how* scientists develop and defend those fascinating claims, they would make their greatest possible contribution to public understanding.

3 Consider three ideas, proposed in perfect seriousness to explain that greatest of all titillating puzzles—the extinction of dinosaurs. Since these three notions invoke the primarily fascinating themes of our culture—sex, drugs, and violence—they surely reside in the category of fascinating claims. I want to show why two of them rank as silly speculation, while the other represents science at its grandest and most useful.

4 Science works with testable proposals. If, after much compilation and scrutiny of data, new information continues to affirm a hypothesis, we may accept it provisionally and gain confidence as further evidence mounts. We can never be completely sure that a hypothesis is right, though we may be able to show with confidence that it is wrong. The best scientific hypotheses are also generous and expansive: they suggest extensions and implications that enlighten related, and even far distant, subjects. Simply consider how the idea of evolution has influenced virtually every intellectual field.

5 Useless speculation, on the other hand, is restrictive. It generates no testable hypothesis, and offers no way to obtain potentially refuting evidence. Please note that I am not speaking of truth or falsity. The speculation may well

---

[2] Kuhn, T. S., *The Structure of Scientific Revolutions,* 2nd ed. Chicago: U. of Chicago Press, 1970, 10.

be true; still, if it provides, in principle, no material for affirmation or rejection, we can make nothing of it. It must simply stand forever as an intriguing idea. Useless speculation turns in on itself and leads nowhere; good science, containing both seeds for its potential refutation and implications for more and different testable knowledge, reaches out. But, enough preaching. Let's move on to dinosaurs, and the three proposals for their extinction.

1 Sex: Testes function only in a narrow range of temperature (those of mammals hang externally in a scrotal sac because internal body temperatures are too high for their proper function): A worldwide rise in temperature at the close of the Cretaceous period caused the testes of dinosaurs to stop functioning and led to their extinction by sterilization of males.

2 Drugs: Angiosperms (flowering plants) first evolved toward the end of the dinosaurs' reign. Many of these plants contain psychoactive agents, avoided by mammals today as a result of their bitter taste. Dinosaurs had neither means to taste the bitterness nor livers effective enough to detoxify the substances. They died of massive overdoses.

3 Disasters: A large comet or asteroid struck the earth some 65 million years ago, lofting a cloud of dust into the sky and blocking sunlight, thereby suppressing photosynthesis and so drastically lowering world temperatures that dinosaurs and hosts of other creatures became extinct.

Before analyzing these three tantalizing statements, we must establish a basic ground rule often violated in proposals for the dinosaurs' demise. *There is no separate problem of the extinction of dinosaurs.* Too often we divorce specific events from their wider contexts and systems of cause and effect. The fundamental fact of dinosaur extinction is its synchrony with the demise of so many other groups across a wide range of habitats, from terrestrial to marine.

6 The history of life has been punctuated by brief episodes of mass extinction. A recent analysis by University of Chicago paleontologists Jack Sepkoski and Dave Raup, based on the best and most exhaustive tabulation of data ever assembled, shows clearly that five episodes of mass dying stand well above the "background" extinctions of normal times (when we consider all mass extinctions, large and small, they seem to fall in a regular 26-million-year cycle . . .). The Cretaceous debacle, occurring 65 million years ago and separating the Mesozoic and Cenozoic eras of our geological time scale, ranks prominently among the five. Nearly all the marine plankton (single-celled, floating creatures) died with geological suddenness; among marine invertebrates, nearly 15 percent of all families perished, including many previously dominant groups, especially the ammonites (relatives of squids in coiled shells). On land, the dinosaurs disappeared after more than 100 million years of unchallenged domination.

7 In this context, speculations limited to dinosaurs alone ignore the larger phenomenon. We need a coordinated explanation for a system of events that

includes the extinction of dinosaurs as one component. Thus it makes little sense, though it may fuel our desire to view mammals as inevitable inheritors of the earth, to guess that dinosaurs died because small mammals ate their eggs (a perennial favorite among untestable speculations). It seems most unlikely that some disaster peculiar to dinosaurs befell these massive beasts—and that the debacle happened to strike just when one of history's five great dyings had enveloped the earth for completely different reasons.

8 The testicular theory, an old favorite from the 1940s, had its root in an interesting and thoroughly respectable study of temperature tolerances in the American alligator, published in the staid *Bulletin of the American Museum of Natural History* in 1946 by three experts on living and fossil reptiles—E. H. Colbert, my own first teacher in paleontology; R. B. Cowles; and C. M. Bogert.

9 The first sentence of their summary reveals a purpose beyond alligators: "This report describes an attempt to infer the reactions of extinct reptiles, especially the dinosaurs, to high temperatures as based upon reactions observed in the modern alligator." They studied, by rectal thermometry, the body temperatures of alligators under changing conditions of heating and cooling. (Well, let's face it, you wouldn't want to try sticking a thermometer under a 'gator's tongue.) The predictions under test go way back to an old theory first stated by Galileo in the 1630s—the unequal scaling of surfaces and volumes. As an animal, or any object, grows (provided its shape doesn't change), surface areas must increase more slowly than volumes—since surfaces get larger as length squared, while volumes increase much more rapidly, as length cubed. Therefore, small animals have high ratios of surface to volume, while large animals cover themselves with relatively little surface.

10 Among cold-blooded animals lacking any physiological mechanism for keeping their temperatures constant, small creatures have a hell of a time keeping warm—because they lose so much heat through their relatively large surfaces. On the other hand, large animals, with their relatively small surfaces, may lose heat so slowly that, once warm, they may maintain effectively constant temperatures against ordinary fluctuations of climate. (In fact, the resolution of the "hot-blooded dinosaur" controversy that burned so brightly a few years back may simply be that, while large dinosaurs possessed no physiological mechanism for constant temperature, and were not therefore warm-blooded in the technical sense, their large size and relatively small surface area kept them warm.)

11 Colbert, Cowles, and Bogert compared the warming rates of small and large alligators. As predicted, the small fellows heated up (and cooled down) more quickly. When exposed to a warm sun, a tiny 50-gram (1.76-ounce) alligator heated up one degree Celsius every minute and a half, while a large alligator, 260 times bigger at 13,000 grams (28.7 pounds), took seven and a half minutes to gain a degree. Extrapolating up to an adult 10-ton dinosaur, they concluded that a one-degree rise in body temperature would take eighty-six hours. If large animals absorb heat so slowly (through their relatively small surfaces), they will also be unable to shed any excess heat gained when temperatures rise above a favorable level.

12 The authors then guessed that large dinosaurs lived at or near their optimum temperatures; Cowles suggested that a rise in global temperatures just before the Cretaceous extinction caused the dinosaurs to heat up beyond their optimal tolerance—and, being so large, they couldn't shed the unwanted heat. (In a most unusual statement within a scientific paper, Colbert and Bogert then explicitly disavowed this speculative extension of their empirical work on alligators.) Cowles conceded that this excess heat probably wasn't enough to kill or even to enervate the great beasts, but since testes often function only within a narrow range of temperature, he proposed that this global rise might have sterilized all the males, causing extinction by natural contraception.

13 The overdose theory has recently been supported by UCLA psychiatrist Ronald K. Siegel. Siegel has gathered, he claims, more than 2,000 records of animals who, when given access, administer various drugs to themselves—from a mere swig of alcohol to massive doses of the big H. Elephants will swill the equivalent of twenty beers at a time, but do not like alcohol in concentrations greater than 7 percent. In a silly bit of anthropocentric speculation, Siegel states that "elephants drink, perhaps, to forget . . . the anxiety produced by shrinking rangeland and the competition for food."

14 Since fertile imaginations can apply almost any hot idea to the extinction of dinosaurs, Siegel found a way. Flowering plants did not evolve until late in the dinosaurs' reign. These plants also produced an array of aromatic, amino-acid-based alkaloids—the major group of psychoactive agents. Most mammals are "smart" enough to avoid these potential poisons. The alkaloids simply don't taste good (they are bitter); in any case, we mammals have livers happily supplied with the capacity of detoxify them. But, Siegel speculates, perhaps dinosaurs could neither taste the bitterness nor detoxify the substances once ingested. He recently told members of the American Psychological Association: "I'm not suggesting that all dinosaurs OD'd on plant drugs, but it certainly was a factor." He also argued that death by overdose may help explain why so many dinosaur fossils are found in contorted positions. (Do not go gentle into that good night.)

15 Extraterrestrial catastrophes have long pedigrees in the popular literature of extinction, but the subject exploded again in 1979, after a long lull, when the father-son, physicist-geologist team of Luis and Walter Alvarez proposed that an asteroid, some 10 km in diameter, struck the earth 65 million years ago (comets, rather than asteroids, have since gained favor. . . . Good science is self-corrective).

16 The force of such a collision would be immense, greater by far than the megatonnage of all the world's nuclear weapons. . . . In trying to reconstruct a scenario that would explain the simultaneous dying of dinosaurs on land and so many creatures in the sea, the Alvarezes proposed that a gigantic dust cloud, generated by particles blown aloft in the impact, would so darken the earth that photosynthesis would cease and temperatures drop precipitously. (Rage, rage against the dying of the light.) The single-celled photosynthetic oceanic plankton, with life cycles measured in weeks, would perish outright, but land plants might survive through the dormancy of their seeds (land plants were not much

affected by the Cretaceous extinction, and any adequate theory must account for the curious pattern of differential survival). Dinosaurs would die by starvation and freezing; small, warm-blooded mammals, with more modest requirements for food and better regulation of body temperature, would squeak through. "Let the bastards freeze in the dark," as bumper stickers of our chauvinistic neighbors in sunbelt states proclaimed several years ago during the Northeast's winter oil crisis.

17 All three theories, testicular malfunction, psychoactive overdosing, and asteroidal zapping, grab our attention mightily. As pure phenomenology, they rank about equally high on any hit parade of primal fascination. Yet one represents expansive science, the others restrictive and untestable speculation. The proper criterion lies in evidence and methodology; we must probe behind the superficial fascination of particular claims.

18 How could we possibly decide whether the hypothesis of testicular frying is right or wrong? We would have to know things that the fossil record cannot provide. What temperatures were optimal for dinosaurs? Could they avoid the absorption of excess heat by staying in the shade, or in caves? At what temperatures did their testicles cease to function? Were late Cretaceous climates ever warm enough to drive the internal temperatures of dinosaurs close to this ceiling? Testicles simply don't fossilize, and how could we infer their temperature tolerances even if they did? In short, Cowles's hypothesis is only an intriguing speculation leading nowhere. The most damning statement against it appeared right in the conclusion of Colbert, Cowles, and Bogert's paper, when they admitted: "It is difficult to advance any definite arguments against this hypothesis." My statement may seem paradoxical—isn't a hypothesis really good if you can't devise any arguments against it? Quite the contrary. It is simply untestable and unusable.

19 Siegel's overdosing has even less going for it. At least Cowles extrapolated his conclusion from some good data on alligators. And he didn't completely violate the primary guideline of siting dinosaur extinction in the context of a general mass dying—for rise in temperature could be the root cause of a general catastrophe, zapping dinosaurs by testicular malfunction and different groups for other reasons. But Siegel's speculation cannot touch the extinction of ammonites or oceanic plankton (diatoms make their own food with good sweet sunlight; they don't OD on the chemicals of terrestrial plants). It is simply a gratuitous, attention-grabbing guess. It cannot be tested, for how can we know what dinosaurs tasted and what their livers could do? Livers don't fossilize any better than testicles.

20 The hypothesis doesn't even make any sense in its own context. Angiosperms were in full flower ten million years before dinosaurs went the way of all flesh. Why did it take so long? As for the pains of a chemical death recorded in contortions of fossils, I regret to say (or rather I'm pleased to note for the dinosaurs' sake) that Siegel's knowledge of geology must be a bit deficient: muscles contract after death and geological strata rise and fall with motions of the earth's crust after burial—more than enough reason to distort a fossil's pristine appearance.

21 The impact story, on the other hand, has a sound basis in evidence. It can be tested, extended, refined and, if wrong, disproved. The Alvarezes did not just construct an arresting guess for public consumption. They proposed their hypothesis after laborious geochemical studies with Frank Asaro and Helen Michael had revealed a massive increase of iridium in rocks deposited right at the time of extinction. Iridium, a rare metal of the platinum group, is virtually absent from indigenous rocks of the earth's crust; most of our iridium arrives on extraterrestrial objects that strike the earth.

22 The Alvarez hypothesis bore immediate fruit. Based originally on evidence from two European localities, it led geochemists throughout the world to examine other sediments of the same age. They found abnormally high amounts of iridium everywhere—from continental rocks of the western United States to deep sea cores from the South Atlantic.

23 Cowles proposed his testicular hypothesis in the mid-1940s. Where has it gone since then? Absolutely nowhere, because scientists can do nothing with it. The hypothesis must stand as a curious appendage to a solid study of alligators. Siegel's overdose scenario will also win a few press notices and fade into oblivion. The Alvarezes' asteroid falls into a different category altogether, and much of the popular commentary has missed this essential distinction by focusing on the impact and its attendant results, and forgetting what really matters to a scientist—the iridium. If you talk about asteroids, dust, and darkness, you tell stories no better and no more entertaining than fried testicles or terminal trips. It is the iridium—the source of testable evidence—that counts and forges the crucial distinction between speculation and science.

24 The proof, to twist a phrase, lies in the doing. Cowles's hypothesis has generated nothing in thirty-five years. Since its proposal in 1979, the Alvarez hypothesis has spawned hundreds of studies, a major conference, and attendant publications. Geologists are fired up. They are looking for iridium at all other extinction boundaries. Every week exposes a new wrinkle in the scientific press. Further evidence that the Cretaceous iridium represents extraterrestrial impact and not indigenous volcanism continues to accumulate. As I revise this essay in November 1984 (this paragraph will be out of date when the book is published), new data include chemical "signatures" of other isotopes indicating unearthly provenance, glass spherules of a size and sort produced by impact and not by volcanic eruptions, and high-pressure varieties of silica formed (so far as we know) only under the tremendous shock of impact.

25 My point is simply this: Whatever the eventual outcome (I suspect it will be positive), the Alvarez hypothesis is exciting, fruitful science because it generates tests, provides us with things to do, and expands outward. We are having fun, battling back and forth, moving toward a resolution, and extending the hypothesis beyond its original scope. . . .

26 As just one example of the unexpected, distant cross-fertilization that good science engenders, the Alvarez hypothesis made a major contribution to a theme that has riveted public attention in the past few months—so-called nuclear winter. . . . In a speech delivered in April 1982, Luis Alvarez calculated the energy that a ten-kilometer asteroid would release on impact. He compared

such an explosion with a full nuclear exchange and implied that all-out atomic war might unleash similar consequences.

27 This theme of impact leading to massive dust clouds and falling temperatures formed an important input to the decision of Carl Sagan and a group of colleagues to model the climatic consequences of nuclear holocaust. Full nuclear exchange would probably generate the same kind of dust cloud and darkening that may have wiped out the dinosaurs. Temperatures would drop precipitously and agriculture might become impossible. Avoidance of nuclear war is fundamentally an ethical and political imperative, but we must know the factual consequences to make firm judgments. I am heartened by a final link across disciplines and deep concerns—another criterion, by the way, of science at its best. A recognition of the very phenomenon that made our evolution possible by exterminating the previously dominant dinosaurs and clearing a way for the evolution of large mammals, including us, might actually help to save us from joining those magnificent beasts in contorted poses among the strata of the earth.

QUESTIONS FOR WRITING AND DISCUSSION

OBSERVING

1. Identify as many statements by Gould as you can find that echo Popper's or Kuhn's criteria for what constitutes good science. Note that although Gould cites neither source, to accuse him of plagiarism would be unfair. Popper's and Kuhn's criteria have become such well-accepted approaches to the current scientific paradigm that such references are no longer necessary—anymore than a scientist would think it necessary today to cite Darwin when using the model of biological evolution.
2. Briefly summarize the major reasons why the sex and drugs theories for dinosaur extinction are not good science, and why the disaster hypothesis is.

EVALUATING

1. In addition to sex, drugs, and disasters, Gould briefly mentions another and older theory to explain dinosaur extinction, competition with mammals. What kind of presuppositions and ideologies prevalent during the first half of this century made this explanation seem plausible, even preferable despite the fact that it offered no help in explaining the well-known and simultaneous mass extinction of so much of marine life? Notice that the mammalian competition hypothesis required the view that dinosaurs were inferior in important ways to mammals.
2. Argue that the dismissal of the mammalian competition theory is part of the reason many generally assumed features of dinosaurs, including their

cold-bloodedness and lack of intelligence, are currently being radically revised. Does this suggest further ideological connections?

3. What reasons, other than purely scientific ones, can explain why some scientists may prefer any of the three major theories discussed by Gould? Argue that prejudices in themselves will or will not render these theories invalid.
4. Among the questions asked at the end of the Darwin selection was this: "What is the usefulness of a theory like evolution that cannot ever be fully proven?" Having read the Gould selections and the introduction to them, explain whether you find yourself better equipped to answer this question.

RESPONDING AND APPLYING

1. How satisfied are you with Gould's explanation of the best choice? Are you disturbed by his acknowledgment that an untestable hypothesis, *even if true*, is still bad science?
2. Choose any body of knowledge that is generally considered marginally scientific or pseudoscientific—telekinesis, telepathy, UFOs, creationism, astrology, palmistry, and so on. Assess the "scientific" basis and the approach in these bodies of knowledge according to Popper's and Kuhn's criteria and according to your own criteria.
3. As stated in the introduction to this selection, learning a science is an initiation into the current scientific paradigm, which is often ignored in our science classes. How important is it that your teachers introduce a concept with something like, "This is the current model"?

JOEL CRACRAFT, "THE SCIENTIFIC RESPONSE TO CREATIONISM"

Creationism in its broadest sense, the belief that a divine being is ultimately responsible for the coming into existence of the cosmos, is certainly a legitimate topic for philosophic and theologic debate. So-called scientific creationism, the vast majority of professional scientists believe, is not. *Joel Cracraft,* curator of ornithology at the American Museum of Natural History who has published extensively in major zoological journals, explains why in the essay below. He was inspired to speak to this issue by the case of "The Balanced Treatment for Creation-Science and Evolution-Science Act" passed into law in Arkansas in 1981. After a two-week trial in federal court, this act was declared unconstitutional early in 1982 on the grounds that "(1) it has been passed with the specific purpose of advancing religion, (2) it had as a major effect 'the advancement of particular religious beliefs,' and (3) it created for Arkansas an 'excessive and prohibited entanglement with religion'" (*Creationism, Science, and the Law,* Marcel C.

La Follette, ed., Cambridge: MIT Press, 1983). Part of the basis for these findings, expressed in the opinion rendered by U.S. District Judge William R. Overton, is that "'creation science' as defined in that section [of the act] is simply not science." Though seemingly settled, the issue has risen again in 1996 in Tennessee, the state where in 1925 John Scopes was convicted of teaching evolution. In March, the Tennessee Legislature passed an act that requires firing any teacher who presents evolution as fact.

Scientific Response to Creationism

Joel Cracraft

INTRODUCTION

1 The rising public awareness of Creationism during the past several years derives not only from the creationists' highly efficient public-relations program, but also from a vigorous response by scientists, philosophers, and theologians. No new tactics were needed to persuade conservative evangelicals that Creationism deserved a wider hearing within secular society, particularly in the public school system; the tenets of Creationism have always been acceptable to these and similar fundamentalist religious groups. But the creationists have also had considerable success in persuading a substantial "uncommitted" portion of Americans—many as unaware of contemporary thinking on science, philosophy, and theology as of the content of Creationism—that Creationism possesses sufficient merit to warrant public support, however marginal. The creationists have accomplished this success primarily through well-placed political pressure, but their major argument has been that Creationism is at least as scientific as the present-day scientific disciplines and thus should be treated with fairness, an open mind, and a willingness to consider equally all "alternative" scientific ideas.

2 For educated persons without formal training in the sciences, many creationist statements—cloaked by the jargon of science and pronounced with conviction by people with Ph.D.'s from reputable universities—have an authoritative ring. Especially when such statements are made in the forum of public debate, the opposing scientist, rarely as skilled in forensics as the creationist, often appears to be on the defensive. The success of the campaign to persuade the public that Creationism has legitimate scientific content has had nothing to do with the normal process of evaluating the merits of competing scientific ideas. The creationists ask the public to arbitrate what is claimed to be a sci-

entific debate while scientists seek judgment of their ideas primarily within the scientific community.

3 In this essay I will examine the proposition that Creationism is legitimate science. To do that, I must first consider, at least briefly, the philosophical basis of that claim, including the methods the creationists use to discredit contemporary scientific thought. Most of my essay, however, will be directed at evaluating the six "scientific" claims most often asserted by the creationists in their writings and public debates.

The Philosophical Position of Creationism

4 Because they accept the Bible as a true, factual account of the history of the universe, earth, and life, the creationists are compelled logically to redefine the philosophical and methodological foundations of science. No longer is science characterized solely by naturalistic explanations of natural phenomena—the creationists place supernatural explanations within the legitimate domain of science. No longer can science construct explanatory hypotheses about events having a time dimension—to creationists, science must study only the observable, only that which can be verified in a laboratory experiment. No longer must scientific ideas, or conjectures, be subject to criticism and eventual rejection—some statements, such as those derived from revelation, are not only to be considered scientific in their content, but also impervious to criticism. In public forums, the creationists are very reluctant to admit that the aim of creation-science is to fit observations about nature into a literal Biblical framework. But in their writings, the creationists (including such leaders as Henry M. Morris, Director of the Institute for Creation Research) are often quite candid about their motives:

> The Bible is the Word of God, absolutely inerrant and verbally inspired . . . The Bible gives us the revelation we need, and it will be found that all the known facts of science or history can be very satisfactorily understood within this Biblical framework.[1]

5 It is impossible, therefore, to evaluate the "science" in Creationism as if this were a typical scientific debate. The creationist world view dictates suspension of commonly accepted canons of science. Moreover, in their criticisms of contemporary science, the creationists rarely attempt to support their claims on merit alone. Rather, they promote a form of dualism: evidence *against* a contemporary scientific idea is evidence *for* a creationist interpretation. Of course, finding evidence against any important scientific idea is not difficult. Real science—particularly "important" science—is full of debate. By choosing the side they wish to discredit and then selectively quoting opposing scientists, the creationists attempt to construct their case. Consider two among many examples.

6 In *Creation: The Facts of Life,* Gary Parker of the Institute for Creation Research emphasizes the design apparent in life as evidence of a supernatural designer. He even cites Harvard biologist Richard C. Lewontin to that effect:

> Then there's the "marvelous fit of organisms to the environment," the special adaptations of cleaner fish, woodpeckers, bombardier beetles, etc., etc.,—what Darwin called "Difficulties with the Theory," and what Harvard's Lewontin (1978) called "the chief evidence of a Supreme Designer." Because of their "perfection of structure," he says, organisms "appear to have been carefully and artfully designed."[2]

What Parker fails to tell his readers is that Lewontin was, in truth, describing the cultural milieu that Darwin faced as he struggled with the problem of adaptation. Here are Lewontin's words in his *Scientific American* article:

> It was the marvelous fit of organisms to the environment, much more than the great diversity of forms, that was the chief evidence of a Supreme Designer. Darwin realized that if a naturalistic theory of evolution was to be successful, it would have to explain the apparent perfection of organisms and not simply their variations.[3]

Yet another example involves Thomas G. Barnes, member of the Institute for Creation Research. Writing in 1973, he claims that the earth's magnetic field does not reverse its polarity (with the North Pole becoming the South, and vice versa).[4] By 1973, of course, geologists and geophysicists had demonstrated conclusively the actuality of reversals. To support his case, Barnes cited one of the leaders in the field, J. A. Jacobs, as expressing doubts about the validity of the reversal hypothesis.[5] The Jacobs' book on which Barnes relied, however, was published in 1963, several years *before* crucial experiments finally demonstrated the reversals, and thus it is no wonder that he was cautious at that time.[6] The Parker and Barnes methods of argumentation are typical of those in all creationist writings.

The Scientific Case Against Creationism

7 Every scientist who becomes engaged in the creation-evolution controversy experiences a sense of frustration over the constant necessity to defend well-established scientific knowledge against the creationists' claims to the contrary. The creationist challenge has not been formulated from a rigorous debate within the scientific literature. This challenge is strictly external to the scientific community and arises within organizations whose stated purposes are avowedly religious.

8 In this section I will briefly discuss six of the major arguments that the creationists raise against the findings of modern science. It is impossible within this brief essay to provide references to the vast technical literature concerning these issues. Instead, I will attempt to explain both the nature of the creationists' assertions and the scientific evidence against them.

The Second Law of Thermodynamics

9 Perhaps no scientific claim is so important to the creationists as their assertion that the laws of physics, especially as embodied in thermodynamics, are more in accord with Creationism than with contemporary physics, chemistry, or biology. They state this repeatedly:

> The Second Law of Thermodynamics is especially significant in its support of the creation model and, correspondingly, its contradiction of the evolution model . . . Evolution requires a universal principle of upward change; the entropy law is a universal principle of downward change.[7]

> We are warranted, then, in concluding that the evolutionary process . . . is completely precluded by the Second Law of Thermodynamics. There seems no way of modifying the basic evolutionary model to accommodate this Second Law.[8]

10 The creationists argue that the inherent tendency of thermodynamic systems to pass from states of high order (low entropy) to those less ordered is opposite to and necessarily precludes a long, continuous history of increasing diversification and complexity of life forms, as interpreted by evolutionary biology. The controversy is easily illustrated by an example. Consider a closed container with a mixture of two different gases subjected to a thermal gradient. At the start, let molecules of one kind be in the right half, of the other kind in the other. This would represent a highly ordered configuration for these molecules. If the system is kept closed to outside energy flow, the gases will soon mix completely and the entire system will reach a configuration of least order, or maximum entropy.

11 When the creationists state that evolution is impossible because it violates the second law, they accept the premise that the system comprising biological materials is a *closed* system. One of the first things taught in elementary biology courses is that the biosphere is, in fact, an open system, receiving a continuous flow of energy from the outside in the form of sunlight. The biosphere, a small region of the universe, may manifest high degrees of order at the expense of the surroundings, ultimately connected to the huge and continuing increase of the entropy of our sun. When this point is brought to the attention of the creationists, they simply respond that it makes no difference. Even an open system, they claim, must have a "program" to direct the increase in order and a "converter" to change the energy needed to build that order. These arguments are, however, straw men manufactured by the creationists. Changes in open systems are predicated upon the configurations already present, and the work applied to systems to drive the change arises inherently from the conversion of one form of energy to another.

12 During the last thirty or forty years a whole branch of thermodynamics has arisen which treats the irreversible processes within nonequilibrium systems, such as the biosphere.[9] Few scientists today believe that we can use the second law to imply, as do the creationists, that regions of open systems cannot

become more organized through time. A closed thermodynamic system is an idealized concept, its closest approximation being a highly controlled experimental situation. Numerous recent studies have successfully applied thermodynamics, properly understood, directly to the question of biological evolution.[10] Not a single creationist has ever challenged this research within the scientific literature.

The Improbability of the Evolution of Life

13 The second most important argument raised by the creationists actually is closely tied to the question of irreversible thermodynamics. The "laws of probability," the creationists assert, rule out the evolution of life. They pose the question this way:

> Assume a "sea" of freely available components, each uniquely capable of performing a specific useful function. What is the probability that two or more of them can come together by chance to form an integrated functioning organism?[11]

> The real problem for evolutionists is explaining how a cell in all of its complexity could arise suddenly from simple inorganic atoms . . . The sudden "poof!" formation of a cell would demand a supernatural act by an agent with supernatural power and intelligence.[12]

14 An extensive body of scientific research exists on the origin of large macromolecules and the cellular origin of life.[13] The creationists have never appeared to be cognizant of this literature, at least on an intellectual and scientific level; instead, they have chosen to re-define the scientific question in a manner that best suits their own polemics. They refer consistently to the origin of complex organic molecules, or to life itself, by characterizing this evolution as being "sudden," "random," and entirely due to "chance." They go to great lengths to calculate the "improbability" that simple molecules could have united spontaneously to form life.

15 The creationists' probability argument is a caricature of science, not a careful consideration of the complicated problems surrounding this issue. The common elements comprising organic molecules here on earth—hydrogen, oxygen, nitrogen, and carbon—are also characteristic of all bodies of the universe. One of these elements' basic properties is their strong affinity for one another to form compounds of varying complexity. Thousands of scientific papers have addressed the physics and chemistry of these chemical reactions. Many scientists have investigated the kinetics of these reactions—how larger and larger molecules are synthesized naturally—and attempted to relate these reactions to the conditions postulated to have been present on the primitive earth 4 to 4.5 billion years ago. No scientist claims that life arose "spontaneously" from non-life, nor does any scientist profess to having certain knowledge of the

precise sequence of chemical reactions leading to macromolecules, such as nucleic acids, characteristic of life.

16 The creationists' argument is a flagrant misapplication of probability analysis. To determine the combined probability for a series of events, one must know the probability of each event in the series. The creationists arbitrarily designate the probabilities of a series of chemical events, with no regard to scientific relevance. Moreover, they assume that the changes from one state to another occur at random, independent of preceding events, even though it is well-known in the scientific literature that these chemical sequences do not take place randomly. Viewed within the framework of an open thermodynamic system, the second law prescribes an inherent increase in the complexity of the chemical reactions leading to life. A large literature exists on the problem of "self-organization" in molecular evolution, all of which the creationists apparently ignore.

The Age of the Earth

17 The creationists make two substantive claims about the age of the earth and the methods used to measure it. First, they declare that the geologists' universally accepted dating techniques, in particular radiometric dating, are invalid. Second, they assert that the age of the earth is very much younger (on the order of 10,000 to 20,000 years) than the age supposed by modern science.

18 Geologists have established, virtually beyond scientific doubt, that the earth is approximately 4.5 to 4.6 billion years old. That the stratigraphic record of sediments can be sequentially dated by radiometric decay rates is not now a matter of question among geologists who study dating techniques. Each radioactive element decays at a unique and constant rate and these rates are not influenced by external factors such as extremes of temperature or pressure. The creationists simply assert that these rates are not constant. Yet, at the Arkansas creation trial, every one of the creationists' geological witnesses—including Robert Gentry, their chief expert on radioactivity—testified that no scientific evidence exists which questions the constancy of these decay rates.

19 The creationists sometimes invoke a "singularity" at about 6,000 years corresponding to their suggested time for the Noachian "Flood"; at this singularity, the decay rates slowed down significantly—more or less to their present level. Prior to that time, the rates were much higher, thus giving the appearance that the earth is billions of years old, when actually it is only thousands. James Hopson of the University of Chicago has suggested to me a simple response to this supposition of a supernatural event: if the creationists are correct in believing that the earth is only thousands of years old, and that the decay rates at one time accelerated, then the amount of heat released from that amount of radioactive decay would have been sufficient—by a large margin—to have vaporized the earth.

20 By their own admission, the creationists cannot provide any scientific evidence for such dramatic changes in radioactive decay rates or their assertion that these rates do not measure the true age of the earth. The creationists turn to a supernatural "singularity," which is a belief derived from religion, not from the evidence of science.

The Geological Record

21 For over two hundred years, geologists have investigated the history of the earth. Many of these workers in the eighteenth and early nineteenth centuries realized that the rate of sedimentary processes observable in nature was too slow to account for the thickness of the earth's strata within the time specified in the Bible. Moreover, they recognized that strata could be correlated with one another over great distances. Surely, they reasoned, the earth is much older than previously believed.

22 Out of this inquiry arose different schools of thought: The "Neptunists" interpreted the geological data in terms of a universal ocean or flood, whereas the "Vulcanists" believed volcanic action was instrumental in shaping the earth's surface. But many workers, notably Charles Lyell, saw geological processes operating less catastrophically, and the hypothesis of a very old earth could not be denied much longer. Notably, this transition in thinking about the age of the earth was accomplished by scientists with deeply-held religious convictions. Nevertheless, many of them were willing to be led by empirical science rather than by recourse to supernatural explanation.

23 In contrast, the modern creationists wish to return to a time when Scripture was considered the final arbiter of knowledge about earth history. The creationist positions on geological issues are so firmly imbedded in religion that it is difficult to address them in rational, scientific terms. Consider the following statement from *The Genesis Flood,* easily the most important creationist publication on geology:

> We believe that the Bible . . . gives us the true framework of historical and scientific interpretation . . . This framework is one of special creation of all things, complete and perfect in the beginning, followed by the introduction of a universal principle of decay and death into the world after man's sin, culminating in a worldwide cataclysmic destruction . . . by the Genesis Flood. We take this revealed framework of history as our basic datum, and then try to see how all the pertinent data can be understood in this context.[14]

24 There is no accepted body of scientific evidence supporting the idea that a universal flood covered all the earth about 6,000 years ago. Recent advances in geology centered around plate tectonics and continental drift, in fact, create special dilemmas for the creationists because of the mass of empirical data supporting a new interpretation of geological history. In dealing with such

data, the creationists merely demur, saying that the results *are* compatible with the "Flood," which they see as providing the energy for continental drift.[15] Such a statement is representative of religious apologetics, not rational scientific inquiry.

Fossil Transitions and Patterns of Descent

25 The strongest argument for the "fact" of evolution—the highly corroborated notion that there exists a historical record of descent with modification—is the non-random stratigraphic sequences of fossil organisms. The creationists make two main attacks on evolutionary interpretation of this record: first, they deny ipso facto that there are fossil transitions between the different kinds of organisms; second, they argue that the stratigraphic sequences of fossil forms are more easily explained by a "Flood" geology than by the accumulation of these remains over a long period of time. Both arguments are demonstrably false.

26 If you do not want to believe in something, the easiest solution is to deny its existence, and, when that fails, to define it such that it cannot exist. The creationists have done just that with the idea of transitional forms:

> Transitional series *must* have existed in the past, if evolution is true, and the fossil record should reveal at least some of these . . . The fact is, however, that no such transitional series—or even occasional transitional forms—have ever been found in the fossil record.[16]

Because there are no transitions between major groups, the creationists conclude, gaps exist just as predicted by the creation model.[17] In making this statement, however, the creationists confuse the idea of "transitional" form and obscure the scientific issue by defining "transitional form" in a way unacceptable to any knowledgeable evolutionist. The creationists argue that a transitional form is one in which all characters are intermediate between two groups. Evolutionists know that characters do not transform simultaneously, but evolve instead at very uneven rates. This variability in rate produces organisms who possess some characteristics (primitive ones) similar to those of their ancestors and others (derived) shared with closely related forms, including possibly their descendants. Each species, then, is an intermediate in some sense of the word; all species possess primitive and derived characters.

27 The fossil record provides abundant documentation of transitional forms. Many of these fossils yield information about characters shared with earlier forms and those shared with species found later in the fossil record. A comparison among these similarities allows the detection of a pattern of phylogenetic relationships which closely approximates the stratigraphic sequences of fossils. For example, the famous fossil bird *Archaeopteryx* shares many primitive skeletal characters with small bipedal dinosaurs; but it also has some features,

such as feathers and a fused "wishbone," that are characteristic of birds. *Archaeopteryx* supplies scientists with a wealth of data about the evolutionary connections between birds and a particular group of reptiles—the dinosaurs. Most evolutionists would not claim, of course, that these intermediate forms are necessarily the direct ancestors of a later group.

28 The creationists' second assertion about the fossil record is that it accords well with an interpretation based on the "Flood." Creationists point out that, after the "Flood" waters receded, the simpler ocean-dwelling forms would have been buried first, followed by fish and other organisms living near the surface, and then by the terrestrial organisms.[18] But religious apologetics such as this hardly does justice to the complexities of the fossil record in which successively more primitive forms—determined on the basis of morphology and not on their position in time—are found correspondingly lower in the stratigraphic column. If there had been a flood of the proportions described by the creationists, then it is inconceivable that the fossil organisms would have their present distribution in the geological record. A scenario based on the "Flood" predicts that there would be samples of fossil deposits containing mixtures of primitive and advanced organisms such as dinosaurs and modern mammals. This does not happen.

The Argument of Design

29 Perhaps none of the creationists' arguments is as beguiling as the argument of design. Does not the presence of design stand as evidence of a designer? In their lectures and writings, the creationists frequently cite William Paley's famous watch-maker example, as it appeared in his *Natural Theology* (1802): "The care with which the parts have been made and the fineness of their adjustment can have only one implication, namely, that the watch must have had a maker who understood its construction and who designed it for the use for which it is fitted." Paley, of course, was arguing for the existence of God. Creationists adopt the same argument in what is ostensibly a scientific debate. Of course, design is evidence for God—if one starts with the premise that only God can produce design. In this case, rather than seek to understand the implications of apparent design from a scientific point of view, the creationists turn the problem into an exercise in religious apologetics.

30 Darwin's solution to the problem of design in nature was his famous theory of adaptation by natural selection. Most evolutionists still subscribe to that explanation, although a growing number are expressing doubts. Hence, the search for an explanation of how organisms come to have the form they do has once again become the subject of considerable research. That science might not be able to provide an entirely satisfactory answer to this question at this time is not, as creationists imply, evidence against an evolutionary point of view, but merely representative of the fact that science never stops questioning.

Conclusion

31 I have tried to present a brief summary of the nature of the creationists' "science" and how the scientific community responds to it. Even a cursory glance at the creationists' literature demonstrates their religious motives. For example, this passage from a book by Henry Morris:

> If we expect to learn anything more than this about the Creation, then God above can tell us. And He has told us! In the Bible, which is the Word of God, He has told us everything we need to know about the Creation and earth's primeval history.[19]

By rejecting the normal goals and methods of science and accepting revelation as a valid way to acquire scientific knowledge, the creationists seek to reinterpret currently accepted scientific knowledge through the eyes of religious Fundamentalism.

References

1. Henry M. Morris, *Evolution and the Modern Christian* (Philadelphia: Presbyterian and Reformed Publishing Co., 1967), p. 55.
2. Gary Parker, *Creation: The Facts of Life* (San Diego: Creation-Life Publishers, 1980), p. 144.
3. Richard C. Lewontin, "Adaptation," 239 *Scientific American* 3 (1978): 212-230.
4. Thomas G. Barnes, "Origin and Destiny of the Earth's Magnetic Field," *Institute for Creation Research Technical Monograph No. 4* (1973): 1-64.
5. J. A. Jacobs, *The Earth's Core and Geomagnetism* (New York: The Macmillan Company, 1963).
6. I am grateful to G. Brent Dalrymple for bringing this example to my attention.
7. Henry M. Morris, *The Scientific Case for Creationism* (San Diego: Creation-Life Publishers, 1977), pp. 13-16.
8. Henry M. Morris, ed., *Scientific Creationism* (San Diego: Creation-Life Publishers, 1974), p. 45.
9. See I. Prigogine, *From Being to Becoming* (San Francisco: W. H. Freeman and Company, 1980).
10. See J. S. Wicken, "The Generation of Complexity in Evolution: A Thermodynamic and Information-Theoretical Discussion," 77 *Journal of Theoretical Biology* (1979): 349-365; J. S. Wicken, "A Thermodynamic Theory of Evolution," 87 *Journal of Theoretical Biology* (1980): 9-23; and D. R. Brooks and E. O. Wiley, "Nonequilibrium Evolution: A Theory of Organismic Change," *Nature* (in press, 1982).
11. Henry M. Morris (1974), *op. cit.,* p. 59.
12. R. L. Wysong, *The Creation-Evolution Controversy* (Midland, MI: Inquiry Press, 1976), pp. 410-411.
13. See, for example, H. Noda, ed., *Origin of Life, Proceedings of the Second ISSOL Meeting* (Tokyo, Japan: Japan Scientific Societies Press, 1978): J. F. Fredrick, ed., "Origins and Evolution of Eukaryotic Intracellular Organelles," 361 *Annals of the New York Academy of Sciences* (1981): 1-512.

14. J. C. Whitcomb, Jr., and H. M. Morris, *The Genesis Flood* (Grand Rapids: Baker Book House, 1961), p. xxvi.
15. Henry M. Morris (1974), *op. cit.*, p. 128.
16. Henry M. Morris. *The Scientific Case for Creation* (San Diego: Creation-Life Publishers, 1977), p. 30.
17. Duane T. Gish, *Evolution? The Fossils Say No!* [Public School Edition] (San Diego: Creation-Life Publishers, 1978), p. 65.
18. Whitcomb and Morris, *op. cit.*, pp. 265–276.
19. Henry M. Morris (1967), *op. cit.*, p. 54.

QUESTIONS FOR WRITING AND DISCUSSION

OBSERVING

1. In what ways, according to Cracraft, does creationism seek "to redefine the philosophical and methodological foundations of science"? Does this in fact make it "impossible . . . to evaluate the 'science' in Creationism as if this were a typical scientific debate"?
2. Summarize any one or two of the six " 'scientific' claims most often asserted by creationists," according to Cracraft.
3. Cracraft reveals how a scientist who works in historical fields like paleontology conducts an "experiment": given the scenario of a worldwide flood responsible for laying down the fossil history of life, how should such a fossil record look, how would it, as it were, stack up? How does that compare with how fossil deposits as you understand them in fact look?

EVALUATING

1. What are some of the differences between forensics, apologetics, and polemics on the one hand and scientific debate on the other? How does this distinction apply to debates about creationism?
2. Cracraft brings up again "the 'fact' of evolution." Why does he render "fact" in quotation marks? Consider this definition of "a scientific fact" framed by Stephen Gould: "a proposition that is confirmed to such a high degree that it would be perverse to withhold one's provisional assent." How could you apply this definition to the distinction both Halstead and Cracraft make between evolution as a phenomenon observable in the historical record displayed by rocks and fossils as opposed to the specific mechanisms by which evolution occurs?

RESPONDING AND APPLYING

1. In your own experience, how consistent have the scientists you have known been in defining and distinguishing clearly between such concepts

as fact, hypothesis, theory, confirmation, or proof? How has their practice shaped your attitude toward scientific enterprise?

2. Do you feel qualified to make a judgment when two or more individuals with claims to be experts argue starkly opposed positions? Are you aware of ways to assess the validity of their claims to expertise apart from their specific arguments, such as consideration, where it applies, of academic association, publishing venues, reviews of their work, the degree of acknowledgment of their work accorded within their discipline? Are there contexts in which such considerations might be irrelevant or misleading? What degree of confidence do you have in science as a community of scholars who keep each other reasonably honest? What factors in history, in the news, in your personal experience have influenced that attitude?
3. Creationists like to argue that students ought to be presented "both sides" of the creation vs. evolution issue and then be allowed to decide for themselves. Putting aside the question of whether creationism constitutes a valid side (most scientists do not believe that it does), how practical is this solution? Do you think most high school students are prepared to make that decision intelligently? What do you think the results would be?

CHAPTER WRITING ASSIGNMENTS

1. Choose some area of scientific development—the discovery of the atom, relativity, quantum theory, the full extent of the electromagnetic spectrum, red shift and the expanding universe, DNA—and examine whether and why it may be considered a scientific revolution. Explore not only the technological implications, but also the impact on culture. What fundamental assumptions or values has the new idea forced us to rethink?
2. Consider again the list Brockman provides of "scientific topics receiving prominent play in newspapers and magazines over the past several years." Choose one to explore in terms of its potential for impact on culture. What fundamental assumptions or values is this topic forcing us to rethink?
3. Some scientific controversies like the extinction of dinosaurs we can be content to let the experts decide, but some like teaching creationism in the schools or global warming have direct consequences on public policy and demand answers now. And while many scientists believe that science is not democratic—Earth revolves around the Sun, not the other way, no matter how many people believe otherwise—the fact is that science in America has to operate in a democratic society. What obligations do these circumstances impose on us as members of such a society?
4. Argue whether science ought to be seen as in conflict with, complementary to, or irrelevant to rationalism. You might look again at Mill's essay and note that while he was demolishing the idea that the benevolence of the Creator is apparent in his creation, he also demolished the idea that the study of nature can in any way improve our moral understanding.
5. Pursue the same question in terms of the relation between science and religion.

6. Write an imaginary dialog that explores the argument in question 4 or 5 by using any two representative writers.
7. Explore the relation between science and morality by choosing one of the situations outlined below and explaining how you would behave, why, and to what extent your knowledge—or ignorance—of science might affect your decision, if at all:
   A. Your close relative suffers from an incurable and excruciatingly painful disease but can be kept alive at great expense by mechanical means. Do you turn off the machines? Say you have them turned off and he doesn't die; he asks you to help him commit suicide, or he asks you to stop feeding him so he can die "naturally."
   B. In the second month of your pregnancy you are told by your doctor that your fetus will be born with Down syndrome and that she is willing to perform an abortion. At this time there is no way to correct the problem. Or you are this woman's husband and you strongly disagree with her decision to have or not have the abortion.
   C. You are a surgeon just notified that a kidney is available for and is equally compatible physiologically with three of your patients. One is a 48-year-old man of considerable wealth who can pay you well for your services. One is an attractive young adult whose parents have widely publicized their child's case and attracted sufficient contributions to pay for the operation, which promises to give your clinic especially good press. One is an eight-year-old Hispanic child from a poor family. What priorities and standards do you apply in deciding who gets the kidney?
8. The possibility of somehow, in Leon Kass' phrase, "re-creating humanity" raises fundamental questions about what is distinctly human about us, what is the minimally human that must be preserved? In addition to humans with higher intelligence and beauty, with gene splicing we could not only eliminate aberrant behavior like genetically based sociopathological tendencies, but we might instill stronger capacities for cooperative behavior. Or we could create sexless or bisexual humans. Or perhaps we could create humans with gills and webbed extremities for survival under water as is suggested in Pohl's story, or with even greater adaptations for survival on other planets. Would you draw the line somewhere on such practices? Based on what principle?
9. Other moral issues of bioengineering are more pressing. We are already able to identify far more genetic defects than we know how to fix, and serious questions are being raised about how this information might be used. Some insurance companies are already calling such problems "pre-existing conditions" that they are not responsible for covering, and some employers are turning down job applicants on the basis of genetic information about them. If young people are identified as genetically prone to addiction or to sociopathic behavior, will schools and law enforcement officials treat them in ways that make this knowledge a self-fulfilling prophecy? Already some people are refusing to be tested out of fear of these kinds of consequences, and some as a result are missing the opportunity for early

identification of and therapy for treatable conditions. What ought to be done about these situations?

10. Choose some source of science news intended for a general audience—the science section of *Newsweek* or *Time,* for example, or if you want more variety, *Science News* or the "Science and the Citizen" feature of *Scientific American*—and read their recent offerings over a period of a few weeks or months. Note the items you find especially interesting and those you think are important or significant, and with that information report why the general public should make an effort to stay informed on scientific matters.

CHAPTER PREVIEW

Chapter Prelude
P. J. O'Rourke, "What Our Original 'Dads' Knew—and Didn't Know—About Democracy"

Introductory Essay

Readings
Edmund Burke, "They Have the Rights of Man"
Thomas Jefferson, "The Declaration of Independence"
The Bill of Rights
Elizabeth Cady Stanton and Lucretia Mott, "Declaration of Sentiments"

Story
Kurt Vonneut, "Harrison Bergeron"

Perspectives
THE CHALLENGES OF DEMOCRACY
Martin Luther King, "Letter from Birmington Jail"
Nadine Gordimer, "Something for the Time Being"

Chapter Writing Assignments

Chapter 7

DEMOCRACY: THE PURSUIT OF LIBERTY AND PUBLIC VIRTUE

What Our Original "Dads" Knew—and Didn't Know—about Democracy

P. J. O'Rourke

1 Our Founding Fathers lacked the special literary skills with which modern writers on the subject of government are so richly endowed. When they wrote the Declaration of Independence, the Constitution and the Bill of Rights, they found themselves more or less forced to come to the point. So clumsy of thought and pen were the Founders that even today, seven generations later, we can tell what they were talking about.

2 They were talking about having a good time:

> We hold these Truths to be self-evident, that all Men are created equal, that they are endowed by their Creator with certain unalienable Rights, that among these are Life, Liberty and the Pursuit of happiness. . . .

3 "This is living!" "I gotta be me!" "Ain't we got fun!" It's all there in the Declaration of Independence. We are the only nation in the world based on happiness. Search as you will the sacred creeds of other nations and peoples, read the Magna Carta, the Communist Manifesto, the Ten Commandments, the Analects of Confucius, Plato's Republic, the New Testament or the UN Charter, and find me any happiness at all. America is the Happy Kingdom. . . .

4 As it is with us, so it was with the Original Dads. Their beef with Triple George? He was no fun:

> He is, at this Time, transporting large Armies of foreign Mercenaries to complete the works of Death, Desolation, and Tyranny, already begun with circumstances of Cruelty and Perfidity, scarcely paralleled in the most barbarous Ages, and totally unworthy the Head of a civilized Nation.

5 Totally.

6 There are twenty-seven specific complaints against the British Crown set forth in the Declaration of Independence. To modern ears they still sound reasonable. They still sound reasonable, in large part, because so many of them can be leveled against the present federal government of the United States. Maybe not the "Death, Desolation, and Tyranny" complaint (unless you're deeply opposed, on fight-for-your-right-to-party grounds, to coca-plant eradication in Bolivia and Peru), but how about:

> . . . has erected a Multitude of new Offices, and sent hither Swarms of Officers to harass our People, and eat out their Substance.

George III was a piker compared with FDR or LBJ.

Or:

> . . . has called together Legislative Bodies at Places unusual, uncomfortable, and distant . . . for the sole Purpose of fatiguing them into Compliance with his Measures.

Every American president does that to the House and the Senate.

> . . . has refused his Assent to Laws, the most wholesome and necessary for the public Good.

7 Our Congress won't pass a balanced-budget constitutional amendment or any legislation banning people over thirty from wearing spandex bicycle shorts.

> . . . has endeavored to prevent the Population of these States; for that Purpose obstructing the Laws for Naturalization of Foreigners; refusing . . . to encourage their Migrations hither. . . .

8 Tell a Vietnamese boat person, a Hong Kong shopkeeper or a migrant worker from Mexico that this doesn't describe U.S. immigration policy.

> . . . has kept among us, in Times of Peace, Standing Armies. . . .

Certainly.

> . . . has combined with others to subject us to a Jurisdiction foreign to our Constitution, and unacknowledged by our Laws, . . .

Federal regulatory agencies, for instance.

> . . . Depriving us, in many Cases, of the Benefits of Trial by Jury.

If we cross one of those regulatory agencies.

> . . . Cutting off our Trade with all Parts of the World

is what our trade quotas and tariffs do.

> . . . Imposing Taxes on us without our Consent.

Nobody asked me if I wanted a 1040 Form.

> . . . Taking away our Charters, abolishing our most valuable Laws, and altering fundamentally the Forms of our Governments.

So say states rights conservatives.

> . . . has plundered our Seas, ravaged our Coasts . . . and destroyed the Lives of our People.

All the tree huggers believe this.

And lastly:

> . . . has excited domestic Insurrections amongst us. . . .

9 In Watts, Bensonhurst, that Mohawk reservation in upstate New York and my house since I married into a family full of Democrats. . . .

10 The Constitution is an equally forthright piece of work and quite succinct—twenty-one pages (in the American civics E-Z-reader large-type version) giving the complete operating instructions for a nation of 250 million people. The manual for a Toyota Camry, which only seats five, is four times as long. And, thanks to the pro-growth economic policies of the vigorously libertarian—not to say completely impotent—Continental Congress, the Constitution is not translated from Japanese.

11 An hour's perusal of our national charter makes it hard to understand what the argle-bargle is about. The First Amendment forbids any law "abridging the freedom of speech." It doesn't say, "except for commercials on children's television" or "unless somebody says . . . 'chick' on a college campus."

12 The Second Amendment states that "the right of the people to keep and bear arms, shall not be infringed," period. There is no mention of magazine size, rate of fire or to what extent these arms may resemble assault rifles. All rifles were assault rifles in those days. Furthermore, if the gun laws that Massachusetts has now had been in force in 1776, we'd all be Canadians, and you know what kind of weather Canada has.

13 There is no reference to abortion whatsoever in the Constitution, not so much as an "I'll pull out in time, honey, honest." The Tenth Amendment tells us that "the powers not delegated to the United States by the Constitution, nor prohibited by it to the States, are reserved to the States respectively, or to the people." This means the power to drive the nation crazy over a gob of meiotic cells that wouldn't fill a coke spoon and, on the other hand, the power to murder innocent babies that haven't even been born as yet are—just as the amendment says—"reserved to the States respectively, or to the people."

14 The Constitution is not hard to understand. Although the quality of reasoning degenerates in the later amendments. The Sixteenth Amendment is particularly awful:

> The Congress shall have the power to lay and collect taxes on incomes, from whatever source derived. . . .

And Section 4 of the Fourteenth is very silly:

> The validity of the public debt of the United States, authorized by law, . . . shall not be questioned.

15 The Twenty-Sixth Amendment, giving the vote to eighteen-year-olds, must have been drafted by people who'd never met any eighteen-year-olds, or, worse, by people who were eighteen.

16 And then there is the—from a male point of view—tactically foolish Nineteenth Amendment:

> The right of citizens of the United States to vote shall not be denied or abridged by the United States or any State on account of sex.

17 This made women stop protesting a trivial wrong to their gender—exclusion from the electoral process—and allowed them to focus their indignation or more serious forms of injustice, such as the fact that women suffer discrimination and harassment in the workplace, are paid less than men, are rarely promoted to the highest levels of corporate or professional responsibility and this year's hemlines make their legs look fat.

18 There are also a few gimmicks and dodges in the Constitution, such as Section 4 of the presidential disability and succession amendment, which says that the vice president "and a majority of either the principal officers of the executive departments or *of such other body as Congress may by law provide*" (italics my own) can declare the president incompetent. If I'm reading this right, it means that with the help of pals in the House and Senate, Dan Quayle and the principal officers of the Fort Wayne, Indiana, Elks Club can send George Bush to the bughouse and declare a national golf emergency.

19 But, on the whole, the text is easily glossed. The single exception being Article Two, Section 1:

> The electors shall . . . vote by ballot for two persons. . . . The person having the greatest number of votes shall be the President; . . . and if there be more than one who have such majority, and have an equal number of votes, then the House of Representatives shall immediately choose by ballot one of them. . . .

This was later modified by the rather more confusing Twelfth Amendment:

> . . . The person having the greatest number of votes for President, shall be the President, if such number be a majority of the whole number of Electors appointed; and if no person have such majority, then from the persons having the highest numbers not exceeding three on the list of those voted for as President, the House of Representatives shall choose immediately, by ballot, the President.

20 The idea seems to be to make the election of a president so complicated and annoying that no one with an important job or a serious avocation—that is, no one presently making any substantial contribution to society—would be tempted to run for the office. So far, it's worked.

21 Otherwise, only one important question is raised by the Constitution, a question implicit in its preamble:

> We the people of the United States, in order to form a more perfect Union, establish justice, insure domestic tranquility, provide for the common defense, promote the general welfare, and secure the blessings of liberty to ourselves and our posterity . . .

The question being, "Are we done yet?" . . .

22 So when can we quit passing laws and raising taxes? When can we say of our political system, "Stick a fork in it, it's done?" When will our officers, officials and magistrates realize their jobs are finished and return, like Cincinnatus, to the plow or, as it were, to the law practice or the car dealership?

23 The mystery of government is not how Washington works but how to make it stop.

QUESTIONS FOR WRITING AND DISCUSSION

OBSERVING

1. What is it exactly that humorist P. J. O'Rourke is saying in this brief, satirical essay about the founding documents of the American nation and their authors? What topics related to the Declaration of Independence and the Constitution does he find to poke fun at? Why?
2. How far do you have to read before you discover he might be "just kidding"? Are any of his examples—the "mistake" of women's suffrage, the freedom to use the word "chick" on campus, or "all the tree huggers believe this"—offensive?

EVALUATING

1. Do you agree with him when he says America "is the only nation in the world based on happiness?" In what ways is this a good reading or a misreading of Thomas Jefferson's well-known opening statement in the Declaration of Independence?
2. O'Rourke goes out of his way to dramatize how absolute he thinks the amendments to the Constitution are by citing several examples. Which of them strike you as important as they do him? Which ones seems frivolous?

RESPONDING AND APPLYING

1. As you reflect upon O'Rourke's humorous interpretation of the value of living in a democratic nation, how much of the content of these founding documents do you yourself understand and consciously appreciate?
2. How many of your peers know of and can recite specifics from the Declaration of Independence or the Constitution (or whatever founding documents that may be analogous in your country)? Should it matter whether

the majority of citizens in a nation trust in, and have a working knowledge of, these key documents? Why or why not?

3. To what extent does the continuation of a democratic tradition, of the individual freedoms, depend upon its citizens' continual and self-conscious renewal and ratification—or reinterpretation and new application—of such original manifestoes?
4. O'Rourke's essay concludes with a series of rhetorical questions, which he then answers with a final jab at the federal government: "The mystery of government is not how Washington works but how to make it stop." What is the purpose of the questions? Why does he answer them as he does? For what reason would one want "Washington" or any government to "stop"?

Balancing Individual and Communal Needs

While O'Rourke's essay may be a tongue-in-cheek inquiry into the history and vitality of the founding documents of the United States, it nevertheless raises some important issues about how much Americans—or any people—know about their nation's founding and its principal values or traditions. It draws our attention to the central problem of any group that assembles to live together, whether a family, a tribe, a neighborhood, a society, or a nation: how do we balance the conflicting claims of freedom and authority, of individual liberty and communal need, and still preserve safety, security, and order? All government starts by recognizing the validity of these claims and then by attempting to resolve the conflicts rising among them. One example of this conflicting claim is the issue of school prayer—how can the interests of those who do not want to pray and those who do want to pray be simultaneously respected? Should any faith be given "official" status in a nation? Another such issue is capital punishment—is the community protected and is it justified in denying the "right to life" to the few who may have committed a capital offense? The fact is, a society earns its right to call itself successful and civilized when it works out an optimal balance between these conflicting claims. Among its greatest challenges then is maximizing individual liberties while maintaining community stability. The history of the nations and communities that tried to reach these goals—what we call "democracy"—in the last 2500 years reveals both effective and ineffective ways of working out this balance of rights and reasonable order.

To even attempt democracy, societies must appeal to differing kinds of values and virtues in its people that they wish to pass on to subsequent generations. This has usually meant as well an appeal to differing kinds of authority to identify and monitor these "public" virtues. While the early Jews, first-century Christians, and seventh-century Muslims appealed to revelation and the word of God as their authority, the ancient Greeks appealed to reason, dialogue, and debate. Rather than kings and rulers dictating what was acceptable, the freemen of Athens, through a representative council of free male citizens, governed the city. They gained the right to do this through heredity (by virtue of being free Athenian males), and chaotic as the system was, taxes, laws, wars, and the rights and obligations of citizenship were debated regularly by hundreds of men in the assembly or town square. Thus, the institution of the city-state that was governed by principle and reason was born. The Greek "democracy," sadly though, only lasted several hundred years. From our standpoint today, it may seem oppressive and intolerable that the great majority of ancient Greeks, that is, slaves, women, and subject peoples, were effectively excluded from the decision-making processes. Even so, the dominant governance systems throughout the West up until the seventeenth century, until the beginning of the Enlightenment, limited participation even further. For women, the oppression lasted longer: suffrage, the issue of voting rights for women which O'Rourke's opening piece playfully notes, did not come for women in this country until 1920. And it was delayed even longer for African Americans: the civil rights movement of the late 1950s and early 1960s was the real beginning of liberation and participation in democratic society for them.

There are a number of reasons that explain why earlier civilizations continued to prefer a hierarchical system of obedience to some higher authority, rather than to experiment with democratic models, for so many hundreds of years. First, obedience to the authority of priest or king, or some combination of these roles, was easy for the masses of peasants, serfs, and slaves, for such obedience was a habit. It required little thought or risk and depended on the identification and patronage of a few strong male leaders who claimed or invested themselves with special powers. In fact, kings and nobles successfully claimed they were closer to God than were the common classes and, therefore, represented God on earth; thus, they ruled with "divine right."

Second, the political benefits, rights, and privileges accruing to the masses were few by our standards, but there was still a modicum of order and the opportunity of some meagre gains, such as protection from starvation. Two things had to happen before obedience to higher authority was no longer practiced by the common classes, which would lead to their full participation in government. First, the authority of the old institutions of church and state had to come into question. The power of religious and secular rulers was grounded in revelation and/or based on heredity, and before that power could be shared with greater numbers of people, a fundamental shift in thinking had to occur. People's concerns regarding life were typically focused on preparation for heaven, not earth; therefore, before any change in political order could occur, it would have to be preceded by a change in this perspective, a change that would emphasize life on earth. Second, a new form of authority would have to recognize the rights and powers of the people, replacing the powers vested in priests and kings. As the growing middle classes began to place more faith in their own rights, as well as in reason and change, they demanded more liberties and political freedoms and eventually the right of rebellion. The first great rebellion of the common classes against a tyrannical central power was the

French Revolution of 1789. Although surely an act of brutish violence and force, the French Revolution was ultimately about ideas, ideas that changed the prevailing thought about the individual's relationship to society. (A number of smaller peasant revolts and what is referred to as the Glorious Revolution preceded the French Revolution, but these did not have the long-standing impact of the more important French Revolution.) According to Vartan Gregoran, president of Brown University:

> The French Revolution espoused for the first time in the history of the West a truly universal civilization, transcending cultural, national, ethnic, social and racial boundaries by proclaiming the fundamental and inviolable rights of all the peoples of the world to freedom and equality. Insofar as it translated those ideals into a living reality, the French Revolution can be said to have founded the modern era and to have given shape for the first time to the principles and institutions by which we now define our purposes and measure our achievements in public life. (*New York Times,* 12 March 1989: 26.)

The combined efforts of three political philosophers would lay the foundation for the ideas just described and, ultimately, for the French and American Revolutions. In the seventeenth and eighteenth centuries, Thomas Hobbes, John Locke, and Jean-Jacques Rousseau helped to establish the basic vocabulary and principles that changed the thinking about government—though it is important to note that not all intellectuals of the time, especially Edmund Burke, whose "Reflections on the French Revolution" is excerpted in this chapter, found the tenets of this revolutionary mind-set fruitful for true human freedom. Hobbes introduced the idea of people living in a state of nature, and though all were equal, all were selfish and innately brutish and needed controls imposed upon them, if, for nothing else, at least for self-preservation. Thus, Hobbes justified the absolute rule of the monarch, which though it protected people, also deprived them of many rights. Locke and Rousseau also believed in the equality of man, but were not as cynical. They also believed that people lived in a state of nature but that this nature was not a jungle that illicited only savage instincts. Rather, it was a political society based on natural laws and rights stemming from God. In such a society, agreements could be arrived at through forms of state governance established to protect all citizens: thus, a social contract, much like God's covenant with the early Jews. Shaping ideas from the Judeo-Christian tradition, as expressed in Genesis and Exodus, would guide relations in a society (except the new covenants became agreements among people, not between people and God). It should become clear that democracies, especially those in the last 200 years, have worked out the institutions and practices to balance individual rights with the public good much more effectively than the Greeks had. The success of the democratic government, in fact, accounts in large part for the changes we have recently seen in the Soviet Union and Eastern Europe.

Thomas Jefferson and other "founding fathers" of the United States codified these principles in three documents that would not only stand the severe test of more than 200 years, but also serve as the governance model for numerous other countries, many in the Third World. Our Declaration of Independence laid out the basis by which a government or state is entitled to govern. Importantly, the Declaration established that the consent and the human rights of the governed take precedence over the will and whims of the state. The Constitution, which is not included as a reading in this text, defines the structure and operation of that government, establishing a division of power into three branches and a system of checks and balances that has somewhat effectively ensured a fair distribution of wealth and power. Last, the Bill of Rights, the first 10 amendments of the Constitution, defines and protects individual rights.

Our readings begin with Edmund Burke's critique of the French Revolution's notion of the "rights of man," and proceed through to two founding documents of American democracy, the Declaration of Independence and the Bill of Rights, and then to Stanton and Mott's "Declaration of Sentiments," which identified in nineteenth-century America certain tension points and challenges to the evolving democratic tradition as it related to the participation of women.

From there we move onto a provocative short story and a "perspectives" case study of two texts: a poignant story and one famous letter, each of which explores the meaning and the contours of contemporary democracy, here and elsewhere, and the endeavor to be inclusive of all peoples and groups in a balance of individual freedom and social order.

EDMUND BURKE (1729–1797), "THEY HAVE THE RIGHTS OF MAN"

Edmund Burke was one of the most colorful and influential figures in the political history of England during King George III's reign, the monarch whose action sparked the American Revolution. As a member of the House of Commons, Burke determinedly defended the American colonies, condemned those who violated the rights of persecuted Catholics in England and Ireland, and opposed the exploitation of the Indian subcontinent by English imperialists. Burke stands out in his own time as a man unafraid of defending tradition and the role of established institutions such as the church in preserving human dignity and freedom and as an ardent opponent of the excesses of democracy. In our time, he has emerged as a prominent philosophical influence on the so-called conservative movement in American politics, which began in the 1950s. He is perhaps most famous for his dissenting view on the value and the legitimacy of the principles of the French Revolution. In a time when many European intellectuals—and Americans like Thomas Paine as well—were championing its merits, Burke denounced them.

In this excerpt from his quite long and passionate work, *Reflections on the Revolution in France,* Burke critiques the notion of the "rights of man," and particularly the use of "abstractions" and self-serving platitudes as building blocks in constructing a new society. Burke contrasts this emergent "rights of man" concept and other tenets of the new French constitution with its refusal to seek mere independence, or unrestrained freedom for their own sake. Prompted by a sermon by Richard Price, an English clergyman sympathetic to the revolution, Burke wrote *Reflections* in 1790, *before* the Reign of Terror. This event took countless lives and ushered in a period of new tyranny in France, dashing the naive hopes of the early enthusiasts of the revolution for a new model of society. The dreadful events that transpired in France served to make the American Revolution seem that much more civil, principled, and sane.

They Have the Rights of Man

Edmund Burke

1 It is no wonder, therefore, that with these ideas of everything in their constitution and government at home, either in church or state, as illegitimate and usurped, or at best as a vain mockery, they look abroad with an eager and passionate enthusiasm. Whilst they are possessed by these notions, it is vain to talk to them of the practice of their ancestors, the fundamental laws of their country, the fixed form of a constitution whose merits are confirmed by the solid test of long experience and an increasing public strength and national prosperity. They despise experience as the wisdom of unlettered men; and as for the rest, they have wrought underground a mine that will blow up, at one grand explosion, all examples of antiquity, all precedents, charters, and acts of parliament. They have "the rights of men." Against these there can be no prescription, against these no agreement is binding; these admit no temperament and no compromise; anything withheld from their full demand is so much of fraud and injustice. Against these their rights of men let no government look for security in the length of its continuance, or in the justice and lenity of its administration. The objections of these speculatists, if its forms do not quadrate with their theories, are as valid against such an old and beneficent government as against the most violent tyranny or the greenest usurpation. They are always at issue with governments, not on a question of abuse, but a question of competency and a question of title. I have nothing to say to the clumsy subtilty of their political metaphysics. . . .

2 Far am I from denying in theory, full as far is my heart from withholding in practice (if I were of power to give or to withhold) the *real* rights of men. In denying their false claims of right, I do not mean to injure those which are real, and are such as their pretended rights would totally destroy. If civil society be

made for the advantage of man, all the advantages for which it is made become his right. It is an institution of beneficence; and law itself is only beneficence acting by a rule. Men have a right to live by that rule; they have a right to do justice, as between their fellows, whether their fellows are in public function or in ordinary occupation. They have a right to the fruits of their industry and to the means of making their industry fruitful. They have a right to the acquisitions of their parents, to the nourishment and improvement of their offspring, to instruction in life, and to consolation in death. Whatever each man can separately do, without trespassing upon others, he has a right to do for himself; and he has a right to a fair portion of all which society, with all its combinations of skill and force, can do in his favor. In this partnership all men have equal rights, but not to equal things. He that has but five shillings in the partnership has as good a right to it as he that has five hundred pounds has to his larger proportion. But he has not a right to an equal dividend in the product of the joint stock; and as to the share of power, authority, and direction which each individual ought to have in the management of the state, that I must deny to be amongst the direct original rights of man in civil society, for I have in my contemplation the civil social man, and no other. It is a thing to be settled by convention.

3 If civil society be the offspring of convention, that convention must be its law. That convention must limit and modify all the descriptions of constitution which are formed under it. Every sort of legislative, judicial, or executory power are its Features. They can have no being in any other state of things; and how can any man claim under the conventions of civil society rights which do not so much as suppose its existence—rights which are absolutely repugnant to it? One of the first motives to civil society, and which becomes one of its fundamental rules, *is that no man should be judge in his own cause.* By this each person has at once divested himself of the first fundamental right of uncovenanted man, that is, to judge for himself and to assert his own cause. He abdicates all right to be his own governor. He inclusively, in a great measure, abandons the right of self-defense, the first law of nature. Men cannot enjoy the rights of an uncivil and of a civil state together. That he may obtain justice, he gives up his right of determining what it is in points the most essential to him. That he may secure some liberty, he makes a surrender in trust of the whole of it.

4 Government is not made in virtue of natural rights, which may and do exist in total independence of it, and exist in much greater clearness and in a much greater degree of abstract perfection; but their abstract perfection is their practical defect. By having a right to everything they want everything. Government is a contrivance of human wisdom to provide for human *wants.* Men have a right that these wants should be provided for by this wisdom. Among these wants is to be reckoned the want, out of civil society, of a sufficient restraint upon their passions. Society requires not only that the passions of individuals should be subjected, but that even in the mass and body, as well as in the individuals, the inclinations of men should frequently be thwarted, their will controlled, and their passions brought into subjection. This can only be done by *a*

power out of themselves, and not, in the exercise omits function, subject to that will and to those passions which it is its office to bridle and subdue. In this sense the restraints on men, as well as their liberties, are to be reckoned among their rights. But as the liberties and the restrictions vary with times and circumstances and admit to infinite modifications, they cannot be settled upon any abstract rule; and nothing is so foolish as to discuss them upon that principle.

5 The moment you abate anything from the full rights of men, each to govern himself, and suffer any artificial, positive limitation upon those rights, from that moment the whole organization of government becomes a consideration of convenience. This it is which makes the constitution of a state and the due distribution of its powers a matter of the most delicate and complicated skill. It requires a deep knowledge of human nature and human necessities, and of the things which facilitate or obstruct the various ends which are to be pursued by the mechanism of civil institutions. The state is to have recruits to its strength, and remedies to its distempers. What is the use of discussing a man's abstract right to food or medicine? The question is upon the method of procuring and administering them. In that deliberation I shall always advise to call in the aid of the farmer and the physician rather than the professor of metaphysics.

6 The science of constructing a commonwealth, or renovating it, or reforming it, is, like every other experimental science, not to be taught *a priori.* Nor is it a short experience that can instruct us in that practical science, because the real effects of moral causes are not always immediate; but that which in the first instance is prejudicial may be excellent in its remoter operation, and its excellence may arise even from the ill effects it produces in the beginning. The reverse also happens: and very plausible schemes, with very pleasing commencements, have often shameful and lamentable conclusions. In states there are often some obscure and almost latent causes, things which appear at first view of little moment, on which a very great part of its prosperity or adversity may most essentially depend. The science of government being therefore so practical in itself and intended for such practical purposes—a matter which requires experience, and even more experience than any person can gain in his whole life, however sagacious and observing he may be—it is with infinite caution that any man ought to venture upon pulling down an edifice which has answered in any tolerable degree for ages the common purposes of society, or on building it up again without having models and patterns of approved utility before his eyes.

7 These metaphysic rights entering into common life, like rays of light which pierce into a dense medium, are by the laws of nature refracted from their straight line. Indeed, in the gross and complicated mass of human passions and concerns the primitive rights of men undergo such a variety of refractions and reflections that it becomes absurd to talk of them as if they continued in the simplicity of their original direction. The nature of man is intricate; the objects of society are of the greatest possible complexity; and, therefore, no simple disposition or direction of power can be suitable either to man's nature or to the quality of his affairs. When I hear the simplicity of contrivance aimed at and

boasted of in any new political constitutions, I am at no loss to decide that the artificers are grossly ignorant of their trade or totally negligent of their duty. The simple governments are fundamentally defective, to say no worse of them. If you were to contemplate society in but one point of view, all these simple modes of polity are infinitely captivating. In effect each would answer its single end much more perfectly than the more complex is able to attain all its complex purposes. But it is better that the whole should be imperfectly and anomalously answered than that, while some parts are provided for with great exactness, others might be totally neglected or perhaps materially injured by the overcare of a favorite member.

8 The pretended rights of these theorists are all extremes; and in proportion as they are metaphysically true, they are morally and politically false. The rights of men are in a sort of *middle,* incapable of definition, but not impossible to be discerned. The rights of men in governments are their advantages; and these are often in balances between differences of good, in compromises sometimes between good and evil, and sometimes between evil and evil. Political reason is a computing principle: adding, subtracting, multiplying, and dividing, morally and not metaphysically, or mathematically, true moral denominations.

9 By these theorists the right of the people is almost always sophistically confounded with their power. The body of the community, whenever it can come to act, can meet with no effectual resistance; but till power and right are the same, the whole body of them has no right inconsistent with virtue, and the first of all virtues, prudence. Men have no right to what is not reasonable and to what is not for their benefit.

QUESTIONS FOR WRITING AND DISCUSSION

OBSERVING

1. According to Burke, what is the doctrine of "the rights of man"? What are the "real rights of men" with which he contrasts this notion? Why does he believe the French version is faulty and potentially devastating to true freedom?
2. What is the concept of *convention,* and how is it all important to Burke's argument that the French have tried to construct a society that ultimately undermines its own existence?
3. Burke says "one of the fundamental motives to civil society . . . is *that no man should be judge in his own cause.*" What does he mean by this and how are the framers of the French Revolution guilty of it?
4. *A priori* is a term used to describe an idea or behavior that is "determined beforehand," that is, is not tested or testable before it is expected to be believed. When Burke observes that constructing or reforming a "commonwealth" or government cannot be *taught a priori,* what is he suggesting? What is his counsel for "the science of government"?

EVALUATING

1. How persuasive is Burke's argument that human freedom must originate in and be tempered by "convention" and a basic respect for traditional institutions? Is there a place for convention in the American Revolution as you read the Declaration of Independence? Where do you see this notion at work in contemporary America?
2. Earlier in his attack on the revolution, Burke says the French "despise experience as the wisdom of unlettered men"; what "experience" or "unlettered men" is he speaking of? Why does Burke himself admire or trust this "wisdom" more than the intellectuals who have provided the theory for the revolution?
3. "The nature of man is intricate," Burke says, contrasting his view of human society as filtered through his experience as a British subject with the "simplistic" view of the French revolutionaries. How does one's theory of what it means to be human determine her or his view of government? Do you believe people are born basically good or basically evil—or neutral? How might your theological or philosophical view—Burke calls this a "metaphysical" view—shape or influence how you vote, respond to trends in society, support or oppose one policy or another? Can you think of an example of a stand you have taken that is based in large part on "the nature of man/woman"?

RESPONDING

1. What do you see as the true foundation of personal liberty? Is it something as fundamental as being human? Is it something bestowed upon individuals by a government or other authority? Is it earned through achievement or financial status? On what basis can you or anyone justify the claim that they are or should be "free"?
2. In your view, where do individual rights stop and community rights prevail? Are you comfortable with the libertarian view that a person ought to be able to do anything that does not directly impinge on another person's freedom? How does one determine that line?
3. Can you conceive of a society based upon "absolute" human freedom? Should I be able to do "whatever I want"? Where would such a society begin to "leak"? At what point is the fabric of a society threatened by the unrestrained choices of free individuals? Is it the government's job to provide those restraints? Should the government be authorized to ban smoking? To regulate the production and sale of marijuana? To "discover" or articulate rights in documents like the Constitution that were formerly left unarticulated, like abortion? Why or why not?

THOMAS JEFFERSON, "THE DECLARATION OF INDEPENDENCE"

Thomas Jefferson (1743 - 1826) was the third president of the United States, primary author of the Declaration of Independence, American statesman here and abroad, and lifelong advocate of agrarian democracy. A graduate of William and Mary College in 1762, he studied law and helped to form the Virginia Committee of Correspondence, for which, as a member, he prepared a paper opposing the British Parliament's authority over the colonists. Never an effective public speaker, he nevertheless won respect as a skilled rhetorician and wrote numerous addresses and resolutions.

As a delegate to the Second Continental Congress in 1775, Jefferson served on the committee drafting the Declaration of Independence, which was wholly his work except for minor alterations from Adams, Franklin, and others on the floor of Congress. In spirit and detail, it reflects the writings of John Locke, with whose work Jefferson was familiar.

The version of the Declaration reprinted here is taken from Jefferson's autobiography. You will note the indication of changes made as the document was being discussed and edited by the delegates of the Second Continental Congress. In particular, the bracketed sections in italics were the parts stricken by the delegates, and the sections in small capital letters were the parts they substituted.

Some of the changes suggest that Jefferson was rather a firebrand, perhaps overstating the case for effect. For instance, "unremitting injuries and usurpations" was changed to "repeated injuries and usurpations," and to the charge that the king had been "depriving us of the benefits of trial by jury" was added the qualifier "in many cases." One can see the concern of members of Congress for the image this document would project. As angry and determined as many no doubt were, they did not want to exaggerate their claims and thereby leave themselves open to the charge of being a group of crazy radicals. It is the reasoned restraint that gives the final document its strength, and it is the suggestions of people like Adams and Franklin that helped to keep its tone dignified.

Of especial importance is the Congress' excision of Jefferson's declaration against slavery. It is refreshing to realize that there were individuals like Jefferson at this time who, when he declared that all men were created equal, did not exclude people of darker skin from humanity. Indeed, when he refers to slavery as a "cruel war against human nature itself," to its perpetrator as "the CHRISTIAN [his caps] king of Great Britain," and to its victims as "MEN" [also his caps] who are "bought and sold," Jefferson leaves no room for doubt that he is condemning the practice on both rational and religious grounds. Yet this entire section was removed by the Congress—no doubt for sound political reasons. Because so many of the colonies were economically dependent on slavery, a declaration of independence that condemned slavery would not have passed, and if an attempt had been made to fight out the slavery issue at this time, there might not have been a United States of America. One might well wonder whether the price was worth paying. In any case, the issue was swept under the rug, a decision for which this nation would suffer for a long time.

Generally, Jefferson worked against the aristocracy of wealth and birth. He denied the originality of his work on the Declaration when he wrote "I did not consider it any part of my charge to invent new ideas, but to place before mankind the common sense of the subject, in terms so plain and firm as to command their assent." Nevertheless, the Declaration represents a primary historical document of great power and interest.

The Declaration of Independence

Thomas Jefferson

[JULY 4, 1776]

1 When, in the course of human events, it becomes necessary for one people to dissolve the political bands which have connected them with another, and to assume among the powers of the earth the separate and equal station to which the laws of nature and of nature's God entitle them, a decent respect to the opinions of mankind requires that they should declare the causes which impel them to the separation.

2 We hold these truths to be self evident: that all men are created equal; that they are endowed by their Creator with CERTAIN [*inherent and*] inalienable rights; that among these are life, liberty, and the pursuit of happiness; that to secure these rights, governments are instituted among men, deriving their just powers from the consent of the governed; that whenever any form of government becomes destructive of these ends, it is the right of the people to alter or to abolish it, and to institute new government, laying its foundation on such principles, and organizing its powers in such form, as to them shall seem most likely to effect their safety and happiness. Prudence, indeed, will dictate that governments long established should not be changed for light and transient causes; and accordingly all experience hath shown that mankind are more disposed to suffer while evils are sufferable, than to right themselves by abolishing the forms to which they are accustomed. But when a long train of abuses and usurpations, [*begun at a distinguished period and*] pursuing invariably the same object, evinces a design to reduce them under absolute despotism, it is

their right, it is their duty to throw off such government, and to provide new guards for their future security. Such has been the patient sufferance of these colonies; and such is now the necessity which constrains them to ALTER [*expunge*] their former systems of government. The history of the present king of Great Britain is a history of REPEATED [*unremitting*] injuries and usurpations, ALL HAVING [*among which appears no solitary fact to contradict the uniform tenor of the rest, but all have*] in direct object the establishment of an absolute tyranny over these states. To prove this, let facts be submitted to a candid world [*for the truth of which we pledge a faith yet unsullied by falsehood*].

3 He has refused his assent to laws the most wholesome and necessary for the public good.

4 He has forbidden his governors to pass laws of immediate and pressing importance, unless suspended in their operation till his assent should be obtained; and, when so suspended, he has utterly neglected to attend to them.

5 He has refused to pass other laws for the accommodation of large districts of people, unless those people would relinquish the right of representation in the legislature, a right inestimable to them, and formidable to tyrants only.

6 He has called together legislative bodies at places unusual, uncomfortable, and distant from the depository of their public records, for the sole purpose of fatiguing them into compliance with his measures.

7 He has dissolved representative houses repeatedly [*and continually*] for opposing with manly firmness his invasions on the rights of the people.

8 He has refused for a long time after such dissolutions to cause others to be elected, whereby the legislative powers, incapable of annihilation, have returned to the people at large for their exercise, the state remaining, in the meantime, exposed to all the dangers of invasion from without and convulsions within.

9 He has endeavored to prevent the population of these states; for that purpose obstructing the laws for naturalization of foreigners, refusing to pass others to encourage their migrations hither, and raising the conditions of new appropriations of lands.

10 He has OBSTRUCTED [*suffered*] the administration of justice BY [*totally to cease in some of these states*] refusing his assent to laws for establishing judiciary powers.

11 He has made [*our*] judges dependent on his will alone for the tenure of their office, and the amount and payment of their salaries.

12 He has erected a multitude of new offices, [*by a self-assumed power*] and sent hither swarms of new officers to harass our people and eat out their substance.

13 He has kept among us in times of peace standing armies [*and ships of war*] without the consent of our legislatures.

14 He has affected to render the military independent of, and superior to, the civil power.

15 He has combined with others to subject us to a jurisdiction foreign to our constitutions and unacknowledged by our laws, giving his assent to their acts of

pretended legislation for quartering large bodies of armed troops among us; for protecting them by a mock trial from punishment for any murders which they should commit on the inhabitants of these states; for cutting off our trade with all parts of the world; for imposing taxes on us without our consent; for depriving us IN MANY CASES of the benefits of trial by jury; for transporting us beyond seas to be tried for pretended offenses; for abolishing the free system of English laws in a neighboring province, establishing therein an arbitrary government, and enlarging its boundaries, so as to render it at once an example and fit instrument for introducing the same absolute rule into these COLONIES [*states*]; for taking away our charters, abolishing our most valuable laws, and altering fundamentally the forms of our governments; for suspending our own legislatures, and declaring themselves invested with power to legislate for us in all cases whatsoever.

16 He has abdicated government here BY DECLARING US OUT OF HIS PROTECTION, AND WAGING WAR AGAINST US [*withholding his governors, and declaring us out of his allegiance and protection*].

17 He has plundered our seas, ravaged our coasts, burnt our towns, and destroyed the lives of our people.

18 He is at this time transporting large armies of foreign mercenaries to complete the works of death, desolation and tyranny already begun with circumstances of cruelty and perfidy SCARCELY PARALLELED IN THE MOST BARBAROUS AGES, AND TOTALLY unworthy the head of a civilized nation.

19 He has constrained our fellow citizens taken captive on the high seas, to bear arms against their country, to become the executioners of their friends and brethren, or to fall themselves by their hands.

20 He has EXCITED DOMESTIC INSURRECTION AMONG US, AND HAS endeavored to bring on the inhabitants of our frontiers, the merciless Indian savages, whose known rule of warfare is an undistinguished destruction of all ages, sexes and conditions [*of existence*].

21 [*He has incited treasonable insurrection of our fellow citizens, with the allurements of forfeiture and confiscation of our property.*

22 *He has waged cruel war against human nature itself, violating its most sacred rights of life and liberty in the persons of a distant people who never offended him, captivating and carrying them into slavery in another hemisphere, or to incur miserable death in their transportation hither. This piratical warfare, the opprobrium of INFIDEL powers, is the warfare of the CHRISTIAN king of Great Britain. Determined to keep open a market where MEN should be bought and sold, he has prostituted his negative for suppressing every legislative attempt to prohibit or to restrain this execrable commerce. And that this assemblage of horrors might want no fact of distinguished die, he is now exciting those very people to rise in arms among us, and to purchase that liberty of which he has deprived them, by murdering the people on whom he also obtruded them: thus paying off former crimes committed against the LIBERTIES of one people, with crimes which he urges them to commit against the LIVES of another.*]

23 In every stage of these oppressions we have petitioned for redress in the most humble terms: our repeated petitions have been answered only by repeated injuries.

24 A prince whose character is thus marked by every act which may define a tyrant is unfit to be the ruler of a FREE people [*who mean to be free. Future ages will scarcely believe that the hardiness of one man adventured, within the short compass of twelve years only, to lay a foundation so broad and so undisguised for tyranny over a people fostered and fixed in principles of freedom.*]

25 Nor have we been wanting in attentions to our British brethren. We have warned them from time to time of attempts by their legislature to extend AN UNWARRANTABLE [*a*] jurisdiction over US [*these our states*]. We have reminded them of the circumstances of our emigration and settlement here, [*no one of which could warrant so strange a pretension: that these were effected at the expense of our own blood and treasure, unassisted by the wealth or the strength of Great Britain: that in constituting indeed our several forms of government, we have adopted one common king, thereby laying a foundation for perpetual league and amity with them: but that submission to their parliament was no part of our constitution, nor ever in idea, if history may be credited: and,*] WE HAVE appealed to their native justice and magnanimity AND WE HAVE CONJURED THEM BY [*as well as to*] the ties of our common kindred to disavow these usurpations which WOULD INEVITABLY [*were likely to*] interrupt our connection and correspondence. They too have been deaf to the voice of justice and of consanguinity. WE MUST THEREFORE [*and when occasions have been given them, by the regular course of their laws, of removing from their councils the disturbers of our harmony, they have, by their free election, reestablished them in power. At this very time too, they are permitting their chief magistrate to send over not only soldiers of our common blood, but Scotch and foreign mercenaries to invade and destroy us. These facts have given the last stab to agonizing affection, and manly spirit bids us to renounce forever these unfeeling brethren. We must endeavor to forget our former love for them, and hold them as we hold the rest of mankind, enemies in war, in peace friends. We might have a free and a great people together; but a communication of grandeur and of freedom, it seems, is below their dignity. Be it so, since they will have it. The road to happiness and to glory is open to us, too. We will tread it apart from them, and*] acquiesce in the necessity which denounces our [*eternal*] separation AND HOLD THEM AS WE HOLD THE REST OF MANKIND, ENEMIES IN WAR, IN PEACE FRIENDS!

26 We, therefore, the representatives of the United States of America in General Congress assembled, appealing to the supreme judge of the world for the rectitude of our intentions, do in the name, and by the authority of the good people of these COLONIES, SOLEMNLY PUBLISH AND DECLARE, THAT THESE UNITED COLONIES ARE, AND OF RIGHT OUGHT TO BE FREE AND INDEPENDENT STATES; THAT THEY ARE ABSOLVED FROM ALL ALLEGIANCE TO THE BRITISH CROWN, AND THAT ALL POLITICAL CONNECTION BETWEEN THEM AND THE STATE OF GREAT BRITAIN IS, AND OUGHT TO BE,

TOTALLY DISSOLVED; [*states reject and renounce all allegiance and subjection to the kings of Great Britain and all others who may hereafter claim by, through or under them; we utterly dissolve all political connection which may heretofore have subsisted between us and the people or parliament of Great Britain: and finally we do assert and declare these colonies to be free and independent states,*] and that as free and independent states, they have full power to levy war, conclude peace, contract alliances, establish commerce, and to do all other acts and things which independent states may of right do.

And for the support of this declaration, with a firm reliance on the protection of divine providence, we mutually pledge to each other our lives, our fortunes, and our sacred honor.

QUESTIONS FOR WRITING AND DISCUSSION

OBSERVING

1. The "laws of nature and of nature's God entitle" us to "separate and equal station [with the British]." Briefly explain what Jefferson and his coauthors mean.
2. According to Jefferson and his coauthors, what are the functions of government?
3. In the Declaration, what statements are made based primarily on faith? What is meant by the claim that some things are "self-evident"?
4. In what ways does Jefferson defend the revolution on the same grounds as the French, whom Edmund Burke opposed? In what ways might Burke have approved of the American version?
5. Note the places in the Declaration that O'Rourke refers to in our opening text to this chapter; why do you think he focused on these?

EVALUATING

1. The members of Congress were mostly landed gentry and from the upper class. Argue that despite this class distinction, the seeds of democracy planted in the Declaration made its framers significantly different from the aristocratic British.
2. Argue that Jefferson's revolutionary vision has or has not been achieved in contemporary America.
3. The Declaration was written and published well after the Revolutionary War had started. Argue that the publication of the document served another purpose other than merely justifying to England the outbreak of war.

RESPONDING AND APPLYING

1. Explain the important differences and similarities between Jefferson's conception of independence and your own.
2. What contemporary circumstances could you imagine that would justify your joining in civil disobedience or outright rebellion against your government?
3. When does the end justify the means? For example, in the case of the American colonies, a variety of circumstances justified, in their eyes, the risk of death, war, civil chaos, and social disruption. How should one determine when the end of a conflict is of sufficient benefit to justify the means of such cost and suffering?

"The Bill of Rights"

It may be said that there are only three great ideas behind democracy. One can be called the "majoritarian principle." According to this principle, the majority of people should have the largest representation in government and the largest control over how that government operates. Thus, by having significant access to the governing powers, the majority can exert some control over the decisions that affect their daily lives. This idea is often called "majority rule."

The second great idea behind democracy can be called the "minority principle" and is generally much less understood but certainly is just as important as the majoritarian principle. This is the principle that protects the minority against the majority's domination of central government and against unjust laws gaining too much power over individuals and small interest groups.

The third great idea behind democracy is the principle of individual and property rights. All individuals have the right to a fair slice of the national pie, a right to a livelihood, a family, and participation in the larger gains of a society.

What is unique about this country, in fact, is not the first principle, which was established in our Constitution, however important that is. Most countries today have documents very similar to our own that guarantee and define citizen representation by a majority principle and that define government operation and the balance of its various powers. Instead, what is unique about our form of democracy and what inspires countless individuals living in repressive regimes to risk their lives in coming here is the minority principle embodied in the Bill of Rights and our courts' willingness to defend it.

The Bill of Rights is the first ten amendments to the Constitution. These amendments were added in 1791, soon after ratification of the Constitution because during the debate over ratification many of the delegates expressed their dissatisfaction with the general assurances and supposed common agreement over what exactly those "natural rights of man" were that a government, in Locke's terms, was supposed to protect. They wanted those natural rights clearly defined and appended to the Constitution. In fact, many delegates were concerned that the Constitution would not have been ratified if the early addition of these amendments had not been assured.

The Bill of Rights is important because it embodies the foundation of our liberties. In the words of attorney Ira Glasser, "It's the idea that even in a democracy, the majority doesn't get to rule everything; that there are certain individual rights and individual liberties that are protected from the tyranny of the majority; that just because there are more whites than blacks doesn't mean that whites can take away from blacks the right to vote or the right to live."[1]

In the Bill of Rights, most of the ten amendments are expressed in the negative ("no law," "not be infringed," and "No soldier"). Many of these are responses to grievances expressed in the Declaration of Independence and are attempts to protect the individual from an intrusive or tyrannical government or even from an overweening or tyrannical majority.

Bill of Rights

ARTICLES IN ADDITION TO, AND AMENDMENT OF, THE CONSTITUTION OF THE UNITED STATES OF AMERICA, PROPOSED BY CONGRESS, AND RATIFIED BY THE LEGISLATURES OF THE SEVERAL STATES PURSUANT TO THE FIFTH ARTICLE OF THE ORIGINAL CONSTITUTION.

Amendment I [1791]

Congress shall make no law respecting an establishment of religion, or prohibiting the free exercise thereof; or abridging the freedom of speech, or of the press; or the right of the people peaceably to assemble, and to petition the Government for a redress of grievances.

Amendment II [1791]

A well regulated Militia, being necessary to the security of a free state, the right of the people to keep and bear Arms, shall not be infringed.

---

[1] Glasser, I. From *Presidential Politics and the ACLU,* 2.

Amendment III [1791]

No Soldier shall, in time of peace be quartered in any house, without the consent of the Owner, nor in time of war, but in a manner to be prescribed by law.

Amendment IV [1791]

The right of the people to be secure in their persons, houses, papers, and effects, against unreasonable searches and seizures, shall not be violated and no Warrants shall issue, but upon probable cause, supported by Oath or affirmation, and particularly describing the place to be searched, and the persons or things to be seized.

Amendment V [1791]

No person shall be held to answer for a capital, or otherwise infamous crime, unless on a presentment or indictment of a Grand Jury, except in cases arising in the land or naval forces, or in the Militia, when in actual service in time of War or public danger; nor shall any person be subject for the same offence to be twice put in jeopardy of life or limb; nor shall be compelled in any criminal case to be a witness against himself, nor be deprived of life, liberty, or property, without due process of law; nor shall private property be taken for public use, without just compensation.

Amendment VI [1791]

In all criminal prosecutions, the accused shall enjoy the right to a speedy and public trial, by an impartial jury of the State and district wherein the crime shall have been committed, which district shall have been previously ascertained by law, and to be informed of the nature and cause of the accusation; to be confronted with the witnesses against him; to have compulsory process for obtaining witnesses in his favor, and to have the Assistance of Counsel for his defence.

Amendment VII [1791]

In Suits at common law, where the value in controversy shall exceed twenty dollars, the right of trial by jury shall be preserved, and no fact tried by jury, shall be otherwise re-examined in any Court of the United States, than according to the rules of the common law.

Amendment VIII [1791]

Excessive bail shall not be required, nor excessive fines imposed, nor cruel and unusual punishments inflicted.

Amendment IX [1791]

The enumeration in the Constitution, of certain rights, shall not be construed to deny or disparage others retained by the people.

Amendment X [1791]

The powers not delegated to the United States by the Constitution, nor prohibited by it to the States, are reserved to the States respectively, or to the people.

QUESTIONS FOR WRITING AND DISCUSSION

OBSERVING

1. Identify one particular issue each amendment deals with. For this issue, describe the potential form of government intrusion into and abuse of individual rights and liberties that made the writing of each amendment necessary.
2. What does the First Amendment appear to be saying about the separation of church and state, the abridging of freedom of speech and press, the right of assembly, and the right to petition for redress of grievances?

EVALUATING

1. Choose a social issue like abortion, capital punishment, gun control, the sale of pornography, requiring the Pledge of Allegiance in schools, the right of hate groups like Neo-Nazis to march or use the Internet, or the right to fly the Confederate flag (to many a symbol of racial segregation) from a statehouse building. Defend your position on one of these issues, basing it on your reading of the Bill of Rights.
2. Which one of the first 10 amendments seems to have been most abused or most subject to abuse? Do you think the individual liberty it protects is important enough to justify the potential abuse?

RESPONDING AND APPLYING

1. Which of the rights enumerated in the Bill of Rights do you think is most crucial to maintaining personal liberty? Why?
2. Discuss one freedom described in the Bill of Rights that you would be most unwilling to give up for the benefit of the community at large.
3. Are people today excessively interested in self at the cost of family and community interests? Explain your position on this question.
4. Describe your relationship to your federal, state, or local government in terms of the freedom you believe you have. Where are the points of contact where any one of your personal freedoms might be under attack or scrutiny? How do you preserve them?

ELIZABETH CADY STANTON AND LUCRETIA MOTT, "DECLARATION OF SENTIMENTS AND RESOLUTIONS, SENECA FALLS"

The Seneca Falls Declaration represents the most important event in the nineteenth-century women's movement, really the beginning of the modern struggle for women's equality. The motivating event for the gathering in Seneca Falls, New York, in 1848 was the attendance eight years earlier of Elizabeth Cady Stanton and Lucretia Mott at the World's Anti-Slavery Convention in London, where they were witness to the exclusion of women as delegates, solely on the basis of their gender. The two women agreed there and then to do something about the discrimination.

Stanton was the central force behind the meeting convened at Seneca Falls. She later wrote:

> My experiences at the World's Anti-Slavery Convention, all I had read of the legal status of women, and the oppression I saw everywhere, together swept across my soul, intensified now by many personal experiences . . . In this tempest-tossed condition of mind I received an invitation to spend the day with Lucretia Mott. . . . I poured out the torrent of my long-accumulating discontent with such vehemence and indignation that I stirred myself, as well as the rest of the party.

Stanton, with the assistance of Mott and others, drafted the Declaration, using the Declaration of Independence with a deliberate irony. This imitation was fitting, especially because political reforms in working conditions were very much in the air at the time as people demanded that the democratic principles of the American and French Revolutions be upheld; it is also more than coincidental that Marx and Engels wrote and presented the *Communist Manifesto* to the world that very same year, in 1848.

Declaration of Sentiments and Resolutions, Seneca Falls

Elizabeth Cady Stanton and Lucretia Mott

". . . In this tempest-tossed condition of mind I received an invitation to spend the day with Lucretia Mott. . . . I poured out the torrent of my long-accumulating discontent with such vehemence and indignation that I stirred myself, as well as the rest of the party."

Then and there the decision was made to call a woman's rights meeting. Only a few days before the convention was scheduled to begin, Stanton, with Lucretia Mott and others, drew up the Seneca Falls Declaration of Sentiments and Resolutions, using the Declaration of Independence as a model.

This use of the Declaration of Independence was particularly appropriate to the time. For in 1848, in England, France, Germany, Austria and elsewhere, people were taking to the streets, seeking the fulfillment of liberal democratic rights, proclaimed in the great documents of the French and American Revolutions and, in many instances, demanding new economic rights for workers. Presaging the political and social storms of the future, that very same year Marx and Engels penned and issued the *Communist Manifesto.*

About three hundred persons appeared at the chapel in Seneca Falls on the appointed day. James Mott, husband of Lucretia, chaired the convention. The Declaration of Sentiments was read to the assembly and adopted. Eleven resolutions were adopted unanimously; a twelfth—that pertaining to granting women elective franchise—passed by a narrow margin only after Frederick Douglass stoutly defended it from the floor.

1 When, in the course of human events, it becomes necessary for one portion of the family of man to assume among the people of the earth a position different from that which they have hitherto occupied, but one to which the laws of nature and of nature's God entitle them, a decent respect to the opinions of mankind requires that they should declare the causes that impel them to such a course.

2 We hold these truths to be self-evident: that all men and women are created equal; that they are endowed by their Creator with certain inalienable rights; that among these are life, liberty, and the pursuit of happiness; that to secure these rights governments are instituted, deriving their just power from the consent of the governed. Whenever any form of government becomes destructive of these ends, it is the right of those who suffer from it to refuse allegiance to it, and to insist upon the institution of a new government, laying its foundation on such principles, and organizing its powers in such form, as to them shall seem most likely to effect their safety and happiness. Prudence, indeed, will dictate that governments being established should not be changed for light and transient causes; and accordingly all experience hath shown that mankind are more disposed to suffer, while evils are sufferable, than to right themselves by abolishing the forms to which they were accustomed. But when a long train of abuses and usurpations, pursuing invariably the same object evinces a design to reduce them under absolute despotism, it is their duty to throw off such government, and to provide new guards for their future security. Such has been the patient sufferance of the women under this government, and such is now the necessity which constrains them to demand the equal station to which they are entitled.

3 The history of mankind is a history of repeated injuries and usurpations on the part of man toward woman, having in direct object the establishment of an absolute tyranny over her. To prove this, let facts be submitted to a candid world.

4 He has never permitted her to exercise her inalienable right to the elective franchise.

5 He has compelled her to submit to laws, in the formation of which she had no voice.

6 He has withheld from her rights which are given to the most ignorant and degraded men—both natives and foreigners.

7 Having deprived her of this first right of a citizen, the elective franchise, thereby leaving her without representation in the halls of legislation, he has oppressed her on all sides.

8 He has made her, if married, in the eye of the law, civilly dead.

9 He has taken from her all right in property, even to the wages she earns.

10 He had made her, morally, an irresponsible being, as she can commit many crimes with impunity, provided they be done in the presence of her husband. In the covenant of marriage, she is compelled to promise obedience to her husband, he becoming, to all intents and purposes, her master—the law giving him power to deprive her of her liberty, and to administer chastisement.

11 He has so framed the laws of divorce, as to what shall be the proper causes, and in case of separation, to whom the guardianship of the children shall be given, as to be wholly regardless of the happiness of women—the law, in all cases, going upon a false supposition of the supremacy of man, and giving all power into his hands.

12 After depriving her of all rights as a married woman, if single, and the owner of property, he has taxed her to support a government which recognizes her only when her property can be made profitable to it.

13 He has monopolized nearly all the profitable employments, and from those she is permitted to follow, she receives but a scanty remuneration. He closes against her all the avenues to wealth and distinction which he considers most honorable to himself. As a teacher of theology, medicine, or law, she is not known.

14 He has denied her the facilities for obtaining a thorough education, all colleges being closed against her.

15 He allows her in Church, as well as State, but a subordinate position, claiming Apostolic authority for her exclusion from the ministry, and, with some exceptions, from any public participation in the affairs of the Church.

16 He has created a false public sentiment by giving to the world a different code of morals for men and women, by which moral delinquencies which exclude women from society, are not only tolerated, but deemed of little account in man.

17 He has usurped the prerogative of Jehovah himself, claiming it as his right to assign for her a sphere of action, when that belongs to her conscience and to her God.

18 He has endeavored, in every way that he could, to destroy her confidence in her own powers, to lessen her self-respect, and to make her willing to lead a dependent and abject life.

19 Now, in view of this entire disfranchisement of one-half the people of this country, their social and religious degradation—in view of the unjust laws

above mentioned, and because women do feel themselves aggrieved, oppressed, and fundamentally deprived of their most sacred rights, we insist that they have immediate admission to all the rights and privileges which belong to them as citizens of the United States.

20 In entering upon the great work before us, we anticipate no small amount of misconception, misrepresentation, and ridicule; but we shall use every instrumentality within our power to effect our object. We shall employ agents, circulate tracts, petition the State and National legislatures, and endeavor to enlist the pulpit and the press in our behalf. We hope this Convention will be followed by a series of Conventions embracing every part of the country.

Resolutions

21 Whereas, The great precept of nature is conceded to be, that "man shall pursue his own true and substantial happiness." Blackstone in his Commentaries remarks, that this law of Nature being co-eval with mankind, and dictated by God himself, is of course superior in obligation to any other. It is binding over all the globe, in all countries and at all times; no human laws are of any validity if contrary to this, and such of them as are valid, derive all their force, and all their validity, and all their authority, mediately and immediately, from this original; therefore,

22 *Resolved,* That such laws as conflict, in any way, with the true and substantial happiness of woman, are contrary to the great precept of nature and of no validity, for this is "superior in obligation to any other."

23 *Resolved,* That all laws which prevent woman from occupying such a station in society as her conscience shall dictate, or which place her in a position inferior to that of man, are contrary to the great precept of nature, and therefore of no force or authority.

24 *Resolved,* That woman is man's equal—was intended to be so by the Creator, and the highest good of the race demands that she should be recognized as such.

25 *Resolved,* That the women of this country ought to be enlightened in regard to the laws under which they live, that they may no longer publish their degradation by declaring themselves satisfied with their present position, nor their ignorance, by asserting that they have all the rights they want.

26 *Resolved,* That inasmuch as man, while claiming for himself intellectual superiority, does accord to woman moral superiority, it is pre-eminently his duty to encourage her to speak and teach, as she has an opportunity, in all religious assemblies.

27 *Resolved,* That the same amount of virtue, delicacy, and refinement of behavior that is required of woman in the social state, should also be required of man, and the same transgressions should be visited with equal severity on both man and woman.

28 *Resolved,* That the objection of indelicacy and impropriety, which is so often brought against women when she addresses a public audience, comes with

a very ill-grace from those who encourage, by their attendance, her appearance on stage, in the concert, or in feats of the circus.

29 *Resolved,* That woman has too long rested satisfied in the circumscribed limits which corrupt customs and a perverted application of the Scriptures have marked out for her, and that it is time she should move in the enlarged sphere which her great Creator has assigned her.

30 *Resolved,* That it is the duty of the women of this country to secure in themselves their sacred right to the elective franchise.

31 *Resolved,* That the equality of human rights results necessarily from the fact of the identity of the race in capabilities and responsibilities.

32 *Resolved, therefore,* That, being invested by the Creator with the same capabilities, and the same consciousness of responsibility for their exercise, it is demonstrably the right and duty of woman, equally with man, to promote every righteous cause by every righteous means; and especially in regard to the great subjects of morals and religion, it is self-evidently her right to participate with her brother in teaching them, both in private and in public, by writing and by speaking, by any instrumentalities proper to be used, and in any assemblies proper to be held; and this being a self-evident truth growing out of the divinely implanted principles of human nature, any custom or authority adverse to it, whether modern or wearing the hoary sanction of antiquity, is to be regarded as a self-evident falsehood, and at war with mankind.

33 [At the last session Lucretia Mott offered and spoke to the following resolution:]

Resolved, That the speedy success of our cause depends upon the zealous and untiring efforts of both men and women, for the overthrow of the monopoly of the pulpit, and for the securing to woman an equal participation with men in the various trades, professions, and commerce.

QUESTIONS FOR WRITING AND DISCUSSION

OBSERVING

1. Based on what specific democratic principles does the Declaration justify taking steps to institute a "new government" or severe social reforms? From whom does Stanton take "the great precept of nature"?
2. Which of the "facts" submitted to support the claim of male oppression seem most important? Which of these grievances seem to have been the most resistant to change in the last century and a half?
3. Why do you think Stanton used the Declaration of Independence as a model? How closely does she imitate the earlier document? What kind of authority, if any, is gained by the imitation?
4. Are there any assumptions about gender behavior here? Traditionally, of course, women have been considered to be more emotional, more sensitive, more artistic, and more compassionate than men, even though these

traits are not likely theirs by nature. To what degree do these assumptions hold up here? Is Stanton using these behaviors in particular rhetorical ways to make a point?

EVALUATING

1. How are men pictured here? Assuming Stanton's claims are accurate, what kind of morality have men followed? How is Stanton using "male" behavior as a persuasive device? Argue your position.
2. There are a number of different references to church and God in the Declaration. Argue that this is merely a rhetorical ploy or that Stanton, in fact, bases her call for equality on traditional Judeo-Christian principles.
3. For thousands of years the word "man" was assumed to mean "thinking person" and was used interchangeably for male or female. The generic noun and pronouns used in the Seneca Falls Declaration are "man" and "he/him," something that would upset many modern feminists. Why do you think these early feminists did not focus on such language issues? What advantages or disadvantages do you see in using language that is gender neutral, such as "person" or "his/her"? Argue that gender-neutral language is or is not important.

RESPONDING AND APPLYING

1. Where do you personally draw the lines when fighting for women's rights? Of these issues, which do you support and why: affirmative action, equal pay for equal work, equal service in the armed services, reproductive rights, child care facilities at work, and maternity leave and benefits.
2. To what degree do you think that the resolutions stated in the Declaration have been successfully achieved today? Is the feminist struggle largely won?

KURT VONNEGUT, JR., "HARRISON BERGERON"

Kurt Vonnegut, Jr. (1922–) is a celebrated and prolific American novelist and essayist who began his writing career primarily as an author of science fiction, having studied science and technology as an undergraduate at Carnegie-Mellon University in Pittsburgh and anthropology at the University of Chicago. In his early career, he suffered from the general lack of critical appreciation for science fiction and a profound misunderstanding of his dark, sardonic humor. With the publication of his novel *Cat's Cradle* in 1962, which revered British novelist Graham Greene referred to as "one of the three best novels of the year by one of the most able living writers," Vonnegut began to evolve from an obscure cult figure to a best-selling, critically acclaimed author. This work exemplified all of Vonnegut's gifts as a writer: a respect for families as the laboratory for human growth, an eye for modern foibles, a ready sense of the absurd, and a keen evocation of his favorite theme, "the frailty of human beings as their greatest asset." He is profoundly interested in reminding the modern, and now post-modern, world that human beings will not find redemption or community merely in superior technology; the human questions remain the same, regardless of one's scientific sophistication.

In the short story, "Harrison Bergeron," Vonnegut raises the question of how far a democracy can go in defining and "prescribing" equality as an operating principle in a society with the help of technology. One can read this story as a wry reflection or commentary on the meaning of Jefferson's "self-evident truth" about "all men being created equal."

Harrison Bergeron

Kurt Vonnegut, Jr.

1 The year was 2081, and everybody was finally equal. They weren't only equal before God and the law. They were equal every which way. Nobody was smarter than anybody else. Nobody was better looking than anybody else. Nobody was stronger or quicker than anybody else. All this equality was due to the 211th, 212th, and 213th Amendments to the Constitution, and to the unceasing vigilance of agents of the United States Handicapper General.

2 Some things about living still weren't quite right, though. April, for instance, still drove people crazy by not being springtime. And it was in that clammy month that the H-G men took George and Hazel Bergeron's fourteen-year-old son, Harrison, away.

3 It was tragic, all right, but George and Hazel couldn't think about it very hard. Hazel had a perfectly average intelligence, which meant she couldn't think about anything except in short bursts. And George, while his intelligence was way above normal, had a little mental handicap radio in his ear. He was required by law to wear it at all times. It was tuned to a government transmitter. Every twenty seconds or so, the transmitter would send out some sharp noise to keep people like George from taking unfair advantage of their brains.

4 George and Hazel were watching television. There were tears on Hazel's cheeks, but she's forgotten for the moment what they were about.

5 On the television screen were ballerinas.

6 A buzzer sounded in George's head. His thoughts fled in panic, like bandits from a burglar alarm.

7 “That was a real pretty dance, that dance they just did,” said Hazel.

8 “Huh?” said George.

9 “That dance—it was nice,” said Hazel.

10 “Yup,” said George. He tried to think a little about the ballerinas. They weren’t really very good—no better than anybody else would have been, anyway. They were burdened with sashweights and bags of birdshot, and their faces were masked, so that no one, seeing a free and graceful gesture or a pretty face, would feel like something the cat drug in. George was toying with the vague notion that maybe dancers shouldn’t be handicapped. But he didn’t get very far with it before another noise in his ear radio scattered his thoughts.

11 George winced. So did two out of the eight ballerinas.

12 Hazel saw him wince. Having no mental handicap herself, she had to ask George what the latest sound had been.

13 “Sounded like somebody hitting a milk bottle with a ball peen hammer,” said George.

14 “I’d think it would be real interesting, hearing all the different sounds,” said Hazel, a little envious. “All the things they think up.”

15 “Um,” said George.

16 “Only, if I was Handicapper General, you know what I would do?” said Hazel. Hazel, as a matter of fact, bore a strong resemblance to the Handicapper General, a woman named Diana Moon Glampers. “If I was Diana Moon Glampers,” said Hazel, “I’d have chimes on Sunday—just chimes. Kind in honor of religion.”

17 “I could think, if it was just chimes,” said George.

18 “Well—maybe make ’em real loud,” said Hazel. “I think I’d make a good Handicapper General.”

19 “Good as anybody else,” said George.

20 “Who knows better’n I do what normal is?” said Hazel.

21 “Right,” said George. He began to think glimmeringly about his abnormal son who was now in jail, about Harrison, but a twenty-one-gun salute in his head stopped that.

22 “Boy!” said Hazel, “That was a doozy, wasn’t it?”

23 It was such a doozy that George was white and trembling, and tears stood on the rims of his red eyes. Two of the eight ballerinas had collapsed to the studio floor, were holding their temples.

24 “All of a sudden you look so tired,” said Hazel. “Why don’t you stretch out on the sofa, so’s you can rest your handicap bag on the pillows, honeybunch.” She was referring to the forty-seven pounds of birdshot in a canvas bag, which was padlocked around George’s neck. “Go on and rest the bag for a little while,” she said. “I don’t care if you’re not equal to me for a while.”

25 George weighed the bag with his hands. “I don’t mind it,” he said. “I don’t notice it any more. It’s just a part of me.”

26 “You been so tired lately—kind of wore out,” said Hazel. “If there was just some way we could make a little hole in the bottom of the bag, and just take out a few of them lead balls. Just a few.”

27 "Two years in prison and two thousand dollars fine for every ball I took out," said George. "I don't call that a bargain."

28 "If you could just take a few out when you came home from work," said Hazel. "I mean—you don't compete with anybody around here. You just set around."

29 "If I tried to get away with it," said George, "then other people'd get away with it—and pretty soon we'd be right back to the dark ages again, with everybody competing against everybody else. You wouldn't like that, would you?"

30 "I'd hate it," said Hazel.

31 "There you are," said George. "The minute people start cheating on laws, what do you think happens to society?"

32 If Hazel hadn't been able to come up with an answer to this question, George couldn't have supplied one. A siren was going off in his head.

33 "Reckon it'd fall all apart," said Hazel.

34 "What would?" said George blankly.

35 "Society," said Hazel uncertainly. "Wasn't that what you just said?"

36 "Who knows?" said George.

37 The television program was suddenly interrupted for a news bulletin. It wasn't clear at first as to what the bulletin was about, since the announcer, like all announcers, had a serious speech impediment. For about half a minute, and in a state of high excitement, the announcer tried to say, "Ladies and gentlemen—"

38 He finally gave up, handed the bulletin to a ballerina to read.

39 "That's all right—" Hazel said of the announcer, "he tried. That's the big thing. He tried to do the best he could with what God gave him. He should get a nice raise for trying so hard."

40 "Ladies and gentlemen—" said the ballerina, reading the bulletin. She must have been extraordinarily beautiful, because the mask she wore was hideous. And it was easy to see that she was the strongest and most graceful of all the dancers, for her handicap bags were as big as those worn by two-hundred-pound men.

41 And she had to apologize at once for her voice, which was a very unfair voice for a woman to use. Her voice was a warm, luminous, timeless melody. "Excuse me—" she said, and she began again, making her voice absolutely uncompetitive.

42 "Harrison Bergeron, age fourteen," she said in a grackle squawk, "has just escaped from jail, where he was held on suspicion of plotting to overthrow the government. He is a genius and an athlete, is under-handicapped, and should be regarded as extremely dangerous."

43 A police photograph of Harrison Bergeron was flashed on the screen—upside down, then sideways, upside down again, then right side up. The picture showed the full length of Harrison against a background calibrated in feet and inches. He was exactly seven feet tall.

44 The rest of Harrison's appearance was Halloween and hardware. Nobody had ever borne heavier handicaps. He had outgrown hindrances faster than the

H-G men could think them up. Instead of a little ear radio for a mental handicap, he wore a tremendous pair of earphones, and spectacles with thick wavy lenses. The spectacles were intended to make him not only half blind, but to give him whanging headaches besides.

45 Scrap metal was hung all over him. Ordinarily, there was a certain symmetry, a military neatness to the handicaps issued to strong people, but Harrison looked like a walking junkyard. In the race of life, Harrison carried three hundred pounds.

46 And to offset his good looks, the H-G men required that he wear at all times a red rubber ball for a nose, keep his eyebrows shaved off, and cover his even white teeth with black caps at snaggle-tooth random.

47 "If you see this boy," said the ballerina, "do not—I repeat, do not—try to reason with him."

48 There was the shriek of a door being torn from its hinges.

49 Screams and barking cries of consternation came from the television set. The photograph of Harrison Bergeron on the screen jumped again and again, as though dancing to the tune of an earthquake.

50 George Bergeron correctly identified the earthquake, and well he might have—for many was the time his own home had danced to the same crashing tune. "My God—" said George, "that must be Harrison!"

51 The realization was blasted from his mind instantly by the sound of an automobile collision in his head.

52 When George could open his eyes again, the photograph of Harrison was gone. A living, breathing Harrison filled the screen.

53 Clanking, clownish, and huge, Harrison stood in the center of the studio. The knob of the uprooted studio door was still in his hand. Ballerinas, technicians, musicians, and announcers cowered on their knees before him, expecting to die.

54 "I am the Emperor!" cried Harrison. "Do you hear? I am the Emperor! Everybody must do what I say at once!" He stamped his foot and the studio shook.

55 "Even as I stand here—" he bellowed, "crippled, hobbled, sickened—I am a greater ruler than any man who ever lived! Now watch me become what I *can* become!"

56 Harrison tore the straps of his handicap harness like wet tissue paper, tore straps guaranteed to support five thousand pounds.

57 Harrison's scrap-iron handicaps crashed to the floor.

58 Harrison thrust his thumbs under the bar of the padlock that secured his head harness. The bar snapped like celery. Harrison smashed his headphones and spectacles against the wall.

59 He flung away his rubber-ball nose, revealed a man that would have awed Thor, the god of thunder.

60 "I shall now select my Empress!" he said, looking down on the cowering people. "Let the first woman who dares rise to her feet claim her mate and her throne!"

61 A moment passed, and then a ballerina arose, swaying like a willow.

62 Harrison plucked the mental handicap from her ear, snapped off her physical handicaps with marvelous delicacy. Last of all, he removed her mask.

63 She was blindingly beautiful.

64 "Now—" said Harrison, taking her hand, "shall we show the people the meaning of the word dance? Music!" he commanded.

65 The musicians scrambled back into their chairs, and Harrison stripped them of their handicaps, too. "Play your best," he told them, "and I'll make you barons and dukes and earls."

66 The music began. It was normal at first—cheap, silly, false. But Harrison snatched two musicians from their chairs, waved them like batons as he sang the music as he wanted it played. He slammed them back into their chairs.

67 The music began again and was much improved.

68 Harrison and his Empress merely listened to the music for a while—listened gravely, as though synchronizing their heartbeats with it.

69 They shifted their weights to their toes.

70 Harrison placed his big hands on the girl's tiny waist, letting her sense the weightlessness that would soon be hers.

71 And then, in an explosion of joy and grace, into the air they sprang!

72 Not only were the laws of the land abandoned, but the law of gravity and the laws of motion as well.

73 They reeled, whirled, swiveled, flounced, capered, gamboled, and spun.

74 They leaped like deer on the moon.

75 The studio ceiling was thirty feet high, but each leap brought the dancers nearer to it.

76 It became their obvious intention to kiss the ceiling.

77 They kissed it.

78 And then, neutralizing gravity with love and pure will, they remained suspended in air inches below the ceiling, and they kissed each other for a long, long time.

79 It was then that Diana Moon Glampers, the Handicapper General, came into the studio with a double-barreled ten-gauge shotgun. She fired twice, and the Emperor and the Empress were dead before they hit the floor.

80 Diana Moon Glampers loaded the gun again. She aimed it at the musicians and told them they had ten seconds to get their handicaps back on.

81 It was then that the Bergerons' television tube burned out.

82 Hazel turned to comment about the blackout to George. But George had gone out into the kitchen for a can of beer.

83 George came back in with the beer, paused while a handicap signal shook him up. And then he sat down again. "You been crying?" he said to Hazel.

84 "Yup," she said.

85 "What about?" he said.

86 "I forget," she said. "Something real sad on television."

87 "What was it?" he said.

88 "It's all kind of mixed up in my mind," said Hazel.

89 "Forget sad things," said George.

90 "I always do," said Hazel.

91 "That's my girl," said George. He winced. There was the sound of a rivetting gun in his head.

92 "Gee—I could tell that one was a doozy," said Hazel.

93 "You can say that again," said George.

94 "Gee—" said Hazel. "I could tell that one was a doozy."

QUESTIONS FOR WRITING AND DISCUSSION

OBSERVING

1. How does Vonnegut force us to think about the meaning(s) of "equality" in this short story?
2. How does "equality" seem to be defined in this futuristic tale? What is the role of "average" in the society he depicts?
3. In what ways does Vonnegut deliberately change the culture in his story to match his imagined future? In what ways does it resemble ours at the end of the twentieth century?
4. What is the point of his reference to "211th, 212th, and 213th Amendments" to the Constitution?

EVALUATING

1. In this imagined society, what does Vonnegut suggest about how good intentions and laudable goals can result in less freedom overall or more obstruction to individual rights and aspirations?
2. What is the role of the "Handicapper General" in the story? Is there a comparable role in today's society for such a person?
3. What is the role of a democratic government in recognizing and rewarding achievement or in privileging certain kinds of achievement over others? What is its role in making access to opportunities for achievement more equal, or to enhance the opportunities of some at the expense of others?

RESPONDING AND APPLYING

1. What is Vonnegut saying about the power of laws (and their interpreters and enforcers) to maintain, balance, or distort the relative freedom and individual rights in a society?
2. Vonnegut makes his hero a 14-year-old. Why is this effective or strategic? What would the difference have been if he had made him 34 or a young woman instead of a teenage male?
3. In your view, what is the general attitude in society toward people of exceptional ability, intelligence, or physical strength? In what ways does the

presence of achieving individuals enhance a sense of democracy and individual freedom? In what ways does it inhibit it or undermine it?

4. Have you personally ever felt you were given privilege because of your gender, skin color, national origin, sexual orientation, age, or innate abilities? Have you ever personally felt discriminated against because of any of these personal attributes or life circumstances? Write a personal essay that explores these events.

PERSPECTIVES

The Challenges of Democracy

In this Perspectives section, you will be asked to consider two texts dealing with the problems inherent in creating or living within a democracy. The first text is a famous letter written in 1963 by Dr. Martin Luther King, Jr., while incarcerated in Birmingham, Alabama, for his participation in a public protest against segregation. In this letter, King astutely relies heavily on the American tradition of peaceful civil disobedience, the fairness and equality reflected in the documents of the white founders and framers of the American political order, and the Biblical authority so often evoked in the Bible-belt South in its justification of an American "apartheid." The second text is a short story by South African writer Nadine Gordimer, which skillfully dramatizes the predicament of a recently freed, black political prisoner who attempts to navigate his way back into a culture supposedly but, in fact, selectively democratic, and his encounter with ineffectual "do-gooders" troubled by his plight but apparently unable to empower him.

MARTIN LUTHER KING, "LETTER FROM BIRMINGHAM JAIL"

Martin Luther King (1929–1968) has become synonymous with the struggle of black people and the poor to overcome oppression and to gain civil rights. He was born the son of a Baptist minister, was graduated from Morehouse College and Grover Theological Seminary, and he earned his Ph.D. from Boston University. Influenced by Mahatma Gandhi's philosophy of nonviolent change, he became pastor at a church in Montgomery, Alabama in 1955, where he used the tactics of economic boycott and civil disobedience to protest the segregation of public bus transportation. In 1957, King moved to Atlanta, where he served with his father as pastor of the Ebeneezer Baptist Church. At that time, he also organized the influential civil rights organization, the Southern Christian Leadership Conference.

In the decade that followed, King led demonstrations against segregation throughout the South. His marches were often met with violence, and sometimes he was arrested and jailed. Although he was successful in changing many of the oppressive Jim Crow laws and conditions in the country at the time (Jim Crow refers to the system of legal and traditional sanctions, most notably segregation against black people in the American South), King's importance extended far beyond the mere opening up of public buses and accommodations.

In 1963 from a Birmingham jail, King wrote the letter that follows on margins of newspapers and on toilet paper and smuggled it to an aide. It was his response to a statement signed by eight clergymen, who criticized him for his "unwise and untimely" demonstrations. A year later, he was awarded the Nobel Peace Prize. He was assassinated in 1968.

Letter from Birmingham Jail

Martin Luther King, Jr.

My Dear Fellow Clergymen:

1 While confined here in the Birmingham city jail, I came across your recent statement calling my present activities "unwise and untimely." Seldom do I pause to answer criticism of my work and ideas. If I sought to answer all the criticisms that cross my desk, my secretaries would have little time for anything other than such correspondence in the course of the day, and I would have no time for constructive work. But since I feel that you are men of genuine good will and that your criticisms are sincerely set forth, I want to try to answer your statement in what I hope will be patient and reasonable terms.

2 I think I should indicate why I am here in Birmingham, since you have been influenced by the view which argues against "outsiders coming in." I have the honor of serving as president of the Southern Christian Leadership Conference, an organization operating in every southern state, with headquarters in Atlanta, Georgia. We have some eighty-five affiliated organizations across the South, and one of them is the Alabama Christian Movement for Human Rights. Frequently we share staff, educational, and financial resources with our affiliates. Several months ago the affiliate here in Birmingham asked us to be on call to engage in a nonviolent direct-action program if such were deemed necessary. We readily consented, and when the hour came we lived up to our promise. So I, along with several members of my staff, am here because I was invited here. I am here because I have organizational ties here.

3 But more basically, I am in Birmingham because injustice is here. Just as the prophets of the eighth century B.C. left their villages and carried their "thus saith the Lord" far beyond the boundaries of their home towns, and just as the

Apostle Paul left his village of Tarsus and carried the gospel of Jesus Christ to the far corners of the Greco-Roman world, so am I compelled to carry the gospel of freedom beyond my own home town. Like Paul, I must constantly respond to the Macedonian call for aid.

4 Moreover, I am cognizant of the interrelatedness of all communities and states. I cannot sit idly by in Atlanta and not be concerned about what happens in Birmingham. Injustice anywhere is a threat to justice everywhere. We are caught in an inescapable network of mutuality, tied in a single garment of destiny. Whatever affects one directly, affects all indirectly. Never again can we afford to live with the narrow, provincial "outside agitator" idea. Anyone who lives inside the United States can never be considered an outsider anywhere within its bounds.

5 You deplore the demonstrations taking place in Birmingham. But your statement, I am sorry to say, fails to express a similar concern for the conditions that brought about the demonstrations. I am sure that none of you would want to rest content with the superficial kind of social analysis that deals merely with effects and does not grapple with underlying causes. It is unfortunate that demonstrations are taking place in Birmingham, but it is even more unfortunate that the city's white power structure left the Negro community with no alternative.

6 In any nonviolent campaign there are four basic steps: collection of the facts to determine whether injustices exist; negotiations; self-purification; and direct action. We have gone through all these steps in Birmingham. There can be no gainsaying the fact that racial injustice engulfs this community. Birmingham is probably the most thoroughly segregated city in the United States. Its ugly record of brutality is widely known. Negroes have experienced grossly unjust treatment in the courts. There have been more unsolved bombings of Negro homes and churches in Birmingham than in any other city in the nation. These are the hard, brutal facts of the case. On the basis of these conditions, Negro leaders sought to negotiate with the city fathers. But the latter consistently refused to engage in good-faith negotiation.

7 Then, last September, came the opportunity to talk with leaders of Birmingham's economic community. In the course of the negotiations, certain promises were made by the merchants—for example, to remove the stores' humiliating racial signs. On the basis of these promises, the Reverend Fred Shuttlesworth and the leaders of the Alabama Christian Movement for Human Rights agreed to a moratorium on all demonstrations. As the weeks and months went by, we realized that we were the victims of a broken promise. A few signs, briefly removed, returned; the others remained.

8 As in so many past experiences, our hopes had been blasted, and the shadow of deep disappointment settled upon us. We had no alternative except to prepare for direct action, whereby we would present our very bodies as a means of laying our case before the conscience of the local and the national community. Mindful of the difficulties involved, we decided to undertake a process of self-purification. We began a series of workshops on nonviolence, and we repeatedly asked ourselves: "Are you able to accept blows without retaliating?" "Are you able to endure the ordeal of jail?" We decided to schedule

our direct-action program for the Easter season, realizing that except for Christmas, this is the main shopping period of the year. Knowing that a strong economic-withdrawal program would be the by-product of direct action, we felt that this would be the best time to bring pressure to bear on the merchants for the needed change.

9 Then it occurred to us that Birmingham's mayoral election was coming up in March, and we speedily decided to postpone action until after election day. When we discovered that the Commissioner of Public Safety, Eugene "Bull" Connor, had piled up enough votes to be in the run-off, we decided again to postpone action until the day after the run-off so that the demonstrations could not be used to cloud the issues. Like many others, we wanted to see Mr. Connor defeated, and to this end we endured postponement after postponement. Having aided in this community need, we felt that our direct-action program could be delayed no longer.

10 You may well ask, "Why direct action? Why sit-ins, marches, and so forth? Isn't negotiation a better path?" You are quite right in calling for negotiation. Indeed, this is the very purpose of direct action. Nonviolent direct action seeks to create such a crisis and foster such a tension that a community which has constantly refused to negotiate is forced to confront the issue. It seeks so to dramatize the issue that it can no longer be ignored. My citing the creation of tension as part of the work of the nonviolent-resister may sound rather shocking. But I must confess that I am not afraid of the word "tension." I have earnestly opposed violent tension, but there is a type of constructive, nonviolent tension which is necessary for growth. Just as Socrates felt that it was necessary to create tension in the mind so that individuals could rise from the bondage of myths and half-truths to the unfettered realm of creative analysis and objective appraisal, so must we see the need for nonviolent gadflies to create the kind of tension in society that will help men rise from the dark depths of prejudice and racism to the majestic heights of understanding and brotherhood.

11 The purpose of our direct-action program is to create a situation so crisis-packed that it will inevitably open the door to negotiation. I therefore concur with you in your call for negotiation. Too long has our beloved Southland been bogged down in a tragic effort to live in monologue rather than dialogue.

12 One of the basic points in your statement is that the action that I and my associates have taken in Birmingham is untimely. Some have asked, "Why didn't you give the new city administration time to act?" The only answer that I can give to this query is that the new Birmingham administration must be prodded about as much as the outgoing one, before it will act. We are sadly mistaken if we feel that the election of Albert Boutwell as mayor will bring the millennium to Birmingham. While Mr. Boutwell is a much more gentle person than Mr. Connor, they are both segregationists, dedicated to maintenance of the status quo. I have hoped that Mr. Boutwell will be reasonable enough to see the futility of massive resistance to desegregation. But he will not see this without pressure from devotees of civil rights. My friends, I must say to you that we have not made a single gain in civil rights without determined legal and nonviolent pressure. Lamentably, it is an historical fact that privileged groups seldom give up

their privileges voluntarily. Individuals may see the moral light and voluntarily give up their unjust posture; but, as Reinhold Niebuhr has reminded us, groups tend to be more immoral than individuals.

13 We know through painful experience that freedom is never voluntarily given by the oppressor; it must be demanded by the oppressed. Frankly, I have yet to engage in a direct-action campaign that was "well timed" in the view of those who have not suffered unduly from the disease of segregation. For years now I have heard the word "Wait!" It rings in the ear of every Negro with piercing familiarity. This "Wait" has almost always meant "Never." We must come to see, with one of our distinguished jurists, that "justice too long delayed is justice denied."

14 We have waited for more than 340 years for our constitutional and God-given rights. The nations of Asia and Africa are moving with jetlike speed toward gaining political independence, but we still creep at horse-and-buggy pace toward gaining a cup of coffee at a lunch counter. Perhaps it is easy for those who have never felt the stinging darts of segregation to say, "Wait." But when you have seen vicious mobs lynch your mothers and fathers at will and drown your sisters and brothers at whim; when you have seen hate-filled policemen curse, kick, and even kill your black brothers and sisters; when you see the vast majority of your twenty million Negro brothers smothering in an airtight cage of poverty in the midst of an affluent society; when you suddenly find your tongue twisted and your speech stammering as you seek to explain to your six-year-old daughter why she can't go to the public amusement park that has just been advertised on television, and see tears welling up in her eyes when she is told that Funtown is closed to colored children, and see ominous clouds of inferiority beginning to form in her little mental sky, and see her beginning to distort her personality by developing an unconscious bitterness toward white people; when you have to concoct an answer for a five-year-old son who is asking, "Daddy, why do white people treat colored people so mean"; when you take a cross-country drive and find it necessary to sleep night after night in the uncomfortable corners of your automobile because no motel will accept you; when you are humiliated day in and day out by nagging signs reading "white" and "colored"; when your first name becomes "nigger," your middle name becomes "boy" (however old you are) and your last name becomes "John," and your wife and mother are never given the respected title "Mrs."; when you are harried by day and haunted by night by the fact that you are a Negro, living constantly at tiptoe stance, never quite knowing what to expect next, and are plagued with inner fears and outer resentments; when you are forever fighting a degenerating sense of "nobodiness"—then you will understand why we find it difficult to wait. There comes a time when the cup of endurance runs over, and men are no longer willing to be plunged into the abyss of despair. I hope, sirs, you can understand our legitimate and unavoidable impatience.

15 You express a great deal of anxiety over our willingness to break laws. This is certainly a legitimate concern. Since we so diligently urge people to obey the Supreme Court's decision of 1954 outlawing segregation in the public schools,

at first glance it may seem rather paradoxical for us consciously to break laws. One may well ask: "How can you advocate breaking some laws and obeying others?" The answer lies in the fact that there are two types of laws: just and unjust. I would be the first to advocate obeying just laws. One has not only a legal but a moral responsibility to obey just laws. Conversely, one has a moral responsibility to disobey unjust laws. I would agree with St. Augustine that "an unjust law is no law at all."

16 Now, what is the difference between the two? How does one determine whether a law is just or unjust? A just law is a man-made code that squares with the moral law or the law of God. An unjust law is a code that is out of harmony with the moral law. To put it in the terms of St. Thomas Aquinas: An unjust law is a human law that is not rooted in eternal law and natural law. Any law that uplifts human personality is just. Any law that degrades human personality is unjust. All segregation statutes are unjust because segregation distorts the soul and damages the personality. It give the segregator a false sense of superiority and the segregated a false sense of inferiority. Segregation, to use the terminology of the Jewish philosopher Martin Buber, substitutes an "I-it" relationship for an "I-thou" relationship and ends up relegating persons to the status of things. Hence segregation is not only politically, economically, and sociologically unsound, it is morally wrong and sinful. Paul Tillich has said that sin is separation. Is not segregation an existential expression of man's tragic separation, his awful estrangement, his terrible sinfulness? Thus it is that I can urge men to obey the 1954 decision of the Supreme Court, for it is morally right; and I can urge them to disobey segregation ordinances, for they are morally wrong.

17 Let us consider a more concrete example of just and unjust laws. An unjust law is a code that a numerical or power majority group compels a minority group to obey but does not make binding on itself. This is *difference* made legal. By the same token, a just law is a code that a majority compels a minority to follow and that it is willing to follow itself. This is *sameness* made legal.

18 Let me give another explanation. A law is unjust if it is inflicted on a minority that, as a result of being denied the right to vote, had no part in enacting or devising the law. Who can say that the legislature of Alabama which set up that state's segregation laws was democratically elected? Throughout Alabama all sorts of devious methods are used to prevent Negroes from becoming registered voters, and there are some counties in which, even though Negroes constitute a majority of the population, not a single Negro is registered. Can any law enacted under such circumstances be considered democratically structured?

19 Sometimes a law is just on its face and unjust in its application. For instance, I have been arrested on a charge of parading without a permit. Now, there is nothing wrong in having an ordinance which requires a permit for a parade. But such an ordinance becomes unjust when it is used to maintain segregation and to deny citizens the First-Amendment privilege of peaceful assembly and protest.

20 I hope you are able to see the distinction I am trying to point out. In no sense do I advocate evading or defying the law, as would the rabid segrega-

tionist. That would lead to anarchy. One who breaks an unjust law must do so openly, lovingly, and with a willingness to accept the penalty. I submit that an individual who breaks a law that conscience tells him is unjust, and who willingly accepts the penalty of imprisonment in order to arouse the conscience of the community over its injustice, is in reality expressing the highest respect for law.

21 Of course, there is nothing new about this kind of civil disobedience. It was evidenced sublimely in the refusal of Shadrach, Meschach, and Abednego to obey the laws of Nebuchadnezzar, on the ground that a higher moral law was at stake. It was practiced superbly by the early Christians, who were willing to face hungry lions and the excruciating pain of chopping blocks rather than submit to certain unjust laws of the Roman Empire. To a degree, academic freedom is a reality today because Socrates practiced civil disobedience. In our own nation, the Boston Tea Party represented a massive act of civil disobedience.

22 We should never forget that everything Adolf Hitler did in Germany was "legal" and everything the Hungarian freedom fighters did in Hungary was "illegal." It was "illegal" to aid and comfort a Jew in Hitler's Germany. Even so, I am sure that, had I lived in Germany at the time, I would have aided and comforted my Jewish brothers. If today I lived in a Communist country where certain principles dear to the Christian faith are suppressed, I would openly advocate disobeying that country's antireligious laws.

23 I must make two honest confessions to you, my Christian and Jewish brothers. First, I must confess that over the past few years I have been gravely disappointed with the white moderate. I have almost reached the regrettable conclusion that the Negro's great stumbling block in his stride toward freedom is not the White Citizen's Counciler or the Ku Klux Klanner, but the white moderate, who is more devoted to "order" than to justice; who prefers a negative peace which is the absence of tension to a positive peace which is the presence of justice; who constantly says, "I agree with you in the goal you seek, but I cannot agree with your methods of direct action"; who paternalistically believes he can set the timetable for another man's freedom; who lives by a mythical concept of time and who constantly advises the Negro to wait for a "more convenient season." Shallow understanding from people of good will is more frustrating than absolute misunderstanding from people of ill will. Lukewarm acceptance is much more bewildering than outright rejection.

24 I had hoped that the white moderate would understand that law and order exist for the purpose of establishing justice and that when they fail in this purpose they become the dangerously structured dams that block the flow of social progress. I had hoped that the white moderate would understand that the present tension in the South is a necessary phase of the transition from an obnoxious negative peace, in which the Negro passively accepted his unjust plight, to a substantive and positive peace, in which all men will respect the dignity and worth of human personality. Actually, we who engage in nonviolent direct action are not the creators of tension. We merely bring to the surface the hidden tension that is already alive. We bring it out in the open, where it can be seen and dealt with. Like a boil that can never be cured so long as it is

covered up but must be opened with all its ugliness to the natural medicines of air and light, injustice must be exposed, with all the tension its exposure creates, to the light of human conscience and the air of national opinion, before it can be cured.

25 In your statement you assert that our actions, even though peaceful, must be condemned because they precipitate violence. But is this a logical assertion? Isn't this like condemning a robbed man because his possession of money precipitated the evil act of robbery? Isn't this like condemning Socrates because his unswerving commitment to truth and his philosophical inquiries precipitated the act by the misguided populace in which they made him drink hemlock? Isn't this like condemning Jesus because his unique God-consciousness and never-ceasing devotion to God's will precipitated the evil act of crucifixion? We must come to see that, as the federal courts have consistently affirmed, it is wrong to urge an individual to cease his efforts to gain his basic constitutional rights because the quest may precipitate violence. Society must protect the robbed and punish the robber.

26 I had also hoped that the white moderate would reject the myth concerning time in relation to the struggle for freedom. I have just received a letter from a white brother in Texas. He writes: "All Christians know that the colored people will receive equal rights eventually, but it is possible that you are in too great a religious hurry. It has taken Christianity almost two thousand years to accomplish what it has. The teachings of Christ take time to come to earth." Such an attitude stems from a tragic misconception of time, from the strangely irrational notion that there is something in the very flow of time that will inevitably cure all ills. Actually, time itself is neutral; it can be used either destructively or constructively. More and more I feel that the people of ill will have used time much more effectively than have the people of good will. We will have to repent in this generation not merely for the hateful words and actions of the bad people, but for the appalling silence of the good people. Human progress never rolls in on wheels of inevitability; it comes through the tireless efforts of men willing to be co-workers with God, and without this hard work, time itself becomes an ally of the forces of social stagnation. We must use time creatively, in the knowledge that the time is always ripe to do right. Now is the time to make real the promise of democracy and transform our pending national elegy into a creative psalm of brotherhood. Now is the time to lift our national policy from the quicksand of racial injustice to the solid rock of human dignity.

27 You speak of our activity in Birmingham as extreme. At first I was rather disappointed that fellow clergymen would see my nonviolent efforts as those of an extremist. I began thinking about the fact that I stand in the middle of two opposing forces in the Negro community. One is a force of complacency, made up in part of Negroes who, as a result of long years of oppression, are so drained of self-respect and a sense of "somebodiness" that they have adjusted to segregation; and in part of a few middle-class Negroes who, because of a degree of academic and economic security and because in some ways they profit by segregation, have become insensitive to the problems of the masses. The other

force is one of bitterness and hatred, and it comes perilously close to advocating violence. It is expressed in the various black nationalist groups that are springing up across the nation, the largest and best-known being Elijah Muhammad's Muslim movement. Nourished by the Negro's frustration over the continued existence of racial discrimination, this movement is made up of people who have lost faith in America, who have absolutely repudiated Christianity, and who have concluded that the white man is an incorrigible "devil."

28 I have tried to stand between these two forces, saying that we need emulate neither the "do-nothingness" of the complacent nor the hatred and despair of the black nationalist. For there is the more excellent way of love and nonviolent protest. I am grateful to God that, through the influence of the Negro church, the way of nonviolence became an integral part of our struggle.

29 If this philosophy had not emerged, by now many streets of the South would, I am convinced, be flowing with blood. And I am further convinced that if our white brothers dismiss as "rabblerousers" and "outside agitators" those of us who employ nonviolent direct action, and if they refuse to support our nonviolent efforts, millions of Negroes will, out of frustration and despair, seek solace and security in black-nationalist ideologies—a development that would inevitably lead to a frightening racial nightmare.

30 Oppressed people cannot remain oppressed forever. The yearning for freedom eventually manifests itself, and that is what has happened to the American Negro. Something within has reminded him of his birthright of freedom, and something without has reminded him that it can be gained. Consciously or unconsciously, he has been caught up by the *Zeitgeist,* and with his black brothers of Africa and his brown and yellow brothers of Asia, South America, and the Caribbean, the United States Negro is moving with a sense of great urgency toward the promised land of racial justice. If one recognizes this vital urge that has engulfed the Negro community, one should readily understand why public demonstrations are taking place. The Negro has many pent-up resentments and latent frustrations, and he must release them. So let him march; let him make prayer pilgrimages to the city hall; let him go on freedom rides—and try to understand why he must do so. If his repressed emotions are not released in nonviolent ways, they will seek expression through violence; this is not a threat but a fact of history. So I have not said to my people, "Get rid of your discontent." Rather, I have tried to say that this normal and healthy discontent can be channeled into the creative outlet of nonviolent direct action. And now this approach is being termed extremist.

31 But though I was initially disappointed at being categorized as an extremist, as I continued to think about the matter I gradually gained a measure of satisfaction from the label. Was not Jesus an extremist for love: "Love your enemies, bless them that curse you, do good to them that hate you, and pray for them which despitefully use you, and persecute you." Was not Amos an extremist for justice: "Let justice roll down like waters and righteousness like an ever-flowing stream." Was not Paul an extremist for the Christian gospel: "I bear in my body the marks of the Lord Jesus." Was not Martin Luther an extremist: "Here I stand;

I cannot do otherwise, so help me God." And John Bunyan: "I will stay in jail to the end of my days before I make a butchery of my conscience." And Abraham Lincoln: "This nation cannot survive half slave and half free." And Thomas Jefferson: "We hold these truths to be self-evident, that all men are created equal. . . ." So the question is not whether we will be extremists, but what kind of extremists we will be. Will we be extremists for hate or for love? Will we be extremists for the preservation of injustice or for the extension of justice? In that dramatic scene on Calvary's hill three men were crucified. We must never forget that all three were crucified for the same crime—the crime of extremism. Two were extremists for immorality, and thus fell below their environment. The other, Jesus Christ, was an extremist for love, truth, and goodness, and thereby rose above his environment. Perhaps the South, the nation, and the world are in dire need of creative extremists.

32 I had hoped that the white moderate would see this need. Perhaps I was too optimistic; perhaps I expected too much. I suppose I should have realized that few members of the oppressor race can understand the deep groans and passionate yearnings of the oppressed race, and still fewer have the vision to see that injustice must be rooted out by strong, persistent, and determined action. I am thankful, however, that some of our white brothers in the South have grasped the meaning of this social revolution and committed themselves to it. They are still all too few in quantity, but they are big in quality. Some—such as Ralph McGill, Lillian Smith, Harry Golden, James McBride Dabbs, Ann Braden, and Sarah Patton Boyle—have written about our struggle in eloquent and prophetic terms. Others have marched with us down nameless streets of the South. They have languished in filthy, roach-infested jails, suffering the abuse and brutality of policemen who view them as "dirty nigger-lovers." Unlike so many of their moderate brothers and sisters, they have recognized the urgency of the moment and sensed the need for powerful "action" antidotes to combat the disease of segregation.

33 Let me take note of my other major disappointment. I have been so greatly disappointed with the white church and its leadership. Of course, there are some notable exceptions. I am not unmindful of the fact that each of you has taken some significant stands on this issue. I commend you, Reverend Stallings, for your Christian stand on this past Sunday, in welcoming Negroes to your worship service on a nonsegregated basis. I commend the Catholic leaders of this state for integrating Spring Hill College several years ago.

34 But despite these notable exceptions, I must honestly reiterate that I have been disappointed with the church. I do not say this as one of those negative critics who can always find something wrong with the church. I say this as a minister of the gospel, who loves the church; who was nurtured in its bosom; who has been sustained by its spiritual blessings and who will remain true to it as long as the cord of life shall lengthen.

35 When I was suddenly catapulted into the leadership of the bus protest in Montgomery, Alabama, a few years ago, I felt we would be supported by the white church. I felt that the white ministers, priests, and rabbis of the South

would be among our strongest allies. Instead, some have been outright opponents, refusing to understand the freedom movement and misrepresenting its leaders; all too many others have been more cautious than courageous and have remained silent behind the anesthetizing security of stained glass windows.

36 In spite of my shattered dreams, I came to Birmingham with the hope that the white religious leadership of this community would see the justice of our cause and, with deep moral concern, would serve as the channel through which our just grievances could reach the power structure. I had hoped that each of you would understand. But again I have been disappointed.

37 I have heard numerous southern religious leaders admonish their worshipers to comply with a desegregation decision because it is the law, but I have longed to hear white ministers declare: "Follow this decree because integration is morally right and because the Negro is your brother." In the midst of blatant injustices inflicted upon the Negro, I have watched white churchmen stand on the sideline and mouth pious irrelevancies and sanctimonious trivialities. In the midst of a mighty struggle to rid our nation of racial and economic injustice, I have heard many ministers say: "Those are social issues, with which the gospel has no real concern." And I have watched many churches commit themselves to a completely otherworldly religion which makes a strange, un-Biblical distinction between body and soul, between the sacred and the secular.

38 I have traveled the length and breadth of Alabama, Mississippi, and all the other southern states. On sweltering summer days and crisp autumn mornings I have looked at the South's beautiful churches with their lofty spires pointing heavenward. I have beheld the impressive outlines of her massive religious-education buildings. Over and over I have found myself asking: "What kind of people worship here? Who is their God? Where were their voices when the lips of Governor Barnett dripped with words of interposition and nullification? Where were they when Governor Wallace gave a clarion call for defiance and hatred? Where were their voices of support when bruised and weary Negro men and women decided to rise from the dark dungeons of complacency to the bright hills of creative protest?"

39 Yes, these questions are still in my mind. In deep disappointment I have wept over the laxity of the church. But be assured that my tears have been tears of love. There can be no deep disappointment where there is not deep love. Yes, I love the church. How could I do otherwise? I am in the rather unique position of being the son, the grandson, and the great-grandson of preachers. Yes, I see the church as the body of Christ. But, oh! How we have blemished and scarred that body through social neglect and through fear of being non-conformists.

40 There was a time when the church was very powerful—in the time when the early Christians rejoiced at being deemed worthy to suffer for what they believed. In those days the church was not merely a thermometer that recorded the ideas and principles of popular opinion, it was a thermostat that transformed the mores of society. Whenever the early Christians entered a town, the people in power became disturbed and immediately sought to convict the

Christians for being "disturbers of the peace" and "outside agitators." But the Christians pressed on, in the conviction that they were "a colony of heaven," called to obey God rather than man. Small in number they were big in commitment. They were too God-intoxicated to be "astronomically intimidated." By their effort and example they brought an end to such ancient evils as infanticide and gladiatorial contests.

41 Things are different now. So often the contemporary church is a weak, ineffectual voice with an uncertain sound. So often it is an archdefender of the status quo. Far from being disturbed by the presence of the church, the power structure of the average community is consoled by the church's silent—and often even vocal—sanction of things as they are.

42 But the judgment of God is upon the church as never before. If today's church does not recapture the sacrificial spirit of the early church, it will lose its authenticity, forfeit the loyalty of millions, and be dismissed as an irrelevant social club with no meaning for the twentieth century. Every day I meet young people whose disappointment with the church has turned into outright disgust.

43 Perhaps I have once again been too optimistic. Is organized religion too inextricably bound to the status quo to save our nation and the world? Perhaps I must turn my faith to the inner spiritual church, the church within the church, as the true *ekklesia* and the hope of the world. But again I am thankful to God that some noble souls from the ranks of organized religion have broken loose from the paralyzing chains of conformity and joined us as active partners in the struggle for freedom. They have left their secure congregations and walked the streets of Albany, Georgia, with us. They have gone down the highways of the South on tortuous rides for freedom. Yes, they have gone to jail with us. Some have been dismissed from their churches, have lost the support of their bishops and fellow ministers. But they have acted in the faith that right defeated is stronger than evil triumphant. Their witness has been the spiritual salt that has preserved the true meaning of the gospel in these troubled times. They have carved a tunnel of hope through the dark mountain of disappointment.

44 I hope the church as a whole will meet the challenge of this decisive hour. But even if the church does not come to the aid of justice, I have no despair about the future. I have no fear about the outcome of our struggle in Birmingham, even if our motives are at present misunderstood. We will reach the goal of freedom in Birmingham and all over the nation, because the goal of America is freedom. Abused and scorned though we may be, our destiny is tied up with America's destiny. Before the pilgrims landed at Plymouth, we were here. Before the pen of Jefferson etched the majestic words of the Declaration of Independence across the pages of history, we were here. For more than two centuries our forebears labored in this country without wages; they made cotton king; they built the homes of their masters while suffering gross injustice and shameful humiliation—and yet out of a bottomless vitality they continued to thrive and develop. If the inexpressible cruelties of slavery could not stop us, the opposition we now face will surely fail. We will win our freedom because

the sacred heritage of our nation and the eternal will of God are embodied in our echoing demands.

45 Before closing I feel impelled to mention one other point in your statement that has troubled me profoundly. You warmly commended the Birmingham police force for keeping "order" and "preventing violence." I doubt that you would have so warmly commended the police force if you had seen its dogs sinking their teeth into unarmed, nonviolent Negroes. I doubt that you would so quickly commend the policemen if you were to observe their ugly and inhumane treatment of Negroes here in the city jail; if you were to watch them push and curse old Negro women and young Negro girls; if you were to see them slap and kick old Negro men and young boys; if you were to observe them, as they did on two occasions, refuse to give food because we wanted to sing our grace together. I cannot join you in your praise of the Birmingham police department.

46 It is true that the police have exercised a degree of discipline in handling the demonstrators. In this sense they have conducted themselves rather "nonviolently" in public. But for what purpose? To preserve the evil system of segregation. Over the past few years I have consistently preached that nonviolence demands that the means we use must be as pure as the ends we seek. I have tried to make clear that it is wrong to use immoral means to attain moral ends. But now I must affirm that it is just as wrong, or perhaps even more so, to use moral means to preserve immoral ends. Perhaps Mr. Connor and his policemen have been rather nonviolent in public, as was Chief Pritchett in Albany, Georgia, but they have used the moral means of nonviolence to maintain the immoral end of racial injustice. As T. S. Eliot has said, "The last temptation is the greatest treason. To do the right deed for the wrong reason."

47 I wish you had commended the Negro sit-inners and demonstrators of Birmingham for their sublime courage, their willingness to suffer, and their amazing discipline in the midst of great provocation. One day the South will recognize its real heroes. They will be the James Merediths, with the noble sense of purpose that enables them to face jeering and hostile mobs, and with the agonizing loneliness that characterizes the life of the pioneer. They will be old, oppressed, battered Negro women, symbolized in a seventy-two-year-old woman in Montgomery, Alabama, who rose up with a sense of dignity and with her people decided not to ride segregated buses, and who responded with ungrammatical profundity to one who inquired about her weariness: "My feets is tired, but my soul is at rest." They will be the young high school and college students, the young ministers of the gospel and a host of their elders, courageously and nonviolently sitting in at lunch counters and willingly going to jail for conscience sake. One day the South will know that when these disinherited children of God sat down at lunch counters, they were in reality standing up for what is best in the American dream and for the most sacred values in our Judeo-Christian heritage, thereby bringing our nation back to those great wells of democracy which were dug deep by the founding fathers in their formulation of the Constitution and the Declaration of Independence.

48 Never before have I written so long a letter. I'm afraid it is much too long to take your precious time. I can assure you that it would have been much shorter if I had been writing from a comfortable desk, but what else can one do when he is alone in a narrow jail cell, other than write long letters, think long thoughts, and pray long prayers?

49 If I have said anything in this letter that overstates the truth and indicates an unreasonable impatience, I beg you to forgive me. If I have said anything that understates the truth and indicates my having a patience that allows me to settle for anything less than brotherhood, I beg God to forgive me.

50 I hope this letter finds you strong in the faith. I also hope that circumstances will soon make it possible for me to meet each of you, not as an integrationist or a civil-rights leader but as a fellow clergyman and a Christian brother. Let us all hope that the dark clouds of racial prejudice will soon pass away and the deep fog of misunderstanding will be lifted from our fear-drenched communities, and in some not too distant tomorrow the radiant stars of love and brotherhood will shine over our great nation with all their scintillating beauty.

Yours for the cause of Peace and Brotherhood,
MARTIN LUTHER KING, JR.

QUESTIONS FOR WRITING AND DISCUSSION

OBSERVING

1. How does King use the Judeo-Christian heritage and American history to buttress his argument?
2. How does King define a "just law"? What is an unjust law? How does King apply these definitions to segregation?
3. What rhetorical devices and techniques does King use to express his concern for oppressed people? How do these affect you as a reader? Note such techniques as direct address of the second person "you" and the use of question and answer or "call and response" (a standard form of dialogue in black churches) sections.
4. On what basis does King strongly criticize the white moderate?

EVALUATING

1. Argue that "injustice anywhere is a threat to justice everywhere." Explain, in your argument, the basis for such an observation and to what degree you think it is valid.
2. What is King's attitude toward the institutional church? How does he see the separation of moral and social issues from the gospel? Argue that religious institutions are or are not generally culpable for their inaction in this regard.

RESPONDING AND APPLYING

1. In the more than 25 years since King's assassination, do you think the optimism he expressed in the letter (paragraph 44) is justified? From what you have seen, has there been progression in such areas as integration of the races and the elimination of poverty? Consider what has happened to African Americans regarding unemployment, family, and education.
2. Describe the racial climate on your campus. Reflect on it, as would King, in terms of the values central to the Judeo-Christian tradition that he represented and the tradition of democracy originating in our founding documents.
3. How do you think King would respond to attitudes and practices associated with more recent African American political leadership, such as Louis Farrakhan or Colin Powell? How do you respond to them? Does King seem more conservative or more radical than these leaders?
4. Do you personally feel that King has deserved the recognition that he has received in terms of a national holiday and his prominent place in American history? Why or why not?

NADINE GORDIMER, "SOMETHING FOR THE TIME BEING"

Nadine Gordimer (1923 -) was born to Jewish emigrants from London who settled in South Africa. Born in Johannesburg and well-acquainted with the system of apartheid that divided white from black society for nearly a century, Gordimer is a novelist who has a keen eye for the contradictions inherent in and the profound failures of the privileged class in its attempt to democratize and/or create equal opportunity for blacks and "coloureds" (the term for people of mixed ancestry in South Africa) in a society based on supremacist assumptions about race. She was awarded the Nobel Prize in literature in 1991; her novels including *The Lying Days* (1953), a semi-autobiographical account of a young South African woman growing up at the beginning of the twentieth century.

In this story, Gordimer explores through the eyes and circumstances of two couples, one white, one black, the depressing political climate in South Africa that existed before the end of apartheid and the rise of Nelson Mandela as an indigenous, democratically elected leader.

Something for the Time Being

Nadine Gordimer

1 He thought of it as discussing things with her, but the truth was that she did not help him out at all. She said nothing, while she ran her hand up the ridge of bone behind the rim of her child-sized yellow-brown ear, and raked her fingers tenderly into her hairline along the back of her neck as if feeling out some symptom in herself. Yet her listening was very demanding; when he stopped at the end of a supposition or a suggestion, her silence made the stop inconclusive. He had to take up again what he had said, carry it—where?

2 "Ve vant to give you a tsance, but you von't let us," he mimicked; and made a loud glottal click, half-angry, resentfully amused. He knew it wasn't because Kalzin Brothers were Jews that he had lost his job at last, but just because he had lost it, Mr. Solly's accent suddenly presented to him the irresistibly vulnerable. He had come out of prison nine days before, after spending three months as an awaiting-trial prisoner in a political case that had just been quashed—he was one of those who would not accept bail. He had been in prison three or four times since 1952; his wife Ella and the Kalzin Brothers were used to it. Until now, his employers had always given him his job back when he came out. They were importers of china and glass and he was head packer in a team of black men who ran the dispatch department. "Well, what the hell, I'll get something else," he said. "Hey?"

3 She stopped the self-absorbed examination of the surface of her skin for a slow moment and shrugged, looking at him.

4 He smiled.

5 Her gaze loosened hold like hands falling away from grasp. The ends of her nails pressed at small imperfections in the skin of her neck. He drank his tea and tore off pieces of bread to dip in it; then he noticed the tin of sardines she had opened and sopped up the pale matrix of oil in which ragged flecks of silver were suspended. She offered him more tea, without speaking.

6 They lived in one room of a decent, three-roomed house belonging to someone else; it was better for her that way, since he was often likely to have to be away for long stretches. She worked in a factory that made knitted socks; there was no one at home to look after their one child, a girl, and the child lived with a grandmother in a dusty, peaceful village a day's train-journey from the city.

7 He said, dismissing it as of no importance, "I wonder what chance they meant? You can imagine. I don't suppose they were going to give me an office with my name on it." He spoke as if she would appreciate the joke. She had known when she married him that he was a political man; she had been proud of him because he didn't merely want something for himself, like the other young men she knew, but everything, and for *the people.* It had excited her,

under his influence, to change her awareness of herself as a young black girl to awareness of herself as belonging to the people. She knew that everything wasn't like something—a handout, a wangled privilege, a trinket you could hold. She would never get something from him.

8 Her hand went on searching over her skin as if it must come soon, come anxiously, to the flaw, the sickness, the evidence of what was wrong with her; for on this Saturday afternoon all these things that she knew had deserted her. She had lost her wits. All that she could understand was the one room, the child growing up far away in the mud house, and the fact that you couldn't keep a job if you kept being away from work for weeks at a time.

9 "I think I'd better look up Flora Donaldson," he said. Flora Donaldson was a white woman who had set up an office to help political prisoners. "Sooner the better. Perhaps she'll dig up something for me by Monday. It's the beginning of the month."

10 He got on all right with those people. Ella had met Flora Donaldson once; she was a pretty white woman who looked just like any white woman who would automatically send a black face round to the back door, but she didn't seem to know that she was white and you were black.

11 He pulled the curtain that hung across one corner of the room and took out his suit. It was a thin suit, of the kind associated with holiday-makers in American clothing advertisements, and when he was dressed in it, with a sharp-brimmed grey hat tilted slightly back on his small head, he looked a wiry, boyish figure, rather like one of those boy-men who sing and shake before a microphone, and whose clothes admirers try to touch as a talisman.

12 He kissed her good-bye, obliging her to put down, the lowering of a defense, the piece of sewing she held. She had cleared away the dishes from the table and set up the sewing-machine, and he saw that the shapes of cut material that lay on the table were the parts of a small girl's dress.

13 She spoke suddenly. "And when the next lot gets tired of you?"

14 "When that lot gets tired of me, I'll get another job again, that's all."

15 She nodded, very slowly, and her hand crept back to her neck.

16 "Who was that?" Madge Chadders asked.

17 Her husband had been out into the hall to answer the telephone.

18 "Flora Donaldson. I wish you'd explain to these people exactly what sort of factory I've got. It's so embarrassing. She's trying to find a job for some chap, he's a skilled packer. There's no skilled packing done in my workshop, no skilled jobs at all done by black men. What on earth can I offer the fellow? She says he's desperate and anything will do."

19 Madge had the broken pieces of a bowl on a newspaper spread on the Persian carpet. "Mind the glue, darling! There, just next to your foot. Well, anything is better than nothing. I suppose it's someone who was in the Soganiland sedition case. Three months awaiting trial taken out of their lives, and now they're chucked back to fend for themselves."

20 William Chadders had not had any black friends or mixed with coloured people on any but master-servant terms until he married Madge, but his views on the immorality and absurdity of the colour bar were sound; sounder, she often felt, than her own, for they were backed by the impersonal authority of a familiarity with the views of great thinkers, saints and philosophers, with history, political economy, sociology and anthropology. She knew only what she felt. And she always did something, at once, to express what she felt. She never measured the smallness of her personal protest against the establishment she opposed; she marched with Flora and eight hundred black women in a demonstration against African women being forced to carry passes; outside the university where she had once been a student, she stood between sandwich-boards bearing messages of mourning because a Bill had been passed closing the university, for the future, to all but white students; she had living in the house for three months a young African who wanted to write and hadn't the peace or space to get on with it in a location. She did not stop to consider the varying degree of usefulness of the things she did, and if others pointed this out to her and suggested that she might make up her mind to throw her weight on the side either of politics or philanthropy, she was not resentful but answered candidly that there was so little it was possible to do that she simply took any and every chance to get off her chest her disgust at the colour bar. When she had married William Chadders, her friends had thought that her protestant activities would stop; they underestimated not only Madge, but also William, who, although he was a wealthy businessman, subscribed to the view of absolute personal freedom as strictly as any bohemian. Besides he was not fool enough to want to change in any way the person who had enchanted him just as she was.

21 She reacted upon him, rather than he upon her: she, of course, would not hesitate to go ahead and change anybody. (But why not? she would have said, astonished. If it's to the good?) The attitude she sought to change would occur to her as something of independent existence, she would not see it as a cell in the organism of personality, whose whole structure would have to regroup itself round the change. She had the boldness of being unaware of these consequences.

22 William did not carry a banner in the streets, of course; he worked up there, among his first principles and historical precedents and economic necessities, but now they were translated from theory to practice of an anonymous, large-scale and behind-the-scenes sort—he was the brains and part of the money in a scheme to get Africans some economic power besides consumer power, through the setting up of an all-African trust company and investment corporation. A number of Madge's political friends, both white and black (like her activities, her friends were mixed, some political, some do-gooders), thought this was putting the middle-class cart before the proletarian horse, but most of the African leaders welcomed the attempt as an essential backing to popular movements on other levels—something to count on outside the unpredictability of mobs. Sometimes it amused Madge to think that William, mak-

ing a point at a meeting in a boardroom, fifteen floors above life in the streets, might achieve in five minutes something of more value than she did in all her days of turning her hand to anything—from sorting old clothes to roneoing[1] a manifesto or driving people during a bus boycott. Yet this did not knock the meaning out of her own life, for her; she knew that she had to see, touch and talk to people in order to care about them, that's all there was to it.

23 Before she and her husband dressed to go out that evening she finished sticking together the broken Chinese bowl and showed it to him with satisfaction. To her, it was whole again. But it was one of a set, that had belonged together, and whose unity had illustrated certain philosophical concepts. William had bought them long ago, in London; for him, the whole set was damaged for ever.

24 He said nothing to her, but he was thinking of the bowls when she said to him as they drove off, "Will you see that chap, on Monday, yourself?"

25 He changed gear deliberately, attempting to follow her out of his preoccupation. But she said, "The man Flora's sending. What was his name?"

26 He opened his hand on the steering wheel, indicating that the name escaped him.

27 "See him yourself?"

28 "I'll have to leave it to the works manager to find something for him to do," he said.

29 "Yes, I know. But see him yourself, too?"

30 Her anxious voice made him feel very fond of her. He turned and smiled at her suspiciously. "Why?"

31 She was embarrassed at his indulgent manner. She said, frank and wheedling. "Just to show him. You know. That you know about him and it's not much of a job."

32 "All right," he said. "I'll see him myself."

33 He met her in town straight from the office on Monday and they went to the opening of an exhibition of paintings and on to dinner and to see a play, with friends. He had not been home at all, until they returned after midnight. It was a summer night and they sat for a few minutes on their terrace, where it was still mild with the warmth of the day's sun coming from the walls in the darkness, and drank lime juice and water to quench the thirst that wine and the stuffy theatre had given them. Madge made gasps and groans of pleasure at the release from the pressures of company and noise. Then she lay quiet for a while, her voice lifting now and then in fragments of unrelated comment on the evening—the occasional chirp of a bird that has already put its head under its wing for the night.

34 By the time they went in, they were free of the evening. Her black dress, her ear-rings and her bracelets felt like fancy-dress; she shed the character and sat on the bedroom carpet, and, passing her, he said, "Oh—that chap of Flora's

[1] A kind of duplicating.

came today, but I don't think he'll last. I explained to him that I didn't have the sort of job he was looking for."

35 "Well, that's all right, then," she said enquiringly. "What more could you do?"

36 "Yes," he said, deprecating. "But I could see he didn't like the idea much. It's a cleaner's job; nothing for him. He's an intelligent chap. I didn't like having to offer it to him."

37 She was moving about her dressing table, piling out upon it the contents of her handbag. "Then I'm sure he'll understand. It'll give him something for the time being, anyway, darling. You can't help it if you don't need the sort of work he does."

38 "Huh, he won't last. I could see that. He accepted it, but only with his head. He'll get fed up. Probably won't turn up tomorrow. I had to speak to him about his Congress[2] button, too. The works manager came to me."

39 "What about his Congress button?" she said.

40 He was unbuttoning his shirt and his eyes were on the unread evening paper that lay folded on the bed. "He was wearing one," he said inattentively.

41 "I know, but what did you have to speak to him about it for?"

42 "He was wearing it in the workshop all day."

43 "Well, what about it?" She was sitting at her dressing-table, legs spread, as if she had sat heavily and suddenly. She was not looking at him, but at her own face.

44 He gave the paper a push and drew his pyjamas from under the pillow. Vulnerable and naked, he said authoritatively, "You can't wear a button like that among the men in the workshop."

45 "Good heavens," she said, almost in relief, laughing, backing away from the edge of tension, chivvying him out of a piece of stuffiness. "And why can't you?"

46 "You can't have someone clearly representing a political organization like Congress."

47 "But he's not there *representing* anything, he's there as a workman?" Her mouth was still twitching with something between amusement and nerves.

48 "Exactly."

49 "Then why can't he wear a button that signifies his allegiance to an organization in his private life outside the workshop? There's no rule about not wearing tie-pins or club buttons or anything, in the workshop, is there?"

50 "No, there isn't, but that's not quite the same thing."

51 "My dear William," she said, "it is exactly the same. It's nothing to do with the works manager whether the man wears a Rotary button,[3] or an Elvis Presley button, or an African National Congress button. It's damn all his business."

52 "No, Madge, I'm sorry," William said, patient, "but it's not the same. I can give the man a job because I feel sympathetic towards the struggle he's in, but

[2] African National Congress. South African anti-apartheid organization.

[3] A civic organization.

I can't put him in the workshop as a Congress man. I mean that wouldn't be fair to Fowler. That I can't do to Fowler." He was smiling as he went towards the bathroom, but his profile, as he turned into the doorway, was incisive.

53 She sat on at her dressing-table, pulling a comb through her hair, dragging it down through knots. Then she rested her face on her palms, caught sight of herself and became aware, against her fingers, of the curving shelf of bone, like the lip of a strong shell, under each eye. Everyone has his own intimations of mortality. For her, the feel of the bone beneath her face, in any living creature, brought her the message of the skull. Once hollowed out of this, outside the world, too. For what it's worth. It's worth a lot, the world, she affirmed, as she always did, life rising at once in her as a fish opens its jaws to a fly. It's worth a lot; and she sighed and got up with the sigh.

54 She went into the bathroom and sat down on the edge of the bath. He was lying there in the water, his chin relaxed on his chest, and he smiled at her. She said, "You mean you don't want Fowler to know."

55 "Oh," he said, seeing where they were again. "What is it I don't want Fowler to know?"

56 "You don't want your partner to know that you slip black men with political ideas into your workshop. Cheeky kaffir agitators. Specially a man who's been in jail for getting people to defy the government!—What was his name; you never said?"

57 "Daniel something. I don't know. Mongoma or Ngoma. Something like that."

58 A line like a cut appeared between her eyebrows. "Why can't you remember his name?" Then she went on at once, "You don't want Fowler to know what you think, do you? That's it? You want to pretend you're like him, you don't mind the native in his place. You want to pretend that to please Fowler. You don't want Fowler to think you're cracked or Communist or whatever it is that good-natured, kind, jolly rich people like old Fowler think about people like us."

59 "I couldn't have less interest in what Fowler thinks outside our boardroom. And inside it, he never thinks about anything but how to sell more earth-moving gear."

60 "I don't mind the native in his place. You want him to think you go along with all that." She spoke aloud, but she seemed to be telling herself rather than him.

61 "Fowler and I run a factory. Our only common interest is the efficient running of that factory. Our *only* one. The factory depends on a stable, satisfied black labour-force, and that we've got. Right, you and I know that the whole black wage standard is too low, right, we know that they haven't a legal union to speak for them, right, we know that the conditions they live under make it impossible for them really to be stable. All that. But the fact is, so far as accepted standards go in this crazy country, they're a stable, satisfied labour-force with better working conditions than most. So long as I'm a partner in a business that lives by them, I can't officially admit an element that represents dissatisfaction with their lot."

62 "A green badge with a map of Africa on it," she said.

63 "If you make up your mind not to understand, you don't, and there it is," he said indulgently.

64 "You give him a job but you make him hide his Congress button."

65 He began to soap himself. She wanted everything to stop while she inquired into things, she could not go on while a remark was unexplained or a problem unsettled, but he represented a principle she subscribed to but found so hard to follow, that life must go on, trivially, commonplace, the trailing hem of the only power worth clinging to. She smoothed the film of her nightgown over the shape of her knees, over and over, and presently she said, in exactly the flat tone of statement that she had used before, the flat tone that was the height of belligerence in her, "He can say and do what he likes, he can call for strikes and boycotts and anything he likes, outside the factory, but he mustn't wear his Congress button at work."

66 He was standing up, washing his body that was full of scars; she knew them all, from the place on his left breast where a piece of shrapnel had gone in, all the way back to the place under his arm where he had torn himself on barbed wire as a child. "Yes, of course, anything he likes."

67 "Anything except his self-respect," she grumbled to herself. "Pretend, pretend. Pretend he doesn't belong to a political organization. Pretend he doesn't want to be a man. Pretend he hasn't been to prison for what he believes." Suddenly she spoke to her husband: "You'll let him have anything except the one thing worth giving."

68 They stood in uncomfortable proximity to each other, in the smallness of the bathroom. They were at once aware of each other as people who live in intimacy are only when hostility returns each to the confines of himself. He felt himself naked before her, where he had stepped out onto the towelling mat, and he took a towel and slowly covered himself, pushing the free end in round his waist. She felt herself an intrusion and, in silence, went out.

69 Her hands were tingling as if she were coming round from a faint. She walked up and down the bedroom floor like someone waiting to be summoned, called to account. I'll forget about it, she kept thinking, very fast. I'll forget about it again. Take a sip of water. Read another chapter. Don't call a halt. Let things flow, cover up, go on.

70 But when he came into the room with his wet hair combed and his stranger's face, and he said, "You're angry," it came from her lips, a black bird in the room, before she could understand what she had released—"I'm not angry. I'm beginning to get to know you."

71 Ella Mngoma knew he was going to a meeting that evening and didn't expect him home early. She put the paraffin lamp on the table so that she could see to finish the child's dress. It was done, buttons and all, by the time he came in at half past ten.

72 "Well, now we'll see what happens. I've got them to accept, *in principle,* that in future we won't take bail. You should have seen Ben Tsolo's face when

I said that we lent the government our money interest-free when we paid bail. That really hit him. That was language he understood." He laughed, and did not seem to want to sit down, the heat of the meeting still upon him. "*In principle.* Yes, it's easy to accept in principle. We'll see."

73 She pumped the primus[4] and set a pot of stew to warm up for him. "Ah, that's nice." He saw the dress. "Finished already?" And she nodded vociferously in pleasure; but at once she noticed his forefinger run lightly along the braid round the neck, and the traces of failure that were always at the bottom of her cup tasted on her tongue again. Probably he was not even aware of it, or perhaps his instinct for what was true—the plumb line, the coin with the right ring—led him absently to it, but the fact was that she had botched the neck.

74 She had an almost Oriental delicacy about not badgering him and she waited until he had washed and sat down to eat before she asked, "How did the job go?"

75 "Oh that," he said. "It went." He was eating quickly, moving his tongue strongly round his mouth to marshal the bits of meat that escaped his teeth. She was sitting with him, feeling, in spite of herself, the rest of satisfaction in her evening's work. "Didn't you get it?"

76 "It got *me.* But I got loose again, all right."

77 She watched his face to see what he meant. "They don't want you to come back tomorrow?"

78 He shook his head, no, no, no, to stem the irritation of her suppositions. He finished his mouthful and said, "Everything very nice. Boss takes me into his office, apologizes for the pay, he knows it's not the sort of job I should have and so forth. So I go off and clean up in the assembly shop. Then at lunchtime he calls me into the office again: they don't want me to wear my A.N.C. badge at work. Flora Donaldson's sympathetic white man, who's going to do me the great favour of paying me three pounds a week." He laughed. "Well, there you are."

79 She kept on looking at him. Her eyes widened and her mouth tightened; she was trying to prime herself to speak, or was trying not to cry. The idea of tears exasperated him and he held her with a firm, almost belligerently inquiring gaze. Her hand went up round the back of her neck under her collar, anxiously exploratory. "Don't do that!" he said. "You're like a monkey catching lice."

80 She took her hand down swiftly and broke into trembling, like a sweat. She began to breathe hysterically. "You couldn't put it in your pocket, for the day," she said wildly, grimacing at the bitterness of malice towards him.

81 He jumped up from the table. "Christ! I knew you'd say it! I've been waiting for you to say it. You've been wanting to say it for five years. Well, now it's out. Out with it. Spit it out!" She began to scream softly as if he were hitting her. The impulse to cruelty left him and he sat down before his dirty plate,

---

[4] Portable stove which requires oil as fuel.

where the battered spoon lay among bits of gristle and potato-eyes. Presently he spoke. "You come out and you think there's everybody waiting for you. The truth is, there isn't anybody. You think straight in prison because you've got nothing to lose. Nobody thinks straight, outside. They don't want to hear you. What are you all going to do with me, Ella? Send me back to prison as quickly as possible? Perhaps I'll get a banishment order next time. That'd do. That's what you've got for me. I must keep myself busy with that kind of thing."

82 He went over to her and said, in a kindly voice, kneading her shoulder with spread fingers, "Don't cry. Don't cry. You're just like any other woman."

QUESTIONS FOR WRITING AND DISCUSSION

OBSERVING

1. Describe the Mngoma household. What are their dreams and aspirations as individuals? As a couple? What is their relationship?
2. Describe the Chadders household. What is their place in society? How do the two of them relate as a couple? In what ways does Gordimer use them as a foil or contrast to the Mngomas?
3. Why has Daniel Mngoma been in prison? How does it affect his ability to gain and hold onto a job?
4. What is the ANC? And why would it be a source of conflict between the Mngoma's, and particularly between William Chadder and Daniel Mngoma?
5. Whose story is this? Why does it first begin at the Mngoma's, them move to Chadders? What is the central conflict of the story? What is the essential theme of the story?
6. Explain the significance of Gordimer's title for the story in view of its ending.

EVALUATING

1. What kind of "democracy" exists in the South Africa depicted in the story? Who benefits by it? What "rights" are evident? For whom?
2. What does Daniel mean when he says "you think straight in prison because you've got nothing to lose"? Compare the fictional Daniel Mngoma with Dr. King in Birmingham Jail; how is their struggle parallel? How might Dr. King's words and reasoning have been useful in Daniel Mngoma's encounter with William Chadders? With his wife, Ella?
3. Is Madge Chadders a sympathetic character in the story? To what extent does she seem the conscience of her household as depicted? Who has more "power" to effect change in white South African society—William or Madge? Why?
4. Argue whether or not the last line of the story—"You're just like any other woman"—is true. Why does Daniel say this to Ella?

RESPONDING AND APPLYING

1. Does Gordimer's story evoke hope for racial equality and eventual reconciliation in South Africa? Why or why not?
2. How difficult is it for you to believe that a regime like that depicted in Gordimer's story could exist at the end of the twentieth century? To what extent does the story make you more sensitized to the values of democracy in the West that you may take for granted? To what extent is the Mngomas' experience in South Africa similar to that of African Americans in the United States?
3. Have you ever worn a button or other clothing as a symbol of protest? If so, what was it, and what was your motive for doing it? How did it affect the people around you? Did you feel pressure to remove it? Why or why not? How effective do you think such symbolic protests generally are?
4. How do you generally respond to social protest? What kinds do you find acceptable and "within reason"? What is "going too far"?

CHAPTER WRITING ASSIGNMENTS

1. Examine the "ways of knowing" that were used to demonstrate humanity's fundamental rights as citizens under democratic rule. In the readings from Burke, Jefferson, Stanton and Mott, King, and others in this chapter, to what degree are equal rights "self-evident"? To what degree are faith, reason, and observation used to demonstrate the importance of individual rights?
2. Examine carefully the Declaration and Bill of Rights and attempt your own parody like P. J. O'Rourke's, noting any excesses of behavior or perspective you discover in contemporary life. In what way are they related to "the pursuit of happiness"? How do they result from taking these "freedoms" to an extreme that threatens the public good?
3. Jefferson, Stanton and Mott, and others in American history identified the most dangerous form of tyranny in America as the abuse of power by the majority through legislative action; do you agree with them? What abuses of legislative power have you witnessed? In what ways do the executive (presidential or gubernatorial) or judicial (court system) branches have the same power to abuse—or balance—as the legislature?
4. Interview an articulate person regarding his or her political life. What are the reasons for this person's political activity or inactivity? What is his notion of a democracy and of citizen freedom and responsibility in that system? What political positions does she hold? Which has she taken public?
5. What political position—liberal, conservative, libertarian, or reactionary—has this chapter turned you toward or away from? What significant conflicts or questions about democracy have been raised in your mind? How has your political consciousness changed as a result of this chapter?
6. Compare King's "Letter from Birmingham Jail" with Jefferson's "Declaration of Independence." Granting whatever major differences there may be

in the situations (for example, King was responding to an unjust set of laws, whereas Jefferson was responding to an unjust government), are the principles that each appeals to similar or different? Given the responses of each, which do you think was the more extreme? How would Stanton and Mott respond to King?

7. What do you find to be the single greatest idea in democracy? What makes it a great idea, and what are its shortcomings?
8. To what extent are stories like Gordimer's and Vonnegut's useful in helping you deliberate over political issues? How do literary treatments of the problems of democracy succeed where straightforward political commentary and debate do not? Write an essay that explores the effective use of literature in wrestling with political issues.
9. How, in a democracy built upon the kinds of documents that are represented in the history of the United States, can the competing claims and aspirations of members of a pluralistic society be resolved? Choose several examples from contemporary life and propose a way to address these sources of tension or conflict in society.
10. "Public" seems to be a dirty word today; private schools, prisons, suburbs, roads, money, and police are "in." Does this signify that citizenship and commitment to the greater good have died? Do you think there should be a form of mandatory public service? Would you consider volunteering in a literacy program or soup bank? For a career in Americorps or the Peace Corps? Write an essay that explains why or why not.

Chapter Preview

Chapter Prelude
Deborah Lutterbeck, "Falling Wages: Why Salaries Keep Sinking When Corporate Profits are Soaring"

Introductory Essay

Readings
Karl Marx, *from* The Communist Manifesto
Charles Beard, *from* The Economic Origins of Jeffersonian Democracy
Frithjof Benjamin, "The Future of Work"

Story
Toni Cade Bambara, "The Lesson"

Perspectives
MORALITY, THE FREE MARKET, AND CLASS
Paul Johnson, "The Capitalism and Morality Debate"
Benjamin DeMott, "Public Policy in the Classless State"

Chapter Writing Assignments

Chapter 8

ECONOMICS AND SOCIAL CLASS

Falling Wages: Why Salaries Keep Sinking When Corporate Profits Are Soaring

Deborah Lutterbeck

1 Nursing used to offer secure, well-paying jobs. But nowadays nurses like Melinda Bagby worry about lay-offs and are afraid to ask for a raise. A coronary-care nurse with 15 years' experience at Audubon Regional Medical Center in Louisville, Ky., Bagby is at the top of her pay scale, earning $21 an hour. But since 1989 her pay has gone up only 60 cents an hour. Audubon, owned by the country's largest for-profit hospital chain, Columbia/HCA Healthcare, is being restructured. Nurses worry that their ranks will be cut and that less-qualified nurses' aides will take over many of their patient-care duties.

2 It's not that Audubon can't afford to pay loyal employees like Bagby, but that corporate executives have put their growing profits elsewhere—including their own pockets. Columbia/HCA's profits increased by almost 25 percent last year, but Bagby's salary has increased less than 3 percent in *six* years, meaning that in real dollars her paycheck is worth less than it was in 1989. The company's CEO, meanwhile, saw his salary more than double from 1992 to '94, and investors in Columbia/HCA have watched the value of their stock holdings increase 129 percent in three years.

3 Neither Bagby nor her employer is unique in today's economy. While profits for all types of industries have soared to a 25-year high, employees' wages and living standards are actually backsliding. The median salary for a full-time worker is $475 a week, down 1 percent from a year ago and 4.6 percent below its 1979 level. Median family income dropped 7 percent, from $39,696 in 1989 to $36,959 in 1993, while the stock market rose almost 50 percent over the period.

4 The two trends are not unconnected. "One reason corporate profits are rising and stock prices have been soaring is that companies have managed to keep a lid on employee costs," says Labor Secretary Robert Reich.

5 Indeed, while companies used to go after the best-educated, most-competent person for the job and pay them what the market demanded, these days corporations are more likely to seek the candidate that can get the job done for the lowest cost. Sometimes that means a computer, sometimes an overseas worker, sometimes a temporary employee and sometimes simply the least-experienced person.

6 Today's rising economic tide is not lifting all boats. Robust stock gains have not trickled down as pay raises or new jobs. Instead, in many industries fewer people are doing more work for the same pay—or less, in inflation-adjusted dollars—rarely complaining for fear they'll be fired. "There is a pervasive sense out there in the American workforce that [workers] are lucky to have a job," Reich says. And this job insecurity makes workers more likely to settle for low wage growth, he says.

7 Job creation is centered primarily in the service sector and high-tech computer firms. But it's hard to raise a family on money earned serving gourmet coffee, and no one learns computer programming overnight.

8 Layoffs add to workers' worries. "Every time an American worker hears about another mass layoff involving thousands of employees, he or she is further deterred from asking for a raise," Reich says. Over the summer some 96,920 workers were laid off or told they would be, and when those people try to find new jobs, they'll have a hard time matching their old salaries. Between 1991 and 1993, 4.5 million workers with at least three years on the job were put out of work, according to the Bureau of Labor Statistics (BLS). In that same period 47 percent of the workers who found new jobs took a pay cut; for 30 percent of them the cut was at least 20 percent.

9 During the 1980s job losses were the factory workers' saga. America's manufacturing base collapsed, taking 3.2 million goods-producing jobs with it from 1979 to 1993. By the 1990s these blue-collar blues had also become white-collar worries. Managerial and professional positions accounted for 24 percent of all permanent layoffs from 1991 to '93.

10 The proliferation of mutual funds and influential institutional investors is demanding higher stock returns, and that trend, in turn, drives corporate executives to pursue a stocks- and investors-first management philosophy. One of the easiest and quickest ways for companies to boost their stock prices is to announce that massive layoffs are part of a restructuring plan, and the strategy is a popular one. In recent years some 80 percent of U.S. companies have "downsized," or cut their staffing levels; among Fortune 500 industrial companies more than a quarter of all employees have been laid off. According to the American Management Association, employment has become a zero-sum game: for every person who lands a new job someone else has been let go.

11 In fact, it's become much easier to find a place to invest in corporate Amer-

ica than a place to work. Bank stocks, for example, have never looked better. This year they've outperformed the elite S&P 500 stock index, rising 41 percent, according to Keefe, Bruyette & Woods, a Wall Street firm that follows the banking industry. No longer burdened with bad real estate loans, money-losing Third World debt write-offs and junk bonds, banks' balance sheets now glitter.

12 Mergers are also creating higher returns. This summer two behemoths, Chase Manhattan Bank and Chemical Bank, linked to become the country's largest bank. But 12,000 people—from stock clerks to senior vice presidents—will lose jobs in the deal. And it's going to get worse. By the year 2005 some 450,000 banking-sector jobs will be gone, according to the accounting firm Deloitte & Touche. And Wall Street's retrenchment goes beyond the banking sector; since the 1987 stock market crash, some 14,000 securities- and commodities-trading jobs have been eliminated.

13 Telecommunications, the much-hyped industry of the future, isn't producing as much employment as news copy. Cellular phone sales and interfacing on the information superhighway don't create many jobs. When phone giant AT&T announced its voluntary break-up this summer, it said it would be cutting more than 8,500 jobs. In October GTE said it would eliminate 4,700 jobs by the end of the year. Last year Bell Atantic announced a plan to cut 5,600 jobs.

14 The manufacturing sector continues to erode. From March to September, 200,000 factory jobs were eliminated. People in their "fifties and sixties are losing their jobs," says Mary Anne Sedey, president of the National Employment Lawyers Association, and the jobs being offered to recent high-school graduates pay 25 percent less than they did in 1989.

15 For many workers lucky enough to still have jobs, wages have declined in real, inflation-adjusted terms. Lasty year factory workers were earning an average of $7.96 an hour, 66 cents less than their hourly wage in 1983. Wages for construction workers dropped from $11.24 an hour in '83 to $9.77 last year, the BLS reports. The sinking-salary trend has also hit many professions: accountants, underwriters, architects and aerospace engineers all earned less in inflation-adjusted dollars in '94 than they did in '84. And workers left in the Wall Street money business are making less of it; their average salaries have dropped roughly 14 percent since 1992.

16 Despite the depth and breadth of employment-related problems facing American voters, the issue gets short shrift on Capitol Hill. The new Congress has focused on cutting government spending and deregulating business while reducing taxes for the wealthiest Americans.

17 Voters are left feeling as if all they can do to improve their standard of living is vote for someone to cut their taxes, says Dean Baker, an economist at the labor-funded Economic Policy Institute—even though the government's share of Gross Domestic Product hasn't increased in decades. "The real issue is not how much the government takes out of your paycheck," Baker says, "but how little your employer puts into it."

Low-Wage Work If You Can Get It

18 The level of industry-wide layoffs approaches that seen in recessionary times, but business hasn't done this well since 1970. So what's keeping the lid on wages? Economists point to several culprits. Among them: computers and other high-tech equipment, which is replacing many low-skilled workers; free trade policies, which allow companies to cross borders and oceans for cheaper labor; a low minimum wage, which creates a cut-rate pool of U.S. workers; chief executives who help themselves to larger shares of the profit pie; and the declining size and muscle of labor unions.

19 ▪ A visit to the bank provides one example of how technology impacts jobs. In 1984 the BLS counted 385,000 bank-teller jobs; last year there were 265,000. It's no coincidence that the number of automated teller machines (ATMs) is moving in the opposite direction; where there were roughly 102,000 ATMs last year, some 158,000 will be operating by the turn of the century. And there's more than customer service and convenience behind the switch; an ATM transaction costs the bank 80 cents less than one made at a teller's window.

20 Computers are becoming more and more a part of the work force. In 1984 almost a quarter of workers used computers; by 1993 half of all full-time workers were plugged in. And while computers make some workers more productive, they send others to the unemployment office. "Technology has benefited those who have a high level of skills at the same time it has replaced those with less skill," says Alan Krueger, a former Labor Department economist now at Princeton University.

21 ▪ In 1993 National Basketball Association star Michael Jordan made $20 million endorsing Nike products—exactly what Nike spent to make 19 million pairs of shoes in Malaysian factories, where workers earn less than $3.50 a day. With pay scales like that U.S. workers aren't even in the running for jobs with their country's No. 1 seller of athletic footwear. Job prospects aren't good with other shoe makers, either. While Nike has never made its shoes in the United States, more than half of all U.S.-based shoe manufacturers closed up shop over the past 25 years, according to the International Trade Commission.

22 And this is just one industry. Foreign competition in the auto and steel industries led to the loss of high-paying jobs that were never replaced by others that paid as well, says George Borjas, an economics professor at the University of California at San Diego. He estimates that losses in those two industries are responsible for roughly one fifth of the decline in U.S. wages. While the government doesn't keep track of the number of American jobs lost because of open trade policies, economists say tens of thousands of workers have been displaced by cheap overseas labor. According to the BLS, since January 1994 some 42,000 workers have signed up for job-loss benefits related to the NAFTA agreement.

23 Federal Reserve Board Chair Alan Greenspan disagrees, saying foreign competition "affects only a relatively small part of our work force—factory jobs, which account for 15 percent of total employment—and some service activities."

24 ▪ Not that wages or working conditions are that great for workers in U.S. factories. The 850 workers at General Foam Plastics Corp. in Norfolk, Va., get only 16 minutes off during an eight-hour shift, and when their job absences add up to 100 hours they get fired. The company makes seasonal products like Christmas trees and children's swimming pools; its workers make the minimum wage of $4.25 an hour year-round.

25 "They are disadvantaged people; they take what they can get," says Randall Rice, an organizer with the Machinists union. "They put up with conditions in order to earn what they can."

26 Sales for General Foam were more than $115 million in 1994, up 10 percent from 1993, according to newspaper accounts. Despite its healthy earnings, the company gets a helping hand from government. The city of Virginia Beach recently granted General Foam a $400,000 expansion subsidy, which should help finance 1,000 new low-wage jobs.

27 But jobs at the minimum wage don't go far in the marketplace; a full-time worker earning the minimum wage makes less than $9,000 a year, far below the poverty level for a family of four. The real-dollar value of the minimum wage is even lower; while living costs continue to increase, the minimum wage hasn't been raised since 1991. In 1960 the minimum wage was worth today's equivalent of $6.40 an hour. And contrary to the conventional wisdom, which has most minimum-wage jobs going to high school students, 84.1 percent of minimum-wage earners were adults in 1991 and 42.6 percent of them were working full time.

28 President Clinton's proposal to raise the minimum wage to $5.15 an hour has gone nowhere. Businesses balked at the proposed increase, warning that its ripple effect would result in higher prices for just about everything. "Everyone who is making more than minimum wage is going to say we want 90 cents too," says Peter Eide, manager of labor law policy at the U.S. Chamber of Commerce. "Do you think it will come out of corporate profits? No. Everything is going to cost more," he says.

29 ▪ But for corporate executives, things are looking up. Along with annual compensation packages worth more than $1 million, Columbia/HCA's top two executives own almost $900 million worth of company stock. The company's recent third-quarter earnings increased 40.5 percent over last year's, to $267 million.

30 Overall, CEOs are doing exceptionally well. While the average worker's earnings were barely keeping pace with inflation last year, the average CEO earned $4.34 million in total compensation, up 15.9 percent from the previous year, according to executive compensation expert Graef Crystal, an adjunct professor at the University of California's Haas School of Business.

31 On average CEOs are earning six times more money than they were in 1980, and the gap between worker and executive earnings has grown dramatically. Twenty years ago the average CEO made about 35 times what the average production worker did; last year the CEO-to-worker earnings ratio was 120-to-1.

32 And as long as stock prices keep skyrocketing, corporate directors and investors are unlikely to question the CEO's compensation package. "A CEO who shows boldness by dramatically cutting payrolls in one fell swoop often gets rewarded [with] an uptick in the price of the shares of the company," says Labor Secretary Reich.

33 On top of that, corporate boards are filled with other CEOs who are unlikely to challenge a peer's pay. "Corporate boards have become even more buddy-buddy than they used to be," says Martin Mayer, guest scholar at the Brookings Institution. "The people on the inside aren't going to argue with you; after all, they're getting theirs." Employees, meanwhile, are getting next to nothing.

34 ▪ Despite the difficult and insecure working conditions for the 627 nurses at the Audubon Regional Medical Center, last year they voted against joining the Nurses Professional Association (NPO), a union. Why? Columbia/HCA officials made it clear to the nurses that becoming unionized would only put further strains on their relationship with management.

35 While the NPO received outside help from the American Federation of State, County and Municipal Employees (AFSCME), Columbia/HCA hired a consulting firm to help block the union. It put up anti-union signs and held meetings, deploying top executives to talk to the nurses. Chief Operating Officer David Vandewater told two nurses that Audubon would not negotiate with a union, according to a complaint the NPO filed with the National Labor Relations Board (NLRB). Talk like this scared the nurses, Bagby says, and they voted 366-220 against union representation. The union is contesting the legitimacy of the vote before the NLRB.

36 The hiring of consultants is just one of the newer tactics corporations employ to block unions. And shrinking union membership—down to roughly 13 percent of the workforce last year—is another reason the average wage is falling. The average hourly compensation for a union worker is $16.47; non-union workers average $12.31.

Money for Campaigns, But Not for Jobs

37 Money can't buy happiness, but it certainly helps grease the skids on Capitol Hill. "Those companies and those individuals with the greatest resources have the most clout in Washington," says Labor's Reich.

38 Money helps shape who wins office, gives special interests access to congressmembers and helps explain why the wage issue isn't on the political agenda. The $41.6 million that labor PACs contributed to congressional candi-

dates in the 1993–94 election cycle is a lot of money, but it's much less than the $73.6 million contributed by corporate and business PACs.

39 And corporate interests have fared very well in the new Congress. The Republican plan to balance the federal budget in seven years barely touched 120 corporate welfare programs, for example, estimated by the Cato Institute and the Progressive Policy Institute to cost taxpayers more than $100 billion a year.

40 And the GOP plan to reduce the capital gains tax is only the latest pro-business tax reduction passed by Congress. The largest tax break government gives business is an accelerated depreciation schedule, which allows corporations to take bigger tax write-offs sooner for their investments in capital assets such as plants and equipment. This tax break will be worth about $32.2 billion to corporations this year, according to the Congressional Budget Office. This and other tax breaks have lowered the average corporate tax rate to 31 percent, down significantly from an average of 44.3 percent from 1952 to 1979.

41 Special interests also give soft money, unregulated contributions to the political parties, and they're giving record amounts. In just the first six months of this year, an off-election year, soft money contributions to both parties totaled $30.6 million, far more than the parties raised in the first half of 1992, a presidential election year.

42 A lot of that money comes from business interests. Businesses ranging from oil and gas companies to bed-sheet makers contributed almost $15.9 million to Republican party committees and $6.7 million to Democratic party committees in the first half of this year. Soft-money contributions made by labor unions totaled $35,000 to Republicans and $896,000 to Democrats during the same period.

The Rich Get Richer

43 While median earnings have declined 15 percent overall since 1973, it's the middle and lower classes that have taken the hardest hits. More than 40 percent of all increases in earnings in recent years have gone to the wealthiest 1 percent of American households. This increasing income inequality alarms Labor's Reich.

44 "We are heading rapidly toward a two-tiered society composed of a relative minority of people who are extremely wealthy and a much larger number who are experiencing downward mobility and greater and greater job insecurity," he says. "That's not good for America. Ultimately it threatens our prosperity and our stability."

45 Edward Leamer, a Yale University economist, wonders if this growing wage inequality will lead to unthinkable class divisions in the 21st century, with "walled communities and police that separate these high-wage people from these low-wage people." An estimated 4 million Americans already live in so-called gated communities, says Mary Gail Snyder, co-author of the forthcoming book *Fortress America.*

46 For nurses like Bagby it's not so much the next century that concerns her as the next few years. "In the old days companies would go to their employees and say, 'We aren't doing as well as we should be. What are we going to do about it?' " she says. But now it's stockholders and wealthy company directors who call the shots, managing and restructuring with stock prices in mind.

47 Bagby wonders how much longer she'll have a job—not because her company is doing poorly, but because it's doing so very, very well.

QUESTIONS FOR WRITING AND DISCUSSION

OBSERVING

1. What are some of the major reasons Lutterbeck offers to explain the rise in recent years in corporate profits and stock prices?
2. To what factors does she attribute the fall in wages?

EVALUATING

1. Lutterbeck points out what might seem to be an impossible situation, that in recent years, during a time of unprecedented economic growth measured in terms of stock market growth and corporate profits, median family income has fallen in spite of the fact that the proportion of two-paycheck families has risen markedly. This is a situation that you may already be aware of since it has been reported with increasing alarm over the last decade. What opinions, if any, have you formulated about why this is happening?
2. Whether or not you have such opinions of your own, Lutterbeck offers her own answers as to why. Do you think her answers are adequate? Are there possible answers you think she might have missed, or answers she has offered that need further explanation or justification? Explain. Are there any significant changes in the economic picture you know of that might affect the judgments voiced here? For example, Congress passed a bill raising the minimum wage in 1996.
3. One reason for falling wages amid rising corporate profits offered here is this: "The proliferation of mutual funds and influential institutional investors is demanding higher stock returns, and that trend, in turn, drives corporate executives to pursue a stocks- and investors-first philosophy." The language here suggests that management *philosophy* is "driven" by economic forces and conditions. Is the choice implied here as to who will profit a philosophical or moral choice, or is it a recognition of and necessary surrender to irresistable economic forces? Is that a choice at all?
4. Among our democratic ideals is the belief that our system creates a society in which wealth is widely and equitably distributed among a population that is almost entirely middle class, yet current trends, Lutterbeck points

out, are producing "increasing income inequality," heading us toward "a two-tiered society" of an increasingly wealthy minority and an increasingly poor majority, a society of "unthinkable class divisions." Do you see these as real possibilities, and if so why?

RESPONDING AND APPLYING

1. To what extent do you think a nation's economy has anything to do with a people's concern for creating or maintaining a just society? Does economics have anything to do with justice, with morality?
2. To what extent do you think a nation's economy—or the world's, for that matter—can or should be controlled?
3. If it can at least to some extent be controlled, can you imagine any principles in terms of which that control should be exerted?

ECONOMICS AND SOCIAL CLASS

The Industrial Revolution and the Rise of Economics

Economics is often called "the dismal science," even by many who would dispute whether it is a science at all. But whether or not it is dismal or a science, economic ideas have had and continue to have enormous impact on our lives, not only in terms of the choices we make about our personal lives, but more importantly in terms of how we view most matters of public policy. "It's the economy, stupid!" is a slogan that bears on far more than the strategy of a 1990 political campaign.

Like all the ideas we deal with in this text, economics has a history that provides a context helpful in understanding its concerns, its claims, and its controversies. As a condition of human life, economics is as old as human society, but as a study or discipline, a science if you will, it is only some 200 years old, emerging during the last quarter of the eighteenth century during a time of major economic change and resulting class struggle. The major trigger of that change was the Industrial Revolution, the discovery and application in the late eighteenth century of new and highly efficient systems of power and production. This resulted in not only greater production, but profound social and political dislocations. We can get a quick idea of the changes occurring in the nineteenth century by contrasting England in 1800 and 1900. In 1800, the nation's major area of production was agricultural, its major population was rural, and its political system was a somewhat parliamentary structure largely managed by a landed aristocracy. By 1900, England had become an industrial urban democracy, and its population had quadrupled. But to understand the dislocations these changes wrought, what they meant for the day-to-day lives and the toll they exacted in human misery, demands a closer look.

The vast majority of those masses that left the country were driven to the cities by joblessness and hunger, but what they found there was little better. Some of England's largest cities at mid-century had been little more than villages in 1800, having grown at a rate approaching 50% each decade. The established systems by which communities cared for their poor and sick and managed their public services were based on village economics and perspectives and were ill-adapted to handling teeming urban masses. Simple things like housing, roads, sewerage, lighting, and crime control became problems of unprecedented proportions. Effective ways of managing these problems were much slower in developing than were more efficient ways to manufacture pins or weave textiles. Indeed, any real sense of community was slow to develop in the new industrial cities, and the laboring poor, isolated in slums remote from the notice of more prosperous citizens, became an alienated and anonymous mass.

The working poor, the "lucky" ones who had jobs, were indeed the "wage slaves" of Karl Marx's descriptions. In the 1830s and 1840s, before the first regulatory laws were passed, men, women, and children, some as young as five years, were working in mines, factories, and workshops from 12 to 16 hours a day. They labored in the most appalling conditions of heat, cold, and bodily peril, without any job security, worker's compensation, unemployment benefits, social security, or any opportunity for education. Women and children had to work because wages were barely enough to provide for one person's sustenance, much less a family. The sick, the injured, and the few who survived the workplace into anything like old age were simply cast off to die. It is a measure of how bad things were that the Ten Hours Bill of 1847, which limited only the labor of women and children and only in some industries to 10 hours each day and which included grossly inadequate enforcement provisions, was considered unusually progressive.

More progressive legislation came slowly, partly because of the limited sense of compassion of the prosperous, but also because industrial owners and managers were running scared. A constant theme of pro-business spokesmen, in the 1840s as much as in the 1990s, was that the nation's economic survival hung in the balance under the threat of foreign competition for world markets. Higher wages would mean higher prices and lost trade, and indeed many companies failed in that volatile economy, putting many out of work. And since the laboring classes were effectively cut off from political power, their plight was little known or acknowledged. Although the franchise was gradually expanded, property qualifications for voting remained throughout the century (for example, Birmingham, one of England's growing industrial cities, in 1851 had a population of nearly a quarter million, some 8000 of whom could vote in Parliamentary elections). In the labor market the individual worker had no bargaining power whatsoever, while for most of the century labor unions, considered conspiracies in restraint of trade, were outlawed and strikes were brutally put down. As a result, although the trade union movement began in the 1820s, unions in England were not effective until the Parliamentary acts of 1875 fully recognized the right of collective bargaining (similar legislation was not passed in the United States until 1913). As bad as all this may seem, England, in terms of its attitude toward labor, was the most progressive industrialized nation in the world.

Certainly, some parts of England became reasonably prosperous, whereas other parts remained relatively untouched by the Industrial Revolution. Howerver, where economic growth did occur, it generally carried with it some redistribution of wealth. The middle class was growing, and the center of wealth was shifting away from the old aristocracy toward the new industrial rich, but the gap between the moneyed classes and the growing numbers of abjectly poor widened. Growth in trade resulted in the development of a truly international economy, but the fever of unregulated growth also resulted in the first series of great world depressions, referred to in the nineteenth century as financial panics. In the half century before Marx's *Communist Manifesto* (1848), there were three such disasters, in 1825 - 1826, 1836 - 1837, and 1847, in which everyone suffered, as in all depressions, but in which the working classes suffered the most.

Along with economic dislocations came political revolution, in France in 1830 and then in virtually every European capital in 1848, but these were mainly manifestations of nationalism or of liberalism, and were largely middle-class revolts against the old aristocracies, *les anciens regimes,* as they were called. Help for the working poor would be a long time in coming.

Despite these problems, however, a spirit of optimism prevailed among the educated classes, sometimes wildly enthusiastic, sometimes guarded. The Victorian world looks to us in many ways as rather placid, but the sense of change that world experienced was unprecedented. As well as providing new and more products, the Industrial Revolution changed the land itself; it removed the barriers of distance and time with the invention of the railroad and telegraph. The mechanization of the textile industry not only made it possible to clothe the century's exploding population, but its waste cloth provided the raw material for paper, which helped fuel the world's first information explosion. As a result of such changes, Thomas Babington Macaulay, as early as the 1820s, spoke of his time as "an age of transition," a time on the brink of some great and far-reaching historical change. The intellectual life of the century was filled with a sense that the old world, the old order, was passing, yielding place to some new as yet unknown world. It was a time, therefore, that both fostered and resisted the spirit of revolution.

The Industrial Revolution and the Great Ideas

The problems engendered by economic change persisted partly because, as we have seen, established social systems were slow to respond to changing conditions. Also slow to respond effectively were most of Western humanity's intellectual and spiritual traditions. Whether this was because some or all of those traditions were fundamentally flawed is debatable, but a historical perspective can help to provide well-informed and cautious judgments.

Consider the issue of child labor for example. Until the nineteenth century, Western economy was based primarily on agriculture. In most lands, the fundamental unit of agricultural labor was the family, and from time immemorial, all members contributed to the needs of their family, which often required hard labor. Although undoubtedly child abuse occurred in such a system, no one objected to child labor itself, and state interference in such practices was unthinkable. Such attitudes, however, had to be radically rethought in the new industrial society. It was not that the old systems had no sense of social responsibility, but that the new systems required new definitions of that responsibility and new social and political mechanisms for safeguarding it, and that took time. The same again was true of attitudes toward the spiritual and intellectual traditions.

The Judeo-Christian Tradition

Christianity, the dominant religion in Western culture, had always concerned itself more with the soul than with the body, more with the next life than with this one. Although the pulpit inveighed against materialism, what came to be popularly known as the Protestant Work Ethic, especially by the middle classes, tended to identify wealth and prosperity with God's reward for virtue and hard work, and poverty with idleness and vice. To many Christians and their various leaders, then, social reform simply meant repentance, and caring for the poor meant only charity. The idea of instituting new social programs to take care of these problems, especially state-sponsored ones, seemed to go against all popular notions of God's plan for society. Judaism seems always to have been more socially responsive, but as a minority religion that was discriminated against, its impact on society as a whole was relatively small during the nineteenth century.

In most European states, established religions allied themselves with the political status quo and taught that the social order was ordained by God and that proper humility meant accepting one's ordained position in society. Thus, most established religions neglected the spiritual, as well as the physical, needs of the poor; the urban slums had few churches and fewer clergy willing to serve there.

Nevertheless, some seeds of social consciousness could be found among nineteenth-century religious groups, especially some of the Scriptural Protestants, which were denominations advocating that individuals establish personal relationships with God based on their readings of the Bible. These religious groups stood committed to evangelizing, in part, through teaching all believers to read, and a few of the groups made significant attempts to reach the poor. Among the best examples of the Scriptural Protestants were the Evangelicals in England who became active early in the century. They not only established

Bible schools, but they publicized the lot of the working poor and promoted legislation to improve their education and working conditions. In the latter third of the century, William Booth, founder of the Salvation Army, argued forcefully for what is the basis of Christian socialism, that delivering humanity from sin was tied to delivering humanity from material degradation. He advocated a plan of social reform that included shelters for "lost women," prevention homes for girls in moral danger, employment bureaus, vocational training programs, legal assistance and bank services for the poor, missing persons bureaus, and model suburban villages. His ideas, however, met great opposition, both religious and secular, and in the popular mind, he was categorized as someone between a harmless fanatic and a subversive.

Rationalism and Humanism

Like the church, the mainstream of the humanistic tradition was not sensitive to the conditions of the poor, and it too lagged behind events in providing solutions or in awakening social consciousness. Poets like William Blake, John Keats, and Percy Shelley early in the century and Alfred Tennyson and Robert Browning later brought attention to the over-simplifications of the new science and the dehumanizing effects of the new commercialism; they called for a revolution of the human heart, but few paid any heed to poets. Essayists like John Ruskin and Thomas Carlyle attacked the industrial systems that transformed workers into machines. Even so, the solutions they offered were too rooted in the past to effectively deal with the social problems caused by industrialism. For example, Ruskin advocated a return to a handcraft economy; Carlyle called for the reform of society through a "new" kind of feudal leadership to be exerted by those he called "captains of industry." The first solution was impractical, for the population had already grown to the point where reversion to less-efficient means of production would be disastrous, and the second solution was unpopular because of its promotion of elitism and militaristic control (such a plan would later be associated with Nazism). Popular novelists like Charles Dickens, Benjamin Disraeli, and Elizabeth Gaskell attacked with realistic fiction many of the same problems the poets and essayists had, inspiring sympathy and promoting reform through vivid and compassionate portraits of the poor, but the mainstream of the humanistic tradition disdained popular writers.

The Democratic Revolution

An obvious solution to the problems of industrialization would seem to have been democracy, especially as the nineteenth century progressed and the great American experiment proved its own permanence. However, Europe generally was less encouraged by the American Revolution than it was frightened by the results of the French (1789): the Reign of Terror and the guillotine, the transformation of what began as a republic into an autocratic empire, and the years of Napoleonic wars. Moreover, democratic systems were far more difficult to establish in the old world. Class structures were more firmly established, and Europe did not have America's frontier, with seemingly unlimited resources and opportunities both for escape from potential oppression and for individual advancement. Political and economic power in Europe, the wealth and the means of production, were solidly in the hands of the aristocracy and the middle class; and the moneyed classes were less willing to trust the working class with any kind of political power. Even in America, such a step was not taken until the 1820s, when the franchise was expanded, making possible the era of Jacksonian democracy in the 1830s.

Thus, the French Revolution, though based on the declared ideals of liberty, equality, and fraternity, became essentially a revolt of the middle class against the old aristocracy, and the lot of the working class showed no improvement. Indeed, to those more sympathetic to the lower classes, the ideals of the French Revolution seemed to have been betrayed, and from before 1800 through the middle of the nineteenth century, early socialist reformers, especially in France, were attacking bourgeois society. (We shift now to the terminology associated with Marx, which he adopted from the French reformers: *bourgeoisie* and *proletariat* are simply the French words for "middle class" and "working class.")

Indeed, in the early nineteenth century thinkers like Henri de Saint-Simon, Charles Fourier, and Pierre-Joseph Proudhon established a pattern of attack that Marx would adopt and expand. Bourgeois society, they believed, was rapaciously acquisitive and hypocritical, exploiting the labor of the proletariat while conspiring to keep them ignorant. Bourgeois liberalism, while advocating personal liberty, defended mainly the right to keep the profits earned by "free" exchange in the market, a position that ignored the great mass of those without property. Those with only their labor to sell in a subsistence labor market had no opportunity for profit. For them, the market was in no way free, and liberty defined in these terms was to the laboring poor a cruel joke. Bourgeois religion perpetuated social ills by attributing human misery to Adam's curse, God's just response for human sinfulness, rather than to inadequate social systems. The principles of competition and private property seemed to stand in the way of any kind of real equality, and to many reformers, a more radical kind of revolution, one that would overthrow the bourgeoisie as well as the last remnants of the old aristocracy and that would eliminate private property altogether, seemed the only way to a just and democratic society.

The Scientific Revolution

Science bred the faith in humanity's power to control nature that in many ways was the force behind the Industrial Revolution, and science through technological applications improved transportation and communication and increased production. Unfortunately, too many people did not share in these benefits. It was in the quest for solutions to this problem that the scientific spirit had its greatest impact on Marx, a quest beginning with a group of thinkers in the late eighteenth and early nineteenth centuries who tried to find laws as simple as

Newton's laws of motion to describe human economic behavior. They included the creators of the new science of economics, Adam Smith, Thomas Malthus, and David Ricardo.

Smith argued in *Wealth of Nations* (1776) that economic life is shaped by a number of natural developments, the most important of which is the division of labor, which is the notion that the best goods can be created by specialists, individuals dedicating themselves to producing what they can do best and trading the fruits of their labor for their other needs. Social classes developed, and property was distributed as each kind of labor and product found its own market value. Indeed, for Smith, the perception that the best possible economic relations developed naturally was a kind of revelatory wonder. It suggested, as Newton's laws had suggested to others, the rationality and care of the divine law giver: to compete in an open market and to earn the most profit, each individual strove to make the best possible goods; thus, as each person pursued one's own selfish ends, the sum of those efforts, as though guided by what Smith called an "invisible hand," naturally served the whole community. In the past, these processes had too often been misunderstood and misapplied, especially as expressed by nationalistic and militaristic ambitions, but Smith imagined utopian consequences of the implementation of his ideas. Allowed to develop naturally, aggressiveness and competition would be turned to productive rather than destructive ends; the energy of human selfishness would, by the natural laws of economics, be harnessed to trade instead of war; and the prosperity and wealth of all nations and peoples would result. This theory came to be called *laissez faire,* a French phrase meaning "to let alone." It became the dominant economic theory of industrialized nations of the nineteenth century and is the origin of modern market economic theory. In the nineteenth century, it also became mixed up in a number of moral and social controversies.

The great beauty of laissez faire theory for many was that by pursuing one's own selfish ends the good of the larger community would follow. Nature would take care of one's responsibilities to humanity. This tendency to exalt selfishness as a virtue was given a peculiar impetus by Malthus and Ricardo. As noted in the introduction to Darwin in Chapter 5, Malthus argued in his *Essay on the Principle of Population* (1798) that while the technological means of subsistence in human society tend to increase at an arithmetic rate, the population tends to increase geometrically. This meant that the great mass of humanity is inescapably condemned to a life at the level of bare subsistence. Rather than destroy laissez faire theory, however, Malthus only undermined Smith's utopian hopes. Laissez faire was now thought able to deliver only the best possible world, but that one would be far from ideal.

Ricardo developed Smith's and Malthus' ideas further in his *Principles of Political Economy and Taxation* (1817), in which he worked out his own system of "natural" laws regulating the distribution of wealth. The most notable of his formulations was the Law of Wages: the natural price of labor is the amount necessary to enable the worker to subsist and to perpetuate his species "without increase or dimunition." To lower wages below this point was to starve the worker, but to raise wages would create only temporary prosperity; workers would simply have more children, and the new wage would again become the "natural" one of mere subsistence. Another of Ricardo's laws, derived also from Malthus, stated that as population increases and less-productive resources are forced into use, profits must necessarily decline; thus, a more compassionate employer who raises wages above the subsistence level will risk losing his business, and likewise a national policy of compassion will threaten the economic fabric of society.

Such "laws" now seem far less certain—people who are better paid and educated seem to become more concerned with the quality of their lives and tend to have fewer children, not more; despite dire predictions, and notwithstanding periods of financial panic, profits in England rose throughout the century. However, to the hard-headed economists and the clear-eyed capitalists of the nineteenth century, a more benevolent attitude toward the working class was simply foolish sentimentality. In fact, in the second half of the century, Darwin's theories would be expropriated to further support these ideas: according to what came to be called "social Darwinism," the wealthy were so because of their natural superiority and energy, and the poor were so because of their natural inferiority and laziness. Economic classes demonstrated that in the struggle for economic survival the fittest had survived; the upper classes were, therefore, justified in their lack of concern for the lower classes. To work for the betterment of the poor would be to violate the laws of nature and imperil not only one's own survival and that of the nation, but perhaps that of the human race as well.

Other explorations of the science of the first half of the nineteenth century, however, seemed to hold the potential for more hopeful results. At least one thinker began to wonder if something like the materialistic, developmental models sought by geologists and biologists to account for the natural world might account for history. That thinker was Karl Marx.

KARL MARX, *FROM* THE COMMUNIST MANIFESTO

Karl Marx (1818-1883) may have had more impact—directly or indirectly—on life and thought than any other thinker of the past two centuries. More than half the people of the world live in political and economic systems modeled in some sense after his ideas, and most of the rest live in systems strongly influenced and affected by Marxian thought. Yet until recently, Marx has been little studied in the United States except by historians and political scientists. The reasons for this neglect are many and complex, but all are related to the extremes of opinion about his life and works. Many of Marx's supporters have treated him as the prophet of a new order, almost a god, and approached his works as if they were sacred texts. Many of his opponents have considered him as satanic and his ideas as subversive of all that is decent and virtuous. In the United States, anticommunism has become so ingrained that many people consider the mere reading of Marx a dangerous and revolutionary act. However, anyone interested in ideas in general and modern thought in particular cannot afford to neglect him.

The study of Marx is no less important today even though it seems that Marxism as a political philosophy has demonstrated its failure. The last century and a half has seen similar exaggerated predictions of the death of democracy, of capitalism, and even of God, all since proved to be at least highly premature. Likewise, to predict that Marx will end up in the dustbin of history would be premature at the time. For the present, however, an understanding of Marx and his heritage is essential for a proper assessment of the historical events rapidly unfolding before us: the collapse of the Berlin wall, the abolition of the exclusive power of Communist parties throughout Eastern Europe and Russia, the stalled democratic movement in China, and perhaps most important, the continuing revolutionary struggles in underdeveloped countries throughout the world.

Achieving such an understanding, however, is not easy. Part of the reason is the specialized terminology Marx introduced, like "bourgeoisie," "proletariat," "class struggle," and "dialectical materialism." Even more confusing are the many differences between Marx's own ideas and "Marxism," that is, the subsequent and practical applications of Marx's thought by others such as Lenin and Mao. An additional form of his name, "Marxian," denotes approaches to any kind of intellectual or artistic endeavor influenced by Marx but not necessarily "Marxist."

Marx was born in Trier in Rhineland Prussia, now part of Germany, of middle-class Jewish parents. His father had converted to Christianity the year before Karl's birth, and the young Marx exhibited a strong sense of Christian devotion and self-sacrifice in his adolescent years. After one academic year (1835 - 1836) at the University of Bonn, he went on to the University of Berlin to study philosophy and law. While there, he lost his Christian faith, though not his sense of devotion and self-sacrifice, and discovered the work of the German philosopher G. F. W. Hegel (1770 - 1831). He decided to abandon his father's ambitions for his own law career, dedicated himself to philosophy, earned a Ph.D. at the University of Jena, and developed into a political radical. In 1842, he accepted the editorship of a newspaper and discovered his own power as a political journalist. He was so effective, in fact, that the authorities shut him down. He emigrated to Paris in 1843, where he pursued his career as a radical journalist and came in contact with some of the major radical thinkers of his time. Also, in Paris in 1844, he met the young Friedrich Engels (1820 - 1895), the son of a rich Prussian manufacturer, who became his lifelong friend, collaborator, and a major source of financial support, which Marx sorely needed. From 1845 to 1849, he suffered a series of expulsions because of his ideas, which took him to Brussels, then to Germany, and finally to London, where he lived in exile for the rest of his life. In the meantime, he had become associated in 1847 with a

London-based radical group known as the Communist League, which commissioned Marx to draft, in German, a manifesto declaring its doctrines. The result was the now-famous *Communist Manifesto* (1848).

Marx's theories represent a continuation and expansion of the scientific revolution. His approach is based on the belief that history can be understood scientifically as a rational and coherent process. Marx recognized, however, that historical change was far more complicated than anything that could be described in terms of Newtonian mathematics or the laws of the "classical economists," a term coined by Marx to describe the founders of that science. To analyze history scientifically, Marx like Darwin needed a developmental model. To find one, he turned to a method developed by Hegel called "dialectic."

Dialectic is a method of inquiry derived from Plato. The Platonic dialectic arrives at truth by critically exposing the contradictions in opposing arguments. Hegel expanded the term to apply to the contradictions, the contending forces, inherent in reality and the processes by which those forces develop in relation to each other. His most famous formulation is the description of change in a pattern of thesis, antithesis, and synthesis. In simple terms, this means that every idea (thesis) generates its opposite (antithesis); the clash of these ideas results not in the victory of one, but in a new idea or set of ideas (synthesis), which in turn becomes a new thesis, generating an antithesis, and so on in a continuous process of development. Thus, dialectic in this modern sense is a way of looking at reality as process.

Hegel saw this process as the progressive manifestation of Spirit in matter, a development driven by God or the Absolute. Marx saw the process in empirical terms, as the natural way in which complex systems of any kind develop—not as a simple, unidirectional chain of causes and effects, but as a multidirectional network of causation. Indeed, this concept of dialectical empiricism is among the most seminal of Marx's ideas. When we look at any portion of reality as a complex system of interacting parts, where changes in one part affect all the other parts and where the system itself evolves, we are thinking dialectically. Many scientists and thinkers who may be far from Marx philosophically or politically may still have been profoundly influenced by this aspect of Marxian thought. This view is inherent, for example, in such divergent areas as modern applications of evolutionary theory, the latest approaches to literary criticism and linguistics, systems approaches to a wide variety of phenomena from ecology to industrial management, and even to quantum theory, the new mathematical study of chaos, and in many fields that study complex adaptive systems.

Marx is distinguished from other dialectical thinkers in two general ways. First, his major historical concern was political economy. Second, he is philosophically a materialist. That is, in the tradition going back to the ancient Greek philosophers Democritus and Epicurus, he believed that the material world was the ultimate reality. That is why his philosophy has been called "dialectical materialism," although Marx never used this phrase himself.

Studying history in dialectic terms, however, led Marx to many profoundly disturbing conclusions. First, history is a series of revolutions or changes driven by economic forces. Alterations in the means of production or in the mediums of exchange inspire class struggles, which in turn lead to political revolutions. That is why the first major division of the *Manifesto* opens with the declaration, "The history of all hitherto existing society is the history of class struggle." That is, classes have always existed in society, divisions between those who possess economic power and those who do not, between oppressors and oppressed, exploiters and exploited, often including several levels of relative power and powerlessness.

Second, to Marx, class struggle in itself is not wrong. In fact, he considered class structures of various sorts a historical necessity, natural ways that social organisms have adapted to the economic conditions of their life just as biological organisms adapt to their environment. This is the key to why Marx rejected the classical economists. For them, the basic factors that determine economic life are simple and eternal and the laws derived from them are universal; such a view provided no accounting for change, for history. On the other hand, Marx's sense of change leads to the disturbing conclusion that not only economic conditions, but right and wrong are products of historical necessity. Thus, moral law is no more an absolute than is political law for both are defined by the classes in power to maintain social and political stability in ways that also maintain their own power.

Marx does not suggest that the powerful cynically create moral law to serve their own interests; they may sincerely believe in the absolute truth of their sense of law, and a given view of "truth" or "good" may be entirely appropriate for its time. For instance, as mentioned in the introduction to this chapter, child labor in an agricultural economy is a viable, in fact a necessary, practice; however, the definition of what constitutes appropriate child labor was modified throughout the eighteenth and nineteenth centuries as the conditions of labor changed and as people became more socially conscious. In a dialectic view of history, change is inevitable, new economic conditions develop, and those changes cause social change, which in turn force political change. Political change, however, can only take place in the form of revolution, because a privileged class never surrenders its power voluntarily. Thus "wrong" becomes redefined by revolutionary factions to mean resistance to the forces of historical change.

In his own time, Marx saw signs of the processes of historical change accelerating and of the class struggle coming to an end. With the final defeat of the old aristocracy by the bourgeoisie, class struggle was reduced to a final conflict between the two remaining classes, the bourgeoisie and the proletariat. At the same time, the bourgeoisie, in its victory over the aristocracy, was forging the conditions of its own ultimate defeat. Industrialization was itself creating a massive proletariat and concentrating them in cities where they could organize and become a political force. The financial crises of the time were clear indications that bourgeois dominance was weakening, and in establishing a world market, the bourgeoisie was breaking down national boundaries and loyalties, creating a new sense of world culture, and setting the stage for a worldwide communist revolution.

from The Communist Manifesto

Karl Marx

1 A spectre is haunting Europe—the spectre of Communism. All the Powers of old Europe have entered into a holy alliance to exorcise this spectre: Pope and Czar, Metternich and Guizot, French Radicals and German police-spies.

2 Where is the party in oppositon that has not been decried as Communistic by its opponents in power? Where the Opposition that has not hurled back the branding reproach of Communism, against the more advanced opposition parties, as well as against its reactionary adversaries?

3 Two things result from this fact.

I. Communism is already acknowledged by all European Powers to be itself a Power.

II. It is high time that Communists should openly, in the face of the whole world, publish their views, their aims, their tendencies, and meet this nursery tale of the Spectre of Communism with a Manifesto of the party itself.

4 To this end, Communists of various nationalities have assembled in London, and sketched the following Manifesto, to be published in the English, French, German, Italian, Flemish and Danish languages.

I

Bourgeois and Proletarians

5 The history of all hitherto existing society is the history of class struggles.

6 Freeman and slave, patrician and plebeian, lord and serf, guild-master and journeyman, in a word, oppressor and oppressed, stood in constant opposition

to one another, carried on an uninterrupted, now hidden, now open fight, a fight that each time ended, either in a revolutionary re-constitution of society at large, or in the common ruin of the contending classes.

7 In the earlier epochs of history, we find almost everywhere a complicated arrangement of society into various orders, a manifold gradation of social rank. In ancient Rome we have patricians, knights, plebeians, slaves; in the Middle Ages, feudal lords, vassals, guild-masters, journeymen, apprentices, serfs: in almost all of these classes, again, subordinate gradations.

8 The modern bourgeois society that has sprouted from the ruins of feudal society has not done away with class antagonisms. It has but established new classes, new conditions of oppression, new forms of struggle in place of the old ones.

9 Our epoch, the epoch of the bourgeoisie, possesses, however, this distinctive feature: it has simplified the class antagonisms. Society as a whole is more and more splitting up into two great hostile camps, into two great classes directly facing each other: Bourgeoisie and Proletariat. . . .

10 The bourgeoisie, wherever it has got the upper hand, has put an end to all feudal, patriarchal, idyllic relations. It has pitilessly torn asunder the motley feudal ties that bound man to his "natural superiors," and has left remaining no other nexus between man and man than naked self-interest, than callous "cash payment." It has drowned the most heavenly ecstacies of religious fervour, of chivalrous enthusiasm, of philistine sentimentalism, in the icy water of egotistical calculation. It has resolved personal worth into exchange value, and in place of the numberless indefeasible chartered freedoms, has set up that single, unconscionable freedom—Free Trade. In one word, for exploitation, veiled by religious and political illusions, it has substituted naked, shameless, direct, brutal exploitation.

11 The bourgeoisie has stripped of its halo every occupation hitherto honoured and looked up to with reverent awe. It has converted the physician, the lawyer, the priest, the poet, the man of science, into its paid wage-labourers.

12 The bourgeoisie has torn away from the family its sentimental veil, and has reduced the family relation to a mere money relation. . . .

13 The bourgeoisie cannot exist without constantly revolutionising the instruments of production, and thereby the relations of production, and with them the whole relations of society. Conservation of the old modes of production in unaltered form, was, on the contrary, the first condition of existence for all earlier industrial classes. Constant revolutionising of production, uninterrupted disturbance of all social conditions, everlasting uncertainty and agitation distinguish the bourgeois epoch from all earlier ones. All fixed, fast-frozen relations, with their train of ancient and venerable prejudices and opinions, are swept away, all new-formed ones become antiquated before they can ossify. All that is solid melts into air, all that is holy is profaned, and man is at last compelled to face with sober senses, his real conditions of life, and his relations with his kind.

14 The need of a constantly expanding market for its products chases the bourgeoisie over the whole surface of the globe. It must nestle everywhere, settle everywhere, establish connexions everywhere.

15 The bourgeoisie has through its exploitation of the world-market given a cosmopolitan character to production and consumption in every country. To the great chagrin of Reactionists, it has drawn from under the feet of industry the national ground on which it stood. All old-established national industries have been destroyed or are daily being destroyed. They are dislodged by new industries, whose introduction becomes a life and death question for all civilised nations, by industries that no longer work up indigenous raw material, but raw material drawn from the remotest zones; industries whose products are consumed, not only at home, but in every quarter of the globe. In place of the old wants, satisfied by the productions of the country, we find new wants, requiring for their satisfaction the products of distant lands and climes. In place of the old local and national seclusion and self-sufficiency, we have intercourse in every direction, universal inter-dependence of nations. And as in material, so also in intellectual production. The intellectual creations of individual nations become common property. National one-sidedness and narrow-mindedness become more and more impossible, and from the numerous national and local literatures, there arises a world literature.

16 The bourgeoisie, by the rapid improvement of all instruments of production, by the immensely facilitated means of communication, draws all, even the most barbarian, nations into civilisation. The cheap prices of its commodities are the heavy artillery with which it batters down all Chinese walls, with which it forces the barbarians' intensely obstinate hatred of foreigners to capitulate. It compels all nations, on pain of extinction, to adopt the bourgeois mode of production; it compels them to introduce what it calls civilisation into their midst, *i.e.,* to become bourgeois themselves. In one word, it creates a world after its own image.

17 The bourgeoisie has subjected the country to the rule of the towns. It has created enormous cities, has greatly increased the urban population as compared with the rural, and has thus rescued a considerable part of the population from the idiocy of rural life. Just as it has made the country dependent on the towns, so it has made barbarian and semi-barbarian countries dependent on the civilised ones, nations of peasants on nations of bourgeois, the East on the West.

18 The bourgeoisie keeps more and more doing away with the scattered state of the population, of the means of production and of property. It has agglomerated population, centralised means of production, and has concentrated property in a few hands. The necessary consequence of this was political centralisation. Independent, or but loosely connected provinces, with separate interests, laws, governments and systems of taxation, became lumped together into one nation, with one government, one code of laws, one national class-interest, one frontier and one customs-tariff.

19 The bourgeoisie, during its rule of scarce one hundred years, has created more massive and more colossal productive forces than have all preceding generations together. Subjection of Nature's forces to man, machinery, application of chemistry to industry and agriculture, steam-navigation, railways, electric telegraphs, clearing of whole continents for cultivation, canalisation of rivers, whole populations conjured out of the ground—what earlier century had even a presentiment that such productive forces slumbered in the lap of social labour? . . .

20 Modern bourgeois society with its relations of production, of exchange and of property, a society that has conjured up such gigantic means of production and of exchange, is like the sorcerer, who is no longer able to control the powers of the nether world whom he has called up by his spells. For many a decade past the history of industry and commerce is but the history of the revolt of modern productive forces against modern conditions of production, against the property relations that are the conditions for the existence of the bourgeoisie and of its rule. It is enough to mention the commercial crises that by their periodical return put on its trial, each time more threateningly, the existence of the entire bourgeois society. In these crises a great part not only of the existing products, but also of the previously created productive forces, are periodically destroyed. In these crises there breaks out an epidemic that, in all earlier epochs, would have seemed an absurdity—the epidemic of over-production. Society suddenly finds itself put back into a state of momentary barbarism; it appears as if a famine, a universal war of devastation had cut off the supply of every means of subsistence; industry and commerce seem to be destroyed; and why? Because there is too much civilisation, too much means of subsistence, too much industry, too much commerce. The productive forces at the disposal of society no longer tend to further the development of the conditions of bourgeois property; on the contrary, they have become too powerful for these conditions, by which they are fettered, and so soon as they overcome these fetters, they bring disorder into the whole of bourgeois society, endanger the existence of bourgeois property. The conditions of bourgeois society are too narrow to comprise the wealth created by them. And how does the bourgeoisie get over these crises? On the one hand by enforced destruction of a mass of productive forces; on the other, by the conquest of new markets, and by the more thorough exploitation of the old ones. That is to say, by paving the way for more extensive and more destructive crises, and by diminishing the means whereby crises are prevented.

21 The weapons with which the bourgeoisie felled feudalism to the ground are now turned against the bourgeoisie itself.

22 But not only has the bourgeoisie forged the weapons that bring death to itself; it has also called into existence the men who are to wield those weapons—the modern working class—the proletarians.

23 In proportion as the bourgeoisie, *i.e.,* capital, is developed, in the same proportion is the proletariat, the modern working class, developed—a class of

labourers, who live only so long as they find work, and who find work only so long as their labour increases capital. These labourers, who must sell themselves piecemeal, are a commodity, like every other article of commerce, and are consequently exposed to all the vicissitudes of competition, to all the fluctuations of the market.

24 Owing to the extensive use of machinery and to division of labour, the work of the proletarians has lost all individual character, and, consequently, all charm for the workman. He becomes an appendage of the machine, and it is only the most simple, most monotonous, and most easily acquired knack, that is required of him. Hence, the cost of production of a workman is restricted, almost entirely, to the means of subsistence that he requires for his maintenance, and for the propagation of his race. But the price of a commodity, and therefore also of labour, is equal to its cost of production. In proportion, therefore, as the repulsiveness of the work increases, the wage decreases. Nay more, in proportion as the use of machinery and division of labour increases, in the same proportion the burden of toil also increases, whether by prolongation of the working hours, by increase of the work exacted in a given time or by increased speed of the machinery, etc.

25 Modern industry has converted the little workshop of the patriarchal master into the great factory of the industrial capitalist. Masses of labourers, crowded into the factory, are organised like soldiers. As privates of the industrial army they are placed under the command of a perfect hierarchy of officers and sergeants. Not only are they slaves of the bourgeois class, and of the bourgeois State; they are daily and hourly enslaved by the machine, by the overlooker, and, above all, by the individual bourgeois manufacturer himself. The more openly this despotism proclaims gain to be its end and aim, the more petty, the more hateful and the more embittering it is.

26 The less the skill and exertion of strength implied in manual labour, in other words, the more modern industry becomes developed, the more is the labour of men superseded by that of women. Differences of age and sex have no longer any distinctive social validity for the working class. All are instruments of labour, more or less expensive to use, according to their age and sex. . . .

27 But with the development of industry the proletariat not only increases in number; it becomes concentrated in greater masses, its strength grows, and it feels that strength more. The various interests and conditions of life within the ranks of the proletariat are more and more equalised, in proportion as machinery obliterates all distinctions of labour, and nearly everywhere reduces wages to the same low level. The growing competition among the bourgeois, and the resulting commercial crises, make the wages of the workers ever more fluctuating. The unceasing improvement of machinery, ever more rapidly developing, makes their livelihood more and more precarious; the collisions between individual workmen and individual bourgeois take more and more the character of collisions between two classes. Thereupon the workers begin to form combinations (Trades' Unions) against the bourgeois; they club together in or-

der to keep up the rate of wages; they found permanent associations in order to make provision beforehand for these occasional revolts. Here and there the contest breaks out into riots.

28 Now and then the workers are victorious, but only for a time. The real fruit of their battles lies, not in the immediate result, but in the ever-expanding union of the workers. This union is helped on by the improved means of communication that are created by modern industry and that place the workers of different localities in contact with one another. It was just this contact that was needed to centralise the numerous local struggles, all of the same character, into one national struggle between classes. But every class struggle is a political struggle. And that union, to attain which the burghers of the Middle Ages, with their miserable highways, required centuries, the modern proletarians, thanks to railways, achieve in a few years.

29 This organisation of the proletarians into a class, and consequently into a political party, is continually being upset again by the competition between the workers themselves. But it ever rises up again, stronger, firmer, mightier. It compels legislative recognition of particular interests of the workers, by taking advantage of the divisions among the bourgeoisie itself. Thus the ten-hours' bill in England was carried.

30 Altogether collisions between the classes of the old society further, in many ways, the course of development of the proletariat. The bourgeoisie finds itself involved in a constant battle. At first with the aristocracy; later on, with those portions of the bourgeoisie itself, whose interests have become antagonistic to the progress of industry; at all times, with the bourgeoisie of foreign countries. In all these battles it sees itself compelled to appeal to the proletariat, to ask for its help, and thus, to drag it into the political arena. The bourgeoisie itself, therefore, supplies the proletariat with its own elements of political and general education, in other words, it furnishes the proletariat with weapons for fighting the bourgeoisie. . . .

II

Proletarians and Communists

31 In what relation do the Communists stand to the proletarians as a whole?

32 The Communists do not form a separate party opposed to other working-class parties.

33 They have no interests separate and apart from those of the proletariat as a whole.

34 They do not set up any sectarian principles of their own, by which to shape and mould the proletarian movement.

35 The Communists are distinguished from the other working-class parties by this only: 1. In the national struggles of the proletarians of the different countries, they point out and bring to the front the common interests of the entire

proletariat, independently of all nationality. 2. In the various stages of development which the struggle of the working class against the bourgeoise has to pass through, they always and everywhere represent the interests of the movement as a whole.

36 The Communists, therefore, are on the one hand, practically, the most advanced and resolute section of the working-class parties of every country, that section which pushes forward all others; on the other hand, theoretically, they have over the great mass of the proletariat the advantage of clearly understanding the line of march, the conditions, and the ultimate general results of the proletarian movement.

37 The immediate aim of the Communists is the same as that of all the other proletarian parties: formation of the proletariat into a class, overthrow of the bourgeois supremacy, conquest of political power by the proletariat.

38 The theoretical conclusions of the Communists are in no way based on ideas or principles that have been invented, or discovered, by this or that would-be universal reformer.

39 They merely express, in general terms, actual relations springing from an existing class struggle, from a historical movement going on under our very eyes. The abolition of existing property relations is not at all a distinctive feature of Communism.

40 All property relations in the past have continually been subject to historical change consequent upon the change in historical conditions.

41 The French Revolution, for example, abolished feudal property in favour of bourgeois property.

42 The distinguishing feature of Communism is not the abolition of property generally, but the abolition of bourgeois property. But modern bourgeois private property is the final and most complete expression of the system of producing and appropriating products, that is based on class antagonisms, on the exploitation of the many by the few.

43 In this sense, the theory of the Communists may be summed up in the single sentence: Abolition of private property.

44 We Communists have been reproached with the desire of abolishing the right of personally acquiring property as the fruit of a man's own labour, which property is alleged to be the groundwork of all personal freedom, activity and independence.

45 Hard-won, self-acquired, self-earned property! Do you mean the property of the petty artisan and of the small peasant, a form of property that preceded the bourgeois form? There is no need to abolish that; the development of industry has to a great extent already destroyed it, and is still destroying it daily.

46 Or do you mean modern bourgeois private property?

47 But does wage-labour create any property for the labourer? Not a bit. It creates capital, *i.e.,* that kind of property which exploits wage-labour, and which cannot increase except upon condition of begetting a new supply of wage-labour for fresh exploitation. Property, in its present form, is based on the antagonism of capital and wage-labour. Let us examine both sides of this antagonism.

48 To be a capitalist, is to have not only a purely personal, but a social *status* in production. Capital is a collective product, and only by the united action of many members, nay, in the last resort, only by the united action of all members of society, can it be set in motion.

49 Capital is, therefore, not a personal, it is a social power.

50 When, therefore, capital is converted into common property, into the property of all members of society, personal property is not thereby transformed into social property. It is only the social character of the property that is changed. It loses its class-character.

51 Let us now take wage-labour.

52 The average price of wage-labour is the minimum wage, *i.e.,* that quantum of the means of subsistence, which is absolutely requisite to keep the labourer in bare existence as a labourer. What, therefore, the wage-labourer appropriates by means of his labour, merely suffices to prolong and reproduce a bare existence. We by no means intend to abolish this personal appropriation of the products of labour, an appropriation that is made for the maintenance and reproduction of human life, and that leaves no surplus wherewith to command the labour of others. All that we want to do away with, is the miserable character of this appropriation, under which the labourer lives merely to increase capital, and is allowed to live only in so far as the interest of the ruling class requires it. . . .

53 But don't wrangle with us so long as you apply, to our intended abolition of bourgeois property, the standard of your bourgeois notions of freedom, culture, law, &c. Your very ideas are but the outgrowth of the conditions of your bourgeois production and bourgeois property, just as your jurisprudence is but the will of your class made into a law for all, a will, whose essential character and direction are determined by the economical conditions of existence of your class.

54 The selfish misconception that induces you to transform into eternal laws of nature and of reason, the social forms springing from your present mode of production and form of property—historical relations that rise and disappear in the progress of production—this misconception you share with every ruling class that has preceded you. What you see clearly in the case of ancient property, what you admit in the case of feudal property you are of course forbidden to admit in the case of your own bourgeois form of property.

55 Abolition of the family! Even the most radical flare up at this infamous proposal of the Communists.

56 On what foundation is the present family, the bourgeois family, based? On capital, on private gain. In its completely developed form this family exists only among the bourgeoisie. But this state of things finds its complement in the practical absence of the family among the proletarians, and in public prostitution.

57 The bourgeois family will vanish as a matter of course when its complement vanishes, and both will vanish with the vanishing of capital.

58 Do you charge us with wanting to stop the exploitation of children by their parents? To this crime we plead guilty.

59 But, you will say, we destroy the most hallowed of relations, when we replace home education by social.

60 And your education! Is not that also social, and determined by the social conditions under which you educate, by the intervention, direct or indirect, of society, by means of schools, &c.? The Communists have not invented the intervention of society in education; they do but seek to alter the character of that intervention, and to rescue education from the influence of the ruling class.

61 The bourgeois clap-trap about the family and education, about the hallowed co-relation of parent and child, becomes all the more disgusting, the more, by the action of Modern Industry, all family ties among the proletarians are torn asunder, and their children transformed into simple articles of commerce and instruments of labour.

62 But you Communists would introduce community of women, screams the whole bourgeoisie in chorus.

63 The bourgeois sees in his wife a mere instrument of production. He hears that the instruments of production are to be exploited in common, and, naturally, can come to no other conclusion than that the lot of being common to all will likewise fall to the women.

64 He has not even a suspicion that the real point aimed at is to do away with the status of women as mere instruments of production.

65 For the rest, nothing is more ridiculous than the virtuous indignation of our bourgeois at the community of women which, they pretend, is to be openly and officially established by the Communists. The Communists have no need to introduce community of women; it has existed almost from time immemorial.

66 Our bourgeois, not content with having the wives and daughters of their proletarians at their disposal, not to speak of common prostitutes, take the greatest pleasure in seducing each other's wives.

67 Bourgeois marriage is in reality a system of wives in common and thus, at the most, what the Communists might possibly be reproached with, is that they desire to introduce, in substitution for a hypocritically concealed, an openly legalised community of women. For the rest, it is self-evident that the abolition of the present system of production must bring with it the abolition of the community of women springing from that system, *i.e.*, of prostitution both public and private. . . .

68 When, in the course of development, class distinctions have disappeared, and all production has been concentrated in the hands of a vast association of the whole nation, the public power will lose its political character. Political power, properly so called, is merely the organised power of one class for oppressing another. If the proletariat during its contest with the bourgeoisie is compelled, by the force of circumstances, to organise itself as a class, if, by means of a revolution, it makes itself the ruling class, and, as such, sweeps away by force the old conditions of production, then it will, along with these conditions, have swept away the conditions for the existence of class antagonisms and of classes generally, and will thereby have abolished its own supremacy as a class.

69 In place of the old bourgeois society, with its classes and class antagonisms, we shall have an association, in which the free development of each is the condition for the free development of all. . . .

70 The Communists disdain to conceal their views and aims. They openly declare that their ends can be attained only by the forcible overthrow of all existing social conditions. Let the ruling classes tremble at a Communistic revolution. The proletarians have nothing to lose but their chains. They have a world to win.

WORKING MEN OF ALL COUNTRIES, UNITE!

QUESTIONS FOR WRITING AND DISCUSSION

OBSERVING

1. "The bourgeoisie cannot exist without constantly revolutionising the instruments of production, and thereby the relations of production, and with them the whole relations of society." Explain this chain of causes. How in Marx's view does changing the instruments of production lead to changes in the relations of society?
2. Why do labor unions arise and what is their place in Marx's view of the development of the proletariat? Does Marx consider whether they may become a sufficient force to balance the power of the bourgeoisie?
3. What reasons does Marx give for his declaration "that the bourgeoisie is unfit any longer to be the ruling class in society"?
4. In his discussion of the family, Marx raises the question of education. What is the connection?
5. What are some of the specific assumptions that form the basis of Marx's dream of a society in which "the free development of each is the condition for the free development of all"?

EVALUATING

1. Marx claimed that "national one-sidedness and narrow-mindedness" would break down as a result of the developing world market, paving the way for a world state. Argue the accuracy of this claim in the light of recent resurgences of nationalism in the Middle East and Eastern Europe. Consider also that in 1992, nearly a century and a half after the *Manifesto,* Europe began to function, in terms of trade, like a single nation, ostensibly to be more competitive in the world market. Was Marx simply wrong or did he underestimate the time required for the predicted changes? Consider this question in larger terms by selecting several of Marx's predictions about economic changes: are there more that either have already or seem about to come true than have not?

2. Marx was not alone in noting that one result of industrialization during the nineteenth century was the dehumanization of labor itself: no joy remained in the work, as the worker "becomes an appendage of the machine, and it is only the most simple, most monotonous, and most easily acquired knack that is required of him." Argue that this is or is not still a problem in modern industry.
3. The forces of labor, as Marx predicted, have coalesced politically into a labor party in nearly all the industrialized nations of Europe but not in the United States. Why not?
4. How different is Marx's concern for the material bases of society, value, and institutions from Smith's and Ricardo's insistence on the role of greed in creating an ideal—or at least the best possible—system? Who is more materialistic?
5. Compare and contrast the *Manifesto* with the Declaration of Independence in terms of the ideologies that lie behind each. Which do you think offers a more adequate view of human nature and human relationships?

RESPONDING AND APPLYING

1. Marx claims that the triumph of bourgeois values "has put an end to all feudal, patriarchal, idyllic relations . . . and has left remaining no other nexus between man and man than naked self-interest, than callous 'cash payment.'" Many people today who are not Marxists may agree with this statement and argue that the phrase "business ethics" is a contradiction in terms. How much room do you think capitalism has left for the operation of values and ideals other than making money?
2. Marx believed that individuality and freedom, the great ideals of the bourgeoisie, are limited by the economic conditions of capitalism to the freedom and individuality of only a privileged class. Explain why this might have seemed true in mid-nineteenth-century Europe, and argue what degree of truth you can see in this belief now in the last decade of the twentieth century.
3. Consider Marx's argument that a "selfish misconception" we share "with every ruling class" induces us "to transform into eternal laws of nature and reason, the social forms springing from [our] present mode of production and form of property." From your own understanding of history, how true has this been? Do you think Marx himself fell into his own version of this "selfish misconception"? Do you think any truths or values remain apart from any historical context?
4. Marx advocated public education for all children, which many opposed because they believed it would undermine the family. Today, though public education is generally advocated for all, many Americans are still concerned that it may be undermining the values on which the institution of the family is based. What are the central issues in those arguments? Has our society dealt adequately with the issue of what values should be taught in our schools? How do today's arguments in favor of public education differ from or resemble Marx's?

CHARLES BEARD, *FROM* ECONOMIC ORIGINS OF JEFFERSONIAN DEMOCRACY

By 1900, the original versions of both capitalism and communism had begun to change. Capitalist economies in industrialized nations were beginning to solve some of their worst abuses, recognizing in deed, if not in theory, that even a "free" market required some government control. Contrary to both Ricardo's and Marx's predictions, profits for capitalists and real wages for the working class had increased, at least enough to keep unrest at the level of the strike or riot but short of outright revolution. Marx had been established as the major voice of socialist theory, but numerous controversies had risen over how he was to be interpreted and applied. Among the most notable critics near the turn of the century was a young Russian revolutionary calling himself Lenin, who argued that Marx was "wrong" mainly because he failed to anticipate how colonial imperialism would both mask and delay the developments he predicted: working men in industrialized nations were not miserable enough to rise because they were not in fact the lowest class; they and their bourgeois Western economies were being supported by the exploited colonial masses of Africa, China, Latin America, and elsewhere. But while these battles concerning interpretation were being fought both theoretically and in the streets, Marx's ideas were influencing, in subtle ways, Western thought, including the academic disciplines and especially history.

History is not the past, but an interpretation of the past. Therefore, every work of history has behind it a historian's assumptions about what drives events: divine will; some racial, ethnic, or national destiny; powerful personalities; the force of great ideas; or the pressures of economics. The last of these is among the least-popular approaches to history because it may depress a reader to conceive of great human events being caused primarily by crass materialistic forces like money, property, the means of production, and class conflict, and because to look at history this way may seem too much like Marxism. Yet one measure of Marx's significance is the extent to which both Marxist and non-Marxist students of society began to stress the importance of economic conditions and to use much of his basic terminology for their studies.

Charles Beard (1874-1948) was not a Marxist. He was, however, an eminent American historian and political scientist who pursued a system of interpreting history inspired to a significant degree by Marx. In his *Economic Interpretation of the Constitution* (1913), he upset cherished, popular notions about the origins of the Federal government by calling attention to the role of property and class conflict in the ratification of the U.S. Constitution. In Beard's hands, the story of the Constitution's origins was not so much one of the emergence of great political ideals as it was a conflict over concrete economic interests. "The financiers, public creditors, traders, commercial men, manufacturers, and allied groups, centering mainly in the larger seaboard towns," supported ratification while "the farmers, particularly in the inland regions, and the debtors" mainly opposed it. It was in short a conflict "between the capitalistic and agrarian classes."

To Beard, the result of his discovery was neither dismaying nor evidence of the need for a proletarian dictatorship. If the origins of the American government were less than idyllic and if America in his lifetime was still less than perfect, Beard nevertheless believed that American history demonstrated the feasibility of the gradual emergence of a true social democracy. In *The Rise of American Civilization* (1927), written with his wife Mary Beard, he positioned the Golden Age of American Democracy in the future, not the past. In his attempt to promote that future, however, he did more than write; he functioned as a reformer and gadfly. A professor of history at Columbia University from 1904 to 1917, he resigned in protest over the dismissal of two colleagues for their opposition to the United States' entry into World War I. In 1918, he helped organize the New School for Social Research in New York City. Although strongly supporting the New Deal in the 1930s and 1940s, he attacked Franklin Delano Roosevelt's foreign policy, arguing in his last book that Roosevelt had forced Japan to war. He was one of the earliest and most eminent of American historians to argue the point, now considered a commonplace and implied earlier in this introduction, that a historian's view of history is "not a purely objective discovery."

Following is an excerpt from the opening chapter of Beard's *Economic Origins of Jeffersonian Democracy* (1915), in which he briefly summarizes the bases for his conclusions in the *Economic Interpretation of the Constitution,* before carrying on the argument to show how the same class conflict continued in the early decades under the new Constitution.

from Economic Origins of Jeffersonian Democracy

Charles A. Beard

CHAPTER I

The Federalist-Republican Antagonism and the Conflict Over the Constitution

1 An examination into the origins of Jeffersonian Democracy naturally opens with an inquiry whether there was any connection between that party and the large body of citizens who opposed the establishment of the Constitution of the United States. In the struggle over the adoption of that instrument, there appeared, it is well known, a sharp antagonism throughout almost the entire country. The views of competent contemporary observers and of modern students of the period are in accord on that point. Of this there can be no doubt. Chief Justice Marshall, a member of the Virginia ratifying convention and a Federalist of high standing, who combined with his unusual opportunities for personal observation his mastery of President Washington's private correspondence, informs us that the parties to the conflict over the Constitution were in some states evenly balanced, that in many instances the majority in favor of the new system was so small that its intrinsic merits alone would not have carried the day, that in some of the adopting states a majority of the people were in the opposition, and that in all of them the new government was accepted with reluctance only because a dread of dismemberment of the union overcame hostility to the proposed fundamental law.[1]

2 A half a century after Marshall thus described the contest over the ratification of the Constitution, Hildreth, a patient and discriminating student of the Federalist period, on turning over the sources in a fresh light, came to the same conclusion.[2] He frankly declared that it was exceedingly doubtful whether, upon a fair canvass, a majority of the people, in several of the states which ratified the Constitution, actually favored its adoption; that in the powerful states of Massachusetts, New York, Pennsylvania, and Virginia, the majority in favor of the new frame of government was very uncertain, so uncertain, in fact, as to raise the question whether there had been any majority at all; and that everywhere the voters of the states were sharply divided into two well-marked political parties. Bancroft, whose devotion to the traditions of the Constitution is never to be questioned, was no less emphatic than Hildreth in

[1] *Life of Washington* (2d ed.), Vol. II, 127.

[2] Hildreth, *History of the United States* (1856), Vol. IV, 25 ff.

his characterization of the contest for the new political order as a hard-fought battle ending in victory snatched from the very jaws of defeat.[3] From the day of Hildreth and Bancroft to this, no serious student of the eighteenth century has doubted at least the severity and even balance of the conflict over the Constitution. Only those publicists concerned with the instant need of political controversies have been bold enough to deny that the fundamental law of the land was itself the product of one of the sharpest partisan contests in the history of the country.

3 This stubbornly fought battle over the Constitution was in the main economic in character, because the scheme of government contemplated was designed to effect, along with a more adequate national defence, several commercial and financial reforms of high significance, and at the same time to afford an efficient check upon state legislatures that had shown themselves prone to assault acquired property rights, particularly of personality, by means of paper money and other agrarian measures. To speak more precisely, the contest over the Constitution was not primarily a war over abstract political ideals, such as state's rights and centralization, but over concrete economic issues, and the political division which accompanied it was substantially along the lines of the interests affected—the financiers, public creditors, traders, commercial men, manufacturers, and allied groups, centering mainly in the larger seaboard towns, being chief among the advocates of the Constitution, and the farmers, particularly in the inland regions, and the debtors being chief among its opponents. That other considerations, such as the necessity for stronger national defence, entered into the campaign is, of course, admitted, but with all due allowances, it may be truly said that the Constitution was a product of a struggle between capitalistic and agrarian interests.

4 This removal of the Constitution from the realm of pure political ethics and its establishment in the dusty way of earthly strife and common economic endeavor is not, as some would have us believe, the work of profane hands. It has come about through the gathering of the testimony of contemporary witnesses of undoubted competency and through the researches of many scholars. Although in the minds of some, the extent of the economic forces may be exaggerated and the motives of many leaders in the formation and adoption of the Constitution may be incorrectly interpreted, the significant fact stands out with increasing boldness that the conflict over the new system of government was chiefly between the capitalistic and agrarian classes.

5 Occupying an influential position in the former of these classes were the holders of the state and continental debt amounting to more than all the rest of the fluid capital in the United States. No less an important person than Washington assigned the satisfaction of the claims of the public creditors as the chief reason for the adoption of the Constitution, for he held that unless provisions were made for the payment of the debt, the country might as well continue under the old order of the Articles of Confederation. "I had endulged the expecta-

[3] *History of the Constitution of the United States* (1882), Vol. II, *passim.*

tion," he wrote to Jefferson, "that the New Government would enable those entrusted with its administration to do justice to the public creditors and retrieve the National character. But if no means are to be employed but requisitions, that expectation will be in vain and we may well recur to the old Confederation."[4]

6 Without doubting the fact that the standard of honor which Washington here set up was a consideration in the minds of many, it is no less a fact that the numerous holders of the public debt themselves formed a considerable centre corps in the political army waging the campaign for the adoption of the Constitution. For instance, a prominent Federalist of Connecticut, Chauncey Goodrich, a man placed by his connections and experience in a position to observe closely the politics of that and surrounding states, wrote, in 1790, that "perhaps without the active influence of the creditors, the government could not have been formed, and any well-grounded dissatisfaction on their part will make its movements dull and languid, if not worse."[5] The willingness of a number of Northern men to break up the Union before the new government was fairly launched because they could not secure a satisfactory settlement of the debt is proof that Goodrich had correctly gauged the weight of the public creditors in the battle for the Constitution.

7 To the testimony of Virginia and Connecticut in this matter of the influence of public creditors and allied interests in the formation and ratification of the Constitution we may add that of New York, then as now one of the first financial centres, speaking through a witness of such high authority that the most incredulous would hardly question it,—Alexander Hamilton, the first Secretary of the Treasury under the new system. He had been a member of the Convention which drafted the Constitution. He was intimately associated with the leaders in the movement for ratification. He shared in the preparation of that magnificent polemic, *The Federalist.* But above all, he was, as Secretary of the Treasury, in full possession of the names of those who funded continental and state securities after the Constitution was adopted. No one in all the United States, therefore, had such excellent opportunities to know the real forces which determined the constitutional conflict. What Goodrich could surmise, Hamilton could test by reference to the Treasury ledgers at his elbow. That the public creditors were "very influential" and the allied property interests, that is, in the main, capitalistic interests, were "very weighty" in securing the adoption of the Constitution, he distinctly avowed, although he wisely refrained from estimating exactly their respective values in the contest. In an unfinished manuscript on the funding system, he considered this matter at length, saying: "The public creditors, who consisted of various descriptions of men, a large proportion of them very meritorious and very influential, had had a considerable agency in promoting the adoption of the new Constitution, for this peculiar reason, among the many weighty reasons which were common to them as citizens and proprietors, that it exhibited the prospect of a government able to do

[4] *Documentary History of the Constitution,* Vol. IV, 40.

[5] Gibbs, *Administrations of Washington and Adams,* Vol. I, 37.

justice to their claims. Their disappointment and disgust quickened by the sensibility of private interest, could not but have been extreme [if the debt had not been properly funded]. There was also another class of men, and a very weighty one, who had had great share in the establishment of the Constitution, who, though not personally interested in the debt, considered maxims of public credit as of the essence of good government, *as intimately connected by the analogy and sympathy of principles with the security of property in general,* and as forming an inseparable portion of the great system of political order. These men, from sentiment, would have regarded their labors in supporting the Constitution as in a great measure lost; they would have seen the disappointment of their hopes in the unwillingness of the government to do what they esteemed justice, and to pursue what they called an honorable policy; and they would have regarded this failure as an augury of the continuance of the fatal system which had for some time prostrated the national honor, interest, and happiness. The disaffection of a part of these classes of men might have carried a considerable reinforcement to the enemies of the government."[6]

8 Other contemporaries stressed other features in the conflict, but nevertheless agreed that it had been primarily economic in character. For instance, Fisher Ames, of Massachusetts, who had been a member of the state ratifying convention, laid emphasis upon the commercial rather than the financial aspects of the constitutional battle. Speaking in the House of Representatives, on March 28, 1789, he said: "I conceive, sir, that the present Constitution was dictated by commercial necessity more than any other cause. The want of an efficient government to secure the manufacturing interests and to advance our commerce, was long seen by men of judgment and pointed out by patriots solicitous to promote our general welfare."[7] The inevitable inference from this remark is that, in Ames's opinion, men of commercial and manufacturing interests must have seen the possibilities of economic advantage in the adoption of the Constitution, and naturally arrayed themselves on its side.

9 More than a decade after the conflict over the Constitution, when many of the great actors in that drama had passed away, and there had been ample time and opportunity to reflect deeply upon the nature and causes of that struggle, Chief Justice Marshall described it, in effect, though not in exact terms, as a war between mercantile, financial, and capitalistic interests generally, on the one hand, and the agrarian and debtor interests, on the other.[8] Half a century later, Hildreth, whose work has been cited above, came to substantially identical conclusions. He declared that "in most of the towns and cities, and seats of trade and mechanical industry, the friends of the Constitution formed a very decided majority. Much was hoped from the organization of a vigorous national government and the exercise of extensive powers vested in it for the regulation of

---

[6] Hamilton, *Works* (Lodge ed.), Vol. VII, 418. The smaller edition, not the Federal edition, is cited throughout this volume.

[7] P. W. Ames, *Speeches of Fisher Ames,* 12.

[8] Beard, *Economic Interpretation of the Constitution,* 296.

commerce." In North Carolina and Rhode Island, the states which first rejected the Constitution, Hildreth continued, the trouble was the state paper money which destroyed the rights of creditors. In Massachusetts he found the "weight of talent, wealth, and influence" on the Federal side. In Virginia, the opponents of the Constitution included many of the great planters and "the backwoods population almost universally," and the opposition of the planters was to be, in part, ascribed to the fear of having to pay their debts due to British merchants in case the Constitution went into effect. In New York it was the City and the southern counties, not the interior agricultural regions, that supported the new scheme of national government.[9]

10 By a strange coincidence, Charles Francis Adams gave to the world the same economic interpretation of the Constitution in the very year that Hildreth published his history. In his life of his grandfather, the President, Mr. Adams, who enjoyed the unrivalled advantage of having access to documents closed to all his contemporaries, represented the adoption of the fundamental law of the United States as a triumph of property over the propertyless. The social disorder which preceded the federal Convention of 1787, Mr. Adams attributed to "the upheaving of the poorest classes to throw off all law of debtor and creditor," and the Convention itself, he declared, "was the work of commercial people in the seaport towns, of the planters of the slave-holding states, of the officers of the revolutionary army, and the property holders everywhere. . . . That among the opponents of the Constitution are to be ranked a great majority of those who had most strenuously fought the battle of independence of Great Britain is certain. . . . Among the federalists, it is true, were to be found a large body of the patriots of the Revolution, almost all the general officers who survived the war, and a great number of the substantial citizens along the line of the seaboard towns and populous regions, all of whom had heartily sympathized in the policy of resistance. But these could never have succeeded in effecting the establishment of the Constitution, had they not received the active and steady cooperation of all that was left in America of attachment to the mother country, as well as of the moneyed interest, which every points to strong government as surely as the needle to the pole."[10]

11 That which representative men of the eighteenth century definitely understood, and Hildreth implied in a somewhat rambling fashion was completely demonstrated by Professor O. G. Libby in his study of the *Geographical Distribution of the Vote on the Constitution in the Thirteen States:* the support for the Constitution came from the centres of capitalistic interst and the opposition came from the agrarians and those burdened with debts. To adduce further evidence in support of Professor Libby's thesis is merely to add documentation to that which has been satisfactorily established.[11]

---

[9] *Op. cit.,* Vol. IV, 25 ff.

[10] C. F. Adams, *The Works of John Adams,* Vol. 1, 441.

[11] Beard, *Economic Interpretation of the Constitution.* It is curious that this volume raised such a storm of criticism in certain quarters when the leading ideas set forth in it had long been accepted by students of the economic aspects of American history.

QUESTIONS FOR WRITING AND DISCUSSION

OBSERVING

1. What authorities does Beard cite in making his case for the economic forces behind the Constitutional debate? Are they reliable sources that effectively support his argument?
2. In waging the Revolutionary War, the new nation had incurred a considerable public debt, and the Articles of Confederation, the document that empowered the government before the Constitution was ratified, provided no means by which the central government could raise the money to pay that debt. How do Washington and Hamilton characterize the state of the government operating under the Articles?
3. The Preamble to the Constitution declares that "We the People of the United States" ordained and established that document. According to Beard, to what extent is this true?

EVALUATING

1. Consider the full text of the Preamble, where the reasons for establishing the Constitution are listed: "We the People of the United States, in order to form a more perfect union, establish Justice, insure domestic tranquility, provide for the common defence, promote the general Welfare, and secure the Blessings of Liberty to ourselves and our Posterity, do ordain and establish this Constitution of the United States of America." It does not mention anything much like the words quoted by Beard of Washington, "to do justice to the public creditors," or of Hamilton, to maintain "the security of property." Why not? Argue that the Preamble is or is not biased.
2. Review the selections from Alexis de Tocqueville's *Democracy in America,* which appear in Chapter 6. What indications did he see of class conflict as described by Beard in America, and how did they enter into his assessment of the internal dangers facing the young nation?

RESPONDING AND APPLYING

1. The Bill of Rights, as you know, was not part of the original Constitution. Was this an indication, do you think, that the original framers of the Constitution thought of "liberty" in terms more of the security of property than of free speech, a free press, or even freedom of religion?
2. It has long been popular for the people of the United States to conceive of the national character in terms of images drawn from both agrarian and frontier experience, where the central struggle was with the land or its aboriginal inhabitants. Yet, if Beard is correct, farmers, planters, and backwoodsmen, who according to President John Quincey Adams' grandson (and President John Adams' great-grandson) C. F. Adams, were "a great majority of those who had most strenuously fought the battle of independence of Great Britain" and were the interests most opposed to

acceptance of the Constitution. How does this knowledge affect your conception of the national character?

3. Are there other popular ways of conceiving of the national character that reveal a knowledge of class consciousness? Choose a popular film—*Evita, Jerry McGuire, Michael, Independence Day,* or *Ferris Bueller's Day Off,* for example—and examine it as a Marxian drama.
4. Do you see any economic, geographic, and class divisions as significant in today's Democratic and Republican parties as those Beard found among the Federalists and anti-Federalists?

FRITHJOF BERGMANN, "THE FUTURE OF WORK"

The development of world markets and of more efficient means of agricultural production produced the hordes of rural unemployed that fueled the industrial revolution of the eighteenth and nineteenth centuries. The potential for massive unemployment in developed countries created during the twentieth century by increasing mechanization of industry was averted by growing world markets and a burgeoning service economy, fueling the post-industrial age. In the last quarter of this century, we have entered into an age as yet unnamed in which global markets are increasingly competitive, while new technologies not only continue the process of reducing employment in agriculture and industry but have begun to cut deeply into employment in the service sector, and this time there seem to be no new areas of work likely to even begin to absorb those displaced.

Frithjof Bergmann, who teaches philosophy and anthropology at the University of Michigan, also works with auto workers in Flint, Michigan, a center of the auto industry especially hard hit by corporate downsizing and plant closings and movings, with their attendant effects of layoffs and unemployment. There, the Center for New Work, which Bergmann helped establish, is trying to solve the many problems generated by this situation. In the essay which follows, he explores the causes and parameters of our impending economic crisis, anticipating when he wrote this in the early 1980s many of the problems Deborah Lutterbeck, in the prelude to this chapter, sees coming to a head in the mid-1990s. Bergmann offers a kind of solution that asks us to reevaluate our ideas about work and its relation to our humanity. Indeed, the Industrial Revolution, Bergmann argues, has already brought about major changes in the way people think about work, changes that were forced upon the population in an atmosphere of periodic crisis generated by the kinds of economic development they little understood. The same thing seems to be happening again in the post-industrial age, but perhaps we can understand it better this time and turn these changes to more positive effects.

The Future of Work

Frithjof Bergmann

1 At the moment we have no picture of a future—certainly we do not have an image of a more attractive, better, maybe even nobler social order that we could aim for, for which it would make sense to exert ourselves, let alone to struggle. One by one, like lights, the visions have gone out.

2 Consider then, simply as an opening proposition, the idea that half of the sum total of the now existing jobs could be soon eliminated; and do not take this primarily as a prediction, but think of it instead as the summation of a technological capacity which we already possess now, though we, for social reasons, might use it in very different ways. Our first reaction is apt to be a panic. If this were the case, then the kind of unemployment we have had so far might only be a hint at the severity of what is still to come, and unemployment on such a scale evokes the image of a downward spiral on which we might turn at an even faster pace.

3 Certainly we cannot simply say that enough jobs will of course be found just because this has always been the case, and why should it be different now? The large, and panoramic picture is more nearly that up until about two hundred years ago ninety percent of the total population lived on farms and therefore did not have jobs at all in our sense. From that perspective one could say that the very notion that everyone could or should have a job came into being only with the Industrial Revolution, and that the brief span in which that idea had any viability may now be past. The last 200 years represented perhaps only a transition or rather a tooling-up period—which are notoriously wasteful and cumbersome—but now that full-grown technology has finally arrived there is no presumption whatsoever that 40 hours of every week for 45 years of everybody's life should be filled by a job. On the contrary: the basic purpose of technology from its first beginnings was the elimination of human labor. This is the common denominator that extends all the way back to the first wheel and from there forwards to the loom and the steam engine and now to the computer. If there will not be enough jobs in the future it will only mean that we at long last have succeeded!

4 Agriculture is one enormously large example that illustrates the extent of our great achievement. We have turned the situation on its head: up until as recently as 180 years ago approximately 80 to 90% of the population was required to grow sufficient surplus for the remaining 10 or 20. Now, a mere 5% grows all our food, and in addition the large quantities which we export. So machines really can make human labor obsolete! Still, the other side of this coin is of course that somewhere between 75 and 85% of the entire workforce was displaced. On one level this bears on the much-repeated mindless adage that it will take as many people to run the computers, and to keep them in repair as

these computers will displace. In response to this one can only ask: how many people does it take to maintain and to repair the whole array of our farm machines? The ratio of the jobs "created" by the maintaining of these machines, relative to those that were displaced may well be 1:10,000, and with computers the proportion could easily be in that same range.

5 On another level, this fact about agriculture evokes more than any other a comprehensive image of the larger epic in which we are perhaps involved: Starting out with between 80 and 90% of the entire population living and working on farms, we evacuated all but 5% of these. It was machines that made their presence on the land no longer necessary and that drove them off the land. Ever since then this great mass has looked for a new place to settle—like refugees after a war—and for a time they did find a space in manufacturing; but as it turned out that phase was short-lived. Technology developed further and encroached progressively into the area of manufacturing. So people moved again: this time from manufacturing into service. (The standard definition of the much-used word "post-industrial" is that more than 50% of the workforce is in service jobs.) And this brings the drama to its head, for the question is: *What comes after service?* Given the three categories of agriculture, manufacturing and service, it is not at all obvious that there is yet another, fourth such category—let alone one that could have the required breadth. And that makes very vivid one interpretation of the situation we have reached: It is like a Dunkirk with no place to go. And here it is important that progress is still in full swing. New forms of mechanization and labor-saving are still constantly being introduced even into agriculture, and it is of course the same with factories. More overwhelming still, however, is the fact that the service sector may be the area that is under greatest pressure: virtually all of the examples from which we began, from the checking out of groceries, to working as a waiter, right across to being a rental or a travel agent would be classified as "service": so the large new wave of just arriving technological innovations runs precisely into this last and already overcrowded space.

6 One could add that those who hope that the "Third World" will provide us with jobs by being the great market for which we can boundlessly produce are fearfully deluded. Everything moves and points in exactly the opposite direction: the "Third World" has itself millions of workers looking for jobs—much of the time they are in straits which make them ready to labor for a fraction of our customary wages: So, if anything, the "Third World" represents yet another loss in jobs. For in the same way in which whole blocks of jobs are lost to technology, they are also lost to other, still poorer regions of the world, and not just because parts of the still remaining manufacturing are moved to areas where labor is less costly, but also because these areas are rapidly acquiring technological capacities of their own, so that the tables are gradually being turned: it is not they who are our market, but the reverse: it is we who import what their labor makes.

7 And this brings yet one further factor on the scene: the steadily increasing and tightening international competition. The fashion in which this affects the

availability of jobs involves in some instances strange turns that give it an odd indirectness, but that in no way diminishes the seriousness or the quantity of the result. That we lose jobs because many prefer Japanese cars to Fords has been emphasized quite enough. But a less apparent aspect has to do with the much improved quality of *our* goods. We are *forced* to manufacture products that will need much less repair and that will be far more durable—that in short will no longer have all the attributes of the once notorious built-in obsolescence—and though this is naturally to the good from a point of view that has regard for the scarcity of raw materials, it all the same is from the point of view of labor yet another threat.

8 This is connected to still another element which also has its origin in the escalated international competition. There are a great number of technological devices and new materials and machines that we do *not* use often, but by no means always, because unions have fought against them to protect their jobs. Similarly, there are hundreds of thousands of jobs that are protected mainly by hard-won regulations, of which those that regulate the speed of work are only the most obvious surface example. Under the impact of intensified international competition much of this is already in the process of a softening and contraction, if not in a full-scale retreat.

9 It would be extremely difficult to estimate the implications of just this one development, even if it could be isolated. For if the union movement, together with the very conceptions which underlie it, is seriously damaged and crushed or circumvented (and the sheer magnitude and diversity and particularly the internationality of many corporations is apt to have this effect) then a whole series of cautiously erected channels and safeguards is bound to collapse. This will bring on, among many other things, an intensification of the competition for each job to a degree that is now quite unimagined. With one hand one will be clinging to one's job, while one will use the other to fend others off and this would bring about not just a great compression of the number of those who work, but it would also wholly change the ethos that now still surrounds work.

10 With all this said one could nonetheless still add an entire second level to this perspective: many will lose their jobs just because others have lost theirs. One could call this "domino unemployment" since the falling of one single job can trigger a longish chain where each in succession brings down the next. To this it is once more relevant that the preponderance of jobs are already involved in the rendering of service. Many people are likely to forego many services soon after they lose their jobs, some from poverty, but many also because they now have the time to perform these services themselves. So this factor, like the other general shifts which we have just enumerated will have effects so large that our normal instruments of quantitative measure can no longer comprehend them.

11 If we now step away from the array of factors which we have just rehearsed and try to gain an overview, to what more general outlook are we led? It should be put down firmly that no simplistic and oracular predictions either can or should be made. Certainly it would be foolish and pretentious to say any-

thing about what exactly will happen exactly where and when. But with that set aside there nonetheless are some assertions which can be made, and these even with considerable force. For we can know a good deal about what will *not* occur and what will *not* work and that may be very much more useful than at first appears.

12 Nothing, for instance, indicates that merely the invention and the selling of new products could possibly reverse the general trend that we so far defined. Without any question new goods will naturally be invented, maybe even at a sharply accelerating rate, but there is first the consideration that many of these new products or services will advance the process we have been describing and will themselves still further eliminate the need for human labor. So the fact that we will of course continue to invent may not resolve, but could on the contrary still further aggravate the situation.

13 But apart from that there is the even more basic matter of the sheer magnitude or size. Nothing at all, as far as we can see, would justify the expectation that even the wildest outburst of the engineering imagination or of a newly rising productivity could hope to outweigh or even just to balance the *combined* might of the factors that we have just detailed. It goes without saying that new jobs will be constantly created, but the simple question is, How many? So far there is not a shred of evidence that the two could be balanced, and much suggests that the ratio could be one new job for every 80 or 100 that are lost.

14 A closely analogous kind of thinking applies to the notion that a simple upturn of the economy will somehow set everything to rights again. An upturn will of course occur, but there, too, one could first point out that no significant upswing could conceivably materialize unless a higher technology (one competitive with the Germans and the Japanese) were put into place. But if so, then that technology would itself cancel out whatever increase in employment any putative upswing might have made. For individual industries estimates along these lines have been variously made, and one telling instance came to the conclusion that the workforce of the automobile industry would be cut in half even if five years from now car sales exceeded the previous high point of '76 and '77. But the major consideration would again be from the magnitudes involved: as with products before, it seems inconceivable that an upswing in economic activity could balance, let alone reverse, the technologically produced decline in the quantity of needed labor.

15 (Throughout—and it is crucial that this is not misunderstood—we are of course not discussing "work." "Work" will naturally always exist in limitless abundance; there is no end of things that any of us can always do. But that is not the issue: we are considering *Jobs;* and that means work which someone else is *willing* but also *able* to pay for.)

16 The political implications of this are intensely serious. Everybody knows that a very large number concurred with the two most basic Reagan measures, of reducing the programs for the poor, and of increasing the money that would go to the rich, only because they considered these bitter medicines that despite

their awful side effects were the only way to regain health. In essence, people were willing to give money to the rich because they had been persuaded that this would eventually lead to an increase in jobs. But the key link in this calculation may no longer hold: the hope is that putting the rich in the position to buy will ultimately help, because it will give work to those who make the things which the rich will acquire. But that nostrum leaves technology totally out of the picture. In some isolated village in the Middle Ages this might have been true, but it should have been put into a museum after the invention of the first machine, for this already created the very plain alternative that the rich with their money would buy *machines*—which would make them even less dependent on all others than they were before.

17 The progress of technology has slowly brought about a condition where a conjunction of machines can turn out finished products with a bare minimum of human help. This self-sufficiency of the technological apparatus created the situation where the rich can put their money into a set of machines and can eventually receive much more money in return, but now they no longer need to include anyone else in this small cycle: it is all between them and their machines and themselves. Thereby technology has among many other things also changed our most basic political equations: it is now eminently possible that money given to the rich will benefit them and them alone. And it is possible with the same ease for the economy to swing up high, and to improve while the number of those that this still effects progressively decreases.

18 Analogous implications hold on still a different level. Not just the cooked-up pablum of supply side economics turns pivotally on the fiction of these jobs, the same is true for the tradition of respected conservative economic thought all the way back to Adam Smith. For, in one way or another the notion of wealth or benefits "trickling down" was the main claim on which its appeal to a rational and disinterested public rested; more than that: its very status as a genuine "theory" of economics or as a "doctrine" stands and falls with this. And mere technology may well have brought it to its fall. For the "trickling down" is surely just a metaphor. Mere gravity alone will certainly not bring about the wider distribution. If anything is able to put substance behind this veil then it is only work and jobs. But it seems that this one avenue has now been blocked. Thanks to technology, wealth can now produce goods and beget more wealth—without labor. This has a side which is truly marvelous but it also flattens much of the carefully constructed architecture of previous thought, and forces us to grasp the quite new situation which we ourselves have managed to create.

19 The consequences of persisting in our current infatuation with the antiquated are neither unimaginable nor unthinkable. A somewhat realistic picture of the degree and of the magnitude that unemployment could soon reach, and of the destitution that it would entail, is fairly close at hand. A number of South American countries have endured unemployment of 50 or 60 or even 70 percent over extended periods of time. In most of these countries multitudes of peasants left the land for many reasons, and no one, as far as anyone can tell,

ever assumed that all of them would find full employment in the developing economies. Each city is half surrounded with a shanty town that holds perhaps five times the population of the city which we know by name. Yet that version of the "South Americanization" of the United States is probably too picturesque. We know the deterioration that we should expect from almost any city close to us. There are the blocks or streets that can be easily identified by the windows which have neither glass nor frames, and in which "bums" or "drifters" or "down-and-outs" live. Nothing guarantees that this will stay localized. We already know that whole districts and quarters can easily become like that. And there are many towns in Mexico, for instance, that have their three or four very fashionable, very modern, very expensive-looking streets, but where the three or six or ten remaining *miles* of town are like a camp after a natural disaster or in a war—so crowded are the sidewalks with the drunken and the sleeping and the dying and the sick. If we cannot invent a social order and an economy and above all a way to work that reckons with the technology and takes advantage of it, then St. Louis, and Chicago and San Francisco may become like this.

20 Our most central problem is ambivalent to a degree that is downright comic: our greatest shortage seems to be a shortage of slow, mechanical, hard labor. It is easy to imagine how much sympathy coolies and water-carriers and peasant women from previous generations might have felt for us. But that it is laughable from one side in no way detracts from the terror that it presents from the other side. The fact is that our social order and our individual lives are quite obviously organized around the spine of work. But it seems that technology can undercut and decimate and crush out of existence large quantities of this one commodity on which we utterly depend. The conflict therefore is as basic as that between our need for work—and this need is economical and social and psychological—and the whole arsenal of forces which together constitute technology whose basic purpose is the elimination of the need for human work.

21 The depth of this problem requires a thoroughgoing and maybe radical rethinking, and first on the agenda must perhaps be the revision of what for many is a kind of first and axiomatic premise: the notion that "less work inevitably means less money." Some portion of most of us seems conditioned in an almost Pavlovian way to assent to this patently mistaken proposition. Major shortages of labor invoke in our minds at once images of long lines of people waiting for soup, or bread, or jobs: even the idea of shorter hours evokes in most people at once a corresponding inward calculation, that cuts the paycheck in the same proportion as the hours. This association is so false and so paralyzing that we cannot hope to advance any further unless that crude reflex is somehow interrupted.

22 The image of factories producing with a minimum of human labor should be a help. For better or worse we have reached the point where it is not totally misleading to think of a factory as analogous to a large mill, into which we pour fifteen or twenty different kinds of raw materials at one end, while the finished product drops out at the other. The quantity and the diversity and the sheer

wealth of things has almost no relationship at all to quantities of labor. Like it or not, the secret of grinding out infinite quantities of *things*—till they shove up against each other and rise up in heaps—*that* we have found. No one would have to be deprived of any of our recently developed comfort-giving niceties just because we collectively did less work. The exact opposite seems to be our problem: namely, that we seem unable to invent contraptions that would be complex enough to require the expense of our multiplying energies.

23 In a different, for us more authoritative and reassuring language: we do not have a problem of production, but only one of distribution. This much is clear enough; technology does not spell poverty or destitution to us as a whole or as a culture. From that point of view precisely the reverse is far more true. (Think of the proverbial agrarian republics!)

24 In the past two centuries work functioned as our main instrument of exchange. Not all, but many, could give foundations to the claim that they receive their share only in and through their work. What we are witnessing, therefore, is the collapse of our main means of distribution. But as with other currencies—and this is what work was for us—a revision in the measure, or a *revaluation* might be enough to rectify the situation.

25 One possible procedure through which we could adjust to the sudden drop in the need and the demand for labor is simply to let things take their course. This was the method of the Reagan administration, and in our view this is the worst course *both* for the 30 or 40% who might manage to defend their jobs and for the 60 to 70% who might eventually be unemployed. An alternative approach would basically move in the direction of cutting the working hours of every present job roughly in half; which might mean that one would go through a progression, from the four day workweek, to three days, and perhaps from there down to two. What would be some of the advantages of this different course?

26 In the present context we shall set the moral superiority of this approach deliberately to the side. That it would be fairer and more equitable and more humane is so blantantly evident that embellishing this with many words would only weaken that categorical consideration. That it would be more just is however far from the only claim that it could make. It may in addition have very practical and material benefits and some of these it is important to rehearse. For one, there probably would be very much less of the resistance to technology which we have just discussed, and one could argue that this by itself is very major; that this country cannot possibly regain its preeminence unless advanced technology can be moved in more quickly than has so far been the case, and that this reduction is therefore the only hope we have to regain our former place. But there also is the need for buyers and for markets. If the rich are not by any means the most reliable and fertile buyers, since high technology has brought extreme wealth closer to a barren self-enclosement, then the thought that halving people's jobs might provide us with twice as many persistent buyers than we would have otherwise cannot be ignored.

27 A third consideration is not entirely economical, but it also is not mainly moral. A continuing and escalating struggle over the shrinking quantity of jobs would not just soon pass the point of diminishing returns—it would be worse: more like the cliché of the exit from a theater through which all could safely pass if they were only calm, which, however, instead is blocked shut by a mad onrush in which people die. To work only half as much would *not* hurt us; it would not even mean that we would have to live a much more frugal life. It would make room for a more effective and efficient technology that in all likelihood would more than compensate us for the loss—and there would be no unemployed. But if we cannot move intelligently and quietly through the transition period, then we may gradually work our way up into a frenzied and ferocious and yet wholly pointless struggle.

28 Despite these advantages there is one respect in which this second course would still be senseless and clumsy and debilitating, and though this one respect at first seems minor it is actually decisive, like the short span of a railroad switch that in itself seems brief and that yet makes the difference between our ending up in Canada if it is set in one way, or our arriving in Mexico if it points to the other. This crucial difference concerns the timing. To work on a schedule where one would have three and one half days work and then three and one half days off would be flagrantly wasteful and demoralizing for those who do the work. One would be perpetually in a state of transition, just finding one's stride when one again would be interrupted, and again barely adjusting to one's work-free time when one would again be going back to work. But the worst absurdity involved in giving to one's life this structure is that it makes it virtually impossible to undertake anything either purposeful or productive in these short bits of work-free time.

29 Most people's work takes place in a powerful and established external order which gives at once content and structure to that portion of their lives. The work-free time, however, has been gradually drained and emptied as we became more modern and more atomized, and everything that gave content to traditional life, from the rituals and ceremonies of religion down to the larger and more coherent family was slowly undermined and weakened.

30 This is a large part of the problem that our way of dealing with the sudden implosion of the quantity of labor seeks to address. We should turn away sharply from the parcelling out of both work and free time in small crouton-sized bits. Instead we should compress and pull together the chips of each until life would be structured into larger and more satisfying blocks. One could work intensely and concentratedly for six months for example and then have six months of work-free time; and for many it might be better to divide the time by years, or even into stretches of two or three or still more years.

31 On the surface this might seem like a marginal and not far-reaching difference. But that is seriously deceptive. How very large a change this rearranging of a schedule, of the bare slots of time would actually bring about is hard to imagine or to convey. One way of doing it might be to propose that we now face a vastly more complex and deeper problem than the one which we

addressed so far. The current antiquated mode of parcelling work out managed to paper this second problem over, but now that cover has been torn. As long as people's work-free time came in small frustrating bits, the uselessness of it, the fact that it was for many people not much more than a morose and sullen waiting, a stretch of "quiet desperation," could be hidden. But if one pictures a life in which the sum total of job time is reduced from forty or forty-five to twenty years and where these twenty years come perhaps in two or three or four concentrated blocks, then one is forced to ask: and what will people do in their work-free time? How will it be filled and used, what meaning will we give to it; and what ends will it be made to serve? . . .

32 If the question is what people will do in the large stretches of work-free time, one could as part of a preliminary shorthand answer say:

33 1) That it is of course true that many people now spend their leisure time in sad and silly ways, but that this may in considerable part be the *result* of the kind of work they do (or rather, of what their work does to them)—and crucially may be the effect of the timing and scheduling that we arrange. Many people would probably do much better—if they had a whole year instead of many three-day weekends, and importantly also if they had stretches of job-free time earlier in life and not only after they are 65.

34 2) Giving people empty time is no different from surrounding them with empty space—one can suffocate in both. Yet there also is no reason why this would have to occur. If one seriously wanted to create a culture that fostered individuality one would have to devise a gamut of institutions which encourage and support people in the enterprises and endeavors that they would pursue in their job-free times. These institutions might give information, and counsel, and help organize, and much more. More broadly and more basically, one certainly would need a wholly different system of education. (One of the grossest absurdities of our present course is that we tailor education more and more to jobs, just at the point at which jobs occupy an ever smaller portion of our lives.) But these would only be first steps. So much more beyond this could be done that one in effect would be creating a new culture: Culture after the Elimination of Labor.

35 3) There should be no confusion: we are in the beginning of a great scarcity of jobs—but not of work. If people had rotating jobs they perhaps at last would have time to do some of the work that has not been gotten done: maybe they would have time to rebuild the cities and the roads, time to care for the old and to raise children, and time to make a saner world.

36 If the question is what actions we can take to bring about the transition to rotating work schedules, then one could perhaps suggest:

37 1) The notion of rotating work schedules is not new and not untried. In the last ten years many companies in many different countries (in Sweden, Germany, and Yugoslavia, for example, but also in the United States) have experimented with alternatives to the rote 8-hour day and 40-hour week. By now there exists a large literature on the subject. Many have pointed out that some of the various rotating work schedules have in addition to the large societal ad-

vantages which we surveyed, a good number of diverse, more fine-grained "operational" benefits. These include: increased productivity, better morale, the capacity to attract a more qualified workforce, reduced absenteeism, fewer burnouts, greater flexibility in relation to one's personnel during high and low work seasons, and more of the like. This means that many companies may make the transition to rotating work schedules with much less resistance than one might expect, and that the providing of information and of explanations in the transition is quite particularly important. (In a few cases that by itself may be sufficient.)

38 2) No discussion with either union members or union leaders should pretend that everyone is sitting calmly in their studies—the unions are fighting for their lives, and there are many kinds of conversations for which they now have, understandably, neither the time nor the inclination. But with that understanding one could nonetheless propose that the current situation will almost certainly become much worse, and that therefore deep and serious reconsiderations are entirely practical and needed. Unions might conduct new kinds of negotiations for new and different contracts. These contracts could provide that there are no further layoffs; that the job time from here on in will be divided equitably among union members, and that a transition will be made to rotating work schedules. (One could think in terms of 3 or 4 shifts where one shift is "rotated out" for 3 or 6 or 12 months.) Crucial to these contracts would be that reliable provision would be made for the job-free times. Most obviously these could of course be used for retraining, but as one would grow more accustomed to rotating work schedules one could include "Community Service Projects." (In cooperation with other unions one could work on hospitals, roads, recreation parks, and much else.) In a city like Detroit or a town like Flint the automobile companies must improve their public relations, and the companies might therefore be receptive to such a proposal. In addition one could make provisions that would encourage and allow the workers to be economically productive in their job-free times. (Included in this would be a variety of projects that would make life more economical: one could undertake to reduce the cost of heat [in one's own house], or the cost of one's housing, or of one's food and the like.)

39 An individual worker would derive his or her income during a job-free period from at least five different sources: a) The profits of the company might be higher, since higher technology could be introduced with less resistance. Some of these profits might be shared. b) The companies might contribute—as they do now to health insurance and the like. c) Workers might pay contributions—as they do now to Social Security. d) Various levels of government should pay since funds otherwise needed to support the unemployed, and to cover the costs which they create, would be freed. e) Quite significantly: indirect income might be derived from the activities engaged in during job-free times.

40 3) At the present moment the idea of a rotating work schedule is still strange, but conceivably that could change rather quickly. (In principle it is no different from rationing gasoline or food.) If it were possible to familiarize

people with the justification for, and the reasoning behind this innovation then political candidates could include rotating work schedules into the measures which they advocate. All candidates will be asked with increasing insistence for their answer to unemployment, and rotating work schedules might be part of the answer that some candidates could soon give. The more particular and specific ways in which either the city, or the state, or the federal government could promote the institution of rotating work schedules can be easily imagined. (A program involving "model companies" that had such schedules would be one example.)

41 4) There could and should be a major effort to "organize the unemployed." The difficulties that stand in the way of this are evident, but as the number of the unemployed increases the need to give them political voice and force will of course grow commensurately—and with that also the possibilities of achieving this. An organization of the unemployed could demand and exercise pressure for the institution of rotating work schedules.

42 The transition will be gradual even under the best of circumstances. But the fact that one could work towards the realization of this goal in so many forms and also in so many places makes it more likely that it can be reached.

QUESTIONS FOR WRITING AND DISCUSSION

OBSERVING

1. Bergmann calls attention to a number of trends (changes in the status of labor unions and in attitudes toward work regulations are two examples) visible to him when he published this essay in 1983. List as many as you can and, looking at them from your perspective a decade and a half later, comment on the accuracy of ones you know something about.
2. Why is it, according to Bergmann, that the "Third World" is not likely to provide us with jobs by offering new markets?
3. Bergmann says he makes "no simplistic and oracular predictions," by which apparently he means we will find no words like "looming disaster," not even the words used in our headnote: "impending economic crisis." But do you find his analysis disturbing? Why? What is the effect of his not using such loaded language? Or would you argue that his description of the possible "South Americanization" of the United States is at least a veiled oracular prediction?

EVALUATING

1. Bergmann associates the notion of a "trickle down" economic effect with Adam Smith. This is not, of course, Smith's metaphor, but how is it similar, and how different from Smith's "invisible hand"?

2. Compare Bergmann's claim in 1983 that "a simple upturn of the economy" or "simply to let things take their course" will not solve the problems he outlines with Lutterbeck's description in the chapter prelude of the state of our economy at the end of 1995? Where do you think Bergmann was right, where wrong?
3. How practical do you think Bergmann's proposed solution is? Analyze its strengths and weaknesses and make your own recommendation about whether it ought to be pursued.

RESPONDING AND APPLYING

1. Are there practical ways Bergmann's notion of rethinking our attitude toward work could be initiated? Investigate the possibility by finding out about Bergmann's work with the Center for New Work, which he helped establish in Flint, Michigan, a city especially hard hit by industrial unemployment.
2. The results of an international study by the Paris-based Organization for Economic Cooperation and Development show that the gap between rich and poor was greater in the United States during the 1980s than in any other industrialized nation. This study was released too late in 1995 to be used by Lutterbeck, but it is consistent with her data and with Bergmann's conclusion: "We do not have a problem of production, but only one of distribution." While very few Americans today would advocate Marxist ideas of abolition of private property, most would agree that a reasonably equitable distribution of available wealth, however we define "reasonably equitable," is an indication of a just society, and that where that distribution is weighted too far in one direction, we are not likely to find a land of equal opportunity. What are some of the ways societies, including our own, have controlled the distribution of wealth? Are there any that we aren't already doing that seem to you worth trying in the United States?
3. Many economists do not agree that the degree of inequality of income distribution in the United States is a problem, especially if the rich invest their wealth productively. They argue instead thar our increase in poverty is the result of other factors like the breakdown of the American family and the rise in the number of unwed mothers. Do you find this a better or worse explanation of the problem? What assumptions about the nature of humanity and of economics lie behind these two views?

TONI CADE BAMBARA, "THE LESSON" *FROM* GORILLA MY LOVE

Whether Marx was right that the history of all society is the history of class struggle, it is impossible to doubt that class struggle is an important aspect of history. Charles Beard has shown that this so even in America, where class divisions are usually assumed to be less important and less well defined than in the so-called old world. It is also clear that Marxist thought has had its greatest appeal where class divisions have been most pronounced, and Clifford Odets has shown how frustrating it can be for one who believes himself oppressed in what is supposed to be a freely competitive society: the cards are stacked against him, and when he loses, "the money man . . . says, what's the matter you can't win—no stuff on the ball." This frustration is even worse when the class divisions are defined in terms of visibly ethnic differences like skin color. Injustice seems inescapable and becomes so much a part of life that for many it is not even seen as injustice. But once perceived, there is released the kind of anger that breeds revolutionary thought. This is the kind of situation Toni Cade Bambara deals with in her short story "The Lesson."

Bambara was born Toni Cade in New York City in 1939; in 1970, she added Bambara, a name she learned was associated with her grandmother's family. She grew up in the New York City boroughs of Harlem, Bedford-Stuyvesant, Queens, and Jersey City, New Jersey. Her education was an unusually rich combination of the informal and the formal. Of her informal education she has said, "As a kid with an enormous appetite for knowledge and a gift for imagining myself anywhere in the universe, I always seemed to be drawn to the library or to some music spot or to 125th Street and Seventh Avenue, Speaker's Corner, to listen to Garveyites, Father Diviners, Rastafarians, Muslims, trade unionists, communists, Pan-Africanists." Her formal education included a B.A. in theater arts and English from Queens College, City University of New York (1959), and an M.A. in modern American fiction from City College of New York (1964). In between, she managed to study most of one year in Europe at the University of Florence and the Ecole de Mime Etienne Decroux in Paris, to work in New York as a social worker and as a recreational and occupational therapist for a hospital psychiatric division, to volunteer her time directing or coordinating numerous local neighborhood programs, and to write.

She has gone on to teach at several colleges and universities, including positions as associate professor at Livingston College in New Jersey and writer in residence at Spellman College in Atlanta. During this time, she continued her involvement in civil rights and community issues, especially those related to blacks and women. She has also edited two first-of-their-kind anthologies, *The Black Woman* (1970) and *Tales and Stories for Black Folks* (1971); has published two short story collections, from the first of which, *Gorilla My Love* (1972), the story below is taken; and has written a novel, *The Salt Eaters* (1980).

"The Lesson" takes place in the late 1940s or early 1950s, certainly before the mid-century civil rights movement began in America. The story illustrates how oppression breeds its greatest ally, ignorance, which deprives its victims not only of the means of improving themselves, but even of the knowledge of that oppression. Mrs. Moore, one of the two central characters, is one of those heroic black women who struggled against that ignorance to pass on her own sense of dignity and purpose and create the basis in awareness for change.

The Lesson

Toni Cade Bambara

1 Back in the days when everyone was old and stupid or young and foolish and me and Sugar were the only ones just right, this lady moved on our block with nappy hair and proper speech and no makeup. And quite naturally we laughed at her, laughed the way we did at thc junk man who went about his business like he was some big-time president and his sorry-ass horse his secretary. And we kinda hated her too, hated the way we did the winos who cluttered up our parks and pissed on our handball walls and stank up our hallways and stairs so you couldn't halfway play hide-and-seek without a goddamn gas mask. Miss Moore was her name. The only woman on the block with no first name. And she was black as hell, cept for her feet, which were fish-white and spooky. And she was always planning these boring-ass things for us to do, us being my cousin, mostly, who lived on the block cause we all moved North the same time and to the same apartment then spread out gradual to breathe. And our parents would yank our heads into some kinda shape and crisp up our clothes so we'd be presentable for travel with Miss Moore, who always looked like she was going to church, though she never did. Which is just one of the things the grownups talked about when they talked behind her back like a dog. But when she came calling with some sachet she'd sewed up or some gingerbread she'd made or some book, why then they'd all be too embarrassed to turn her down and we'd get handed over all spruced up. She'd been to college and said it was only right that she should take responsibility for the young ones' education, and she not even related by marriage or blood. So they'd go for it. Specially Aunt Gretchen. She was the main gofer in the family. You got some ole dumb shit foolishness you want somebody to go for, you send for Aunt Gretchen. She been screwed into the go-along for so long, it's a blood-deep natural thing with her. Which is how she got saddled with me and Sugar and Junior in the first place while our mothers were in a la-de-da apartment up the block having a good ole time.

2 So this one day Miss Moore rounds us all up at the mailbox and it's puredee hot and she's knockin herself out about arithmetic. And school suppose to let up in summer I heard, but she don't never let up. And the starch in my pinafore

scratching the shit outta me and I'm really hating this nappy-head bitch and her goddamn college degree. I'd much rather go to the pool or to the show where it's cool. So me and Sugar leaning on the mailbox being surly, which is a Miss Moore word. And Flyboy checking out what everybody brought for lunch. And Fat Butt already wasting his peanut-butter-and-jelly sandwich like the pig he is. And Junebug punchin on Q.T.'s arm for potato chips. And Rosie Giraffe shifting from one hip to the other waiting for somebody to step on her foot or ask her if she from Georgia so she can kick ass, preferably Mercedes'. And Miss Moore asking us do we know what money is, like we a bunch of retards. I mean real money, she say, like it's only poker chips or monopoly papers we lay on the grocer. So right away I'm tired of this and say so. And would much rather snatch Sugar and go to the Sunset and terrorize the West Indian kids and take their hair ribbons and their money too. And Miss Moore files that remark away for next week's lesson on brotherhood, I can tell. And finally I say we oughta get to the subway cause it's cooler and besides we might meet some cute boys. Sugar done swiped her mama's lipstick, so we ready.

3 So we heading down the street and she's boring us silly about what things cost and what our parents make and how much goes for rent and how money ain't divided up right in this country. And then she gets to the part about we all poor and live in the slums, which I don't feature. And I'm ready to speak on that, but she steps out in the street and hails two cabs just like that. Then she hustles half the crew in with her and hands me a five-dollar bill and tells me to calculate 10 percent tip for the driver. And we're off. Me and Sugar and Junebug and Flyboy hangin out the window and hollering to everybody, putting lipstick on each other cause Flyboy a faggot anyway, and making farts with our sweaty armpits. But I'm mostly trying to figure how to spend this money. But they all fascinated with the meter ticking and Junebug starts laying bets as to how much it'll read when Flyboy can't hold his breath no more. Then Sugar lays bets as to how much it'll be when we get there. So I'm stuck. Don't nobody want to go for my plan, which is to jump out at the next light and run off to the first bar-b-que we can find. Then the driver tells us to get the hell out cause we there already. And the meter reads eighty-five cents. And I'm stalling to figure out the tip and Sugar say give him a dime. And I decide he don't need it bad as I do, so later for him. But then he tries to take off with Junebug foot still in the door so we talk about his mama something ferocious. Then we check out that we on Fifth Avenue and everybody dressed up in stockings. One lady in a fur coat, hot as it is. White folks crazy.

4 "This is the place," Miss Moore say, presenting it to us in the voice she uses at the museum. "Let's look in the windows before we go in."

5 "Can we steal?" Sugar asks very serious like she's getting the ground rules squared away before she plays. "I beg your pardon," say Miss Moore, and we fall out. So she leads us around the windows of the toy store and me and Sugar screamin, "This is mine, that's mine, I gotta have that, that was made for me, I was born for that," till Big Butt drowns us out.

6 "Hey, I'm goin to buy that there."

7 "That there? You don't even know what it is stupid."

8 "I do so," he say punchin on Rosie Giraffe. "It's a microscope."

9 "Whatcha gonna do with a microscope, fool?"

10 "Look at things."

11 "Like what, Ronald?" ask Miss Moore. And Big Butt ain't got the first notion. So here go Miss Moore gabbing about the thousands of bacteria in a drop of water and the somethinorother in a speck of blood and the million and one living things in the air around us is invisible to the naked eye. And what she say that for? Junebug go to town on that "naked" and we rolling. Then Miss Moore ask what it cost. So we all jam into the window smudgin it up and the price tag say $300. So then she ask how long'd take for Big Butt and Junebug to save up their allowances. "Too long," I say, "Yeh," adds Sugar, "outgrown it by that time." And Miss Moore say no, you never outgrow learning instruments. "Why, even medical students and interns and," blah, blah, blah. And we ready to choke Big Butt for bringing it up in the first damn place.

12 "This here costs four hundred eighty dollars," says Rosie Giraffe. So we pile up all over her to see what she pointin out. My eyes tell me it's a chunk of glass cracked with something heavy, and different-color inks dripped into the splits, then the whole thing put into a oven or something. But for $480 it don't make sense.

13 "That's a paperweight made of semi-precious stones fused together under tremendous pressure," she explains slowly, with her hands doing the mining and all the factory work.

14 "So what's a paperweight?" asks Rosie Giraffe.

15 "To weigh paper with, dumbbell," say Flyboy, the wise man from the East.

16 "Not exactly," say Miss Moore, which is what she say when you warm or way off too. "It's to weigh paper down so it won't scatter and make your desk untidy." So right away me and Sugar curtsy to each other and then to Mercedes who is more the tidy type.

17 "We don't keep paper on top of the desk in my class," say Junebug, figuring Miss Moore crazy or lyin one.

18 "At home, then," she say. "Don't you have a calendar and pencil case and a blotter and a letter-opener on your desk at home where you do your homework?" And she know damn well what our homes look like cause she nosys around in them every chance she gets.

19 "I don't even have a desk," say Junebug. "Do we?"

20 "No. And I don't get no homework neither," says Big Butt.

21 "And I don't even have a home," say Flyboy like he do at school to keep the white folks off his back and sorry for him. Send this poor kid to camp posters, is his specialty.

22 "I do," says Mercedes. "I have a box of stationery on my desk and a picture of my cat. My godmother bought the stationery and the desk. There's a big rose on each sheet and the envelopes smell like roses."

23 "Who wants to know about your smelly-ass stationery," say Rosie Giraffe fore I can get my two cents in.

24 "It's important to have a work area all your own so that . . ."

25 "Will you look at this sailboat, please," say Flyboy, cuttin her off and pointin to the thing like it was his. So once again we tumble all over each other to gaze at this magnificent thing in the toy store which is just big enough to maybe sail two kittens across the pond if you strap them to the posts tight. We all start reciting the price tag like we in assembly. "Handcrafted sailboat of fiberglass at one thousand one hundred ninety-five dollars."

26 "Unbelievable," I hear myself say and am really stunned. I read it again for myself just in case the group recitation put me in a trance. Same thing. For some reason this pisses me off. We look at Miss Moore and she lookin at us, waiting for I dunno what.

27 "Who'd pay all that when you can buy a sailboat set for a quarter at Pop's, a tube of glue for a dime, and a ball of string for eight cents? It must have a motor and a whole lot else besides," I say. "My sailboat cost me about fifty cents."

28 "But will it take water?" say Mercedes with her smart ass.

29 "Took mine to Alley Pond Park once," say Flyboy. "String broke. Lost it. Pity."

30 "Sailed mine in Central Park and it keeled over and sank. Had to ask my father for another dollar."

31 "And you got the strap," laugh Big Butt. "The jerk didn't even have a string on it. My old man wailed on his behind."

32 Little Q.T. was staring hard at the sailboat and you could see he wanted it bad. But he too little and somebody'd just take it from him. So what the hell. "This boat for kids, Miss Moore?"

33 "Parents silly to buy something like that just to get all broke up," say Rosie Giraffe.

34 "That much money it should last forever," I figure.

35 "My father'd buy it for me if I wanted it."

36 "Your father, my ass," say Rosie Giraffe getting a chance to finally push Mercedes.

37 "Must be rich people shop here," say Q.T.

38 "You are a very bright boy," say Flyboy. "What was your first clue?" And he rap him on the head with the back of his knuckles, since Q.T. the only one he could get away with. Though Q.T. liable to come up behind you years later and get his licks in when you half expect it.

39 "What I want to know is," I says to Miss Moore though I never talk to her, I wouldn't give the bitch that satisfaction, "is how much a real boat costs? I figure a thousand'd get you a yacht any day."

40 "Why don't you check that out," she says, "and report back to the group?" Which really pains my ass. If you gonna mess up a perfectly good swim day least you could do is have some answers. "Let's go in," she say like she got something up her sleeve. Only she don't lead the way. So me and Sugar turn the

corner to where the entrance is, but when we get there I kinda hang back. Not that I'm scared, what's there to be afraid of, just a toy store. But I feel funny, shame. But what I got to be shamed about? Got as much right to go in as anybody. But somehow I can't seem to get hold of the door, so I step away from Sugar to lead. But she hangs back too. And I look at her and she looks at me and this is ridiculous. I mean, damn, I have never ever been shy about doing nothing or going nowhere. But then Mercedes steps up and then Rosie Giraffe and Big Butt crowd in behind and shove, and next thing we all stuffed into the doorway with only Mercedes squeezing past us, smoothing out her jumper and walking right down the aisle. Then the rest of us tumble in like a glued-together jigsaw done all wrong. And people looking at us. And it's like the time me and Sugar crashed into the Catholic church on a dare. But once we got in there and everything so hushed and holy and the candles and the bowin and the handkerchiefs on all the drooping heads, I just couldn't go through with the plan. Which was for me to run up to the altar and do a tap dance while Sugar played the nose flute and messed around in the holy water. And Sugar kept givin me the elbow. Then later teased me so bad I tied her up in the shower and turned it on and locked her in. And she'd be there till this day if Aunt Gretchen hadn't finally figured I was lying about the boarder takin a shower.

41 Same thing in the store. We all walkin on tiptoe and hardly touchin the games and puzzles and things. And I watched Miss Moore who is steady watchin us like she waitin for a sign. Like Mama Drewery watches the sky and sniffs the air and takes note of just how much slant is in the bird formation. Then me and Sugar bump smack into each other, so busy gazing at the toys, specially the sailboat. But we don't laugh and go into our fat-lady bump-stomach routine. We just stare at that price tag. Then Sugar run a finger over the whole boat. And I'm jealous and want to hit her. Maybe not her, but I sure want to punch somebody in the mouth.

42 "Watcha bring us here for, Miss Moore?"

43 "You sound angry, Sylvia. Are you mad about something?" Givin me one of them grins like she tellin a grown-up joke that never turns out to be funny. And she's lookin very closely at me like maybe she planning to do my portrait from memory. I'm mad, but I won't give her that satisfaction. So I slouch around the store bein very bored and say, "Let's go."

44 Me and Sugar at the back of the train watchin the tracks whizzin by large then small then getting gobbled up in the dark. I'm thinkin about this tricky toy I saw in the store. A clown that somersaults on a bar then does chin-ups just cause you yank lightly at his leg. Cost $35. I could see me askin my mother for a $35 birthday clown. "You wanna who that costs what?" she'd say, cocking her head to the side to get a better view of the hole in my head. Thirty-five dollars could buy new bunk beds for Junior and Gretchen's boy. Thirty-five dollars and the whole household could go visit Granddaddy Nelson in the country. Thirty-five dollars would pay for the rent and the piano bill too. Who are these people that spend that much for performing clowns and $1000 for toy sailboats? What

kinda work they do and how they live and how come we ain't in on it? Where we are is who we are, Miss Moore always pointin out. But it don't necessarily have to be that way, she always adds then waits for somebody to say that poor people have to wake up and demand their share of the pie and don't none of us know what kind of pie she talking about in the first damn place. But she ain't so smart cause I still got her four dollars from the taxi and she sure ain't gettin it. Messin up my day with this shit. Sugar nudges me in my pocket and winks.

45 Miss Moore lines us up in front of the mailbox where we started from, seem like years ago, and I got a headache for thinkin so hard. And we lean all over each other so we can hold up under the draggy-ass lecture she always finishes us off with at the end before we thank her for borin us to tears. But she just looks at us like she readin tea leaves. Finally she say, "Well, what did you think of F. A. O. Schwarz?"

46 Rosie Giraffe mumbles, "White folks crazy."

47 "I'd like to go there again when I get my birthday money," says Mercedes, and we shove her out the pack so she has to lean on the mailbox by herself.

48 "I'd like a shower. Tiring day," say Flyboy.

49 Then Sugar surprises me by sayin, "You know, Miss Moore, I don't think all of us here put together eat in a year what that sailboat costs." And Miss Moore lights up like somebody goosed her. "And?" she say, urging Sugar on. Only I'm standin on her foot so she don't continue.

50 "Imagine for a minute what kind of society it is in which some people can spend on a toy what it would cost to feed a family of six or seven. What do you think?"

51 "I think," say Sugar pushing me off her feet like she never done before, cause I whip her ass in a minute, "that this not much of a democracy if you ask me. Equal chance to pursue happiness means an equal crack at the dough, don't it?" Miss Moore is besides herself and I am disgusted with Sugar's treachery. So I stand on her foot one more time to see if she'll shove me. She shuts up, and Miss Moore looks at me, sorrowfully I'm thinkin. And somethin weird is goin on, I can feel it in my chest.

52 "Anybody else learn anything today?" lookin dead at me. I walk away and Sugar has to run to catch up and don't even seem to notice when I shrug her arm off my shoulder.

53 "Well, we got four dollars anyway," she says.

54 "Uh hunh."

55 "We could go to Hascombs and get half a chocolate layer and then go to the Sunset and still have plenty money for potato chips and ice cream sodas."

56 "Uh hunh."

57 "Race you to Hascombs," she say.

58 We start down the block and she gets ahead which is O.K. by me cause I'm going to the West End and then over to the Drive to think this day through. She can run if she want to and even run faster. But ain't nobody gonna beat me at nuthin.

QUESTIONS FOR WRITING AND DISCUSSION

OBSERVING

1. Notice the physical features of Mrs. Moore that Sylvia, the narrator, dislikes: "nappy hair and proper speech and no makeup . . . [and] black as hell." Why are these features significant to Sylvia? What do they reveal about Mrs. Moore?
2. Describe Sylvia's attitude toward education. What specific elements of her environment account for that attitude?
3. The $35.00 toy clown becomes an economic yardstick for Sylvia. Compare the toy clown with all the other things the $35.00 could pay for, and consider what that clown would cost in today's dollars.

EVALUATING

1. What is the significance of the lady dressed in a fur coat in the summer and of Sylvia's response, "White folks crazy"? Argue that the story is or is not critical of "white" behaviors and attitudes. Why is the same response being spoken by another of the youngsters near the end of the story?
2. What is Mrs. Moore trying to teach the youngsters about "real money," and why is it important? How does it relate to what Bambara considers the root cause of injustice in her society?
3. Trace the development of Sylvia's emotional responses. Why is she surly, then bored, ashamed as she starts to enter toy store, and then angry? Why is so much of her anger directed at her cousin Sugar? Is another kind of emotion emerging at the end of the story when she says, "But ain't nobody gonna beat me at nuthin"?
4. Argue that Mrs. Moore is either an educator or agitator. Is it possible to work among a deprived group as an educator without being an agitator?

RESPONDING AND APPLYING

1. Argue whether America's racial problems are really problems of class. Might our society better handle racial problems if they were approached as class problems?
2. On the basis of this story (admittedly a small sample on which to base a generalization) would you describe Bambara as Marxist, Marxian, or something else? To what extent do you think Marx can help us deal with the social problems revealed in the story?
3. It is common to hear from the pulpit and to read in magazines and newspapers of the disintegration of the American family. Review some you have heard, and consider how often poverty is described as a major cause of this problem. What do you conclude about the state of social consciousness in America?

4. It is sometimes said that anticapitalist arguments are basically arguments for the redistribution of wealth, that is, taking from the wealthy and giving to the poor. It is also sometimes said that all arguments for the redistribution of wealth are basically pro-Marxist. Is either statement fair? Would you consider government-sponsored social relief programs or the graduated income tax as means of redistributing wealth?
5. Faced with the problem of injustice as it is presented in Bambara's story, how would you define the difference between the ideal response of a Jew or Christian, a humanist, and a Marxist? Describe what you think is the best response (one or some combination of these three, or something entirely your own), making clear your criteria for what you consider "best."

PERSPECTIVES

Morality, the Free Market, and Class

The struggle we have seen developing over the last two and a half centuries between the advocates of classical economics and those who question whether the "free market" is in fact free continues raging today. The essays that follow take opposite sides on this issue which, perhaps more than any other, affects people's positions on the wide variety of social policy questions facing us today and likely to be facing us for the next several decades. Most significantly, both consider the relation between economics and morality.

PAUL JOHNSON, "THE CAPITALISM & MORALITY DEBATE"

Paul Johnson (1928–) is a distinguished British historian and chronicler of the history of ideas whose works on Judaism, *A History of the Jews* (1987), and Christianity, *The History of Christianity* (1985), have received plaudits internationally for their careful historical accuracy and sensitivity. His *Modern Times* (1983) is considered by many a classic historical overview of the twentieth century, its major events and ideas, and its links to the past. A more recent and more controversial book, *Intellectuals* (1988), surveys the lives of prominent thinkers—among them Jean-Jacques Rousseau, Karl Marx, and Ernest Hemingway—in a provocative philosophical critique of what Johnson believes are their dubious intellectual contributions.

In this essay, Johnson confronts the moral dilemmas that capitalism seems to raise. If one grants that the free enterprise and market system is indeed best suited to creating wealth for the majority of a society's citizens, how then does one deal with the apparent gap between the standard of living of the rich and the poor in such a society? In accepting the premise that Marxist and socialist governments and economic systems are on the wane worldwide, Johnson asks how we may confront the issue of whether capitalism's arguably amoral stance can yield equitable and ethical relationships in society at large.

The Capitalism & Morality Debate

Paul Johnson

1 The decade of the 1980s has proved to be an ideological watershed. It has been marked by a huge resurgence of the power and efficacy of the capitalist market system and a corresponding collapse of confidence in the capacity of socialist "command economies." This loss of confidence in collectivism is the culmination of many decades of trial and misfortune. The truth is that, during the twentieth century, large parts of the world have given the collectivist alternative to capitalism a long, thorough, and staggeringly costly trial, and it seems to have failed absolutely everywhere. It was during the 1980s that this realization dawned even in the quarters most reluctant to admit it—among the rulers of the socialist-style states. Many of them are turning back—in despondency, almost in despair—to the despised market disciplines they had rejected.

2 Meanwhile the capitalist world is racing ahead and is creating wealth on a scale never before dreamed of. It is clear that capitalism, being a natural force rather than a contrived ideology, springing from instincts deep in our human natures, is modifying itself all the time, and we cannot foresee how it will evolve over the next century. But I am willing to predict, as a result of our experiences in this one, that never again will any considerable body of opinion seriously doubt its wealth-producing capacity or seek to replace it with something fundamentally different. We are near the end of an historical epoch in which capitalism has survived the collectivist assault and is now firmly reestablished as the world's primary way of conducting its economic business.

3 So where does this leave us? It leaves us, I suggest, with a considerable moral dilemma. I can state the dilemma in one sentence: how do we give a moral dimension to this triumphant reassertion of capitalism? For one thing we know: whereas wealth creation is essential to men's well-being, especially in a world where population is expanding so rapidly, it cannot in itself make men and women happy. We are creatures of the spirit as well as of the flesh, and we cannot be at ease with ourselves unless we feel we are fulfilling, however vaguely or imperfectly, a moral purpose. It is in this respect that capitalism, as such, is inadequate.

4 It is not that capitalism is immoral. Clergymen who insist that it is and preach against it are themselves confused, as were their predecessors a hundred years ago who insisted that any form of socialism was immoral. One can be a good Christian and a capitalist, just as one can be a good Christian and practice collectivism.

5 The trouble with capitalism is quite otherwise. It lies in its moral neutrality, its indifference to the notion of moral choices. Capitalism and the market system which gives it its efficiency and its power is single-minded in its thrust—that is why it is so productive. It is blind to all other factors: blind to class, race, and color, to religion and sex, to nationality and creed, to good and evil. It is materialist, impersonal, and nonhuman. It responds with great speed and accuracy to all the market factors. In a way it is like a marvelous natural computer. But it cannot make distinctions for which it is not programmed. It does not and cannot possess a soul and it therefore lacks a moral inclination one way or the other.

6 Indeed it is precisely because capitalism is morally indifferent—and so productive of great miseries as well as great blessings—that many idealists early in the nineteenth century saw it as evil, rejected it entirely, and sought to replace it. We have come to the end of that line of argument. We have discovered there is no effective substitue for the market. We have to accept capitalism as the primary means whereby wealth is produced and begin the process of moralization within its terms of reference. I say "begin," but in a sense we have been doing it for two hundred years—by factories acts, mines acts, by monopoly and fair-trading legislation, and by all the countless laws we devise to restrict ways in which the market system can be distorted by man's cupidity.

7 But these are merely negative attempts to correct the excesses of capitalism. They do not in themselves give capitalism a positive moral purpose. That is a quite different and much more difficult matter. The moment you start trying to give capitalism a moral purpose, you risk interfering with the basic market mechanism which provides its wealth-creating power. If, for instance, you try to use capitalism to promote greater equality of wealth by imposing on it a steeply progressive, redistributive system of taxation, you frustrate the way in which it rewards its chief dynamic force, the acquisitive impulse, and you are liable to end by making everyone poorer. Or if, to take another example, you try to redistribute power within capitalism by balancing managerial authority by trade union privileges, you either choke the entrepreneurial spirit or you eliminate profits—the system's life-blood—or, as a rule, you do both, and so again you end by making everyone poorer.

8 Almost all efforts to provide capitalism itself with a positive moral purpose run into the same difficulty. Great Britain, between 1945 and the end of the 1970s, was a classic case where repeated and often ingenious attempts were made to cudgel capitalism into a system of national redistribution of wealth. It was part socialism, part corporatism, and wholly inefficient. It was baptized by the moral-sounding name of "the mixed economy." In fact, by the end of the

1970s, it had come to resemble an ancient piece of do-it-yourself machinery, constructed by amateurs, held together by adhesive tape and emitting old-fashioned steam from every joint. The British economy had become one of the least efficient and productive in the Western world. In 1979 Mrs. Thatcher and her government began the return to true capitalism, but even after a decade of common sense reforms and rapid improvements in productivity, we calculate it will still take us another ten years or so to catch up with Germany and France, while the United States and Japan are still further beyond our reach.

9 That is the price of trying to make capitalism do something which is not in its nature to do—promote equality. The price is paid in the shape of reduced national wealth and income—lower general living standards, inadequate health care, a run-down transport system, impoverished social services, underfunded schools. These results have been repeated, in varying degrees, everywhere else in the world where attempts to invest capitalism with positive moral functions have been made. We have to accept that the market system, while exceedingly robust when left to itself, rapidly becomes sick and comatose once you try to force it to do things contrary to its nature. The more you interfere with its mechanism by imposing moral objectives the less efficiently it works. Indeed, under a sufficient weight of moral obligation, it will seize up altogether.

10 How do we escape from this difficulty? How can we practice capitalism, with its unrivaled capacity to produce wealth, within the framework of a society that recognizes moral objectives? To put it another way: is it possible to harness the power of market capitalism to moral purposes without destroying its dynamism? That is the real, practical question that faces humanity. And I often wish our Christian theologians would address themselves to it, instead of peremptorily dismissing capitalism as intrinsically evil, as so many of them thoughtlessly do.

11 I do not pretend the problem is easily solved. On the other hand, I think it is defeatist to regard it as inherently insoluble. It is a mistake to try to turn capitalism itself into a moral animal. But I think it is possible to run it in tandem with public policies that make use of its energy while steering it in a moral direction. Let me indicate a number of ways in which I believe this can happen.

12 First, and in some ways the most important, is to provide the capitalist economy with an overall legal framework which has a moral basis. This can only be done if we accept that a fundamental object of the just society is to establish, so far as is humanly possible, absolute equality before the law. Equality of wealth is a utopian fantasy whose hopeless pursuit usually leads to tyranny. But equality before the law is a reasonable objective, whose attainment—albeit in an imperfect form—is well within the reach of civilized modern societies. Moreover, this form of equality responds to a strong human need: for whereas few of us really want equality of possessions, or believe it possible, all of us want fairness. The notion of a fair society is an attractive concept, and one toward which progress can undoubtedly be made. Moreover equality before the

law is a necessary adjunct to the competitive nature of capitalism: the end result cannot be equality, but from start to finish the rules must apply equally to all.

13 What do we mean by equality before the law? We mean that the law must make no distinction of birth or caste, race or color, sex or tribe, wealth or poverty. It must hold the scales of justice blindfolded. In a curiously paradoxical way, the capitalist system similarly makes no distinction about the nature of men and women. Hence for the law so to distinguish is a gross interference with the market mechanism and makes it less efficient. Equality before the law reinforces the natural power of capitalism, so that in this case moral purpose and wealth creation go hand in hand. Inequality before the law takes many forms, some of them grotesque, as in the Republic of South Africa or the Soviet Union, some more subtle. Even in advanced Western societies like the United States, where the principle is well understood and established, the ability to buy more law than your neighbor is a ubiquitous source of inequality. In no society that I know is full equality before the law established in practice, and I do not say that it can be realized perfectly and overnight anywhere. But it is one form of equality that can be broadly attained without destructive side effects, and systematic progress toward it is an essential object of any society that wishes to place capitalism in a context of justice.

14 Another way to combine capitalism with moral purpose is for society to endorse the related but broader concept of equality of opportunity. It is one of the miracles of the human condition that all of us, however humble, possess talents of one kind or another, waiting to be of service. The notion that all of us have something to contribute is God-given and stands at the heart of the Judeo-Christian tradition. The range of talents is as infinite as human variety itself, and the society that is swiftest to identify them in each, and put them to use, will certainly be the most efficient (as well as just). Here again, capitalism and justice pursue the same ends, for capitalism thrives on meritocracy—one of the prime functions of the market is to identify and reward objective merit—and it creates wealth most rapidly when all obstacles to equality of opportunity, social and historic as well as purely legal, are removed. This aspect of equality is a vital element in the moral legitimation of capitalism, for an economic structure in which every man and woman, in theory at least, can progress from the lowest to the highest place cannot be held to be intrinsically unjust.

15 I say "in theory." What about in practice? It is unrealistic to talk of equality of opportunity without taking drastic measures to make high-quality education generally available to those who can profit from it. I know that in practice we are not going to get a society where all will be able to benefit from the standards of the best schools and colleges. To begin with, throughout human history the most gifted teachers have always been in limited supply—there are never enough to go around. In any case, the culture and habits of industry, which parents transmit to their children, make absolute equality of opportunity unattainable. But it is one thing to concede the difficulties, quite another to accept the present system of educational inequality, which exists to some degree

in every country in the world. There is no single way, in my view, more likely to make capitalism morally acceptable, to anchor its functions in justice, than by giving the poor access, by merit, to high quality education of every kind and at every stage. And it is implicit in this objective that we identify merit, of every variety, at the earliest possible age—another respect in which we tend to be woefully inept.

16 Of course, to educate the poor, according to aptitude, to the highest standards is enormously expensive. But it is the great merit of capitalism that it does produce wealth in immense quantities for such necessary purposes; and the more people we educate efficiently, the more wealth the system will produce. The matter is increasingly urgent for, as capitalism advances itself, it demands ever more refined skills at each level. If training in them is not available for all who can benefit, inequalities—both within societies and between them—will increase instead of diminish, and the moral credentials of the system will inevitably be subjected to growing challenge. We have, in short, to educate ourselves into justice, and to do so with all deliberate speed.

17 But we must not stop at access to education. We must see to it that there is more readiness of access to the capitalist system itself. I believe that the notion of "democratic capitalism" is a genuine one, and that its realization, to some degree at least, is within our grasp. There are many ways in which it can be brought about. Some are old. Some we have only recently discovered. Some are yet to be devised.

18 In the last half-century and more, we have found that to take an industry into public ownership in no way democratizes it—quite the contrary. Nationalization, whether in the form of a monolithic public corporation, as in the old British system, or through so-called "workers' control," as in Yugoslavia, for example, merely puts the business firmly into the hands of bureaucratic or union elites, or indeed both. But it is now possible, as has been found in Britain and elsewhere, to float public corporations so that they become the property of millions of small stockholders.

19 Let us not deceive ourselves that this conveys control of them to the masses. But it does spread ownership widely, and it does introduce an element of mass financial participation in the system that is new and healthy. It gives millions of humble, ordinary people a sense that they are no longer entirely victims of the system: that they act, as well as are acted upon; that to some small degree they have a stake in society. It is a source of pride, of reassurance, even of security, and it is thus morally significant.

20 Democratic capitalism also lends itself to the old but unrealized idea of co-ownership by giving the workforce easy entry into the purchase of stock. Over 90 percent, for instance, of those who work for the recently privatized British corporation British Telecom now hold stock in the firm—thus bridging the destructive and needless chasm that separates owners and workers and that promotes class warfare. In any great capitalist enterprise, the community of interest between those who own, run, and work for it is, or ought to be, far

greater than any conflict of interest. Access of workers to stock is the surest way of demonstrating this fundamental truth, which is often obscured by political sloganeering. This is particularly important in industries where the work is hard and dangerous and the profits high, such as mining and offshore oil extraction, to give two obvious examples. Democratic capitalism, and especially the worker-stock ownership aspect of it, serves to refute one of the gravest charges against capitalist practice—that it is, by its very nature, exploitative.

21 Stock ownership is not, however, the only or even the best way in which the notion of democratic capitalism can be pursued. One of the most important but least-understood disadvantages of the so-called "mixed economy" is that, in its inevitable drift to corporatism, it involves tripartite deals between government, labor unions, and large-scale capital. Such deals invariably leave out small businesses. In Britain, for instance, it is only since we have begun to dismantle mixed-economy corporatism that the needs of small businesses, and equally important, of those wishing to start them, have played any part in the formation of government policy.

22 Why have we been so remiss? Now that most of the world is necessarily turning its back on the soil, to start one's own business has replaced that fundamental human urge to farm one's own land—it is an expression of the natural creativity in man, and as such a profoundly moral impulse. Sensible, practical assistance in helping people to set up their own businesses, and to ensure a climate of fairness in which they operate, is the best way to promote, at one and the same time, equality of opportunity, democratic capitalism, and, not least, the efficiency and acceptability of the system as a whole. There is almost invariably a strong correlation between the number of small business starts and soundly based economic expansion. So here again the interests of justice and the process of wealth creation coincide.

23 Popular access to capitalism at a national level has its international counterpart in access to markets. The vigorous promotion of free trade is an important way in which capitalism is legitimized morally. Protectionism in any form tends to undermine capitalist efficiency by creating privileged industries, and it is unacceptable morally because it deprives the consumer of the full fruits of the market. It always appears to have advantages for new, small, and weak economies—or for old established ones meeting new and ruthless competition. But in the long term, and often in the short term too, these advantages are greatly outweighed by the drawbacks. Equally objectionable are barter deals between states, or deals between states and big international corporations. All these attempts to escape the rigors of competition invariably produce corruption and fraud and bring out the worst aspects both of big government and of capitalism itself. One might put it this way: international free trade is the global version of equality of opportunity.

24 But just as equal opportunities within a society are unlikely to become reality without general access to high-quality education, so free trade will not in practice be generally accepted, especially among the poorer countries, until the

huge discrepancies between nations in technical and commercial skills are diminished. I do not think that the normal workings of the international market will be recognized as just and reasonable until we narrow this gap, so much more important in the long run than any more obvious gap in living standards or financial resources. Yet here, perhaps, is the best way in which richer nations can effectively help the poorer ones.

25 Old-style aid is now discredited, and I think rightly so, for certainly there are few more foolish things than for a rich nation to salve its conscience by transferring cash to the government of a poor one, thus as a rule keeping an inefficient and unpopular tyranny in power. But it is another matter to use our resources to train the disadvantaged masses of the Third World—and indeed the emerging ex-communist world too—in the skills of market capitalism. By widening the availability of such skills, we do many things simultaneously: we benefit the poorer countries by enabling them to compete; we benefit ourselves by making it possible for them to open their markets to us; we strengthen the system by giving it universality as well as fairness; and consumers everywhere find goods cheaper as competition increases. Here again, the process of placing capitalism in a moral context has the additional advantage of adding to its wealth-creating power. To sum up my case: doing the right thing morally usually proves to be commercially the right thing to do as well.

26 However, I willingly concede that there is an important flaw in my argument. And it applies whether one looks at individual societies or at the global community—within nations and between them. However thoroughly one applies the principle of equality before the law, however ingeniously one provides equality of opportunity and universal access to high-quality education, bitter experience seems to show that a great many people remain in deprivation, misery, and hopelessness. It is not enough to provide individuals with an exit from this underclass. Its very existence, as a class, perpetuating itself from generation to generation, is or at least seems to be a categorical indictment of the capitalist market system itself.

27 In fact it does not truly reflect upon the market. The market can be made fair—to give it moral legitimacy it *must* be made fair—but what it cannot be made to do, at least not without wrecking it, is to discriminate in favor of failure. And we have to face the fact that many human beings, in any society, will fail however fair the rules and however wide the opportunities. There is overwhelming evidence that market capitalism can conquer mass want and create a very general affluence anywhere in the world. What we now have to demonstrate is that the societies in which capitalism is the energizing force can cope with the minority problem of failure. It is, in my judgment, the biggest single task our societies face today: a problem which is at one and the same time moral, economic, and political.

28 It is *moral* because we cannot accept, on a permanent basis, the exclusion of perhaps a fifth of society from a life of modest decency. Earlier ages had to reconcile themselves to permanent mass poverty. We *know* a solution can be found, and we have an inescapable moral obligation to find it.

29 It is *economic* because it is waste on a colossal scale. Often up to 50 percent of budgets are absorbed by coping with poverty. And it is not just material waste but waste of minds and hearts.

30 It is *political* because the percentage involved is too small to effect change through the democratic process. Thus, there is an inherent tendency to resort to violence, often with racial overtones—and a violence which possesses a kind of moral authority all its own.

31 The solutions tried up to now have been collectivist ones, so they have all failed. I believe we must now turn to entrepreneurial solutions and seek to use—the problem-solving mechanism of market capitalism, which has never failed us yet, to provide the answers.

32 The need is urgent, because the problem is already reproducing itself at the international level. It is right, as I have argued, to press steadily for the expansion of free trade, and for the richer nations to finance training programs and other devices to make such expansion fair and profitable to all. The majority of the global population can be progressively drawn into such a system.

33 But it would be misleading to suggest that all the nations are at present eligible. Indeed an underclass of nations, mainly but not exclusively in Africa, is developing too. What we observe in large parts of Africa is what might be called the Haiti Syndrome: entities nominally classified as states which have virtually fallen out of the international economy and which seemingly cannot provide for their citizens elementary justice or allow them to provide for themselves the basic necessities of life. In many cases, the miseries of these underclass nations are envenomed by civil war and frontier disputes among themselves. As they are at present organized and governed, there is nothing that capitalism can do for them—and socialism, to which most have resorted, merely compounds their problems. Indeed such underclass states seem inevitably to attract the worst exponents both of capitalism at its most unscrupulous and socialism at its most destructive. Where lies the remedy? Indeed, is there a remedy?

34 Certainly there is no obvious remedy within the common assumptions of the late twentieth century—that all states, whatever their origins and nature, are equally sovereign. In the nineteenth century, the existence of such failed societies, with abysmally low and falling living standards exacerbated by chronic violence, would have attracted the attentions of one or other of the colonial powers. Sooner or later a colonial power would have moved in, from moral motives as well as from hope of commercial and political gain. That would be inconceivable now.

35 Or would it? Has not the failure of decolonization, in some areas at least, been as spectacular and tragic as the general failure of collectivism? And is it unthinkable to revive the notion of national trusteeship, once so important a part of the League of Nations' work in the 1920s and 1930s? And if trusteeship is a valid concept, worth discussing in the international context, is it, or something like it, a useful idea to mull over in the context of the intractable problem of the internal underclass?

36 What I am suggesting is that in exploring the future potentialities of the capitalist market system and in devising ways in which society can consolidate its moral acceptability, we should keep an open mind to fresh ideas. We are at the end of one ideological era, the era in which collectivism was tried and found wanting. One thing history surely teaches is that when old ideas die, others rush in to fill the vacuum. For men and women need ideas as much as they need food and drink. If sensible and creative ideas are not forthcoming, we can be certain that dangerous and destructive ones will emerge to exert their spell. It is essential that those of us whose roots are still within the Judeo-Christian system of ethics, who value freedom, who strive for the just society, and who recognize the enormous productive potential of market capitalism should be fertile in ideas in the coming battle for minds. For if we get the ideas right, the opportunities for mankind in the next century are almost without limit.

QUESTIONS FOR WRITING AND DISCUSSION

OBSERVING

1. Explain Johnson's claim that capitalism is morally neutral.
2. According to Johnson, why do efforts to "provide capitalism itself with a positive moral purpose" fail?
3. The market, Johnson posits, can be made "fair," but it cannot be asked to "discriminate in favor of failure." What does he mean by this? Must "democratic capitalism" always be willing to accept a certain measure of individual failure so that the vast majority may reasonably prosper?

EVALUATING

1. Capitalism cannot "promote equality," says Johnson, if by that we mean something other than equality "before the law." What does *equality* entail: equal opportunity, equal legal status, preferred status for underrepresented groups, or something else? Do you agree with Johnson's basic understanding of how equality must work in a free market society? In what sense might his view of "equality" differ from that defined in the Declaration of Independence? Argue your position.
2. According to Johnson, how can capitalism be "combined with moral purpose"? Argue that these attempted adjustments would or would not avoid the same trap that plagues noncapitalist or anticapitalist societies, that is, the eventual state control of individual lives.
3. How may Johnson's concessions about capitalism's "failure" to provide moral guidance within a society serve the Marxist critique of the "bourgeoisie"? Argue whether such objections can be made against capitalism without subscribing to Marxist economics? Does opposition to capitalism's "excesses" commit one to a socialist or centrally planned economy?

4. Johnson argues on the one hand that capitalism is morally neutral, and on the other that "doing the right thing morally usually proves to be commercially the right thing to do as well." Argue whether these views are contradictory or compatible.

RESPONDING AND APPLYING

1. At one point in his argument, Johnson links "the notion that all of us have something to contribute" to society to the Judeo-Christian tradition. What is his basis for attributing this social platitude to the Biblical worldview? Do you find it plausible to credit the Bible for this notion?
2. While talking about some of capitalism's weaknesses, Johnson primarily focuses upon the problems of socialist economies and their typical "nationalization," a system wherein an economy—its means of production, its jobs, prices of goods, the training of workers and diversity of occupations available—is controlled by the state. Is there any middle ground between the totalitarian state and modern democracies? Or does any semblance of economic control by the state lend itself to totalitarian control in the lives of individuals?
3. Johnson describes capitalism as "immoral," "materialist, impersonal, and non-human," yet it "thrives on meritocracy—one of the prime functions of the market is to identify and reward objective merit." What kind of "merit" does this suggest that capitalism rewards in Johnson's view? He also says that "doing the right thing usually proves to be commercially the right thing to do as well." Are Johnson's views contradictory or compatible?
4. Johnson speaks of "democratic capitalism." Can there not also be "democratic socialism"? How would such a society be structured, and do any such societies exist now?
5. Although Johnson sees capitalism as a "natural force," "the primary means whereby wealth is produced," he concedes that some "underclass nations" are not at present capable of appreciating its benefits. Reminding us to "keep an open mind to fresh ideas," he suggests a modified form of colonialism as a possible solution to this problem. Explore what you think to be the ethics of this solution from a perspective based on your notion of one of the Great Ideas you have studied so far.
6. The degree of capitalist individualism or of socialist collectivism found to be appropriate to any given country is likely to be more a matter of national or regional cultural traditions than of universal law, whether the source of that law is some notion of morality or of historical necessity. How would Marx and Johnson each respond to this statement? How do you?
7. Imagine yourself to be Toni Cade Bambara. Having read Johnson's essay, how satisfied would you be with his analysis of the relation between capitalism and morality and the solutions he offers for the problem of the underclass?

Benjamin DeMott, "Public Policy in the Classless State"

Benjamin DeMott, who teaches at Amherst College in Massachusetts, has authored two novels, four books of social commentary, and numerous columns for magazines such as *The Atlantic, Harper's, The American Scholar, Change,* and *Entertainment Weekly.* In his book *The Imperial Middle: Why Americans Can't Think Straight about Class* (1990), he argues that public policy in America is "locked in distortion and lies" by the belief that ours is a classless society, that independence, individualism, and choice operate freely among a population "of men and women of the middle united as strivers and self-betterers." It is a belief that encourages, he maintains, a policy of acceptance of social wrong on the grounds that those who do not succeed are losers who have simply failed to take advantage of opportunities we all share equally and who therefore deserve their misery. It is a belief, moreover, that fosters self-loathing among some, a sense of being cheated among others—the rising tide of people who feel they are not cashing in on what the American dream claims all have an equal opportunity to achieve. This chapter from his book printed below shows how this attitude has manifested itself in public policy, but DeMott presents this discussion in the context of his thesis that class is very much a part of American society, and until we face that fact and deal with it honestly, we will not begin to solve the many problems of inequity that exist among us.

Public Policy in the Classless State

Benjamin DeMott

1 What exactly does it mean to say that American public policy is everywhere infected with the influence of the myth of classlessness? It means that publicly financed options, advantages, and programs theoretically available to all are in fact restricted, by official rulings and by the social distribution of civic and other competencies, to a favored few. It means that social problems resulting in significant measure from government-sanctioned or administered inequities are metamorphosed into incidents in a grand struggle between good and evil—a struggle represented by "realists" as lying beyond government intervention. It means that an endless succession of program failures is blamed on "bureaucracy," instead of upon the obscurantist, legislatively consecrated definitions of problems with which bureaucracy is obliged to work. It means the spread of doubt, by the media, concerning the feasibility of rational management of

public affairs. It means a descent by leaders into sentimental stoicism. And it means the threat of near-total governmental surrender to socioeconomic crisis.

2 In every situation American public policy displays obligatory solicitude for . . . the unconditioned individual, the person of will and ambition who builds identity solely from a moral core within and is in no significant measure socially determined. The beliefs underlying the solicitude are by now entirely familiar: individualistic choosing is the definitively American activity; citizens who don't participate in this central activity are found only on the margins of society; the differences between non-choosers (the tiny minority) and choosers (the often embattled but still vast majority) are moral and characterological in nature, not socioeconomic. Talk and decisions based on these beliefs can be moderate or extreme; the tone is adjusted to economic and political weather. The state negotiates accords between champions of social provision and proponents of strict observance of personal responsibility and self-discipline; its own official discourse includes both panegyric on moral individuals and the unconditioned self, and arguments for federal help for the helpless.

3 But no turn of political weather—no "emergency," no "problem"—ever lifts from the state the burden that the myth of classlessness imposes upon it: that of insisting on the representativeness—the place at center stage—of the unconditioned American. And from this felt obligation stem the consequences just named. Commitment to the legend of the average American as unfettered chooser makes it impossible for the state to take adequate account of the complex actualities of a class society. More than once in recent times the resulting state-administered class injustice has been not less than appalling in its human cost. And the longer-range consequences—the undermining of belief in the possibility of reasoned collective action—are yet more serious. Structured authority comes to be viewed as incapable of defending the interests of decency and fairness; suspicion mounts that nothing on earth can long stand in the path of brutality and fraud; a sense of futility and impotence becomes the norm.

4 By far the worst recent episode of state-administered class injustice occurred during the Vietnam war. Between America's formal entry into the war, in 1964, and the taking of Saigon by Viet Cong troops in 1973, 27 million men came of draft age; 60 percent of them—about 16 million—escaped military service. Then as now it was often assumed that the majority of the escapees were draft evaders who took flight to Canada, Sweden, or elsewhere; actually only about 3 percent of the 16 million (570,000) were draft offenders. Nine out of ten escapees missed the war because officially deferred, exempted, or disqualified on grounds of mental or physical handicap; most of these were sons of the imperial middle. And the inequities were directly traceable to the myth of classlessness—the influence ultimately responsible for official wrongheadedness in dealings with the draftee population.

5 During the war and after, the inequities were underpublicized; no formal hearings were held. But the story was no secret. General officers observing rifle companies rotating out of the line noted the absence of a cross section of Amer-

ican youth. "In the average rifle company," wrote General S. L. A. Marshall, "the strength was 50% composed of Negroes, Southwestern Mexicans, Puerto Ricans, Guamanians, Nisei, and so on." A Chicago-based wartime study, unofficial but methodologically sound, established that "youths from neighborhoods with low educational levels [were] four times as likely to die in Vietnam as youths from better-educated neigborhoods." A Wisconsin Congressman polled a randomly selected one hundred inductees from his district—unlucky youngsters, that is, who had missed out on deferments—and found that *all* belonged to families with incomes under $5,000. A Harvard *Crimson* editor learned—also by polling—that of the 1,200 members of the class of 1970, only two went to Vietnam. The Defense Department was apprised that a quarter of the Americans killed in combat in 1965 were blacks, and subsequently took steps to alter the racial balance of casualties; no action was ever taken to alter the class balance of casualties.

6 Social commentators with middle class bases were remarking, as early as 1972, that they "had never known a single family that had lost a son in Vietnam, or indeed, one with a son wounded, missing in action, or held prisoner of war." And by the mid-Seventies article writers had begun describing Vietnam explicitly as a "class war." . . .

7 Doctors, dentists, and psychiatrists who became specialists in draft avoidance labored chiefly for the advantaged. "The people we saw," said one doctor, "were all middle class. [The others] just never thought of going for professional help." Low-income youngsters knew nothing about the more exotic modes of help available to would-be draft avoiders—such as the infamous "order of call" defense employed by thousands. This scheme involved mathematical investigation of draft board records in search of evidence that boards had called up registrants out of the order specified by their lottery numbers; one mathematician formed a corporation called Draft Research Associates to run the investigations, charging each client $250. As for less exotic ways out (the National Guard, the reserves): these modes of service, in which "duty" often consisted of golf and bridge, were class preserves. "Reservists and guardsmen were better connected, better educated, more affluent, and whiter than their peers in the active forces," and minorities knew better than to apply.

8 What lay behind the multitude of imperial middle ploys, scams, hideouts? Mainly the ignorance of officialdom. Officials didn't know (or didn't know it mattered) that some young men are taught the location, name, and nature of the levers of power, and that some are not, and that class holds the key to this difference. They didn't know (or didn't know it mattered) that some young men are taught that city hall can't be fought, and that some are taught ways of outwitting city hall instead of fighting or capitulating, and that class holds the key to this difference. They didn't know (or didn't know it mattered) that, for these and related reasons, trusting a theoretically uniform physical examination or uniform appeals process to insure equality of treatment was naive. . . .

9 And, to judge from official Selective Service papers, the root cause of the mistakes was obsession with the average American as individualistic chooser.

Public statements and testimony by the Service's head, General Lewis B. Hershey, argued that the draft system could be made distinctively American by stressing individualistic choice; they implied that potential draftees who were in a position to make choices constituted the majority. "The psychology of granting wide choice under pressure to take action," Selective Service declared in 1965, "is the American or indirect way of achieving what is done by direction in foreign countries where choice is not permitted." It's also the best way, because "an individual generally applies himself better to something he has decided to do rather than something he has been told to do." Our system exerts "'pressurized guidance' to encourage young people to enter and remain in study, in critical occupations, and in other activities in the national health, safety and interest. . . ." The statement added: "From the individual's viewpoint, he is standing in a room which has been made uncomfortably warm. Several doors are open, but they all lead to various forms of recognized, patriotic service to the Nation. Some accept the alternatives gladly—some with reluctance. The consequence is approximately the same. . . ."

10 Who were the individuals in the "uncomfortably warm" room? In introducing them the policy statement described a recent shift of opinion regarding occupational deferments—an emerging belief that "for the mentally qualified man there is a special order of patriotism other than service in uniform . . . For the man having the capacity, dedicated service as a civilian in such fields as engineering, the sciences and teaching constitutes the ultimate in their expression of patriotism." Clearly the individuals in the warm room were people who benefited from this new perspective on deferment—"mentally qualified" professionals or pre-professionals in training who could express their patriotism best by choosing to stay out of uniform.

11 But both the policy statement and later Selective Service pronouncements spoke as though the world of "pressurized guidance" familiar to those individuals was the same as that known by youth generally. When officials used such phrases as "young people" and "the young man," they were referring to persons in position to choose occupational deferments, and imagining the pre-professional as Everyman. Describing the psychology of potential draftees, Selective Service wrote: "The young man registers at age 18 and pressure begins to force his choice. He does not have the inhibitions that a philosophy of universal service in uniform would engender. The door is open for him as a student to qualify if capable in a skill badly needed by his nation. He has many choices and he is prodded to make a decision."

12 Fusing "the young man" about to make a choice with young men who knew nothing of choices . . . made the job of assuring fair treatment for the whole draftee population look easy. . . .

13 This was worse than nonsense. The planners' absorption with choosers left their system vulnerable to the scams that involved millions. It made them assume that fairness for 483,000 choice-making, deferred professionals and pre-professionals—one thirtieth of those who escaped the draft—meant fairness to all. And beyond question, their mistakes flowed directly from commitment to the muddy, unexamined substance of Americanism: the middle as all, equal op-

portunity guaranteed, social differences as moral differences in disguise. Because the state was in thrall to the myth of classlessness, "the great bulk of . . . Americans deeply scarred by Vietnam were those already economically, socially, and educationally disadvantaged"; the waging of the dirty war was left to the boys from Chelsea and to blacks.

14 Unusual both because statistically verifiable and because based on articulated assumptions, this particular episode of class injustice is in few other respects atypical. Decisions of state taken in fields remote from that of wartime manpower policy show the influence of the same habits of oversimplification and the same ruling assumptions and themes—choice, the individual, the single sector construed as the social whole. Peacetime tax exemptions parallel wartime draft exemptions, with inequities arising because one group within the population—comparable to that composed of pre-professional potential draftees in the warm room—is seen not as a group but as the whole.

15 Consider, for example, the treatment of mortgage interest. Officialdom distributes a huge subsidy to homeowners; the subsidy bears no trace of the stigma attached, say, to food stamps. The implicit justification is that home ownership is universal and socially stabilizing, and that those not now sharing the benefit could share it if they chose. In reality, because of the nature of the urban housing stock, an enormous number of working class urban families can never make that choice, and are excluded from the benefit. But their inability is often viewed as a characterological defect (renters don't *save*), and, in any case, the habit of deleting the factor of social difference renders the families in question relatively invisible (like the boys from Chelsea). When the matter of urban housing needs is raised, the state pleads lacks of funds, and the head of state produces one-liners. (After reading that the city of New York paid $37,000 to support a family in a welfare hotel for a year, President Reagan remarked: "I wonder why somebody doesn't build them a house for $37,000.")

16 The links between the myth of classlessness and the major areas of class injustice—housing, education, health care, Social Security taxes, the court system, and the rest—warrant meticulous inquiry. And the methods of inquiry themselves demand the same. Conventional approaches to social injustice—not excluding the so-called multi-leveled approach taken, a generation ago, during the War on Poverty—often emerge as misdirected efforts to seal off problems that are in fact beyond enclosure. "Nutrition problems" are dealt with in isolation from "literacy problems," and vice versa; dropout problems, teen pregnancy problems, homeless problems, jobless problems, drug problems—all are fenced and bounded, in contempt not only of their obvious interrelationships but of the direct bearing on each of tax-supported arrangements and bonanzas in other sectors of the population. And inevitably the frustrations arising from the "failures" of programs conceived in these terms leads to the practice of moralizing, minoritizing, and biologizing socio-economic realities.

17 The effect of the latter practice is to transform difficult but comprehensible problems into mysteries involving dark forces and defying rational search for solutions. The lack of decent rental housing, in cities, for working class and

lower middle class families, is in no small measure the result of the bestowal of federal largesse on some classes and the withholding of it from others. And this philanthropy involves much more than mortgage interest, of course. Five hundred billion is spent to bail out well-heeled savings and loan bankers, while pieties about the "inexorable laws of the free market" are preached to *bodega* owners in bankruptcy and to foreclosed family farmers. And at state and city levels huge handouts are distributed to Sears and other corporations in the form of "tax increment financing" arrangements under which inner city locations are abandoned and glossy new corporate headquarters in suburbs are subsidized with public funds.

18 But when housing shortages are set in a moral context, the class aspect of the problem disappears, memories of class bailouts fade, and mystification enters. The mortgage interest tax exemption and related tax breaks become rewards for the virtuous and circumspect; the absence of a mortgage is subtly converted into a sign of recklessness; the collapse of urban housing becomes entangled with the problem of the nature of man; government can only turn up its hands.

19 Moral and even metaphysical entanglements—distractions leading minds away from clear issues of class advantage into murky jungles of casuistry—figure regularly in the history of American public policy planning. Well before the turn of the last century, one historian writes, the prevailing elite ideology identified "the fundamental division in American society not [as that] between rich and poor, but [as] between industrious and idle, virtuous and vicious, community-minded and selfish." This conception of difference played a role in shaping the first functional equivalent, in America, of an old age and disability pension system—the benefits that were paid to a million and a half Civil War veterans and their survivors. According to Ann Shola Orloff, writing on "The Political Origins of America's Belated Welfare State," Civil War pension benefits "flowed primarily to members of the middle class and the upper strata of the working class, rather than to the neediest Americans." From the time of those first pensions to the present, when, as Theda Skocpol argues, "social security" for "deserving workers" is bifurcated from "welfare" for "barely deserving poor people," the distinction between the decent and indecent, virtuous and vile, has dogged American social provision. But lately the theorists of dark forces have grown more aggressive in attributing program failures to moral corruption, and in dismissing the notion that improved public policy could ever succeed at the task of moderating inequity.

20 In support of that notion a large arsenal of weapons is deployed, including the weapon of pseudo-science—the branch represented by inventors and promoters of what is termed the "pathology of poverty." These promoters purport to provide objective, penetrating, social-scientific accounts of things as they humanly are. The manner of the descriptions is candid and unflinching; a claim is made for the respect awarded those whose thankless task is to face the worst. But the substance induces feelings of despair—a sense that the crises of the age are biologically foreordained and that utopians alone dream of abating them through human intervention. Who among us knows the answer to Evil?

21 Among the best-known promoters of the pathological fallacy is Edward C. Banfield, a professor of government at Harvard and head of President Nixon's Task Force on Cities. In *The Unheavenly City* (1970) Professor Banfield presents himself as "a social scientist [thinking] about the problems of cities in the light of scholarly findings." ("Facts are facts, however unpleasant.") His thesis is that American cities are in ruins because the underclass individual isn't normal—is mentally ill, pathologically sick:

22 > [He] lives from moment to moment . . . Impulse governs his behavior, either because he cannot discipline himself to sacrifice a present for a future satisfaction or because he has no sense of the future. He is therefore radically improvident: whatever he cannot consume immediately he considers valueless. His bodily needs (especially for sex) and his taste for "action" take precedence over everything else—and certainly over any work routine. He works only as he must to stay alive and drifts from one unskilled job to another, taking no interest in the work . . . He feels no attachment to community, neighbors, or friends (he has companions, not friends), resents all authority (for example, that of policemen, social workers, teachers, landlords, employers), and is apt to think that he has been "railroaded" and to want to "get even" . . . Much of [his] violence is probably more an expression of mental illness than of class culture.

23 Here he is, the unconditioned American individual, in new guise. *I am what I am. I am myself alone.* In accounts such as Banfield's the man of the underclass is a person crossing an open field, making free choices as he goes. He can decide in favor of the long view—decide, say, to follow the example of his father (a Bell Labs engineer) and develop a science hobby in junior high (taking over the basement rumpus room for a lab); decide to develop a research focus on robotics under the guidance of Mr. Herman, the brilliant young senior high chem department chair (Herman has already had two GE Young Scientist finalists); decide at Cal Tech that space robotics is where he wants to go; decide to take the Lockheed/NASA post-doc offer, etc., etc.

24 Or he can decide to "live from moment to moment" in West Harlem, opting to work as a steerer-lookout for his dealing brother at age nine and ten, opting to heist car batteries at twelve, opting to drop out at thirteen, opting thereafter for dealing and pimping. Life is options. It's up to him whether he respects authority or despises it; immaterial that authority from his first encounter with it assumed that he would despise it. It's up to him—to his free choice—whether to work at a skilled or an unskilled job, whether to study and train or drift and steal.

25 If a street kid opts for joblessness when straight before him lies the rumpus room/robotics/Cal Tech option, what can this mean except that moral sickness has gripped his soul?

26 An effective labor movement might have done much to counter the claim that unemployed people, such as Banfield's inner city alienated, are sick; it could also, through its backing, provide activist legislators and policymakers with reason for seeing themselves not as isolated do-gooders but as representatives answerable to lively, demanding, expectant constituencies. But owing to

factors ranging from right-to-work laws to a century of Red-baiting, no such labor movement exists. Nor does any political party with a disposition to challenge the assumption that social problems are, in essence, problems of morality and pathology. Perceiving themselves as omni-entities, American political parties express horror at the prospect of "polarization" of business and labor; they compete with each other for business alms ("Republicans represent corporate oil; Democrats, independent oil; Republicans represent commercial finance; Democrats, the savings and loan associations"); they deny that class exists.

27 In the course of their careers few policymakers at work today have heard even the beginnings of a serious public discussion, by political leaders with unfickle constituencies, of the impact of the American class system. What they have heard, almost ceaselessly, is criticism—murmured or shouted—of "government interference" in the affairs of individuals, and denunciations of "special interest lobbies." (Equal rage is directed—democratically—at oil lobbies and lobbies for coalminers.) And the result is that critics and criticized alike arrive—by different methods of reckoning—at quasi-agreement that such interference is not only unavailing but at least partly responsible for nourishing the dark forces.

28 In the past quarter-century federal initiatives in the areas of poverty and welfare have joined federal regulation of business as chief targets of opportunity for enemies of "government interference." No initiative in the welfare and poverty areas was ever shaped on the basis of accurate understanding of the pertinent class differences in education, expectation, housing, and family structure. And, not surprisingly, most of the initiatives passed swiftly through a cycle beginning in optimism and ending in chaos. Office of Economic Opportunity programs were condemned early for waste, unfairness, and "coddling," and later for worsening the situations they were intended to rectify. ("Poverty programs cause poverty," as Sidney Blumenthal mockingly summarized the standard indictment in *The Rise of the Counter-Establishment,* 1986.)

29 As for expanded welfare programs: first a famous white paper discovered that their unanticipated consequence was the destruction of the black family, then the dark force theorists developed the point into an indictment of government itself. Charles Murray, the Reagan Administration's welfare theorist, claimed in 1983 that the "liberal ascendancy" was blind to the real cause of anguish in Harlem and comparable communities. The real cause is government; the new welfare programs are actually responsible for the moral collapse of the poor; all such programs must go. Let government be mindful henceforth of the consequences of ignoring the ineluctable individuality of each of its citizens. Let the nation ponder the costs of deleting the moral substance from "conditions" and pretending that life is a "social problem" soluble by technical means. Let men and women remember the truth of original sin—most especially the sins of working people and the poor.

30 Viewed in these terms, inequity—even inequity traceable to specific, misconceived government action in the past—takes on the status of nature: appears weighty and irreversible. The elements of the basic situation are these:

there are people of light and people of darkness, and although the former may send their rays—their hope—toward the latter, they can do no more. Nor can government itself; it cannot function as the locus of purposive action on the side of sound human values. As awareness of this basic situation takes hold, a sense of powerlessness and self-elevating moral stoicism settles over the capitols and statehouses—disbelief that the intricate interrelationships among problems can or perhaps should be clarified, doubt that alliances necessary to create public support for legislative solutions can or perhaps should be forged. Vying for the crown of *a*politicality, leaders tell themselves and their constituents that hope resides nowhere save in individual impulses of benevolence—the kindness of one person to the next. And *we* the imperial middle are the kind; the capital of benevolence, as of light itself, is in our sole charge. . . .

31 The language that needs desperately to be spoken—the only language in which the interconnectedness of bad schools, bad housing, bad nutrition, and horrific family life can be grasped, and strong but hidden joint interests can be defined—is the indispensable language of class, and that language is proscribed. And the proscription is, finally, most devastating because, as I said, it extends the influence of the myth of classlessness well beyond the mere enforcement of consent to inequity. By legitimizing the claims of the middle as sole moral exemplar, it lifts all restraints on ruling class ego. And by depriving government of its own power to imagine a complex response, it insures that government can never be equal to complex problems. State and citizenry alike stand forth as victims of that deprivation because both are robbed of the only resource on which either can afford for long to rely: the resource of *mind.*

QUESTIONS FOR WRITING AND DISCUSSION

OBSERVING

1. What does DeMott mean by the belief in "the unconditioned individual"?
2. What is the relation in the American mind, according to DeMott, between social differences and moral differences?
3. What is it about the American attitude toward the "middle," according to DeMott, that makes it "imperial"?

EVALUATING

1. Do you think it is just or unjust that the fighting—and dying—in Vietnam was done by a disproportionate number of persons of lower economic class?
2. Cite some of the examples DeMott calls attention to of special privileges some Americans enjoy that they see as rights even though many others of their countrymen do not share them. To explore some of the ways this

question applies to public policy, substitute "entitlements" for "rights." Why is a tax deduction for mortgage interest looked upon differently than unemployment compensation or food stamps? Should it be?

RESPONDING AND APPLYING

1. Examine carefully the conditions of your own life and identify in what ways you may be said to be privileged in comparison to others of your contemporaries. Try to consider the many things you are in the habit of taking for granted as well as the things you may feel you have earned that others may never have had a chance to compete for. Or do you conceive of yourself as an unconditioned American individual?
2. If DeMott is correct, it may be that many of those who complain most about programs like affirmative action, which attempt to remedy social injustice, are individuals who fail to recognize that what they feel they are losing is not their equal rights but their special privileges. Do you agree or disagree with this speculation?
3. DeMott claims that those who insist on seeing social differences as moral differences support that notion with a variety of weapons including pseudo-science. Compare this claim with Johnson's that capitalism is "a natural force" that "thrives on meritocracy." Do you agree with Johnson that capitalism as it operates in America is "blind to class, race, and color, to religion and sex, to nationality and creed," as well as "to good and evil"?

CHAPTER WRITING ASSIGNMENTS

1. History seems to have shown that although Adam Smith and David Ricardo oversimplified the laws of economics there is a good bit of truth in what they said: free market economies have been the most successful. However, the development of the free market system, and even the definition of what constitutes a free market economy, has changed over the years. Indeed, today, most operate under controls that early in this century would have been considered Marxist. Marx, too, oversimplified the laws of economics in projecting the disappearance of capitalism and the emergence of a classless society, but much of what he said remains true, even in the face of recent changes in major socialist economies. Argue some variation on this thesis: modern economic and political history can be seen as the working out of a Marxian dialectic between a capitalist thesis and a Marxist antithesis; the result has been a synthesis that neither old style capitalists or Marxists anticipated.
2. Some economists today see even more truth in the classic economic theories, especially in Ricardo's Malthusianism. Only in the last third of this century has much of the world become aware that world population is increasing while resources are dwindling. We could well be moving toward a Malthusian world of bare subsistence for the vast majority. Do you think we will revert again to some of the abuses of nineteenth-century capitalism or of twentieth-century collectivism, or do you think we can solve

such problems more equitably and humanely? Given the possibility of worldwide want, what values do you think will most sustain us, those embodied in the Judeo-Christian, the humanistic, the Marxian, some other (for example, science), or some combination of traditions like Christian socialism?

3. Some people may argue that we are already in a Malthusian world. As citizens of one of the wealthiest nations, we are simply too far removed from world hunger to realize that we are a small minority, a privileged class. Because of our wealth, we have operated in a "free" world market with all sorts of advantages. Already, though, that seems to be changing. How do you think we will maintain our privileged status? Or if not, how are we likely to accommodate its loss?
4. According to *Forbes Magazine*, the number of billionaires in the United States has been nearly doubling on a yearly basis in recent years: 14 in 1985, 26 in 1986, 49 in 1987. This and the fact that during the 1980s the real median income of the top 40% of U.S. households has risen substantially while the real median income of the bottom 40% has fallen have suggested to many economists that the middle class is disappearing and we are moving toward a two-tiered society, as in many Third-World countries in which society comprises an affluent minority and a desperately poor majority. What signs, if any, do you see of this trend? Do you think it is a serious trend? If the trend should continue, do you think that some elements of Marxism will become appealing to Americans?
5. Marxism has always had the strongest appeal and has been most feared in noncommunist societies where class divisions have been the greatest—prerevolutionary Russia, China, and Cuba, for example, or many present underindustrialized countries. Do you think that the kind of revisions that socialist governments have undergone recently in Eastern Europe will substantially change that appeal? Is it possible to bring such societies to a state of more equitable distribution of wealth without some form of socialism?
6. A major argument of the feminist movement has been the Marxian one that the traditional family is based on the exploitation of women. If true, can this situation be altered in ways other than Marx's prediction of the disappearance of the family as a social institution? Can the family be reaffirmed in ways that provide women full equality with men? How do economic factors affect these possibilities? For example, if economic changes are making it increasingly necessary for most families to have two primary wage earners to achieve or maintain their desired standard of living, is it not true that an adjustment becomes necessary in the direction of equality in household and parental duties?
7. Johnson argues that capitalism is distinguished from collectivism in that the former is "a natural force rather than a contrived ideology." What ideas derived from Adam Smith do you recognize in this statement? How would Bergmann or DeMott respond to this statement? Define "ideology" and examine what grounds Johnson has for claiming that capitalism is not an ideology.
8. If we think of a business as a political structure, it is a curious fact that the classic model, especially for big business, is an oriental despotism in which

the owner is the absolute ruler. Corporations represent an advance in that they operate on the model of a feudal kingdom in which the chief executive officer holds power with the backing of a property-holding nobility of stockholders who support the CEO as long as it profits them. Do you think it possible that in a democratic society something more like a democracy might serve as a model for business? Would it be a violation of natural law to conceive of a management system that owed some responsibility for and accountability to the workers—and to the community? Do such management models exist, and are they at all viable?

CHAPTER PREVIEW

Chapter Prelude
Kurt Vonnegut, "Address to P.E.N. Conference"

Introductory Essay

Readings
Dylan Thomas, *from* "Notes on the Art of Poetry"
Joyce Cary, "The Artist and the World"
Doug Blandy, "Art, Social Action, and the Preparation of Democratic Citizens"
W. H. Auden, from "Squares and Oblongs" and from *The Dryer's Hand*

Story
Walter Van Tilburg Clark, "The Portable Phonograph"

Perspectives
SHOULD THE GOVERNMENT SUBSIDIZE ART?
George Will, "Washington's Works of Art"
Douglas Davis, "Multicultural Wars"

Chapter Writing Assignments

Chapter 9

THE ARTS AND HUMANITIES

Address to P.E.N. Conference in Stockholm, 1973

Kurt Vonnegut

1 Journalists and teachers are often bullied or fired in my country—for saying this or that. But writers of novels and plays and short stories and poems have never been hurt or hampered much. They haven't even been noticed much by federal, state, or local governments, no matter how insolent or blasphemous or treasonous those writers may be. This has been going on now for nearly two hundred years.

2 If tyranny comes to my country, which is an old one now (and tyranny can come anywhere, anytime, as nearly as I can tell), I expect to go on writing whatever I please, without putting myself in danger, as long as what I write is fiction. The experience of American power structures with fiction since 1776 would appear to validate what is perhaps the first poem I ever learned by heart. A playmate must have taught it to me. It goes like this:

Sticks and stones
May break my bones,
But words can never hurt me.

3 It is the feeling in several countries, I know, that fiction can hurt a social order a lot. And by fiction I mean any person's written report of what is going on in his head, as opposed to the daily news. Writers of such stuff, as Heinich Böll[1] can tell us, have been jailed, put into lunatic asylums, exiled, or even killed

[1] Heinrich Böll (1917–1985) was a German writer who emerged after the collapse of Hitler's Germany. Awarded the Nobel Prize for Literature, he was one of the best-known and most controversial writers of his time.

sometimes—for putting certain words in a certain order. Politicians who do things like that to fiction writers should learn from the American experience that they are not merely being cruel. They are being preposterous, too. Fiction is harmless. Fiction is so much hot air.

4 The Vietnam war has proved this. Virtually every American fiction writer was against our participation in that civil war. We all raised hell about the war for years and years—with novels and poems and plays and short stories. We dropped on our complacent society the literary equivalent of a hydrogen bomb.

5 I will now report to you the power of such a bomb. It has the explosive force of a very large banana-cream pie—a pie two meters in diameter, twenty centimeters thick, and dropped from a height of ten meters or more.

6 My own feeling is that we should turn this awesome weapon over to the United Nations, or to some other international peacekeeping organization, such as the C.I.A.

7 What can tyrants, large and small, learn from my speech so far? That fiction writers are harmless. They may safely be allowed all the freedoms which birds have—to sing as they please, to hop about, to fly. Harsh authorities everywhere should learn this poem by heart, and recite it joyfully at the start of every day;

Sticks and stones
May break my bones,
But fiction can never hurt me.

8 Thus ends the public part of my speech.

9 I have a few additional words for you, my colleagues. Please don't repeat them outside this room. While it is true that we American fiction writers failed to modify the course of the war, we have reason to suspect that we have poisoned the minds of thousands or perhaps millions of American young people. Our hope is that the poison will make them worse than useless in unjust wars.

10 We shall see.

11 Unfortunately, that still leaves plenty of Americans who don't read or think much—who will still be extremely useful in unjust wars. We are sick about that. We did the best we could.

12 Most writers I know, all over the world, do the best they can. They must. They have no choice in the matter. All artists are specialized cells in a single, huge organism, mankind. Those cells have to behave as they do, just as the cells in our hearts or our fingertips have to behave as they do.

13 We here are some of those specialized cells. Our purpose is to make mankind aware of itself, in all its complexity, and to dream its dreams. We have no choice in the matter.

14 And there is more to our situation than that. In privacy here, I think we can acknowledge to one another that we don't really write what we write. We

don't write the *best* of what we write, at any rate. The best of our stuff draws information and energy and wholeness from outside ourselves. Sculptors feel this more strongly than we do, incidentally. Every sculptor I ever knew felt that some spook had taken possession of his hands.

15 Where do these external signals come from? I think they come from all the other specialized cells in the organism. Those other cells contribute to us energy and little bits of information, in order that we may increase the organism's awareness of itself—and dream its dream.

16 But if the entire organism thinks that what we do is important, why aren't we more influential than we are? I am persuaded that we are tremendously influential, even though most national leaders, my own included, probably never heard of most of us here. Our influence is slow and subtle, and it is felt mainly by the young. They are hungry for myths which resonate with the mysteries of their own times.

17 We give them those myths.

18 We will become influential when those who have listened to our myths have become influential. Those who rule us now are living in accordance with myths created for them by writers when *they* were young. It is perfectly clear that our rulers do not question those myths for even a minute during busy day after busy day. Let us pray that those terribly influential writers were humane.

19 Thank you.

QUESTIONS FOR WRITING AND DISCUSSION

OBSERVING

1. Vonnegut writes of the power of fiction writers and of artists in general. How does he see the relationship between the arts and morality? Why does he say the artists' attack on our involvement in the Vietnam War had the effect of dropping a large banana cream pie if he believes that artists have so much influence?
2. Vonnegut gave this speech in 1973 to a group of writers in Stockholm as the Vietnam War was winding down. What significance does the time and setting have to Vonnegut's message?
3. What do you think Vonnegut means when he claims that artists are "cells in a single, huge organism"? How does he use this metaphor to convey his message?

EVALUATING

1. This speech is divided into two parts, one that Vonnegut calls "the public part," and one he describes as "for you, my colleagues." Which of these two audiences do you identify with? What is the point of this division—especially since both parts are in fact public? Do you think this is an effective rhetorical strategy?
2. How would you characterize the way our society sees artists and writers? Is Vonnegut right that most of our national leaders probably don't know our national artists? If you answered yes, why do you think this is true?

RESPONDING AND APPLYING

1. What do you think Vonnegut means by the "myths" artists give to the young? Do you think the poetry and fiction young people read may have had something to do with what drove a generation in the 1960s and early 1970s to reject an "unjust war"? What myths embodied in what poetry and fiction do you think may have inspired the older generation that pursued that war? How much of that poetry and fiction do you think students encountered in school, how much in other contexts? Even though many say that schools should not teach morality, what moral messages do you think you may have absorbed from the works of literature and art you have dealt with in school?

THE IMAGINATION AND HUMAN CULTURE

It is difficult to think about art as an "idea" since it is so fundamentally human an activity, but it is among the earliest indicators of real humanity that anthropologists recognize. Toolmaking is one indicator. Another is signs of spirituality like the making of fetishes (objects believed to have supernatural powers) or burial practices that suggest the expectation of some kind of continuing existence after death. Art is another, the earliest examples of which are the fashioning or decorating of objects in a way that suggests a sense of the beautiful.

Though art is the most recent of these developments, the last century of archeological discovery seems to keep pushing back its earliest appearances. It is certainly questionable whether a sense of beauty may have entered into the fashioning of paleolithic tools, but sophisticated cave paintings were discovered in 1879 at Altamira in Spain, indicating that ancient humanity was far less primitive than supposed; in 1940, even more beautiful cave paintings were discovered in Lascaux cave in France, which carbon-14 dating (a technology discovered in 1946) revealed to be some 17,000 years old; then in 1994, explorers discovered the Chavet Cave in the Ardèche Valley of southeast France, with paleolithic paintings as good as but 15,000 years older—some 30,000 to 32,000 years old.

Words like "beautiful," "more beautiful," "sophisticated," "art" carry with them all sorts of assumptions and questions about what we are really talking about. Does a sense of beauty enter into the perception of a toolmaker—or user—when the form is seen as elegantly reflecting the function of the tool? Is the spiritual effectiveness of a religious object seen to be greater if that object is itself apprehended as beautiful? Is Beauty Truth, Truth Beauty, as Keats' "Ode on a Grecian Urn" declares? What are the differences between that great triad of human concern, Truth, Goodness, and Beauty, or are they really simply different words for the same thing? How does the art of a culture express or reflect that culture?

The answers to such questions are complicated by the fact that they are based on distinctions that come both historically and experientially after the event. The philosophical word for the study of beauty, *aesthetics,* is derived from a Greek word for perception, and it refers first to a special kind of perceptual event usually described as a moment of illumination, vision, or epiphany evoked by a perceived object, image, or set of sounds or words. Medieval philosopher Thomas Aquinas described a key feature of this experience as *claritas,* which twentieth-century novelist James Joyce translated as "radiance." However we wish to describe that sense of fullness, of pleasure, of satisfaction, of relatedness to the perceived other, we can be sure it existed in human beings long before anyone tried to analyze or explain it, though it may well be a major root of the human senses of spirituality, love, reverence, and even those of order and law.

In modern times, however, we have tended to divide and compartmentalize such senses and instincts. Speaking of the ancient character of poetry, long considered the ultimate form of human art, anthropologist Jan Huizinga argues that to understand this form we must:

> discard the idea that poetry has only an aesthetic function or can only be explained in terms of aesthetics. In any flourishing, living civilization, above all in archaic cultures, poetry has a vital function that is both social and liturgical. All antique poetry is at one and the same time ritual, entertainment, artistry, riddle-making, doctrine, persuasion, sorcery, soothsaying, prophecy, and competition. . . . The true appellation of the poet is *vates* [Latin, usually translated as prophet or seer], the possessed, the God-smitten. . . . Gradually the poet-seer splits up into the figures of the prophet, the priest, the soothsayer, the mystagogue and the poet as we know him; even the philosopher, the legislator, the orator, the demagogue, the sophist and the rhetor spring from that primordial composite type, the *vates.* The early Greek poets all show traces of their common progenitor. Their function is eminently a social one; they speak as the educators and monitors of their people. (*Homo Ludens: A Study of the Play-Element in Culture,* 1938)

But have these several original functions of the poet been in effect replaced? Certainly the long history of attack upon the arts is linked to the fact that these attacks come, in effect, from rivals, specialists, we might say, who lay claim to some of the functions first associated with the poet, especially philosophers (Plato's is among the first recorded attacks upon the arts) and religious and political leaders of all kinds. Is there any function left for the artist to perform that is uniquely or necessarily her own? Or has poetry become an extinct species of human activity? Indeed, what is perhaps the major modern philosophical attack on the arts, Utilitariansim, asserted late in the eighteenth century that there was no longer any useful function for art, that poetry especially was a symptom of culture in a childish stage of development, that as civilization advances, poetry must necessarily decline, and that the arts in general, as well as older philosophies, are expensive luxuries, affectations we would do well to dispense with. It is an indication of how alive the Utilitarian argument is today that a standard argument among defenders of the arts, including National Endowment for the Arts chairperson Jane Alexander, is that they promote economic development.

Historically, however, arguments justifying the arts have tended to be less utilitarian, though they have certainly included a belief that the arts perform some kind of service for humanity, satisfy some essential human need. Percy Bysshe Shelley (1792-1822), for example, in his *A Defense of Poetry* called poets "the unacknowledged legislators of the world" and saw poetry as acting "to produce the moral improvement of man":

> The great secret of morals is Love; or a going out of our own nature, and an identification of ourselves with the beautiful which exists in thought, action, or person, not our own. A man, to be greatly good, must imagine intensely and comprehensively; he must put himself in the place of another and of many others; the pains and pleasures of his species must become his own. The great instrument of moral good is the imagination; and poetry administers to the effect by acting upon the cause.

In facing the modern crisis of faith, in which all traditions, creeds, and dogmas seemed to be falling, writers and poets like Matthew Arnold (1822-1888) and Wallace Stevens (1879-1955) have looked to poetry to satisfy our continuing need for a spirituality which they believed religion could no longer supply. But whether or not art can be an adequate substitute for religion, its defenders would all agree that it ministers significantly to important aspects of our sense of self, our sense of relation to our natural and human environments, and on some level our sense of spirituality.

In the selections which follow, modern British poet Dylan Thomas emphasizes the artist's preoccupation with her medium. The medium is words in Thomas' case, but in the case of other artists it could be colors, forms, sounds, images, or whatever the artistic form involved. Joyce Cary deals with art as a creative act that brings meaning into the world, but he deals also with the paradox that this creation is based on a discovery of something that is really out there, not just in the artist's imagination—what he calls "certain constants" present in "human nature and its social relations." While many artists see themselves in relation to their society in a role something like Socrates' notion of the gadfly, even as enemies of the state, Doug Blandy is concerned with art as an expression of its community. The tendency for the production and distribution of the arts to be controlled by an elite group of specialists he sees as contrary to the spirit of participation that ought to characterize a democratic society. W. H. Auden seems to take a more jaundiced view, distrusting the traditional claims about the great virtue of the poet or the power of the poet or of poetry to change the world; he sees poetry more as a kind of game, "a game of knowledge." Though poetry is better understood, according to Auden, as a form of play, it is nevertheless serious play which requires considerable skill; the poet's greatness lies more in his mastery of his medium, and, writing in the context of the rise of Hitler, Auden is concerned that a concentration on the poetic message can be turned to dangerous ends.

The story by Walter Van Tilburg Clark speculates on what it would be like if we were deprived of the arts, while the "perspectives" section looks in morc detail at the kind of cultural civil war that is currently ranging about the state of the arts and its place in relation to government.

DYLAN THOMAS, *FROM* "NOTES ON THE ART OF POETRY"

What makes an artist? Is it divine inspiration, training, discipline, special kinds of sensitivity or awareness, genius, a special kind of vision? All of these perhaps, but poet *Dylan Thomas* (1914–1953) focuses in this selection on what started the process for him: a kind of love affair with a particular artistic medium, words.

Given his background, this may not be so surprising. Thomas was born and grew up in South Wales, in a picturesque corner that had been left relatively untouched by the mining, foundries, and general industrialization that changed the face of most of that land during the nineteenth and early twentieth centuries. Wales has long been conducive to poets, since poetry and music have for centuries been elements of culture of enormous importance. Nearly everyone in Wales sings, choral groups of all sorts abound, and poets and preachers are among the most respected members of the community, drawn not from an aristocratic class but from the shopkeepers and small farmers that have for so long remained the backbone of Welsh society. Nevertheless, love of the medium is a notion often voiced by artists, and not at all peculiar to Thomas.

Dylan Thomas is among the most admired of modern British poets. His poetry is now most readily available in the *Collected Poems* (1953), but he is also well known for his autobiographical *Portrait of the Artist as a Young Dog,* his radio play *Under Milk Wood,* and the short story, "A Child's Christmas in Wales."

from Notes on the Art of Poetry[1]

Dylan Thomas

1 You want to know why and how I just began to write poetry, and which poets or kinds of poetry I was first moved and influenced by.

2 To answer the first part of this question, I should say I wanted to write poetry in the beginning because I had fallen in love with words. The first poems I knew were nursery rhymes, and before I could read them for myself I had come to love just the words of them, the words alone. What the words stood for, symbolised, or meant, was of very secondary importance. What mattered was the *sound* of them as I heard them for the first time on the lips of the remote and incomprehensible grown-ups who seemed, for some reason, to be living in my world. And these words were, to me, as the notes of bells, the sounds of musical instruments, the noises of wind, sea, and rain, the rattle of milkcarts, the clopping of hooves on cobbles, the fingering of branches on a window pane, might be to someone, deaf from birth, who has miraculously found his hearing. I did not care what the words said, overmuch, nor what happened to Jack and Jill and the Mother Goose rest of them; I cared for the shapes of sound that their names, and the words describing their actions, made in my ears; I cared for the colours the words cast on my eyes. I realise that I may be, as I think back all the way, romanticising my reactions to the simple and beautiful words of those pure poems; but that is all I can honestly remember, however much time might have falsified my memory. I fell in love—that is the only expression I can think of—at once, and am still at the mercy of words, though sometimes now, knowing a little of their behaviour very well, I think I can influence them slightly and have even learned to beat them now and then, which they appear to enjoy. I tumbled for words at once. And, when I began to read the nursery rhymes for myself, and, later, to read other verses and ballads, I knew that I had discovered the most important things, to me, that could be ever. There they were, seemingly lifeless, made only of black and white, but out of them, out of their own being, came love and terror and pity and pain and wonder and all the other vague abstractions that make our ephemeral lives dangerous, great, and bearable. Out of them came the gusts and grunts and hiccups and heehaws of the common fun of the earth; and though what the words meant was, in its own way, often deliciously funny enough, so much funnier seemed to me, at that almost forgotten time, the shape and shade and size and noise of the words as they hummed, strummed, jugged and galloped along. That was the time of innocence; words burst upon me, unencumbered by trivial or portentous association; words were their spring-like selves, fresh with Eden's dew, as they flew

[1] Written in the summer of 1951, at Laugharne, in reply to questions posed by a student.

out of the air. They made their own original associations as they sprang and shone. The words, "Ride a cock-horse to Banbury Cross," were as haunting to me, who did not know then what a cock-horse was nor cared a damn where Banbury Cross might be, as, much later, were such lines as John Donne's, "Go and catch a falling star, Get with child a mandrake root," which also I could not understand when I first read them. And as I read more and more, and it was not all verse, by any means, my love for the real life of words increased until I knew that I must live *with* them and *in* them always. I knew, in fact, that I must be a writer of words, and nothing else. The first thing was to feel and know their sound and substance; what I was going to do with those words, what use I was going to make of them, what I was going to *say* through them, would come later. I knew I had to know them most intimately in all their forms and moods, their ups and downs, their chops and changes, their needs and demands. (Here, I am afraid, I am beginning to talk too vaguely. I do not like writing *about* words, because then I often use bad and wrong and stale and wooly words. What I like to do is to treat words as a craftsman does his wood or stone or what-have-you, to hew, carve, mould, coil, polish and plane them into patterns, sequences, sculptures, fugues of sound expressing some lyrical impulse, some spiritual doubt or conviction, some dimly-realised truth I must try to reach and realise). It was when I was very young, and just at school, that, in my father's study, before homework that was never done, I began to know one kind of writing from another, one kind of goodness, one kind of badness. My first, and greatest, liberty was that of being able to read everything and anything I cared to. I read indiscriminately, and with my eyes hanging out. I could never have dreamt that there were such goings-on in the world between the covers of books, such sandstorms and ice-blasts of words, such slashing of humbug, and humbug too, such staggering peace, such enormous laughter, such and so many blinding bright lights breaking across the just-awaking wits and splashing all over the pages in a million bits and pieces all of which were words, words, words, and each of which was alive forever in its own delight and glory and oddity and light (I must try not to make these supposedly helpful notes as confusing as my poems themselves.) I wrote endless imitations, though I never thought them to be imitations but, rather, wonderfully original things, like eggs laid by tigers. They were imitations of anything I happened to be reading at the time: Sir Thomas Browne, de Quincey, Henry Newbolt, the Ballads, Baroness Orczy, Marlowe, Chums, the Imagists, the Bible, Poe, Keats, Lawrence, Anon., and Shakespeare. A mixed lot, as you see, and randomly remembered. I tried my callow hand at almost every poetical form. How could I learn the tricks of a trade unless I tried to do them myself? I learned that the bad tricks come easily; and the good ones, which help you to say what you think you wish to say in the most meaningful, moving way, I am still learning. (But in earnest company you must call these tricks by other names, such as technical devices, prosodic experiments, etc.)

3 The writers, then, who influenced my earliest poems and stories were, quite simply and truthfully, all the writers I was reading at the time, and, as you

see from a specimen list higher up the page, they ranged from writers of schoolboy adventure yarns to incomparable and inimitable masters like Blake. That is, when I began, bad writing had as much influence on my stuff as good. The bad influences I tried to remove and renounce bit by bit, shadow by shadow, echo by echo, through trial and error, through delight and disgust and misgiving, as I came to love words more and to hate the heavy hands that knocked them about, the thick tongues that (had) no feel for their multitudinous tastes, the dull and botching hacks who flattened them out into a colourless and insipid paste, the pedants who made them moribund and pompous as themselves. Let me say that the things that first made me love language and want to work *in* it and *for* it were nursery rhymes and folk tales, the Scottish Ballads, a few lines of hymns, the most famous Bible stories and the rhythms of the Bible, Blake's Songs of Innocence, and the quite incomprehensible magical majesty and nonsense of Shakespeare heard, read, and near-murdered in the first forms of my school.

QUESTIONS FOR WRITING AND DISCUSSION

OBSERVING

1. Thomas suggests a difference between his first attraction to the mere sound of words and his later attraction to other effects of language. What are some of those other effects he mentions?
2. In his comments about good and bad writing, what indication of how Thomas defines kinds of goodness and badness in writing do you see?

EVALUATING

1. Do you think it is really possible to be "haunted" by words like "Ride a cock-horse to Banbury Cross"? Why do you suppose some of the earliest stories that children are told are in verse?
2. Do you think it is possible to enjoy a poem or a picture you can't understand? What, for example, is the basis for the appeal—to adults as well as children—of nonsense verse? Consider examples like "Jabberwocky" from Lewis Carroll's *Through the Looking Glass* or many of the Dr. Suess stories by Theodor Geisel.

RESPONDING AND APPLYING

1. Many people can remember something of the stories they first heard, but do you remember any of the actual words and phrases with which any were told to you? Do you remember any of your early experiences with sounds and music, with colors and forms? Think about these kinds of

experience in a variety of contexts: from the radio, the television, records, tapes, or live performances, street or neighborhood sounds, playmates, kindergarten and Sunday school, your parents or relatives. Is it ideas you mostly remember, or more concrete sounds and images?

2. Do you think your education up to now has equipped you to appreciate or to pursue the arts? In which ways, positively or negatively, has your attitude toward the arts been shaped by your education?
3. Has it ever occurred to you to wonder what first inspires an individual to become an artist or what makes an artist? Have you had such aspirations yourself? If so, how do your motivations compare with those of Thomas? Did you pursue or are you pursuing those aspirations? Why or why not? Judging from Thomas' experience, if you have artistic tendencies, the odds are that the memories you thought of in answer to the first "Responding and Applying" question were of concrete things like specific images or sounds, not abstract ideas. Does your own experience bear this out or not?

JOYCE CARY, "THE ARTIST AND THE WORLD"

Whatever may initially inspire the artist, she creates in part because she has something to share. She may or may not work alone, but the end result of that work is a product designed to communicate somehow with an audience, to move or illuminate, to delight or change the members of that audience. *Joyce Cary* (1888-1957) offers some insight into this end of the artistic process.

Cary has been called one of the most significant of midtwentieth-century writers. He is best known for his novel *The Horse's Mouth* (1944), the central character of which is an outrageous and outrageously creative modern painter, but he has also written on aesthetics, most noteably his study *Art and Reality: Ways of the Creative Process,* from which the following selection is taken.

The Artist and the World

Joyce Cary

1 This is an attempt to examine the relation of the artist with the world as it seems to him, and to see what he does with it. That is to say, on the one side with what is called the artist's intuition, on the other with his production, or the work of art.

2 My only title to discuss the matter is some practical knowledge of two arts. I know very little about aesthetic philosophy, so I shall try, as far as possible, to speak from practical experience.

3 It is quite true that the artist, painter, writer or composer starts always with an experience that is a kind of discovery. He comes upon it with the sense of a discovery; in fact, it is truer to say that it comes upon *him* as a discovery. It surprises him. This is what is usually called an intuition or an inspiration. It carries with it always the feeling of directness. For instance, you go walking in the fields and all at once they strike you in quite a new aspect: you find it extraordinary that they should be like that. This is what happened to Monet as a young man. He suddenly saw the fields, not as solid flat objects covered with grass or useful crops and dotted with trees, but as colour in astonishing variety and subtlety of gradation. And this gave him a delightful and quite new pleasure. It was a most exciting discovery, especially as it was a discovery of something real. I mean, by that, something independent of Monet himself. That, of course, was half the pleasure. Monet had discovered a truth about the actual world.

4 This delight in discovery of something new in or about the world is a natural and primitive thing. All children have it. And it often continues until the age of twenty or twenty-five, *even* throughout life.

5 Children's pleasure in exploring the world, long before they can speak, is very obvious. They spend almost all their time at it. We don't speak of their intuition, but it is the same thing as the intuition of the artist. That is to say, it is direct knowledge of the world as it is, direct acquaintance with things, with characters, with appearance, and this is the primary knowledge of the artist and writer. This joy of discovery is his starting point.

6 Croce, probably the most interesting of the aesthetic philosophers, says that art is simply intuition. But he says, too, that intuition and expression are the same thing. His idea is that we can't know what we have intuited until we have named it, or given it a formal character, and this action is essentially the work of art.

7 But this is not at all the way it seems to an artist or a writer. To him, the intuition is quite a different thing from the work of art. For the essential thing about the work of art is that it is work, and very hard work too. To go back to the painter. He has had his intuition, he has made his discovery, he is eager to explore it, to reveal it, to fix it down. For, at least in a grown, an educated man, intuitions are highly evanescent. This is what Wordsworth meant when he wrote of their fading into the light of common day.

8 I said the joy of discovery often dies away after twenty years or so. And this is simply a truth of observation; we know it from our own experience. The magic object that started up before our eyes on a spring day in its own individual shape, is apt, in the same instant, to turn into simply another cherry tree, an ordinary specimen of a common class. We have seen it and named it pretty often already. But Housman, as poet, fixed his vision of the cherry tree before it had changed into just another tree in blossom.

9 Housman fixed it for himself and us, but not by an immediate act, indistinguishable from the intuition. He had to go to work and find words, images, rhyme, which embodied his feeling about the tree, which fixed down its meaning for him, so that he could have it again when he wanted it, and also give it to us. He made a work of art, but he made it by work.

10 So for the painter, when he has his new, his magic landscape in front of him; he has to fix it down. And at once he is up against enormous difficulties. He has only his paints and brushes, and a flat piece of canvas with which to convey a sensation, a feeling, about a three-dimensional world. He has somehow to translate an intuition from real objects into a formal and ideal arrangement of colours and shapes, which will still, mysteriously, fix and convey his sense of the unique quality, the magic of these objects in their own private existence. That is to say, he has a job that requires thought, skill, and a lot of experience.

11 As for the novelist, his case is even worse. He starts also with his intuition, his discovery; as when Conrad, in an Eastern port, saw a young officer come out from a trial, in which he had been found guilty of a cowardly desertion of his ship and its passengers after a collision. The young man had lost his honour and Conrad realised all at once what that meant to him, and he wrote *Lord Jim* to fix and communicate that discovery in its full force.

12 For that he had to invent characters, descriptions, a plot. All these details, as with the painter, had to enforce the impression, the feeling that he wanted to convey. The reader had to *feel,* at the end of the tale, 'That is important, that is true'. It's no good if he says, 'I suppose that is true, but I've heard it before'. In that case Conrad has failed, at least with that reader. For his object was to give the reader the same discovery, to make him feel what it meant to that young man to lose his honour, and how important honour is to men.

13 And to get this sharp and strong feeling, the reader must not be confused by side issues. All the scenes and characters, all the events in the book, must contribute to the total effect, the total meaning. The book must give the sense of an actual world with real characters. Otherwise they won't engage the reader's sympathy, his feelings will never be concerned at all.

14 But actual life is not like that, it doesn't have a total meaning, it is simply a wild confusion of events from which we have to select what we think significant for ourselves. Look at any morning paper. It makes no sense at all—it means nothing but chaos. We read only what we think important; that is to say, we provide our own sense to the news. We have to do so because otherwise it wouldn't be there. To do this, we have to have some standard of valuation, we have to know whether the political event is more important than a murder, or a divorce than the stock market, or the stock market than who won the Derby.

15 The writer, in short, has to find some meaning in life before he gives it to us in a book. And his subject matter is much more confused than that of a painter. Of course, in this respect, everyone is in the same boat. Everyone, not only the writer, is presented with the same chaos, and is obliged to form his own idea of

the world, of what matters and what doesn't matter. He has to do it, from earliest childhood, for his own safety. And if he gets it wrong, if his idea does not accord with reality, he will suffer for it. A friend of mine, as a child, thought he could fly, and jumped off the roof. Luckily he came down in a flower-bed and only broke a leg.

16 This seems to contradict what I said just now about the chaos which stands before us every morning. For the boy who failed to fly did not suffer only from bad luck. He affronted a law of gravity, a permanent part of a reality objective to him. As we know very well, underneath the chaos of events, there are laws, or if you like consistencies, both of fact and feeling. What science calls matter, that is to say, certain fixed characteristics of being, presents us with a whole framework of reality which we defy at our peril. Wrong ideas about gravity or the wholesomeness of prussic acid are always fatal.

17 So, too, human nature and its social relations present certain constants. Asylums and gaols are full of people who have forgotten or ignored them. On the other hand, we can still comprehend and enjoy palaeolithic art and Homer. Homer's heroes had the same kind of nature as our own.

18 These human constants are also a part of reality objective to us, that is, a permanent character of the world as we know it. So we have a reality consisting of permanent and highly obstinate facts, and permanent and highly obstinate human nature. And human nature is always in conflict with material facts, although men are themselves most curious combinations of fact and feeling, and actually require the machinery of their organism to realise their emotions, their desires and ambitions. Though the ghost could not exist without the machine which is at once its material form, its servant, its limitation, its perfection and its traitor, it is always trying to get more power over it, to change it.

19 Men have in fact obtained more power over matter, but to change it is impossible. It may be said that all works of art, all ideas of life, all philosophies are 'As if,' but I am suggesting that they can be checked with an objective reality. They might be called propositions for truth and their truth can be decided by their correspondence with the real. Man can't change the elemental characters. If you could, the world would probably vanish into nothing. But because of their very permanence, you can assemble them into new forms. You can build new houses with the bricks they used for the oldest Rome, because they are still bricks. For bricks that could stop being bricks at will would be no good to the architect. And a heart that stopped beating at its own will would be no good to the artist. The creative soul needs the machine, as the living world needs a fixed character, or it could not exist at all. It would be merely an idea. But by a paradox we have to accept, part of this fixed character is the free mind, the creative imagination, in everlasting conflict with facts, including its own machinery, its own tools.

QUESTIONS FOR WRITING AND DISCUSSION

OBSERVING

1. In what way, according to Cary, is the intuition of a child the same thing as the intuition of an artist?
2. How does Cary describe the relation between intuition and expression?
3. What important difference between life and art does Cary suggest? What important similarities? Do you agree?

EVALUATING

1. Cary speaks of the artist starting with a kind of discovery. How does he characterize that discovery? How, for example, does it differ from other kinds of discovery—a scientist's, for example? Are there such things, do you think, as "laws . . . both of fact and feeling"? How does the scientific discovery of "certain fixed characteristics of being" compare to the artist's discovery of "certain constants" in "human nature and its social relations"?
2. Amid all our concern for multiplicity and multiculturalism, is there such a thing as "permanent and highly obstinate human nature," and if so, how do you think we are most likely to discover it, through disciplines like psychology, sociology, and anthropology, or through art?
3. How do you understand Cary's claim that "the creative soul needs the machine"?

RESPONDING AND APPLYING

1. If each of us, as Cary suggests, "is obliged to form his own idea of the world," are we not all to that extent creative artists? Is it valid or useful to compare creating a poem, a painting, a musical composition to creating one's own life? Do Cary's comments on the need for work apply to both as well? In what sense?
2. To what extent do you think art can aid us in the process of creating our lives?

DOUG BLANDY, "ART, SOCIAL ACTION, AND THE PREPARATION OF DEMOCRATIC CITIZENS"

Doug Blandy (1951–), born in Springfield, Ohio, and educated at Ohio University and Ohio State University, began his teaching career at Bowling Green State University as assistant professor of art education. He has since taught at the University of Oregon, where he is active in Oregon's Folklore and Folkarts Program and in ARTS

Unlimited. Blandy is the author of several articles and the editor of several books, including *Directory of Accessible Arts* (1986), *Art in a Democracy* (1987), and *Pluralistic Approaches to Art Criticism* (1991). He is especially interested in the community arts movement in the United States. As he told *Contemporary Authors,* "I firmly believe that the right to access and celebrate one's own culture is a basic human right. This belief is the primary motivation for my research and teaching."

Art, Social Action, and the Preparation of Democratic Citizens

Doug Blandy

1 Citizens living in a democratic community have the responsibility of making judicious decisions on moral, ethical, artistic, and practical issues that affect the common good. Voting in national or regional elections is only one way in which citizens participate in a democracy. Other participatory activities include holding opinions as members of institutions such as schools, businesses, and cultural centers. Decisions will also be made on a personal level as family members, friends, casual acquaintances, and strangers are encountered. Integral to the decision-making process is public dialogue in the form of discussion, argumentation, and conflict resolution.

2 The presence or absence of public dialogue will define the success or failure of a democracy. John Stuart Mill (1859-1966) underlined the importance of public dialogue to a democracy when he recognized that women and men are not infallible; "that their truths, for the most part, are only half-truths; that unity of opinion, unless resulting from the fullest and freest comparison of opposite opinions, is not desirable, and diversity not an evil, but a good, until [humankind] are much more capable than at present of recognizing all sides of the truth" (p. 73). Philosopher Paul Feyerabend (1978) supports Mill's perceptions of humankind in the present day when he argues for the necessity of public debate and the participation of all people in decision making. I concur with Feyerabend's opinion that the need for this public debate is so great that it should occur even if it jeopardizes the ultimate success of the final decision.

3 Several approaches to public discourse are possible. Habermas (1983) identifies three interactive approaches that characterize discourse on the common good. These approaches are the cognitive, the moral-practical, and the aesthetic-expressive. The cognitive approach is exemplified in the empirical methods of science, the moral-practical in ethical theory. The aesthetic-expressive approach is primarily evidenced in the creations of artists who participate in public discourse through their art. The Art Workers' Coalition (AWC), Artists for

Nuclear Disarmament (AND), the Political Art Documentation/Distribution group (PADD), and the Bread and Puppet Theatre are four visual artists' collectives that exemplify this approach in the fine-arts context. The 1985 Peace Ribbon Project was a grassroots example of aesthetic-expressive discourse independent of a specific art world. Organized by Justine Merritt, the Peace Ribbon Project involved thousands of women, children, and men in the successful effort of crafting a 13-mile pictorial ribbon exhibited in the streets of Washington, D.C., for the purpose of commemorating the fortieth anniversary of the nuclear attacks on Hiroshima and Nagasaki.

4 In Habermas's view (1983), the aesthetic-expressive, moral-practical, and cognitive approaches to public discourse are of equal value. It is his opinion that, in those situations where one approach continually takes precedence over the other two, the result is terrorism. Aestheticized politics, moral rigorism, or doctrinaire politics result from the imbalance.

5 A democratic community is nurtured by a mature and experienced citizenry prepared through active democratic participation to govern themselves. Democracy will continue in a community only as long as the mature members act personally and through social and cultural institutions to prepare children and youth to be competent members of the community. The ability of children and youth to participate in public dialogue and democratic decision making will require an experiential education in which cognitive approaches can interact with the moral-practical and the aesthetic-expressive. This will insure the continuation of the tradition. According to Habermas (McCarthy, 1981), experience with these approaches is at the heart of identification with the community and contributes to that aspect of ego development that encourages social action and moral consciousness.

6 There is a substantial body of research that attests to the political awareness of children and youth. A significant recent contribution to this record is *The Political Life of Children* (Coles, 1986), in which Coles chronicles his political conversations with children and youth over the past decade. This cross-cultural investigation clearly indicates that children and youth, worldwide, are astute in their understanding of the larger and smaller issues affecting their lives, the lives of other family members, their community, nation, and the world. Consequently it might seem reasonable to assume that American school teachers, along with parents and significant others, are participating in the experiential education of young people that prepares them to participate democratically. If this were true, teachers would be acting as responsive members of their community who are teaching others to be the same. Unfortunately this is not the current situation. Students are indicating that their teachers are failing in this task and not properly preparing them, for example, to participate in a modern world dominated by the complexities of nuclear politics (Macy, 1983).

7 There are exceptions. It is one of these exceptions that will spur our discussion in this chapter. This exceptional case exemplifies the contribution that aesthetic-expressive discourse can make to a democracy and one context of many in which such discourse can be effective. The type of environment that

can nurture such discourse and some of the forces currently working against public debate and decision making are considered.

A Lima, Ohio, Demonstration

8 Lima is a small city of approximately 46,000 residents located in northwestern Ohio. A booming city in the early twentieth century, it now suffers the malaise of unemployment and economic hardship typical of many midwestern industrial communities. Lima residents have almost deserted the original business district and adjacent residential areas in favor of the surrounding suburbs. However, in recent years there has been a concentrated effort by the city government to revitalize the inner city through the building of a convention center and the refurbishment of existing buildings. The Lima Art Association, a publicly funded arts organization, assists in this effort by operating an art gallery in the mezzanine of a mid-city auditorium.

9 In 1985 the Lima Art Association sponsored a sculpture competition for the town square. A committee of leading Lima citizens and Art Association bureaucrats awarded $25,000 to Cincinnati, Ohio, sculptor Stuart Fink for the design and installation of a 12-foot high, fluted-columned, double-arched, cast concrete fantasy mounted on a two-tiered base. Fink calls this work "Trinity" and describes it as a representation of the Lima Community (M. Huffman, personal communication, September 21, 1986).

10 On May 31, 1985, at mid-day, students enrolled in Mike Huffman's Art II class at Lima Senior High School walked a seven-foot papier-maché milkshake, a three-foot hamburger, and several six-foot french fries through the streets of mid-city Lima to the town square where "Trinity" will be installed. The monumental fast food that they carried was marked with the logo of the Kewpee restaurant chain. The students and their teacher stayed several hours in the town square. During this time they discussed with interested passersby the Lima Art Association Sculpture Competition, "Trinity," and the students' alternative to the choice funded by the Association. These discussions were videotaped for later reference. A local art critic covered the event for the city's newspaper, and a subsequent article was published.

11 This public demonstration by Mike Huffman and his students was motivated by their dissatisfaction with the process and results of the sculpture competition. According to Huffman (personal communication, January 2, 1986), he and his students felt that it was ludicrous for the sculpture competition committee to commission a public sculpture, purportedly reflective of the Lima community, from an artist who would visit the city on only one or two occasions. One student spoke for all when he said, "Who does this guy think he is? He comes here for one day and tells us who we are, what we like, and what we are about!" Writing about the students' alternative, Huffman states, "Our 'Kewpee Piece' was a direct image from the community. Unlike the artist in question, we had a longstanding relationship with Lima. That relationship allowed us to focus on a single aspect common to almost everyone at every social and

economic level in the community. We merely repeated expressively a beloved image as subject and theme for our public sculpture."

12 The action taken by Huffman and his students ended as it began. They walked their sculpture back to the high school. The readily apparent results of their action were not dramatic, although Huffman believes the temporary installation of his students' sculpture "spurred the Lima Art Association sponsors to attempt to include collaboration and participation in their public piece called 'Trinity.' The base will include concrete work, flat slabs of drawings by area school children" (personal communication, March 19, 1986).

13 The impact and importance of this instance of public action, however, should not be considered in terms of immediate results, but through the example and implications of its challenge to the Lima community. These Lima High School students and their teacher exemplify the means by which young people can be prepared to be competent members of a democratic community. The public debate that they initiated with the Lima Art Association and the citizenry on the square experientially reaffirms for them the importance of free public dialogue. These individuals exercised their rights as citizens to voice their concerns with public policy in an aesthetic-expressive manner, free of intimidation by the educational backgrounds, economic status, or social standing of those with whom they were in conflict. These activists trusted their ability to make their points known to the community and accepted the fact that this same community would pass judgment on the merits of their argument.

A Challenge to Specialization

14 The conduct of Mike Huffman and his collaborators is commendable for the challenge that it presents to all of the citizens of Lima. Despite the fact that the history of democratic ideas supports public debate, social critics are currently suggesting that this principle is severely threatened or has been eliminated by economic, educational, cultural, sexual, and political prejudices (Gans, 1977; Mann, 1977; Truitt, 1977). It appears that John Stuart Mill's warning on the fallibility of the singular opinions of men and women is no longer being heeded. Fortunately, there are some individuals, like those from the Lima Senior High School, who repudiate this current situation by periodically reaffirming that public dialogue does exist as a responsibility of the ordinary citizen. This reaffirmation of public debate reacts to the current trend in which decision making by citizens is discouraged and replaced by decision making by specialists in narrow fields of endeavor. In the case of the Lima sculpture competition, decisions were made by art specialists schooled in a fine-art or high-art tradition as interpreted and reinforced by Art Association bureaucrats. On this situation in Lima, Mike Huffman states that

> the open question of what is public art is what we wrestled with and continue to discuss. Of course, what always seemed to amaze my students and nearly incites to riot individual groups was the fact that there are those art managerial types in the community who not only know exactly what public

art is, but what it looks like and where it shall go. (Personal communication, January 7, 1986)

15 Wendell Berry (1977) describes specialization of the type evidenced in the Lima sculpture competition as the "disease of the modern character" (p. 19). Symptomatic of this disease is the willingness of ordinary citizens to relinquish their personal responsibility to govern, understand law, maintain health, engineer, educate, and define a personal aesthetic. Citizens have relinquished these rights to specialists who are trained in very specialized fields and who make decisions for others based upon a narrow perspective.

16 The extent to which citizens have done this is so great that the National Art Education Association (NAEA) can go on record as stating that the purpose of education is not to prepare citizens to make geopolitical decisions, record history, or make important artistic decisions. The NAEA sees such decision making as being in the realm of the "professional." These endeavors, once open to public debate, are now recognized as the tasks of specialists. The NAEA uses this rationale to support an approach to art education that negates students' ability to make and respond to art in favor of students' accepting, understanding, and modeling their responses to conform to the methodologies and judgments of aestheticians, critics, and art educators (NAEA, 1986). The NAEA approach to art education implies that aesthetic discourse is now the specialization of the art expert. Consequently, the ordinary citizen can no longer recognize art without the expert's assistance. Ultimately art is validated by these art specialists or their appointees.

17 The consequences of this state of specialization are dire. Berry (1977) recognizes the citizenry of America as fragmented by their singular competencies and multiple incompetencies. Citizens are confined to narrow realms of influence and have virtually no voice or ability to make known their opinions in the vast majority of decisions that affect their lives. This incompetence includes the selection of objects chosen for their aesthetic contemplation, as in the Lima example. The Lima Art Association assumed that the citizens of Lima were largely willing to accept that they could not perceive, contemplate, and appreciate the aesthetic in objects or in their day-to-day activities. Berry (1983) does not recognize democracy in this state, but sees totalitarianism in its singularity and fragmentation. It is because of circumstances like those witnessed in Lima, that Habermas (cited in Bottomore, 1984) can decry the influence of technical experts and call for the readdressing of social policy in public debate.

18 Educational systems contribute to cultural alienation and fragmentation. It is primarily school systems that are responsible for the perpetualization of specialization, through their curricula. A recent study of American life entitled *Habits of the Heart* (Bellah, Madsen, Sullivan, Swidler, & Tipton, 1985) reveals that educators are failing to teach individuals to recognize and actualize a place for themselves in the community. This same study found, however, that educators are succeeding at communicating specialized information and technical skills. An erosion of personal meaning and coherence typifies the findings.

19 The problem of social fragmentation, described by Berry (1977) and corroborated by Bellah et al. (1985), has been gestating in America since its discovery by white men bringing an industrial economy from the western fringes of Europe (Berry, 1977). Walt Whitman, in the latter part of the nineteenth century, recognized social fragmentation in his own time and optimistically proposed that societal cohesiveness could be regained through art. In his view the artist is the one person who can process and create images that transcend the individual and speak to all (cited in Hyde, 1983).

20 Art is not the panacea for social fragmentation. Habermas (1983) argues persuasively that singular approaches are terroristic. Consequently, in order for art to achieve Whitman's purposes it must be paired with social purpose and connectedness. This is what Huffman and his students achieved in Lima. . . .

References

Bellah, R. N., Madsen, R., Sullivan, W. M. Swidler, A., & Tipton, S. M. (1985). *Habits of the heart.* Berkeley, CA: University of California Press.

Berry, W. (1977). *The unsettling of America: Culture and agriculture.* San Francisco: Sierra Club Books.

Berry, W. (1983). *Standing by words.* San Francisco, CA: North Point Press.

Bottomore, T. (1984). *The Frankfurt school.* Chichester, England: Ellis Horwood Limited.

Boyte, H. C., Evans, S. M. (1986). The sources of democratic change. *Tikkun, 1* (1), 49-55.

Coles, R. (1986). *The political life of children.* Boston, MA: The Atlantic Monthly Press.

Davis, C. (1980). *Theology and political society.* London: Cambridge University Press.

Feyerabend, P. (1978). *Science in a free society.* London: Verso.

Gans, H. J. (1977). Democracy and the arts: Adversary or ally? In D. A. Mann (Ed.), *The arts in a democratic society* (pp. 98-117). Bowling Green, OH: Popular Press.

Habermas, J. (1972). *Knowledge and human interest.* (Jeremy J. Shapiro, Trans.). Boston, MA: Beacon Press.

Habermas, J. (1983). Modernity: An incomplete project. (S. Ben-Habib, Trans.). In H. Foster (Ed.), *The anti-aesthetic: Essays on postmodern culture* (pp. 3-15). Port Townsend, WA: Bay Press.

Hyde, L. (1983). *The gift.* New York: Vintage Books.

Macy, J. R. (1983). *Despair and personal power in the nuclear age.* Philadelphia, PA: New Society Publishers.

Mann, D. A. (1977). Introduction: The arts in a democratic society. In D. A. Mann (Ed.), *The arts in a democratic society* (pp. 3-17). Bowling Green, OH: Popular Press.

McCarthy, T. (1981). *The critical theory of Jurgen Habermas.* Cambridge, MA: MIT Press.

Mill, J. S. (1966). On liberty. In J. M. Robson (Ed.), *John Stuart Mill: A selection of his works.* Toronto: Macmillan of Canada.(Original work published 1859)

National Art Education Association. (1986). *Quality art education: Goals for schools.* Reston, VA: The National Art Education Association.

Truitt, W. H. (1977). Art for the people. In D. A. Mann (Ed.), *The arts in a democratic society* (pp. 58-69). Bowling Green, OH: Popular Press.

QUESTIONS FOR WRITING AND DISCUSSION

OBSERVING

1. Blandy identifies three approaches to public discourse. Explain what each of these is and how each affects and shapes public consciousness. City examples where you can.
2. Blandy cites Habermas' claim that terrorism results when one of the three approaches to public discourse takes precedence over the others. At the end of paragraph 4 he gives general examples. Can you identify a specific example? Consider political or religious groups, or art and cultural movements. How does Blandy's example of Lima, Ohio, fit here?
3. How would you describe Blandy's view of the ideal education? What would the role of the arts be? How would education connect to the community? In what ways does Blandy think that schools are failing?

EVALUATING

1. Describe Mike Huffman's view of art. In what sense can a papier mache milkshake and a three foot hamburger be art? If you think it is not art, what is your definition of art? What are examples of what you would call art in your community? How do these function in your life?
2. Blandy condemns what he calls our society's "specialists," who he claims discourage citizen decision making in favor of control by the few. The result, he says, is "cultural alienation and fragmentation." Cite examples of specialists in the arts, in politics, in the working world, and reflect on their comparative advantages and disadvantages to our society.
3. The Lima school situation was, for Blandy, a happy exception to the role of specialists, in schools and out. Can you think of other exceptions where citizens act out of their own imaginations and sensibilities, in ways that affect their communities?

RESPONDING AND APPLYING

1. Do you agree that the experience of the Lima students is an exception to the general quality of education today? What do you think schools or communal art associations could learn from Mike Huffman's Art II class?
2. What is your own view of art? Do you find the "fine" arts to be too elitist, too ephemeral, too delicate for your tastes? Describe your own art education. How does it compare to what Blandy advocates?
3. What is "public art"? What function does it serve in the community? What are examples in your own school or community? Is public art the same thing as public memorials?

W. H. AUDEN, *FROM* "SQUARES AND OBLONGS" AND *FROM* THE DYER'S HAND

A major train of thought about the nature of art is the notion that it possesses a special kind of autonomy, that it derives its power from its being separate from the world, however it may comment on it. W. H. Auden (1907-1973), expressed something of this notion in a passage of his poem "In Memory of W. B. Yeats," which he wrote shortly after the death of that great poet in 1939:

> For poetry makes nothing happen: it survives
> In the valley of its making where executives
> Would never want to tamper, flows on south
> From ranches of isolation and the busy griefs,
> Raw towns that we believe and die in; it survives,
> A way of happening, a mouth.

In the selections which follow, however, we will discover that while Auden may believe that poetry "makes nothing happen" in a utilitarian sense, he nevertheless believes that it can profoundly affect us. This is revealed as well in the poem quoted above, which concludes with the living poet invoking the dead one whose work still remains:

> Follow, poet, follow right
> To the bottom of the night,
> With your unconstraining voice
> Still persuade us to rejoice;
>
> With the framing of a verse
> Make a vineyard of the curse, . . .
> In the prison of his days
> Teach the free man how to praise.

Auden was born in England, educated at Oxford, taught school for five years, and like many young intellectuals of his generation became involved in leftist movements that led him to volunteer to aid the Republican forces in Spain's Civil War, something American writer Ernest Hemingway did as well. In 1939, he came to the United States, became a citizen in 1946, and taught at a number of American universities before he returned to England to be a professor of poetry at Oxford, 1956-1960. His poetry is noted for its irreverence, its combining the diction and rhythms of popular speech and popular arts like the English music hall and American blues with a full awareness of traditional poetics and a high degree of technical skill. In the prose selections which follow, he displays something of the freshness and experimentalism of his poetry in that he writes in a form that Winston Weathers defines in his book *On Alternate Style* (Rochelle Park, NJ: Hayden Book Co., 1980) as *the crot:*

> A crot is an obsolete word meaning "bit" or "fragment." The term was given new life by Tom Wolfe in his "Introduction" to a collection of *Esquire* magazine fiction, *The Secret Life of Our Times,* edited by Gordon Lish (New York: Doubleday, 1973) . . . The crot may range in length from one sentence to twenty of thirty sentences. It is fundamentally an autonomous unit, characterized by the absence of any transitional devices that might relate it to preceding or subsequent crots. . . . In its most intense form it is characterized by a certain abruptness in its termination: "As each crot breaks off," Tom Wolfe says, "it tends to make one's mind search for some point that must have just been made—*presque vu*—almost seen! In the hands of a writer who really understands the device, it will have you making crazy leaps of logic, leaps you never dreamed of before."

from "Squares and Oblongs"

W. H. Auden

1 A poet is, before anything else, a person who is passionately in love with language. Whether this love is a sign of his poetic gift or the gift itself—for falling in love is given not chosen—I don't know, but it is certainly the sign by which one recognizes whether a young man is potentially a poet or not.

2 "Why do you want to write poetry?" If the young man answers: "I have important things I want to say," then he is not a poet. If he answers: "I like hanging around words listening to what they say," then maybe he is going to be a poet.

3 Two theories of poetry. Poetry as a magical means for inducing desirable emotions and repelling undesirable emotions in oneself and others, or Poetry as a game of knowledge, a bringing to consciousness, by naming them, of emotions and their hidden relationships.

4 The first view was held by the Greeks, and is now held by MGM, Agit-Prop,[1] and the collective public of the world. They are wrong.

---

[1] *Agit-Prop,* slang popular around 1930–1960 for "agitation and propaganda," a term applied to the systems perfected by Adolf Hitler and his propaganda minister Paul Joseph Goebbels and used by many others since for manipulating and directing public opinion.

5 The girl whose boy-friend starts writing her love poems should be on her guard. Perhaps he really does love her, but one thing is certain: while he was writing his poems he was not thinking of her but of his own feelings about her, and that is suspicious. Let her remember St. Augustine's[2] confession of his feelings after the death of someone he loved very much: "I would rather have been deprived of my friend than of my grief."

6 Everyone in his heart of hearts agrees with Baudelaire[3]: "To be a useful person has always seemed to me something particularly horrible," for, subjectively, to be useful means to be doing not what one wants to do, but what someone else insists on one's doing. But at the same time, everyone is ashamed to admit in public that he is useless. Thus if a poet gets into conversation with a stranger in a railway coach and the latter asks him: "What is your job?", he will think quickly and say: "A schoolteacher, a beekeeper, a bootlegger," because to tell the truth would cause an incredulous and embarrassing silence.

7 How glad I am that the silliest remark ever made about poets, "the unacknowledged legislators of the world," was made by a poet whose work I detest.[4] Sounds more like the secret police to me.

8 It is a sobering experience for any poet to read the last page of the Book Section of the Sunday *Times* where correspondents seek to identify poems which have meant much to them. He is forced to realize that it is not his work, not even the work of Dante or Shakespeare, that most people treasure as magic talismans in times of trouble, but grotesquely bad verses written by maiden ladies in local newspapers; that millions in their bereavements, heartbreaks, agonies, depressions, have been comforted and perhaps saved from despair by appalling trash while poetry stood helplessly and incompetently by.

9 The frightful falsehood which obsessed the Greeks and Romans and for which mankind has suffered ever since, was that government is a similar activity to art, that human beings are a medium like language out of which the gifted politician creates a good society as the gifted poet creates a good poem.

10 A society which really was like a poem and embodied all the esthetic values of beauty, order, economy, subordination of detail to the whole effect, would

---

[2] Augustine (354-430) was a Christian theologian most famous for his autobiography *Confessions.*

[3] Charles Baudelaire (1821-1867) was a French poet, critic, and leader in the Aesthetic Movement, often associated with the phrase "art for art's sake." The Aesthetes reacted against the dominant expectations among public and critics that art was supposed to embody and promote conventional morality, which Baudelaire called "the didactic heresy"; the sole purpose of art, he insisted, was to be beautiful: "poetry . . . does not have truth for its objects, but only itself."

[4] This quotation from Shelley you will recognize if you recall the reference to it in the introductory essay to this chapter.

be a nightmare of horror, based on selective breeding, extermination of the physically or mentally unfit, absolute obedience to its Director, and a large slave class kept out of sight in cellars.

11 All poets adore explosions, thunderstorms, tornadoes, conflagrations, ruins, scenes of spectacular carnage. The poetic imagination is therefore not at all a desirable quality in a chief of state.

12 The democratic idea that anyone should be able to become president is right. For to talk of the profession of politics or a gifted politician ought to be nonsense. A good politician ought to mean someone who loves his neighbor and, with God's help, anyone can do that if he choose.

13 The old superstition that it is dangerous to love a poet is perhaps not without some foundation. Given the opportunity, a poet is perhaps more tempted than others to drop his old innocent game of playing God with words, and take up that much more exciting but forbidden game of creating a human being, that game which starts off with such terrific gusto but always ends sooner or later in white faces and a fatal accident.

14 Orpheus who moved stones is the archetype, not of the poet, but of Goebbels. The archetype, not of the poet as such, but of the poet who loses his soul for poetry, is Narcissus.[5]

15 Being esthetes, the Greeks were naive psychologists. Narcissus does not fall in love with his reflection because it is beautiful but because it is like himself. In a later version of the myth, it is a hydrocephalic idiot who gazes entranced into the pool, saying: "On me it looks good." In another, still more sophisticated version, Narcissus is neither beautiful nor ugly but as completely average as a Thurber[6] husband, and instead of addressing his image with the declarative "I love you," he puts to it over and over again the same question, "Haven't we met before someplace?"

---

[5] Orpheus and Narcissus are characters from Greek mythology. The former was reputed to be the most famous poet and musician who ever lived, so accomplished that he could not only tame wild beasts but make trees and rocks move from their places to follow his music. The latter is the beautiful young man who fell in love with his own reflection in a pond. Narcissus' neglected lover was the nymph Echo, who in her grief pined away into only a distant sound.

[6] James Thurber (1894–1961) was a Pulitzer Prize winning writer and cartoonist.

from The Dyer's Hand

1 In our age, the mere making of a work of art is itself a political act. So long as artists exist, making what they please and think they ought to make, even if it is not terribly good, even if it appeals to only a handful of people, they remind the Management of something managers need to be reminded of, namely, that the managed are people with faces, not anonymous members, that *Homo Laborans* is also *Homo Ludens.*[1]

2 If a poet meets an illiterate peasant, they may not be able to say much to each other, but if they both meet a public official, they share the same feeling of suspicion; neither will trust one further than he can throw a grand piano. If they enter a government building, both share the same feeling of apprehension; perhaps they will never get out again. Whatever the cultural differences between them, they both sniff in any official world the smell of an unreality in which persons are treated as statistics. The peasant may play cards in the evening while the poet writes verses, but there is one political principle to which they both subscribe, namely, that among the half dozen or so things for which a man of honor should be prepared, if necessary, to die, the right to play, the right to frivolity, is not the least.

QUESTIONS FOR WRITING AND DISCUSSION

OBSERVING

1. How does the example of St. Augustine illustrate why a girl should be suspicious of a boyfriend who writes her love poems?
2. Auden seems to suggest that poetry is useless, yet his description of poetry as a game of knowledge seems useful in some sense. Can you imagine a way of defining usefulness that makes sense of this? How does it relate to the liberal humanistic idea that knowledge is valuable for its own sake?
3. Auden uses Orpheus as a type of what the poet is often thought to be but is not, and Narcissus as a particular kind of poet. Explain.

[1] *Homo Laborans / Homo Ludens:* Man the worker / Man the player. The implication of the Latin and the association of this phrasing with the human genus is to describe humans as beings as much defined by their need and capacity to play as to work.

EVALUATING

1. Auden implies that poets are embarrassed about their occupation because it is useless, but he seems to associate the poet's kind of uselessness with freedom, "doing what one wants to do." What do you make of this? Is this poet's response determined more by his feelings about his art or by his concern about the reaction of the common man, the "stranger in a railway coach"?
2. Do you agree with Auden's describing as silly Shelley's statement that poets are "the unacknowledged legislators of the world"? Why?

RESPONDING AND APPLYING

1. Why do you think it should be a sobering experience for a poet (the implication is, a "real" poet) to discover that people feel most comforted and supported, even "saved from despair," by bad poetry? Is poetry not supposed to be uplifting? What do you think poetry, art in general, is supposed to do? Think of this in terms of the variety of things it might do, and consider whether there ought to be any priorities among that variety. It might be useful for you to think of this question in terms of the lyrics of the songs you listen to. In ancient times, poetry was most often sung or chanted, and it became common to speak of poetry as song even in times and places where it was most commonly read silently rather than heard; today it seems that for most people, at least in America, as in ancient times the only poetry they are exposed to is what comes to them by way of music.
2. In what ways do you see the imaginative process of creating form, order, coherence in a work of art as related to the imaginative process all of us need to be engaged in, that of creating a society? Why is Auden disturbed by this relation? Aside from the historical context that may have influenced him, to what extent do you think his ideas may have been shaped by his engagement in the very individual art of poetry? Might his opinion have been different if he were more involved in collaborative arts like theater, film, or television (Auden was involved in theater as well, but to a relatively minor degree)? To what extent are your attitudes toward art shaped by whether you see it as a private or a collaborative endeavor?
3. In what sense can "the mere making of a work of art" be considered "a political act," regardless, Auden implies, of its content? Could this explain the uneasiness many people feel about the arts? To what extent might this determine the minimal support in our country for art education (communities would much sooner support a high school football or basketball team than art classes)? To what extent might this be a motive behind censorship?

Walter Van Tilburg Clark, "The Portable Phonograph"

Born in Maine, Walter Van Tilburg Clark moved to Nevada at age 8 when his father was appointed president of the state university. Though he moved back East 15 years later to pursue an advanced degree and taught high school English in central New York state for some 10 years, until 1945, he managed to become best known as a writer of Western fiction. He is especially famous for *The Oxbow Incident* (1940), which concerns the lynching of a group of innocent men; this novel was also turned into a classic Western film.

The story which follows, though set in the West, deals with a common science fiction theme, the aftermath of an apocalyptic end of civilization. Keep in mind that the story was first published in 1942, before the public—or Clark—knew much of anything about nuclear weapons. He is not being especially prophetic on that score, since numerous writers had been seeing the possibility of a war with what we call conventional weapons causing the end of civilization for a century before the dawn of the nuclear age. Clark's focus, however, is not so much on what brought about this destruction as on what was lost as a result.

The Portable Phonograph

Walter Van Tilburg Clark

1 The red sunset, with narrow, black cloud strips like threads across it, lay on the curved horizon of the prairie. The air was still and cold, and in it settled the mute darkness and greater cold of night. High in the air there was wind, for through the veil of the dusk the clouds could be seen gliding rapidly south and changing shapes. A sensation of torment, of two-sided, unpredictable nature, arose from the stillness of the earth air beneath the violence of the upper air. Out of the sunset, through the dead, matted grass and isolated weed stalks of the prairie, crept the narrow and deeply rutted remains of a road. In the road, in places, there were crusts of shallow, brittle ice. There were little islands of an old oiled pavement in the road too, but most of it was mud, now frozen rigid. The frozen mud still bore the toothed impress of great tanks, and a wanderer on the neighboring undulations might have stumbled, in this light, into large, partially filled-in and weed-grown cavities, their banks channeled and beginning to spread into badlands. These pits were such as might have been made by falling meteors, but they were not. They were the scars of gigantic bombs, their rawness already made a little natural by rain, seed and time. Along the road

there were rakish remnants of fence. There was also, just visible, one portion of tangled and multiple barbed wire still erect, behind which was a shelving ditch with small caves, now very quiet and empty, at intervals in its back wall. Otherwise there was no structure or remnant of a structure visible over the dome of the darkling earth, but only, in sheltered hollows, the darker shadows of young trees trying again.

2 Under the wuthering arch of the high wind a V of wild geese fled south. The rush of their pinions sounded briefly, and the faint, plaintive notes of their expeditionary talk. Then they left a still greater vacancy. There was the smell and expectation of snow, as there is likely to be when the wild geese fly south. From the remote distance, toward the red sky, came faintly the protracted howl and quick yap-yap of a prairie wolf.

3 North of the road, perhaps a hundred yards, lay the parallel and deeply intrenched course of a small creek, lined with leafless alders and willows. The creek was already silent under ice. Into the bank above it was dug a sort of cell, with a single opening, like the mouth of a mine tunnel. Within the cell there was a little red of fire, which showed dully through the opening, like a reflection or a deception of the imagination. The light came from the chary burning of four blocks of poorly aged peat, which gave off a petty warmth and much acrid smoke. But the precious remnants of wood, old fence posts and timbers from the long-deserted dugouts, had to be saved for the real cold, for the time when a man's breath blew white, the moisture in his nostrils stiffened at once when he stepped out, and the expansive blizzards paraded for days over the vast open, swirling and settling and thickening, till the dawn of the cleared day when the sky was a thin blue-green and the terrible cold, in which a man could not live for three hours unwarmed, lay over the uniformly drifted swell of the plain.

4 Around the smoldering peat four men were seated cross-legged. Behind them, traversed by their shadows, was the earth bench, with two old and dirty army blankets, where the owner of the cell slept. In a niche in the opposite wall were a few tin utensils which caught the glint of the coals. The host was rewrapping in a piece of daubed burlap, four fine, leather-bound books. He worked slowly and very carefully, and at last tied the bundle securely with a piece of grass-woven cord. The other three looked intently upon the process, as if a great significance lay in it. As the host tied the cord, he spoke. He was an old man, his long, matted beard and hair gray to nearly white. The shadows made his brows and cheekbones appear gnarled, his eyes and cheeks deeply sunken. His big hands, rough with frost and swollen by rheumatism, were awkward but gentle at their task. He was like a prehistoric priest performing a fateful ceremonial rite. Also his voice had in it a suitable quality of deep, reverent despair, yet perhaps, at the moment, a sharpness of selfish satisfaction.

5 "When I perceived what was happening," he said, "I told myself, 'It is the end. I cannot take much; I will take these.' "

6 "Perhaps I was impractical," he continued. "But for myself, I do not regret, and what do we know of those who will come after us? We are the doddering

remnant of a race of mechanical fools. I have saved what I love; the soul of what was good in us here; perhaps the new ones will make a strong enough beginning not to fall behind when they become clever."

7 He rose with slow pain and placed the wrapped volumes in the niche with his utensils. The others watched him with the same ritualistic gaze.

8 "Shakespeare, the Bible, *Moby-Dick, The Divine Comedy,*" one of them said softly. "You might have done worse; much worse."

9 "You will have a little soul left until you die," said another harshly. "That is more than is true of us. My brain becomes thick, like my hands." He held the big, battered hands, with their black nails, in the glow to be seen.

10 "I want paper to write on," he said. "And there is none."

11 The fourth man said nothing. He sat in the shadow farthest from the fire, and sometimes his body jerked in its rags from the cold. Although he was still young, he was sick, and coughed often. Writing implied a greater future than he now felt able to consider.

12 The old man seated himself laboriously, and reached out, groaning at the movement, to put another block of peat on the fire. With bowed heads and averted eyes, his three quests acknowledged his magnanimity.

13 "We thank you, Doctor Jenkins, for the reading," said the man who had named the books.

14 They seemed then to be waiting for something. Doctor Jenkins understood, but was loath to comply. In an ordinary moment he would have said nothing. But the words of *The Tempest,* which he had been reading, and the religious attention of the three, made this an unusual occasion.

15 "You wish to hear the phonograph," he said grudgingly.

16 The two middle-aged men stared into the fire, unable to formulate and expose the enormity of their desire.

17 The young man, however, said anxiously, between suppressed coughs, "Oh, please," like an excited child.

18 The old man rose again in his difficult way, and went to the back of the cell. He returned and placed tenderly upon the packed floor, where the firelight might fall upon it, an old, portable phonograph in a black case. He smoothed the top with his hand, then opened it. The lovely green-felt-covered disk became visible.

19 "I have been using thorns as needles," he said. "But tonight, because we have a musician among us"—he bent his head to the young man, almost invisible in the shadow—"I will use a steel needle. There are only three left."

20 The two middle-aged men stared at him in speechless adoration. The one with the big hands, who wanted to write, moved his lips, but the whisper was not audible.

21 "Oh, don't," cried the young man, as if he were hurt. "The thorns will do beautifully."

22 "No," the old man said. "I have become accustomed to the thorns—but they are not really good. For you, my young friend, we will have good music tonight.

23 "After all," he added generously, and beginning to wind the phonograph, which creaked, "they can't last forever."

24 "No, nor we," the man who needed to write said harshly. "The needle, by all means."

25 "Oh, thanks," said the young man. "Thanks," he said again, in a low, excited voice, and then stifled his coughing with a bowed head.

26 "The records, though," said the old man when he had finished winding, "are a different matter. Already they are very worn. I do not play them more than once a week. One, once a week, that is what I allow myself.

27 "More than a week I cannot stand it; not to hear them," he apologized.

28 "No, how could you?" cried the young man. "And with them here like this."

29 "A man can stand anything," said the man who wanted to write, in his harsh, antagonistic voice.

30 "Please, the music," said the young man.

31 "Only the one," said the old man. "In the long run we will remember more that way."

32 He had a dozen records with luxuriant gold and red seals. Even in that light the others could see that the threads of the records were becoming worn. Slowly he read out the titles, and the tremendous, dead names of the composers and the artists and the orchestras. The three worked upon the names in their minds, carefully. It was difficult to select from such a wealth what they would at once most like to remember. Finally the man who wanted to write named Gershwin's "New York."

33 "Oh, no," cried the sick young man, and then could say nothing more because he had to cough. The others understood him, and the harsh man withdrew his selection and waited for the musician to choose.

34 The musician begged Doctor Jenkins to read the titles again, very slowly, so that he could remember the sounds. While they were read, he lay back against the wall, his eyes closed, his thin, horny hand pulling at his light beard, and listened to the voices and the orchestras and the single instruments in his mind.

35 When the reading was done he spoke despairingly. "I have forgotten," he complained. "I cannot hear them clearly."

36 "There are things missing," he explained.

37 "I know," said Doctor Jenkins. "I thought that I knew all of Shelley by heart. I should have brought Shelley."

38 "That's more soul than we can use," said the harsh man. *"Moby-Dick* is better.

39 "By God, we can understand that," he emphasized.

40 The doctor nodded.

41 "Still," said the man who had admired the books, "we need the absolute if we are to keep a grasp on anything.

42 "Anything but these sticks and peat clods and rabbit snares," he said bitterly.

43 "Shelley desired an ultimate absolute," said the harsh man. "It's too much," he said. "It's no good; no earthly good."

44 The musician selected a Debussy nocturne. The others considered and approved. They rose to their knees to watch the doctor prepare for the playing, so that they appeared to be actually in an attitude of worship. The peat glow showed the thinness of their bearded faces, and the deep lines in them, and revealed the condition of their garments. The other two continued to kneel as the old man carefully lowered the needle onto the spinning disk, but the musician suddenly drew back against the wall again, with his knees up, and buried his face in his hands.

45 At the first notes of the piano the listeners were startled. They stared at each other. Even the musician lifted his head in amazement, but then quickly bowed it again, strainingly, as if he were suffering from a pain he might not be able to endure. They were all listening deeply, without movement. The wet, blue-green notes tinkled forth from the old machine, and were individual, delectable presences in the cell. The individual, delectable presences swept into a sudden tide of unbearably beautiful dissonance, and then continued fully the swelling and ebbing of that tide, the dissonant inpourings, and the resolutions, and the diminishments, and the little, quiet wavelets of interlude lapping between. Every sound was piercing and singularly sweet. In all the men except the musician, there occurred rapid sequences of tragically heightened recollection. He heard nothing but what was there. At the final, whispering disappearance, but moving quietly, so that the others would not hear him and look at him, he let his head fall back in agony, as if it were drawn there by the hair, and clenched the fingers of one hand over his teeth. He sat that way while the others were silent, and until they began to breathe again normally. His drawn-up legs were trembling violently.

46 Quickly Doctor Jenkins lifted the needle off, to save it, and not to spoil the recollection with scraping. When he had stopped the whirling of the sacred disk, he courteously left the phonograph open and by the fire, in sight.

47 The others, however, understood. The musician rose last, but then abruptly, and went quickly out at the door without saying anything. The others stopped at the door and gave their thanks in low voices. The doctor nodded magnificently.

48 "Come again," he invited, "in a week. We will have the 'New York.'"

49 When the two had gone together, out toward the rimmed road, he stood in the entrance, peering and listening. At first there was only the resonant boom of the wind overhead, and then, far over the dome of the dead, dark plain, the wolf cry lamenting. In the rifts of clouds the doctor saw four stars flying. It impressed the doctor that one of them had just been obscured by the beginning of a flying cloud at the very moment he heard what he had been listening for, a sound of suppressed coughing. It was not near by, however. He believed that down against the pale alders he could see the moving shadow.

50 With nervous hands he lowered the piece of canvas which served as his door, and pegged it at the bottom. Then quickly and quietly, looking at the piece of canvas frequently, he slipped the records into the case, snapped the lid shut, and carried the phonograph to his couch. There, pausing often to stare at

the canvas and listen, he dug earth from the wall and disclosed a piece of board. Behind this there was a deep hole in the wall, into which he put the phonograph. After a moment's consideration, he went over and reached down his bundle of books and inserted it also. Then, guardedly, he once more sealed up the hole with the board and the earth. He also changed his blankets, and the grass-stuffed sack which served as a pillow, so that he could lie facing the entrance. After carefully placing two more blocks of peat on the fire, he stood for a long time watching the stretched canvas, but it seemed to billow naturally with the gusts of a lowering wind. At last he prayed, and got in under his blankets, and closed his smoke-smarting eyes. On the inside of the bed, next the wall, he could feel with his hand, the comfortable piece of lead pipe.

QUESTIONS ON STORY

OBSERVING

1. Why is Dr. Jenkins, the aged host of the story, described as "like a prehistoric priest performing a fateful ceremonial rite" as he rewraps the books from which he has been reading?
2. Why is the piece of lead pipe Jenkins feels at the end of the story described as "comfortable"? Why is this statement ironic?

EVALUATING

1. After you have read the story, read its first paragraph again. Can you recognize why in this descriptive passage Clark chose some of the details he did? Why, for example, are the cloud strips "like threats"? Why is there "a sensation of torment" in the conflict between the still lower air and the upper winds that are driving those clouds? What other details suggest kinds of significance that are appropriate to the situation and action the story will develop? Are there details later in the story that seem especially appropriate? Why out of all of Shakespeare's plays should the group have been listening to Dr. Jenkins read from *The Tempest?* Why is the musical form they listen to a nocturne?
2. In what sense can the books Dr. Jenkins has saved, "Shakespeare, the Bible, *Moby-Dick, the Divine Comedy,*" be described as "the soul of what was good in us here"?
3. Dr. Jenkins describes the group he is hosting (probably including himself) as "the doddering remnant of a race of mechanical fools." Do you find it ironic that part of what was good about those fools is transmitted by the mechanical device of a phonograph? Was the fault of these people in their machines, in their souls, in their stars, or what?

RESPONDING AND APPLYING

1. Clark has built his story around an old game, usually based on the question of what books one would like to have if she were indefinitely stranded on a desert island. How would your choices compare with Clark's? Defend your choices. Would your choices be any different if, like Dr. Jenkins, you felt compelled to take upon yourself the task of preserving "the soul" of civilization? Assume that you have access to museums, libraries, and churches, but you are limited to a total of items that is portable.
2. Speaking of the books Dr. Jenkins has saved, the guest identified as "the harsh man" says that *Moby-Dick* was a good choice: "By God, we can understand that," he says. Do you know what he could mean by that? Some students may be unable to guess because they are unfamiliar with Melville's novel. If so, do you see that as a serious gap in knowledge or not? Can or should the soul of a culture be defined, at least in part, in terms of an identifiable body of literary, musical, and plastic arts—a so-called canon?
3. If humanity's attitude toward and use of machines caused the failure of civilization in Clark's story, do you see any suggestion in the story that some greater emphasis on the arts would have made any difference? Does Clark suggest that the arts serve only to make life more endurable? In your own mind, are the arts a source of kinds of satisfaction we want to preserve, or are they a force that somehow helps us survive?

PERSPECTIVES

Should the Government Subsidize Art?

In times like the present, when words like *downsizing, cutbacks, retrenchment, belt-tightening,* and *taxpayer revolt* constantly reverberate in the media, in legislative halls, on political stumps, and in corporate boardrooms, the arts seem to be among the easiest targets for elimination. Two of the ablest spokespersons on both sides of this issue are presented next.

GEORGE F. WILL, "WASHINGTON'S WORKS OF ART"

George F. Will (1941–) has been described as "one of the strongest and most constructive conservative voices addressing contemporary issues" (Nelson W. Polsby writing in *Fortune*) and as "the most widely read and heard political commentator in America" (Sally Bedell Smith in the *New York Times*). No doctrinaire partisan, however, he is noted for arguing that most conservatives are hopelessly wrong about what conservativism is. He won the Pulitzer Prize in 1977 for distinguished commentary; has been a columnist for the *Washington Post, Newsweek,* and the *New York Daily News;* has been a regular panelist or commentator on major television news programs, including NBC's "This Week with David Brinkley" and ABC's "World News Tonight"; and has published several books, including *The Pursuit of Virtue, and Other Tory Notions* (1982) and *Statecraft as Soulcraft: What Government Does* (1983).

Washington's Works of Art

George F. Will

1 The selection of Jane Alexander to be chairman of the National Endowment for the Arts was itself a work of art, of sorts. Of course nowadays almost anything may, without serious challenge, be said to be a work of art. But more about that problem anon.

2 After a hearing that lasted barely an hour, the Senate confirmed Alexander with a unanimous swoon. Her confirmation process proved that chivalry is not dead and that she, although an altogether modern woman, knows the usefulness of male gallantry. The Senate asked her no searching questions about spending $175 million a year to shape public sensibilities. It vibrated like a tuning fork to her vision that "every man, woman and child find the song in his or her heart." She has mastered the arts-speak that passes for, and suffices for, argument on behalf of the NEA. It is a sugary patois that calls to mind Joseph Epstein on Carl Sandburg: "Clichés run through his verse like calories through cheesecake."

3 The NEA was created in 1965, at the high tide of Great Society hubris about the competence of government. Today Alexander presides over one of the most secure federal spending programs. It is instructive to note why it is that.

4 Alexander correctly says that it is a mistake to focus attention entirely on the NEA's involvement with what she delicately describes as "controversial" art. The NEA was born just as the last remnants of consensus about the nature of art and its public purposes were dying. By 1972 the NEA was funding, for example, "Dinner Party," a triangular table with 39 place settings of vaginas on dinner plates. NEA money was involved with the "performance artist" who inserted a speculum into her vagina and invited members of the audience on stage to view her cervix with a flashlight. The NEA funded a Chicago film project that was advertised with a poster announcing "Sister Serpents F— a Fetus." The theme was: "For all you folks who consider a fetus more valuable than a woman, have a fetus cook for you, have a fetus affair, go to a fetus house to ease

your sexual frustration." Recently NEA funds went to three Wyoming women for an exhibit of 70 cows inscribed (painted; why not branded?) with feminist thoughts. Well, not everyone has the same song in his or her heart.

5 Such sophomoric attempts to shock the bourgeoisie confirm Paul Valéry's axiom that "everything changes but the avant-garde." But Alexander is right that "controversial" art should not monopolize the attention given to the NEA. Most of what the NEA does is popular, particularly with the political class.

6 Alexander notes that government subsidizes science and she says the arts deserve equal treatment. But suppose government wants to cause the production of a large-scale scientific instrument that private market forces could never produce—say, a space telescope. Government knows how to assemble relevant experts, to measure their progress and to know when the goal has been reached. Baptists and atheists, liberals and conservatives can collaborate. Now, try to develop an analogy with arts projects.

7 Arguing that the arts "always have been subsidized," she elides a lot of distinctions, such as those between state subventions and private patronage. She even notes, in justification of the NEA, that without the help of his brother Theo, Vincent Van Gogh "would have drifted into obscurity." She also is gifted at the Washington art of arguing that her programs pay for themselves.

8 In a speech in Indiana, Pa., she sounded like a member of Congress, reciting the blessings the NEA has bestowed on western Pennsylvania. It brought the Ballet Hispánico and the Pittsburgh Ballet to Johnstown, enabled the American Theater Arts for Youth to perform in Indiana and Ford City, helped the Indiana Arts Council (the NEA is just the top of an enormous pyramid of government involvement in the arts) to hire a director. The NEA supported a playhouse in Ebensburg, and the Johnstown symphony, and the Southern Allegheny Museum of Art in Loretto, and gave $800,000 last year to support the state arts agency, and so on. She asserted that Pittsburgh's tax revenues from the arts have more than doubled since 1990, and she vaguely associated the arts with the creation of 6,300 permanent new jobs "projected" by the end of the decade. She said the arts in Pittsburgh are outdrawing that city's professional baseball, football and hockey teams combined. She did not explain why, if Pittsburgh's arts are so popular, they need federal subsidies.

9 She tells of her travels, marveling that she is greeted everywhere by outpourings of gratitude: "I can't tell you how many people came up to me and said how glad they are . . ." Yes, of course. But only Washington believes that expressions of gratitude justify federal activities requiring one group to pay for another group's pleasures.

10 In Washington the best defense is a brazen offense. She asserts that the NEA is "probably the most successful agency in the federal government." Its success is, she says, "unparalleled." Well. If a government agency exists to encourage, say, the production of corn or electric power or highways or housing, it is relatively easy to formulate standards for measuring the agency's success or failure. But the NEA cannot help but be a huge success. Using money to do the summoning, the NEA summons "art" from the vasty deep. Lots of stuff called

"art" comes. Not surprisingly: the summoner is not particular about what can be called art.

11 Alexander stressed the NEA's role in "leveraging" money from the private sector. She says NEA grants generate an elevenfold return in private money. But some NEA grants give a patina of legitimacy to foolishness, or worse, and enable highly political and lightly talented organizations to milk support from well-meaning but inattentive people in the private sector.

12 There was a time when the question of what constitutes serious art was answered by patrons and the educated public, perhaps influenced by philosophers. Today the question "Is it art?" is considered an impertinence and even a precursor of "censorship," understood as a refusal to subsidize. Today art is whatever the "arts community" says it is, and membership in that community involves no exacting entrance requirements. (A familiar Washington rhetorical trope: "You are a *lobby,* we are a *community.*") the "arts community" is characterized by strident insistence that any attempt to distinguish serious from philistine art is bad because it is both elitist and populist. It is impermissibly elitist because it assumes that a few are more talented than most. It is impermissibly populist because it implies that the arts ought to try to be marginally popular—that they generally should pay for themselves by attracting audiences, rather than by attracting government grants.

13 Alexander hopes people will "look to the NEA for a vision for the arts in the 21st century." But given what is known about both the behavior of government and the history of art, it is passing strange to suppose that a government bureaucracy is suited to the business of such vision-making. Alexander speaks of the arts as being often "prophetic." A similar bromide of arts-speak is that art should discomfort, provoke, disturb, etc. This conceit gives an arts bureaucracy a bias toward novelty, the political and "the new." This means a tilt against standards of taste because, as a character says in Alan Bennett's play, "Forty Years On," "Standards are always out of date. That is what makes them standards."

14 The NEA says that "peer review" ensures proper standards in the disbursement of funds. But as we have seen, the screening process often is, to say no more, porous. Besides, would "the arts community" agree to a system whereby defense contracts were approved by "peer review" panels composed of defense contractors? Of course defense contractors constitute a lobby, not a "community."

15 New York City shells out $87.3 million a year to 431 arts groups. An aide to the new mayor speculates that there are a lot of "clubhouse-type political handouts." Good guess. The New York Times reports that plans to increase—yes, increase—support for the city's premier arts institutions, "possibly" by cutting support for lesser ones, "was met with anger and trepidation" by politicians and "members of the arts community."

16 Any plan for supporting only the best is reflexively denounced as "elitist." That epithet comes awkwardly from the directors of museums and dance troupes and other things that claim to deserve subsidies because they have scant popular support. But this is the residual argument for public television in

an era of rapidly proliferating cable choices: some programming should be subsidized precisely because it cannot earn an audience sufficient to make it commercially viable. Finally, it is said that refusal to subsidize the most marginal art is a sin against "diversity."

17 Subsidized arts are pork for the articulate, for people nimble and noisy in presenting their employment or entertainment as an entitlement. So the subsidies are secure, as is the right of everyone to have federal support in finding the song in his or her heart.

QUESTIONS FOR WRITING AND DISCUSSION

OBSERVING

1. Why does Will seem to agree with NEA chairperson Jane Alexander that "it is a mistake to focus attention entirely on the NEA's involvement with what she delicately describes as 'controversial' art"? What does he mean by stating that "Most of what the NEA does is popular, particularly with the political class"?
2. Will characterizes the arts community as being unwilling "to distinguish serious from philistine art." Why, according to Will, is this the case? Do you see any indication of how Will would make that distinction?

EVALUATING

1. Will describes the NEA as "one of the most secure federal spending programs." Do you think this claim is justified?
2. Do you think it is valid to argue as Will does that it is more appropriate for government to subsidize science than art because the goals and results of scientific endeavors can be more clearly defined? Why?
3. Will suggests that subsidizing the arts constitutes one group paying for another group's pleasures. Operating on the principle that this is objectionable, what other government programs can you think of that might be equally ripe for cutting?

RESPONDING AND APPLYING

1. Attempt to define your position on government involvement in the arts. Consider not just Federal support for the NEA, but national, state, and local government support for such art-related institutions and programs as museums, libraries, special exhibits, and art fairs. Would the effects of letting all such vehicles for the arts be market driven be mainly good or bad? Is it possible to make reasonable distinctions between kinds of artistic activity that should be supported—perhaps art education, for example—and kinds that should not be?

DOUGLAS DAVIS, *FROM* "MULTICULTURAL WARS"

Douglas Davis (1933-) was born in Washington, DC, and educated at Abbott Art School (1948-1950), American University (1956), and Rutgers University (1958). His career has been wonderfully eclectic. A practicing artist, educator, and writer, Davis exhibits widely. The author of numerous books, most recently *The Museum Transformed* and *The Five Myths of Television Power,* he founded the National Task Force of Cultural Policy in the Public Interest with Anthony Keller, Martha Wilson, and others. His recent exhibition, "Inter Actions (1997-81)" traveled the United States by both internet and conventional means.

Davis has especially been fascinated by the interactions of art and the new technologies, commenting, "The one characteristic that sets contemporary art apart from virtually every mode of plastic or visual expression prior to 1900 is its extensive physical and intellectual collaboration with the new technology and information."

Multicultural Wars

Douglas Davis

1 There is no longer much doubt that we face a cultural revolution in the last decade of this century. It is signaled within the arts community by deep disagreements among artists, performers, critics, art dealers, museum professionals, cultural bureaucrats and the public. It is signaled in the larger community by seismic changes in the society itself, some of which fed the Republican resurgence in the fall 1994 elections. A month before the elections, Irving Kristol announced in a little-noticed *Wall Street Journal* editorial that henceforth all political wars will be primarily "cultural" in nature, pitting "the higher-paid and more economically secure professions" against "cultural conservatives . . . in the working and lower-middle classes."[1] Though Kristol's discussion centered primarily on religion, he also targeted "professors and those in the art world," joining the anti-art hyperbole lately employed by both politicians and commentators. The enemies of art now seem to include the Speaker of the House of Representatives, Newt Gingrich, who shortly after the election called for the

[1] Irving Kristol, "The New Face of American Politics," *Wall Street Journal,* Aug. 26, 1994.

destruction of the National Endowment for the Arts—an outcome widely assumed to be possible as this essay goes to press.[2]

2 In the past, "revolution" has often been metaphorically daubed "red," but we face an entirely different palette of ideological colors now. If critical exchange was once bounded by the pieties of the Cold War and formalist esthetics, we currently face, as Kristol says, a welter of cultural policy issues—some of them explosive and few of them fitting into the old left-right categories. They include the perennial struggle over federal funding for the arts; the alleged blasphemies of content occurring in art galleries and performance-art spaces throughout the U.S.; the rewriting of history and art history in books, exhibitions and wall labels; the demands by women, gays, persons of color and ethnic minorities for recognition and inclusion; and the phenomenal redistributive power of telecommunications. Each of these issues promises to have an impact on art-making and the critical discussion surrounding it. Collectively, they will certainly change the relationship of art to its public.

3 Much of today's cutting-edge, socially engaged art is—inescapably—provocative. It's quite likely to explore both sexuality and technology, two themes that are controversial in very different ways. The unclad body and the gleaming computer terminal are fast becoming icons of the mid-'90s. A spectrum of this work came to broad public attention in the 1993 Whitney Biennial and, later, in the two-part exhibition "Bad Girls" at Manhattan's New Museum in the spring of 1994 (which had a California counterpart, "Bad Girls West," simultaneously seen at UCLA). "Black Male," which opened last fall at the Whitney on the heels of the Republican landslide, is still on view. Each of these shows prompted caustic criticism from the mainstream media. But they are simply the tip of the iceberg which shows itself in museums of contemporary art, commercial galleries, universities and performance spaces throughout the U.S. This activity has already prompted the proponents both of reaction and of innovation to progressively heighten the pitch of argument. If the fate of the entire culture is currently seen to be at stake in politics, both sides now claim that it's at risk, as well, in the new art. . . .

4 While politicians and the popular press deliver sensationalized anti-art rhetoric to a large, diffuse public, the neoconservative elite offers cooler but equally aggressive critical verbiage to what might be called the attentive "new center"—the educated general public as well as the university-professional class. The key targets in 1993 and most if 1994 were—and are—wavering liberal humanists. Bestsellers like Allan Bloom's *The Closing of the American Mind* (1987) and William Bennett's *Book of Virtues* (1994) dramatize the notion that the "classics" of Western thought are losing their hold. Arthur Schlesinger's tract on the

---

[2] Jacqueline Trescott, "A Dole-ful Day at the NEA?: GOP Victory Sparks Fear at Arts Agencies," *Washington Post,* Nov. 27, 1994. This article was representative of several that appeared across the U.S.

risks of multiculturalism, *The Disuniting of America* (1993), reached a similar constituency.

5 Robert Hughes targeted this center, too. In his lectures and books, Hughes's witty aphorisms, honed by his long tenure at *Time,* have engaged swarms of apolitical art fans. In his polemic, *The Culture of Complaint* (1993), Hughes recited a familiar litany of Neo-Con anecdotes, from feminists hooting down male lecturers to NEA panels hunting through applications to find "persons of color" to receive grants. These are sad, tired stories but they clearly stir deep fears of impending cultural chaos, and demean the legitimacy of serious social and cultural "complaint," particularly when it is leveled at the engines of authority.

6 Let no one underestimate the effectiveness of a similar campaign being conducted on a higher academic level. Here the goal is to distort the complex, many-sided implications of what has come to be called "postmodernism" or "post-structuralism," depending on the journal and genre of the writer. Gertrude Himmelfarb's *On Looking Into the Abyss,* a broad-based assault on postmodernism and post-structuralism, is a prominent example. Widely quoted, it takes little serious account contemporary criticism and theory. Rather, Himmelfarb unaccountably views contemporary theory, as well as contemporary art in general as deeply hostile to the very historicity it indulges. She writes about it the way vested tradition has so often viewed fresh ideas—as a threat to received standards of "quality" and indeed to morality itself. In her view, these yoked "ideologies" (postmodernism and post-structuralism) will soon replace an "objective" body of thought—that is, the received body of traditional culture—with whining, petulant subjectivity, leveling high art down to "P.C." crudities. With a shuffling here and there of names, places and dates, Himmelfarb's laments could be mistaken for the vintage roars against the "decadent" Impressionism of the 1870s, the "godless" Matisses and Duchamps of the 1913 Armory Show or "Jack the Dripper" (*Time's* memorable description of Jackson Pollock).

7 No mainstream journal or medium of communication has yet chosen to reply in kind to the Neo-Con attacks. As a result, they stand unchallenged in the public mind. By force of repetition alone—evidenced clearly in Gingrich's post-election bravura—they carry a certain weight. This is precisely why our inoffensive moderates court disaster when they fail to carry the fight to the opposition.

8 Yet there is an impassioned body of ideas flourishing beyond the borders of the mass media, though very little of this intellectual fervor or creative ferment has been tapped by the administration or its supporters. There is a major intellectual debate underway that is far from one-sided. As Kristol or Himmelfarb could eagerly testify, today's innovative activity permeates dozens of art magazines, desktop-published manifestos, small-press books and college seminars. But it takes more "establishment" forms as well, in numerous volumes published by trade and university presses, as well as academic journals in a variety of fields. The art world plays a particularly active role in this debate. Our art galleries and museums continue to attract a large, growing audience for contemporary art of an adventurous cast.

9 The paradox buried beneath the continuing muteness of the mainstream liberal-left is that even today's politically fraught contemporary art could be easily defended. Long ago, proponents of today's avant-gardists should have argued that this democracy, or any democracy worth its name, thrives on dissent. Such is the eloquent message of Gordon S. Wood's *The Radicalism of the American Revolution* (1991) and Ronald Takaki's *A Different Mirror: A History of Multicultural America* (1993). Wood forcefully reminds us that the Declaration of Independence is the purest example of the "cultural complaint" genre, based as it is in widespread disaffection on the part of the colonists with the social and cultural inequities of the old European monarchical system. *The Radicalism of the American Revolution* documents endless protesting throughout the 17th and 18th centuries. Every known ethnic and racial group among us has at some time complained, raged, demonstrated, published pamphlets and made insurgent art. Often with just cause. The revisionist art and history now flowing from the hands of whites, blacks, feminists, gays, Latinos and Asian-Americans does not threaten, or claim to supplant "high modernism." Rather, it offers important information neglected by earlier artists and writers. Such revisionism is prompted by the same impulses of self-determination that animated the Declaration of Independence.

10 Since today's new art is a rainbow product, and since it embodies a broad range of changing attitudes, it becomes vulnerable on a myriad of levels. The flood of conservative rhetoric that is so much in evidence at present trades on deep-seated cultural, racial and sexual anxieties. Add to this a widespread resistance to attempts at finding innovative means to express new thoughts or attitudes (in the manner of science, say, or philosophy): it sometimes seems we are forbidden even to research the premises of art that may appear offensive or merely obscure.[3]

11 Two books that might permit us to think freshly about the patterns before us were recently written by black scholars. Both Stephen Carter, author of *The Culture of Disbelief* (1993)[4] and Cornel West, author of *Race Matters* (1993), present eloquent testimonies to the virtues of diversity and innovation. They see in the complexity of our multilayered cultural a salutary liberation from single-minded views of history—and of culture, including art. In place of ideals of assimilation and homogeneity, West reminds his readers (as the Whitney Biennial might have reminded a calmer media) of our "culturally hybrid

---

[3] Robert Hughes's *The Shock of the New,* New York, Knopf, 1980, Hilton Kramer's *The Age of the Avant-Garde. An Art Chronicle of 1956–1972,* New York, Farrar Straus and Giroux, 1978; Frederic Jameson's *Postmodernism, or, the Cultural Logic of Late Capitalism,* Durham, Duke University Press, 1992, and Willibald Sauderlander's "Un-German Activities," *New York Review of Books,* Apr. 7, 1994, are all examples of anti-innovation, "endgame" rhetoric in modes varying from entrenched Augustan humanism to Marxism. These positions are discussed in Douglas Davis's "The Avant-Garde is Dead! Long Live the Avant-Garde!" in *Art in America,* April 1982, 11–19.

[4] Carter's book, subtitled "How American Law and Politics Trivialize Religious Devotion," has been unjustly labeled "conservative" because it defends the validity of religious belief and assails the limitations of a secular society disposed to doubt professions of mysticism or spirituality.

character." He argues that the hybrid (like jazz, which is rooted in both European and African music) flies in the face of any policing of cultural boundaries. Faced as we are with a global intermingling of peoples, products, art and ideas, it would seem rational to follow the lead of Carter and West, not those who insist on the perpetuation against all odds of a Eurocentric world and a WASP culture no longer predominant. . . .

12 Since the world at large has literally turned itself inside out, economically as well as politically, it is impossible to take seriously either academic or political attacks on avant-gardism in art. The case for change in form, content and manner of address is based in the society that generates both the makers and the receivers of art. This case is stronger than the desire to cleave to the "objective" verities proclaimed by the neoconservatives (or their fearful liberal allies), particularly regarding issues of family, sexuality or technology, the ones that seem to pain the mainstream establishment most of all.

13 No informed observer ought to demand that the contemporary arts and humanities stand still in the midst of profound societal change. Despite the anti-counterculture (read: anti-avant-garde) rhetoric that accompanied the Republican midterm sweep, now is precisely the moment to seek a definitive picture of where our cultural institutions should be heading as the year 2000 approaches. Without that research, it's clearly impossible to invent a reformed cultural policy—that is, to adjust the categories, methods and goals of the Endowments, as well as rethink the rest of the immense federal cultural and educational monolith, which includes the Smithsonian and the Library of Congress. . . .

14 What's finally at stake is much more than the Endowments, whose form and structure could be improved. It is the creative freedom of all Americans that should concern us, currently under attack as it is by school boards across the U.S.[5] Thomas Jefferson warned us in 1798 that censorship damages everyone—artists, humanists, scientists, citizens of any political party. The report Clinton has requested from the President's Committee therefore deserves spirited, forceful language and a working definition of culture that is inclusive, not exclusive.

QUESTIONS FOR WRITING AND DISCUSSION

OBSERVING

1. Davis describes a cultural revolution that appears especially within the arts and education communities. What do the two sides of this war represent?

[5] See (among many similar recent reports) Virginia Witt, "School Censorship Attempts Hit Twelve-Year High," *People for the American Way News*, Fall 1994, 1.

What are examples of this war? How are the cuts undertaken in the budgets of the National Endowment for the Arts and the National Endowment for the Humanities (NEA and NEH) examples of this war?

2. Davis mentions "blasphemies of content," the rewriting of history, and demands for inclusion by the marginalized. Can you cite examples of these? Can you think of artists or writers who are seen as offensive by the mainstream culture?
3. What defense of new developments in art and education does Davis offer? How does he see these developments, as well as our Declaration of Independence, as parts of what he calls the genre of "cultural complaint"? What is "revisionist art"?

EVALUATING

1. Davis cites the books of Stephen Carter and Cornel West as presenting "eloquent testimonies to the virtues of diversity and innovation." They defend our "culturally hybrid character" against more "single-minded views of history." What values are these authors championing? Is there a limit to these values?
2. Davis takes some very consciously political stands here. Explain them and consider the numerous surveys that support moves for various kinds of art censorship, at least in the form of curtailing the federal support for the arts. What are Davis' politics? Do you think he is right in going against the mainstream?
3. True to George Will's claim that the art community tends to brand attempts to define serious art as elitist, Davis refers to Will as one of the neoconservative elite. Do you think this descriptive phrase is accurate or justified? What do you think it means?

RESPONDING AND APPLYING

1. Davis claims that the neoconservative attacks on some forms of expression "stand unchallenged" in the public mind. Where do you stand on the issue of support for controversial art? Of public support? Like King in his "Letter from Birmingham Jail," Davis attacks moderates who remain silent. What do you think he means by this?
2. Davis claims that the "creative freedom of all Americans" is under attack. What do you think he means? Do you agree with him? What could one do to take a stand?

CHAPTER WRITING ASSIGNMENTS

1. What group would you rather have making decisions about which art ought to be supported: people like George Will who have a clear idea of what "serious" art is, people like Douglas Davis who are open to a wide variety of ideas about what could be called art, some system like that

suggested by Doug Blandy that involves the community as a whole, the free market of purchasers, the support of art patrons, or some other means? Keep in mind that in a modern society, the development of an audience for the arts depends on access to the means of disseminating it.

2. To what extent is the art we are exposed to determined by the group or groups that control its distribution? How is your answer affected by Auden's statement that "the mere making of a work of art is itself a political act"? To what extent is the control of art the control both of expression and of information?
3. The kinds of art that are produced in a given time are determined not only by changing fashions in art but by technological developments, economic changes, and social and political movements. What factors do you think are currently having the greatest impact on what you personally are exposed to and think of as art? Are they the same as what you think are having the greatest impact on American society as a whole?
4. Describe the kinds of art education you have been exposed to in your life up to now. Consider all the forms of art—literary, musical, dramatic, and plastic—that you have been exposed to as well as all the major sources of that exposure such as home, schools, church, community programs, local museums and libraries, friends, etc. Do you think that exposure has been adequate? If so, to which of these sources of exposure do you feel most indebted? If not, which of these sources do you feel is most responsible for that inadequacy?
5. What do you think of when you hear the phrase "artistic community"? Have you had any real contact or involvement with such a group? What are the features or characteristics of such a group as you conceive of it that attract or repulse you? Do you think it necessary or helpful to involve yourself with such a group in order to appreciate or engage in art? Can one be said to belong to such a community by the mere fact of appreciating or engaging in art?
6. We often speak of various kinds of "literacy" as being necessary or desirable for members of a democratic society, such as cultural or scientific or historical or political literacy (mathematicians have their own word for the concept, numeracy). In this context, would you describe artistic literacy (perhaps a subset of cultural literacy, but then aren't they all?) as necessary, desirable, trivial, or something else? Defend your position.
7. Write a series of short comments in the form of crots (see the introduction to the Auden selection) about any aspects of art that occur to you.

Chapter Preview

Chapter Prelude

Affirmative Action: A Debate
White House Staff, "Review of Affirmative Action"
Ernest Pasour, "Affirmative Action: A Counter-Productive Policy"
John Mongan, "UC-Berkeley Looks to Replace Affirmative Action"

Introductory Essay

Readings

James Baldwin, *from* The Fire Next Time
Suzanne Pharr, "Homophobia: A Weapon of Sexism"
Carolyn Merchant, "Women and Nature"
Susan Griffin, "The Sacrifical Lamb"

Story

Ann Petry, "Like a Winding Sheet"

Perspectives

A BLURRING OF IDENTITIES
Gloria Anzaldua, "La Donciencia de la mestiza/Towards a New Consciousness"
Ishmael Reed, "What's American About America?"

Chapter Writing Assignments

Chapter 10

MULTICULTURALISM: RACE, ETHNICITY, GENDER, AND THE DEMOCRATIC IDEAL

AFFIRMATIVE ACTION: A DEBATE

The White House Review of Affirmative Action[1]

The Clinton White House Staff

1 On March 7, 1995, President Clinton directed that a review be conducted of the Federal government's affirmative action programs. The President asked the following questions:

> **Descriptions.** What kinds of Federal programs and initiatives are now in place, and how are they designed?
>
> **Performance.** What is known about their effects—benefits and costs, direct and indirect, intended and unintended—both to the specified beneficiaries and to others? In short, how are they run? Do they work? Are they fair?

2 In preparing this report, we analyzed federal programs that might be categorized as affirmative action. These programs range from outreach efforts that encourage grantmakers to seek out members of disadvantaged groups, to procurement regulations that set aside particular contracts for competitive bidding limited largely to minority-owned, economically disadvantaged small businesses.

---

[1] (http://www.whitehouse.gov/WH/EOP/OP/html/aa/aa01.html)

3 The report first sets forth the framework we used to analyze these programs. It then describes the evolution of affirmative action, as policymakers sought to make real the promises of the civil rights legal breakthroughs. It then summarizes the evidence of discrimination and exclusion today, followed by a brief review of the overall effectiveness of affirmative action and antidiscrimination measures. All of this provides the context for considering current affirmative action programs in more detail. Several sections describe the government's major affirmative action programs, and apply to those programs the policy test set forth by the President.

4 We conclude that these programs have worked to advance equal opportunity by helping redress problems of discrimination and by fostering the inclusion needed to strengthen critical institutions, professions and the economy. In addition, we have examined concerns about fairness. The evidence shows that, on the whole, the federal programs are fair and do not unduly burden nonbeneficiaries. Finally, we conclude that some reforms would make the programs work better and guarantee their fairness.

Basic Premise: Equal Opportunity

5 The tests that we apply are based on a fundamental premise: the goal of any affirmative action program must be to promote equal opportunity. Offering every American a fair chance to achieve success is a central tenet of our constitutional and political system, and is a bedrock value in our culture. It is the fundamental goal of the civil rights statutes—and of affirmative action as well. More particularly, affirmative action is only one of several tools used in the public and private sectors to move us away from a world of lingering biases and the poisons of prejudice, toward one in which opportunity is equal. Affirmative action measures recognize that existing patterns of discrimination, disadvantage and exclusion may require race- or gender-conscious measures to achieve that equality of opportunity.

6 Because our ultimate goal is to perfect and realize this American ideal of opportunity, affirmative action cannot supersede the concept of merit—because to do so would unfairly deprive others of opportunity that is their due. In other words, we believe it is wrong if an unqualified person receives a preference and is thereby, chosen for a job, a scholarship, or a federal contract over a qualified person in the name of affirmative action. However, the review of federal programs and broader practices demonstrates that affirmative action, when used properly, is consistent with merit. It also demonstrates that "merit" must be properly defined in terms of the needs of each organization, and not in arbitrary ways that are, in their effect, exclusionary. A demonstrated or predicted ability to get the job done is a merit test; "old-boy" connections and cronyism are not.

The First Test: Does It Work?

7 More specifically, the President's first charge was to determine whether the federal government's affirmative action programs work.

8 Whether a program "works" depends on what goal it seeks to achieve. Above all else, the overriding goal of affirmative action must be to provide equal opportunity for all citizens. In pursuit of that goal, affirmative action has two general justifications—remediation of discrimination, and promoting inclusion—both of which are consistent with the traditional American values of opportunity, merit and fairness.

Expanding Opportunity by Fighting and Preventing Discrimination

9 The primary justification for the use of race- and gender-conscious measures is to eradicate discrimination, root and branch. Affirmative action, therefore, is used first and foremost to remedy specific past and current discrimination or the lingering effects of past discrimination—used sometimes by court order or settlement, but more often used voluntarily by private parties or by governments. Affirmative action is also used to prevent future discrimination or exclusion from occurring. It does so by ensuring that organizations and decisionmakers end and avoid hiring or other practices that effectively erect barriers. In undertaking such efforts, however, two wrongs don't make a right. Illegal discrimination includes reverse discrimination; reverse discrimination is discrimination, and it is wrong. Affirmative action, when done right, is not reverse discrimination.

Expanding Opportunity Through Inclusion

10 Vigorous prosecution of proven instances of discrimination will not by itself close the opportunity gap; bias and prejudice have proven too varied and subtle for that. Therefore, to genuinely extend opportunity to all, we must take affirmative steps to bring underrepresented minorities and women into the economic mainstream. The consequences of years of officially sanctioned exclusion and deprivation are powerfully evident in the social and economic ills we observe today. In some circumstances, therefore, race- and gender-conscious measures can also be justified by the compelling importance of inclusion. Affirmative action is sometimes used simply to open institutions and opportunities because doing so will move minorities and women into the economic mainstream, with benefits to them, to those institutions, and to our society as a whole. For example:

- Virtually all educators acknowledge that a college is a better academic enterprise if the student body and faculty are diverse.
- A police department will be more effective in protecting and serving its community if its officers are somewhat reflective of that community.
- The military recognized years ago that sharp imbalances in the representation of minorities and women in the leadership grades of enlisted and commissioned personnel undermined the cohesion and effectiveness of military units, and effectively deprived the armed forces of full use of a portion of our nation's pool of talent. Most major corporations recognize this same challenge.

- Judges and government policymakers must be able to reflect the concerns, aspirations and experiences of the publics they serve in order to do their jobs well and enjoy legitimacy.

11 Ultimately, therefore, the test of whether an affirmative action program works is whether it hastens the eradication of discrimination, and promotes inclusion of everyone in the opportunities America promises us all. As a general matter, increases in the numbers of employees, or students or entrepreneurs from historically underrepresented groups are a measure of increased opportunity. It is very difficult, however, to separate the contribution of affirmative action from the contribution of antidiscrimination enforcement, decreasing prejudice, rising incomes and other forces. At the same time, the fact that we observe so much continuing socioeconomic division and inequality of opportunity does not imply that affirmative action is a failure. It is merely one tool among many that must play a part in creating opportunity.

The Second Test: Is the Program Fair?

12 For each federal program, at the President's direction, the Review team asked the agency head to apply the following test of essential fairness, stated here with regard to race:

1 **Not quotas.** Quotas are intrinsically rigid, and intrinsically relegate qualifications and other factors to secondary status. Does the program effectively avoid quotas for inclusion of racial minorities?

2 **Race-Neutral Options.** In a program's design or reconsideration, have options for using various race-neutral decision factors been analyzed? Were options reasonably rejected, given the available information and experience, because those alternatives are unlikely to be acceptably effective in advancing the program objectives?

3 **Flexible.** If race-neutral measures will not work, is the measure applied in a flexible manner, and were less extensive or intrusive uses of race analyzed and rejected based on a determination that they would not have been acceptably effective?

4 **Transitional.** Is the measure limited in duration, and does the administering agency periodically review the continuing need for the measure?

5 **Balanced.** Is the effect on nonbeneficiaries sufficiently small and diffuse so as not to unduly burden their opportunities? In other words, are other jobs or other similar benefits available, or is the result of the program to close off an irreplaceable benefit?

Affirmative Action: The Right Way and the Wrong Way

13 In short, we believe that there is a right way to do affirmative action, and a wrong way. This review conducts a preliminary policy analysis of many of the

existing programs to assess whether they represent the "right way." This means two things: they must actually work to effectuate the goals of fighting discrimination and encouraging inclusion; and they must be fair—i.e., no unqualified person can be preferred over another qualified person in the name of affirmative action, decisions will not be made on the basis of race or gender except when there is a special justification for doing so, and these measures will be transitional. Only by applying these principles can we aggressively and simultaneously pursue remedies to discrimination, the inclusion we need in order to strengthen our institutions and our economy, and essential fairness to all.

The Adarand Review

14 On June 12, 1995, in the case of Adarand Constructors, Inc. v. Peña, the United States Supreme Court held that many federal affirmative action programs, under the equal protection component of the Fifth Amendment's Due Process Clause, must be reviewed by the courts using "strict scrutiny." To surmount this hurdle, the program must be shown to meet a "compelling governmental interest," and must be "narrowly tailored to meet that interest." This is a more demanding legal test than had previously been applied to federal affirmative action programs, and as a practical matter it will require a searching analysis of many federal programs. The specific dimensions of that inquiry, as best can be discerned from federal caselaw, are described in Appendix B to this Report, which is the memorandum to agency general counsels from Assistant Attorney General Walter Dellinger, Office of Legal Counsel, Department of Justice.

15 The Court's decision concerned what is constitutionally permissible, which is a necessary but not sufficient consideration in judging whether a measure is wise public policy. We have recommended, therefore, that the President issue a directive to agency heads which not only instructs them to conduct the thorough analysis required by Adarand as a matter of constitutional law, but also instructs them to apply a set of basic policy principles. Specifically, after emphasizing the President's commitment to affirmative action, the President instructs agency heads:

16 In all programs for which you are responsible that use race, ethnicity or gender as a consideration in order to expand opportunity or provide benefits to members of groups that have suffered discrimination, I ask you to take steps to ensure adherence to the following policy principles. Any program must be eliminated or reformed if it:

- creates a quota;
- creates preferences for unqualified individuals;
- creates reverse discrimination; or
- continues even after its purposes have been achieved.

Affirmative Action: A Counter-Productive Policy

Ernest Pasour

1 "That teacher was selected for affirmative action reasons." That is how I first heard the term used—implying a lack of ability on the part of a teacher at my high school.

2 The phrase "affirmative action" was first used in a racial discrimination context in Executive Order No. 10,925 issued by President John F. Kennedy in 1961. This executive order indicated that federal contractors should take affirmative action to ensure that job applicants and employees are treated "without regard to their race, creed, color, or national origin." The civil rights legislation of the 1960s followed in the same vein.

3 Kennedy's executive order implied equal access and nothing else. The system that has evolved since is a perversion of the original intent of affirmative action.

4 A shift in emphasis from equality of prospective opportunity toward statistical measures of results was already under way by the time the Civil Rights Act of 1964 was debated in Congress. Quotas and the right of minorities and women to have a "correct" percentage of their population employed have since become rallying cries for civil rights activists. Affirmative action as it has been applied is detrimental to the operation of the job market, to white males, and to the groups it is supposed to benefit.

5 First, affirmative action promotes the hiring of less skilled workers. It sometimes forces employers to choose the best of the minority workers they can find, regardless of whether they have the required job skills. For example, Duke University recently adopted a resolution requiring each department to hire at least one new black for a faculty position by 1993. However, only six blacks received Ph.D.s in mathematics in 1987 in all of the U.S., casting doubts as to whether it would be possible for each department to find a well-qualified black, much less hire one.

6 Colleges and universities frequently also have quotas for how many blacks it is necessary to admit to "round out" their freshman classes. An example is the admission practices at Berkeley. Only 40 percent of the entering class in 1988 were selected solely on the basis of academic merit. While whites or Asian-Americans need at least a 3.7 grade point average in high school to be considered for admission, most minority candidates who meet a much lower standard are automatically admitted. Berkeley continues this practice of preferential admissions for minorities even though the graduation rate of minorities is very low. Sixty-six percent of whites or Asian-Americans graduate while only 27 percent of blacks graduate.

7 Affirmative action also causes reverse discrimination. Discrimination against white males is just as bad as discrimination against minorities. Some people say

that affirmative action is justified as a way of making up for past discrimination. Although discrimination still exists in the U.S., as it does in the rest of the world, most blacks entering the job market today were born after the Civil Rights Act of 1964 and have suffered little or no prejudice in terms of salary.

8 When this Civil Rights Act was passed, its spirit was not one of reverse discrimination but of getting employers to consider applicants objectively in filling jobs within their companies. Hubert Humphrey, a major sponsor of the Act, swore that he would eat the bill if it were ever used for discrimination of any sort. The past cannot be changed and we should stop compensating people who were never hurt at the expense of people who have done them no harm.

9 Another problem caused by affirmative action is that it places a stigma on groups which receive preferential treatment, especially on individuals who earn their positions because of their ability. Consider an employer who hires a member of a minority group for a high position on the basis of merit, not for affirmative action reasons. Other employers, however, are likely to assume that it was an affirmative action hiring, as are many other minority hirings.

10 The increase in racial tensions between whites and blacks at U.S. colleges is also related to preferential admission policies. It is not surprising that racial tensions have grown worse since affirmative action policies were implemented. At colleges in North Carolina, for example, black students recently stated that they were treated like affirmative action cases even if they were not. Professors, seeking to help, asked them if they needed tutoring or other assistance, already assuming the black students' lack of qualifications.

11 Affirmative action as originally conceived may have been a constructive policy, but it has been counter-productive in practice. I hope by the time I am in college that students, teachers, and others will be selected on the basis of ability—not according to quotas based on race or sex. If so, we will have finally achieved true civil rights for everyone.

UC-Berkeley Looks to Replace Affirmative Action

John Mongan

1 The University of California-Berkeley is taking new steps to keep the number of its black and Latino students from being cut in half.

2 To counter the recent elimination of affirmative action in admissions throughout the University of California system, Berkeley Chancellor Chang-Lin Tien yesterday announced the creation of the "Berkeley Pledge" program. The

program is designed to maintain or raise the number of students from "under-represented" racial and ethnic groups.

3 The Pledge seeks to accomplish its goals by improving the academic standards of California students in kindergarten through 12th grade.

4 According to the Pledge proposals, students who "show potential, yet face major obstacles" will be put into outreach programs to "build their academic records," a Berkeley press release issued yesterday said. The Pledge will also attempt to make Berkeley more affordable, including new financial aid packages and a vow to raise $60 million in scholarships in the next five years.

5 The release also announced the founding of the Berkeley Recruitment Corps to encourage more students to apply, as well as the Berkeley Academy, a summer program at the university to help high school students prepare for the school's academic rigors. Part of the Academy will provide training to high school teachers as well.

6 The Pledge is a response to a decision by the UC Board of Regents in July to eliminate "race, ethnicity, and gender from consideration in student admissions by 1997," according to yesterday's release.

7 The UC decision joins recent statewide legislation against affirmative action. California Governor and presidential hopeful Pete Wilson proposed a state government measure to end all affirmative action policies in California by 1996, and the anti-immigrant Proposition 187 is currently making its way through the federal court system.

8 Ending affirmative action in admissions could drastically alter the racial and ethnic balance of the University, Berkeley Spokeswoman Marie Felde said.

9 Statistics provided by Berkeley's Office of Public Affairs indicate that, had Berkeley's affirmative action policy not been used with the class of 1998, the number of black and Latino students at the University would have been halved.

10 The projections for a class chosen with no affirmative action considerations show an increase in Asian-American students from the current 42 percent to between 49 and 52 percent of the class. White students would increase from 30 percent to between 32 and 37 percent. Other minority students, including black and Latino students, would fall from the current 23 percent to between 13 and 7 percent of the class.

11 Issuing the Pledge does not mean the UC system is accepting the destruction of affirmative action without a fight.

12 "All nine UC school presidents have spoken out against this decision," Felde said. A faculty petition opposing the decision has been circulated around the schools, and has gained more than 500 signatures, she added.

13 A "fair number of protests and rallies," including one on the first day of school that drew 700 people, have already taken place, Felde said. At a school with more than 30,000 students and a reputation for campus activism, 700 is a small showing, Felde added.

14 Student protest has so far been limited to Berkeley, the only UC school which has started classes.

15 "Protests are going to be on hold until the entire system starts," said *Daily Californian News* Editor Risa Goldberg, a Berkeley senior.

16 Opposition at Berkeley is led mainly by Diversity in Action, a "mainstream" alliance of ethnically-based groups on campus. The group intends to start system-wide protests in October, Goldberg said.

17 But student opinion is not unified. Campus Republicans have organized rallies in support of ending affirmative action, Goldberg said.

18 Other students said they are taking compromise positions, advocating changing affirmative action without abolishing it.

19 "Basing [affirmative action] on socioeconomics has been discussed, and it sounds like a good idea," Berkeley freshperson Rob Maguire said. "I'm not sure replacing it altogether is a good idea."

QUESTIONS FOR WRITING AND DISCUSSION

OBSERVING

1. Based on the three documents above, formulate a definition of affirmative action. Try to guard against any bias in the way you choose your words and ideas to describe the government program. Also be sure you include a statement of purpose and some suggestions of the means public and private groups use to execute affirmative action's goals.
2. What assumptions about race and gender undergird an affirmative action program? Is it fair, for example, to claim that "we" have discriminated against "others" on the basis of race and gender? What does "discriminate" mean in this context? What do we mean by race and gender?

EVALUATING

1. Is it fair to claim that taking the race- and gender-balance of a school or business into account when hiring is reasonable? Is it reasonable to think that present actions like affirmative action can make up for past instances of discrimination? Can you think of other ways to deal with past acts of discrimination?
2. Identify the strengths and weaknesses of affirmative action as you see them. As an attempt to "move us away from a world of lingering biases and the poisons of prejudice," affirmative action uses "race- and gender-conscious measures" to achieve equal opportunity. Why is such action toward such an admirable goal so fraught with difficulty?

RESPONDING AND APPLYING

1. Identify personal experiences you've had with affirmative action, including things you've heard or witnessed. Be careful to separate rumor from fact

by identifying the sources of your information carefully. How have these experiences shaped your attitudes?

2. What is "reverse discrimination"? Some say it is impossible for those without general power in a society to discriminate against those with power. Do you agree? What does the Clinton government document defending affirmative action say about reverse discrimination? Do you agree?
3. Carefully analyze the arguments behind the UC-Berkeley and the Freeman articles. What important similarities and differences do you find? What kinds of evidence does each writer cite? What are the underlying reasons each takes the position he does? Which side comes closer to your thinking?

OUTSIDERS AND THE SEARCH FOR GENUINE MULTICULTURALISM

The Scientific and Democratic Revolutions of the sixteenth, seventeenth, and eighteenth centuries overturned the ancient cosmology and spawned new ways of looking at human rights, at social and economic organization, at governance, at the ownership of property, and at the distribution of goods and power. The civil monarchy and church authority, all parts of the old cosmology, were questioned and radically rethought, leading the way to modern revolutions such as the civil rights and women's rights movements. But the ideal of genuine equality for all individuals has stubbornly eluded us. What accounts for the fact that many of the same groups have consistently been excluded from the bounties of the Industrial Revolution and the benefits of a market economy? How will we identify those ways of thinking and the historical patterns of inclusion and exclusion that result from them that might then give us a hint of a cause? This chapter searches for patterns of thought that explain systemic behaviors which determine how truly multicultural our world will be.

Cultures divide people by many means, including religion, nationality, ethnicity, race, ability, appearance, occupation, age, economic class, sexual preference/orientation, and gender. When we examine all these categories, the broadest patterns that appear suggest three kinds of groups by which we tend to divide people: economic class, gender, and race/ethnicity. Most of the other categories can be subsumed under these more general classifications.

Scholars have singled out these three categories to gain insight into what causes some groups or cultures to be included in a region's wealth and others to be treated as "other" or outsider. The ways we view class, gender, and race/ethnicity can work to divide people, and too often such divisions create inequities. Since we deal with the first of these three categories in the chapter Economics and Social Class, this chapter singles out the two remaining, gender and race/ethnicity—not surprisingly categories by which dominant groups have separated themselves from others for thousands of years. Race and gender were also the subject of numerous nineteenth-century "scientific studies," using the supposedly reliable tool of the scientific method to generalize about racial and gender characteristics. As Gould points out in "Women's Brains" (page 250), researchers like Paul Broca seemed unaware of the extent to which their prejudices and presuppositions shaped the questions they asked and the alternatives they considered, kinds of blindness that gave them a false sense of confidence in the "scientific" conclusions they drew that women and black people were biologically inferior. Indeed, the confidence of a scientist like Broca indicates how deeply ingrained these prejudices were in Western culture and the extent to which gender and racial equality have been in fact new ideas to the nineteenth and twentieth centuries. The strength of the old prejudices, moreover, helps account for Hitler's success in making racism and sexism parts of a national policy he extended to degrade the largest and most visible minority ethnic group in his own country, the Jews, claiming they were genetically inferior and therefore a threat to a greater Germany. In fact, almost every time a group is targeted for exclusion from the dominant society, some theory is advanced to give the appearance of legitimacy. Very often, since the scientific revolution, that theory has been supported by some sort of pseudoscience, with claims made about a group's physical and biological inferiority. Recently, Oregon's Proposition 9, defeated by a narrow margin, claimed homosexuals were inferior; the seemingly scholarly book *The Bell Curve* (1994) by Charles Murray and Richard J. Hernstein made similar claims about blacks.

The advantage of looking at the treatment of more than one group at a time is the opportunity to see patterns of thought, judgment, and inference. By studying race/ethnicity and gender together, we can see ways of thinking, values assumptions that have stubbornly persisted through history, such as the assumption that the husband's rule over his wife is just part of the natural order, as is God's rule of his people. All the readings in this chapter deal with such patterns, forms of power, perception, and discrimination as they apply to questions of gender and race/ethnicity. Whether it be the systematic exclusion of women written into the annals of our government (Stanton and Mott, page 321), the brutal treatment of the slaves and then "free" blacks in our urban ghettos (Baldwin, page 510), the prejudicial bias against homosexuals (Pharr, page 515), or the gendered biases by which we see and treat nature (Merchant, page 520), each behavior is undergirded by a set of ideas (Griffin, page 524). Even this chapter's story, Ann Petry's "Like a Winding Sheet," artfully examines the interaction of race and gender for a black man whose loving wife becomes the ironic victim of his rage. Finally, the "perspective section" examines two writers' views of our blurring identities, a welcome alternative to the dangerously narrow goals of a "purer racial" self.

The discussion of the theoretical patterns by which we include or exclude people is often bound up in a search for appropriate terminology that describes the situation and plight of victims of discrimination. The term *minority,* for instance, once used to describe groups who were numerically underrepresented in a population, is no longer regarded as an appropriate designation, chiefly because it defines groups in terms of who they *are not* instead of who they *are,* and it connotes inferiority for those not deemed in the *majority.* Likewise, the terms *prejudice* and *bigotry* have now given way to more global terms like *racism* and *ethnocentricity.* This semantic problem, in fact, illustrates the difficulty of confronting the issue of equality among groups objectively and sensitively; the very words one uses to describe the disadvantaged predicament of groups within a society may alienate or malign the groups even when the intention is to seek their welfare. The majority in a society naturally struggles with the rights of its excluded members, if only to articulate the threat they feel to their standing or power. "What do 'they,' 'those people' want? Can't 'they' get a job or go to school or quit having children?" It is the experience of the "other," the underprivileged, the marginalized, that many of us lack and need to be informed of.

The social scientist Joe R. Feagin helpfully places the terms *race* and *ethnic group* in perspective. He points out that while a phrase like *Black race* is popularly used, *race* is an inaccurate and potentially dangerous concept when interpreted as a distinct category of human being based on physical or psychological characteristics transmitted by descent. As Feagin points out:

> A racial group is not something which is naturally generated as part of the self-evident order of the universe, but is a social group which persons inside or outside the groups have decided is important to single out as inferior or superior, typically on the basis of real or alleged physical characteristics subjectively selected. (*Racial and Ethnic Relations,* Princeton, NJ: Prentice Hall, 1976, 7)

Consequently, we can view "race" and "racism" as social constructions, intellectual fabrications which consider a group's unchangeable physical characteristics to be linked in a direct, causal way to psychological or intellectual characteristics, and which on this basis distinguishes between superior and inferior groups. When transplanted Europeans, who had rarely thought of black men and women as other than primitives and slaves, encountered them—as well as Native Americans in the New World—they could rarely overcome this association to treat them with dignity and mutual respect. Immigrants from Ireland and Italy were once widely defined by white, Anglo-Saxons as an inferior "racial" group. In Nazi Germany, the hatred directed at Jews was in part based on the identification of Jews as a "race" with supposedly inferior genetic characteristics—an example of a loathsome and dogmatic social theory denying not only the *civil* but the *human* right to live. Judaism, of course, defines not a "race," or biological entity, but a culture, a faith, and one of the oldest on earth.

Increasingly social scientists, and sensitive and sympathetic citizens in general, are moving away from *race*-oriented terms and concepts that are clearly based on culturally biased or biologically unsound notions that extend, instead of end, discriminatory thinking. Potentially more useful as a descriptive term is *ethnicity,* or ethnic group. All human beings, regardless of skin color, physical structure, or religious heritage, belong to an ethnic group. The term "ethnic" comes from the Greek word *ethnos,* which means simply "nation." There presently are broad and narrow uses of the term, and frankly, "ethnic" can also be misused for the sake of making distinctions or exclusions that deprive persons of their civil rights.

Feagin's definition, however, is a helpful one to use in furthering our understanding of the dynamics of civil rights and the idea of ethnic heritage: "an ethnic group [is] a group which is socially distinguished or set apart, by others and/or by itself, primarily on the basis of cultural or nationality characteristics." Ethnicity means a "shared sense of peoplehood" that transcends mere biology or geography and that includes one's native language, literature, and the cultural experiences of a shared past. Such an identity has meaning, however, only when it is *self-defined,* that is, defined from within the context of the group. To impose an external identity or set of cultural values on a group is potentially an excuse to further deprive the group of its sense of social importance and relevance and to alienate that group. For instance, to categorize an ethnic group as intellectually inferior to another, or to regard one ethnic group's language, literature, or music as "more primitive" or "less prestigious" than another only perpetuates a social and ethnocentric discrimination. The meaning, relevance, and pride in an ethnic identity must arise authentically from the people who comprise that ethnic group.

Another intellectual revolution stemming from the Enlightenment occurred as the result of the way we examine history through the lens of gender and sexuality, and the radically new ways we think about gender and sexual roles in our own lives. By *gender* we mean not the sexual categories of male and female but the ways in which a culture constructs or prescribes behaviors of both sexes. Traditionally, this has meant that men are strong, rational, and assertive, while women are intuitive, emotional, and nurturing. Men work outside the home and exercise authority over women, while women work in the home and raise the children. By *sexual roles,* we refer to the biological functions assigned to individuals. The best way to examine the changes spawned by rethinking these matters is by looking at the feminist revolution of the last 150 years, since feminism employed just those categories, gender and sexuality, to unravel traditional assumptions about our thinking and behaving.

While feminism as an organized system of thought is a relatively recent phenomenon, it is a far-reaching and revolutionary idea that touches every significant part of modern life. Because feminism forces us to reexamine the role gender plays in our personal, political, and even spiritual lives and because so many people feel so strongly about it, studying feminism can be especially difficult.

Whether we want to admit it, we are in the midst of a feminist revolution. Unlike most of the other ideas in this text, whose initial impact occurred in the relatively distant past, feminism is very much happening now. Once we accept this as a given, it becomes apparent that the newer a revolutionary idea is, the more controversial the idea may seem. Somehow, the passing of time helps us to adjust to new ideas. Even though new ideas about gender may make us very uncomfortable, they may also challenge and improve our lives; thus, it becomes incumbent on us to examine the new ways of thinking about being male or female, about sexual orientation and preference, and test them against traditional ways. Doing this, we may find ourselves admitting that many ways of seeing gender and sex roles have been ill-informed and harmful. Often the conflict appears in playful ways and is, therefore, harmless; but too frequently, it ends in abuse and pain, as in rape, divorce, wife battering, and attacks on gays and lesbians. Sometimes the conflict has political, ideological, and religious dimensions, as with abortion, child custody laws, and state-supported child care.

The difficulty in studying feminism does not derive just from the fact that the revolution is still occurring. It also stems from the fact that feminism is a complex idea that seeks to combine the personal, the religious, and the political. Because that combination can invoke our defenses and personal prejudices, the best stance to take in studying feminism may be to step outside the present, at least outside our strongest opinions on the subject, and examine feminism as a historical phenomenon, much as this textbook has approached each of the previous six ideas.

At its simplest, feminism is both an organized system of thought and the struggle for social, economic, and educational equality for women. Feminism views most societies as "patriarchal," an organizational scheme that grants greater power to men than to women by denying women equal status, power, and access to those resources needed to develop full lives. Feminists generally believe that the power of patriarchy derives from its gender system, which assigns particular traits to men and women on the basis of their sex. Once this assignment is made, a number of conclusions follow. First, the seeming "fact" that it is "natural" for women to be sensitive, emotional, cooperative, submissive, and nurturing. Second, that men "should be" aggressive, logical, and unemotional. If one accepts these premises, it follows that men are more suitable for doing the business of the world, whereas women are more suitable for work in the home. The world outside the home is where so much of the power resides, so women find themselves at a disadvantage. As a result, a majority of the poor in this country are women and children. Most feminists believe that biological differences do not explain these roles or the inequality of the genders. Rather, it is the traditional social and political makeup of society that gives importance and autonomy to men. Thus, the power of patriarchy stems from its pervasiveness: it is so hard to change because many people assume it is anchored in our biology as well as all previous ideas, religion, humanism, science, and so on, that have shaped who we are. Because it is central to what we do and how we think, it begins to seem unalterable.

Clearly, feminism is not just the attempt to understand and eliminate exploitation or subordination of females by males; feminism is also a new perspective on the kind of authority that establishes truth, a way of knowing (like revelation, reason, and science) that uses gender as a category of analysis. Such a new way of knowing would point out that most history has been written by men, that history has been shaped by the male viewpoint and male values, that the "great books of the western world" are written mostly by white men of

European descent not because women are incapable of such feats, that male dominance has affected the way we view history and shape reality, and that so much writing by women has been systematically suppressed. Such a way of knowing would describe a feminist epistemology (an approach to knowledge shaped by a consciousness of gender) dramatically different from one shaped by men. It would explain why so many women, especially in the last century, who tried to compete with men outside the home, thereby violating the conventions of "female decorum," found themselves driven to depression and suicide.

Although the feminist struggle for equality has occurred mainly in the last 150 years in the United States and Great Britain, its roots are ancient. There are pro-female texts from ancient Greece (Sappho's poetry and some of Aristophanes' plays) and from the Middle Ages (Lilith is often considered the first feminist). Women's resistance was strengthened in the Enlightenment and through the humanism of the eighteenth century, both of which asserted the dignity and equality of all persons. Wherever and whenever feminist struggles are occurring, it is clear that massive historical forces have helped to determine the relative success or failure of the idea. Specifically, as social conditions changed from feudal monarchy to industrial democracy, women began in the late eighteenth and nineteenth centuries to demand full equality and opportunity in all walks of life.

The power and importance of struggle for women's equality stems from the fact that with all the rhetoric of equality apparent in such works as Plato's *Republic,* Locke's *Treatise on Government,* and Jefferson's declaration that "all men are created equal," women were still, over the last 4000 or more years, regarded by many as physically, emotionally, and intellectually inferior to men. Traditionally tied to the home as child bearers and by the division of labor that sent men into the external world while women stayed in the home, women were further subjugated to men by law and theology. Legally, women could not own property, participate in business, or gain control over the lives of their children. Theologically, men have often used the Fall, as well as other portions of scripture, to justify women's subordination; as early as in Genesis 3:16, God says to Eve, "I will greatly multiply thy sorrow and thy conception; in sorrow thou shalt bring forth children; and thy desire *shall be* to thy husband and he shall rule over thee."

To this day most feminists believe that biased attitudes persist, that males do control a grossly disproportionate amount of economic and political power in the world, and we are facing in the feminist movement a monumental power struggle. What Martin Luther King, Jr. (1929-1968) said in regard to race surely applies as well to sex: "Lamentably, it is an historical fact that privileged groups seldom give up their privileges voluntarily."

Although many rights have been secured in the advanced countries of the Western world, most feminists believe that the feminist revolution is by no means complete. While suffrage was won in the United States in 1920 through ratification of the 19th Amendment, the first wave of feminism did not have the impact the suffragettes had hoped for. Even with the vote for women, little seemed to change. Still treated as the weaker sex, for women little changed in the way of politics, economics, or their role in society. The 1960s, 1970s, and 1980s have witnessed a rebirth of feminism, often referred to as the "second wave" of the "Women's Liberation Movement." Two important works that paved the way for the second wave are Simone de Beauvoir's (1908–1986) *The Second Sex* (1952) and Betty Friedan's *The Feminine Mystique* (1963). French writer, existentialist, and companion of philosopher Jean-Paul Sartre (1908–1980) and filmmaker Claude Lanzmann, de Beauvoir spent her life in revolt against bourgeois values she had been raised to respect. Her fight for women's rights was a natural outgrowth of that conflict. Critic Liliane Lazar summarizes the essential message of *The Second Sex,* which "postulates that man conceived of himself as the essential being and has made the woman the unessential being, the other, the second." Beauvoir's other main postulate is that there is no biological law that determines feminine nature, and all notions of feminine nature are, therefore, cultural or artificial. "One is not born, but rather one becomes a woman."

Friedan's groundbreaking early work was a similar attack on the expectations that women could succeed only through childbearing and domestic life. Three years after she wrote *The Feminine Mystique,* Friedan founded the National Organization for Women (NOW) and served as its president until 1970. By the 1970s NOW had over 400 local chapters, pressing for reform legislation in such areas as abortion rights, child care centers, equal pay for equal work, the elimination of gender bias in educational testing, and for elimination of cultural stereotyping of women and men in the media and in education. By the 1980s, NOW had grown dramatically, and the National Women's Political Caucus, organized in 1971 to strengthen the position of women in politics, had 73,000 members. Other women's groups, such as the Black Feminist Organization (1973) and the Coalition of Labor Union Women (1974), abound. As feminist Ellen Berry writes, "Today, it is possible to describes a world in which the idea of a woman working seriously at a career is no longer laughable, in which the choice to remain single no longer makes a woman an old maid, and in which contraception and a degree of sexual freedom are taken for granted." Nevertheless, feminists believe those gains are no reason for complacency, because deeply engrained attitudes of male superiority, which privilege men, still exist.

The second wave of feminism is a single, unified movement only in its goal of equality for women. Clearly, feminists differ in how they think equality should be achieved. One basic division has to do with whether they believe that change can occur within our system, or whether the system itself needs changing. "Liberal" feminists think that liberal democracy and its principles of individual rights guaranteeing freedom to all do not need changing. They just want these principles applied fairly and equally to women. They argue for better enforcement of current employment laws regarding equal opportunity, sexual harrassment on the job, equal pay for equal work, and sexually balanced application of the laws concerning divorce and child support.

An important group among feminists is people of color. This is a growing and important movement, especially in the United States, where black, Hispanic, Native American, and Asian women have too often been excluded from the mainstream of feminist thought. The fact that the "patriarchy" assailed by feminists is in large measure white and Western makes the inclusion of these women critical. (The bias of patriarchy is often referred to as its Eurocentric quality because the men who shaped the ideas of Western society were mostly white Europeans.)

Clearly, such classification systems are never universally agreed on. Some feminists may consider reproductive rights, including legalized abortion, as an essential part of liberal feminism. Those who believe in the "right to life," on the other hand, may fully agree with the economic issues like equal pay but oppose abortion and consider those who support it as "radical" feminists.

Feminism stirs deep feelings, and it remains the subject of one of the great debates of contemporary life. More recently, feminism has become more of a worldwide movement. In September 1995, the Fourth World Wide Conference on Women (the first was in Mexico in 1975) was held in Beijing, China. Basing its 38-paragraph Declaration and Platform for Action on a U.N. study called *The World's Women 1995: Trends and Statistics,* the conference reviewed the differential treatment of men and women around the world, using comparative data on economic, political and social differences. These are some of the highlights of the report:

- In the last few decades women have made significant educational gains though there are marked regional contrasts. High rates of illiteracy prevail among women in much of Africa and in part of Asia. High illiteracy is accompanied by large differences between men and women.
- Women's increased access to education, employment, and contraception has contributed to nearly worldwide decline in fertility. But country differences are wide: in developed regions, women bear 1.9 children, while African women still have an average of 6 children.
- While adolescent fertility rates declined in developing and developed countries in the last 20 years, they remain high. In Central America and sub-Saharan Africa, rates are five to seven times higher than in developed regions. Among developed countries, the highest rates of adolescent fertility are found in Bulgaria and the United States.
- Too many women still have no access to reproductive health care.
- Women still face major obstacles entering top levels of influence in their societies. Women in the highest levels of government are the exception in all regions. At the end of 1994, only 10 women were heads of state. Though their participation in the labor force is increasing, women rarely account for more than 1% or 2% percent of top executive positions. (gopher:'gopher.uundp.org:70/00/95_07/84/)

The 38-paragraph Declaration is accessible on the World Wide Web at this address: http://www.iisd.ca/linkages/women.html

Sadly, this conference on women removed "sexual orientation" from the antidiscrimination clauses of its platform. (*NYT,* 10 October 1995, A12) Given that fact, and the high rates of abuse and harassment gays and lesbians are subject to, not to mention teen suicide, it appears that discrimination based on sexual orientation-preference is the last form that is widely tolerated in the United States.

Thus, feminism emerges as a concept and plan of action contributing powerfully to the overall fomentation of multiculturalism that animates much of our social and political life as we enter a new century. The complex and interrelated ways that race, color, ethnic background, and gender inform our discussion of equality, fair educational standards, and the meaningfulness of "life, liberty, and the pursuit of happiness" is the underlying subject of the selections for this chapter.

JAMES BALDWIN, *FROM* THE FIRE NEXT TIME

James Baldwin, arguably more than any other writer this century, has reminded Americans of our long and continuing history of racism. Born in Harlem in 1924, raised by a tyrannical father, "Jimmy" served as a preacher in his father's church, where he first practiced the rhythmical cadences that became famous in his prose. Eulogizing him at his death, the *New York Times* referred to his "insistent, passionate voice, as an essayist, novelist and playwright," which "helped to inform and transform the debate on civil rights. . . . His deeply generous spirit nourished a generation of writers, black and white, who benefited from his personal warmth and were inspired by the incisive, articulate anger that distinguished his writings." Nobel Laureate Toni Morrison commented that he "gave us ourselves to think about, to cherish" in describing the astonishing gift of his art and friendship. Many critics feel that his finest writing occurred in his essays; what follows is an excerpt from "Letter from a Region of My Mind" which is a section of *The Fire Next Time,* first published in *The New Yorker* in 1962.[1]

from The Fire Next Time

James Baldwin

1 I underwent, during the summer that I became fourteen, a prolonged religious crisis. I use the word "religious" in the common, and arbitrary sense, meaning

[1] *Letter from a Region of My Mind,* of which the first half is printed here, was originally published in the *New Yorker* in 1962, then combined with a shorter essay to make up *The Fire Next Time*

that I then discovered God. His saints and angels, and His blazing Hell. And since I had been born in a Christian nation, I accepted this Deity as the only one. I supposed Him to exist only within the walls of a church—in fact, of *our* church—and I also supposed that God and safety were synonymous. The word "safety" brings us to the real meaning of the word "religious" as we use it. Therefore, to state it in another, more accurate way, I became, during my fourteenth year, for the first time in my life, afraid—afraid of the evil within me and afraid of the evil without. What I saw around me that summer in Harlem was what I had always seen; nothing had changed. But now, without any warning, the whores and pimps and racketeers on the Avenue[2] had become a personal menace. It had not before occurred to me that I could become one of them, but now I realized that we had been produced by the same circumstances. Many of my comrades were clearly headed for the Avenue, and my father said that I was headed that way, too. My friends began to drink and smoke, and embarked—at first avid, then groaning—on their sexual careers. Girls, only slightly older than I was, who sang in the choir or taught Sunday school, the children of holy parents, underwent, before my eyes, their incredible metamorphosis, of which the most bewildering aspect was not their budding breasts or their rounding behinds but something deeper and more subtle, in their eyes, their heat, their odor, and the inflection of their voices. Like the strangers on the Avenue, they became, in the twinkling of an eye, unutterably different and fantastically *present.* Owing to the way I had been raised, the abrupt discomfort that all this aroused in me and the fact that I had no idea what my voice or my mind or my body was likely to do next caused me to consider myself one of the most depraved people on earth. Matters were not helped by the fact that these holy girls seemed rather to enjoy my terrified lapses, our grim, guilty, tormented experiments, which were at once as chill and joyless as the Russian steppes and hotter, by far, than all the fires of Hell.

2 Yet there was something deeper than these changes, and less definable, that frightened me. It was real in both the boys and the girls, but it was, somehow, more vivid in the boys. In the case of the girls, one watched them turning into matrons before they had become women. They began to manifest a curious and really rather terrifying single-mindedness. It is hard to say exactly how this was conveyed: something implacable in the set of the lips, something farseeing (seeing what?) in the eyes, some new and crushing determination in the walk, something peremptory in the voice. They did not tease us, the boys, any more; they reprimanded us sharply, saying, "You better be thinking about your soul!" For the girls also saw the evidence on the Avenue, knew what the

(1963). In the second half of the *Letter* Baldwin describes in detail his impressions of the Black Muslims and their leader, Elijah Muhammad. The book's epigraph—"God gave Noah the rainbow sign, 'No more water, the fire next time!' "—alludes to what Baldwin terms at the book's conclusion "the fulfilment of that prophecy, recreated from the Bible in song by a slave," which we will suffer if we do not "end the racial nightmare, and achieve our country."

[2] Lenox Avenue, the main street running through Harlem.

price would be, for them, of one misstep, knew that they had to be protected and that we were the only protection there was. They understood that they must act as God's decoys, saving the souls of the boys for Jesus and binding the bodies of the boys in marriage. For this was the beginning of our burning time, and "It is better," said St. Paul—who elsewhere, with a most unusual and stunning exactness, described himself as a "wretched man"—"to marry than to burn."[3] And I began to feel in the boys a curious, wary, bewildered despair, as though they were now settling in for the long, hard winter of life. I did not know then what it was that I was reacting to; I put it to myself that they were letting themselves go. In the same way that the girls were destined to gain as much weight as their mothers, the boys, it was clear, would rise no higher than their fathers. School began to reveal itself, therefore, as a child's game that one could not win, and boys dropped out of school and went to work. My father wanted me to do the same. I refused, even though I no longer had any illusions about what an education could do for me: I had already encountered too many college-graduate handymen. My friends were now "downtown," busy, as they put it, "fighting the man." They began to care less about the way they looked, the way they dressed, the things they did; presently, one found them in twos and threes and fours, in a hallway, sharing a jug of wine or a bottle of whiskey, talking, cursing, fighting, sometimes weeping; lost, and unable to say what it was that oppressed them, except that they knew it was "the man"—the white man. And there seemed to be no way whatever to remove this cloud that stood between them and the sun, between them and love and life and power, between them and whatever it was that they wanted. One did not have to be very bright to realize how little one could do to change one's situation; one did not have to be abnormally sensitive to be worn down to a cutting edge by the incessant and gratuitous humiliation and danger one encountered every working day, all day long. The humiliation did not apply merely to working days, or workers; I was thirteen and was crossing Fifth Avenue on my way to the Forty-second Street library, and the cop in the middle of the street muttered as I passed him, "Why don't you niggers stay uptown where you belong?" When I was ten, and didn't look, certainly, any older, two policemen amused themselves with me by frisking me, making comic (and terrifying) speculations concerning my ancestry and probable sexual prowess, and for good measure, leaving me flat on my back in one of Harlem's empty lots. Just before and then during the Second World War, many of my friends fled to the service, all to be changed there, and rarely for the better, many to be ruined, and many to die. Others fled to other states and cities—that is, to other ghettos. Some went on wine or whiskey or the needle, and are still on it. And others, like me, fled into the church.

3 For the wages of sin were visible everywhere, in every wine-stained and urine-splashed hallway, in every clanging ambulance bell, in every scar on the

---

[3]1 Corinthians 7:8–9.

faces of the pimps and their whores, in every helpless, newborn baby being brought into this danger, in every knife and pistol fight on the Avenue, and in every disastrous bulletin: a cousin, mother of six, suddenly gone mad, the children parcelled out here and there; an indestructible aunt rewarded for years of hard labor by a slow, agonizing death in a terrible small room; someone's bright son blown into eternity by his own hand; another turned robber and carried off to jail. It was a summer of dreadful speculations and discoveries, of which these were not the worst. Crime became real, for example—for the first time—not as *a* possibility but as *the* possibility. One would never defeat one's circumstances by working and saving one's pennies; one would never, by working, acquire that many pennies, and, besides, the social treatment accorded even the most successful Negroes proved that one needed, in order to be free, something more than a bank account. One needed a handle, a lever, a means of inspiring fear. It was absolutely clear that the police would whip you and take you in as long as they could get away with it, and that everyone else—housewives, taxidrivers, elevator boys, dishwashers, bartenders, lawyers, judges, doctors, and grocers—would never, by the operation of any generous human feeling, cease to use you as an outlet for his frustrations and hostilities. Neither civilized reason nor Christian love would cause any of those people to treat you as they presumably wanted to be treated; only the fear of our power to retaliate would cause them to do that, or to seem to do it, which was (and is) good enough. There appears to be a vast amount of confusion on this point, but I do not know many Negroes who are eager to be "accepted" by white people, still less to be loved by them; they, the blacks, simply don't wish to be beaten over the head by the whites every instant of our brief passage on this planet. White people in this country will have quite enough to do in learning how to accept and love themselves and each other, and when they have achieved this—which will not be tomorrow and may very well be never—the Negro problem will no longer exist, for it will no longer be needed.

4 People more advantageously placed than we in Harlem were, and are, will no doubt find the psychology and the view of human nature sketched above dismal and shocking in the extreme. But the Negro's experience of the white world cannot possibly create in him any respect for the standards by which the white world claims to live. His own condition is overwhelming proof that white people do not live by these standards. Negro servants have been smuggling odds and ends out of white homes for generations, and white people have been delighted to have them do it, because it has assuaged a dim guilt and testified to the intrinsic superiority of white people. Even the most doltish and servile Negro could scarcely fail to be impressed by the disparity between his situation and that of the people for whom he worked: Negroes who were neither doltish nor servile did not feel that they were doing anything wrong when they robbed white people. In spite of the Puritan-Yankee equation of virtue with well-being, Negroes had excellent reasons for doubting that money was made or kept by any very striking adherence to the Christian virtues; it certainly did not work that way for black Christians. In any case, white people, who had

robbed black people of their liberty and who profited by this theft every hour that they lived, had no moral ground on which to stand. They had the judges, the juries, the shotguns, the law—in a word, power. But it was a criminal power, to be feared but not respected, and to be outwitted in any way whatever. And those virtues preached but not practiced by the white world were merely another means of holding Negroes in subjection.

QUESTIONS FOR WRITING AND DISCUSSION

OBSERVING

1. What changes does Baldwin identify in himself during his summer when he became 14? What changes does he see outside himself at the same time?
2. What happened to the Harlem boys and girls around Baldwin? What effect did their "situation" and the white man have on them?
3. What is Baldwin saying about life in Harlem?

EVALUATING

1. What does Baldwin mean by the "wages of sin"?
2. What role does fear play in Baldwin's essay? How was it a tool that both perpetrator and victim used?
3. What is Baldwin's attitude toward white people? Toward "Christian virtues" and the Church? What is his view of human nature?

RESPONDING AND APPLYING

1. Baldwin wrote *The Fire Next Time,* the work from which this excerpt is drawn, in 1962; much of the description in the essay is about the time he turned 14, which would have been 1938. In that 25-year period before the fury of the civil rights movement, the roots of many current urban problems (violence, drugs, poverty, out-of-wedlock children) may have taken root. What seems to have changed since then?
2. How do you react to Baldwin's characterization of the white man?

SUZANNE PHARR, "HOMOPHOBIA: A WEAPON OF SEXISM"

Suzanne Pharr has led antidiscrimination groups and workshops on homophobia for 14 years in the South. Pharr founded and has been active in the Women's Project in Arkansas since 1981. More recently, she has been active in the Oregon "Measure Nine" campaign. "Measure Nine" is a statewide initiative that defined homosexuals as "abnormal, wrong, unnatural, and perverse."

Homophobia: A Weapon of Sexism

Suzanne Pharr

1 Homophobia—the irrational fear and hatred of those who love and sexually desire those of the same sex. Though I intimately knew its meaning, the word homophobia was unknown to me until the late 1970s, and when I first heard it, I was struck by how difficult it is to say, what an ugly word it is, equally as ugly as its meaning. Like racism and anti-Semitism, it is a word that calls up images of loss of freedom, verbal and physical violence, death.

2 In my life I have experienced the effects of homophobia through rejection by friends, threats of loss of employment, and threats upon my life; and I have witnessed far worse things happening to other lesbian and gay people: loss of children, beatings, rape, death. Its power is great enough to keep ten to twenty percent of the population living lives of fear (if their sexual identity is hidden) or lives of danger (if their sexual identity is visible) or both. And its power is great enough to keep the remaining eighty to ninety percent of the population trapped in their own fears.

3 Long before I had a word to describe the behavior, I was engaged in a search to discover the source of its power, the power to damage and destroy lives. The most common explanations were that to love the same sex was either abnormal (sick) or immoral (sinful).

4 My exploration of the sickness theory led me to understand that homosexuality is simply a matter of sexual identity, which, along with heterosexual identity, is formed in ways that no one conclusively understands. The American Psychological Association has said that it is no more abnormal to be homosexual than to be lefthanded. It is simply that a certain percentage of the population *is.* It is not healthier to be heterosexual or righthanded. What is unhealthy—and sometimes a source of stress and sickness so great it can lead to suicide—is homophobia, that societal disease that places such negative messages, condemnation, and violence on gay men and lesbians that we have to struggle throughout our lives for self-esteem.

5 The sin theory is a particularly curious one because it is expressed so often and with such hateful emotion both from the pulpit and from laypeople who rely heavily upon the Bible for evidence. However, there is significant evidence that the approximately eight references to homosexuality in the Bible are frequently

read incorrectly, according to Dr. Virginia Ramey Mollenkott in an essay in *Christianity and Crisis:*

> Much of the discrimination against homosexual persons is justified by a common misreading of the Bible. Many English translations of the Bible contain the word homosexual in extremely negative contexts. But the fact is that the word *homosexual* does not occur anywhere in the Bible. No extant text, no manuscript, neither Hebrew nor Greek, Syriac, nor Aramaic, contains the word. The terms *homosexual* and *heterosexual* were not developed in any language until the 1890's, when for the first time the awareness developed that there are people with a lifelong, constitutional orientation toward their own sex. Therefore the use of the word *homosexuality* by certain English Bible translators is an example of the extreme bias that endangers the human and civil rights of homosexual persons. (pp. 383–4, Nov. 9, 1987)

6 Dr. Mollenkott goes on to add that two words in I Corinthians 6:9 and one word in Timothy 1:10 have been used as evidence to damn homosexuals but that well into the 20th century the first of these was understood by everyone to mean masturbation, and the second was known to refer to male prostitutes who were available for hire by either women or men. There are six other Biblical references that are thought by some to refer to homosexuals but each of these is disputed by contemporary scholars. For instance, the sin in the Sodom and Gommorah passage (Genesis 19:1–10) is less about homosexuality than it is about inhospitality and gang rape. The law of hospitality was universally accepted and Lot was struggling to uphold it against what we assume are heterosexual townsmen threatening gang rape to the two male angels in Lot's home. While people dwell on this passage as a condemnation of homosexuality, they bypass what I believe is the central issue or, if you will, *sin:* Lot's offering his two virgin daughters up to the men to be used as they desired for gang rape. Here is a perfectly clear example of devaluing and dehumanizing and violently brutalizing women.

7 The eight Biblical references (and not a single one by Jesus) to alleged homosexuality are very small indeed when compared to the several hundred references (and many by Jesus) to money and the necessity for justly distributing wealth. Yet few people go on a rampage about the issue of a just economic system, using the Bible as a base.

8 Finally, I came to understand that homosexuality, heterosexuality, bi-sexuality are *morally neutral.* A particular sexual identity is not an indication of either good or evil. What is important is not the gender of the two people in relationship with each other but the content of that relationship. Does that relationship contain violence, control of one person by the other? Is the relationship a growthful place for the people involved? It is clear that we must hold all relationships, whether opposite sex or same sex, to these standards.

9 The first workshops that I conducted were an effort to address these two issues, and I assumed that if consciousness could be raised about the invalidity of these two issues then people would stop feeling homophobic and would understand homophobia as a civil rights issue and work against it. The workshops

took a high moral road, invoking participants' compassion, understanding, and outrage at injustice.

10 The eight-hour workshops raised consciousness and increased participants' commitment to work against homophobia as one more oppression in a growing list of recognized oppressions, but I still felt something was missing. I felt there was still too much unaccounted for power in homophobia even after we looked at the sick and sinful theories, at how it feels to be a lesbian in a homophobic world, at why lesbians choose invisibility, at how lesbian existence threatens male dominance. All of the pieces seemed available but we couldn't sew them together into a quilt.

11 As I conducted more workshops over the years I noticed several important themes that led to the final piecing together:

1 Women began to recognize that economics was a central issue connecting various oppressions;

2 Battered women began talking about how they had been called lesbians by their batterers;

3 Both heterosexual and lesbian women said they valued the workshops because in them they were given the rare opportunity to talk about their own sexuality and also about sexism in general.

12 Around the same time (1985–86), the National Coalition Against Domestic Violence (NCADV) entered into a traumatic relationship with the U.S. Department of Justice (DOJ), requesting a large two-year grant to provide domestic violence training and information nationally. At the time the grant was to be announced, NCADV was attacked by conservative groups such as the Heritage Foundation as a "pro-lesbian, pro-feminist, anti-family" organization. In response to these attacks, the DOJ decided not to award a grant; instead they formulated a "cooperative agreement" that allowed them to monitor and approve all work, and they assured conservative organizations that the work would not be pro-lesbian and anti-family. The major issue between NCADV and the DOJ became whether NCADV would let an outside agency define and control its work, and finally, during never-ending concern from the DOJ about "radical" and "lesbian" issues, the agreement was terminated by NCADV at the end of the first year. Throughout that year, there were endless statements and innuendoes from the DOJ and some members of NCADV's membership about NCADV's lesbian leadership and its alleged concern for only lesbian issues. Many women were damaged by the crossfire, NCADV's work was stopped for a year, and the organization was split from within. It was lesbian baiting at its worst.

13 As one of NCADV's lesbian leadership during that onslaught of homophobic attacks, I was still giving homophobia workshops around the country, now able to give even more personal witness to the virulence of the hatred and fear of lesbians and gay men within both institutions and individuals. It was a time of pain and often anger for those of us committed to creating a world free of violence, and it was a time of deep distress for those of us under personal

attack. However, my mother, like many mothers, had always said, "All things work for the good," and sure enough, it was out of the accumulation of these experiences that the pieces began coming together to make a quilt of our understanding.

14 On the day that I stopped reacting to attacks and gave my time instead to visioning, this simple germinal question came forth for the workshops: "What will the world be like without homophobia in it—for everyone, female and male, whatever sexual identity?" Simple though the question is, it was at first shocking because those of us who work in the anti-violence movement spend most of our time working with the damaging, negative results of violence and have little time to vision. It is sometimes difficult to create a vision of a world we have never experienced, but without such a vision, we cannot know clearly what we are working toward in our social change work. From this question, answer led to answer until a whole appeared of our collective making, from one workshop to another.

15 Here are some of the answers women have given:

- Kids won't be called tomboys or sissies; they'll just be who they are, able to do what they wish.
- People will be able to love anyone, no matter what sex; the issue will simply be whether or not she/he is a good human being, compatible, and loving.
- Affection will be opened up between women and men, women and women, men and men, and it won't be centered on sex; people won't fear being called names if they show affection to someone who isn't a mate or potential mate.
- If affection is opened up, then isolation will be broken down for all of us, especially for those who generally experience little physical affection, such as unmarried old people.
- Women will be able to work whatever jobs we want without being labeled masculine.
- There will be less violence if men do not feel they have to prove and assert their manhood. Their desire to dominate and control will not spill over from the personal to the level of national and international politics and the use of bigger and better weapons to control other countries.
- People will wear whatever clothes they wish, with the priority being comfort rather than the display of femininity or masculinity.
- There will be no gender roles.

16 It is at this point in the workshops—having imagined a world without homophobia—that the participants see the analysis begin to fall into place. Someone notes that all the things we have been talking about relate to sexual gender roles. It's rather like the beginning of a course in Sexism 101. The next question is "Imagine the world with no sex roles—sexual identity, which may be in flux, but no sexual gender roles." Further: imagine a world in which opportunity is not determined by gender or race. Just the imagining makes women alive with

excitement because it is a vision of freedom, often just glimpsed but always known deep down as truth. Pure joy.

17 We talk about what it would be like to be born in a world in which there were no expectations or treatment based on gender but instead only the expectation that each child, no matter what race or sex, would be given as many options and possibilities as society could muster. Then we discuss what girls and boys would be like at puberty and beyond if sex role expectations didn't come crashing down on them with girls' achievement levels beginning to decline thereafter; what it would be for women to have the training and options for economic equity with men; what would happen to issues of power and control, and therefore violence, if there were real equality. To have no prescribed sex roles would open the possibility of equality. It is a discussion women find difficult to leave. Freedom calls.

QUESTIONS FOR WRITING AND DISCUSSION

OBSERVING

1. How does Pharr define homophobia? How does she characterize its effects? How does she explain the way it is formed? Why is its source, and whether it is genetic or learned, so important? Why does she call homosexuality "normal" (and not sick) and "morally neutral"?
2. What does Pharr mean by the sin theory? How does she see the Biblical accounts that are often used to condemn homosexuals?
3. What does Pharr see as most important in relationships? What role does gender play?

EVALUATING

1. Pharr is obviously disturbed by the conservative and Department of Justice attack on the National Coalition Against Domestic Violence. What was the basis of the attack? Why was NCADV not given the grant? Is it possible to be "pro-lesbian" and "pro-feminist" without being anti-family?
2. How does Pharr turn the conflict with the Justice Department into something good? Do you think she capitulated?
3. Why does Pharr think sex roles are at the core of the problem of homophobia?

RESPONDING AND APPLYING

1. Where do you stand on the question of homophobia? Do you think NCADV should have gotten the grant? Why?
2. How do you react to the eight points of Pharr's vision? Which make the most or least sense to you?

CAROLYN MERCHANT, "WOMEN AND NATURE"

Carolyn Merchant is a professor of philosophy at the University of California at Berkeley. Her book *The Death of Nature* has become a pivotal document in the Green Movement, one of the most important social, political, and scientific events of our age and the successor to traditional environmentalism. The Green Movement seeks to define a new world order which starts with the assumption, stated by E. F. Schumacher, that "Modern man does not experience himself as part of nature but as an outside force destined to dominate and conquer it." The ecology movement finds many of its central anti-development, anti-hierarchy, anti-science, and anti-capitalism values and attitudes in the ecofeminism, the blend of the women's and ecology movements, that Merchant presents. Merchant is also editor of *Major Problems in American Environmental History: Documents and Essays* (1993) which, according to her publisher D. C. Heath, "traces the history of the United States environment through examinations of 14 critical issues and is ideal for courses in environmental history and related fields."

Women and Nature

Carolyn Merchant

1 Women and nature have an age-old association—an affiliation that has persisted throughout culture, language, and history. Their ancient interconnections have been dramatized by the simultaneity of two recent social movements—women's liberation, symbolized in its controversial infancy by Betty Friedan's *Feminine Mystique* (1963), and the ecology movement, which built up during the 1960s and finally captured national attention on Earth Day, 1970. Common to both is an egalitarian perspective. Women are struggling to free themselves from cultural and economic constraints that have kept them subordinate to men in American society. Environmentalists, warning us of the irreversible consequences of continuing environmental exploitation, are developing an ecological ethic emphasizing the interconnectedness between people and nature. Juxtaposing the goals of the two movements can suggest new values and social structures, based not on the domination of women and nature as resources but on the full expression of both male and female talent and on the maintenance of environmental integrity.

2 New social concerns generate new intellectual and historical problems. Conversely, new interpretations of the past provide perspectives on the pres-

ent and hence the power to change it. Today's feminist and ecological consciousness can be used to examine the historical interconnections between women and nature that developed as the modern scientific and economic world took form in the sixteenth and seventeenth centuries—a transformation that shaped and pervades today's mainstream values and perceptions.

3 Feminist history in the broadest sense requires that we look at history with egalitarian eyes, seeing it anew from the viewpoint not only of women but also of social and racial groups and the natural environment, previously ignored as the underlying resources on which western culture and its progress have been built. To write history from a feminist perspective is to turn it upside down—to see social structure from the bottom up and to flip-flop mainstream values. An egalitarian perspective accords both women and men their place in history and delineates their ideas and roles. The impact of sexual differences and sex-linked language on cultural ideology and the use of male, female, and androgynous imagery will have important places in the new history.

4 The ancient identity of nature as a nurturing mother links women's history with the history of the environment and ecological change. The female earth was central to the organic cosmology that was undermined by the scientific revolution and the rise of a market-oriented culture in early modern Europe. The ecology movement has reawakened interest in the values and concepts associated historically with the premodern organic world. The ecological model and its associated ethics make possible a fresh and critical interpretation of the rise of modern science in the crucial period when our cosmos ceased to be viewed as an organism and became instead a machine.

5 Both the women's movement and the ecology movement are sharply critical of the costs of competition, aggression, and domination arising from the market economy's *modus operandi* in nature and society. Ecology has been a subversive science in its criticism of the consequences of uncontrolled growth associated with capitalism, technology, and progress—concepts that over the last two hundred years have been treated with reverence in western culture. The vision of the ecology movement has been to restore the balance of nature disrupted by industrialization and overpopulation. It has emphasized the need to live within the cycles of nature, as opposed to the exploitative, linear mentality of forward progress. It focuses on the costs of progress, the limits to growth, the deficiencies of technological decision-making, and the urgency of the conservation and recycling of nature resources. Similarly, the women's movement has exposed the costs for all human beings of competition in the marketplace, the loss of meaningful productive economic roles for women in early capitalist society, and the view of both women and nature as psychological and recreational resources for the harried entrepreneur-husband. . . .

6 Women's place in the order of nature. At the root of the identification of women and animality with a lower form of human life lies the distinction between nature and culture fundamental to humanistic disciplines such as history, literature, and anthropology, which accept that distinction as an unquestioned

assumption. Nature-culture dualism is a key factor in western civilization's advance at the expense of nature. As the unifying bonds of the old hierarchical cosmos were severed, European culture increasingly set itself above and apart from all that was symbolized by nature. Similarly, in America the nature-culture dichotomy was basic to the tension between civilization and the frontier in westward expansion and helped to justify the continuing exploitation of nature's resources. Much of American literature is founded on the underlying assumption of the superiority of culture to nature. If nature and women, Indians and blacks are to be liberated from the strictures of this ideology, a radical critique of the very categories *nature* and *culture,* as organizing concepts in all disciplines, must be undertaken.

7 Anthropologists have pointed out that nature and women are both perceived to be on a lower level than culture, which has been associated symbolically and historically with men. Because women's physiological functions of reproduction, nurture, and child rearing are viewed as closer to nature, their social role is lower on the cultural scale than that of the male. Women are devalued by their tasks and roles, by their exclusion from community functions whence power is derived, and through symbolism.

8 In early modern Europe, the assumption of a nature-culture dichotomy was used as a justification for keeping women in their place in the established hierarchical order of nature, where they were placed below the men of their status group. The reaction against the disorder in nature symbolized by women was directed not only at lower-class witches, but at the queens and noblewomen who during the Protestant Reformation seemed to be overturning the order of nature. . . .

9 An allegorical tale, reputedly sent to Paul Schneevogel, a professor at Leipzig about 1490–5, expressed opposition to mining encroachments into the farmlands of Lichtenstat in Saxony, Germany, an area where the new mining activities were developing rapidly. Reminiscent of Alain of Lille's *Natura* and her torn gown and illustrative of the force of the ancient strictures against mining is the following allegorical vision of an old hermit of Lichtenstat. Mother Earth, dressed in a tattered green robe and seated on the right hand of Jupiter, is represented in a court case by "glib-tongued Mercury" who charges a miner with matricide. Testimony is presented by several of nature's deities:

> Bacchus complained that his vines were uprooted and fed to the flames and his most sacred places desecrated. Ceres stated that her fields were devastated; Pluto that the blows of the miners resound like thunder through the depths of the earth, so that he could hardly reside in his own kingdom; the Naiad, that the subterranean waters were diverted and her fountains dried up; Charon that the volume of the underground waters had been so diminished that he was unable to float his boat on Acheron and carry the souls across to Pluto's realm, and the Fauns protested that the charcoal burners had destroyed whole forests to obtain fuel to smelt the miner's ores.

In his defence, the miner argued that the earth was not a real mother, but a wicked stepmother who hides and conceals the metals in her inner parts instead of making them available for human use.

10 The final judgment, handed down by Fortune, stated that if men deign "to mine and dig in mountains, to tend the fields, to engage in trade, to injure the earth, to throw away knowledge, to disturb Pluto and finally to search for veins of metal in the sources of rivers, their bodies ought to be swallowed up by the earth, suffocated by its vapours . . . intoxicated by wine . . . afflicted by hunger and remain ignorant of what is best. These and many other dangers are proper of men. Farewell."

QUESTIONS FOR WRITING AND DISCUSSION

OBSERVING

1. How does Merchant see the relationship between women and nature? How does she relate the women's and ecology movements?
2. What assumptions about gender do you see in the writing? What is the writer's attitude toward men? Towards women?
3. What does Merchant mean by writing "history from a feminist perspective"?
4. To what end does Merchant retell the allegory at the end of the article?

EVALUATING

1. What is Merchant's view of science and the scientific revolution? What about capitalism and free market economics?
2. What difference does Merchant see between our cosmos as an organism and as a machine? What are the implications of this distinction?
3. Describe and assess Merchant's speculations on the relationship of nature and culture (see paragraph 5).

RESPONDING AND APPLYING

1. What does living "within the cycles of nature" (paragraph 5) mean to you? What examples of indifference to nature do you see in our culture? What steps are you willing to take to limit "growth" and "progress"? Consider such things as industrial pollution controls, acid rain, mass transport, automobile emission controls, and the ozone layer.
2. Do you buy the argument that we as a culture have destroyed or are in the process of destroying nature and that such destruction is related to gender?

SUSAN GRIFFIN, "THE SACRIFICIAL LAMB"

Born in Los Angeles in 1943, poet, editor, writer, and feminist Susan Griffin is probably best known for her book *Pornography and Silence: Culture's Revolt Against Nature* (1981). In it she sees pornography as a manifestation of the male desire to separate himself from feeling and emotion. Instead of confronting his emotion, he projects it onto women. Griffin commented, "All the qualities that women are accused of—passivity, wantonness or prudery, both the fear of sex and nymphomania—all of these qualities are human qualities . . . and they are projected onto women." In "The Sacrificial Lamb," a chapter in *Pornography and Silence,* Griffin broadens the definition of pornography to include projections of male inadequacies not just on women, but on African Americans, homosexuals, and Jews.

The Sacrificial Lamb

Susan Griffin

Therefore, I saw my own task especially in extracting those nuclear ideas from the extensive and unshaped substance of a general world view and remolding them into more or less dogmatic forms which in their clear delineation are adapted for holding solidly together those men who swear allegiance to them.

—ADOLF HITLER, *Mein Kampf*

1 There are two kinds of delusion which it is possible for the civilized mind to embrace. The first delusion is a private one. The mind possessed by such a delusion is often perceived as mad. Certainly as strange. For the private delusion sets the one who believes in it apart from the rest of humanity. But exactly the opposite is true of the second delusion. This is the *mass delusion:* it consists of a *shared* set of beliefs which are untrue and which distort reality. A whole nation, for example, decides to believe that "the Jew" is evil. This type of delusion brings the man or woman who believes in it into a common circle of humanity. And because the mass delusion is a shared delusion, the mind which shares it is perceived as normal, while the same society perceives as mad the mind which sees reality.

2 Pornography is a mass delusion and so is racism. In certain periods of history, both of these mass delusions have been accepted as sane views of the world, by whole societies or certain sectors of society. The pornographic ideology, for instance, is perceived as a reasonable world view by parts of American and European societies today. And various forms of racism have been the

official ideologies of societies, political parties, and even governments. Most notably, we remember the official racism of the Third Reich. But are we arguing that because of the prevalence of these delusional systems they are an inevitable outcome of civilization? This is indeed what the delusional mind would have us believe. And when we grow up inside a culture of denial, a culture which embodies and expresses delusion, we begin to think of this distortion as part of human nature.

3 We see a film in which a woman is murdered. Or a series of women are murdered, or beaten, or raped. The next day, we read in the newspaper that a woman has been shot to death by a stranger. We hear that the man next door has several times "broken down" and threatened the life of his wife, his son. An advertisement for a novel depicts a woman's throat cut open and bleeding. And in our minds all this is woven into a fabric which we imagine is inevitable.

4 We begin to look on the violence of men toward women as a kind of natural phenomenon. And slowly, our own behavior becomes a part of this delusion which we have called reality. If we are women, we grow up with a fear which we come to believe is as common as hunger, or thirst, or anger. This fear becomes so much a part of us that it forms a background to all our movements, and we begin to believe this fear is a part of ourselves, born at the same moment as our souls. If we are men, acts of violence toward women become part of a range of behavior which we think of as human.

5 And in this way, we cease to realize that culture has a profound influence on our minds and on human behavior. For in fact, it is not inevitable that the human mind choose delusion over reality. It is a choice which temporarily solves the human feeling of powerlessness before nature. Yet it is not the only choice which might solve that dilemma. For example, one can imagine that a child might, for a period of time, believe in the fantasy of mind over matter and culture over nature, and then grow beyond such a delusion, just as the child does in fact, in our society, come to understand that his infant body is separate from his mother's body, which in an earlier state of mind he did not perceive.

6 But in this society an event intervenes in the child's life and helps to determine what choice he or she will make. And this event is culture. Our culture offers to the mind of the child socially acceptable forms through which to hold on to delusion. These are the mass delusional forms which we know as racism and the pornographic sensibility. Through these systems of thought, the mind learns to deny the natural part of its own being. It learns to project this denied part of its own being onto another, playing out against this other its own ambivalence toward the natural self. So a woman is hated and loved, ridiculed, sought after, possessed, raped. And so, also, the black or the Jew is captured and brought into slavery, or exiled; owned or dispossessed; humiliated, excluded, attacked, and murdered.

7 For the pornographic mind and the racist mind are really identical, both in the symbolic content and in the psychological purposes of the delusionary systems they express. And now, if we undertake to study this mind, we shall begin to see precisely how a cultural delusion gradually shapes itself into such

devastating social events as the mass murder of European Jewry, which we have come to know as the Holocaust.

8 Finally one comes to recognize that the contents of the racist mind are fundamentally pornographic. And with this recognition, it can be seen how the pornographic images of racism provide social forms through which private disturbances may be expressed as public conflicts. In this way, the pornographic sensibility affects history even more deeply than one would have suspected. And when one examines the dynamic shape of racist propaganda, one can see that it, too, has the same shape as the movement of the pornographic mind. Indeed, there is a classic mental pattern by which images must accelerate in their violence until they become actual events, events which devastate countless human lives.

The Chauvinist Mind

> *Among our secrecies, not to despite Jews (that is, ourselves) or our darknesses, our blacks, or in our sexuality where it takes us . . .*
>
> —Muriel Mukeyzer, *"The Despisals"*

9 On the leaflet are two familiar figures. A monstrous black man menaces a voluptuous white woman. Her dress is cut low, her skirt torn so that a thigh shows through; the sleeves of her dress fall off her shoulders. She looks over her shoulder in fear and runs. The man's body is huge and apelike. The expression on his face is the personification of bestiality, greed, and lust. Under the words "Conquer and Breed," and above a text which warns the reader against intermarriage, these two figures act out an age-old drama.

10 At the heart of the racist imagination we discover a pornographic fantasy: the specter of miscegenation. This image of a dark man raping a fair woman embodies all that the racist fears. The fantasy preoccupies his mind. A rational argument exists which argues that the racist simply uses pornographic images to manipulate the mind. But these images seem to belong to the racist. They are predictable in a way that suggests a more intrinsic part in the genesis of this ideology.

11 And when we turn to pornography, we discover that just as the racist is obsessed with a pornographic drama, the pornographer is obsessed with racism. In Juvenal, for example, we read about the "trusty Jewess" who will "tell you dreams of any kind you please for the minutest of coins." *Hustler* magazine displays a cartoon called *Chester the Molester* (part of a series depicting child molestation as humor), in which a man wearing a swastika on his arm hides behind a corner, holds a bat, and dangles a dollar bill on a wire to entice a little girl away from her parents. The child and her parents all wear yellow stars of David; each member of the family is drawn with a stereotypical hooked nose of anti-Semitic caricature. In another cartoon, a young black man dressed in a yellow polka-dot shirt and eating watermelon stands outside the bars of a cage in which a money dressed in the same yellow shirt eats watermelon and listens to

a transistor radio. A film called *Slaves of Love* is advertised with a portrait of two black women, naked and in chains. A white man stands over them with a whip. Nazi memorabilia, helmets, SS uniforms, photographs of the atrocities of concentration camps, swords, knives, are sold as pornography along with books and films. Pornographic films bear the titles *Golden Boys of the SS, Ilse the She-Wolf of the SS, Leiben Camp.*

12 Writing of the twin traditions of anti-Semitism and obscenity, Lucy Dawidowicz tells us of a rock group called "The Dictators," who declare "we are the members of the master race," and she lists for us a mélange of articles found in the apartment of a Hell's Angel: devices of torture, a Nazi flag, a photograph of Hitler, Nazi propaganda, and of course, pornography. She writes "Pornography and propaganda have reinforced each other over the decades."

13 Indeed, the association between pornographic thought and racist ideology is neither casual nor coincidental. As Hannah Arendt points out, both Gobineau and Houston Chamberlain (anti-Semitic ideologies who had a great influence on the philosophy of the Third Reich and on Hitler himself) were deeply influenced by the writing of the Marquis de Sade. Like de Sade, they "elevated cruelty to a major virtue."

14 We know that the sufferings women experience in a pornographic culture are different in kind and quality from the sufferings of black people in a racist society, or of Jewish people under anti-Semitism. (And we know that the hatred of homosexuality has again another effect on the lives of women and men outside of the traditional sexual roles.[1]) But if we look closely at the portrait which the racist draws of a man or a woman of color, or that the anti-Semite draws of the Jew, or that the pornographer draws of a woman, we begin to see that these fantasized figures resemble one another. For they are the creations of one mind. This is the chauvinist mind, a mind which projects all it fears in itself onto another: a mind which defines itself by what it hates.

15 The black man as stupid, as passive, as bestial; the woman as highly emotional, unthinking, a being closer to the earth. The Jews as a dark, avaricious race. The whore. The nymphomaniac. Carnal lust in a woman insatiable. The virgin. The docile slave. The effeminate Jew. The usurious Jew. The African, a "greedy eater," lecherous, addicted to uncleanness. The black woman as lust: "These sooty dames, well vers'd in Venus' school / Make love an art, and boast they kiss by rule." As easy. The Jew who practices sexual orgies who practices cannibalism. The Jewish and the black man with enormous sexual endowment.

16 The famous materialism of the Jew, the black, the woman. The woman who spends her husband's paychecks on hats. The black who drives a Cadillac while his children starve. The Jewish moneylender who sells his daughter. "There is nothing more intolerable than a wealthy woman," we read in Juvenal.

[1] Homophobia is a clear mass delusional system. Yet to draw an analogy between this system and racism and pornography would require another chapter. Suffice it to mention here that the fear of homosexuals historically accompanies racism, sexism, facism, and all forms of totalitarian or authoritarian rule.

(And in an eighteenth-century pornographic work, the pornographer writes that his heroine had "a natty little bourgeois brain." And in a contemporary pornographic novel, the hero murders a woman because she prefers "guys who drives Cadillacs.") The appetite which swallows. The black man who takes away the white man's job or the woman who takes a man's job.

17 Over and over again the chauvinist draws a portrait of the other which reminds us of that part of his own mind he would deny and which he has made dark to himself. The other has appetite and instinct. The other has a body. The other has an emotional life which is uncontrolled. And in the wake of this denied self, the chauvinist constructs a false self with which he himself identifies.

18 Whereover we find the racist idea of another being as evil and inferior, we also discover a racial *ideal,* a portrait of the self as superior, good, and righteous. Such was certainly the case with the white Southern slave owner. The Southern white man imagined himself as the heir to all the best traditions of civilization. He thought of himself as the final repository of culture. In his own mind, he was an aristocrat. Thus Southern life was filled with his pretensions, his decorum, his manners, and his ceremonies of social ascension.

19 Just as he conferred the black men and women he enslaved with inferior qualities, so also he blessed himself with superiorities. He was "knightly" and "magnanimous," filled with "honesty" which emanated from the "flame of his strong and steady eye." He was honorable, responsible and above all, noble.

20 And the anti-Semite frames himself in the same polarity. Against his portrait of the Jew, he poses himself as the ideal, the Aryan: fair, courageous, honest, physically and morally stronger.

21 But this is a polarity deeply familiar to us. We learn it almost at birth from our mothers and fathers. Early in our lives, the ideal of masculinity is opposed to the idea of femininity. We learn that a man is more intelligent, that he is stronger than a woman. And in pornography, the male hero possesses an intrinsic moral rightness which, like Hitler's Aryan, allows him to behave toward women in ways outside morality. For according to this ideology, he is the more valuable member of the species. As the Marquis de Sade tells us, "the flesh of women," like the "flesh of all female animals," is inferior.

22 It is because the chauvinist has used the idea that he is superior as a justification to enslave and exploit the other, whom he describes as inferior, that certain historians of culture have imagined the ideology of chauvinism exists only to justify exploitation. But this ideology has a raison d'être intrinsic to the mind itself. Exploring this mind, one discovers that the chauvinist values his delusion for its own sake, that above all, the chauvinist mind needs to believe in the delusion it has created. For this delusion has another purpose than social exploitation. Indeed, the delusions of the chauvinist mind are born from the same condition which gives birth to all delusion, and this condition is the mind's desire to escape truth. The chauvinist cannot face the truth that the other he despises is himself.

23 This is why one so often discovers in chauvinist thinking a kind of hysterical denial that the other could possibly be like the self. The chauvinist insists

upon an ultimate and defining difference between himself and the other. This insistence is both the starting point and the essence of all his thinking. Thus, Hitler writes on the beginnings of his own anti-Semitism:

> One day, when passing through the Inner City, I suddenly came across an apparition in a long caftan and wearing black sidelocks. My first thought was: is this a Jew? . . . but the longer I gazed at this strange countenance and examined it section by section, the more the first question took another shape in my brain: is this a German. . . . For the first time in my life I bought myself some anti-Semitic pamphlets for a few coins.

24 In this way, by inventing a figure different from itself, the chauvinist mind constructs an allegory of self. Within this allegory, the chauvinist himself represents the soul, and the knowledge of culture. Whoever is the object of his hatred represents the denied self, the natural self, the self which contains the knowledge of the body. Therefore this other must have no soul.

25 From the chauvinist ideology we learn, for example, that a woman's soul is smaller than a man's. The misogynist and anti-Semite Otto Weiniger tells us that a woman "can have no part in the higher, transcendental life." The church tells that in order for a woman to get into heaven she must assume the shape of a man. Her body is incapable of spirituality. She is called the "devil's gateway." She brings evil into the world.

QUESTIONS FOR WRITING AND DISCUSSION

OBSERVING

1. How does Griffin distinguish between private and mass delusion? What is society's role in confirming the delusion? Cite examples in your explanation.
2. How does Griffin define pornography? What does she mean by racism? In what ways are pornography and racism similar? How do they interact in practice?
3. In what sense are the delusions Griffin speaks of not inevitable? What is her purpose in making the point that the virulence of these scourges can be controlled?

EVALUATING

1. Griffin draws a psychological profile of the pornographic, racist mind, calling it the "chauvinist mind." In choosing delusion over reality, it "solves the human feeling of a powerlessness before nature" and "projects all it fears in itself onto another: a mind which defines itself by what it hates." Explain this with an example.

2. How does the "racial ideal," "a portrait of the self as superior" function?
3. What do racism, sexism, homophobia, and anti-Semitism have in common for Griffin? What significant differences exist in these forms of "the other" when it comes to Griffin's analysis?

RESPONDING AND APPLYING

1. Griffin focuses on only four other groups. Why do you think she chooses these particular ones? Can you think of other groups that have fallen victim to what she calls the chauvinist mind?
2. Do you think Griffin is being too unfair to males?
3. Can you think of other explanations for what is behind the chauvinist mind? Consider how a Marxist might explain it, or a Freudian, or an evolutionary biologist.

ANN PETRY, "LIKE A WINDING SHEET"

Born in Old Saybrook, Connecticut, in 1908, Ann Petry has written three novels, one collection of stories, and five books for children. Considered the first black woman to write successfully about the problems of poor black women, Petry's first notable achievement was the novel *The Street* (1946), which one critic called an "unflinching portrayal of violence and degradation" in the black community of New York City. Petry is too often dismissed by critics and readers, perhaps because she was overshadowed by Richard Wright, whose novel *Native Son* came out in 1940 to rave reviews, six years before *The Street.* But Petry shouldn't be overlooked, as the power of the following story indicates.

Like a Winding Sheet

Ann Petry

1 He had planned to get up before Mae did and surprise her by fixing breakfast. Instead he went back to sleep and she got out of bed so quietly he didn't know she wasn't there beside him until he woke up and heard the queer soft gurgle of water running out of the sink in the bathroom.

2 He knew he ought to get up but instead he put his arms across his forehead to shut the afternoon sunlight out of his eyes, pulled his legs up close to his body, testing them to see if the ache was still in them.

3 Mae had finished in the bathroom. He could tell because she never closed the door when she was in there and now the sweet smell of talcum powder was drifting down the hall and into the bedroom. Then he heard her coming down the hall.

4 "Hi, babe," she said affectionately.

5 "Hum," he grunted, and moved his arms away from his head, opened one eye.

6 "It's a nice morning."

7 "Yeah." He rolled over and the sheet twisted around him, outlining his thighs, his chest. "You mean afternoon, don't ya?"

8 Mae looked at the twisted sheet and giggled. "Looks like a winding sheet," she said. "A shroud—" Laughter tangled with her words and she had to pause for a moment before she could continue. "You look like a huckleberry—in a winding sheet—"

9 "That's no way to talk. Early in the day like this," he protested.

10 He looked at his arms silhouetted against the white of the sheets. They were inky black by contrast and he had to smile in spite of himself and he lay there smiling and savoring the sweet sound of Mae's giggling.

11 "Early?" She pointed a finger at the alarm clock on the table near the bed and giggled again. "It's almost four o'clock. And if you don't spring up out of there, you're going to be late again."

12 "What do you mean 'again'?"

13 "Twice last week. Three times the week before. And once the week before and—"

14 "I can't get used to sleeping in the daytime," he said fretfully. He pushed his legs out from under the covers experimentally. Some of the ache had gone out of them but they weren't really rested yet. "It's too light for good sleeping. And all that standing beats the hell out of my legs."

15 "After two years you oughta be used to it," Mae said.

16 He watched her as she fixed her hair, powdered her face, slipped into a pair of blue denim overalls. She moved quickly and yet she didn't seem to hurry.

17 "You look like you'd had plenty of sleep," he said lazily. He had to get up but he kept putting the moment off, not wanting to move, yet he didn't dare let his legs to completely limp because if he did he'd go back to sleep. It was getting later and later but the thought of putting his weight on his legs kept him lying there.

18 When he finally got up he had to hurry, and he gulped his breakfast so fast that he wondered if his stomach could possibly use food thrown at it at such a rate of speed. He was still wondering about it as he and Mae were putting their coats on in the hall.

19 Mae paused to look at the calendar. "It's the thirteenth," she said. Then a faint excitement in her voice, "Why, it's Friday the thirteenth." She had one arm in her coat sleeve and she held it there while she stared at the calendar. "I oughta stay home," she said. "I shouldn't go outa the house."

20 "Aw, don't be a fool," he said. "Today's payday. And payday is a good luck day everywhere, any way you look at it." And as she stood hesitating he said, "Aw, come on."

21 And he was late for work again because they spent fifteen minutes arguing before he could convince her she ought to go to work just the same. He had to talk persuasively, urging her gently, and it took time. But he couldn't bring himself to talk to her roughly or threaten to strike her like a lot of men might have done. He wasn't made that way.

22 So when he reached the plant he was late and he had to wait to punch the time clock because the day-shift workers were streaming out in long lines, in groups and bunches that impeded his progress.

23 Even now just starting his workday his legs ached. He had to force himself to struggle past the outgoing workers, punch the time clock, and get the little cart he pushed around all night, because he kept toying with the idea of going home and getting back in bed.

24 He pushed the cart out on the concrete floor, thinking that if this was his plant he'd make a lot of changes in it. There were too many standing-up jobs for one thing. He'd figure out some way most of 'em could be done sitting down and he'd put a lot more benches around. And this job he had—this job that forced him to walk ten hours a night, pushing this little cart, well, he'd turn it into a sitting-down job. One of those little trucks they used around railroad stations would be good for a job like this. Guys sat on a seat and the thing moved easily, taking up little room and turning in hardly any space at all, like on a dime.

25 He pushed the cart near the foreman. He never could remember to refer to her as the forelady even in his mind. It was funny to have a white woman for a boss in a plant like this one.

26 She was sore about something. He could tell by the way her face was red and her eyes were half-shut until they were slits. Probably been out late and didn't get enough sleep. He avoided looking at her and hurried a little, head down, as he passed her though he couldn't resist stealing a glance at her out of the corner of his eyes. He saw the edge of the light-colored slacks she wore and the tip end of a big tan shoe.

27 "Hey, Johnson!" the woman said.

28 The machines had started full blast. The whirr and the grinding made the building shake, made it impossible to hear conversations. The men and women at the machines talked to each other but looking at them from just a little distance away, they appeared to be simply moving their lips because you couldn't hear what they were saying. Yet the woman's voice cut across the machine sounds—harsh, angry.

29 He turned his head slowly. "Good evenin', Mrs. Scott," he said, and waited.

30 "You're late again."

31 "That's right. My legs were bothering me."

32 The woman's face grew redder, angrier looking. "Half this shift comes in late," she said. "And you're the worst one of all. You're always late. Whatsa matter with ya?"

33 "It's my legs," he said. "Somehow they don't ever get rested. I don't seem to get used to sleeping days. And I just can't get started."

34 "Excuses. You guys always got excuses," her anger grew and spread. "Every guy comes in here late always has an excuse. His wife's sick or his grandmother died or somebody in the family had to go to the hospital," she paused, drew a deep breath. "And the niggers is the worse. I don't care what's wrong with your legs. You get in here on time. I'm sick of you niggers—"

35 "You got the right to get mad," he interrupted softly. "You got the right to cuss me four ways to Sunday but I ain't letting nobody call me a nigger."

36 He stepped closer to her. His fists were doubled. His lips were drawn back in a thin narrow line. A vein in his forehead stood out swollen, thick.

37 And the woman backed away from him, not hurriedly but slowly—two, three steps back.

38 "Aw, forget it," she said. "I didn't mean nothing by it. It slipped out. It was an accident." The red of her face deepened until the small blood vessels in her cheeks were purple. "Go on and get to work," she urged. And she took three more slow backward steps.

39 He stood motionless for a moment and then turned away from the sight of the red lipstick on her mouth that made him remember that the foreman was a woman. And he couldn't bring himself to hit a woman. He felt a curious tingling in his fingers and he looked down at his hands. They were clenched tight, hard, ready to smash some of those small purple veins in her face.

40 He pushed the cart ahead of him, walking slowly. When he turned his head, she was staring in his direction, mopping her forehead with a dark blue handkerchief. Their eyes met and then they both looked away.

41 He didn't glance in her direction again but moved past the long work benches, carefully collecting the finished parts, going slowly and steadily up and down, back and forth the length of the building, and as he walked he forced himself to swallow his anger, get rid of it.

42 And he succeeded so that he was able to think about what had happened without getting upset about it. An hour went by but the tension stayed in his hands. They were clenched and knotted on the handles of the cart as though ready to aim a blow.

43 And he thought he should have hit her anyway, smacked her hard in the face, felt the soft flesh of her face give under the hardness of his hands. He tried to make his hands relax by offering them a description of what it would have been like to strike her because he had the queer feeling that his hands were not exactly a part of him anymore—they had developed a separate life of their own over which he had no control. So he dwelt on the pleasure his hands would have felt—both of them cracking at her, first one and then the other. If he had done that his hands would have felt good now—relaxed, rested.

44 And he decided that even if he'd lost his job for it, he should have let her have it and it would have been a long time, maybe the rest of her life, before she called anybody else a nigger.

45 The only trouble was he couldn't hit a woman. A woman couldn't hit back the same way a man did. But it would have been a deeply satisfying thing to

have cracked her narrow lips wide open with just one blow, beautifully timed and with all his weight in back of it. That way he would have gotten rid of all the energy and tension his anger had created in him. He kept remembering how his heart had started pumping blood so fast he had felt it tingle even in the tips of his fingers.

46 With the approach of night, fatigue nibbled at him. The corners of his mouth drooped, the frown between his eyes deepened, his shoulders sagged; but his hands stayed tight and tense. As the hours dragged by he noticed that the women workers had started to snap and snarl at each other. He couldn't hear what they said because of the sound of machines but he could see the quick lip movements that sent words tumbling from the sides of their mouths. They gestured irritably with their hands and scowled as their mouths moved.

47 Their violent jerky motions told him that it was getting close on to quitting time but somehow he felt that the night still stretched ahead of him, composed of endless hours of steady walking on his aching legs. When the whistle finally blew he went on pushing the cart, unable to believe that it had sounded. The whirring of the machines died away to a murmur and he knew then that he'd really heard the whistle. He stood still for a moment, filled with a relief that made him sigh.

48 Then he moved briskly, putting the cart in the storeroom, hurrying to take his place in the line forming before the paymaster. That was another thing he'd change, he thought. He'd have the pay envelopes handed to the people right at their benches so there wouldn't be ten or fifteen minutes lost waiting for the pay. He always got home ten or fifteen minutes late on payday. They did it better in the plant where Mae worked, brought the money right to them at their benches.

49 He stuck his pay envelope in his pants' pocket and followed the line of workers heading for the subway in a slow-moving stream. He glanced up at the sky. It was a nice night, the sky looked packed full to running over with stars. And he thought if he and Mae would go right to bed when they got home from work they'd catch a few hours of darkness for sleeping. But they never did. They fooled around—cooking and eating and listening to the radio and he always stayed in a big chair in the living room and went almost but not quite to sleep and when they finally got to bed it was five or six in the morning and daylight was already seeping around the edges of the sky.

50 He walked slowly, putting off the moment when he would have to plunge into the crowd hurrying toward the subway. It was a long ride to Harlem and tonight the thought of it appalled him. He paused outside an all-night restaurant to kill time, so that some of the first rush of workers would be gone when he reached the subway.

51 The lights in the restaurant were brilliant, enticing. There was life and motion inside. And as he looked through the window he thought that everything within range of his eyes gleamed—the long imitation marble counter, the tall stools, the white porcelain-topped tables and especially the big metal coffee urn right near the window. Steam issued from its top and a gas flame flickered under it—a lively, dancing, blue flame.

52 A lot of the workers from his shift—men and women—were lining up near the coffee urn. He watched them walk to the porcelain-topped tables carrying steaming cups of coffee and he saw that just the smell of the coffee lessened the fatigue lines in their faces. After the first sip their faces softened, they smiled, they began to talk and laugh.

53 On a sudden impulse he shoved the door open and joined the line in front of the coffee urn. The line moved slowly. And as he stood there the smell of the coffee, the sound of the laughter and of the voices, helped dull the sharp ache in his legs.

54 He didn't pay any attention to the white girl who was serving the coffee at the urn. He kept looking at the cups in the hands of the men who had been ahead of him. Each time a man stepped out of the line with one of the thick white cups the fragrant steam got in his nostrils. He saw that they walked carefully so as not to spill a single drop. There was a froth of bubbles at the top of each cup and he thought about how he would let the bubbles break against his lips before he actually took a big deep swallow.

55 Then it was his turn. "A cup of coffee," he said, just as he had heard the others say.

56 The white girl looked past him, put her hands up to her head and gently lifted her hair away from the back of her neck, tossing her head back a little. "No more coffee for a while," she said.

57 He wasn't certain he'd heard her correctly and he said, "What?" blankly.

58 "No more coffee for a while," she repeated.

59 There was silence behind him and then uneasy movement. He thought someone would say something, ask why or protest, but there was only silence and then a faint shuffling sound as though the men standing behind him had simultaneously shifted their weight from one foot to the other.

60 He looked at the girl without saying anything. He felt his hands begin to tingle and the tingling went all the way down to his finger tips so that he glanced down at them. They were clenched tight, hard, into fists. Then he looked at the girl again. What he wanted to do was hit her so hard that the scarlet lipstick on her mouth would smear and spread over her nose, her chin, out toward her cheeks, so hard that she would never toss her head again and refuse a man a cup of coffee because he was black.

61 He estimated the distance across the counter and reached forward, balancing his weight on the balls of his feet, ready to let the blow go. And then his hands fell back down to his sides because he forced himself to lower them, to unclench them and make them dangle loose. The effort took his breath away because his hands fought against him. But he couldn't hit her. He couldn't even now bring himself to hit a woman, not even this one, who had refused him a cup of coffee with a toss of her head. He kept seeing the gesture with which she had lifted the length of her blond hair from the back of her neck as expressive of her contempt for him.

62 When he went out the door he didn't look back. If he had he would have seen the flickering blue flame under the shiny coffee urn being extinguished. The line of men who had stood behind him lingered a moment to watch the

people drinking coffee at the tables and then they left just as he had without having had the coffee they wanted so badly. The girl behind the counter poured water in the urn and swabbed it out and as she waited for the water to run out, she lifted her hair gently from the back of her neck and tossed her head before she began making a fresh lot of coffee.

63 But he had walked away without a backward look, his head down, his hands in his pockets, raging at himself and whatever it was inside of him that had forced him to stand quiet and still when he wanted to strike out.

64 The subway was crowded and he had to stand. He tried grasping an overhead strap and his hands were too tense to grip it. So he moved near the train door and stood there swaying back and forth with the rocking of the train. The roar of the train beat inside his head, making it ache and throb, and the pain in his legs clawed up into his groin so that he seemed to be bursting with pain and he told himself that it was due to all that anger-born energy that had piled up in him and not been used and so it had spread through him like a poison—from his feet and legs all the way up to his head.

65 Mae was in the house before he was. He knew she was home before he put the key in the door of the apartment. The radio was going. She had it turned up loud and she was singing along with it.

66 "Hello, babe," she called out, as soon as he opened the door.

67 He tried to say 'hello' and it came out half grunt and half sigh.

68 "You sure sound cheerful," she said.

69 She was in the bedroom and he went and leaned against the doorjamb. The denim overalls she wore to work were carefully draped over the back of a chair by the bed. She was standing in front of the dresser, tying the sash of a yellow housecoat around her waist and chewing gum vigorously as she admired her reflection in the mirror over the dresser.

70 "Whatsa matter?" she said. "You get bawled out by the boss or somep'n?"

71 "Just tired," he said slowly. "For God's sake, do you have to crack that gum like that?"

72 "You don't have to lissen to me," she said complacently. She patted a curl in place near the side of her head and then lifted her hair away from the back of her neck, ducking her head forward and then back.

73 He winced away from the gesture. "What you got to be always fooling with your hair for?" he protested.

74 "Say, what's the matter with you anyway?" She turned away from the mirror to face him, put her hands on her hips. "You ain't been in the house two minutes and you're picking on me."

75 He didn't answer her because her eyes were angry and he didn't want to quarrel with her. They'd been married too long and got along too well and so he walked all the way into the room and sat down in the chair by the bed and stretched his legs out in front of him, putting his weight on the heels of his shoes, leaning way back in the chair, not saying anything.

76 "Lissen," she said sharply. "I've got to wear those overalls again tomorrow. You're going to get them all wrinkled up leaning against them like that."

77 He didn't move. He was too tired and his legs were throbbing now that he had sat down. Besides the overalls were already wrinkled and dirty, he thought. They couldn't help but be for she'd worn them all week. He leaned farther back in the chair.

78 "Come on, get up," she ordered.

79 "Oh, what the hell," he said wearily, and got up from the chair. "I'd just as soon live in a subway. There'd be just as much place to sit down."

80 He saw that her sense of humor was struggling with her anger. But her sense of humor won because she giggled.

81 "Aw, come on and eat," she said. There was a coaxing note in her voice. "You're nothing but an old hungry nigger trying to act tough and—" she paused to giggle and then continued, "You—"

82 He had always found her giggling pleasant and deliberately said things that might amuse her and then waited, listening for the delicate sound to emerge from her throat. This time he didn't even hear the giggle. He didn't let her finish what she was saying. She was standing close to him and that funny tingling started in his finger tips, went fast up his arms and sent his fist shooting straight for her face.

83 There was the smacking sound of soft flesh being struck by a hard object and it wasn't until she screamed that he realized he had hit her in the mouth—so hard that the dark red lipstick had blurred and spread over her full lips, reaching up toward the tip of her nose, down toward her chin, out toward her cheeks.

84 The knowledge that he had struck her seeped through him slowly and he was appalled but he couldn't drag his hands away from her face. He kept striking her and he thought with horror that something inside him was holding him, binding him to this act, wrapping and twisting about him so that he had to continue it. He had lost all control over his hands. And he groped for a phrase, a word, something to describe what this thing was like that was happening to him and he thought it was like being enmeshed in a winding sheet—that was it—like a winding sheet. And even as the thought formed in his mind, his hands reached for her face again and yet again.

QUESTIONS ON STORY

OBSERVING

1. Describe Johnson's relationship with Mae at the opening of the story. Trace his feelings and reactions through the scenes that follow, at the factory, the restaurant, and then back home. What is driving his anger?
2. How does Petry characterize Johnson? What kind of man is he? Does Petry mean for us to see him as sympathetic?
3. What symbolism operates in the image of the winding sheet?

EVALUATING

1. In Petry's portrait of a man who loses control, she examines the conditions of his life. What is her purpose in following him through his day?
2. What happens at the restaurant with the white girl? Explain Johnson's thinking.
3. Why do you think Johnson beats his wife?

RESPONDING AND APPLYING

1. Do you blame Johnson for his behavior? Do you excuse it? Who or what do you think is ultimately responsible for his violence?
2. What does this story tell us about family violence? About racism? Sexism?

PERSPECTIVES

A Blurring of Identities

After a decade or more of calls for diversity and multiculturalism in our schools, we still struggle to understand the challenge of leaving a world sharply divided along racial, ethnic, and gendered lines. The 1964 *Brown vs. Board of Education* case that demanded racially balanced schools drew the proverbial line in the sand: we are and must fully become a society of diverse groupings and backgrounds which are free to mix and gather on level ground.

The two essays that follow, on the blurring of our already blurred identities, seem relevant to exploring questions raised by the entrance of multiculturalism in our political and educational systems, questions like these: If we reject "pure racial identities" as fictions, where does that lead us? How do we think of and treat people of mixed-racial and mixed-ethnic and mixed-religious identities? Why is there such resentment in so many places of interracial dating and marriage? How can we gain the diversity without losing the best of our unique heritages? How do we celebrate the diversity of our country and world without appreciating heritages other than our own?

GLORIA ANZALDÚA, "LA CONCIENCIA DE LA MESTIZA"

Editor of *Hacienda Caras: Making Face/Making Soul* (1990) and author of the esteemed *Borderlands/La Frontera: The New Mestiza* (1987), Gloria Anzaldúa explores her own Spanish and Indian heritage in her poetry and prose. In addition, she challenges us to imagine a new consciousness, a new and more universal self, a self that identifies with the species and not just a single national or ethnic group. Anzaldúa describes an evolutionary process whereby new understandings of race, class, and gender develop out of "cultural collisions" of male and female, black and white and Hispanic. Out of such a clash and then bending, a healing and a new identity emerge. Pay special attention to her own blending of languages in what follows.

La conciencia de la mestiza[1]/ Towards a New Consciousness

Glorida Anzaldúa

Por la mujer de mi raza
hablará el espíritu.[2]

1 Jose Vasconcelos, Mexican philosopher, envisaged *una raza mestiza, una mezcla de razas afines, una raza de color—la primera raza síntesis del globo.*[3] He called it a cosmic race, *la raza cósmica,* a fifth race embracing the four major races of the world.[4] Opposite to the theory of the pure Aryan,[5] and to the policy of racial purity that white America practices, his theory is one of inclusivity. At the confluence of two or more genetic streams, with chromosomes constantly "crossing over," this mixture of races, rather than resulting in an inferior being, provides hybrid progeny, a mutable, more malleable species with a rich gene pool. From this racial, ideological, cultural, and biological cross-pollinization, an "alien" consciousness is presently in the making—a new *mestiza* consciousness, *una conciencia de mujer.*[6] It is a consciousness of the Borderlands.

---

[1] *La conciencia de la mestiza: mestiza* consciousness; consciousness of the *mestiza* (a woman of mixed racial heritage).

[2] This is my own "take off" on Jose Vasconcelos' idea. Jose Vasconcelos, *La Raza Cósmica: Misión de la Raza Ibero-Americana* (México: Aguilar S.A. de Ediciones, 1961). [Author's note] *Por la mujer de mi raza . . . :* the spirit shall speak through the women of my race.

[3] *una raza mestiza . . . :* a multiracial race, a mixture of kindred races, a race of color, the first synthetic race of the world.

[4] Vasconcelos. [Author's note]

[5] *the theory of the pure Aryan:* the myth espoused by Adolf Hitler and others of the racial superiority of white northern Europeans.

[6] *una conciencia de mujer:* a female consciousness.

Una lucha de fronteras / A Struggle of Borders

Because I, a *mestiza,*
continually walk out of one culture
and into another,
because I am in all cultures at the same time,
alma entre dos mundos, tres, cuatro,
me zumba la cabeza con lo contradictorio.
Estoy norteada por todas las voces que me hablan
simultáneamente.[7]

2 The ambivalence from the clash of voices results in mental and emotional states of perplexity. Internal strife results in insecurity and indecisiveness. The mestiza's dual or multiple personality is plagued by psychic restlessness.

3 In a constant state of mental nepantilism, an Aztec word meaning torn between ways, *la mestiza* is a product of the transfer of the cultural and spiritual values of one group to another. Being tricultural, monolingual, bilingual, or multilingual, speaking a patois,[8] and in a state of perpetual transition, the *mestiza* faces the dilemma of the mixed breed: which collectivity does the daughter of a darkskinned mother listen to?

4 *El choque de un alma atrapado entre el mundo del espíritu y el mundo de la técnica a veces la deja entullada.*[9] Cradled in one culture, sandwiched between two cultures, straddling all three cultures and their value systems, *la mestiza* undergoes a struggle of flesh, a struggle of borders, an inner war. Like all people, we perceive the version of reality that our culture communicates. Like others having or living in more than one culture, we get multiple, often opposing messages. The coming together of two self-consistent but habitually incompatible frames of reference[10] causes *un choque,* a cultural collision.

5 Within us and within *la cultura chicana,*[11] commonly held beliefs of the white culture attack commonly held beliefs of the Mexican culture, and both attack commonly held beliefs of the indigenous culture. Subconsciously, we see an attack on ourselves and our beliefs as a threat and we attempt to block with a counterstance.

6 But it is not enough to stand on the opposite river bank, shouting questions, challenging patriarchal, white conventions. A counterstance locks one

[7] *alma entre dos mundos . . . :* a soul caught between two, three, four worlds. My head aches with contradictions. I'm led north by all the voices that speak to me simultaneously.

[8] *patois:* nonstandard dialect.

[9] *El choque de una alma atrapado . . . :* The struggle of a soul trapped between the world of the spirit and the world of technology sometimes leaves it paralyzed.

[10] Arthur Koestler termed this "bisociation." Albert Rothenberg, *The Creative Process in Art, Science, and Other Fields* (Chicago, IL: University of Chicago Press, 1979), 12. [Author's note]

[11] *la cultura chicana:* chicana culture. Elsewhere in *Borderlands,* Anzaldúa writes, "*La Cultura chicana* identifies with the mother (Indian) rather than with the father (Spanish). Our faith is rooted in indigenous attributes, images, symbols, magic, and myth" (Chapter 3).

into a duel of oppressor and oppressed; locked in mortal combat, like the cop and the criminal, both are reduced to a common denominator of violence. The counterstance refutes the dominant culture's views and beliefs, and, for this, it is proudly defiant. All reaction is limited by, and dependent on, what it is reacting against. Because the counterstance stems from a problem with authority—outer as well as inner—it's a step towards liberation from cultural domination. But it is not a way of life. At some point, on our way to a new consciousness, we will have to leave the opposite bank, the split between the two mortal combatants somehow healed so that we are on both shores at once and, at once, see through serpent and eagle eyes.[12] Or perhaps we will decide to disengage from the dominant culture, write it off altogether as a lost cause, and cross the border into a wholly new and separate territory. Or we might go another route. The possibilities are numerous once we decide to act and not react.

A Tolerance for Ambiguity

7 The numerous possibilities leave *la mestiza* floundering in uncharted seas. In perceiving conflicting information and points of view, she is subjected to a swamping of her psychological borders. She has discovered that she can't hold concepts or ideas in rigid boundaries. The borders and walls that are supposed to keep the undesirable ideas out are entrenched habits and patterns of behavior; these habits and patterns are the enemy within. Rigidity means death. Only by remaining flexible is she able to stretch the psyche[13] horizontally and vertically. *La mestiza* constantly has to shift out of habitual formations; from convergent thinking, analytical reasoning that tends to use rationality to move toward a single goal (a Western mode), to divergent thinking,[14] characterized by movement away from set patterns and goals and toward a more whole perspective, one that includes rather than excludes.

8 The new *mestiza* copes by developing a tolerance for contradictions, a tolerance for ambiguity. She learns to be an Indian in Mexican culture, to be Mexican from an Anglo point of view. She learns to juggle cultures. She has a plural personality, she operates in a pluralistic mode—nothing is thrust out, the good the bad and the ugly, nothing rejected, nothing abandoned. Not only does she sustain contradictions, she turns the ambivalence into something else.

9 She can be jarred out of ambivalence by an intense, and often painful, emotional event which inverts or resolves the ambivalence. I'm not sure exactly how. The work takes place underground—subconsciously. It is work that the

---

[12] *see through serpent and eagle eyes:* "The eagle symbolizes the spirit (as the sun, the father); the serpent symbolizes the soul (as the earth, the mother). Together, they symbolize the struggle between the spiritual/celestial/male and the underworld/earth/feminine" (*Borderlands,* Chapter 1).

[13] *the psyche:* the soul or self.

[14] In part, I derive my definitions for "convergent" and "divergent" thinking from Rothenberg, 12–13. [Author's note]

soul performs. The focal point or fulcrum, that juncture where the *mestiza* stands, is where phenomena tend to collide. It is where the possibility of uniting all that is separate occurs. This assembly is not one where severed or separated pieces merely come together. Nor is it a balancing of opposing powers. In attempting to work out a synthesis, the self has added a third element which is greater than the sum of its severed parts. That third element is a new consciousness—a *mestiza* consciousness—and though it is a source of intense pain, its energy comes from continual creative motion that keeps breaking down the unitary aspect of each new paradigm.

10 *En unas pocas centurias,*[15] the future will belong to the *mestiza.* Because the future depends on the breaking down of the paradigms, it depends on the straddling of two or more cultures. By creating a new mythos—that is, a change in the way we perceive reality, the way we see ourselves, and the ways we behave—*la mestiza* creates a new consciousness.

11 The work of *mestiza* consciousness is to break down the subject-object duality that keeps her a prisoner and to show in the flesh and through the images in her work how duality is transcended. The answer to the problem between the white race and the colored, between males and females, lies in healing the split that originates in the very foundation of our lives, our culture, our languages, our thoughts. A massive uprooting of dualistic thinking in the individual and collective consciousness is the beginning of a long struggle, but one that could, in our best hopes, bring us to the end of rape, of violence, of war. . . .

El camino de la mestiza
The Mestiza Way

Caught between the sudden contraction, the breath sucked in and the endless space, the brown woman stands still, looks at the sky. She decides to go down, digging her way along the roots of trees. Sifting through the bones, she shakes them to see if there is any marrow in them. Then, touching the dirt to her forehead, to her tongue, she takes a few bones, leaves the rest in their burial place.

She goes through her backpack, keeps her journal and address book, throws away the muni-bart metromaps.[16] The coins are heavy and they go next, then the greenbacks flutter through the air. She keeps her knife, can opener, and eyebrow pencil. She puts bones, pieces of bark, *hierbas,*[17] eagle feather, snakeskin, tape recorder, the rattle and drum in her pack and she sets out to become the complete *tolteca.*[18]

---

[15] *En unas pocas centurias:* in a few centuries.

[16] *muni-bart metromaps:* maps of bus and trail transportation in the San Francisco Bay area.

[17] *hierbas:* herbs.

[18] Gina Valdés, *Puentes y Fronteras: Coplas Chicanas* (Los Angeles, CA: Castle Lithograph, 1982), 2. [Author's note] *tolteca:* the Toltec empire predates the Aztec in ancient Mexico. Anzaldúa associates the Toltecs with more woman-centered culture and religion than those of the warlike, patriarchal Aztecs.

12 Her first step is to take inventory. *Despojando, desgranando, quitando paja.*[19] Just what did she inherit from her ancestors? This weight on her back—which is the baggage from the Indian mother, which the baggage from the Spanish father, which the baggage from the Anglo?

13 *Pero es difiícil*[20] differentiating between *lo heredado, lo adquirido, lo impuesto.*[21] She puts history through a sieve, winnows out the lies, looks at the forces that we as a race, as women, have been a part of. *Luego bota lo que no vale, los desmientos, los desencuentos, el embrutecimiento. Aguarda el juicio, hondo y enraízado, de la gente antigua.*[22] This step is a conscious rupture with all oppressive traditions of all cultures and religions. She communicates that rupture, documents the struggle. She reinterprets history and, using new symbols, she shapes new myths. She adopts new perspectives toward the darkskinned, women, and queers. She strengthens her tolerance (and intolerance) for ambiguity. She is willing to share, to make herself vulnerable to foreign ways of seeing and thinking. She surrenders all notions of safety, of the familiar. Deconstruct, construct. She becomes a *nahual,*[23] able to transform herself into a tree, a coyote, into another person. She learns to transform the small "I" into the total Self. *Se hace moldeadora de su alma. Según la concepción que tiene de sí misma, así será.*[24]

QUE NO SE NOS OLVIDE LOS HOMBRES[25]

> "*Tú no sirves pa'nada*[26]—
> you're good for nothing.
> *Eres pura vieja.*"[27]

14 "You're nothing but a woman" means you are defective. Its opposite is to be *un macho.* The modern meaning of the word "machismo," as well as the concept, is actually an Anglo invention. For men like my father, being "macho" meant being strong enough to protect and support my mother and us, yet being able to show love. Today's macho has doubts about his ability to feed and protect his family. His "machismo" is an adaptation to oppression and poverty and

---

[19] *Despojando, desgranando, quitando paja:* Stripping, removing the grain or the straw.

[20] *Pero es difícil:* But it is difficult.

[21] *lo heredado, lo adquirido, lo impuesto:* the inherited, the acquired, the imposed.

[22] *Luego bota lo que no vale . . . :* Then she discards whatever is useless, falsehoods and brutality. She waits for the deep, probing common sense of the ancient people.

[23] *nahual:* sorceress.

[24] *Se hace moldeadora . . . :* She is able to mold her soul. Whatever image she has of herself, so she will be.

[25] *Que no se nos olvide los hombres:* Let us not forget men.

[26] *Tú no sirves pa'nada:* You're good for nothing.

[27] *Eres pura vieja:* You're nothing but a woman.

low self-esteem. It is the result of hierarchical male dominance. The Anglo, feeling inadequate and inferior and powerless, displaces or transfers these feelings to the Chicano by shaming him. In the Gringo[28] world, the Chicano suffers from excessive humility and self-effacement, shame of self and self-deprecation. Around Latinos he suffers from a sense of language inadequacy and its accompanying discomfort; with Native Americans he suffers from a racial amnesia which ignores our common blood, and from guilt because the Spanish part of him took their land and oppressed them. He has an excessive compensatory hubris[29] when around Mexicans from the other side. It overlays a deep sense of racial shame.

15 The loss of a sense of dignity and respect in the macho breeds a false machismo which leads him to put down women and even to brutalize them. Coexisting with his sexist behavior is a love for the mother which takes precedence over that of all others. Devoted son, macho pig. To wash down the shame of his acts, of his very being, and to handle the brute in the mirror, he takes to the bottle, the snort, the needle, and the fist.

16 Though we "understand" the root causes of male hatred and fear, and the subsequent wounding of women, we do not excuse, we do not condone, and we will no longer put up with it. From the men of our race, we demand the admission/acknowledgment/disclosure/testimony that they wound us, violate us, are afraid of us and of our power. We need them to say they will begin to eliminate their hurtful put-down ways. But more than the words, we demand acts. We say to them: We will develop equal power with you and those who have shamed us.

17 It is imperative that *mestizas* support each other in changing the sexist elements in the Mexican-Indian culture. As long as woman is put down, the Indian and the Black in all of us is put down. The struggle of the *mestiza* is above all a feminist one. As long as *los hombres* think they have to *chingar mujeres*[30] and each other to be men, as long as men are taught that they are superior and therefore culturally favored over *la mujer,*[31] as long as to be *a vieja*[32] is a thing of derision, there can be no real healing of our psyches. We're halfway there—we have such love of the Mother, the good mother. The first step is to unlearn the *puta/virgen*[33] dichotomy and to see *Coatlapopeuh-Coatlicue* in the Mother, *Guadalupe.*[34]

---

[28] *Gringo:* Anglo.

[29] *hubris:* exaggerated pride or self-confidence.

[30] *chingar mujeres:* fuck women.

[31] *la mujer:* the woman.

[32] *vieja:* old woman.

[33] *puta/virgen:* whore/virgin.

[34] *Coatlapopeuh-Coatlicue in the Mother, Guadalupe:* a reference to the dual identity (Indian/pagan and Spanish/Christian) of the Virgin of Guadalupe. Anzaldúa argues that "after the conquest, the Spaniards and their Church . . . desexed Guadalupe, taking Coatlalopeuh, the serpent/sexuality, out of her" (*Borderlands,* Chapter 3).

18 Tenderness, a sign of vulnerability, is so feared that it is showered on women with verbal abuse and blows. Men, even more than women, are fettered to gender roles. Women at least have had the guts to break out of bondage. Only gay men have had the courage to expose themselves to the woman inside them and to challenge the current masculinity. I've encountered a few scattered and isolated gentle straight men, the beginnings of a new breed, but they are confused, and entangled with sexist behaviors that they have not been able to eradicate. We need a new masculinity and the new man needs a movement.

19 Lumping the males who deviate from the general norm with man, the oppressor, is a gross injustice. *Asombra pensar que nos hemos quedado en ese pozo oscuro donde el mundo encierra a las lesbianas. Asombra pensar que hemos, como femenistas y lesbianas, cerrado nuestros corazónes a los hombres, a nuestros hermanos los jotos, desheredados y marginales como nosotros.*[35] Being the supreme crossers of cultures, homosexuals have strong bonds with the queer white, Black, Asian, Native American, Latino, and with the queer in Italy, Australia, and the rest of the planet. We come from all colors, all classes, all races, all time periods. Our role is to link people with each other—the Blacks with Jews with Indians with Asians with whites with extraterrestrials. It is to transfer ideas and information from one culture to another. Colored homosexuals have more knowledge of other cultures; have always been at the forefront (although sometimes in the closet) of all liberation struggles in this country; have suffered more injustices and have survived them despite all odds. Chicanos need to acknowledge the political and artistic contributions of their queer. People, listen to what your *jotería*[36] is saying.

20 The mestizo and the queer exist at this time and point on the evolutionary continuum for a purpose. We are a blending that proves that all blood is intricately woven together, and that we are spawned out of similar souls.

SOMOS UNA GENTE[37]

Hay tantísimas fronteras
que dividen a la gente,
pero por cada frontera
existe también un puente.[38]
—GINA VALDÉS[39]

---

[35] *Asombra pensar que nos hemos quedado, . . . :* It's astonishing to think that we have stayed in that dark well where the world locks up lesbians. It's astonishing to think that as feminist lesbians, we have closed our hearts to men, to our gay brothers, as disinherited and alienated as we are.

[36] *jotería:* gayness.

[37] *Somas una gente:* We are one people.

[38] *Hay tantísimas fronteras . . . :* There are so many borders / dividing people / but through each border there / passes a bridge.

[39] Richard Wilhelm, *The I Ching or Book of Changes,* trans. Cary F. Baynes (Princeton, NJ: Princeton University Press, 1950), 98. [Author's note]

Divided Loyalties

21 Many women and men of color do not want to have any dealings with white people. It takes too much time and energy to explain to the downwardly mobile, white middle-class women that it's okay for us to want to own "possessions," never having had any nice furniture on our dirt floors or "luxuries" like washing machines. Many feel that whites should help their own people rid themselves of race hatred and fear first. I, for one, choose to use some of my energy to serve as mediator. I think we need to allow whites to be our allies. Through our literature, art, *corridos,*[40] and folktales we must share our history with them so when they set up committees to help Big Mountain Navajos[41] or the Chicano farmworkers or *los Nicaragüenses*[42] they won't turn people away because of their racial fears and ignorances. They will come to see that they are not helping us but following our lead.

22 Individually, but also as a racial entity, we need to voice our needs. We need to say to white society: we need you to accept the fact that Chicanos are different, to acknowledge your rejection and negation of us. We need you to own the fact that you looked upon us as less than human, that you stole our lands, our personhood, our self-respect. We need you to make public restitution: to say that, to compensate for your own sense of defectiveness, you strive for power over us, you erase our history and our experience because it makes you feel guilty—you'd rather forget your brutish acts. To say you've split yourself from minority groups, that you disown us, that your dual consciousness splits off parts of yourself, transferring the "negative" parts onto us. (Where there is persecution of minorities, there is shadow projection. Where there is violence and war, there is repression of shadow.) To say that you are afraid of us, that to put distance between us, you wear the mask of contempt. Admit that Mexico is your double, that she exists in the shadow of this country, that we are irrevocably tied to her. Gringo, accept the doppelganger[43] in your psyche. By taking back your collective shadow the intracultural split will heal. And finally, tell us what you need from us.

By Your True Faces We Will Know You

23 I am visible—see this Indian face—yet I am invisible. I both blind them with my beak nose and am their blind spot. But I exist, we exist. They'd like to think I have melted in the pot. But I haven't, we haven't.

24 The dominant white culture is killing us slowly with its ignorance. By taking away our self-determination, it has made us weak and empty. As a people

---

[40] *corridos:* ballads or narrative folk songs of Mexico.

[41] *Big Mountain Navajos:* Big Mountain is an area in New Mexico at the center of a Navaho and Hopi dispute over land rights and treaty conditions.

[42] *los Nicaragüenses:* The Nicaraguans.

[43] *doppelganger:* a double.

we have resisted and we have taken expedient positions, but we have never been allowed to develop unencumbered—we have never been allowed to be fully ourselves. The whites in power want us people of color to barricade ourselves behind our separate tribal walls so they can pick us off one at a time with their hidden weapons; so they can whitewash and distort history. Ignorance splits people, creates prejudices. A misinformed people is a subjugated people.

25 Before the Chicano and the undocumented worker and the Mexican from the other side can come together, before the Chicano can have unity with Native Americans and other groups, we need to know the history of their struggle and they need to know ours. Our mothers, our sisters and brothers, the guys who hang out on street corners, the children in the playgrounds, each of us must know our Indian lineage, our afro-*mestisaje*,[44] our history of resistance.

26 To the immigrant *mexicano* and the recent arrivals we must teach our history. The 80 million *mexicanos* and the Latinos from Central and South America must know our struggles. Each one of us must know basic facts about Nicaragua, Chile, and the rest of Latin America. The Latinoist movement (Chicanos, Puerto Ricans, Cubans, and other Spanish-speaking people working together to combat racial discrimination in the market place) is good but it is not enough. Other than a common culture we will have nothing to hold us together. We need to meet on a broader communal ground.

27 The struggle is inner: Chicano, *indio*,[45] American Indian, *mojado*,[46] *mexicano*, immigrant Latino, Anglo in power, working class Anglo, Black, Asian—our psyches resemble the bordertowns and are populated by the same people. The struggle has always been inner, and is played out in the outer terrains. Awareness of our situation must come before inner changes, which in turn come before changes in society. Nothing happens in the "real" world unless it first happens in the images in our heads.

---

[44] *afro-mestisaje:* mixed-blood Latino people of African descent.

[45] *indio:* Indian (of Mexico/Central America).

[46] *mojado:* wetback.

QUESTIONS FOR WRITING AND DISCUSSION

OBSERVING

1. How does Anzaldúa contrast her idea of *la mestiza* to a policy of "racial purity"? What does she mean by the "*mestiza* consciousness . . . of the Borderlands"?
2. What is the mental state of *la mestiza?* Characterize both the upside and downside of such a state. How does the "cultural collision" affect *la mestiza?*

3. Anzaldúa rejects the stance that shouts its challenges to white patriarchy. Why? She advocates the use of "divergent thinking" and moving "away from set patterns and goals and toward a more whole perspective. . . ." Explain what she means.
4. How is the concept of *mestiza* different from the image of the melting pot?

EVALUATING

1. Tolerating the ambiguity of multiple identities challenges one to operate pluralistically and then to combine one's "several parts" into a new synthesis, "a *mestiza* consciousness." Can you think of examples—in the arts, in entertainment, in politics, in literature—of this?
2. What is Anzaldúa's view of the future? How does she foresee changes in the battles of the races, the sexes, and of various ethnic groups?

RESPONDING AND APPLYING

1. What process of change does Anzaldúa describe as the "*Mestiza* way"? Recognizing that the great majority of us do not belong to a single, pure racial or ethnic group, how can we learn from this?
2. How does Anzaldúa's multilingual voice, with Spanish and English, with poetry and prose, affect your reading? Why do you think she wrote like this?

ISHMAEL REED, "WHAT'S AMERICAN ABOUT AMERICA?"

Teacher, poet, novelist, *Ishmael Reed* was born February 22, 1938, in Chattanooga, Tennessee. The author of six novels and several books of nonfiction, Reed writes to provoke. *New York Times* writer Darryl Pickney claims that "Though variously described as a writer in whose work the black picaresque tradition has been extended, as a misogynist or an heir to both Hurston's folk lyricism and Ellision's irony, he is, perhaps because of this, one of the most underrated writers in America. Certainly no other contemporary black writer, male or female, has used the language and beliefs of folk culture so imaginatively and few have been so stinging about the absurdity of American racism." What may be unique about Reed is his willingness to attack not just the oppressive white, Western, colonialist times, but also the black leaders who claim to want to serve the poor, but in reality wait for a chance to exploit them. Reed's latest book is *Writin' Is Fightin,'* a collection of essays from which "What's American about America?" comes. Recently, Reed has published other volumes of essays and poetry on black life in America, as well as a video soap opera. He is currently senior lecturer at the University of California, Berkeley.

What's American about America?

Ishmael Reed

1 An item from the *New York Times,* June 23, 1983: "At the annual Lower East Side Jewish Festival yesterday, a Chinese woman ate a pizza slice in front of Ty Thuan Duc's Vietnamese grocery store. Beside her a Spanish-speaking family patronized a cart with two signs: 'Italian Ices' and 'Kosher by Rabbi Alper.' And after the pastrami ran out, everybody ate knishes."

2 On the day before Memorial Day, 1983, a poet called me to describe a city he had just visited. He said that one section included mosques, built by the Islamic people who dwelled there. Attending his reading, he said, were large numbers of Hispanic people, 40,000 of whom lived in the same city. He was not talking about a fabled city located in some mysterious region of the world. The city he'd visited was Detroit.

3 A few months before, as I was visiting Texas, I heard the taped voice used to guide passengers to their connections at the Dallas Airport announcing items in both Spanish and English. This trend is likely to continue; after all, for some southwestern states like Texas, where the largest minority is now Mexican-American, Spanish was the first written language and the Spanish style lives on in the western way of life.

4 Shortly after my Texas trip, I sat in a campus auditorium at the University of Wisconsin at Milwaukee as a Yale professor—whose original work on the influence of African cultures upon those of the Americas has led to his ostracism from some intellectual circles—walked up and down the aisle like an old-time Southern evangelist, dancing and drumming the top of the lectern, illustrating his points before some Afro-American intellectuals and artists who cheered and applauded his performance. The professor was "white." After his lecture, he conversed with a group of Milwaukeeans—all who spoke Yoruban, though only the professor had ever traveled to Africa.

5 One of the artists there told me that his paintings, which included African and Afro-American mythological symbols and imagery, were hanging in the local McDonald's restaurant. The next day I went to McDonald's and snapped pictures of smiling youngsters eating hamburgers below paintings that could grace the walls of any of the country's leading museums. The manager of the local McDonald's said, "I don't know what you boys are doing, but I like it," as he commissioned the local painters to exhibit in his restaurant.

6 Such blurring of cultural styles occurs in everyday life in the United States to a greater extent than anyone can imagine. The result is what the above-mentioned Yale professor, Robert Thompson, referred to as a cultural bouillabaisse. Yet members of the nation's present educational and cultural elect still cling to the notion that the United States belongs to some vaguely defined entity they refer to as "Western civilization," by which they mean, presumably, a civilization created by people of Europe, as if Europe can even be viewed in

monolithic terms. Is Beethoven's Ninth Symphony, which includes Turkish marches, a part of Western civilization? Or the late-nineteenth- and twentieth-century French paintings, whose creators were influenced by Japanese art? And what of the cubists, through whom the influence of African art changed modern painting? Or the surrealists, who were so impressed with the art of the Pacific Northwest Indians that, in their map of North America, Alaska dwarfs the lower forty-eight states in size?

7 Are the Russians, who are often criticized for their adoption of "Western" ways by Tsarist dissidents in exile, members of Western civilization? And what of the millions of Europeans who have black African and Asian ancestry, black Africans having occupied several European countries for hundreds of years? Are these "Europeans" a part of Western civilization? Or the Hungarians, who originated across the Urals in a place called Great Hungary? Or the Irish, who came from the Iberian Peninsula?

8 Even the notion that North America is part of Western civilization because our "system of government" is derived from Europe is being challenged by Native American historians who say that the founding fathers, Benjamin Franklin especially, were actually influenced by the system of government that had been adopted by the Iroquois hundreds of years prior to the arrival of Europeans.

9 Western civilization, then, becomes another confusing category—like Third World, or Judeo-Christian culture—as humanity attempts to impose its small-screen view of political and cultural reality upon a complex world. Our most publicized novelist recently said that Western civilization was the greatest achievement of mankind—an attitude that flourishes on the street level as scribbles in public restrooms: "White Power," "Niggers and Spics Suck," or "Hitler was a prophet." Where did such an attitude, which has caused so much misery and depression in our national life, which has tainted even our noblest achievements, begin? An attitude that caused the incarceration of Japanese-American citizens during World War II, the persecution of Chicanos and Chinese Americans, the near-extermination of the Indians, and the murder and lynchings of thousands of Afro-Americans.

10 The Puritans of New England are idealized in our schoolbooks as the first Americans, "a hardy band" of no-nonsense patriarchs whose discipline razed the forest and brought order to the New World (a term that annoys Native American historians). Industrious, responsible, it was their "Yankee ingenuity" and practicality that created the work ethic.

11 The Puritans, however, had a mean streak. They hated the theater and banned Christmas. They punished people in a cruel and inhuman manner. They killed children who disobeyed their parents. They exterminated the Indians, who had taught them how to survive in a world unknown to them. And their encounter with calypso culture, in the form of a servant from Barbados working in a Salem minister's household, resulted in the witchcraft hysteria.

12 The Puritan legacy of hard work and meticulous accounting led to the establishment of a great industrial society, but there was the other side—the strange and paranoid attitudes of that society toward those different from the elect.

13 The cultural attitudes of that early elect continue to be voiced in everyday life in the United States; the president of a distinguished university, writing a letter to the *Times*, belittling the study of African civilizations; the television network that promoted its show on the Vatican art with the boast that this art represented "the finest achievements of the human spirit."

14 When I heard a schoolteacher warn the other night about the invasion of the American educational system by foreign curricula, I wanted to yell at the television set, "Lady, they're already here." It has already begun because the world is here. The world has been arriving at these shores for at least 10,000 years from Europe, Africa, and Asia. In the late nineteenth and early twentieth centuries, large numbers of Europeans arrived, adding their cultures to those of the European, African, and Asian settlers who were already here, and recently millions have been entering the country from South American and the Caribbean, making Robert Thompson's bouillabaisse richer and thicker.

15 North America deserves a more exciting destiny than as a repository of "Western civilization." We can become a place where the cultures of the world crisscross. This is possible because the United States and Canada are unique in the world: The world is here.

QUESTIONS FOR WRITING AND DISCUSSION

OBSERVING

1. In describing the "blurring of cultural styles," Reed punctures categories like "Western civilization." What is his larger purpose in doing this?
2. What kind of attitudes and behaviors does Reed think cause the oppressions and heinous stereotypes listed in paragraphs 9-11?
3. Reed reserves special criticism for the Puritans and "that early elect." What do you think he means by "early elect" and what accounts for his anger?

EVALUATING

1. Characterize Reed's dream of a "place where the cultures of the world crisscross." What institutional and policy changes can you imagine would have to occur before it can become a reality?
2. Closely examine Reed's examples of cultural mixing. To what degree is there a real appreciation, celebration, and understanding for other cultures than the dominant one?

RESPONDING AND APPLYING

1. Examine your own home and school communities. What ideal dominates? Is it true that there's more "cultural bouillabaisse" and mixing "than anyone

can imagine"? Or is such mixing a reality only in a few urban centers in the United States?

2. Is Reed's image of the ideal close to your own? Are you as optimistic as Reed seems to be?

CHAPTER WRITING ASSIGNMENTS

1. One of the themes running through several of the selections in this chapter is the power of literacy, of the command of language to facilitate change among the oppressed. Trace this recognition of the power of language in the careers and writings of persons like James Baldwin, Toni Morrison, Maya Angelou, Richard Rodriguez, Malcolm X, Alice Walker, and Frederick Douglass. Explain how the power of their ideas and skills as readers and writers enhances their personal effectiveness as agents of change.
2. Race has been called our national nightmare in America. Drawing on readings in this chapter, consider the meaning of race in the last decade of the twentieth century. Some see it as having declining significance, given the power of economic and social class to take its place. Some say it's only a mental construction, with no scientific or biological base, and therefore used primarily to confer privilege and power. Others feel it's still a major source of power and ranking in society. How do you see race today?
3. Consider the proposition: a non-white individual in the late 1990s is in a much better position than he or she was at the end of the Civil Rights movement of the 1960s and is approaching full equality and enfranchisement in the political system. Argue for or against it, offering evidence from current events, statistics, and recent history.
4. For some, the Nazi Holocaust, resulting in the deaths of eleven million, six million of whom were Jews, is the best documented study of extreme hatred practiced by a state. Yet some see it as an aberration, unique in history and unrepeatable. To what extent does it represent the result of pseudoscientific policies based on constructed racist categories and state-sponsored discrimination that could happen again? How universal or generalizable is such a phenomenon?
5. Has education as you have known it recognized and celebrated diversity and difference in cultural heritage and background? How would you define ideal diversity in education? Have we fairly represented all groups or overstepped the bounds of fairness? What do you know and think about affirmative action? Argue the case for or against cultural diversity as you've known it in the schools.
6. What does diversity really look and feel like? When we as a culture learn to include those who have traditionally stood outside the mainstream, what will life be like? Draw on your own experiences of diversity and the readings in the "perspectives" section for your answer. Consider genres other than the expository, informative essay, such as narrative, letter, description, dialogue, or monologue.

CHAPTER PREVIEW

Chapter Prelude
Andrew Todhunter, "The Taming of the Saw"

Introductory Essay

Readings
Vaclav Havel, "Civilization's Thin Veneer"
Neil Postman, "Amusing Ourselves To Death"
Michael Ventura, "Inventory of Timelessness"
Steinar Kvale, "Themes of Postmodernity"
Two Cartoons: Bill Watterson, "Calvin and Hobbes"
Garry Trudeau, "Doonesbury"

Story
Ray Bradbury, "The Veldt"

Perspectives
WHERE ARE COMPUTERS TAKING US?
Howard Rheingold, *from* Virtual Community
Bill Gates, *from* The Road Ahead

Chapter Writing Assignments

Chapter 11

Technology, Postmodernism, and the Cyberfuture: Turning in the Widening Gyre

The Taming of the Saw

Andrew Todhunter

1 The problem, clearly, was the cold. The old lodge on the Beaverkill in which we planned to spend the winter was built in the 1920s, before the rising cost of oil created the need for three-paned glass and modern insulation. By today's standards the once four-season lodge was now at best a summer home. There was a furnace of sorts, built for coal and later converted to burn oil at less than 40 percent efficiency. And the fireplace, a great stone maw that devoured all the fire's heat and a good deal more besides, was an even greater liability. When the wind blew across the chimney's mouth, it was like a giant pulling on a corncob pipe, and unless the flue was tightly shut, the pages of your book would flutter in the draw.

2 A wood stove seemed to be the answer.

3 We found a used one quickly enough, a friend's donation, its rusted interior still serving as the lodging for two mice and a decade's worth of shop debris. The mice crept gullibly into Havahart traps set with peanut butter (the rodents' bait of choice) and were bused to a lakeshore some miles to the east.

4 The wood was another matter. There was no shortage on the lot: its forty-odd acres were thick with deadfall and standing maple, beech, and other hardwood, seasoned upright and ready to be felled, split, and stacked. But the bucksaw—a museum piece of my father's childhood, still hanging in the toolroom and sharp enough despite its years—could hardly keep up with the demand of the cold months ahead, which was estimated to be six or eight cords. When our friend the stove donor threw in the offer of a chainsaw for the season, I readily accepted.

5 A chainsaw operator can fell and section a tree for splitting in a fraction of the time required with ax and manual saw. Hard work, of course, was part of the appeal of the place, but we had no hydraulic splitter. All work with wedge and maul would still be done by hand. By my reckoning, splitting six or eight cords over the coming months would constitute an adequate amount of outdoor labor. Sure, I said, I'll borrow your saw.

6 The chainsaw holds a particular position in the average suburban-bred psyche. It wasn't an aspect of daily life in the town of my childhood, where firewood arrived in the back of a dump truck, paused briefly on the back porch, and eventually went into the fire.

7 Instead the tool was a film prop. Who can erase the image of the man-child in *The Texas Chainsaw Massacre?* The tool performs a grisly task in *Scarface—Naow zee leg, hunh?*—and is given a walk-on part in many other movies. Hollywood has branded the chain saw as an embodiment of psychosis and unbridled mayhem. And the machine provides its own sound effects—a roar almost as terrifying and aggressive as images of the blade in contact with flesh.

8 The chainsaw's portrayals in legend do little to allay one's sense of its inherent malevolence. The tale of the logger pinned beneath a tree of impossible diameter, forced to cut one or both legs off with the tool and then drag himself, like Monty Python's Black Knight, legless through thirty miles of icy woods, is subject to infinite and often epic variation.

9 A new bar and chain were required for the beat-up saw, so I took it to the saw dealer, a neighbor who works out of his home. On his mantelpiece stood a row of gleaming figures, each holding high a golden laurel wreath. I read the engraved plaques on marble bases: First Place, County Chainsaw Competition, 1987. Second Place, Third Place, First Place, 1988, 1989, 1990. Chainsaw trophies from one end of his mantelpiece to the other.

10 "All won with this saw right here. The one I work with." He indicated a large German model sitting smugly in its open case.

11 He produced a stack of calendars, each month a different saw, a different champion. He opened one to reveal the present world champ in the custom class. The man held a modified saw the size of a Yugo, huge exhaust pipes sweeping back, the bar three-quarters through a horizontal log. Smoke and sawdust filled the atmosphere behind the champion. Sweat ran down his arms.

12 "Twenty-inch-diameter pine," the dealer said.

13 "How long did he take to make the cut?"

14 "Two seconds. At the outside."

15 He looked down at the pictured saw with unconcealed awe and shook his head.

16 "Nothing like it. I tell you, you should go to one of these saw competitions. It'll change your life."

17 With the new bar and chain came a thin booklet on chainsaw handling, a welcome document that I read carefully twice before setting hand to saw. It warned of the physics of the beast—the infamous kickback, caused by several

possible circumstances but most notably the tip's catching on another surface. This can send the machine careering up and into a face or throat, its power diverted from the chain into the body of the saw. Other possibilities, less vivid but still formidable, were laid out simply, the precautions to be taken clear. To clarify the potential of kickback, the saw dealer had zealously dealt me another anecdote, this one with the legitimacy of a professional source.

18 An acquaintance of his stopped one evening to cut up a tree lying dead by the side of the road. He worked quickly in the dimming light, eager to get home, and didn't see the burl waiting for his blade. With a quick jerk the saw kicked back and fell to the ground from his hands. That was close, he said to himself, and reached down to continue the job. Then he felt the warmth from the severed carotid artery in his torn throat, and he lay down on the roadside to die. The next moment he reconsidered—there were children, a young wife—and with a balled-up rag pressed against the wound he tried to make it into town. He chanced to come up behind an off-duty ambulance and was saved. By the time they got him stitched up, he had lost more than half his blood.

19 I finished the safety booklet and set out with heavy tread for the woodpile. Wearing shatterproof glasses, stout orange silencers, and rawhide gloves, I felt underprepared for an event that seemed to warrant a great heaume, hauberk, and greaves. I started the saw with a tug, ready for a kickback to beeline for my vitals. Spared evisceration in the starting, I poised for the first cut while the engine warmed. Several moments passed. Perhaps I should move the woodpile into the garage first, I mused, what with the coming of rain . . . Coward! Make the damn cut! The teeth nibbled delicately on the bark. Small chips flecked against my boots. The manual had advised that I operate at maximum rpm to reduce the possibility of kickback. With the trigger clenched and the engine howling at full throttle, the teeth took another taste. Bare wood gleamed; the dust blew golden on my pant cuffs. I allowed the saw to take long, steady gulps of the seasoned beech, snarling, vibrating deep into my upper arm, deceptively still, descending slowly and easily through the narrow width.

20 The section tumbled off into the leaves and the saw took a breath. I released the trigger. *Hum-a-ding-ding-ding-a-ding-ding*—it idled pleasantly like any healthy two-stroke motorcycle engine. I examined the chain, now still and wet with oil. The dust that had gathered where the chain slinks into the machine's innards was wet and gummy, like sedimenting grass on the bottom of a lawn mower.

21 Soon the pile was cut to length, the weapon more comfortable, if still unwelcome, in the hand. With the light step of a man who has cheated death, I stacked the hour's quick work and made it back inside as the first raindrops fell. The stove was fed for the night.

22 In the weeks to come I would tame the saw, learn its nature, acknowledge the enormous boost in productivity. I raced the stove and soon outstripped it. The woodpiles climbed faster than they could be devoured. Trees fell by the dozens, suddenly. Deadfall simply disappeared.

23 And now the fear of the machine is gone, leaving only the respect required for safe use. The chainsaw is no longer a film prop but a simple tool that has saved hours of hard work.

24 And how I hate the thing: its roar, its stink, its jarring vibration, its very presence a transgression in the quiet of the woods. Perhaps most of all I dislike its efficiency. I now understand the mulish refusal of Tolstoy's serfs to give up their antiquated tools. It's more than a question of aesthetics, of an offended ear or nose. Nor is it simply stubbornness—that what is new must be worse. I suppose it's the intuitive awareness that what relieves us of our labor removes us from our lives. We grow more frail and dim-witted with each invention that outstrips us. It is this sense of robbery, of loss, that makes us cringe at technology's advance.

25 And yet the bucksaw hangs in the garage. We simply need the wood.

QUESTIONS FOR WRITING AND DISCUSSION

OBSERVING

1. What conditions lead Todhunter to buy a woodstove?
2. Does the way the author speaks of the mice give you a hint about the theme of the article? What is its theme or message?
3. What significance does the title have?
4. What history of the chainsaw does Todhunter give? Why does he give this history? In what way does the chainsaw suggest its "inherent malevolence"?
5. What significance do the chainsaw dealer and the story about his acquaintance have?

EVALUATING

1. The author most dislikes the efficiency of the chainsaw. How can you explain this?
2. What attitudes toward labor, invention, and technology do you see in the article? Do you agree that technologies make us "more frail and dim-witted"?

RESPONDING AND APPLYING

1. What is your attitude toward technology in general? How would you define technology? What technologies play major roles in your life? Can you identify how your life is changed by these devices and how it would be different in their absence?
2. How do you see computers and their increasing domination of our lives? What advantages and disadvantages do you see in them?
3. If you could, would you want to slow down the rate of change in the world? Some futurists like Alvin Toffler coin terms like "future shock" to describe our times. Do you find that an apt description? Why?

Todhunter regretfully uses a modern tool, the chainsaw, even as he reflects on how much of our lives we lose with each new technological wonder. Most likely, Todhunter would be the first to admit to the value of gaining historical perspective, so that we can intelligently choose which technologies to invest our lives in. Such a perspective, such knowledge, we as authors of this text speculated, is the only and, presently, a very threatened foundation on which we can build a hopeful and sound future. We explored what many have called our moral decay and crisis—the rise in violence among the young, the precarious state of the nuclear family and the number of children born out of wedlock, the decay of our inner cities, the struggles for survival in many of our poor and minority communities, and what many see as a retreat from history in our commodified, commercial culture.

It is fitting that this final chapter explore our newest frontier, technology (especially in its electronic form) and the far-reaching effects the newest technologies (television, cable, CD-ROM, email and the Internet) are having on the state of our turbulent world. We are particularly interested in the moral implications of these developments, setting out to answer questions like these: How do these new technologies affect our individual psychologies and psyches, and our beliefs and values? How do they alter our family structures, our religious faiths and systems, and our levels and kinds of civic participation? How do they alter our view of and relation to nature? And, finally, how do the new technologies shape our access to power and justice, and our building of communities, both small and large? But first we must examine this new technological phenomenon and its roots.

The technological frontier, of course, is an extension of another great idea or frontier, science, and of the technologies that arise from the applications of basic science. Societies have always been profoundly shaped by their technologies. From the wheel and the plow to the telescope, the railroad, the car, and the computer, each new technology extends some human faculty. The wheel extends the foot, and the telescope extends the eye. The computer, our most powerful technology, extends our brains and bodies at the same time. With each extension, our control of nature becomes more and more total, until today what we call virtual reality threatens to replace reality itself. In fact, an ad for a computer company reads, "At the rate we're advancing multimedia, soon you won't be flipping through this magazine. You'll be walking through it" (*Newsweek,* 11 December 1995). What the ad suggests is that consumers of multimedia events like CD-ROM and hypertext (links from one document to another) on the Internet are much more "actively" participating than if they "just" were reading.

Through our recorded history, the three greatest waves of technology can be thought of as agriculture, industry, and information, each shaping an epoch. Each wave is essentially technological, because it depends on a collation of separate technologies; in the case of agriculture, these were the wheel, the plow, and various means of disseminating and nurturing seeds. More than any other influence, these three technologies seem to have shaped our lives as individuals, as citizens, as family members, as workers, and as religious beings; in short, they profoundly affect how we work and play, and how we think and feel. In fact, many have correctly observed that we live in an environment bombarded with information, which is the result of sophisticated technologies that feed facts, figures, opinions, and images, almost without stop, to anyone who walks the street, or turns on a radio, a television, or a computer.

The Middle Ages and the Renaissance World Views

To gain a sense of how much life has changed over the last several hundred years, contrast that kind of life immersed in information to the life of a serf who lived 500 years ago, thinking mainly about where his next meal was coming from. Our serf didn't live entirely in uncertainty and fear, however, for in religious and political terms, things were pretty fixed, stable, sometimes boringly routine. During the interval of over a thousand years that we call the Middle Ages, the Christian cosmos was so thoroughly charted that there seemed to be little room for uncertainty about his role and proper conduct in society. As shown in our essay on the origins of democracy in Chapter Seven, obedience and conformity were the very foundations of the lives of the masses. For most of the time from the Middle Ages to the nineteenth century, humans in the Western world lived within one belief system, the Christian cosmos. That belief system was controlled by a lord or bishop, and it existed under the economic control of a manor or the religious control of a priest or minister. Thus, one lived within one's religion or politics as if in a fishbowl; just as the fish is the last to see the water, the serf was the last to think carefully about the rules of the human game. The Bible was interpreted as saying that priests and kings inherited power from God. Such a cosmology was largely unquestioned and therefore unseen. It was assumed that there was a Truth, one Truth, and it was Supreme.

At the same time in artistic and intellectual circles in the fourteenth century, at the beginning of the Renaissance, the Greek optimism toward the perfectibility of the individual was renewed and continued through the seventeenth century Enlightenment, and into the eighteenth century with its emphasis on human reason, in particular the scientific method. Confidence in the supposedly unlimited human capacities to solve problems and the inevitability of progress grew steadily. This confidence continued into the late eighteenth century, when the Industrial Revolution began in England, and into the nineteenth century, with the discovery of the biological principles of evolution. (Some would say it continues today—computer magnate Bill Gates' future looks bright. In his book *The Road Ahead,* he shares his belief that a computer-networked world will make people happier, richer, healthier, and smarter.)

The Global Village

With modern communications making nearly instant worldwide contact readily available, creating what Marshall McLuhan called a "global village," the belief in a fixed and unquestioned Truth in an ordered and fully discoverable cosmos becomes questionable, tentative, and highly unstable. In little towns all over America, where a conservative politics and ethos used to set the controlling tone of life, convenience stores are open 24 hours a day, while CNN and MTV play on cable. Sixteen-year-olds get their first job at McDonalds and soon save enough for their first car. The Playboy channel is available for a few extra dollars a month. Thus, the new technologies make war with the older values of family, church, and state. The more information one gets, the more likely one will reflect on and often question what was blindly accepted before. The Internet, television, the cell phone, the fax, and email lead us to ask, How can my truth, my lifestyle, my beliefs be so right if there are so many others who think so differently, but with equal passion?

Some say that all this saturation of information has given our culture an "appetite for ambiguity" and that we don't seem to know what is right or wrong. Ask people what they think of many of the critical issues of the day: welfare, abortion, illegitimate birth, gun control, and capital punishment. Deep in the American psyche there are conflicts about most of these troubling issues—between mercy and justice, between tradition and a hard-nosed, no-nonsense wish to demand change. Notice the frequency of white-collar crime and the increasing violence among the young. Where has our unambiguous sense of right gone?

These cultural changes, so many of which are brought on by technology, especially the demise of the single belief system, have been charted by many scholars, especially by historians, anthropologists, and linguists. By studying many cultures and language systems, many have concluded that what we once thought of as fixed truths are really "social constructions." (We should emphasize the word *many* here, since there is a backlash among anthropologists against postmodernism.) A social construction is a belief created out of the particular circumstances of a particular culture. Theorists like Thomas Kuhn, Richard Rorty, and Mikhail Bakhtin think of knowing as a process mediated by language and, therefore, believe knowledge is the product of a social consensus. Two fields in particular, semiotics in linguistics and deconstruction in literary criticism, accelerated these changes even more. French scholars like Jacques Derrida and Michel Foucault argued that because we could not depend on a certain, fixed relationship between the word (signifier) and its referent (the signified), the conceptual picture we draw of the world with our minds was at best unreliable and, more likely, a fabrication that fit the circumstances.

We can sum up the effects of rapid technological change this way: if *premodern* societies situated people in one belief system, *modern* societies, beginning in the nineteenth century with the attempted overthrow of the bourgeoisie, pitted one belief system against another. In the *postmodern* world, with so many competing systems inundating us daily, we are bound to question the very nature of belief itself. Many have, then, concluded that belief systems are not coming from and existing "out there," fixed in some Transcendent Reality; rather, beliefs are human creations. And these creations take the form of mata-narratives, all-encompassing stories that cultures use to give themselves purpose and continuity.

You may find much of this unsettling at best, because it sounds too much like an anything-goes form of relativism or a direct road to atheism, agnosticism, permissiveness, and moral emptiness. But it is still helpful to look at life through this postmodern lens, in order to better understand our world. As writer Walter Anderson claims, Humpty Dumpty isn't going to get put back together again and any attempt to impose a single order on all will backfire (*The World Isn't What It Used to Be*).

Drewness: A Fable for Our Times

The story of a recent remake of a popular novel series from the 1940s and 1950s will help us see how dramatic these changes really are. Premiering in fall 1995, "Nancy Drew" is a syndicated television program based on the Nancy Drew mystery novels. A guide was written to help the program staff shape the show's characters, plot, themes, and style. Among other things, the guide pointed out that Nancy should have the "ability to make clear choices." She would live "in a moral universe that is simple and straightforward." What the writer called "Drewness" would demand a wardrobe with "clear saturated colors that reflect her moral certainty." Even though Nancy is young, she "brings order to chaos. The objects in her apartment radiate a feeling of security. They have a timeless quality that is impossible to date" (*Harpers,* November 1995, 28).

This guide provides a moral fable for this chapter, which examines the threats to "Drewness," with its moral clarity, its simple colors, and its clear sense of purpose. While Drewness may appeal to many of us for its ready simplicity and easy answers to the dilemmas that plague us, it still represents a fragment of the old world, quickly being replaced by a new one. The new world is called by many names, among them the information society, the postindustrial society, the global village, and the postmodern world. All of these terms describe a world where individuals, once comfortable with their gods and their world views, are now bombarded with conflicting narratives (e.g., different creation stories or competing value systems) and in search of new certainties. The god of technology and technology's effects on the world's cultures begin to explain some disturbing yet at the same time exhilarating world developments that result from extremely rapid technological change, the widespread development of communications, and an almost ceaseless questioning of the inherited meta-narratives on which we've based our lives.

Four Components of Postmodernism

Writer Walter Anderson sees four aspects to the postmodernism we have been broaching here:

- The self, rather than being based on a fixed role or tradition, is rather a "made identity constructed from many cultural sources."
- Morality, rather than found in one's cultural heritage, is made, and we become relativists (constructivists and ironists) who know that when "we do make our judgments, we're standing on the ever-shifting ground of our own socially constructed world views."
- Rather than one style dominating a period, as it did in modernism, we see an endless parade of improvisations and variations on themes, especially through parody and play. Postmodern architects, for example, are "unabashedly eclectic." People everywhere borrow and combine rituals, traditions and myths.
- Rather than being tied to our own place and time, we live in our first global civilization, one of rapid information exchange and unprecedented mobility. (Anderson, *The Truth of the Truth,* 10)

J. D. Hunter takes us further into postmodernism by differentiating between orthodoxy and progressivism, offering a helpful insight into the nature of our culture. Orthodoxy in any major faith or political system asks us to communicate to "an external, definable and transcendent authority" (James D. Hunter, "The Orthodox and the Progressive," in W. Anderson, *The Truth about the Truth,* 97). In Judaism, that authority is the *Torah;* in Islam, it is the *Qur'an.* In the United States, it is the Constitution. Such an authority tells us what is good and offers a stable world view. For a progressivist, on the other hand, moral authority is defined by the spirit of the modern age, a spirit of pluralism and subjectivity. This latter view is not necessarily pessimistic, one of malaise, fragmentation, and disintegration. Rather, as we see in New Wave lifestyles and New Age philosophies, it can be affirmative and process-oriented. A good reading of Tarot cards demonstrates this. Perhaps, as opposed to a single religious truth or orthodoxy, there is emerging a transcendent pluralism, where individuals will be freer to be their unique selves as there is greater harmony among the world's many cultures. Admittedly, some might see a "transcendent-pluralism" as in conflict with postmodernism's emphasis on the here and now.

In practical terms, we see a number of features of our culture that reflect postmodern themes. One, psychiatrist Robert Jay Lifton describes "Protean man," an infinitely changeable individual, who finds it difficult to commit to one role or persona. How many of us find it hard to commit to one church or one political party? Is the perennial popularity of Ross Perot, in part, the result of the search for alternatives to time-honored traditions in politics? Two, some see a dangerous relativism afoot; the popularity of William Bennett's *The Book of Virtues* speaks to an attempt to stem what many see as an erosion of morality. Three, many observers of the culture see a loss or diminution of distinctions between high and low culture. Museums display street art or the works of unschooled artists next to so-called high art of the masters. Such changes can be traced back to the information explosion in the nineteenth century with the mechanization of the printing press. Matthew Arnold's fear that his high culture, preserving what he called the "best that has been said and thought," would be overthrown, carries over into our century.

Four, as we pointed out above, there has been a collapse of distinctions between reality and virtual reality; note the growth in virtual businesses and schools, in many of which the only geography is a World Wide Web address and the request for credit card numbers. Note also increasingly sophisticated VR machines, and the growing power of the Internet, especially browsers like the web's Netscape, where, as *Wired* magazine's Kevin Kelly writes, "millions of messages are passed between its members without the benefit of a central authority" (*Harpers* debate). Finally, the revolution on computing has seen interactive communications technologies that change our capacities for storing and accessing memory. However, we are only slowly achieving social equity and access to these media.

Contextualizing Postmodernism in History

When all of this is said, one must ground these thoughts in intellectual history in order to appreciate what is new and what isn't. Understanding a cultural movement like postmodernism is paradoxical, especially when one reflects on our recent cultural history. Some readers of this text, for example, might have recognized that morality as a "social construct" was also a Marxist idea, but without the notion that change in certain directions is inevitable. For that matter, morality as a social construct did not originate with Marx. A small group of thinkers and poets we now call the Romantics from England had more than a half century earlier begun to conceive of the world in terms of a developmental model, arguing that change and growth defined both nature and history. One, Percy Shelley, argued that morality was not eternally established by an all-knowing God but was created and progressively developed and recreated by imaginative and visionary individuals, in fact by poets, who he described as the "unacknowledged legislators of the world." Also Marxist, though anticipated by French political reformers before him, is the broader idea within this discussion of postmodernism that new technology can alter values. If, in even broader terms, the essence of postmodernism is that Enlightenment attitudes (of an ordered universe) and gods are breaking down, then postmodernism began toward the end of the eighteenth century.

This does not mean that the term is meaningless. Rather, it reveals that what makes describing accurately any new cultural movement so difficult is precisely the fact that there is nothing new that does not have complicated roots reaching back into the past, *even an idea that claims to reject the past.* We cannot, after all, escape history, not even when we choose to be willfully blind to it.

A Whimsical Model of Culture

It would help, perhaps, if we tried to construct a model of culture that reflects this fact. Let's start with a developmental model that pictures the history of culture as a series of layers, like the geological strata that appear on a cliff face revealing the history of the evolution of life on earth, or, better yet, like the churning of a water spout. Fairly low in this water spout, not by any means the bottom, would be Judaism, and overlaying it would be Greek rationalism, and above that Christianity, and so forth with the many ideas and -isms that have followed.

So far so good, but here is where the analogy breaks down: though most of these layers to some extent grow out of the lower layers (Christianity, for example, includes, with some features that are very new, its own synthesis of Judaism and Greek rationalism), unlike a literal cliff *each new layer does not supersede or bury the lower layers.* The whole of our cultural water spout is alive, not just the top layer, and the newest value system both grows out of older ideas and continues to live not so much above as beside many of those it often claims to have superseded.

Although this is a condition that has always existed, recent advancements in communication technology, in making more information more easily available, have made it less easy for a dominant group to control the means of communication, more easy for minority cultural elements to be expressed, and more possible for us to be aware of the cultural multiplicity—indeed the multiplicity and complexity of life itself—that surrounds us. And certainly it is easier for us to be confused by the resulting sense of information overload. Thus, we characterize our postmodern age as multicultural, fragmented, decentralized, fluid, and nonlinear (against a modernist world that is ordered, logical, and hierarchical), when in fact we have only become dramatically more aware of this multiplicity and other complexities.

But such awareness is no minor factor: our awareness is the essence of what we conceive of as our culture, and our degree of awareness determines both the direction and the rate of our personal growth as well as our development as a culture. Indeed, this may help us understand why to those who identify intellectually with postmodernism the crucial question is whether we will face the present and future with an acceptance of the complexity and diversity that life entails and a commitment to a quest for ways of dealing fairly with that complexity, or retreat into some vision of reality that simplifies, narrows, and distorts the truth.

Vaclav Havel, "Civilization's Thin Veneer"

Born in 1936 in Prague, Chechoslovakia, Vaclav Havel has spent most of his life as a dramatist, writer, and political dissident. Havel's first three plays were praised in his home country for their courageous looks at bureaucracy and its dehumanizing effects on society. After the Soviet invasion of Czechoslovakia in 1968, Havel's works were banned; Havel himself was harassed and finally imprisoned by the government—four times since 1977. Active in a number of human rights and writers' organizations, Havel has won a number of awards, including several Obies, the Erasmus, and the L.A. Drama Critics Circle Award. In 1989, Havel was elected President of Czechoslovakia and of the Czech Republic in 1993.

Civilization's Thin Veneer

Vaclav Havel

1 One evening not long ago I was sitting in an outdoor restaurant by the water. My chair was almost identical to the chairs they have in restaurants by the Vltava River in Prague. They were playing the same rock music they play in most Czech restaurants. I saw advertisements I'm familiar with back home. Above all, I was surrounded by young people who were similarly dressed, who drank familiar-looking drinks, and who behaved as casually as their contemporaries in Prague. Only their complexion and their facial features were different—for I was in Singapore.

2 I sat there thinking about this and again—for the umpteenth time—I realized an almost banal truth: that we now live in a single global civilization. The identity of this civilization does not lie merely in similar forms of dress, or similar drinks, or in the constant buzz of the same commercial music all around the world, or even in international advertising. It lies in something deeper: thanks to the modern idea of constant progress, with its inherent expansionism, and to the rapid evolution of science that comes directly from it, our planet has, for the first time in the long history of the human race, been covered in the space of a very few decades by a single civilization—one that is essentially technological. The world is now enmeshed in webs of telecommunication networks consisting of millions of tiny threads or capillaries that not only transmit information of all kinds at lightning speed, but also convey integrated models of social, political, and economic behavior. . . . The life of the human race is completely interconnected not only in the informational sense, but in the causal sense as well. . . . We are familiar with CNN and Chernobyl, and we know who the Rolling Stones, or Nelson Mandela, or Salman Rushdie are. More than that, the capillaries that have so radically integrated this civilization also convey information about certain modes of human coexistence that have proven their worth, like democracy, respect for human rights, the rule of law, the laws of the marketplace. Such information flows around the world and, in varying degrees, takes root in different places.

3 In modern times this global civilization emerged in the territory occupied by European and ultimately by Euro-American culture. Historically, it evolved from a combination of traditions—classical, Judaic, and Christian. In theory, at

least, it gives people not only the capacity for worldwide communication, but also a coordinated means of defending themselves against many common dangers. It can also, in an unprecedented way, make our life on this earth easier and open up to us hitherto unexplored horizons in our knowledge of ourselves and the world we live in.

4 And yet there is something not quite right about it. . . . I want to focus today on the source of the dangers that threaten humanity in spite of this global civilization, and often directly because of it. Above all, I would like to speak about the ways in which these dangers can be confronted.

5 Many of the great problems we face today, as far as I understand them, have their origin in the fact that this global civilization, though in evidence everywhere, is no more than a thin veneer over the sum total of human awareness. . . . This civilization is immensely fresh, young, new, and fragile, and the human spirit has accepted it with dizzying alacrity, without itself changing in any essential way. Humanity has evolved over long millennia in all manner of civilizations and cultures that gradually, and in very diverse ways, shaped our habits of mind, our relationship to the world, our models of behavior, and the values we accept and recognize. In essence, this new, single epidermis of world civilization merely covers or conceals the immense variety of cultures, of peoples, of religious worlds, of historical traditions and historically formed attitudes, all of which in a sense lie "beneath" it. At the same time, even as the veneer of world civilization expands, this "underside" of humanity, this hidden dimension of it, demands more and more clearly to be heard and to be granted a right to life.

6 And thus, while the world as a whole increasingly accepts the new habits of global civilization, another contradictory process is taking place: ancient traditions are reviving, different religions and cultures are awakening to new ways of being, seeking new room to exist, and struggling with growing fervor to realize what is unique to them and what makes them different from others. Ultimately they seek to give their individuality a political expression.

7 It is often said that in our time, every valley cries out for its own independence or will even fight for it. Many nations, or parts of them at least, are struggling against modern civilization or its main proponents for the right to worship their ancient gods and obey the ancient divine injunctions. They carry on their struggle using weapons provided by the very civilization they oppose. . . . In contrast with these technological inventions, other products of this civilization—like democracy or the idea of human rights—are not accepted in many places in the world because they are deemed to be hostile to local traditions.

8 In other words: the Euro-American world has equipped other parts of the globe with instruments that not only could effectively destroy the enlightened values which, among other things, made possible the invention of precisely these instruments, but which could well cripple the capacity of people to live together on this earth.

9 What follows from all of this?

10 It is my belief that this state of affairs contains a clear challenge not only to the Euro-American world but to our present-day civilization as a whole. It is a challenge to this civilization to start understanding itself as a multicultural and a multipolar civilization, whose meaning lies not in undermining the individuality of different spheres of culture and civilization but in allowing them to be more completely themselves. This will only be possible, even conceivable, if we all accept a basic code of mutual coexistence, a kind of common minimum we can all share, one that will enable us to go on living side by side. Yet such a code won't stand a chance if it is merely the product of a few who then proceed to force it on the rest. It must be an expression of the authentic will of everyone, growing out of the genuine spiritual roots hidden beneath the skin of our common, global civilization. If it is merely disseminated through the capillaries of this skin, the way Coca-Cola ads are—as a commodity offered by some to others—such a code can hardly be expected to take hold in any profound or universal way.

11 But is humanity capable of such an undertaking? Is it not a hopelessly utopian idea? Haven't we so lost control of our destiny that we are condemned to gradual extinction in ever harsher high-tech clashes between cultures . . . ?

12 I don't know. But I have not lost hope.

13 I have not lost hope because I am persuaded again and again that, lying dormant in the deepest roots of most, if not all, cultures there is an essential similarity, something that could be made—if the will to do so existed—a genuinely unifying starting point for that new code of human coexistence that would be firmly anchored in the great diversity of human traditions.

14 Don't we find somewhere in the foundation of most religions and cultures . . . common elements such as respect for what transcends us, whether we mean the mystery of Being, or a moral order that stands above us; certain imperatives that come to us from heaven, or from nature, or from our own hearts; a belief that our deeds will live after us; respect for our neighbors, for our families, for certain natural authorities; respect for human dignity and for nature; a sense of solidarity and benevolence towards guests who come with good intentions?

15 Isn't the common, ancient origin or human roots of our diverse spiritualities, each of which is merely another kind of human understanding of the same reality, the thing that can genuinely bring people of different cultures together?

16 And aren't the basic commandments of this archetypal spirituality in harmony with what even an unreligious person—without knowing exactly why—may consider proper and meaningful?

17 Naturally, I am not suggesting that modern people be compelled to worship ancient deities and accept rituals they have long since abandoned. I am suggesting something quite different. . . . We must recollect our original spiritual and moral substance, which grew out of the same essential experience of humanity. I believe that this is the only way to achieve a genuine renewal of our sense of responsibility for ourselves and for the world. And at the same time, it is the only way to achieve a deeper understanding among cultures that will enable them to work together in a truly ecumenical way to create a new order for the world.

18 The veneer of global civilization that envelops the modern world and the consciousness of humanity, as we all know, has a dual nature, bringing into question, at every step of the way, the very values it is based upon, or which it propagates. The thousands of marvelous achievements of this civilization that work for us so well and enrich us can equally impoverish, diminish, and destroy our lives, and frequently do. . . . How much easier it is today than it was during the First World War to destroy an entire metropolis in a single air raid. And how much easier would it be today, in the era of television, for a madman like Hitler or Stalin to pervert the spirit of a whole nation. When have people ever had the power we now possess to alter the climate of the planet or deplete its mineral resources or the wealth of its fauna and flora [in] a few short decades? . . .

19 In our era, it would seem that one part of the human brain, the rational part which has made all these morally neutral discoveries, has undergone exceptional development, while the other part, which should be alert to ensure that these discoveries really serve humanity and will not destroy it, has lagged behind catastrophically. . . .

20 There is no way back. Only a dreamer can believe that the solution lies in curtailing the progress of civilization in some way or other. The main task in the coming era is something else: a radical renewal of our sense of responsibility. Our conscience must catch up to our reason, otherwise we are lost.

21 It is my profound belief that there is only one way to achieve this: we must divest ourselves of our egoistical anthropocentrism, our habit of seeing ourselves as masters of the universe who can do whatever occurs to us. We must discover a new respect for what transcends us: for the universe, for the earth, for nature, for life, and for reality. Our respect for other people, for other nations, and for other cultures, can only grow from a humble respect for the cosmic order and from an awareness that we are a part of it, that we share in it and that nothing of what we do is lost, but rather becomes part of the eternal memory of Being, where it is judged.

22 A better alternative for the future of humanity, therefore, clearly lies in imbuing our civilization with a spiritual dimension. It's not just a matter of understanding its multicultural nature and finding inspiration for the creation of a new world order in the common roots of all cultures. It is also essential that the Euro-American cultural sphere—the one which created this civilization and taught humanity its destructive pride—now return to its own spiritual roots and become an example to the rest of the world in the search for a new humility. . . .

23 So what specifically is to be done? I do not believe in some universal key or panacea. I am not an advocate of what Karl Popper called "holistic social engineering," particularly because I had to live most of my adult life in circumstances that resulted from an attempt to create a holistic Marxist utopia. I know more than enough, therefore, about efforts of this kind.

24 This does not relieve me, however, of the responsibility to think of ways to make the world better.

25 It will certainly not be easy to awaken in people a new sense of responsibility for the world. . . . But this does not mean that those who wish to work for it cannot begin at once. It is a great task for teachers, educators, intellectuals, the clergy, artists, entrepreneurs, journalists, people active in all forms of public life.

26 Above all it is a task for politicians.

27 Even in the most democratic of conditions, politicians have immense influence, perhaps more than they themselves realize. This influence does not lie in their actual mandates, which in any case are considerably limited. It lies in something else: in the spontaneous impact their charisma has on the public.

28 The main task of the present generation of politicians is not, I think, to ingratiate themselves with the public [or] to go on winning elections. . . . Their role is something quite different: to assume their share of responsibility for the long-range prospects of our world and thus to set an example for the public in whose sight they work. Their responsibility is to think ahead boldly, not to fear the disfavor of the crowd, to imbue their actions with a spiritual dimension (which of course is not the same thing as ostentatious attendance at religious services), to explain again and again—both to the public and to their colleagues—that politics must do far more than reflect the interests of particular groups or lobbies. After all, politics is a matter of serving the community, which means that it is morality in practice. And how better to serve the community and practice morality than by seeking in the midst of the global (and globally threatened) civilization their own global political responsibility: that is, their responsibility for the very survival of the human race?

29 I don't believe that a politician who sets out on this risky path will inevitably jeopardize his or her political survival. This is a wrongheaded notion which assumes that the citizen is a fool and that political success depends on playing to this folly. That is not the way it is. A conscience slumbers in every human being, something divine. And that is what we have to put our trust in. . . .

30 With your permission, I will say a few words on the subject of the politics of a great power. It is obvious that those who have the greatest power and influence also bear the greatest responsibility. Like it or not, the United States now bears probably the greatest responsibility for the direction our world will take. The United States, therefore, should reflect most deeply on this responsibility.

31 Isolationism has never paid off for the United States. Had it entered the First World War earlier, perhaps it would not have had to pay with anything like the casualties it actually incurred.

32 The same is true of the Second World War: when Hitler was getting ready to invade Czechoslovakia, and in so doing finally expose the lack of courage on the part of the western democracies, your president wrote a letter to the Czechoslovak president imploring him to come to some agreement with Hitler. Had he . . . instead shown a few teeth, perhaps the Second World War need not have happened, and tens of thousands of young Americans need not have died fighting in it.

33 Likewise, just before the end of that war, had your president, who was otherwise an outstanding man, said a clear "no" to Stalin's decision to divide the world, perhaps the Cold War, which cost the United States hundreds of billions of dollars, need not have happened either.

34 I beg you: do not repeat these mistakes! You yourselves have always paid a heavy price for them! There is simply no escaping the responsibility you have as the most powerful country in the world.

35 There is far more at stake here than simply standing up to those who would like once again to divide the world into spheres of interest, or subjugate others who are different from them, and weaker. What is now at stake is saving the human race. . . .

36 There is one great opportunity in the matter of coexistence between nations and spheres of civilization, culture and religion, that should be grasped and exploited to the limit. . . . Regional groupings in areas that have common traditions and a common political culture ought to be a natural part of the complex political architecture of the world. . . . As long as the broadening of NATO membership to include countries who feel culturally and politically a part of the region the Alliance was created to defend is seen by Russia, for example, as an anti-Russian undertaking, it will be a sign that Russia has not yet understood the challenge of this era.

37 The most important world organization is the United Nations. I think the fiftieth anniversary of its birth could be an occasion to reflect on how to infuse it with a new ethos, a new strength, and a new meaning, and make it the truly most important arena of good cooperation among all cultures that make up our planetary civilization.

38 But neither the strengthening of regional structures nor the strengthening of the UN will save the world if both processes are not informed by that renewed spiritual charge which I see as the only hope that the human race will survive another millennium.

39 I have touched on what I think politicians should do. There is, however, one more force that has at least as much, if not more, influence on the general state of mind as politicians do. That force is the mass media.

40 Only when fate sent me into the realm of high politics did I become fully aware of the media's double-edged power. Their dual impact is not a specialty of the media. It is merely a part, or an impression of the dual nature of today's civilization of which I have already spoken.

41 Thanks to television the whole world discovered, in the course of an evening, that there is a country called Rwanda where people are suffering beyond belief. Thanks to television it is possible to do at least a little to help those who are suffering. Thanks to television the whole world, in the course of a few seconds, was shocked and horrified about what happened in Oklahoma City, and, at the same time, understood it as a great warning for all. Thanks to television the whole world knows that there exists an internationally recognized country called Bosnia and Herzegovina and that from the moment it recognized

this country, the international community has tried unsuccessfully to divide it into grotesque mini-states according to the wishes of warlords who have never been recognized by anyone as anyone's legitimate representatives.

42 That is the wonderful side of today's mass media, or rather, of those who gather the news. Humanity's thanks belong to all those courageous reporters who voluntarily risk their lives wherever something evil is happening, in order to arouse the conscience of the world.

43 There is, however, another, less wonderful, aspect of television, one that merely revels in the horrors of the world, or unforgivably, makes them commonplace, or compels politicians to become first of all television stars. But where is it written that someone who is good on television is necessarily also a good politician? I never fail to be astonished at how much I am at the mercy of television directors and editors, and how my public image depends far more on them than it does on myself, at how . . . television forces me to express my thoughts as sparsely as possible, in witticisms, slogans, or sound bites, at how easily my television image can be made to seem different from the real me. I am astonished by this and at the same time, I fear it serves no good purpose. I know politicians who have learned to see themselves only as the television camera does. Television has thus expropriated their personalities, and made them into something like television shadows of their former selves. I sometimes wonder whether they even sleep in a way that will look good on television.

44 I am not outraged with television or the press for distorting what I say, or ignoring it. . . . What interests me is something else: the responsibility of those who have the mass media in their hands. They too bear responsibility for the world, and for the future of humanity. Just as the splitting of the atom can immensely enrich humanity in a thousand and one ways and, at the same time, can also threaten it with destruction, so television can have both good and evil consequences. Quickly, suggestively, and to an unprecedented degree, it can disseminate the spirit of understanding, humanity, human solidarity, and spirituality, or it can stupefy whole nations and continents. And just as our use of atomic energy depends solely on our sense of responsibility, so the proper use of television's power to enter practically every household and every human mind depends on our sense of responsibility as well.

45 Whether our world is to be saved from everything that threatens it today depends above all on whether human beings come to their senses, whether they understand the degree of their responsibility and discover a new relationship to the very miracle of Being. The world is in the hands of us all. Yet some have a greater influence on its fate than others. The more influence a person has—be they politician or television announcer—the greater the demands placed on their sense of responsibility and the less they should think merely about personal interests.

46 In conclusion allow me a brief personal remark. I was born in Prague and I lived there for decades without being allowed to study properly or visit other countries. Nevertheless, my mother never abandoned one of her secret and

quite extravagant dreams: that one day I would study at Harvard. Fate did not permit me to fulfill her dream. But something else happened, something that would never have occurred even to my mother: I have received a doctoral degree at Harvard without even having to study here.

47 More than that, I have been given to see Singapore, and countless other exotic places. I have been given to understand how small this world is and how it torments itself with countless things it need not torment itself with if people could find within themselves a little more courage, a little more hope, a little more responsibility, a little more mutual understanding and love.

48 I don't know whether my mother is looking down at me from heaven, but if she is I can guess what she's probably thinking: she's thinking that I'm sticking my nose into matters that only people who have properly studied political science at Harvard have the right to stick their noses into.

49 I hope that you don't think so.

QUESTIONS FOR WRITING AND DISCUSSION

OBSERVING

1. Why does Havel see our world as a "single global civilization"? What contributions does technology make to that "single civilization"? What technologies in particular does Havel have in mind?
2. What values and political ideas undergird this unitary civilization, according to Havel? What does Havel see as the historical roots of these values?
3. What danger does the author see hovering below the "veneer" of civilization? Cite examples of cultures and nations where "ancient traditions are reviving" and "seeking new room to exist." Consider Europe, Asia, and Africa especially.
4. Explain what Havel means when he says we can meet the challenge of conflicting cultures with "a basic code of mutual coexistence." What definition of religion and faith is implicit in Havel's thinking?

EVALUATING

1. Havel describes a duality in our achievements and another in our brains. We have brilliantly created a "morally neutral" advanced civilization at the same time that we have not always guarded humanity against the dangers. How would Havel resolve this conflict? What is "egotistical anthropocentrism"? Do you find Havel's argument convincing?
2. What moves Havel to see politicians as assuming a frontline position in the struggle for civilization? What does he expect of them? Is this reasonable?
3. What role does Havel think mass media should play in our collective future?

RESPONDING AND APPLYING

1. To what degree does Havel's sense of "common elements" of religion coincide with your own religious beliefs or the tenets of your family's faith? Or if you are not religious, can you find meaning and comfort in what Havel calls "this archetypcal spirituality"?
2. How convincing do you find Havel's analysis of our political history from World War II to the present? What mistakes does he identify? What is your prescription for change?

NEIL POSTMAN, "AMUSING OURSELVES TO DEATH"

Born in 1931 and educated at the State University of New York at Fredonia and at Columbia, Neil Postman is professor of Communications Arts and Sciences at New York University and editor of the journal *Et Cetera.* A prolific and controversial writer, Postman initially wrote about language; he has since expanded to investigate communications, schooling, and social theory and history. The speech below was the keynote address at the 1984 Frankfurt Book Fair and was published in *Et Cetera* in Spring 1985. It is important because it signals the tendencies of powerful technologies like television to shape human consciousness in destructive ways.

Books of interest by Postman are *Teaching as a Subversive Activity, Teaching as a Conserving Activity, Amusing Ourselves to Death, Conscientious Objections: Stirring Up Trouble about Language, Technology and Education, The Disappearance of Childhood,* and *Technopoly.* Postman is the recipient of the Christian Lindback Award for Excellence in Teaching and of the George Orwell Award for Clarity in Language given by the National Council of Teachers of English.

Amusing Ourselves to Death

Neil Postman

1 Chancellor Kohl, Lord Mayor Wallmann, Mr. Christiansen, Ladies and Gentlemen:

2 In accepting the honor of delivering this address, I am obliged to say something about the theme of this year's Book Fair, which, as you know, is Orwell in

the year 2000. I trust you will not think me grossly disrespectful if what I say is that the choice of this theme is a mistake. To be precise, it is half of a mistake. There is no doubt that Orwell's prophecies and parables have application to roughly half the governments of the world. If, for example, one were to read both *1984* and *Animal Farm,* and then for good measure, Arthur Koestler's *Darkness at Noon,* one would have a fairly accurate blueprint of the machinery of thought-control as it presently operates in scores of countries, some of them not far distant from where we are meeting.

3 But the fact is that so far as the Western democracies are concerned, Orwell missed the mark almost completely. This obvious point has provided many civil libertarians with a false sense of pride and accomplishment. They were keeping their eye on 1984. And when the year came and the prophecy didn't, they sang songs of praise for themselves and their countries. And they do still. The roots of liberal democracy have not been torn asunder. Wherever else the terror has happened, we, in the West, have not been visited by Orwellian nightmares.

4 But, I fear, some of us have forgotten that alongside Orwell's dark vision, there was another vision—slightly older, slightly less well-known, equally chilling. I refer to Aldous Huxley's *Brave New World.* Contrary to common belief, even among the educated, Huxley and Orwell did not prophesy the same thing. Orwell warned that we will be overcome by an externally imposed oppression. But in Huxley's vision, no Big Brother or Ministry of Truth is required to deprive people of their autonomy, maturity, and history. As Huxley saw it, people will come to love their oppression, to adore the technologies that undo their capacities to think.

5 What Orwell feared were those who would ban books. What Huxley feared was that there would be no reason to ban a book, for there would be no one who wanted to read one. Orwell feared that the truth would be concealed from us. Huxley feared that the truth would be drowned in a sea of irrelevance. Orwell feared we would become a captive people. Huxley feared we would become a trivial people, preoccupied with some equivalent of the feelies, the orgy porgy, and the centrifugal bumblepuppy. As Huxley remarked in *Brave New World Revisited,* freedom lovers who are ever on the alert to oppose tyranny have "failed to take into account man's almost infinite appetite for distractions." In Orwell's book, Huxley added, people are controlled by inflicting pain. In *Brave New World,* they are controlled by inflicting pleasure. In short, Orwell thought we would be marched single-file and manacled into oblivion. Huxley thought we would dance ourselves there, with an idiot smile on our face.

6 In America, Orwell's prophecies are of small relevance but Huxley's are well underway toward being realized. I speak to you of America not only because I know its situation better than any other but also because America is engaged in the world's most ambitious experiment to accommodate itself to the technological distractions made possibly by the electric plug. This is an experiment that began slowly and modestly in the mid-nineteenth century with

the invention of the telegraph, and has now, in the latter half of the twentieth, reached a perverse maturity in America's consuming love affair with television. As nowhere else in the world, Americans have moved far and fast in bringing to a close the age of the slow-moving printed word, and have granted to television sovereignty over all of their institutions. By ushering in the age of television, America has given the world the clearest available glimpse of the Huxleyan future, 2000.

7 To anyone who is unfamiliar with this vast shift in America's symbolic ecology, I offer a few examples. According to the 1983 Nielsen Report on Television, ninety-eight percent of all American homes have a television set. Fifty-one percent have two or more television sets. Seventy-five percent have color television sets. The average household has its television sets on approximately seven hours a day. The average American child watches 5000 hours of television before he or she ever gets to school; about 16,000 hours by high school's end. The only activity that occupies more of an American youth's time than TV-viewing is sleeping. Americans who have reached the age of forty will have seen over one million television commercials, and can expect to see another million before their first retirement check arrives.

8 Television in America, it would appear, is the *soma* of Huxley's *Brave New World.* But let me hasten to say that America's immersion in television is not to be taken as an attempt by a malevolent government or an avaricious corporate state to employ the age-old trick of distracting the masses with circuses. The problem is more serious than that, and far from being age-old. The problem is not that TV presents the masses with entertaining subject matter, but that television presents all subject matter as entertaining. What is dangerous about television is not its junk. Every culture can absorb a fair amount of junk, and, in any case, we do not judge a culture by its junk but by how it conducts its serious public business. What is happening in America is that television is transforming all serious public business into junk.

9 As our politics, our news, our religion, our education, and our commerce are less and less given expression in the form of printed words or even oratory, they are rapidly being reshaped and staged to suit the requirements of the television. And because television is a visual medium; because it does its talking in pictures, not words; because its images are in color and are most pleasurably apprehended when they are fast-moving and dynamic; because television demands an immediate and emotional response; because television is nothing at all like a pamphlet, a newspaper, or a book; because of all this and more, all discourse on television must take the form of an entertainment. Television has little tolerance for arguments, hypotheses, reasons, explanations, or any of the instruments of abstract, expositional thought. What television mostly demands is a performing art. Thinking is not a performing art. Showing is. And so what can be shown rather than what can be thought becomes the stuff of our public consciousness. In all arenas of public business, the image now replaces the word as the basic unit of discourse. As a consequence, television makes the

metaphor of the marketplace of ideas obsolete. It creates a new metaphor: the marketplace of images.

10 Should you need a precise example of what this means, then consider the following: In America, circa 1984, a fat person cannot be elected to high political office. With your indulgence, I shall repeat this, because it captures the sense of the great Huxleyan transformation now taking place: In America, a fat person cannot be elected to high political office. A fat person makes an unpleasant image on television, and such an image easily overwhelms whatever profundities may issue forth from its mouth. If you have not heard any interesting ideas from American political leaders, it is not, I assure you, that they have none. It is because ideas are irrelevant to political success. In the Age of Television, people do not so much agree or disagree with politicians as they like or dislike them, for the image is not susceptible to verification or refutation, only to acceptance or rejection. In 1984, politics in America is not the Federalist Papers. It is not the Lincoln-Douglas Debates. It is not even Roosevelt's fireside chats. Politics is good looks and amiability. It is fast-moving imagery. A quick tempo, a good show, celebrities. Because of this it is even possible that some day a Hollywood movie actor may become President of the United States.

11 What is true of politics is equally true of news, which is transmitted to Americans through the device widely known as a "TV news show." Our newscasters, sometimes referred to as "talking hair-dos," comprise the handsomest class of people in America. Their shows are always introduced and concluded with music. While on camera, they talk to each other with chatty informality. Each of the stories they tell us rarely occupies more than forty-five seconds of our time. And in all cases, coherence and continuity are sacrificed in favor of visual interest. A TV news show is only marginally concerned with public information. What is important is its tempo, the celebrity of its performers, the pleasant familiarity of its ambience. A TV news show is precisely what its name implies: A show is an entertainment, a world of artifice, carefully staged to produce a particular series of effects so that the audience is left laughing or crying or stupified. And that is why each evening at the conclusion of a news show, the newscaster invites us to "join" him or her tomorrow. One would think that thirty minutes of fragmented images of disorder and sorrow would provide enough anxiety for a month of sleepless nights. Not so. We join them tomorrow because we know a good show when we see one.

12 And that is exactly why so many Americans now prefer to get their religious instruction from television rather than church. Church is apt to provide congregants with a serious and austere experience; in any case, not a very amusing one. But television makes religion *fun.* Billy Graham, Oral Roberts, and Robert Schuller are only among the more entertaining of a coven of preachers who do religion regularly on television. Surrounded by singers, celebrities, floral displays, sparkling fountains, exotic locales, and exceedingly handsome people, these evangelists offer a religion that is as simplistic and theatrical as any Las Vegas stage show. No dogma, terminology, logic, ritual, doctrines, or

traditions are called upon to burden the minds of viewers, who are required to respond only to the image of the preacher, to whom God, Himself, must take second billing. For God does not play well on television. In an imagistic medium God is scarcely present; only the relentless and charismatic image of a messenger who, to gain attention and large audiences, turns theology into a vaudeville act.

13 Which, of course, is what has been done to education by "Sesame Street," our highly acclaimed TV show for children. Both its creators and its audiences now accept without qualification the idea that learning and entertainment are indistinguishable, just as businessmen, in spending millions on those mini-entertainments known as commercials, accept the idea that economics is less a science than an adjunct of show business.

14 This shift in the form and content of public discourse is not only manifested in what is *on* television but also in what is *off* television. As TV moves typography to the edges of our culture and takes its place at the center, the television show becomes our most compelling model and metaphor of all communication. How TV stages the world becomes our idea of how the world is properly to be staged. Our newspapers, increasingly, are designed to give readers the feeling they are watching television. Indeed, America's newest national daily, *USA Today,* is sold on the streets in receptacles that look like television screens. Our teachers have increased the visual stimulation of their lessons, and strive to make their classrooms even more entertaining than "Sesame Street." In case you have not heard the news, I fear I must tell you that the Philadelphia public schools have embarked on an experiment in which children will have their curriculum sung to them to the rhythms of rock music. Those ministers who are confined to non-electronic, traditional pulpits are often driven to adopting a show business style to prove, as it were, that one does not have to be serious to be holy. Indeed, some wish to prove that one does not have to be holy at all, as for example, Father John J. O'Connor, who put on a New York Yankees baseball cap in mugging his way through his installation as Archbishop of the Archdiocese of New York. Our universities eagerly award honorary degrees to television and movie stars, some of whom are asked to address the graduates at commencement exercises on subjects about which neither they nor the graduates know anything whatsoever. It is of no matter. In a culture in which one becomes a celebrity by merely appearing on television, the distinction between entertainment and anything else becomes odious.

15 That is why our politicians eagerly make appearances on non-political television shows. Henry Kissinger joined former President Gerald Ford for an appearance on the hit TV show, "Dynasty." Speaker of the House of Representatives Tip O'Neill did a cameo role on the comedy show "Cheers." Consumer advocate Ralph Nader hosted the popular show "Saturday Night Live." So did George McGovern and the Mayor of New York City, Edward Koch, who also played the role of a prize-fight manager on a made-for-TV movie, starring James Cagney. Just as the television commercial freed the entrepreneur from concen-

trating on the quality of his product and, instead, demanded that he concentrate on entertaining the consumer, the format of television frees the politician from the serious confines of the political arena. Political figures may show up anywhere, at any time, doing anything, without being thought odd, presumptuous, or in any way out of place. I can assure you that no American would be surprised if Geraldine Ferraro[1] showed up in a small role as a Queens housewife in a Francis Coppola film.

16 In America, all forms of social life strive to be like television shows or are thought to have potential as TV shows. We are now televising our courtroom trials, most recently and notably a rape trial in New Bedford, Massachusetts, which took audiences away from their favorite soap operas for several weeks. We have also discovered that real-life surgery is, if anything, more engrossing than fictional medical shows. In this connection, perhaps the most significant statement made in America, recently, about the state of our culture was inadvertently uttered by Mr. Bernard Schuler, who became an instant celebrity by allowing Dr. Edward Dietrich to perform triple by-pass surgery on him while on television. Mr. Schuler was uncommonly confident about the operation because, he said, "There is no way in hell they are going to lose me on live TV."

17 That all the world is a stage is hardly an unfamiliar thought. But that all the world is a TV situation comedy has come as quite a surprise—except to Aldous Huxley. We must, in any case, make no mistake about it. Television is not merely an entertainment medium. It is a philosophy of discourse, every bit as capable of altering a culture as was the printing press. Among other things, the printed word created the modern idea of prose, and invested exposition with unprecedented authority as a means of conducting public affairs. Television disdains exposition, which is serious, sequential, rational, and complex. It offers instead a mode of discourse in which everything is accessible, simplistic, concrete, and above all, entertaining. As a result, America is the world's first culture in jeopardy of amusing itself to death.

18 And much of the rest of the world appears eager to join us. While America may no longer be loved, American television certainly is. It is estimated that America exports 250,000 hours of TV programming per year, equally divided among Europe, Asia, and Latin America. Even the People's Republic of China has lately contracted with CBS to assist its people in joining in the fun. Contracts with NBC and ABC are sure to follow. One hopes the Chinese understand that this represents a revolutionary political act. The Gang of Four[2] is as nothing when compared to the Gang of Three.

19 I do not say this merely to achieve an effect, for, in concluding, I wish you to understand me to be saying that there are two ways by which the spirit of

---

[1] Geraldine Ferraro—The Democratic vice-presidential candidate in 1984.

[2] Gang of Four—Jiang Qing (Mao Zedong's second wife), Wang Hongwen, Zhang Chunqiao, and Yao Wenyuan. They were imprisoned, tried, and convicted by the Red Chinese government in 1980-1981 for their harsh policies during the Chinese Cultural Revolution of the 1960s.

a culture may be shrivelled. In the first—the Orwellian—culture becomes a prison. In the second—the Huxleyan—culture becomes a burlesque. The first way is far easier for us to recognize and to oppose. Everything in our background has prepared us to know and resist a prison when the walls begin to close around us. We are not likely to be indifferent to the voices of the Sakharovs and the Timmermans and the Walesas. We take arms against such a sea of troubles, buttressed by the spirit of Luther, Milton, Bacon, Voltaire, Goethe, and Jefferson. But what if there are no cries of anguish to be heard? Who is prepared to take arms against a sea of amusements? To whom do we complain, and when, and in what tone of voice, when serious discourse dissolves into giggles? What is the antidote to a culture dying of laughter? I fear, ladies and gentlemen, that our philosophers have as yet given us no guidance in this matter.

QUESTIONS FOR WRITING AND DISCUSSION

OBSERVING

1. In what sense does Postman claim Orwell "missed the mark"?
2. Why does Postman prefer Huxley's over Orwell's vision? Summarize each vision before answering the question.
3. What role does technology play in Postman's fears? What in particular does Postman find so harmful about television?
4. What are entertainment values and in what ways do they pervade our culture, according to the author? What is Postman's view of democracy in an electronic age?

EVALUATING

1. What has changed in the past decade since Postman gave his talk as it relates to Orwell's prophesies? Note especially events in South and Central America, Asia, and Africa.
2. Do you think Postman has correctly diagnosed the core of our culture's ills? What problems head the list in your thinking? What causes would you assign to them? Do we "love" our "oppression" and "adore the technologies that undo" our capacities for reason?
3. Identify examples of our "distractions" that drive us to be a "trivial people." Do you buy the assumptions that underlie Postman's fears? Can you make a case that Postman needs to lighten up, that he has overestimated the harmful effects of entertainment? What good can you identify that comes from the electronic media? Does the Internet change the situation significantly since it is a two-way medium, where television is one-way?

RESPONDING AND APPLYING

1. If you have read *Brave New World,* how good a match do you find between our world and the one Huxley has painted? Do you think Orwell's *1984* is off the mark in the ways Postman claims?
2. How worried are you that our culture is being undermined by the newest technologies and an ethic of entertainment?
3. Where do you get your news? What biases and flaws are a part of the media you consume for most of your information? If you read *USA Today,* do you find the articles superficial and vulnerable to entertainment values? What media do you think present the best news?

MICHAEL VENTURA, "AN INVENTORY OF TIMELESSNESS"

Michael Ventura was born in 1945 in the Bronx, New York, to Michael, a cab driver, and Celia, a clerical worker. He is the author of several books, including *The Zoo Where You're Fed to God* (1994) and *Letters at Three A.M.: Reports on Endarkenment* (1993), from which the following excerpt is taken. He is also author of a column in the *Austin Chronicle* and the *Los Angeles Village View* called "Letters at Three A.M." Ventura, when asked why he writes, responded: "I write for a country called America, a country that doesn't exist now, a country that never existed. Yet at certain times and through certain souls, American gave (and gives) humanity a dream of the people, for the people, by the people, and this dream will haunt the world from now on. I write in the name of that haunting." Ventura names his heroes: Randolph Bourne, Sherwood Anderson, Emma Goldman, Walt Whitman, James Baldwin, Henry Miller, Nelson Algren, Willa Cather, Charlie Parker, Billie Holiday, John Cassavetes, and Stevie Ray Vaughan.

An Inventory of Timelessness

Michael Ventura

1 We've dispensed with time, so we're lost in space.

2 ITEM: Wells Fargo Bank has introduced a twenty-four-hour-per-day, seven-day-per-week telephone service. You can now pick up the phone at any hour,

anywhere, and talk to a person—not a computer—who can answer any conceivable question about your banking needs. This stretches the term *banking needs* beyond all previous definitions in the eight-hundred-odd-year history of Western banking. Why do my bankers anticipate that I'll need them at three o'clock in the morning? Partly because there's no telling where I'll be: Tokyo, Barcelona, Moscow—desperate to know what my balance is before the market opens in Berlin or Hong Kong. But a hefty percentage of the calls are from Wells Fargo's home time zone and involve personal, not business, accounts. Which means that 'round about midnight in these United States, a number of demographically ordinary people feel the pressing need to question their banker.

3 Twenty-four-hour bank call-ins and automatic tellers speak of a people increasingly coaxed to live without pattern, without boundaries. Such things fuzz the boundaries between intimate time and business time, between home and work, night and day, individual and corporate, public and private, environment and psyche. Yet while, as consumers, we increasingly demand to live without pattern *in terms of services,* we bemoan the loss of pattern in our morality, our love lives, our thought.

4 If one individual demanded to do his/her banking at three in the morning, it would be considered pretty weird. But when a corporation provides the service, and it meets the demands of thousands . . . then despite what even the most conservative people might prefer morally or politically, their patternless consumerism disrupts the sense of time and space that contained, and gave form to, their morality.

5 ITEM: Life in Clarendon, a town of about fourteen hundred in the Texas Panhandle, revolves around its several fundamentalist churches. Like many towns in that part of the country, it's still "dry"—you can't buy alcohol within the city limits. But not too long ago a twenty-four-hour convenience store opened. It never closes. And such stores flourish now in almost every small town in the country. Why do they need such a store, in such a town? Until recently, in that area you could tune in two, sometimes three, television stations—depending on the weather. These stations signed off around midnight, often earlier. Now, with satellite and cable, you can tune in dozens of stations, and they never sign off. Some show porn in the wee hours. And MTV all the time. And constant news. And movies that no one in this area would ever have heard of otherwise. (Clarendon's "picture show" went out of business years back.)

6 So a place that depended for its way of life upon its isolation—upon its strict regulation of what it allowed through its boundaries, upon its rooted connectedness to what it imagines to be the morality of the nineteenth century—has been penetrated by what it views as a service. It is no longer separate in space; it no longer has a farmer's sense of time.

7 ITEM: Utah. A place owned and run by the Mormon Church, a place with no separation of church and state. With satellite and cable late-night porn has

become very, very popular in Utah. Which means Utah is no longer Utah at three in the morning.

8 In America, from big city to tiny town, time and space have become tentative, arbitrary. And this in the most concrete, personal sense. There are instruments in each home eating away at the time and space of people who have become addicted to those instruments. Consciously, these are most often people who see themselves as normal, righteous, and conservative, and they emphatically don't want this to change. Yet something else is operative in them, some hunger that they follow without thought or plan, in which they indulge in activities that subtly but thoroughly undermine their most cherished assumptions. Politically and socially they are demanding more and more boundaries—yet, by choice, they fill their lives with things that cause them to live less and less within those boundaries. They *want* these things, these appliances and services—so much so that they measure their success or failure by whether or not they have these things. But their very wanting is subversive to their way of life. It's fair, then, to assume that something other than consciousness, something deep within them, is doing this subversive wanting.

9 ITEM: The electric light bulb. An invention barely one hundred years old. In general use for roughly fifty years now. The technological beginning of the end of linear time. Before the light bulb, darkness constricted human space. Outside cities especially, night shrank the entire landscape into the space within arm's reach. (The moon figures so greatly in our iconography because it was all that allowed one to go far out into the night—when it was bright enough, and not obscured by clouds.) But now there are few places in North America or Europe that are truly dark at night; the glow of even a small town can be seen for many miles. Light gives us all the space we want, any time we want it. Psychoactive events of monstrous proportions take place, like Hitler's Nuremberg rallies. All those tens of thousands of people in perfect formation are unthinkable without spotlights. Light creates the necessary space, pushing back the boundaries of time. Dream time becomes a time for acting out the nightmare.

10 ITEM: The car is a private space that can go in any direction at any time. The motel room cinched that: anywhere you go, there will be a space for you—a fact unique to contemporary life and alien to every previous society. But the fact that there's a room for you anywhere makes less substantial the place where you actually *are*. Thus you are a transient, without having chosen to be one. Human transience used to be defined almost solely by death. Now the fact of so much choice makes everyone a transient *all* the time—and, for most of us now, makes any single choice almost unbearably tentative. Why be where you are, who you are, when you can just as easily be somewhere else, behaving differently?

11 This is a question that even most demographically "average" people ask often these days. How can it not make them more and more uncertain? So, to compensate, they're craving certainty in all the wrong places. In politics, which

has *always* been uncertain. In metaphysics, which by its nature is uncertain. In love and sex, where certainty breeds boredom and diminishes lovers in each other's eyes. Many of these people blame the uncertain, tentative quality of their lives on "liberalism," "humanism," "relativism," "the sixties"—when what is really going on is that they were once prisoners of time and space, and they will never be prisoners again, and they miss those prisons desperately.

12 How long will it take them to become accustomed to the new timeless, spaceless environment? This has become a crucial historical question. For until they acclimate themselves, they will continue to crave reactionary solutions that can only increase the chaos.

13 This all began, by the way, with Jesus. Boris Pasternak, in *Doctor Zhivago,* saw it clearly:

> In the first [Western] miracle you have a popular leader, the patriarch Moses, dividing the waters by a magic gesture, allowing a whole nation—countless numbers, hundreds of thousands—to go through. . . . In the second miracle you have a girl—an everyday figure who would have gone unnoticed in the ancient world—quietly, secretly, bringing forth a child. . . . What an enormously significant change! How did it come about that an individual human event, insignificant by ancient standards, was regarded as equal in significance to the migration of a whole people? . . . Individual human life became the very story of God, and its contents filled the vast expanses of the universe.

14 We don't know how it came about, but we know the enormity of the result. In Judaism, God redeemed a race. In Christianism, God redeems *you*—an absolute reversal of metaphysics as it was practiced everywhere else in the world. Everywhere else, with the exception of the most highly sophisticated Buddhism, worship was always tribal: people propitiating existence for comparatively small favors. But now Christianism presented an unheard-of demand upon the sacred: that the *individual* is entitled to the full and undivided attention of the universe—a staggering change in individual space and eternal time.

15 It took a long time—the Renaissance, the discovery of America, the elucidation of democratic principles, the technological revolution—but the Christianist sense of the individual being the center of the universe has become our daily reality.

16 Today, through a centuries-long process that culminated in our technological revolution, the West has what it's been praying for since the birth of Christ: every individual is being addressed directly, and constantly, by an infinite universe. It may be a media-conveyed universe, and the voice you hear may be anyone's from Mandela to Madonna; images of sensuality and mayhem may confront us wherever we turn (though they are no more violent or sexy than the images in the Bible); we may have asked for the holy and gotten the profane (complain to the Manufacturer)—but it *is* a universe and it *does* seem to speak to us, even dote on us, individually. In short, we asked for a paradigm and we got it.

17 In biblical mythology, this state of being is followed by apocalypse.

18 But what is apocalypse, exactly? In Revelation it is described as the coming of the beast. Richmond Lattimore's pristine translation from the original Greek reads:

> Then I saw a beast coming up from the sea with ten horns and seven heads, and upon his horns ten diadems, and upon his heads the names of blasphemy. The beast I saw was like a leopard, and his feet as those of a bear, and his mouth as the mouth of a lion. And the dragon gave him his power and his throne and his great authority. . . . Then the whole earth went in wonder after the beast. . . . Who is like the beast, and who can fight with him? (Revelation 13:1-4)

19 From the ancients to Jung, the sea has been the great symbol of the human psyche. So Revelation's beast is the manifestation, in the waking world, of what's deepest in the psyche. And it is given its power by the dragon, the worldwide symbol of the meeting of spiritual and sexual energy. The beast is a multilayered, multiheaded image of dissonant simultaneity—a simultaneity which *in itself* is seen as great power: "And upon his heads the names of blasphemy." The expectation is that when this psychic beast appears it will challenge all morals, all traditions, all laws.

20 These fearful writers of early Christianism sensed what had been started: that the new Christianist focus on the individual would sooner or later bring forth the secrets of the psyche—but in ways that would contradict their conscious morality. And they saw this, literally, as the end of the world.

21 Well, perhaps they were being a mite too concrete. It is the end of *a* world, certainly—the world in which waking and dreaming are rigidly separate. When this "beast" rises from its "sea," the surrealities of dream life become the facts of waking life.

22 In preceding centuries there was a pretty obvious separation between what's called the *subconscious* and the *conscious.* Individual daily life was more or less ordered, however unjust or distasteful. Except for the occasional plague and cathedral gargoyle, lurid phantasms were usually left to the realm of dreams. But now we live in a technologically hallucinogenic culture that behaves with the sudden dynamics of a dream—*an environment that duplicates the conditions of dreaming.*

23 What I'm saying is that we in the late twentieth century live not in a city or country, not on a planet, but in a collective dream. Our everyday world is one of dreamlike instantaneous changes, unpredictable metamorphoses, random violence, archetypal sex, and a threatening sense of multiple meaning. For a quarter of a million years we experienced this only in sleep, or in art, or in carefully structured religious rituals. Now, in our electronic environment, the dream world of sudden transformation and unpredictable imagery greets us when we open our eyes. And our response to it, against all our better judgments, is to want more, more, more—more of the VCRs, PCs, car phones, and faxes that create this new surreality. For the long-suppressed psyche is as outrageous in conservatives as it is in bohemians, in capitalists as in socialists, in evangelicals

as in atheists—and, through our appliances, it is finally free to feed on the outer world, and so to grow.

24 What distinguishes the twentieth century is that each individual life is a daily progression through a concrete but fluctuating landscape of the psyche's projections. Technology projects the subconscious into countless *things,* and thus duplicates the processes of the subconscious's greatest artifact, the dream. The surreality, simultaneity, sexuality, and instantaneous change that once occurred only in our dreams now also occur all around us.

25 So the condition of our subconscious is now also the condition of this physical environment we've built for ourselves.

26 Now we reel between dream and dream. Between the dreams of our sleep that speak to us alone and the dreamscape of the waking world, in which we make our way through millions of dream pieces colliding around us in a collective slam-dance.

27 It was easy (or so it seems now) to love the world as it used to be, the world of rigid boundaries. That world *was* a world, it held still long enough to *be* a world and gave us time to learn to love it. But loving this scary state of flux? We want to love it, we have love in us to give it, but we are frightened and do not know how. Yet daily life hinges on what we are and are not able to love. So this craving not *for* love but *to* love, to be able to love what's around one—it twists itself into a mere, and futile, search for certainty.

28 Still, we made this world. We gobble up its instantaneousness, and we breathlessly want more. Could it be that our collective purpose is to revivify the psyche by making it ideal with its labyrinthine *physical* image at every turn? Have we created this always-shifting multiculture in order to learn to live within, and use, our own immense and cacophonous psyches? Is this the collective thrust of our history, a kind of genetic demand?

29 As individuals, we feel that our contemporary anti-environment has been forced upon us. But I repeat: collectively, we *made* this world. And, both individually and collectively, we've eagerly welcomed each separate manifestation of this collective change. The radio, television, telephone, fax machine, VCR, computer, light bulb, airplane, car—all the building blocks of contemporary life, which manifest in reality what were once only dreams and myths—have been seized upon everywhere in the world. It is not enough to blame this on capitalism or consumerism. The very eagerness of the world's embrace of this hallucinogenic technology by the most different sorts of people is evidence of the deepest longing.

30 Perhaps it is a longing to let the beast out—for the psyche to flood forth. Or a longing, as in love, to be swept away no matter what. But it may be far deeper and more complex than that. It may be an agonized collective molting: five billion people and the planet itself on the same acid trip, creating together a living, inescapable dream (nightmare though it may seem) after which, when we wake up, we will be unimaginably different.

31 Nightmares, remember, are often the most telling and visionary of our dreams, the most useful for insight and change.

32 When I say that at the conclusion of this transformation, if we survive, we will be unimaginably different, please don't mistake that for new-age goo. The pious platitudes of the new agers are pathetic incantations hoping to tame the untamable. Our transformation will leave humankind *different,* not necessarily better. It's just that all of us collectively have decided it's time for the big change—though individually most of us wish it were happening to somebody else in some other space-time.

33 What we now know (whether or not we ever wanted to know it) is that the human psyche is one of the great forces of nature. And what is most frightening about our new technology is that it exposes us to this force within us as nothing else ever has. We are standing in the storm of our own being. So we must face the fact that this, too, is our natural habitat. We have willy-nilly broken through all the old rigidities, all the limits we thought were nature itself, and we can never go back. This is a new nature. Since we, too, are a product of nature, it can be said that this is what nature is doing to itself hereabouts.

34 Dream has become reality. Dream-state metamorphoses have become waking-state conditions of everyday life. And through this fact echoes what may yet be the great axiom of our culture: *In dreams begins responsibility.*

QUESTIONS FOR WRITING AND DISCUSSION

OBSERVING

1. The essay begins with a series of "items" that illustrate the author's opening line, "We've dispensed with time, so we're lost in space." What do each of these "items" tell us about the relationship between time and space?
2. Midway through this essay, the author introduces religion—specifically Judaism and Christianity—into his observations. Which features of these faiths are referenced, and how does the author integrate them into his reflections on time and eternity?
3. What does the essay's last line mean, "In dreams begins responsibility"?

EVALUATING

1. Rhetorically, the author concludes each of the items with a brief summary or epigram of how the objects or incidents cited forced him to reflect on the relationships of time and space. How convincing are these anecdotes? Do you agree, basically, with the author's interpretation?
2. Why does the author coin the terms "Christianism" and "Christianist"? How are these different from Christianity or Christian? Do you think his use of these terms is warranted—or effective?

3. What the does the author claim distinguishes the 20th century from previous ones? What is the next stage in your view? Is the next century full of promise or fear for you?

RESPONDING AND APPLYING

1. "We made this world," the author suggests. Which world is he talking about, and what part did any individual, yourself included, play in creating it? Can you or anyone "uncreate" it, or escape it?
2. What insight or experience can you bring to the themes of this essay? Does life seem "faster" or time "stop" for you at different junctures of your life?
3. What "responsibility" do you wish to take for the "dreams"—in the author's sense—you are living? Are you content that your particular dream "has become a reality"? What would you change?

STEINER KVALE, "THEMES OF POSTMODERNITY"

Steiner Kvale is director of the Centre for Qualitative Research at the Institute of Psychology, Aarhus University, in Denmark, where he is also professor of educational psychology. He is an international authority on postmodernism and psychology. Kvale is the author of many books, including *Psychology and Postmodernism* (1992).

Kvale's survey of the postmodern scene reveals an interesting conflict, between fragmentation, incoherence, the local, and the specific on the one hand, and wholeness, universality, and a larger framework of meaning on the other. Whether these two sides are reconcilable is a difficult question, but one thing is clear: the single human truth or the systemic idea-system that claims a solid and objective sense of the whole is out of reach for Kvale and most postmodernists.

Themes of Postmodernity

Steiner Kvale

1 It is debatable whether postmodernity is actually a break with modernity, or merely its continuation. Postmodern writers may prefer to write history so that their own ideas appear radically new. Postmodern themes were present in the romanticism of the last century, in Nietzsche's philosophy at the turn of the century, with the surrealists and in literature, for instance in Blixen and Borges.

What is new today is the pervasiveness of postmodern themes in culture at large.

2 "Postmodern" does not designate a systematic theory or a comprehensive philosophy, but rather diverse diagnoses and interpretations of the current culture, a depiction of a multitude of interrelated phenomena. Postmodern thought is characterized by a loss of belief in an objective world and an incredulity towards meta-narratives of legitimation. With a delegitimation of global systems of thought, there is no foundation to secure a universal and objective *reality*. There is today a growing public acknowledgement that "Reality isn't what it used to be."

3 In philosophy there is a departure from the belief in one true reality—subjectively copied in our heads by perception or objectively represented in scientific models. There exists no pure, uninterpreted datum; all facts embody theory. In science the notion of an objective reality is an interesting hypothesis, but is not necessary for carrying out scientific work. Knowledge becomes the ability to perform effective actions.

4 The focus is on the social and linguistic construction of a perspectival reality. In society the development of technology, in particular the electronic media, opens up an increased exposure to a multiplicity of perspectives, undermining any belief in one objective reality. In a world of media, the contrast between reality and fantasy breaks down and is replaced by a hyperreality, a world of self-referential signs. What remains is signs referring to other signs, texts referring to other texts.

5 A critique of *legitimation* is central in Lyotard's analysis of the postmodern condition. Legitimacy involves the question of what is valid, what is legal, the issue of whether an action is correct and justifiable. Habermas brought the issue to the fore in his book *Legitimation Crisis,* depicting a general loss of faith in tradition and authority, with a resulting relativity of values.

6 Lyotard identifies "*postmodern* as incredulity towards meta-narratives," as a "paganism," where we pass judgement on truth, beauty and justice without criteria for the judgements. In a comment on the debate between Lyotard and Habermas, Rorty interprets Lyotard as saying that "the trouble with Habermas is not so much that he provides a narrative of emancipation as that he feels the need to legitimize, that he is not content to let the narratives which hold all culture together do their stuff. He is scratching where it does not itch." Rather than continuing the Cartesian attempts of "self-grounding," Rorty advocates a Baconian approach of "self-assertion."

7 A further theme of modernity is the dichotomy of the *universal and the individual,* between society and the unique person, whereby the rootedness of human activity and language in a given social and historical context is overlooked. In modernity the person is an object for a universal will, or for general laws of history or nature. Or the person is overburdened; man has become the centre of the world, the individual self-feeling being the cornerstone of modern thought, a self stretched out between what it is and what it ought to be.

8 If we abstract a human from his or her context, we are trapped between the poles of the universal and the individual—the way out is to study humans

in their cultural and social context. With the collapse of the universal meta-narratives, the local narratives come into prominence. The particular, heterogeneous and changing language games replace the global horizon of meaning. With a pervasive decentralization, communal interaction and local knowledge become important in their own right. Even such concepts as nation and tradition are becoming rehabilitated in a postmodern age.

9 The emphasis upon the local surpasses the modern polarity of the universal and the individual, of the objective and the subjective. The local interaction, the communal network, is the point of departure; universal laws and unique individual selves are seen as abstractions from man's being in the world. Rather than equating universal laws with the objective and the individual with the subjective and relative, valid interpretations of meaning and truth are made by people who share decisions and the consequence of their decisions. Instead of a subjective nihilism, we may here talk of a contextual relativism where legitimation of action occurs through linguistic practice and communicative action.

10 With the collapse of the universal systems of meaning or meta-narratives, a re-narrativization of the culture takes place, emphasizing communication and the impact of a message upon the audience. There is today an interest in *narratives,* on the telling of stories. In contrast to an extrinsic legitimation through appeal to meta-discourses, or Utopia, Lyotard advocates an intrinsic legitimation through a narrative knowledge which "does not give priority to the question of its own legitimation, and . . . certifies itself in the pragmatics of its own transmission without having recourse to argumentation and proof." Narratives themselves contain the criteria of competence and illustrate how they ought to be applied; they are legitimated by the simple fact that they do what they do. A narrative is not merely a transmission of information. In the very act of telling a story the position of the storyteller and the listener, and their place in the social order, is constituted; the story creates and maintains social bonds. The narratives of a community contribute to uphold the values and the social order of that community.

11 Postmodern thought focuses on *heterogeneous* language games, on the non-commensurable, on the instabilities, the breaks and the conflicts. Rather than regarding a conversation as a dialogue between partners, it is seen as a game, a confrontation between adversaries. A universal consensus of meaning is no ideal; the continual effort after meaning is no longer a big deal. The reply to the modern global sense-makers is simply "just let it be" or "stop making sense."

12 There exists no standard method for measuring and comparing knowledge within different language games and paradigms; they are incommensurable. A postmodern world is characterized by a continual change of perspectives, with no underlying common frame of reference, but rather a manifold of changing horizons. Rock music videos capture a world of continually changing perspectives and overlapping contexts.

13 *Language* and knowledge do not copy reality. Rather, language constitutes reality, each language constructing specific aspects of reality in its own way.

The focus is on the linguistic and social construction of reality, on interpretation and negotiation of the meaning of the lived world.

14 Human language is neither universal nor individual, but each language is rooted in a specific culture, as dialects or as national languages. Current philosophy has undergone a linguistic turn, focusing on language games, speech acts, hermeneutic interpretation, textual and linguistic analysis. The language games take place in local communities; they are heterogeneous and incommensurable. Highly refined expressions in one language, such as poetry, cannot be translated into another language without change of meaning. There exists no universal meta-language, no universal commensurability.

15 The focus on language implies a decentralization of the subject. The self no longer uses language to express itself; rather the language speaks through the person. The individual self loses prominence; the author is today less an original genius than a gifted craftsman and mediator of the culture through his or her mastery of language.

16 In postmodern thought there has taken place an *expansion of rationality.* It is not just a "momentary lapse of reason," but a going beyond the cognitive and scientific domain to include also the ethical and aesthetic domains of life in reason. "Modern times" involved a restricted concept of rationality, with a dominance of a technical means-ends rationality. There has been an emphasis on plans and programmes, on calculation, prediction and control. Reason and science have been overburdened with visions of Utopia where all human problems would be solved in the long run by the methods of science and technology.

17 When the presupposed rationality is seldom found in the given reality, another deeper, more essential reality is constructed to account for the disorder we observe in the world around us. The overstressed conception of a rationality has, in its turn, fostered sceptical reactions in the form of romanticist and irrationalist movements.

18 Postmodern thought goes beyond a Kantian split of modern culture into science, morality and art, and involves a rehabilitation of the ethical and aesthetic domains. The positivists' split of facts and values is no longer axiomatic; science is a value-constituted and value-constituting enterprise. Appeals to formal logic recede before a rehabilitated rhetoric of persuasion. With the loss of general systems of legitimation, when actions are not justified by appeal to some higher system or idea of progress, the values and the ethical responsibility of the interacting persons become central.

19 Art is not merely an aesthetic experience, but a way of knowing the world. Rationalist thought has abhorred the non-linear, the imprecise, the unpredictable, and has separated art from science. Mathematicians have been more open to an affinity of science and art, emphasizing the elegance and beauty of models as criteria of truth, cf. for instance *The Beauty of Fractals.*

20 Postmodern art is characterized by *pastiche* and collage. Art in a postmodern world does not belong to a unitary frame of reference, nor to a project or a Utopia. The plurality of perspectives leads to a fragmentation of experience,

the collage becoming a key artistic technique of our time. Styles from different periods and cultures are put together; in postmodern art high-tech may exist side by side with antique columns and romantic ornamentation, the effects being shocking and fascinating. In contrast to modern architecture, tradition is not rejected; nor is it worshipped as in the new classicism. Elements from other epochs are selected and put together in an often ironical recycling of what is usable as decorum. In literature there are collages of texts put together from other texts; the author's individuality and originality are lost in a pervasive use of and references to other texts. Eco's medieval detective novel *The Name of the Rose,* which may be read as a postmodern caricature of the modern meaning hunters, is thus filled with hidden quotes and allusions to other texts.

21 The reaction against modern rationality and functionalism was visible at an early stage in *architecture.* There was a protest against the functional, against straight lines and square blocks, against the cold logic and boredom of a modern architecture where function preceded form. Postmodern architecture is a reaction against what the painter Hundertwasser has called "the tyranny of the straight line." In the new architecture there is an emphasis on the curvilinear, on the unpredictable, on ornamentation and pastiche and on a non-functional beauty. Reflecting surfaces and labyrinths have become main elements.

22 On one side there is a return to the medieval village, with its tight-knit community and complex webs of buildings and places. The atriums of the Hyatt Regency Hotels appear as secularized cathedrals with quiet, closed and labyrinthine internal space, with an ornamentation of mixed styles. On the other side there is the Las Vegas trend of architecture, going to the extreme of learning from the most extravagant expressions of current architecture, as expressed in Venturi et al.'s *Learning from Las Vegas.* There is a collage of styles, as in Caesars Palace with its antique statues and parking valets dressed as Roman legionaries. Here there is dominance of the surface, the immense lighted billboards attracting the customer to the less spectacular interior labyrinths of gambling tables and slot machines.

23 Postmodern thought focuses on the *surface,* with a refined sensibility to what appears, a differentiation of what is perceived. The relation of sign and signified is breaking down; the reference to a reality beyond the sign recedes. In the media, texts and images refer less to an external world beyond the signs than to a chain of signifiers, to other texts and images. A dichotomy of fantasy and reality breaks down or loses interest. There is an intertextuality where texts mainly point to other texts. The TV series *Miami Vice* may refer less to the vice in Miami than to other TV series, imitating and parodying for example the car chases, playing up to the viewer's expectations of a cops-and-robbers series. The image, the appearance, is everything; the appearance has become the essence.

24 The interest in surface, in what manifestly appears, is in contrast to a debunking attitude where nothing is what it seems to be. This hermeneutics of suspicion, inherent in much modern thought, was carried to its extremes in some versions of psychoanalytic and Marxist thought. An action may never be

what it appears to be; rather it is an expression of some deeper, more real reality, a symptom of more basic sexual or economic forces. There is a continual hunt for the underlying plan or rationale, the hidden plot or curriculum, to explain the vicissitudes and disorder of what manifestly appears.

25 The modern quest for a unitary meaning, where there may be none, has as its pathological extreme the suspicion of paranoia. The debunking attitude may lead to conspiracy theories seeking for the mastermind plot; or, less extreme, to a continual search for an underlying order, constructing a deeper rationality where none is visible.

26 A postmodern *attitude* involves a suspicion of suspicion, and a refined sensibility to the surface, an openness to the differences and nuances of what appears. It relates to what is given, rather than what has been or what could be—"be cool," "it is no big deal," "no future." The fervent critical attitude of the 1960s and 1970s—as anti-authoritarianism and anti-capitalism—has dissolved. The idea of progress and development, be it the progress of mankind or the individual pilgrim's progress towards salvation of his or her soul, is out. An attitude of tolerant indifference has replaced the involvement and engagement in the social movements and the inner journeys of the 1960s and 1970s. What is left is a liberating nihilism, a living with the here and now, a weariness and a playful irony. Fascination may take the place of reflection; seduction may replace augmentation. There is an oscillation of an intense sensuous fascination by the media and a cool, ironical distance to what appears.

27 To the existentialists, the discovery of a world without meaning was the point of departure; today a loss of unitary meaning is merely accepted; that is just the way the world is. Postmodern man has stopped waiting for Godot. The absurd is not met with despair; rather it is a living with what is, a making the best of it, a relief from the burden of finding yourself as the goal of life; what remains may be a happy nihilism. With the death of the Utopias, the local and personal responsibility for actions here and now becomes crucial.

QUESTIONS FOR WRITING AND DISCUSSION

OBSERVING

1. What does Kvale mean by a "loss of belief in objective world"? Where and how is this loss felt by the average person, if at all?
2. According to Kvale, what part does language and its use play in this "disintegration" of objective reality?
3. At the end of the essay, Kvale references the play by Irish playwright Samuel Becket, *Waiting for Godot;* what is its relevance to these postmodern themes? (If you're unfamiliar with the play and its theme, look it up in a dictionary or glossary.)

EVALUATING

1. Kvale says postmodernism suggests "Human language is neither universal nor individual, but each language is rooted in a specific culture. . . ." What are the implications of this for community action and more global cooperation? On what basis can human beings "get along" if everything is specific to the culture in which it is situated?
2. Where are the weaknesses in postmodernist premises? Where are its strengths? What are its "uses"?
3. Drawing on your readings in Spirituality, what themes from the Bible or the Qu'ran clash with postmodernist thought? Write a brief Islamic, Christian, or Judaic critique of Kvale's survey.

RESPONDING AND APPLYING

1. With which of the "themes of postmodernism" are you most uncomfortable? Why?
2. Do you believe postmodernism is a "fad"? Why or why not?
3. Are you a "postmodernist"? If so, why? If not, on what basis can you resist it or its influence on your life and times?

BILL WATTERSON, "CALVIN AND HOBBES"

Born in 1958, Bill Watterson's full name is William B. Watterson II. He has spent his recent years as a professional cartoonist. Watterson grew up in Chagrin Falls, Ohio, and graduated from Kenyon College (1980) in Gambier, Ohio, where he received a degree in political science. With his wife, he now lives in Santa Fe, New Mexico. Watterson first drew comics for his secondary school newspaper and then for his hometown journal, *The Chagrin Herald.* At Kenyon, Watterson drew what he calls his "beer-swilling, library allergic, carbohydrate-addicted" peers.

Watterson worked at the *Cincinnati Post* for only a short period before he found the experience "horrible." After several attempts, he succeeded in 1985 at syndication with *Calvin and Hobbes,* something far less political than anything he had previously done. Some describe Watterson as America's hottest comic strip artist, given its recent syndication in over 2,000 papers worldwide. Part of his success may be due to Watterson's commitment to the comic strip as an art form, to "quality over a quick buck." Calvin and Hobbes ceased production on Dec. 31, 1995, because its creator found its work demands too restrictive. A *Chicago Tribune* editorial lamented the disappearance of the *Calvin and Hobbes* comic strip from daily newspapers, saying that those papers will be "emptier absent the companionship of an imaginative but self-centered 6-year-old and his humane, dignified stuffed tiger who comes to life when nobody else is present."

calvin and HOBBES
by WATTERSON
UH-O
OH NO! EVERYTHING HAS SUDDENLY TURNED NEO-CUBIST!
IT ALL STARTED WHEN CALVIN ENGAGED HIS DAD IN A MINOR DEBATE! SOON CALVIN COULD SEE BOTH SIDES OF THE ISSUE! THEN POOR CALVIN BEGAN TO SEE BOTH SIDES OF EVERYTHING!
THE TRADITIONAL SINGLE VIEWPOINT HAS BEEN ABANDONED! PERSPECTIVE HAS BEEN FRACTURED!
THE MULTIPLE VIEWS PROVIDE TOO MUCH INFORMATION! IT'S IMPOSSIBLE TO MOVE! CALVIN QUICKLY TRIES TO ELIMINATE ALL BUT ONE PERSPECTIVE!
IT WORKS! THE WORLD FALLS INTO A RECOGNIZABLE ORDER!
YOU'RE STILL WRONG, DAD.

QUESTIONS FOR WRITING AND DISCUSSION

OBSERVING

1. Explain the reference to cubism and the graphic representations in the cartoon.
2. What happened between Calvin and his dad that fractured perspective? What is a fractured perspective? What is the problem with seeing both sides of an issue, or "both sides of everything"?
3. How does Calvin resolve his problem?

EVALUATING

1. In what ways can various social conflicts and problems be attributed to the abandonment of a single viewpoint? What problems are there that stem from holding multiple views?
2. To what degree is Calvin's solution to his problem satisfactory? Is it reasonable today to think that we can "eliminate all but one perspective"?
3. Some say multiculturalism on college campuses is the result of the fracturing of perspective, of taking too many viewpoints at once. Critics like Alan Bloom attack students for being too accepting and too uncritical. What do you think?

RESPONDING AND APPLYING

1. Describe an experience in which you gained multiple viewpoints and experienced problems as a result. How does "too much information" create immobility?
2. Calvin ends by telling his dad that he's still wrong. Do you think the cartoon is funny?

GARRY TRUDEAU, "DOONESBURY"

In 1984, cartoonist Garry Trudeau drew a comic strip in which a character expresses fear that then-obscure Representative Newt Gingrich would ascend to a position of power. Trudeau's clairvoyance is only one small part of his very popular cartoon *Doonesbury.* Born in 1948, Trudeau draws cartoons that offer trenchant political, social, philosophical and theological commentary on the world's events. Winner of the Spirit of Liberty Award from People for the American Way in 1995, Trudeau has satirized everything from gays in the Catholic church to junk bond king Michael Milkin, fires in Southern California, President Bush's residency and tax payments, and the Apple Newton computer. Recently, newspapers received over

Doonesbury
G. B. TRUDEAU
HEY... HERE COMES CORNELL!
UH-OH... HE'S CARRYING A **NEWSPAPER!**
ANYONE WANT A SECTION OF THE PAPER?
THE PAPER? YOU STILL READ THE PAPER? HOW COME, CORNELL?
NEWS, BOOPSIE. TO FIND OUT WHAT'S GOING ON.
BUT THAT'S WHAT "ENTERTAINMENT TONIGHT" IS FOR.
WHOA... WE'VE REALLY SLIPPED INTO POST-LITERACY, HAVEN'T WE? NO WONDER NEWSPAPERS ARE IN SUCH TROUBLE...
THE TUBE RULES, TOTALLY. PEOPLE BUY PAPERS FOR THE TV AND MOVIE LISTINGS. THEY BUY MAGAZINES FOR THE PICTURES. THEY STILL BUY ACTUAL BOOKS, BUT THEY RARELY FINISH READING THEM.
WOW... THAT'S PRETTY SCARY...
10-16
WILL ANYONE FINISH READING **THIS?**
GOOD QUESTION.
BOYS! GIRLS! DID **YOU** MAKE IT THIS FAR? YOU **MAY** HAVE WON A VALUABLE PRIZE!
CHECK WITH THIS NEWSPAPER!
GBTrudeau

20,000 responses to a questionnaire published in a *Doonesbury* cartoon. It is not uncommon for newspapers to suspend the cartoon, as did the *L.A. Times,* for the fires series.

QUESTIONS FOR WRITING AND DISCUSSION

OBSERVING

1. Boopsie is surprised that Cornell still reads a newspaper. Why?
2. Cornell explains Boopsie's surprise as a phenomenon of "post-literacy." What is "post-literacy"? If we think of reading and writing print as literacy, what kind of experience comes after print, where "the tube rules"? Why is it scary to Boopsie that people rarely finish reading books?

EVALUATING

1. What is the tone of the cartoon? What attitude toward "boys and girls" does the cartoon take? "Did you make it this far?" Do you think the writing is angry and sarcastic, or just whimsical and jocular?
2. What is lost with a diminished valuing of reading print, if anything? Why do so many young people prefer to "see the movie" than "read the book"?
3. What signs of post-literacy do you see in society? How does it affect people's behavior and tastes?

RESPONDING AND APPLYING

1. How do you handle the conflict between books and electronic forms of the media? How were you raised, in terms of television watching? How will you raise your children? Do you think TV should be limited?
2. The Internet has been described as a smart medium, since it is interactive and requires an active reader. Television, on the other hand, is described as a "dumb" medium, a boob tube, for the couch potatoes. Do you accept these key differences?

RAY BRADBURY, "THE VELDT"

Born in 1921, Ray Bradbury is one of America's most popular futurists and science fiction writers. He is known and widely respected as a prodigiously prolific storyteller whose imagination often seems uncontrollable. He has published more than 400 stories and many novels, including *Fahrenheit 451, The Martian Chronicles,* and *Something Wicked This Way Comes.* Bradbury is also famous as a packrat: he noted in an interview that he throws nothing away. "If on ten different mornings I hear (in my head) ten different voices, there might eventually come out of it five short stories, four poems and a one-act play." When Bradbury was young, he grew enchanted by the science fiction of Jules Verne, H. G. Wells, and the fantasies of Poe. He also spent almost every night in his local library, "just taking books off the shelves and falling in love with them."

The Veldt

Ray Bradbury

1 George, I wish you'd look at the nursery."

2 "What's wrong with it?"

3 "I don't know."

4 "Well, then."

5 "I just want you to look at it, is all, or call a psychologist in to look at it."

6 "What would a psychologist want with a nursery?"

7 "You know very well what he'd want." His wife paused in the middle of the kitchen and watched the stove busy humming to itself, making supper for four.

8 "It's just that the nursery is different now than it was."

9 "All right, let's have a look."

10 They walked down the hall of their soundproofed Happy-life Home, which had cost them thirty thousand dollars installed, this house which clothed and fed and rocked them to sleep and played and sang and was good to them. Their approach sensitized a switch somewhere and the nursery light flicked on when they came within ten feet of it. Similarly, behind them, in the halls, lights went on and off as they left them behind, with a soft automaticity.

11 "Well," said George Hadley.

12 They stood on the thatched floor of the nursery. It was forty feet across by forty feet long and thirty feet high; it had cost half again as much as the rest of the house. "But nothing's too good for our children," George had said.

13 The nursery was silent. It was empty as a jungle glade at hot high noon. The walls were blank and two-dimensional. Now, as George and Lydia Hadley stood in the center of the room, the walls began to purr and recede into crystalline distance, it seemed, and presently an African veldt appeared, in three dimensions; on all sides, in colors reproduced to the final pebble and bit of straw. The ceiling above them became a deep sky with a hot yellow sun.

14 George Hadley felt the perspiration start on his brow.

15 "Let's get out of the sun," he said. "This is a little too real. But I don't see anything wrong."

16 "Wait a moment, you'll see," said his wife.

17 Now the hidden odorophonics were beginning to blow a wind of odor at the two people in the middle of the baked veldtland. The hot straw smell of lion grass, the cool green smell of the hidden water hole, the great rusty smell of animals, the smell of dust like a red paprika in the hot air. And now the sounds: the thump of distant antelope feet on grassy sod, the papery rustling of vultures. A shadow passed through the sky. The shadow flickered on George Hadley's upturned, sweating face.

18 "Filthy creatures," he heard his wife say.

19 "The vultures."

20 "You see, there are the lions, far over, that way. Now they're on their way to the water hole. They've just been eating," said Lydia. "I don't know what."

21 "Some animal." George Hadley put his hand up to shield off the burning light from his squinted eyes. "A zebra or a baby giraffe, maybe."

22 "Are you sure?" His wife sounded peculiarly tense.

23 "No, it's a little late to be *sure,*" he said, amused. "Nothing over there I can see but cleaned bone, and the vultures dropping for what's left."

24 "Did you hear that scream?" she asked.

25 "No."

26 "About a minute ago?"

27 "Sorry, no."

28 The lions were coming. And again George Hadley was filled with admiration for the mechanical genius who had conceived this room. A miracle of efficiency selling for an absurdly low price. Every home should have one. Oh, occasionally they frightened you with their clinical accuracy, they startled you, gave you a twinge, but most of the time what fun for everyone, not only your own son and daughter, but for yourself when you felt like a quick jaunt to a foreign land, a quick change of scenery. Well, here it was!

29 And here were the lions now, fifteen feet away, so real, so feverishly and startlingly real that you could feel the prickling fur on your hand, and your mouth was stuffed with the dusty upholstery smell of their heated pelts, and the yellow of them was in your eyes like the yellow of an exquisite French tapestry, the yellows of lions and summer grass, and the sound of matted lion lungs exhaling on the silent noontide, and the smell of meat from the panting, dripping mouths.

30 The lions stood looking at George and Lydia Hadley with terrible green-yellow eyes.

31 "Watch out!" screamed Lydia.

32 The lions came running at them.

33 Lydia bolted and ran. Instinctively, George sprang after her. Outside, in the hall, with the door slammed, he was laughing and she was crying and they both stood appalled at the other's reaction.

34 "George!"

35 "Lydia! Oh, my dear poor sweet Lydia!"

36 "They almost got us!"

37 "Walls, Lydia, remember; crystal walls, that's all they are. Oh, they look real, I must admit—Africa in your parlor—but it's all dimensional superactionary, supersensitive color film and mental tape film behind glass screens. It's all odorophonics and sonics, Lydia. Here's my handkerchief."

38 "I'm afraid." She came to him and put her body against him and cried steadily. "Did you see? Did you *feel?* It's too real."

39 "Now, Lydia . . ."

40 "You've got to tell Wendy and Peter not to read any more on Africa."

41 "Of course—of course." He patted her.

42 "Promise?"

43 "Sure."

44 "And lock the nursery for a few days until I get my nerves settled."

45 "You know how difficult Peter is about that. When I punished him a month ago by locking the nursery for even a few hours—the tantrum he threw! And Wendy too. They *live* for the nursery."

46 "It's got to be locked, that's all there is to it."

47 "All right." Reluctantly he locked the huge door. "You've been working too hard. You need a rest."

48 "I don't know—I don't know," she said, blowing her nose, sitting down in a chair that immediately began to rock and comfort her. "Maybe I don't have enough to do. Maybe I have time to think too much. Why don't we shut the whole house off for a few days and take a vacation?"

49 "You mean you want to fry my eggs for me?"

50 "Yes." She nodded.

51 "And darn my socks?"

52 "Yes." A frantic, watery-eyed nodding.

53 "And sweep the house?"

54 "Yes, yes—oh, yes!"

55 "But I thought that's why we bought this house, so we wouldn't have to do anything?"

56 "That's just it. I feel like I don't belong here. The house is wife and mother now and nursemaid. Can I compete with an African veldt? Can I give a bath and scrub the children as efficiently or quickly as the automatic scrub bath can? I cannot. And it isn't just me. It's you. You've been awfully nervous lately."

57 "I suppose I have been smoking too much."

58 "You look as if you don't know what to do with yourself in this house, either. You smoke a little more every morning and drink a little more every afternoon and need a little more sedative every night. You're beginning to feel unnecessary too."

59 "Am I?" He paused and tried to feel into himself to see what was really there.

60 "Oh, George!" She looked beyond him, at the nursery door. "Those lions can't get out of there, can they?"

61 He looked at the door and saw it tremble as if something had jumped against it from the other side.

62 "Of course not," he said.

63 At dinner they ate alone, for Wendy and Peter were at a special plastic carnival across town and had televised home to say they'd be late, to go ahead eating. So George Hadley, bemused, sat watching the dining room table produce warm dishes of food from its mechanical interior.

64 "We forgot the ketchup," he said.

65 "Sorry," said a small voice within the table, and ketchup appeared.

66 As for the nursery, thought George Hadley, it won't hurt for the children to be locked out of it awhile. Too much of anything isn't good for anyone. And it was clearly indicated that the children had been spending a little too much time on Africa. That *sun.* He could feel it on his neck, still, like a hot paw. And the *lions.* And the smell of blood. Remarkable how the nursery caught the telepathic emanations of the children's minds and created life to fill their every desire. The children thought lions, and there were lions. The children thought zebras, and there were zebras. Sun—sun. Giraffes—giraffes. Death and death.

67 That *last.* He chewed tastelessly on the meat that the table had cut for him. Death thoughts. They were awfully young, Wendy and Peter, for death thoughts. Or, no, you were never too young, really. Long before you knew what death was you were wishing it on someone else. When you were two years old you were shooting people with cap pistols.

68 But this—the long, hot African veldt—the awful death in the jaws of a lion. And repeated again and again.

69 "Where are you going?"

70 He didn't answer Lydia. Preoccupied, he let the lights glow softly on ahead of him, extinguish behind him as he padded to the nursery door. He listened against it. Far away, a lion roared.

71 He unlocked the door and opened it. Just before he stepped inside, he heard a faraway scream. And then another roar from the lions, which subsided quickly.

72 He stepped into Africa. How many times in the last year had he opened this door and found Wonderland, Alice, the Mock Turtle, or Aladdin and his Magical Lamp, or Jack Pumpkinhead of Oz, or Dr. Dolittle, or the cow jumping over a very real-appearing moon—all the delightful contraptions of a make-believe world. How often had he seen Pegasus flying in the sky ceiling, or seen fountains of red fireworks, or heard angel voices singing. But now, this yellow hot Africa, this bake oven with murder in the heat. Perhaps Lydia was right. Perhaps they needed a little vacation from the fantasy which was growing a bit too real for ten-year-old children. It was all right to exercise one's mind with gymnastic fantasies, but when the lively child mind settled on *one* pattern . . . ? It seemed that, at a distance, for the past month, he had heard lions roaring, and smelled their strong odor seeping as far away as his study door. But, being busy, he had paid it no attention.

73 George Hadley stood on the African grassland alone. The lions looked up from their feeding, watching him. The only flaw to the illusion was the open door through which he could see his wife, far down the dark hall, like a framed picture, eating her dinner abstractedly.

74 "Go away," he said to the lions.

75 They did not go.

76 He knew the principle of the room exactly. You sent out your thoughts. Whatever you thought would appear.

77 "Let's have Aladdin and his lamp," he snapped.

78 The veldtland remained; the lions remained.

79 "Come on, room! I demand Aladdin!" he said.

80 Nothing happened. The lions mumbled in their baked pelts.

81 "Aladdin!"

82 He went back to dinner. "The fool room's out of order," he said. "It won't respond."

83 "Or— "

84 "Or what?"

85 "Or it *can't* respond," said Lydia, "because the children have thought about Africa and lions and killing so many days that the room's in a rut."

86 "Could be."

87 "Or Peter's set it to remain that way."

88 "*Set* it?"

89 "He may have got into the machinery and fixed something."

90 "Peter doesn't know machinery."

91 "He's a wise one for ten. That I.Q. of his— "

92 "Nevertheless— "

93 "Hello, Mom. Hello, Dad."

94 The Hadleys turned. Wendy and Peter were coming in the front door, cheeks like peppermint candy, eyes like bright blue agate marbles, a smell of ozone on their jumpers from their trip in the helicopter.

95 "You're just in time for supper," said both parents.

96 "We're full of strawberry ice cream and hot dogs," said the children, holding hands. "But we'll sit and watch."

97 "Yes, come tell us about the nursery," said George Hadley.

98 The brother and sister blinked at him and then at each other. "Nursery?"

99 "All about Africa and everything," said the father with false joviality.

100 "I don't understand," said Peter.

101 "Your mother and I were just traveling through Africa with rod and reel; Tom Swift and his Electric Lion," said George Hadley.

102 "There's no Africa in the nursery," said Peter simply.

103 "Oh, come now, Peter. We know better."

104 "I don't remember any Africa," said Peter to Wendy. "Do you?"

105 "No."

106 "Run see and come tell."

107 She obeyed.

108 "Wendy, come back here!" said George Hadley, but she was gone. The house lights followed her like a flock of fireflies. Too late, he realized he had forgotten to lock the nursery door after his last inspection.

109 "Wendy'll look and come tell us," said Peter.

110 "She doesn't have to tell *me.* I've seen it."

111 "I'm sure you're mistaken, Father."

112 "I'm not, Peter. Come along now."

113 But Wendy was back. "It's not Africa," she said breathlessly.

114 "We'll see about this," said George Hadley, and they all walked down the hall together and opened the nursery door.

115 There was a green, lovely forest, a lovely river, a purple mountain, high voices singing, and Rima, lovely and mysterious, lurking in the trees with colorful flights of butterflies, like animated bouquets, lingering in her long hair. The African veldtland was gone. The lions were gone. Only Rima was here now, singing a song so beautiful that it brought tears to your eyes.

116 George Hadley looked in at the changed scene. "Go to bed," he said to the children.

117 They opened their mouths.

118 "You heard me," he said.

119 They went off to the air closet, where a wind sucked them like brown leaves up the flue to their slumber rooms.

120 George Hadley walked through the singing glade and picked up something that lay in the corner near where the lions had been. He walked slowly back to his wife.

121 "What is that?" she asked.

122 "An old wallet of mine," he said.

123 He showed it to her. The smell of hot grass was on it and the smell of a lion. There were drops of saliva on it, it had been chewed, and there were blood smears on both sides.

124 He closed the nursery door and locked it, tight.

125 In the middle of the night he was still awake and he knew his wife was awake. "Do you think Wendy changed it?" she said at last, in the dark room.

126 "Of course."

127 "Made it from a veldt into a forest and put Rima there instead of lions?"

128 "Yes."

129 "Why?"

130 "I don't know. But it's staying locked until I find out."

131 "How did your wallet get there?"

132 "I don't know anything," he said, "except that I'm beginning to be sorry we bought that room for the children. If children are neurotic at all, a room like that— "

133 "It's supposed to help them work off their neuroses in a healthful way."

134 "I'm starting to wonder." He stared at the ceiling.

135 "We've given the children everything they ever wanted. Is this our reward—secrecy, disobedience?"

136 "Who was it said, 'Children are carpets, they should be stepped on occasionally'! We've never lifted a hand. They're insufferable—let's admit it. They come and go when they like; they treat us as if *we* were offspring. They're spoiled and we're spoiled."

137 "They've been acting funny ever since you forbade them to take the rocket to New York a few months ago."

138 "They're not old enough to do that alone, I explained."

139 "Nevertheless, I've noticed they've been decidedly cool toward us since."

140 "I think I'll have David McClean come tomorrow morning to have a look at Africa."

141 "But it's not Africa now, it's Green Mansions country and Rima."

142 "I have a feeling it'll be Africa again before then."

143 A moment later they heard the screams.

144 Two screams. Two people screaming from downstairs. And then a roar of lions.

145 "Wendy and Peter aren't in their rooms," said his wife.

146 He lay in his bed with his beating heart. "No," he said. "They've broken into the nursery."

147 "Those screams—they sound familiar."

148 "Do they?"

149 "Yes, awfully."

150 And although their beds tried very hard, the two adults couldn't be rocked to sleep for another hour. A smell of cats was in the night air.

151 "Father?" said Peter.

152 "Yes."

153 Peter looked at his shoes. He never looked at his father anymore, nor at his mother. "You aren't going to lock up the nursery for good, are you?"

154 "That all depends."

155 "On what?" snapped Peter.

156 "On you and your sister. If you intersperse this Africa with a little variety—oh, Sweden perhaps, or Denmark or China—"

157 "I thought we were free to play as we wished."

158 "You are, within reasonable bounds."

159 "What's wrong with Africa, Father?"

160 "Oh, so now you admit you have been conjuring up Africa, do you?"

161 "I wouldn't want the nursery locked up," said Peter coldly. "Ever."

162 "Matter of fact, we're thinking of turning the whole house off for about a month. Live sort of a carefree one-for-all existence."

163 "That sounds dreadful! Would I have to tie my own shoes instead of letting the shoe tier do it? And brush my own teeth and comb my hair and give myself a bath?"

164 "It would be fun for a change, don't you think?"

165 "No, it would be horrid. I didn't like it when you took out the picture painter last month."

166 "That's because I wanted you to learn to paint all by yourself, Son."

167 "I don't want to do anything but look and listen and smell; what else *is* there to do?"

168 "All right, go play in Africa."

169 "Will you shut off the house sometime soon?"

170 "We're considering it."

171 "I don't think you'd better consider it any more, Father."

172 "I won't have any threats from my son!"

173 "Very well." And Peter strolled off to the nursery.

174 "Am I on time?" said David McClean.

175 "Breakfast?" asked George Hadley.

176 "Thanks, had some. What's the trouble?"

177 "David, you're a psychologist."

178 "I should hope so."

179 "Well, then, have a look at our nursery. You saw it a year ago when you dropped by; did you notice anything peculiar about it then?"

180 "Can't say I did; the usual violences, a tendency toward a slight paranoia here or there, usual in children because they feel persecuted by parents constantly, but, oh, really nothing."

181 They walked down the hall. "I locked the nursery up," explained the father, "and the children broke back into it during the night. I let them stay so they could form the patterns for you to see."

182 There was a terrible screaming from the nursery.

183 "There it is," said George Hadley. "See what you make of it."

184 They walked in on the children without rapping.

185 The screams had faded. The lions were feeding.

186 "Run outside a moment, children," said George Hadley. "No, don't change the mental combination. Leave the walls as they are. Get!"

187 With the children gone, the two men stood studying the lions clustered at a distance, eating with great relish whatever it was they had caught.

188 "I wish I knew what it was," said George Hadley. "Sometimes I can almost see. Do you think if I brought high-powered binoculars here and— "

189 David McClean laughed dryly. "Hardly." He turned to study all four walls. "How long has this been going on?"

190 "A little over a month."

191 "It certainly doesn't *feel* good."

192 "I want facts, not feelings."

193 "My dear George, a psychologist never saw a fact in his life. He only hears about feelings; vague things. This doesn't feel good, I tell you. Trust my hunches and my instincts. I have a nose for something bad. This is very bad. My

advice to you is to have the whole damn room torn down and your children brought to me every day during the next year for treatment."

194 "Is it that bad?"

195 "I'm afraid so. One of the original uses of these nurseries was so that we could study the patterns left on the walls by the child's mind, study at our leisure, and help the child. In this case, however, the room has become a channel toward—destructive thoughts, instead of a release away from them."

196 "Didn't you sense this before?"

197 "I sensed only that you had spoiled your children more than most. And now you're letting them down in some way. What way?"

198 "I wouldn't let them go to New York."

199 "What else?"

200 "I've taken a few machines from the house and threatened them, a month ago, with closing up the nursery unless they did their homework. I did close it for a few days to show I meant business."

201 "Ah, ha!"

202 "Does that mean anything?"

203 "Everything. Where before they had a Santa Claus now they have a Scrooge. Children prefer Santas. You've let this room and this house replace you and your wife in your children's affections. This room is their mother and father, far more important in their lives than their real parents. And now you come along and want to shut it off. No wonder there's hatred here. You can feel it coming out of the sky. Feel that sun. George, you'll have to change your life. Like too many others, you've built it around creature comforts. Why, you'd starve tomorrow if something went wrong in your kitchen. You wouldn't know how to tap an egg. Nevertheless, turn everything off. Start new. I'll take time. But we'll make good children out of bad in a year, wait and see."

204 "But won't the shock be too much for the children, shutting the room up abruptly, for good?"

205 "I don't want them going any deeper into this, that's all."

206 The lions were finished with their red feast.

207 The lions were standing on the edge of the clearing watching the two men.

208 "Now *I'm* feeling persecuted," said McClean. "Let's get out of here. I never have cared for these damned rooms. Make me nervous."

209 "The lions look real, don't they?" said George Hadley. "I don't suppose there's any way—"

210 "What?"

211 "—that they could *become* real?"

212 "Not that I know."

213 "Some flaw in the machinery, a tampering or something?"

214 "No."

215 They went to the door.

216 "I don't imagine the room will like being turned off," said the father.

217 "Nothing ever likes to die—even a room."

218 "I wonder if it hates me for wanting to switch it off?"

219 "Paranoia is thick around here today," said David McClean. "You can follow it like a spoor. Hello." He bent and picked up a bloody scarf. "This yours?"

220 "No." George Hadley's face was rigid. "It belongs to Lydia."

221 They went to the fuse box together and threw the switch that killed the nursery.

222 The two children were in hysterics. They screamed and pranced and threw things. They yelled and sobbed and swore and jumped at the furniture.

223 "You can't do that to the nursery, you can't!"

224 "Now, children."

225 The children flung themselves onto a couch, weeping.

226 "George," said Lydia Hadley, "turn on the nursery, just for a few moments. You can't be so abrupt."

227 "No."

228 "You can't be so cruel."

229 "Lydia, it's off, and it stays off. And the whole damn house dies as of here and now. The more I see of the mess we've put ourselves in, the more it sickens me. We've been contemplating our mechanical, electronic navels for too long. My God, how we need a breath of honest air!"

230 And he marched about the house turning off the voice clocks, the stoves, the heaters, the shoe shiners, the shoe lacers, the body scrubbers and swabbers and massagers, and every other machine he could put his hand to.

231 The house was full of dead bodies, it seemed. It felt like a mechanical cemetery. So silent. None of the humming hidden energy of machines waiting to function at the tap of a button.

232 "Don't let them do it!" wailed Peter at the ceiling, as if he was talking to the house, the nursery. "Don't let Father kill everything." He turned to his father. "Oh, I hate you!"

233 "Insults won't get you anywhere."

234 "I wish you were dead!"

235 "We were, for a long while. Now we're going to really start living. Instead of being handled and massaged, we're going to *live*."

236 Wendy was still crying and Peter joined her again. "Just a moment, just one moment, just another moment of nursery," they wailed.

237 "Oh, George," said the wife, "it can't hurt."

238 "All right—all right, if they'll only just shut up. One minute, mind you, and then off forever."

239 "Daddy, Daddy, Daddy!" sang the children, smiling with wet faces.

240 "And then we're going on a vacation. David McClean is coming back in half an hour to help us move out and get to the airport. I'm going to dress. You turn the nursery on for a minute, Lydia, just a minute, mind you."

241 And the three of them went babbling off while he let himself be vacuumed upstairs through the air flue and set about dressing himself. A minute later Lydia appeared.

242 "I'll be glad when we get away," she sighed.

243 "Did you leave them in the nursery?"

244 "I wanted to dress too. Oh, that horrid Africa. What can they see in it?"

245 "Well, in five minutes we'll be on our way to Iowa. Lord, how did we ever get in this house? What prompted us to buy a nightmare?"

246 "Pride, money, foolishness."

247 "I think we'd better get downstairs before those kids get engrossed with those damned beasts again."

248 Just then they heard the children calling, "Daddy, Mommy, come quick—quick!"

249 They went downstairs in the air flue and ran down the hall. The children were nowhere in sight. "Wendy? Peter?"

250 They ran into the nursery. The veldtland was empty save for the lions waiting, looking at them. "Peter, Wendy?"

251 The door slammed.

252 "Wendy, Peter!"

253 George Hadley and his wife whirled and ran back to the door.

254 "Open the door!" cried George Hadley, trying the knob. "Why, they've locked it from the outside! Peter!" He beat at the door. "Open up!"

255 He heard Peter's voice outside, against the door.

256 "Don't let them switch off the nursery and the house," he was saying.

257 Mr. and Mrs. George Hadley beat at the door. "Now, don't be ridiculous, children. It's time to go. Mr. McClean'll be here in a minute and . . ."

258 And then they heard the sounds.

259 The lions on three sides of them, in the yellow veldt grass, padding through the dry straw, rumbling and roaring in their throats.

260 The lions.

261 Mr. Hadley looked at his wife and they turned and looked back at the beasts edging slowly forward, crouching, tails stiff.

262 Mr. and Mrs. Hadley screamed.

263 And suddenly they realized why those other screams had sounded familiar.

264 Well, here I am," said David McClean in the nursery doorway. "Oh, hello." He stared at the two children seated in the center of the open glade eating a little picnic lunch. Beyond them was the water hole and the yellow veldtland; above was the hot sun. He began to perspire. "Where are your father and mother?"

265 The children looked up and smiled. "Oh, they'll be here directly."

266 "Good, we must get going." At a distance Mr. McClean saw the lions fighting and clawing and then quieting down to feed in silence under the shady trees.

267 He squinted at the lions with his hand up to his eyes.

268 Now the lions were done feeding. They moved to the water hole to drink.

269 A shadow flickered over Mr. McClean's hot face. Many shadows flickered. The vultures were dropping down the blazing sky.

270 "A cup of tea?" asked Wendy in the silence.

QUESTIONS ON STORY

OBSERVING

1. Describe the Hadley household. What are the relations like among parents and children? What was the original intention of the Nursery? How does the Nursery affect family relations?
2. What is the attitude toward work and leisure in the story?
3. What do the parents learn from the psychologist?

EVALUATING

1. What or who controls the house? The Nursery? The parents? The children?
2. What values are in conflict in the house? What is important to the parents? To the children? What role does permissiveness have in the household? What role does freedom play?
3. What does it mean that the virtual lions have become "real" in the story? How can virtual reality replace reality? Consider virtual business or schools today in your answer.
4. What does the story say about our love affair with technology?

RESPONDING AND APPLYING

1. "Pride, money, foolishness," Lydia says when George asks what prompted them to buy a "nightmare." Do you think they have the whole story?
2. What struggles around control vs. permissiveness did you have or are you having with persons who have authority positions in your life?

PERSPECTIVES

Where Are Computers Taking Us?

Many people tend to take exaggerated positions with regard to the sudden appearance of the digitized, electronic technologies and one of their outgrowths, the information superhighway. What many call a major change in the way we communicate, socialize, work, and play may not carry the weight of the scientific or democratic revolutions, but digitized information will profoundly change most facets of modern life. Howard Rheingold and Bill Gates, the authors of the pieces that follow, are just two of the many cyber-gurus who have offered leadership in this revolution. Both tend to be enthusiasts, but we must approach these new wonders with healthy skepticism. How are they affecting our knowledge of and relationship to our past? Do they offer us a greater or lesser sense of perspective on and understanding of human history? How will we address questions regarding fair distribution of the power that these new tools offer us? How can we take advantage of the global village, the much smaller planet that is within our reach? How can we see the hidden costs in such developments, such as those dramatically identified by author Bill McKibben in his book *The Age of Missing Information* (Plume Penguin, 1993)? Or those in Daniel Quinn's book-length allegory, *Ishmael: An Adventure of the Mind and Spirit* (Bantam, 1992)?

Howard Rheingold, *from* Virtual Community

Internet visionary, pioneer, and promoter, Howard Rheingold is the author of many books including *Virtual Reality,* editor of the *Whole Earth Review* and *The Millennium Whole Earth Catalog,* and a consultant to the U.S. Congress Office of Technology and Assessment. A popular speaker on the computer circuit, Rheingold is also an active participant in the WELL, a computer network based in California. The essay that follows is the beginning of the Introduction to *The Virtual Community: Homesteading on the Electronic Frontier.* As an informed and optimistic tour of the Internet and cyberspace, this book makes an excellent introduction to the many worlds of the information superhighway. Mitch Kapor, founder of Lotus Development Corporation and The Electronic Frontier Foundation, calls the book "a Magical Mystery Tour of the human side of cyberspace." Rheingold's Home Page on the World Wide Web can be found at ⟨http://www.well.com/user/hlr/index.html⟩.

from Virtual Community

Howard Rheingold

1 "Daddy is saying 'Holy moly!' to his computer again!"

2 Those words have become a family code for the way my virtual community has infiltrated our real world. My seven-year-old daughter knows that her father congregates with a family of invisible friends who seem to gather in his computer. Sometimes he talks to them, even if nobody else can see them. And she knows that these invisible friends sometimes show up in the flesh, materializing from the next block or the other side of the planet.

3 Since the summer of 1985, for an average of two hours a day, seven days a week, I've been plugging my personal computer into my telephone and making

contact with the WELL (Whole Earth 'Lectronic Link)—a computer conferencing system that enables people around the world to carry on public conversations and exchange private electronic mail (e-mail). The idea of a community accessible only via my computer screen sounded cold to me at first, but I learned quickly that people can feel passionately about e-mail and computer conferences. I've become one of them. I care about these people I met through my computer, and I care deeply about the future of the medium that enables us to assemble.

4 I'm not alone in this emotional attachment to an apparently bloodless technological ritual. Millions of people on every continent also participate in the computer-mediated social groups known as virtual communities, and this population is growing fast. Finding the WELL was like discovering a cozy little world that had been flourishing without me, hidden within the walls of my house; an entire cast of characters welcomed me to the troupe with great merriment as soon as I found the secret door. Like others who fell into the WELL, I soon discovered that I was audience, performer, and scriptwriter, along with my companions, in an ongoing improvisation. A full-scale subculture was growing on the other side of my telephone jack, and they invited me to help create something new.

5 The virtual village of a few hundred people I stumbled upon in 1985 grew to eight thousand by 1993. It became clear to me during the first months of that history that I was participating in the self-design of a new kind of culture. I watched the community's social contracts stretch and change as the people who discovered and started building the WELL in its first year or two were joined by so many others. Norms were established, challenged, changed, reestablished, rechallenged, in a kind of speeded-up social evolution.

6 The WELL felt like an authentic community to me from the start because it was grounded in my everyday physical world. WELLites who don't live within driving distance of the San Francisco Bay area are constrained in their ability to participate in the local networks of face-to-face acquaintances. By now, I've attended real-life WELL marriages, WELL births, and even a WELL funeral. (The phrase "in real life" pops up so often in virtual communities that regulars abbreviate it to IRL.) I can't count the parties and outings where the invisible personae who first acted out their parts in the debates and melodramas on my computer screen later manifested in front of me in the physical world in the form of real people, with faces, bodies, and voices.

7 I remember the first time I walked into a room full of people IRL who knew many intimate details of my history and whose own stories I knew very well. Three months after I joined, I went to my first WELL party at the home of one of the WELL's online moderators. I looked around at the room full of strangers when I walked in. It was one of the oddest sensations of my life. I had contended with these people, shot the invisible breeze around the electronic watercooler, shared alliances and formed bonds, fallen off my chair laughing with them, become livid with anger at some of them. But there wasn't a recognizable face in the house. I had never seen them before.

8 My flesh-and-blood family long ago grew accustomed to the way I sit in my home office early in the morning and late at night, chuckling and cursing, sometimes crying, about words I read on the computer screen. It might have looked to my daughter as if I were alone at my desk the night she caught me chortling online, but from my point of view I was in living contact with old and new friends, strangers and colleagues:

9 I was in the Parenting conference on the WELL, participating in an informational and emotional support group for a friend who just learned his son was diagnosed with leukemia.

10 I was in MicroMUSE, a role-playing fantasy game of the twenty-fourth century (and science education medium in disguise), interacting with students and professors who know me only as "Pollenator."

11 I was in TWICS, a bicultural community in Tokyo; CIX, a community in London; CalvaCom, a community in Paris; and Usenet, a collection of hundreds of different discussions that travel around the world via electronic mail to millions of participants in dozens of countries.

12 I was browsing through Supreme Court decisions, in search of information that could help me debunk an opponent's claims in a political debate elsewhere on the Net, or I was retrieving this morning's satellite images of weather over the Pacific.

13 I was following an eyewitness report from Moscow during the coup attempt, or China during the Tiananmen Square incident, or Israel and Kuwait during the Gulf War, passed directly from citizen to citizen through an ad hoc network patched together from cheap computers and ordinary telephone lines, cutting across normal geographic and political boundaries by piggybacking on the global communications infrastructure.

14 I was monitoring a rambling real-time dialogue among people whose bodies were scattered across three continents, a global bull session that seems to blend wit and sophomore locker-room talk via Internet Relay Chat (IRC), a medium that combines the features of conversation and writing. IRC has accumulated an obsessive subculture of its own among undergraduates by the thousands from Adelaide to Arabia.

15 People in virtual communities use words on screens to exchange pleasantries and argue, engage in intellectual discourse, conduct commerce, exchange knowledge, share emotional support, make plans, brainstorm, gossip, feud, fall in love, find friends and lose them, play games, flirt, create a little high art and a lot of idle talk. People in virtual communities do just about everything people do in real life, but we leave our bodies behind. You can't kiss anybody and nobody can punch you in the nose, but a lot can happen within those boundaries. To the millions who have been drawn into it, the richness and vitality of computer-linked cultures is attractive, even addictive.

16 There is no such thing as a single, monolithic, online subculture; it's more like an ecosystem of subcultures, some frivolous, others serious. The cutting edge of scientific discourse is migrating to virtual communities, where you can read the electronic pre-printed reports of molecular biologists and cognitive

scientists. At the same time, activists and educational reformers are using the same medium as a political tool. You can use virtual communities to find a date, sell a lawnmower, publish a novel, conduct a meeting.

17 Some people use virtual communities as a form of psychotherapy. Others, such as the most addicted players of Minitel in France or Multi-User Dungeons (MUDs) on the international networks, spend eighty hours a week or more pretending they are someone else, living a life that does not exist outside a computer. Because MUDs not only are susceptible to pathologically obsessive use by some people but also create a strain on computer and communication resources, MUDding has been banned at universities such as Amherst and on the entire continent of Australia.

18 Scientists, students, librarians, artists, organizers, and escapists aren't the only people who have taken to the new medium. The U.S. senator who campaigned for years for the construction of a National Research and Education Network that could host the virtual communities of the future is now vice president of the United States. As of June 1993, the White House and Congress have e-mail addresses.

19 Most people who get their news from conventional media have been unaware of the wildly varied assortment of new cultures that have evolved in the world's computer networks over the past ten years. Most people who have not yet used these new media remain unaware of how profoundly the social, political, and scientific experiments under way today via computer networks could change all our lives in the near future.

20 I have written this book to help inform a wider population about the potential importance of cyberspace to political liberties and the ways virtual communities are likely to change our experience of the real world, as individuals and communities. Although I am enthusiastic about the liberating potentials of computer-mediated communications, I try to keep my eyes open for the pitfalls of mixing technology and human relationships. I hope my reports from the outposts and headquarters of this new kind of social habitation, and the stories of the people I've met in cyberspace, will bring to life the cultural, political, and ethical implications of virtual communities both for my fellow explorers of cyberspace and for those who never heard of it before.

21 The technology that makes virtual communities possible has the potential to bring enormous leverage to ordinary citizens at relatively little cost—intellectual leverage, social leverage, commercial leverage, and most important, political leverage. But the technology will not in itself fulfill that potential; this latent technical power must be used intelligently and deliberately by an informed population. More people must learn about that leverage and learn to use it, while we still have the freedom to do so, if it is to live up to its potential. The odds are always good that big power and big money will find a way to control access to virtual communities; big power and big money always found ways to control new communications media when they emerged in the past. The Net is still out of control in fundamental ways, but it might not stay that way for long. What we know and do now is important because it is still possible

for people around the world to make sure this new sphere of vital human discourse remains open to the citizens of the planet before the political and economic big boys seize it, censor it, meter it, and sell it back to us.

22 The potential social leverage comes from the power that ordinary citizens gain when they know how to connect two previously independent, mature, highly decentralized technologies: It took billions of dollars and decades to develop cheap personal computers. It took billions of dollars and more than a century to wire up the worldwide telecommunication network. With the right knowledge, and not too much of it, a ten-year-old kid today can plug these two vast, powerful, expensively developed technologies together for a few hundred dollars and instantly obtain a bully pulpit, the Library of Congress, and a world full of potential coconspirators.

23 Computers and the switched telecommunication networks that also carry our telephone calls constitute the technical foundation of *computer-mediated communications* (CMC). The technicalities of CMC, how bits of computer data move over wires and are reassembled as computer files at their destinations, are invisible and irrelevant to most people who use it, except when the technicalities restrict their access to CMC services. The important thing to keep in mind is that the worldwide, interconnected telecommunication network that we use to make telephone calls in Manhattan and Madagascar can also be used to connect computers together at a distance, and you don't have to be an engineer to do it.

24 *The Net* is an informal term for the loosely interconnected computer networks that use CMC technology to link people around the world into public discussions.

25 *Virtual communities* are social aggregations that emerge from the Net when enough people carry on those public discussions long enough, with sufficient human feeling, to form webs of personal relationships in cyberspace.

26 *Cyberspace,* originally a term from William Gibson's science-fiction novel *Neuromancer,* is the name some people use for the conceptual space where words, human relationships, data, wealth, and power are manifested by people using CMC technology.

27 Although spatial imagery and a sense of place help convey the experience of dwelling in a virtual community, biological imagery is often more appropriate to describe the way of cyberculture changes. In terms of the way the whole system is propagating and evolving, think of cyberspace as a social petri dish, the Net as the agar medium, and virtual communities, in all their diversity, as the colonies of microorganisms that grow in petri dishes. Each of the small colonies of microorganisms—the communities on the Net—is a social experiment that nobody planned but that is happening nevertheless.

28 We now know something about the ways previous generations of communications technologies changed the way people lived. We need to understand why and how so many social experiments are coevolving today with the prototypes of the newest communications technologies. My direct observations of online behavior around the world over the past ten years have led me to con-

clude that whenever CMC technology becomes available to people anywhere, they inevitably build virtual communities with it, just as microorganisms inevitably create colonies.

29 I suspect that one of the explanations for this phenomenon is the hunger for community that grows in the breasts of people around the world as more and more informal public spaces disappear from our real lives. I also suspect that these new media attract colonies of enthusiasts because CMC enables people to do things with each other in new ways, and to do altogether new kinds of things—just as telegraphs, telephones, and televisions did.

30 Because of its potential influence on so many people's beliefs and perceptions, the future of the Net is connected to the future of community, democracy, education, science, and intellectual life—some of the human institutions people hold most dear, whether or not they know or care about the future of computer technology. The future of the Net has become too important to leave to specialists and special interests. As it influences the lives of a growing number of people, more and more citizens must contribute to the dialogue about the way public funds are applied to the development of the Net, and we must join our voices to the debate about the way it should be administered. We need a clear citizens' vision of the way the Net ought to grow, a firm idea of the kind of media environment we would like to see in the future. If we do not develop such a vision for ourselves, the future will be shaped for us by large commercial and political powerholders.

QUESTIONS FOR WRITING AND DISCUSSION

OBSERVING

1. What does the word "virtual" mean to Rheingold? How does he use it to describe communities he found on the WELL? What does he mean by "authentic community"? What is the net and what are its origins?
2. What is Rheingold's attitude toward the many virtual communities he has joined since 1985, his "global bull session"? In what sense has the Internet made what Marshall McLuhan called "the global village" a reality? What opportunities does Rheingold see stemming from that globalization?
3. What does Rheingold mean when he says that the net is an "ecosystem of subcultures"?

EVALUATING

1. Rheingold writes that "people can feel passionately about e-mail and computer conferences." Is he convincing? Passion and a computer screen would seem to be antithetical. What advantages and disadvantages as a

communications medium do the Internet and e-mail have over other forms such as face-to-face, letters, and the telephone? Why do some people gravitate to the Internet while others resist it?

2. Rheingold suggests the Internet will "profoundly" change our lives and, moreover, that it is doing that now. How is it changing our lives? What seem to be the most important and valuable changes and opportunities it affords? Which seem dangerous to you? Draw on Rheingold's writing. (Consider the Internet's effects on such things as participatory democracy and equal access to tools of power.) What does the author think is the political benefit of the net, for "ordinary citizens"? Do you agree?
3. What does the author say about "big power and big money"? What does he fear in this regard? What inferences can you draw from what Rheingold says about government or business controlling the Internet? What does he think about the "unplanned" and "out of control" nature of today's Internet?
4. Rheingold calls his daily linkage a "ritual." To what extent is it like a religious experience?

RESPONDING AND APPLYING

1. What experiences have you had, in or out of a classroom, with e-mail and the Internet? In what significant ways have the new technologies enhanced or retarded your learning? What has made these good experiences or bad ones? Based on those experiences, what would you predict for our technological future? What is the most important use of the computer, if any, for you personally?
2. Where do you stand on control, free speech, First Amendment issues as they relate to cyber-censorship? You might investigate the situation in Germany, where various contents such as hate-speech are banned, and compare it to our current debates over Internet control. Check into the recent Exon Amendment to ban "indecent" content, from Senator Exon and the reaction of many advocates of free speech such as the Electronic Frontier Foundation.
3. Do you find anything ominous or forbidding about the widening use of computers and networking? Do you feel your privacy threatened? Why or why not?

BILL GATES, *FROM* THE ROAD AHEAD

William H. (Bill) Gates, born in 1956, software wizard, multi-billionaire, and chief executive officer of Microsoft Corporation, is the author of *The Road Ahead* (1995), from which the following reading is drawn. Gates attended Harvard University where he developed BASIC for the MITS Altair, the first microcomputer, which initiated the phenomenon of hobby computing. A few years later, Gates started Microsoft with Paul Allen in 1975 in order to develop software for personal computers. Gates considers himself an avid reader; he also plays golf and bridge. Microsoft's Home Page can be found at <http://www.microsoft.com/corpinfo/>

from The Road Ahead

Bill Gates

1 I wrote my first software program when I was thirteen years old. It was for playing tic-tac-toe. The computer I was using was huge and cumbersome and slow and absolutely compelling. Letting a bunch of teenagers like me and my friend Paul Allen loose on a computer was the idea of the Mothers' Club at Lakeside, the private school I attended. The mothers decided that the proceeds from a rummage sale should be used to install a terminal and buy computer time for students, a pretty amazing choice at the time in Seattle—and one I'll always be grateful for.

2 I realized later part of the appeal was that here was an enormous, expensive, grown-up machine and we, the kids, could control it. We were too young to drive or to do any of the other fun-seeming adult activities, but we could give this big machine orders and it would always obey. It's feedback you don't get from many other things. That was the beginning of my fascination with software. And to this day it still thrills me to know that if I can get the program right it will always work perfectly, every time, just the way I told it to.

3 My parents paid my tuition at Lakeside and gave me money for books, but I had to take care of my own computer-time bills. This is what drove me to the commercial side of the software business. A bunch of us, including Paul, got entry-level software programming jobs. For high school students the pay was extraordinary—about $5,000 each summer, part in cash and the rest in computer time. One of the programs I wrote was the one that scheduled students in classes. I surreptitiously added a few instructions and found myself nearly the only guy in a class full of girls.

4 As a college sophomore, I stood in Harvard Square with Paul and pored over the description of a kit computer in Popular Electronics magazine. As we read excitedly about the first truly personal computer, Paul and I didn't know exactly how it would be used, but we were sure it would change us and the world of computing. We were right. The personal-computer revolution happened and it has affected millions of lives. It has led us to places we had barely imagined.

The Next Revolution

5 Now that computing is astoundingly inexpensive and computers inhabit every part of our lives, we stand at the brink of another revolution. This one will involve unprecedentedly inexpensive communication; all the computers will join together to communicate with us and for us. Interconnected globally, they will form a network, which is being called the information highway. A direct precursor is the present Internet, which is a group of computers joined and exchanging information using current technology.

6 The revolution in communications is just beginning. It will take place over several decades, and will be driven by new "applications"—new tools, often meeting currently unforeseen needs. During the next few years, major decisions will have to be made by governments, companies, and individuals. These decisions will have an impact on the way the highway will roll out and how much benefit those deciding will realize. It is crucial that a broad set of people—not just technologists or those who happen to be in the computer industry—participate in the debate about how this technology should be shaped. If that can be done, the highway will serve the purposes users want. Then it will gain broad acceptance and become a reality.

7 In the United States, the connecting of all these computers has been compared to another massive project: the gridding of the country with interstate highways, which began during the Eisenhower era. This is why the new network was dubbed the "information superhighway." The highway metaphor isn't quite right, though. The phrase suggests landscape and geography, a distance between points, and embodies the implication that you have to travel to get from one place to another. In fact, one of the most remarkable aspects of this new communications technology is that it will eliminate distance. It won't matter if someone you're contacting is in the next room or on another continent, because this highly mediated network will be unconstrained by miles and kilometers.

8 A different metaphor that I think comes closer to describing a lot of the activities that will take place is that of the ultimate market. Markets from trading floors to malls are fundamental to human society, and I believe this new one will eventually be the world's central department store. It will be where we social animals will sell, trade, invest, haggle, pick stuff up, argue, meet new people, and hang out. Think of the hustle and bustle of the New York Stock Exchange or a farmers' market or of a bookstore full of people looking for fascinating stories and information. All manner of human activity takes place, from billion-dollar deals to flirtations.

9 The highway will enable capabilities that seem magical when they are described, but represent technology at work to make our lives easier and better. Because consumers already understand the value of movies and are used to paying to watch them, video-on-demand will be an important application on the information highway. It won't be the first, however. We already know that PCs

will be connected long before television sets and that the quality of movies shown on early systems will not be very high. The systems will be able to offer other applications such as games, electronic mail, and home banking. When high-quality video can be transmitted, there won't be any intermediary VCR; you'll simply request what you want from a long list of available programs.

10 Television shows will continue to be broadcast as they are today for synchronous consumption—at the same time they are first broadcast. After they air, these shows—as well as thousands of movies and virtually all other kinds of video—will be available whenever you want to view them. You'll be able to watch the new episode of "Seinfeld" at 9:00 p.m. on Thursday night, or at 9:13 p.m., or at 9:45 p.m., or at 11:00 a.m. on Saturday. If you don't care for his brand of humor, there will be thousands of other choices. Even if a show is being broadcast live, you'll be able to use your infrared remote control to start, stop, or go to any previous part of the program, at any time. If someone comes to your door, you'll be able to pause the program for as long as you like. You'll be in absolute control.

11 Your television set will not look like a computer and won't have a keyboard, but additional electronics inside or attached will make it architecturally like a PC. Television sets will connect to the highway via a set-top box similar to ones supplied today by most cable TV companies.

A World of 'E-Books'

12 On the information highway, rich electronic documents will be able to do things no piece of paper can. The highway's powerful database technology will allow them to be indexed and retrieved using interactive exploration. It will be extremely cheap and easy to distribute them. In short, these new digital documents will replace many printed paper ones because they will be able to help us in new ways.

13 Ultimately, incremental improvements in computer and screen technology will give us a lightweight, universal electronic book or "e-book," which will approximate today's paperback book. Inside a case roughly the same size and weight as today's hardcover or paperback book, you'll have a display that can show high-resolution text, pictures, and video. You'll be able to flip pages with your finger or use voice commands.

14 The real point of electronic documents is not simply that we will read them on hardware devices. Going from paper book to e-book is just the final stage of a process already well under way. The exciting aspect of digital documentation is the redefinition of the document itself.

15 By the end of the decade a significant percentage of documents, even in offices, won't even be fully printable on paper. They will be like a movie or a song is today. You will still be able to print a two-dimensional view of its content, but it will be like reading a musical score instead of experiencing an audio recording.

16 Electronic documents will be interactive. Request a kind of information, and the document responds. Indicate that you've changed your mind, and the document responds again. Once you get used to this sort of system, you find that being able to look at information in different ways makes that information more valuable. The flexibility invites exploration, and the exploration is rewarded with discovery.

17 You'll be able to get your daily news in a similar way. You'll be able to specify how long you want your newscast to last because you'll be able to have each of the news stories selected individually. The newscast assembled for and delivered only to you might include world news from NBC, the BBC, CNN, or the Los Angeles Times, with a weather report from a favorite local TV meteorologist—or from any private meteorologist who wanted to offer his or her own service. You will be able to request longer stories on the subjects that particularly interest you and just highlights on others. If, while you are watching the newscast, you want more than has been put together, you will easily be able to request more background or detail, either from another news broadcast or from file information.

18 Among all the types of paper documents, narrative fiction is one of the few that will not benefit from electronic organization. Almost every reference book has an index, but novels don't because there is no need to be able to look something up in a novel. Novels are linear. Likewise, we'll continue to watch most movies from start to finish. This isn't a technological judgment—it is an artistic one: Their linearity is intrinsic to the storytelling process.

19 The success of CD-ROM games has encouraged authors to begin to create interactive novels and movies in which they introduce the characters and the general outline of the plot, then the reader/player makes decisions that change the outcome of the story. No one suggests that every book or movie should allow the reader or viewer to influence its outcome. A good story that makes you just want to sit there for a few hours and enjoy it is wonderful entertainment. I don't want to choose an ending for "The Great Gatsby" or "La Dolce Vita." F. Scott Fitzgerald and Federico Fellini have done that for me.

20 Significant investments will be required to develop great on-line content that will delight and excite PC users and raise the number on-line from 10 percent up to 50 percent, or even the 90 percent I believe it will become. Part of the reason this sort of investment isn't happening today is that simple mechanisms for authors and publishers to charge their users or to be paid by advertisers are just being developed.

21 As the fidelity of visual and audio elements improves, reality in all its aspects will be more closely simulated. This "virtual reality," or VR, will allow us to "go" places and "do" things we never would be able to otherwise.

22 In order to work, VR needs two different sets of technology software that creates the scene and makes it respond to new information, and devices that allow the computer to transmit the information to our senses. The software will have to figure out how to describe the look, sound, and feel of the artificial world down to the smallest detail. That might sound overwhelmingly difficult

but actually it's the easy part. We could write the software for VR today, but we need far more computer power to make it truly believable. At the pace technology is moving, though, that power will be available soon.

23 Inevitably, there has been more speculation (and wishful thinking) about virtual sex than about any other use for VR. Sexually explicit content is as old as information itself. If historical patterns are a guide, a big early market for advanced virtual-reality documents will be virtual sex. But again, historically, as each of these markets grew, explicit material became a smaller and smaller factor.

The Importance of Education

24 More than ever, an education that emphasizes general problem-solving skills will be important. In a changing world, education is the best preparation for being able to adapt. As the economy shifts, people and societies who are appropriately educated will tend to do best. The premium that society pays for skills is going to climb, so my advice is to get a good formal education and then keep on learning. Acquire new interests and skills throughout your life.

25 Some fear that technology will dehumanize formal education. But anyone who has seen kids working together around a computer, the way my friends and I first did in 1968, or watched exchanges between students in classrooms separated by oceans, knows that technology can humanize the educational environment. The same technological forces that will make learning so necessary will also make it practical and enjoyable. Just as information technology now allows Levi Strauss & Co. to offer jeans that are both mass-produced and custom fitted, information technology will bring mass customization to learning. Multimedia documents and easy-to-use authoring tools will enable teachers to "mass-customize" a curriculum for each student: computers will fine-tune the product—educational material, in this case—to allow students to follow somewhat divergent paths and learn at their own rates.

26 There is an often-expressed fear that technology will replace teachers. I can say emphatically and unequivocally, IT WON'T. The information highway won't replace or devalue any of the human educational talent needed for the challenges ahead: committed teachers, creative administrators, involved parents, and, of course, diligent students. However, technology will be pivotal in the future role of teachers.

27 Before the benefits of these advances can be realized, though, the way computers in the classroom are thought about will have to change. A lot of people are cynical about educational technology because it has been overhyped and has failed to deliver on its promises. Many of the PCs in schools today are not powerful enough to be easy to use, and they don't have the storage capacity or network connections to permit them to respond to a child's curiosity with much information.

28 When teachers do excellent work and prepare wonderful materials now, only their few dozen students benefit each year. The network will enable teach-

ers to share lessons and materials, so that the best educational practices can spread. The interactive network also will allow students to quiz themselves any time, in a risk-free environment. A self-administered quiz is a form of self-exploration. Testing will become a positive part of the learning process. A mistake won't call forth a reprimand; it will trigger the system to help the student overcome his misunderstanding. The highway will also make home schooling easier. It will allow parents to select some classes from a range of quality possibilities and still maintain control over content.

THE IMPACT ON SOCIETY

29 Just because I'm optimistic doesn't mean I don't have concerns about what is going to happen to all of us. The broad benefits of advancing productivity are no solace for someone whose job is on the line. When a person has been trained for a job that is no longer needed, you can't just suggest he go out and learn something else. Adjustments aren't that simple or fast, but ultimately they are necessary.

30 The fully developed information highway will be affordable—almost by definition. An expensive system that connected a few big corporations and wealthy people simply would not be the information highway—it would be the information private road. The network will not attract enough great content to thrive if only the most affluent 10 percent of society choose to avail themselves of it. There are fixed costs to authoring material; so to make them affordable, a large audience is required. Advertising revenue won't support the highway if a majority of eligible people don't embrace it. If that is the case, the price for connecting will have to be cut or deployment delayed while the system is redesigned to be more attractive. The information highway is a mass phenomenon, or it is nothing.

31 The net effect will be a wealthier world, which should be stabilizing. Developed nations, and workers in those nations, are likely to maintain a sizable economic lead. However, the gap between the have and have-not nations will diminish. Starting out behind is sometimes an advantage. Those who adopt late skip steps, and avoid the mistakes of the trailblazers. Some countries will never have industrialization but will move directly into the Information Age.

32 The information highway is going to break down boundaries and may promote a world culture, or at least a sharing of cultural activities and values. The highway will also make it easy for patriots, even expatriates, deeply involved in their own ethnic communities to reach out to others with similar interests no matter where they may be located. This may strengthen cultural diversity and counter the tendency toward a single world culture.

33 A complete failure of the information highway is worth worrying about. Because the system will be thoroughly decentralized, any single outage is unlikely to have a widespread effect. If an individual server fails, it will be replaced and its data restored. But the system could be susceptible to assault. As the system

becomes more important, we will have to design in more redundancy. One area of vulnerability is the system's reliance on cryptography—the mathematical locks that keep information safe. None of the protection systems that exist today, whether steering-wheel locks or steel vaults, are completely fail-safe. The best we can do is make it as difficult as possible for somebody to break in. Still, popular opinions to the contrary, computer security has a very good record.

34 Loss of privacy is another major concern about the highway. A great deal of information is already being gathered about each of us, by private companies as well as by government agencies, and we often have no idea how it is used or whether it is accurate. As more business is transacted using the highway and the amount of information stored there accrues, governments will consciously set policies regarding privacy and access to information. The potential problem is abuse, not the mere existence of information.

35 These privacy fears revolve around the possibility that someone else is keeping track of information about you. But the highway will also make it possible for an individual to keep track of his or her own whereabouts—to lead what we might call "a documented life." Your wallet PC will be able to keep audio, time, location, and eventually even video records of everything that happens to you. It will be able to record every word you say and every word said to you, as well as body temperature, blood pressure, barometric pressure, and a variety of other data about you and your surroundings. It will be able to track your interactions with the highway—all of the commands you issue, the messages you send, and the people you call or who call you. The resulting record will be the ultimate diary and autobiography, if you want one.

36 I find the prospect of documented lives a little chilling, but some people will warm to the idea. One reason for documenting a life will be defensive. If someone ever accused you of something, you could retort: "Hey, buddy, I have a documented life. These bits are stored away. I can play back anything I've ever said. So don't play games with me." Medical malpractice insurance might be cheaper, or only available, for doctors who record surgical procedures or even office visits. I can imagine proposals that every automobile, including yours and mine, be outfitted not only with a recorder but also with a transmitter that identifies the car and its location. If a car was reported stolen, its location would be known immediately. After a hit-and-run accident or a drive-by shooting, a judge could authorize a query: "What vehicles were in the following two-block area during this thirty-minute period?" The black box could record your speed and location, which would allow for the perfect enforcement of speeding laws. I would vote against that.

37 Even if the model of political decision making does not change explicitly, the highway will bestow power on groups who want to organize to promote causes or candidates. This could lead to an increased number of special-interest groups and political parties. Someone will doubtless propose total "direct democracy," having all issues put to a vote. Personally, I don't think direct voting would be a good way to run a government. There is a place in governance for representatives—middlemen—to add value. They are the ones who understand all the nuances of complicated issues. Politics involves compromise,

which is nearly impossible without a relatively small number of representatives making decisions on behalf of the people who elected them.

38 We are watching something historic happen, and it will affect the world seismically, the same way the scientific method, the invention of printing, and the arrival of the Industrial Age did. Big changes used to take generations or centuries. This one won't happen overnight, but it will move much faster. The first manifestations of the information highway will be apparent in the United States by the millennium. Within a decade there will be widespread effects. If I had to guess which applications of the network will be embraced quickly and which will take a long time, I'd certainly get some wrong. Within twenty years virtually everything I've talked about will be broadly available in developed countries and in businesses and schools in developing countries.

QUESTIONS FOR WRITING AND DISCUSSION

OBSERVING

1. Gates opens by saying his first software program for playing tic-tac-toe gave him a control he couldn't otherwise get at 13. What is the nature of that control and its relationship to traditional forms of authority? Why is the anecdote from his childhood significant to the larger issues he raises later?
2. Why does Gates not like the highway metaphor as it is applied to the Internet? What metaphor does he prefer and why?
3. What opportunities does Gates see in information technology? What does he predict for print technology? What artistic demands does Gates think will dictate the form of the movie and novel?
4. What does Gates mean by virtual reality and what predictions does he make about virtual reality? What does Gates think "the next revolution" will be? What will be its immediate effects?

EVALUATING

1. Gates shows his excitement over electronic developments. Which ones is he most interested in and what do these tell us about his values, about what is important to him? Where do you find Gates persuasive? Where is his logic weak or troubling?
2. What does Gates mean by "mass customization" when he describes the effects of technology on formal education? Isn't "mass customization" an oxymoron, a compact paradox?
3. Gates compares the technological revolution to the development of the scientific method, the invention of printing, and the Industrial Age. How are the new technologies so epoch-making? Is Gates engaging in hyperbole?
4. Gates denies technology will "replace teachers." Do you agree? Why?

RESPONDING AND APPLYING

1. Gates is enthusiastically optimistic when he describes technology's impact on society. He predicts that the gap between the haves and the have-nots will diminish, and that boundaries between persons and countries will break down. What is the basis of his optimism? Do you share it? What assumptions underlie Gates' thinking?
2. Describe your childhood as technologically rich or barren or some place in-between. What effects, positive or negative, has that aspect of your childhood had on you? Did it give you control over a world dominated by adults, as Gates seems to think? Or was the control illusory?

CHAPTER WRITING ASSIGNMENTS

1. In "The Taming of the Saw," Todhunter asserts that the technology that saves our labors also "removes us from our lives." What do you think Todhunter means by this?
2. Defining technology as any tool that extends our human faculties, investigate a single technology: look into its history, the era out of which it first came, its uses, and its impact when it was first invented and now. Who gains from the technology and who loses? What ethical or value problems has the new technology created? Consider such technologies as the alphabet, the internal combustion engine, the pill, the stirrup (for a horse), splitting of the atom, the telescope, the television, the phone, the robot, the computer, the refrigerator and the human or animal clone.
3. Investigate the impact of a new technology such as the Internet, the CD-ROM, telecomputing, distance learning, or e-mail on the discipline you are majoring in or one you might wish to find work in. How has that field changed in the past 30 years? What moral problems or challenges has the technology created?
4. Choose a technological visionary to study: consider such names as Bill Gates, Nicholas Negroponte, Sherry Turkle, Richard Lanham, Howard Rheingold, Steven Jobs, David Bolter. Or investigate a business or university lab that has made pioneering efforts in the new technologies. Consider the Voyager Company, Microsoft, the MIT Media Lab, or Apple Computer.
5. Investigate a science fiction writer who has explored the effects of the newest technologies on society. Consider William Gibson, Pat Cadigan, Bruce Sterling, Neal Stephenson, or Wilhelmina Baird. Look at the cyberpunk movement, asking questions like, What is virtual reality and its effect on the human personality, on government, religion, schooling, and the family?
6. Study the directions the Internet is going in today. Focus on an access provider such as America On Line or Prodigy, or the many small, community-based providers. What effects is the Internet having on small or larger communities? What kinds of services are provided? How are costs covered? Is there consideration of equity and access issues; i.e., are there subsidies for people who cannot afford the costs? Is the Internet changing our

ideas of what a community is? Interview leaders in your town who have been active supporters of such developments.

7. Look into cyberdemocracy. Study the latest efforts of the present administration in Washington to develop technological access. What issues are important to them? What values do you see behind these issues? You might also study the efforts of recent administrations, such as Bush/Quayle or Clinton/Gore, in this regard.
8. Study the profound changes schools are undergoing as a result of the new technologies. What, if any, role will teachers play as computers increasingly take over? What new forms and sources of authority will replace the teachers? What is or will be the effect of hypertext, electronically linked documents, on learning?
9. The easy access to information provided by the Internet seems immensely desirable, but not if information overload reduces that information to babble. In what ways, if any, do the new technologies provide aid in comprehending and synthesizing the information they make available? This question seems important, especially since a major concern in learning, especially where research is required, is the extent to which you are in control of your sources. With the new technologies, especially the Internet, consider these questions: Are you simply parroting the established authorities or who you assume to be authorities? How able are you to evaluate your sources, to deal with controversy among authorities, to fashion a reasonable synthesis of available information? For background, read William Greider's *Who Will Tell the People?* (Simon & Schuster, 1992) and James Follows' *Breaking the News* (Pantheon, 1996).

CREDITS

"This World Is Not This World" from *The Nazi Doctors* by Robert Jay Lifton. Copyright © 1986 by Robert Jay Lifton. Reprinted by permission of BasicBooks, a division of HarperCollins Publishers, Inc.

"Women and Nature" from *The Death of Nature: Women, Ecology, and the Scientific Revolution* by Carolyn Merchant. Copyright © 1980 by Carolyn Merchant. Reprinted by permission of HarperCollins Publishers, Inc.

Harper's: "Secularism's Blind Faith" by Peter Marin. Copyright © 1995 by *Harper's Magazine.* All rights reserved. Reproduced from the September issue by special permission.

Harvard Magazine: "Civilization's Thin Veneer" by Vaclav Havel. The 1995 Harvard Commencement address, as excerpted by the editors of *Harvard Magazine.* Reprinted by permission of Harvard Magazine.

Harvard University Press: Excerpt from "On Natural Law" from *Laws in Cicero in Twenty-Eight Volumes.* Reprinted by permission of the publishers and the Loeb Classical Library from *Cicero: De Republica, De Legibus,* Volume 16, translated by Clinton Walker Keyes, Cambridge, MA: Harvard University Press, 1928.

Houghton Mifflin: "The Challenge of Change" excerpted from *The Cycles of American History* by Arthur M. Schlesinger, Jr. Copyright © 1986 by Arthur M. Schlesinger Jr. Reprinted by permission of Houghton Mifflin Company. All rights reserved. Excerpt published in *The New York Times Magazine.*

ICM: "The Portable Phonograph" from *The Watchful Gods and Other Stories,* by Walter Van Tilburg Clark. Reprinted by permission of International Creative Management, Inc. Copyright © 1941 by Walter Van Tilburg Clark.

"The Great Relearning Heralds the 21st Century" by Tom Wolfe, originally published in *Cleveland Plain Dealer,* 1988.

James Baldwin Estate: Excerpted from "Down at the Cross: Letter from a Region of My Mind" © 1962 by James Baldwin. Copyright renewed. Collected in *The Fire Next Time,* published by Vintage Books. Reprinted with the permission of the James Baldwin Estate.

Linda Simon: "The Naked Source" by Linda Simon, from "Inquiry" in the *Michigan Quarterly Review,* Vol. XXVII, No. 3, Summer 1988. Reprinted by permission of the author.

Michael Ventura: "Inventory of Timelessness" by Michael Ventura. Copyright © 1993 by Michael Ventura, from *Letters at 3AM: Reports on Endarkenment.* Reprinted by permission of the author.

MIT Press: "The Scientific Response to Creationism" by Joel Cracraft, from *Creationism, Science and the Law: The Arkansas Case,* ed. Marcel C. La Follette, copyright © 1983. Reprinted by permission of the MIT Press.

Neil Postman: "Amusing Ourselves to Death" by Neil Postman, from *Et Cetera,* Vol. 42, No. 1. Reprinted by permission of the author.

Newsweek: "The Virtuecrats" by Howard Fineman, from *Newsweek,* June 13, 1994, © 1994 Newsweek, Inc. All rights reserved. Reprinted by permission.

New York Times: "Study Says Society Fails 19 Million Youths" by Peter Applebome, in the *New York Times,* October 12, 1995. Copyright © 1995 by The New York Times Company. Reprinted by permission.

Oxford University Press: "Allegory of the Cave" reprinted from *The Republic of Plato* translated by F. M Cornford (1941) by permission of Oxford University Press.

Patricia King: Dr. King is Professor and Chair of the Department of Higher Education and Student Affairs at Bowling Green State University. This article, "How Do We Know? Why Do We Believe? Learning to Make Reflective Judgments," is reprinted with the permission of the author from *Liberal Education,* Vol. 78, No. 1, 1992.

Penguin USA: "Washington's Works of Art" by George Will, originally published in *Newsweek,* reprinted as "Pork for the Articulate" from *The Leveling Wind: Politics, the Culture and Other News 1990-1994,* Viking Books, © 1994 by George F. Will. Used by permission of Viking Penguin, a division of Penguin Books USA Inc.

Excerpt from *The Road Ahead* by Bill Gates, originally appeared in *Newsweek,* November 27, 1995. Copyright © 1995 by William H. Gates III. Used by permission of Viking Penguin, a division of Penguin USA Inc.

"Something for the Time Being" copyright © 1960, renewed © 1988 by Nadine Gordimer, from *Selected Stories* by Nadine Gordimer. Used by permission of Viking Penguin, a division of Penguin Books USA Inc.

Penn State Press: "What Is the New History?" by Peter Burke, from *New Perspectives on Historical Writings,* from University Park: The Pennsylvania State University Press, pp. 1-6. Copyright by the

Pennsylvania State University. Reproduced by permission of the publisher.

Philosophical Library: "Existentialism" by Jean Paul Sartre, translated by Bernard Frechtman, © 1947.

Questar: "The Two Trees" from *God Came Near* by Max Lucado; Multnomah Books, Questar Publishers; copyright © 1987. Reprinted by permission.

Random House: "The Problem of Our Laws" and "An Old Manuscript" from *Franz Kafka: The Complete Stories* by Franz Kafka, edited by Nahum N. Glatzer. Copyright © 1946, 1947, 1948, 1949, 1954, 1958, 1971 by Schocken Books, Inc. Reprinted by permission of Schocken Books, distributed by Pantheon Books, a division of Random House, Inc.

"The Lesson" from *Gorilla My Love* by Toni Cade Bambara. Copyright © 1972. Excerpt from "The Poet and the City" from *The Dyer's Hand and Other Essays* by W. H. Auden. Copyright © 1989 Vintage International.

Routledge: "What's American about America?" by Ishmael Reed from *Writin' Is Fightin'* in *Ourselves among Others* edited by Carol Verberg. Reprinted by permission.

Russell & Volkening: "Something for the Time Being" from *Selected Stories* by Nadine Gordimer. Copyright © 1975.

"Like a Winding Sheet" from *Miss Muriel and Other Stories* by Ann Petry. Reprinted by permission of Russell & Volkening as agents for the author. Copyright © 1946 by Ann Petry, copyright renewed by Ann Petry. "Like a Winding Sheet" was originally published in *The Crisis* in 1946.

Sage Publications: Steinar Kvale, "Themes of Postmodernism," *Journal of Humanistic Psychology,* Vol. 18, No. 1, 1990. Reprinted by permission of Sage Publications, Inc.

Simon & Schuster: Introduction from *The Book of Virtues* by William J. Bennett, copyright © 1993.

Excerpt from *One by One: Remembering the Holocaust* by Judith Miller, copyright © 1990. Reprinted by permission.

"The Emerging Third Culture" by John Brockman, from *The Third Culture,* copyright © 1995. Reprinted by permission.

St. Martin's Press: "Trying Out One's New Sword" from *Heart and Mind: The Varieties of Moral Experience* by Mary Midgley. Copyright © 1981 by Mary Midgley. Reprinted with permission of St. Martin's Press, Incorporated.

Tanner, Propp, Ferlsom and Sterner: "Harrison Bergeron" from *Welcome to the Monkey House* by Kurt Vonnegut, Jr. copyright © 1968 Delacourt Press.

"Address to P.E.N. Conference" from *Wampeters, Foma, and Granfalloons* by Kurt Vonnegut, Jr. Copyright © 1975 by Delacourt Press.

Teachers College Press: Excerpt from "Art, Social Action, and the Preparation of Democratic Citizens." Reprinted by permission of the publisher from Blandy, D., & Congdon, K. G. (eds.), *Art in a Democracy* (New York: Teachers College Press, © 1987 by Teachers College, Columbia University. All rights reserved.), excerpts from pp. 9–23.

The Crossing Press: "Fourth of July" reprinted with permission from *Zami: A New Spelling of My Name,* by Audre Lorde © 1982. Published by The Crossing Press: Freedom, CA.

University of Illinois Press: "Madagascar" by Steven Schwartz from *Lives of the Fathers.* Copyright © 1991 by Steven Schwartz. Used with the permission of the author and the University of Illinois Press.

University of Notre Dame Press: "The Future of Work" by Frithjof Bergmann from *Working in America: A Humanities Reader,* edited by Robert Sessions and Jack Wortman, © 1992 by the University of Notre Dame Press. Reprinted by permission.

W.W. Norton: "Women's Brains" from *The Panda's Thumb: More Reflections in Natural History* by Stephen Jay Gould. Copyright © 1980 by Stephen Jay Gould. Reprinted by permission of W.W. Norton & Company, Inc.

"Sex, Drugs, Disasters, and the Extinction of Dinosaurs" from *The Flamingo's Smile: Reflections in Natural History* by Stephen Jay Gould. Copyright © 1984 by Stephen Jay Gould. Reprinted by permission of W.W. Norton & Company, Inc.

Watkins/Loomis Agency: "The Greatest Drama Ever Staged" from *Christian Letters to a Post-Christian World* by Dorothy L. Sayers. Copyright © 1949 by Dorothy L. Sayers. Reprinted by permission of the authors' agent.

Wellington House: "Day Million" by Frederick Pohl. Originally appeared in *Rogue Magazine,* © 1966.

William Morrow: "Public Policy in the Classless State" from *The Imperial Middle: Why Americans Can't Think Straight about Class,* by Benjamin DeMott. Copyright © 1990 by Benjamin DeMott. Reprinted by permission of William Morrow & Company, Inc.

INDEX